S0-AHS-233

CURRY

CLASSIC AND CONTEMPORARY

VIVEK SINGH

CURRY

CLASSIC AND CONTEMPORARY

ABSOLUTE PRESS A.

First published in Great Britain in 2008 by Absolute Press, an imprint of Bloomsbury Publishing Plc

Absolute Press
Scarborough House
29 James Street West
Bath BA1 2BT

Phone 44 (0) 1225 316013
Fax 44 (0) 1225 445836
E-mail info@absolutepress.co.uk
Website www.absolutepress.co.uk

Reprinted 2010, 2012

Publisher Jon Croft
Commissioning Editor Meg Avent
Editorial Assistant Andrea O'Connor
Designer Matt Inwood
Design Assistant Claire Siggery
Editor Jane Middleton
Photography Cristian Barnett
Food Styling Vivek Singh and Abdul Yaseen
Props Styling Cynthia Inions

ISBN 13: 9781904573883
Printed in China on behalf of Latitude Press Ltd

A catalogue record of this book is available from the British Library.

Bloomsbury Publishing Plc
50 Bedford Square
London WC1B 3DP
www.bloomsbury.com

A note about the text
This book is set in Sabon and Trajan. Sabon was designed by Jan Tschichold in 1964. The roman design is based on type by Claude Garamond, whereas the italic design is based on types by Robert Granjon. Trajan was designed in 1989 by Carol Twombly, and is based on classic Roman letterforms.

6 INTRODUCTION

14 VEGETARIAN
54 SEAFOOD
98 MEAT
148 POULTRY AND GAME
178 ACCOMPANIMENTS

202 BASICS
205 GLOSSARY
208 INDEX
214 A NOTE FOR AMERICAN READERS
215 ACKNOWLEDGEMENTS

INTRODUCTION

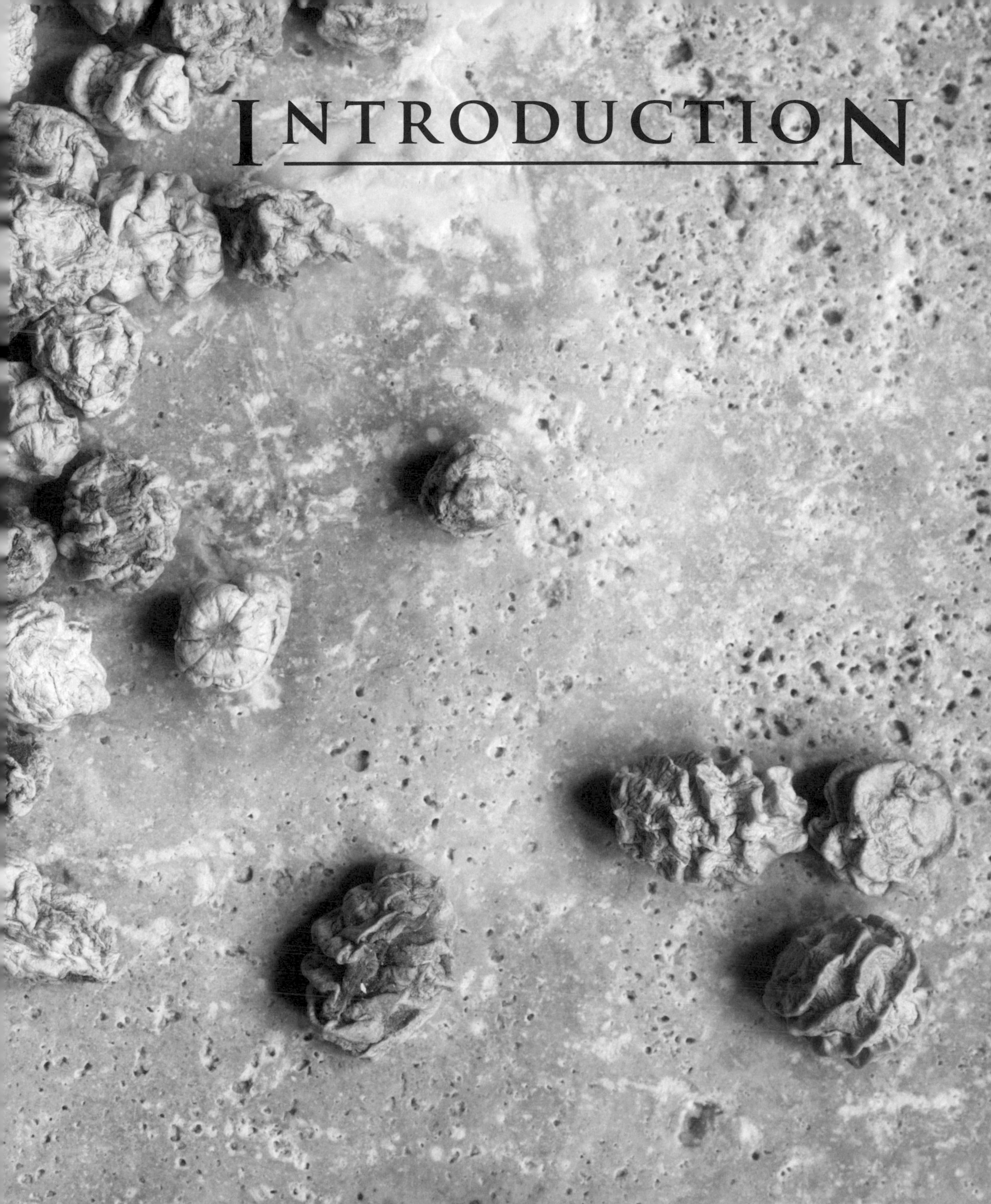

ORIGINS AND MYTHS

Curry is hugely popular throughout the world, yet in India, the place where it all began, the term barely exists. When I finished writing this book, I went through my old Indian menus to make sure I hadn't missed anything out and hardly came across the word at all. I was so surprised – and so concerned to find an authentic definition – that I decided to ask people in India itself, what they understood by curry.

My first port of call was the busy metropolis of Mumbai. Everyone there was very well informed about the latest culinary trends in London and New York, yet when I asked them to define curry there was a palpable hesitation. I looked at menus all over the city and came across just one reference to it. So I headed inland to see if I could find out more there. Bilaspur is a small town at the heart of central India, where most families cook 18 meals a week at home on average. There, too, people struggled to come up with a definition of curry for me; some confused it with kadhai, the Indian wok, while most dismissed the question as absurd, arguing, quite reasonably, that you couldn't possibly group such a large variety of wonderful dishes under a single umbrella. My mother came up with three possible answers: one a soup-style dish made with yoghurt (kadhi); another a style of cooking (kadhai-style) and third a cooking utensil (kadhai again).

Contrast this with the West, and particularly the UK, where the word curry has come to stand for an entire genre of cooking from Southeast Asia. While it mostly refers to meat, seafood or vegetarian dishes, braised with spices in a sauce, it can also describe spicy stir-fries and dry dishes.

One school of thought links curry to the Tamil word *kari*, or *karee*, meaning sauce. A more plausible explanation, however, is that when British officers in the East India Company were stationed in Chennai (known then as Madras), they would ask the local staff what was being cooked and were told 'curry', or, a mixture. Even though the dishes were quite different every day, the description remained the same – curry. This saved the effort of trying to translate and explain individual dishes, and would account for the British understanding of curry as a complete genre. It is possible that what started as an oversimplification was responsible for one of the biggest misunderstandings in culinary history. It seems that there is no such thing as an authentic definition of curry after all.

THE INDIAN ART OF SPICING

I have come to accept that everyone has their own personal expectations of a curry, whether it's a dish in a standard British curry house or a blanket term for the cooking of an entire subcontinent. Although authenticity might be an illusion, however, what is vital is the role that spices have to play.

When I was cooking at the Aberdeen Marina Club in Hong Kong many years ago, I was rather offended to be told that the guests expected the food to be hotter. In revenge, I kept increasing the amount of chillies in each dish until they started begging for milder food! The things one does as a young man...it did not occur to me then that this would have been an ideal opportunity to introduce those guests to sophisticated, balanced and well-rounded Indian cooking, rather than just playing up to their prejudices. Indian food is about far more than chilli heat. There is a huge repertoire of spices to explore, not just for their heat but for other qualities too: coriander for cooling, cloves for flavour and heat of a different kind, saffron for fragrance, mace and cardamom for their aroma. It is the combination of spices that makes each curry unique.

The art of spicing in India is arguably the most sophisticated and complex in the world. In other cuisines, spices tend to be used in isolation or in simple combinations. Indian cooking relies on an intimate knowledge of the way spices work together – not just their flavours but also their textures, the sequence in which they are added to a dish, and how long they are cooked. It is an exciting and challenging way of cooking, and one in which there is always something new to learn. This brings me on to the subject of ready-made curry powders. The very idea of an all-purpose seasoning blend that can be added to any curry is simply outrageous. Most dishes don't need all the spices they contain anyway, and it is always best to grind what you need when you need it rather than buying ready-ground spices, which lose much of their flavour, appearance and aroma within two weeks.

Historically, spices were used in India for a variety of reasons. Foremost among these, of course, was flavour, but they were just as important for preservation. In the days before refrigeration, spices helped to prolong the shelf life of fresh ingredients, and were also used to tenderise meat. Traditional Ayurvedic medicine relies on spices for certain health benefits. Besides using spices to treat various ailments, an Ayurvedic practitioner will assess a person's body type and advise which spices and other foods are beneficial for them to consume and which best avoided. It is common knowledge in India that cumin aids digestion, while coriander is an antipyretic which has a cooling effect on the body and is often used to reduce fever in children. Fennel seeds also aid digestion and are used as a mouth freshener. Turmeric is an effective antiseptic and is frequently used to treat minor cuts, burns and wounds.

Although Indian spicing can be highly complex, the cooking techniques for curry are generally very simple. One of the most common is braising, a slow cooking method that allows spices to be added at various stages, resulting in well-rounded, layered flavours. Some curries rely on a combination of cooking techniques, such as marinating, frying and then roasting. None of these stages is difficult, and often some of them can be done in advance, making life easier for the cook. This ease of preparation and versatility partly account for the success of curry throughout the world, while the magic and intrigue of its spicing mean that one need never get bored. There are hundreds of variations for each dish – a minor nuance changed here or there can create something entirely different.

REGIONAL AND RELIGIOUS INFLUENCES

Far more important than learning recipes is to understand the context in which they developed. It is the context that gives them their soul. In India, region and religion have both had a big impact on the way in which the cuisine has developed.

The majority of the population in India is Hindu and does not eat beef, which is considered sacred. The second most commonly practised religion is Islam, which forbids the consumption of pork. It is because of these two restrictions that you don't often see pork and beef used in curries.

In Punjab, Kashmir and the north of the country, the climate is moderate to cold, while the soil is fertile and wheat is the staple grain, Vegetables and fruit grow in abundance and dairy produce is widely used. In this land of plenty, rich dishes made with milk, butter, lamb and chicken are common. The spicing varies a fair bit; dishes range from creamy butter chicken to rustic, hot, kadhai-style stir-fries, essentially relying on a basic combination of woody spices such as cumin, coriander, cardamom, cinnamon, star anise and cloves. The majority of the population is either Hindu or Muslim, so beef and pork are rarely seen.

In the eastern part of the country, the picture is very different. In Bengal rice is the staple rather than wheat, mustard oil is commonly used for cooking, and the spicing is fairly basic: onion seeds, fennel seeds, carom, mustard seeds, cumin and cardamom being the most common, with few of the more aromatic spices, such as star anise and saffron, ever making an appearance. The Bengalis' love of good food, however, is apparent in the multitude of fish and seafood dishes, which are so different from anywhere else in the country.
As a Communist state, West Bengal is one of only two states in India (Kerala being the other) where it is legal to buy and sell beef. This, together with the British influence during the days of the Raj, means that beef and pork are frequently seen on menus here.

The southern end of the peninsula, consisting of Andhra Pradesh, Tamil Nadu, Kerala and Karnataka, is blessed by a long coastline, and hence a strong bias towards seafood dishes. The population is a mix of all religions and every kind of dish is found, even pork. Rice is the staple in this region and spices are plentiful. So is coconut, and both the oil and the milk are used freely in cooking. The climate is quite tropical and can be very hot and humid. Chillies and spices are added liberally to dishes in order to promote sweating, creating a cooling effect.

On the western coast are Mumbai and Goa – one a melting pot of different cultures and culinary styles, the other a former Portuguese colony with strong European influences. While in Mumbai anything goes, and the food is a heady mix of Maharashtrian, Pan-Indian and world cuisine, Goa is synonymous with fresh seafood cooked with vibrant, bold spicing – very much like the spirit of its residents.

Further west, Gujarat and Rajasthan are predominantly vegetarian, although Rajasthan also has a tradition of cooking with game. Since much of the land is dry and arid, not much grows there and the vegetarian cuisine displays great innovation, with spicy, earthy flavours.

CURRY IN BRITAIN

In the UK, far from the land of its birth and the influences that shaped it, curry is a six-billion-pound industry. Between restaurants, takeaways and supermarkets, a vast amount of curry is sold on a daily basis. For years I believed that the longstanding British love affair with India was the reason Indian food was so popular here. To be honest, I'm now beginning to wonder if it's the other way round!

The British experience of curry has come a long way since the days when it was made with sultanas and curry powder. As more Asians have become part of British society, many people have had the opportunity to eat in their homes and discover genuine Indian food.

Restaurants have become more sophisticated and it is quite common now for them to specialise in regional food from various parts of India. At the same time, a genuinely British-Indian strand of cooking has developed. Much as top Indian chefs might turn up their noses at the typical high-street curry house, an entire generation of British people has grown up with Sylheti kormas, vindaloos and Madras curry and wouldn't have it any other way. I tried jhalfrezi for the first time when I arrived in London and also had my first balti in Birmingham – an experience, to say the least. It was not something I had ever eaten in India but there were several people around me who were completely at ease with the dishes.

Anyone who has ever had a curry understands how addictive it can be, creating a craving for more. The pleasure sensations associated with eating curry come from the release of endorphins, and are known to drive many of us in the UK straight to a curry house when we come back from a holiday abroad. Little wonder, then, that when British officers returned from the subcontinent back in the days of the East India Company, they would bring sacks of spices, and sometimes even their own cooks, in order to be able to enjoy curries at home.

When I first travelled outside India – and particularly when I came to England – my eyes were opened to a phenomenon I had not known existed. The huge community of Indians living abroad, many of them over several generations, had invented new dishes, or adapted traditional curries to suit local ingredients. This new style of Indian food fused with the local cuisine to create an entirely different way of cooking. The results may be frowned upon by people back in India as inauthentic. But the question is, who decides what is authentic?

AUTHENTIC CURRY – YOURS OR MINE?

I recently met a Bori Muslim lady who has lived in Britain for 50 years but whose family originally came from Gujarat. Before they moved to Britain, three generations of her family had lived in East Africa over the course of a century. Effectively, the cooking in this family still drew from traditional Gujarati dishes but has adapted to include local, seasonal ingredients available in their new homes. A slow but constant evolution over 150 years has unquestionably changed their food and eating habits, but try telling this lady that the food she cooks for her family is not authentic!

If authentic cooking comes from the home, then there is no such thing as authentic Indian food, as no two homes ever cook a dish in exactly the same way. The search for authenticity is pointless, since what is the genuine article to me might mean nothing to you, and what is authentic today may be meaningless tomorrow.

Over the last 14 years as a chef, I have on numerous occasions seen authenticity used as an excuse for not doing things rather than the other way round. During the early days of The Cinnamon Club, guests would often tell me that they had loved their meal but weren't sure if they could call it authentic. My response would be, did it matter, as long as they had enjoyed it?

As Masaharu Morimoto describes in his book, *Morimoto: The New Art of Japanese Cooking* (DK Publishing, 2007), he experienced the same confusion in response to his cooking in the USA, which draws inspiration from traditional Japanese cuisine but also uses local produce and influences. His answer to the question of authenticity is: why isn't my food Japanese and why must it be?

I couldn't agree more. So many cuisines are merging and moulding, mixing and changing every day. Very few chefs' larders are restricted to what's local any more and in theory anything goes. Curry, like everything else, is subject to a continual process of change, evolving in order to remain accessible, popular and relevant. This isn't only a recent phenomenon. It may sound blasphemous to say that the tandoor does not belong to India, or that the lovely naan bread we are all so used to ordering in Indian restaurants is not really Indian either, but that is the truth. In the mid-fifteenth century, when Mughal rulers invaded India from Persia via Afghanistan, they brought over many of their culinary influences, including the tandoor. Over the next few hundred years, these gradually blended in with local traditions. Today it has become almost impossible to identify and separate the different influences. And to be honest, why bother?

Tradition is nothing but successful innovation, and innovation today forms the basis of tradition tomorrow. Innovation draws from tradition, as it should. In terms of cooking curries, a sound, deep-rooted understanding of spices and techniques is fundamental to any successful innovation. Part of the joy of cooking at The Cinnamon Club is that I have the opportunity to deconstruct traditional curries into their essential parts and then build them up again, creating layers of flavour and texture and maximising the appreciation of the core ingredients. It's impossible to do this without a deep understanding of traditional dishes.

This book is an attempt to present curry in both its forms – classic and contemporary. It shows what curry has always been and what it could become. It is a celebration of the timeless nature of curry – a tradition that dates back centuries, yet remains popular today. While you will find in its pages some of the greatest recipes from all over the subcontinent, I hope you will also be inspired to create your own modern classics, adapting the recipes to suit your own tastes.

VIVEK SINGH, SEPTEMBER 2008

VEGETARIAN

16 BABY AUBERGINES WITH SESAME AND TAMARIND SAUCE
18 SEARED AUBERGINE STEAKS WITH SESAME TAMARIND SAUCE
20 SEARED BOTTLE GOURD WITH CHICKPEA BREAD AND BOTTLE GOURD COOKED IN MILK
23 PUNJABI CHICKPEA FRITTERS IN YOGHURT CURRY
24 CHICKPEA POLENTA IN YOGHURT SAUCE
25 CHICKPEA DUMPLINGS IN YOGHURT SAUCE
28 WINTER VEGETABLE CURRY WITH CARROTS, PEAS AND TOMATOES
30 HOME-STYLE CURRY OF POTATOES AND CAULIFLOWER
33 STIR-FRIED OKRA
34 OMELETTE CURRY
36 GREEN MOONG TADKA WITH SCRAMBLED EGG
39 PUNJABI SPICED CHICKPEAS
40 MOREL MUSHROOM AND GREEN PEA CURRY
41 PANEER CHEESE IN CREAMY FENUGREEK SAUCE
42 SPICED GRATED PANEER WITH PEPPERS
45 PANEER BUTTER MASALA
46 PUNJABI-STYLE MUSTARD GREENS
47 GUJARATI-STYLE SWEET AND SOUR MIXED VEGETABLES
48 TAWA PALAK METHI MUSHROOM
51 POTATOES FILLED WITH PANEER AND DRIED FRUIT
52 BOTTLE GOURD AND YELLOW SPLIT PEA CURRY

BABY AUBERGINES WITH SESAME AND TAMARIND SAUCE

BAGHARE BAINGAN

There are different versions of this dish all over the country but the most popular one is from Hyderabad. It has rich, deep, earthy notes, and some recipes use fat green chillies alongside the aubergines, or even include lamb's liver in the sauce.

The term *baghare* refers to the tempering of the aubergines.

SERVES 4

12 baby aubergines
1½ teaspoons salt
2 tablespoons vegetable or corn oil
½ teaspoon mustard seeds
2 sprigs of fresh curry leaves
2 teaspoons Ginger-Garlic Paste (see page 202)
1 quantity of Boiled Onion Paste (see page 203)
¼ teaspoon ground turmeric
1 teaspoon red chilli powder
4 tablespoons tamarind paste
500ml (2 cups) water

For the masala paste
50g (½ cup) desiccated coconut
1 tablespoon peanuts
1 tablespoon sesame seeds
1 tablespoon coriander seeds
½ teaspoon cumin seeds
3 green chillies, chopped
2 tablespoons coriander stalks

To finish
a pinch of sugar
a sprig of mint, finely chopped
1 tablespoon Crisp Fried Onions (see page 203)

Make 2 deep slits in each aubergine, forming a cross from the base towards the stalk end but leaving the quarters attached. Leave the calyx and a little of the stalk on to hold the aubergine together. Sprinkle the aubergines with half the salt and set aside for a good 20 minutes.

Meanwhile, make the masala paste. Separately roast the coconut, peanuts, sesame, coriander and cumin seeds in a dry frying pan over a medium heat for a minute or two, then remove from the heat. Blitz them in a small food processor with the chillies and coriander stalks, adding just enough water to make a paste.

To cook the aubergines, heat 1 tablespoon of the oil in a large, heavy-based pan and fry them over a high heat for 2–3 minutes, stirring from time to time, until they are seared on all sides. Remove the aubergines from the pan and heat the remaining oil in it. Add the mustard seeds and curry leaves, let them crackle, then add the ginger-garlic paste and fry for 2–3 minutes, stirring constantly to prevent sticking. Add the onion paste and cook, stirring, until it turns light brown. Stir in the turmeric, red chilli powder and masala paste, reduce the heat and fry for 10–12 minutes, until the oil begins to separate from the mixture at the side of the pan. Now add the remaining salt and the tamarind paste and cook for 3–4 minutes.

Return the fried aubergines to the pan and mix well. Pour in the water and simmer for 10–12 minutes, until the aubergines are soft but still hold their shape. Finish with the sugar, chopped mint and fried onion. Serve with rice or Layered Parathas (see page 196).

Cook's note
Don't stir the aubergines too vigorously when simmering them in the sauce, as they break quite easily.

SEARED AUBERGINE STEAKS WITH SESAME TAMARIND SAUCE

This is a modern version of the previous recipe. Essentially it uses a Hyderabadi-style sauce but the aubergines are fried separately rather than cooked in the sauce. This technique is commonly seen in Bengal, while the spice mix is an adaptation of a housewives' recipe from the hills in Nainital. All in all, the dish uses techniques from various parts of India and combines the flavours beautifully.

SERVES 4

2 large aubergines
1 teaspoon salt
1/2 teaspoon ground turmeric
1/2 teaspoon red chilli powder
1 teaspoon fennel seeds
1/2 teaspoon black onion seeds
2 tablespoons gram (chickpea) flour
2 tablespoons rice flour
3 tablespoons vegetable or corn oil

For the stuffing
2 teaspoons fennel seeds, roasted in a dry frying pan and then coarsely pounded
1 teaspoon ground cumin
2 teaspoons ground coriander
3 teaspoons dried mango powder
1 teaspoon red chilli powder
1/2 teaspoon ground turmeric
1/2 teaspoon salt
1/4 teaspoon sugar
1/2 teaspoon black onion seeds
1/2 teaspoon carom seeds

For the sauce
2 tablespoons coriander seeds
1 tablespoon sesame seeds
1 teaspoon cumin seeds
50g (1/2 cup) desiccated coconut
4 tablespoons vegetable or corn oil
50g (1/2 cup) peanuts or cashew nuts
500ml (2 cups) water
4 dried red chillies
1/2 teaspoon mustard seeds
1/2 teaspoon black onion seeds
2 sprigs of fresh curry leaves
3 tablespoons Boiled Onion Paste (see page 203)
1 teaspoon red chilli powder
1/2 teaspoon ground turmeric
2 tablespoons tamarind paste
1 teaspoon salt
1/2 teaspoon sugar
25g (1/2 cup) fresh coriander, chopped

Combine all the ingredients for the stuffing and set aside.

Slice the aubergines into rounds 2cm (3/4-inch) thick. Make an incision on the side of each 'steak' towards the centre, then insert a small, sharp knife and make a pocket by turning the knife around. Fill the pockets with the dry spice stuffing, then rub the salt, turmeric, chilli powder, fennel seeds and black onion seeds over the outside. Set aside for 30 minutes to remove excess moisture.

For the sauce, roast the coriander, sesame and cumin seeds in a dry frying pan over a medium heat for a minute or so. Tip them out on to a plate and set aside. Roast the coconut in the same pan until golden, then add to the seeds. Heat a tablespoon of the oil in the pan, add the nuts and fry until golden. Put them in a food processor with the seeds and coconut, add the water and blend to a smooth paste.

Heat the remaining oil in a pan, add the red chillies and mustard seeds and let them crackle. Add the onion seeds and curry leaves, followed by the onion paste, and cook for 8–10 minutes, until the oil separates from the mixture. Now add the ground seed and nut paste and stir over a low heat for a couple of minutes. Add the chilli powder, turmeric and tamarind paste and cook gently for 15–18 minutes, until the sauce thickens. Stir in the salt, sugar and coriander, then remove from the heat and keep warm.

To cook the aubergine, mix together the gram flour and rice flour and use to dust the steaks. Heat the 3 tablespoons of oil in a large frying pan, add the aubergines and fry over a medium heat for about 1 1/2 minutes on each side, until golden brown and cooked through.

Divide the sauce between 4 serving plates and put the aubergine steaks on top. Serve with steamed rice, garnished with Tapioca Crisps (see page 190).

SEARED BOTTLE GOURD WITH CHICKPEA BREAD AND BOTTLE GOURD COOKED IN MILK

This was inspired by a dish on the menu at The Cinnamon Club called aubergine cooked three ways. I was toying with the idea of serving slices of bottle gourd filled with paneer and spices when I stumbled across this amazing bottle gourd curry cooked slowly in milk with curry leaves. The textures were superb and it had all the richness I was looking for, so I decided simply to fry some bottle gourd slices to provide another texture. The combination of rich bottle gourd curry with chickpea bread is also an absolute winner.

SERVES 4

For the chickpea bread

150g (1 cup) gram (chickpea) flour
100g (2/3 cup) plain flour
1 teaspoon salt
1cm (1/2-inch) piece of fresh ginger, chopped
1 green chilli, finely chopped
1 tablespoon chopped fresh coriander
1/2 teaspoon carom seeds
1/2 teaspoon red chilli powder
1/4 teaspoon ground turmeric
1 red onion, chopped
1 spring onion, chopped
1 tablespoon vegetable or corn oil
100ml (scant 1/2 cup) water
2 tablespoons ghee or butter

For the seared bottle gourd

500g (1lb 2oz) bottle gourd, peeled and cut into slices 1cm (1/2 inch) thick
1/2 teaspoon ground turmeric
1/2 teaspoon red chilli powder
1/2 teaspoon fennel seeds
1/2 teaspoon black onion seeds
1 teaspoon salt
2 tablespoons vegetable or corn oil
juice of 1/2 lime

For the bottle gourd curry

2 tablespoons vegetable or corn oil
1/2 teaspoon mustard seeds
1 dried red chilli
10 fresh curry leaves
1 onion, chopped
1cm (1/2-inch) piece of fresh ginger, chopped
4 green chillies, slit open lengthwise
500g (1lb 2oz) bottle gourd, peeled and cut into 5mm (1/4-inch) dice
1/2 teaspoon ground turmeric
1 teaspoon salt
250ml (1 cup) milk
juice of 1/2 lime
1 tablespoon chopped fresh coriander

For the sauce

4 tablespoons canned tomato purée
2 tablespoons butter
3 tablespoons single cream
1/2 teaspoon salt
1/2 teaspoon red chilli powder
a pinch of sugar
a pinch of dried fenugreek leaves

To make the bread dough, mix the gram flour and plain flour together in a bowl, then take out 3 tablespoons of the mixture and set aside for dusting. Add all the rest of the ingredients except the ghee and knead to make a stiff dough. Cover with a damp cloth and leave to rest for about 20 minutes.

Rub the bottle gourd slices with the spices and salt and set aside for about 20 minutes to remove excess moisture.

To make the bottle gourd curry, heat the oil in a saucepan and add the mustard seeds, dried chilli and curry leaves. When they crackle, add the onion and sauté until soft. Add the ginger and green chillies, followed by the bottle gourd, turmeric and salt, and sauté for a minute. Add half the milk, reduce the heat and cook, stirring occasionally, for 6–8 minutes, until the sauce thickens. Add the rest of the milk and continue cooking for about 10 minutes, till the bottle gourd is thoroughly tender. Squeeze the lime juice over, sprinkle in the coriander, then remove from the heat and keep warm.

Divide the bread dough into 4 pieces and shape them into balls. On a lightly floured surface, roll out each one into a circle about 15cm (6 inches) in diameter, dusting with the flour you set aside. Heat a large, non-stick frying pan or a flat griddle over a high heat and place a piece of dough on it. Cook for 3–4 minutes, until lightly browned underneath, then turn over and cook the other side. Reduce the heat, brush the top of the bread with some of the ghee or butter, then turn it over and cook until the colour has deepened. Brush the top again and repeat the process. Cook the remaining breads in the same way and keep warm. Clean out the pan with a dry kitchen cloth and heat the 2 tablespoons of oil for the seared bottle gourd in it. Remove any excess moisture from the bottle gourd slices with kitchen paper and place

them in the pan. Cook over a medium heat for 2–3 minutes, turning once, until they are just tender. Remove from the heat and squeeze the lime juice over.

For the sauce, put the tomato purée, butter and cream in a small pan and bring to the boil. Season with the salt, red chilli powder and sugar, then add the fenugreek.

To serve, pour the sauce on to 4 shallow plates or dishes and arrange the fried bottle gourd on top. Serve with the bottle gourd curry and chickpea bread.

Cook's notes

You could use wax gourd or another member of the marrow family instead of bottle gourd.

Any of the components of this dish would be very good on its own.

PUNJABI CHICKPEA FRITTERS IN YOGHURT CURRY

KADHI PAKORA

This is a firm favourite in most North Indian households. There are numerous versions of it, including ones from the Punjab, Rajasthan, Gujarat, Bengal-Orissa and Uttar Pradesh. The recipe below most closely resembles those from Uttar Pradesh.

I love this dish for its simplicity. It uses very basic ingredients yet there is an interesting play of textures and flavours. In a restaurant set-up, the kadhi is incredibly versatile and can easily be transformed into a soup or a sauce.

SERVES 4

For the yoghurt kadhi
500g (2 cups) plain yoghurt
2 tablespoons gram (chickpea) flour
600ml (2½ cups) water
1½ teaspoons salt
1 teaspoon ground turmeric
2 tablespoons ghee
2 dried red chillies
1 teaspoon cumin seeds
a sprig of fresh curry leaves
juice of 1 lemon

For the pakoras
4 red onions, thinly sliced
4 green chillies, finely chopped
½ teaspoon carom seeds
1 teaspoon red chilli powder
1 teaspoon salt
2.5cm (1-inch) piece of fresh ginger, finely chopped
10 large spinach leaves, finely shredded
1 tablespoon finely chopped fresh coriander
2 tablespoons gram (chickpea) flour
vegetable or corn oil for deep-frying

Start with the yoghurt kadhi. Whisk together the yoghurt, gram flour, water, salt and turmeric and pass through a fine sieve to get rid of any lumps. Place the mixture in a saucepan and bring to the boil over a medium heat, whisking constantly. Reduce the heat and simmer for 8–10 minutes, until it turns glossy and thickens enough to coat the back of a wooden spoon lightly. Skim off any scum or impurities that may have come to the surface. In a small pan, heat the ghee to smoking point. Add the dried chillies, cumin seeds and curry leaves and leave for a few seconds, until they splutter and crackle. Tip the contents of the pan over the yoghurt mixture and set aside.

Mix together all the ingredients for the pakoras except the flour and oil and set aside for 10 minutes or so, to allow the salt to draw out moisture from the onions and spinach. Sprinkle with the flour and mix lightly until the mixture just holds together.

In a large saucepan or a deep-fat fryer, heat the oil to 170°C/325°F. Drop in dessertspoonfuls of the batter to form small dumplings. Fry for 3–4 minutes, until crisp and golden, then drain on kitchen paper.

Bring the yoghurt kadhi back to the boil and drop the crisp fritters into it. Serve immediately, accompanied by steamed rice.

CHICKPEA POLENTA IN YOGHURT SAUCE

PITHOD KI SUBZI

Found only in Rajasthan, this is a very unusual vegetarian dish with yoghurt and gram flour as the primary ingredients. The technique is quite similar to that of set polenta or semolina gnocchi, and the combination of an unusual texture with a complex mix of spices provides a very interesting experience. This dish is good for the summer months and is best served with steamed rice.

SERVES 6

750g (3 cups) Greek-style yoghurt
500ml (2 cups) water
100g (2/3 cup) gram (chickpea) flour
1 teaspoon salt
1/2 teaspoon ground turmeric
1/2 teaspoon sugar
1/2 teaspoon garam masala
2.5cm (1-inch) piece of fresh ginger, finely chopped
2 tablespoons ghee
1 teaspoon fennel seeds
a pinch of asafoetida
vegetable or corn oil for frying

For the yoghurt sauce
2 tablespoons vegetable or corn oil
a pinch of asafoetida
1 1/2 teaspoons cumin seeds
4 cloves
1 onion, finely chopped
400g (1 2/3 cups) Greek-style yoghurt
2 tablespoons ground coriander
1/2 teaspoon ground turmeric
1/2 teaspoon red chilli powder
1 teaspoon salt
2 green chillies, slit lengthwise into quarters
200ml (scant 1 cup) water
a pinch of sugar (optional)
1cm (1/2-inch) piece of fresh ginger, cut into fine strips
20g (1/2 cup) fresh coriander, chopped
juice of 1/2 lemon

Whisk the yoghurt and water with the gram flour, salt, turmeric, sugar, garam masala and ginger, then set aside. Heat the ghee in a large, heavy-based pan, add the fennel seeds and sauté briefly, then add the asafoetida and stir for 30 seconds. As the flavours are released, add the yoghurt mixture and cook over a medium heat, stirring constantly, for 20–25 minutes, until the mixture thickens and acquires the consistency of a soft dough. Remove from the heat and transfer to a greased 15cm (6-inch) square baking tin. Chill for about 30 minutes, until set like a cake.

To make the sauce, heat the oil in a saucepan over a moderate heat and add the asafoetida, cumin and cloves. When they begin to crackle, add the onion and cook gently for 8–10 minutes, until soft but not coloured. Whisk the yoghurt with the ground coriander, turmeric, chilli powder and salt. Add to the onion, stirring constantly, and keep stirring until the mixture comes to the boil; this will prevent the yoghurt splitting. Add the green chillies and water, bring back to the boil and simmer for about 5 minutes.
Check the seasoning, adding more salt and the sugar to balance the taste if required. Stir in the ginger, fresh coriander and lemon juice and keep warm.
Cut the gram flour 'cake' into 2.5cm (1-inch) squares. Heat a thin layer of oil in a large frying pan and add the squares a few at a time. Fry for a couple of minutes, until the outside gets a golden brown crust, then turn and cook the other side. Serve the fritters on top of the hot sauce, or mix them into the sauce and bring to a simmer before serving.

Variation
POPPADOM CURRY (PAPAD KI SUBZI)

This imaginative use of the humble poppadom is unique to Rajasthan. Simply make the sauce as above, then cut 6 poppadoms into strips 2.5cm (1 inch) wide and simmer them in the sauce for 30 seconds–1 minute. Serve with Pilau Rice (see page 180).

CHICKPEA DUMPLINGS IN YOGHURT SAUCE

GATTE KI SUBZI

This Rajasthani dish symbolises austerity and creativity like no other. It is based on ingredients that are readily available in the dry, arid terrain of Rajasthan, where little else grows. By simply altering the proportions of these ingredients, the Rajasthanis have created a whole range of different dishes such as Kadhi Pakora (see page 23) and Pithod ki Subzi (see page 24).

These chickpea dumplings are a bit of an acquired taste for many people in the Western world but, as a curry that characterises the originality of Rajasthani vegetarian cuisine, it is quite unrivalled and thus deserves its place in this book.

SERVES 4

For the chickpea dumplings

250g (1⅔ cups) gram (chickpea) flour
½ tablespoon finely chopped fresh ginger
2 green chillies, finely chopped
½ teaspoon ground turmeric
a pinch of asafoetida
½ teaspoon cumin seeds, roasted in a dry frying pan
2 pinches of carom seeds
a pinch of bicarbonate of soda
1 teaspoon finely chopped mint
125g (½ cup) Greek-style yoghurt, tied in a muslin cloth and left hanging up overnight to drain
2 teaspoons ghee
½ teaspoon salt
vegetable or corn oil for deep-frying

For the yoghurt sauce

250g (1 cup) plain yoghurt
½ teaspoon ground turmeric
½ teaspoon ground coriander
1 teaspoon red chilli powder
2.5cm (1-inch) piece of fresh ginger, finely chopped
1 teaspoon salt
1½ tablespoons ghee
1 bay leaf
2 dried red chillies
½ teaspoon cumin seeds
1 onion, finely chopped
2 green chillies, slit open lengthwise
1½ teaspoons dried fenugreek leaves
250ml (1 cup) water
1 teaspoon mint leaves

Mix together all the ingredients for the dumplings except the oil and knead well, adding a very little water to form a firm but pliable dough. Cover with cling film and set aside for 15 minutes.

Divide the dough into 8 pieces and shape them into cylinders about 1cm (½ inch) in diameter, rolling them on the worktop with the palm of your hand. Now cut them into batons 4cm (1½ inches) long. In a large saucepan or a deep-fat fryer, heat the oil to about 120–140°C. Add the dumplings and fry for 6–8 minutes, until golden. Drain on kitchen paper and set aside.

For the yoghurt sauce, whisk the yoghurt, turmeric, coriander, chilli powder, ginger and salt together, then set aside. Heat the ghee in a heavy-based pan over a high heat and add the bay leaf, dried chillies and cumin seeds. When they crackle, add the onion and reduce the heat. Cook gently until the onion is translucent, then pour in the yoghurt mixture. Stir continuously, gradually increasing the heat, until the yoghurt comes to the boil. On no account stop stirring, or the yoghurt will split.

When the yoghurt starts to boil, add the green chillies, fenugreek leaves and water and simmer for 2 minutes. Now add the dumplings and simmer for 6 minutes, until they are heated through and have soaked up some of the sauce to thicken it slightly. Take care to add the dumplings just before you are ready to serve; if you leave them in the sauce for too long, they tend to soak up too much liquid and break up. Scatter with the mint leaves and serve hot, with a bread of your choice or even steamed rice.

Cook's note

If you don't want to fry the dumplings, you could wrap the dough cylinders in foil and poach them in a pan of salted water for 12–15 minutes, then cut them into short lengths and finish cooking in the sauce, as above. This works just as well and is much healthier.

Left to right
Chickpea Dumplings in Yoghurt Sauce (page 25); Chickpea Polenta in Yoghurt Sauce (page 24); Poppadom Curry (page 24).

WINTER VEGETABLE CURRY WITH CARROTS, PEAS AND TOMATOES

GAJJAR MUTTER TAMATAR KI SUBZI

This humble vegetable curry is cooked in almost every household in northern India. Generally considered too mundane to put on restaurant menus, it is an all-time favourite at home, and comes in many guises – made with cauliflower or turnips instead of the vegetables listed below, for example, or served with lots of sauce to accompany rice. If the water is omitted, this semi-dry dish goes down a treat with chapattis. I rather prefer the drier version, as the flavours are more pronounced.

SERVES 4

3 tablespoons vegetable or corn oil
1 bay leaf
4 green cardamom pods
1 teaspoon cumin seeds
3 onions, finely chopped
3 ripe tomatoes, blended to a purée
2.5cm (1-inch) piece of fresh ginger, finely chopped
2 green chillies, cut lengthwise in half
1/2 teaspoon ground turmeric
1/2 teaspoon red chilli powder
1 teaspoon ground cumin
1 teaspoon ground coriander
2 teaspoons salt
4 carrots, peeled and cut into 1cm (1/2-inch) dice
200g (1 1/3 cups) peas
250ml (1 cup) water
juice of 1 lemon
2 tablespoons chopped fresh coriander or dill

Heat the oil in a heavy-based pan, add the bay leaf, cardamom pods and cumin seeds and let them crackle. Add the chopped onions and cook over a fairly high heat until golden brown. Stir in the puréed tomatoes, ginger, green chillies, spices and salt and cook for 8–10 minutes, until the oil begins to separate from the mixture at the sides of the pan. Add the carrots and cook, stirring, for 2 minutes, then add the peas and cook for 3 minutes. Pour in the water and cook till the vegetables are tender but still retain a little bite. Check the seasoning, then stir in the lemon juice and sprinkle with the chopped herbs. Serve hot with with chapattis or Naan Bread (see page 192).

Cook's note

If you cut the carrots even smaller, in 5mm (1/4-inch) dice, and cook the mixture without adding any water, then it could be used as a topping for various canapés or as a filling for wraps (made using supermarket tortillas, if you like). Papdi – wheat crisps, available in Indian supermarkets – topped with this vegetable curry make a good canapé option.

HOME-STYLE CURRY OF POTATOES AND CAULIFLOWER

ALOO GOBHI

This is probably the most common and basic vegetable curry you will find anywhere in India. Cooked pretty much nine months of the year, it is one of those recipes that sparks an intense debate over authenticity. One of the disadvantages of its universal appeal is that there is no such thing as a universal recipe!

SERVES 4

3 tablespoons vegetable or corn oil
1 teaspoon cumin seeds
1 large onion, chopped
1 tablespoon Ginger-Garlic Paste (see page 202)
4 green chillies, slit open lengthwise
2 medium potatoes, peeled and cut into 2.5cm (1-inch) dice
1 cauliflower, divided into florets
1 teaspoon ground turmeric
2 teaspoons salt
2 tomatoes, chopped
$^1/_2$ teaspoon garam masala
1 tablespoon chopped fresh coriander
5cm (2-inch) piece of fresh ginger, cut into fine strips
juice of $^1/_2$ lime

Heat the oil in a wide, shallow pan and add the cumin seeds, followed by the onion. Sauté for about 5 minutes, until the onion is soft, then add the ginger-garlic paste and fry for a few seconds longer. Add the green chillies and potatoes and sauté over a high heat for a couple of minutes. Tip in the cauliflower, turmeric and salt, mix well, then reduce the heat. Cover the pan and cook for about 10 minutes, stirring occasionally to prevent sticking.

Add the tomatoes and garam masala and cook for about 5 minutes, until the vegetables are completely tender. Sprinkle in the chopped coriander and the ginger, squeeze over the lime juice and serve – either with chapattis or as a side dish.

Cook's notes

If you cut the cauliflower florets slightly bigger than the potatoes, they will cook in roughly the same time, rather than overcooking and disintegrating before the potatoes are done.

It's important to use a wide, shallow pan for this dish. If you use a deep pan or a wok instead, don't overcrowd it with the vegetables or they will start to disintegrate.

STIR-FRIED OKRA

A home-style stir-fry of okra, often cooked in North Indian homes in the rainy season when okra is abundant. It's a very simple dish but can be tricky to get right. If the okra is not dried properly after washing, or you add any water during cooking, it can become quite slimy and sticky. Many people don't like okra because they think it will be slimy, but cooked right it's a thing of beauty!

SERVES 4

- 6 tablespoons vegetable or corn oil
- 2 teaspoons cumin seeds
- 1/2 teaspoon fenugreek seeds
- 2 red onions, finely chopped
- 800g (1 3/4lb) okra, topped and tailed, then sliced into 1cm (1/2-inch) rounds
- 1 teaspoon ground cumin
- 1 teaspoon ground coriander
- 1 teaspoon red chilli powder
- 1 tomato, deseeded and cut into 1cm (1/2-inch) dice
- 3cm (1 1/4-inch) piece of fresh ginger, finely chopped
- 1 1/2 teaspoons salt
- 1 teaspoon dried mango powder
- 1/2 teaspoon garam masala (optional)

Heat the oil in a wide frying pan over a medium heat and add the cumin and fenugreek seeds. When they start to crackle, add the onions and fry until golden brown. Add the okra and cook over a fairly high heat for 6–8 minutes, until it is crisp and the juices have dried up. Add the ground cumin, coriander and chilli powder and cook, stirring occasionally, for 2 minutes. Now add the tomato and toss quickly over a high heat. Stir in the ginger, salt and mango powder. For an extra touch of flavour, add the garam masala, then serve immediately.

Cook's note

Stir as little as possible after adding the okra, otherwise the juices will make the dish slimy. The salt is added after the okra has dried up, as it draws out the juices. Plenty of oil and a high heat ensure that the okra becomes crisp.

OMELETTE CURRY

This rather simple dish, made with rolled-up spiced omelette, is quick and easy, yet impressive. You can be really imaginative with the flavourings and try whatever is in season. Serve as a main dish or an accompaniment.

SERVES 4

6 free-range hen or duck eggs
1 red onion, finely chopped
2 green chillies, deseeded and finely chopped
1/2 teaspoon cumin seeds, roasted in a dry frying pan and then coarsely crushed
1/2 teaspoon ground turmeric
1 tablespoon finely chopped chives
1 teaspoon finely chopped fresh coriander
1 1/2 teaspoons salt
1cm (1/2-inch) piece of fresh ginger, finely chopped
2 tablespoons vegetable or corn oil

For the sauce
3 tablespoons vegetable or corn oil
2 green cardamom pods
1 bay leaf
1 large onion, finely chopped
1 tablespoon Ginger-Garlic Paste (see page 202)
1 teaspoon red chilli powder
1/2 teaspoon ground cumin
1/2 teaspoon ground coriander
1/2 teaspoon ground turmeric
1 teaspoon salt
3 ripe tomatoes, puréed
1/2 teaspoon sugar
1/2 teaspoon garam masala
1 tablespoon chopped fresh coriander
1 tablespoon single cream
juice of 1/2 lemon

Break the eggs into a bowl and whisk them lightly with all the other ingredients except the oil. Heat the oil in a large, non-stick frying pan and pour in just enough egg mix to make a thin omelette. Cook, without stirring, over a medium-high heat until it begins to set, then remove from the pan (without turning it over) and roll into a cylinder, like a swiss roll. Repeat with the remaining egg mix. Cut the omelette rolls in slices 1.5cm (2/3 inch) thick and keep warm.

For the sauce, heat the oil in a pan, add the green cardamom and bay leaf and let them crackle for 30 seconds or so. Add the onion and cook until golden brown. Add the ginger-garlic paste and stir for a minute. Add the red chilli powder, cumin, coriander, turmeric and salt and cook for another minute or so. Stir in the puréed tomatoes and cook for 6–8 minutes, until the mixture has reduced by half. Add the sugar and garam masala, then finish with the fresh coriander, single cream and lemon juice.

Pour the sauce into a serving dish and arrange the omelette slices on top. Serve immediately.

Cook's note
You could add finely chopped raw vegetables, such as asparagus, spinach or artichokes, to the beaten egg if you like. Or experiment with the sauce, adding curry leaves and coconut milk if you want to make it more interesting.

GREEN MOONG TADKA WITH SCRAMBLED EGG

In Punjab and the rest of northern India, the term *tadka* refers to tempering cumin, chillies, onions, etc., before using them to finish lentils and similar dishes. The final addition of spices cooked in hot ghee gives them smokiness and a pronounced kick. In roadside cafés along the highways of eastern India, the meaning has become distorted, and *tadka* refers to a dish of green moong lentils. I've seen many variations of this lentil dish, some with a sauce made from chicken, lamb or even egg. This version uses egg.

SERVES 4

200g (1 cup) whole green moong lentils
2.5 litres ($2^1/_2$ quarts) water
1 tablespoon salt
1 tablespoon Ginger-Garlic Paste (see page 202)
1 bay leaf
3 black cardamom pods
4 tablespoons vegetable or corn oil
1 teaspoon cumin seeds
1 tablespoon chopped garlic
2 onions, very finely chopped
$1^1/_2$ teaspoons chilli powder
1 tablespoon ground coriander
3 very ripe tomatoes, puréed
2–3 green chillies, finely chopped
$^1/_2$ teaspoon garam masala
1 tablespoon butter
juice of $^1/_2$ lemon
4 free-range eggs, lightly beaten
1 tablespoon chopped fresh coriander

Wash the lentils, leave them to soak in cold water for 20 minutes, then drain. Put them in a pan with the water, three-quarters of the salt, plus the ginger-garlic paste, bay leaf and black cardamom pods. Bring to the boil and simmer for about 50 minutes, until the lentils are soft but still hold their shape.

Heat 2 tablespoons of the oil in a large, heavy-based pan and add the cumin seeds. When they crackle, add the garlic and fry until golden. Add three-quarters of the onions and cook till golden brown, then stir in the chilli powder and ground coriander. Cook for 3–5 minutes, until the oil starts to separate from the mixture round the edge of the pan. Add the puréed tomatoes and cook for 8–10 minutes. Pour the boiled lentils into this mixture, bring to the boil and simmer for 10–12 minutes. Add the green chillies and garam masala and cook gently until the onion mix and lentils are thoroughly combined and the lentils thicken the mix slightly so it is homogenous. Simmer for another 2–3 minutes, then add the butter and lemon juice. Transfer to a serving bowl.

Heat the remaining oil in a separate pan and sauté the remaining onion in it until translucent. Add the eggs and the remaining salt and cook gently, stirring to scramble the eggs. Pour the eggs over the lentils. Garnish with the coriander and serve hot, accompanied by Layered Parathas (see page 196) or Naan Bread (see page 192).

Cook's note

If you like, you could extend any leftover chicken or lamb curry by adding plain boiled green moong lentils to it and heating through thoroughly.

PUNJABI SPICED CHICKPEAS

PINDI CHOLEY

This classic Punjabi dish is also prepared with minor variations in Pakistan, Delhi and almost the entire north of India. Traditionally served with deep-fried leavened breads called *bhaturey*, it is just as good with steamed rice or served with tamarind chutney as part of *chaats* – a variety of tangy, sweet and sour mixes sold as street snacks in northern India.

Pindi choley refers to a rich, dark and earthy preparation of chickpeas in Rawalpindi style. *Pind* also refers to a Punjabi word for village, making this dish 'village-style chickpeas'. The characteristic colour comes from boiling the chickpeas in tin containers with the addition of dried gooseberries. Some people cheat and use tealeaves to add colour.

My version here is slightly different and does not call for dried gooseberries, which are a bit of an acquired taste. Instead the sourness comes from dried pomegranate seeds, which serve the dual purpose of adding flavour as well as texture.

SERVES 4

200g (1 cup) chickpeas, soaked in plenty of cold water overnight
a pinch of bicarbonate of soda (optional)
6 tablespoons vegetable or corn oil
2 black cardamom pods
1/2 teaspoon cloves
2 bay leaves
1 teaspoon cumin seeds
1/2 teaspoon asafoetida
2 onions, finely chopped
1 tablespoon Ginger Paste (see page 202)
1 teaspoon Garlic Paste (see page 202)
3 tomatoes, finely chopped
3 green chillies, chopped
2 teaspoons salt
2 teaspoons red chilli powder
1 tablespoon ground coriander
1 teaspoon dried mango powder
1 tablespoon dried pomegranate seeds (*anardana*), coarsely pounded
1 teaspoon sugar
juice of 1 lemon
2 tablespoons chopped fresh coriander
2.5cm (1-inch) piece of fresh ginger, cut into fine strips

Drain the chickpeas, put them in a large, heavy-based pan and pour in 2–2.5 litres (2–2 1/2 quarts) of water, or enough to cover the chickpeas generously. You could add a pinch of bicarbonate of soda to reduce the cooking time. Bring to the boil and simmer until the chickpeas are soft enough to give way when pressed between your fingers.

Heat the oil in a separate pan, add the cardamom pods, cloves and bay leaves and cook, stirring, over a high heat for 30 seconds. Add the cumin seeds and asafoetida and cook for 30–60 seconds, until the seeds crackle. Then add the onions and sauté for 6–8 minutes, until golden brown. Stir in the ginger and garlic pastes and sauté for another minute or two. Add the tomatoes and stir-fry them over a high heat for a couple of minutes. Add the green chillies and salt and cook for another 3 minutes. Add the chilli powder and ground coriander and cook for 6–8 minutes, until the mixture turns dark and the oil starts to separate round the edge of the pan.

Drain the chickpeas and add them to the pan. Using the back of a wooden spoon, mash a few chickpeas to thicken the gravy. Add the dried mango powder and crushed pomegranate seeds. Check the seasoning, add the sugar and lemon juice, then garnish with the coriander and ginger. Serve with steamed rice or bread.

Cook's notes

If you can't find dried pomegranate seeds, use 2–3 tablespoons of thick tamarind pulp instead; it works just as well.

If the water evaporates before the chickpeas are tender, add some boiling water from the kettle. It's always better to start with more water than you think will be necessary. Adding cold water to chickpeas just makes them tougher and they take forever to cook!

Rather than using dried chickpeas, you could substitute 2 drained cans of chickpeas.

MOREL MUSHROOM AND GREEN PEA CURRY

GUCHHI MUTTER

This is a once-in-a-while treat that would not be out of place in a five-star restaurant. Morels are extremely difficult to find in India and fresh ones are eaten only by wealthy families on very special occasions. You can use dried or fresh morels in this dish. When peas are in season, the delicate combination of morels with fresh peas is simply delightful. Otherwise, substitute frozen petits pois, which are very nearly as good.

SERVES 4–6

12–16 dried or fresh morel mushrooms
4 tablespoons vegetable oil or ghee
1/4 teaspoon royal (black) cumin seeds
3 green cardamom pods
1cm (1/2-inch) piece of cinnamon stick
2 onions, finely chopped
2.5cm (1-inch) piece of fresh ginger, chopped
3 garlic cloves, chopped
6 tomatoes, blended to a purée
1/2 teaspoon ground turmeric
1 teaspoon red chilli powder
1 teaspoon ground cumin
2 teaspoons salt
300g (2 cups) shelled fresh peas or frozen petits pois
2 tablespoons Crisp Fried Onions (see page 203)
3 tablespoons single cream
1 teaspoon finely chopped mint
1/4 teaspoon Mace and Cardamom Powder (see page 204)
a pinch of sugar (optional)
1 tablespoon butter

Soak the morels in warm water for 15 minutes (30 minutes if they are dried), then drain. Remove the stalks and wash the mushrooms in several changes of water to get rid of any sand or grit. Drain the mushrooms, dry them on kitchen paper and cut them into 2–4 pieces, depending on size. Set aside.

Heat the oil or ghee in a heavy-based pan and add the royal cumin, cardamom and cinnamon. Once they crackle and pop, add the onions and sauté over a moderate heat until golden brown. Add the ginger and garlic and sauté for 2–3 minutes, then add the puréed tomatoes, turmeric, chilli powder, ground cumin and salt. Cook over a medium heat for 10–12 minutes, until the oil starts separating from the mixture at the edge of the pan. Add the morels and sauté for 2 minutes, then add the peas and stir for a minute or so.

Add the fried onions, cream and chopped mint and mix well. Check the seasoning and stir in the mace and cardamom and a pinch of sugar, if necessary. Finally stir in the butter. Serve with Layered Parathas (see page 196) or any other bread.

Cook's note

It's impossible to say how long you should wash the morels. Just keep on washing them until all the grit and small particles have gone. If the morels are very small, it's better to cut them up before washing, as it will be easier to get rid of the dirt.

PANEER CHEESE IN CREAMY FENUGREEK SAUCE

PANEER METHI MALAI

This is one of several hundred paneer curries made in India. I find it interesting, as the combination of creamy paneer works very well with the fragrant, herbaceous fenugreek.

SERVES 4

100g (1 cup) fresh fenugreek leaves, chopped
4 tablespoons ghee or vegetable oil
1/2 teaspoon cumin seeds
1/4 teaspoon asafoetida
1 onion, finely chopped
2.5cm (1-inch) piece of fresh ginger, finely chopped
4 green chillies, slit open lengthwise
150g (2/3 cup) Boiled Cashew Paste (see page 202)
500g (1lb 2oz) paneer, cut into 1cm (1/2-inch) cubes
250ml (1 cup) whole milk
1 1/2 teaspoons salt
1/2 teaspoon sugar
125ml (1/2 cup) single cream
1 tablespoon dried fenugreek leaves
1/2 teaspoon Mace and Cardamom Powder (see page 204)
juice of 1/2 lemon

Bring about 1 litre (4 cups) of salted water to the boil in a saucepan. Add the fresh fenugreek leaves and when the water returns to the boil, drain them immediately and refresh in iced water. Set aside.

Heat the ghee or oil in a heavy-based pan, add the cumin and asafoetida, then the onion, and cook, stirring, until the onion is light golden brown. Add the ginger and green chillies, followed by the cashew paste, and stir for 4–6 minutes. Add the paneer, then the milk, and cook over a medium heat for about 5 minutes. Stir in the salt and sugar, followed by the cream, the fresh and dried fenugreek leaves and the mace and cardamom. Heat through gently, then squeeze in the lemon juice and remove from the heat. Serve with Layered Parathas (see page 196) or Pilau Rice (see page 180).

Cook's note

Do not cook for too long after adding the fresh fenugreek or it will discolour the dish and make it taste bitter.

SPICED GRATED PANEER WITH PEPPERS

PANEER BHURJI

Paneer is probably one of the most popular vegetarian ingredients in India. It is generally cooked in a curry but this way of serving it as a crumble or moist mash is very versatile, lending itself to many different uses. You can spread it on bread, use it as a filling for a wrap, or even as a pizza topping. If you spread it on naan bread and cut it into squares, it makes an excellent yet simple canapé.

SERVES 4

3 tablespoons vegetable or corn oil
1 teaspoon cumin seeds
1 onion, chopped
2.5cm (1-inch) piece of fresh ginger, chopped
4 green chillies, chopped
$^1/_2$ teaspoon ground turmeric
$^1/_2$ red pepper, cut into 5mm ($^1/_4$-inch) dice
$^1/_2$ green pepper, cut into 5mm ($^1/_4$-inch) dice
$^1/_2$ yellow pepper, cut into 5mm ($^1/_4$-inch) dice
$1^1/_2$ teaspoons salt
$^1/_2$ teaspoon sugar
300g ($10^1/_2$oz) paneer, grated
1 tablespoon chopped fresh coriander
juice of $^1/_2$ lemon
2 tablespoons single cream (optional)

Heat the oil in a frying pan and add the cumin seeds, followed by the onion, ginger and green chillies. Sauté until the onion is soft. Add the turmeric, then the peppers, salt and sugar, and sauté for a minute. Stir in the paneer and mix well. Sprinkle the fresh coriander on top and squeeze in the lemon juice. If the mixture feels dry, fold in the cream. Remove from the heat and serve with Naan Bread (see page 192).

PANEER BUTTER MASALA

Similar to chicken tikka masala in the UK, paneer butter masala is the most famous and widely interpreted paneer dish in India. I learned this recipe from contract banquet cooks from Orissa, who cooked at my sister's wedding and prepared this dish for 1,200 people. Needless to say, I've scaled it down several hundred times!

SERVES 4

4 tablespoons ghee or vegetable oil
½ teaspoon cumin seeds
4 green cardamom pods
2 black cardamom pods
1 bay leaf
1 large onion, finely chopped
1½ teaspoons salt
½ teaspoon ground white pepper
1 tablespoon Ginger-Garlic Paste (see page 202)
1½ teaspoons red chilli powder
5 ripe tomatoes, puréed
2 tablespoons whole milk powder
1 tablespoon Greek-style yoghurt
1 tablespoon Boiled Cashew Paste (see page 202)
500g (1lb 2oz) paneer, cut into 2.5cm (1-inch) rounds or dice
1 tablespoon dried fenugreek leaves
½ teaspoon garam masala
½ teaspoon sugar
3 tablespoons single cream
25g (2 tablespoons) cold butter, cut into small dice
1 tablespoon chopped fresh coriander
juice of ½ lemon

Heat the ghee or oil in a large, heavy-based casserole, add the cumin seeds, green and black cardamom pods and bay leaf and let them crackle. Add the onion and sauté over a high heat for 4–5 minutes, stirring constantly to prevent the onion colouring. Add the salt, then reduce the heat, cover and cook for 10–12 minutes, allowing the onion to soften and reduce to bring out its natural sweetness. Stir in the white pepper, ginger-garlic paste and chilli powder and cook for another 5 minutes, stirring constantly.

Now add the puréed tomatoes and cook gently for 10–12 minutes, until the tomatoes have reduced by half and the oil begins to separate from the mixture round the side of the pan. Add the milk powder and mix well, then stir in the yoghurt. Add the cashew paste and cook for 3–5 minutes. Add the paneer and cook, stirring, for a minute or so, taking care not to break it up.

Stir in the dried fenugreek, garam masala and sugar, followed by the cream, and simmer for another minute or two. Finally stir in the cold butter, a few pieces at a time, to emulsify the sauce; be careful not to let it boil. Sprinkle with the fresh coriander, squeeze in the lemon and serve, accompanied by Pilau Rice (see page 180) or Layered Parathas (see page 196).

Cook's note

Cooking the onion on a slow heat with the lid on is the secret to getting a really lovely, silky, velvety sauce that is unique to Paneer Butter Masala. Take your time to get the onion right and you will enjoy the dish that much more.

PUNJABI-STYLE MUSTARD GREENS

SARSON KA SÁAG

This rustic dish is a firm favourite in the winter months, when the fields in Punjab are filled with mustard and their greens are plentiful. The very mention of a rich mustard purée served with dollops of freshly churned homemade butter, jaggery and chickpea bread brings tears to Punjabi men's eyes!

SERVES 4

1 tablespoon vegetable or corn oil
1 small onion, sliced
1 turnip, roughly diced
1/2 carrot, roughly diced
2.5cm (1-inch) piece of fresh ginger, grated
2 garlic cloves, crushed
4 green chillies, slit open lengthwise
300g (10 1/2oz) bunch of mustard greens (available in most Asian supermarkets), roughly chopped
100g (3 1/2 oz) bunch of spinach, roughly chopped
1 teaspoon salt
1/2 teaspoon sugar

For the tempering
4 tablespoons mustard oil or vegetable oil
6 garlic cloves, chopped
1 onion, chopped
1 tablespoon cornmeal
50g (1/4 cup) unsalted butter
1/2 teaspoon garam masala
juice of 1/2 lime

Heat the oil in a heavy-based pan, add the onion, then cover and sweat until soft. Add the turnip and carrot and sweat for 3–4 minutes, until half cooked. Add the ginger, garlic and green chillies and cook for another 3–4 minutes. Now add the mustard greens and spinach to the pot, sprinkle with 2 tablespoons of water and add the salt and sugar. Cover and cook over a low heat until the vegetables are completely cooked in their own steam. Remove from the heat and blend to a smooth purée in a food processor.

To prepare the tempering, heat the oil in a pan and add the garlic, followed by the onion. Sauté until the onion turns golden, then add the purée and stir over a high heat for 4–5 minutes, until the onion and purée are well mixed and the oil is just about to start separating from the mixture. Sprinkle in the cornmeal, mix well and cook for 3–4 minutes. Add the butter and garam masala and mix them in thoroughly. Squeeze the lime juice over and remove from the heat.

Serve hot, accompanied by Chickpea Bread (see page 20), butter and crushed jaggery.

Cook's note
This dish can be served in different guises, as little canapés on squares of bread, as a spread, or as a dip for finger food.

GUJARATI-STYLE SWEET AND SOUR MIXED VEGETABLES

DHAN SAAK

This is probably one of the most popular dishes in any high-street curry house in the UK. The recipe comes from the Parsee community of Mumbai and it may seem like a lot of work but, believe me, this is the real McCoy!

SERVES 4–6

50g ($^1/_4$ cup) toor dal
50g ($^1/_4$ cup) moong dal (split yellow mung beans)
25g ($^1/_8$ cup) urad dal (white urid lentils)
50g ($^1/_4$ cup) masoor dal (red lentils)
25g ($^1/_8$ cup) chana dal (yellow split peas)
2 litres (8 cups) water
1 teaspoon ground turmeric
1$^1/_2$ teaspoons salt

For the dhan saak masala
4 dried red chillies
12 black peppercorns
$^1/_8$ nutmeg
8 cloves
$^1/_4$ teaspoon fenugreek seeds
1 teaspoon sesame seeds
1 tablespoon garam masala

For the vegetables
1 small potato, peeled and diced
1 carrot, diced
1 small onion, diced
1 small aubergine, cut into 2.5cm (1-inch) dice
2 tomatoes, deseeded and diced
200g (7oz) spinach
75g ($^3/_4$ cup) fresh fenugreek leaves
2 tablespoons coriander leaves
10–15 mint leaves
2 tablespoons grated fresh coconut
1 teaspoon salt
1.5 litres (6 cups) water

To finish
1 tablespoon vegetable or corn oil
1 tablespoon Ginger Paste (see page 202)
1 tablespoon Garlic Paste (see page 202)
4 tablespoons tamarind paste
500ml (2 cups) water

First make the dhan saak masala. Roast all the ingredients except the garam masala in a dry frying pan over a medium heat for a minute or so. Grind them in a spice grinder or coffee grinder, then stir in the garam masala and set aside.

Put all the pulses in a sieve and rinse them under cold running water until clean. Place in a heavy-based pan, add the water, turmeric and salt and bring to the boil. Simmer for $^3/_4$–1 hour, until the pulses are very tender. Blitz to a smooth paste in a food processor and set aside.

Put all the ingredients for the vegetables in a pan, bring to the boil, then reduce the heat and simmer until they are tender. Leave to cool, then purée the mixture in the pan, using a hand-held blender.

To finish the dish, heat the oil in a heavy-based pan and add the boiled pulses mixture. Cook over a high heat for 5 minutes, then add the ginger, garlic and tamarind pastes and cook for another 5 minutes, stirring all the while. Now add the puréed vegetables and keep on stirring for 6–8 minutes. Next stir in the dhan saak masala. When the masala is thoroughly incorporated, add the water. Correct the seasoning if required. Let the dhan saak cook for at least half an hour over a very low heat, stirring from time to time. When the mixture acquires the consistency of a thick sauce, remove from the heat. Serve with a chopped salad and rice (see notes below).

Cook's notes
Meat eaters could add pieces of chicken or meat after the masala and water have been added.

Traditionally Parsees prefer to let a little dhan saak stick to the bottom of the pan, which imparts a slightly burnt taste. If it gets too thick, however, add a little water.

Traditional accompaniments are *kachumbar* (a salad made of finely diced cucumber, tomato and onion seasoned with finely chopped coriander and mint leaves, along with a dash of vinegar, salt and pepper) and 'brown rice' (rice cooked with $^1/_4$ teaspoon of caramelised sugar to give it a light brown colour).

TAWA PALAK METHI MUSHROOM

Strictly speaking, this dish could be made in a kadhai, or Indian wok, rather than a tawa, but using a flat iron griddle increases the surface area and therefore makes the cooking much faster and more exciting.

You could add other ingredients to a simple dish like this, such as broccoli, cauliflower, peppers or paneer.

SERVES 4

250g (9oz) young spinach leaves
50g (1/2 cup) fresh fenugreek leaves
4 tablespoons vegetable or corn oil
2 dried chillies
1 teaspoon coriander seeds
1 teaspoon cumin seeds
3 garlic cloves, chopped
2 onions, finely chopped, plus 2 onions, thickly sliced
1/2 teaspoon ground turmeric
6 green chillies, finely chopped
2.5cm (1-inch) piece of fresh ginger, chopped
2 teaspoons ground cumin
1 teaspoon red chilli powder
1 teaspoon fennel seeds
6 tomatoes, chopped, plus 1 tomato, deseeded and cut into wedges
500g (1lb 2oz) chestnut mushrooms, cut in half, or quartered if large
2 teaspoons salt
250g (9oz) baby sweetcorn, cut lengthwise in half
2 teaspoons dried fenugreek leaves, crushed with your fingertips
juice of 1 lime

Wash the spinach leaves and fenugreek leaves separately to get rid of any earth or grit, then drain well. Roughly tear the spinach and set aside. Chop the fenugreek leaves roughly, discarding the stalks.

Heat the oil on a thick, heavy griddle pan and add the dried chillies, coriander seeds and cumin seeds. When they crackle, add the garlic and sauté until golden, then add the finely chopped onions and sauté until brown. Stir in the turmeric, green chillies, chopped ginger, cumin, chilli powder and fennel seeds and cook over a high heat for 2 minutes. Now add the chopped tomatoes and stir until the oil starts to separate from the mixture at the edge of the pan. Toss in the mushrooms over a high heat, add the salt and cook, stirring frequently, for 3 minutes. Add the baby sweetcorn and the thickly sliced onions and stir for a minute. Add the spinach and fresh fenugreek leaves and stir for 30 seconds or so. Add the tomato wedges and crushed dried fenugreek and stir for another minute or two. Finish with the lime juice. Serve with Naan Bread (see page 192) or Layered Parathas (see page 196).

Cook's note

If you don't have a large enough flat griddle for this dish, you could use a Chinese wok. Just take care not to add too much to it all at once, as this will bring down the temperature, causing all the juices to be released. This would make the dish very wet, which is not the point of this style of cooking!

POTATOES FILLED WITH PANEER AND DRIED FRUIT

This would work very well as a starter; just cut the potato shells in half and serve sprinkled with some chat masala and lemon juice. Served in slightly bigger portions, as below, it makes an impressive main dish for vegetarians. You could really substitute pretty much anything you like for the filling.

SERVES 4

8 medium Desiree potatoes, peeled
2 litres (8 cups) water
2 teaspoons salt
1 teaspoon ground turmeric
vegetable or corn oil for deep-frying

For the filling
4 dried figs, cut into 5mm (1/4-inch) dice
1 tablespoon raisins
1 1/2 tablespoons paneer, cut into 5mm (1/4-inch) dice
1/2 tablespoon cashew nuts, fried in a little oil until golden, then lightly crushed
1 poppadom, fried in oil until crisp, then lightly crushed
2.5cm (1-inch) piece of fresh ginger, finely chopped
2 green chillies, finely chopped
1 tablespoon chopped fresh coriander
1/2 teaspoon salt
juice of 1/2 lime

For the sauce
400g (14oz) tomatoes, cut in half
1cm (1/2-inch) piece of fresh ginger, crushed
2 garlic cloves, peeled
2 green cardamom pods
2 cloves
1 bay leaf
125ml (1/2 cup) water
1 teaspoon red chilli powder
25g (2 tablespoons) butter, diced
3 tablespoons single cream
1 teaspoon dried fenugreek leaves, crushed to a powder
1 teaspoon salt
2 teaspoons sugar

For the marinade
2 tablespoons Greek yoghurt
1 tablespoon single cream
1 teaspoon Ginger Paste (see page 202)
1 teaspoon Garlic Paste (see page 202)
1/2 teaspoon ground turmeric
1/2 teaspoon garam masala
1/2 teaspoon salt

Trim the potatoes with a sharp knife until they are an even cylindrical shape. Now scoop out the inside using a pointed peeler or knife to leave a shell about 5mm (1/4-inch) thick that is open at one end. Cut the trimmings into 5mm (1/4-inch) dice and set aside.

Put the water, salt and turmeric in a saucepan and bring to the boil. Add the potatoes and return to the boil, then drain. Dry the potatoes on kitchen paper.

Heat the oil for frying in a deep saucepan or a deep-fat fryer over a low to medium heat, add the potatoes and fry until golden and crisp. Remove and leave to drain on kitchen paper. Now fry the diced potato until golden brown. Drain on kitchen paper.

Mix all the ingredients for the filling with the fried diced potato and carefully use to stuff the potato shells.

For the sauce, put the tomatoes in a large saucepan with the ginger, garlic, cardamom, cloves, bay leaf and water. Bring to the boil and simmer until the tomatoes have completely broken down. Purée in a blender, then strain through a fine sieve into a clean pan. Bring to the boil again, add the chilli powder and simmer until the mixture begins to thicken. Whisk in the butter a little at a time to give a glossy sauce. Add the cream, fenugreek leaves, sugar and salt, mix well, then remove from the heat. Keep warm.

Mix together all the ingredients for the marinade and lightly apply to the outside of the potato shells. Transfer them to a roasting tray, place in an oven preheated to 180°C/350°F/Gas Mark 4 and roast for 10–12 minutes, until the potatoes are heated through and have become slightly coloured and crisp. Remove from the oven and serve with the sauce.

Cook's notes
When frying the potatoes, the trick is to fry them really slowly, so they get cooked properly and do not colour too much.

If you prefer, you could use a slow barbecue to cook the potato shells after filling them.

BOTTLE GOURD AND YELLOW SPLIT PEA CURRY

LAUKI CHANA

This simple dish combining bottle gourd and split peas is popular all over northern India. Some variations finish it with coconut milk, which is just as good.

SERVES 4

200g (1 cup) chana dal (yellow split peas), soaked in cold water for 30 minutes
1 litre (4 cups) water
1/2 teaspoon ground turmeric
2.5cm (1-inch) piece of fresh ginger, finely chopped
1 teaspoon salt
3 bottle gourds (lauki or doodhi), peeled, deseeded and cut into 2.5cm (1-inch) dice
2 teaspoons chopped fresh coriander

For tempering
2 tablespoons ghee or vegetable oil
1 teaspoon cumin seeds
2 red chillies
1/4 teaspoon asafoetida
1 onion, finely chopped
2 teaspoons ground coriander
1 teaspoon salt
1/2 teaspoon garam masala
juice of 1/2 lemon
1/2 teaspoon brown sugar or jaggery
1/2 teaspoon coarsely crushed fennel seeds

Drain the split peas and put them in a saucepan with the water, turmeric, ginger and salt. Bring to the boil, skimming off the scum that rises to the surface, then reduce the heat and simmer for 30 minutes or until the split peas are tender but retain a little bite. Add the diced bottle gourds and continue to simmer for 15–20 minutes, until the split peas are very tender and the bottle gourd is cooked through.

For the tempering, heat the ghee or oil in a heavy-based pan, add the cumin seeds and whole red chillies and fry until brown. Add the asafoetida and onion and sauté until the onion is golden brown. Add the ground coriander and salt and cook for 2–3 minutes.

Pour in the cooked split peas and bottle gourd, add the garam masala and simmer over a low heat for about 5 minutes, until the gourd and split peas come together. If you like the dish thick, simply cook it slightly longer until it reaches the desired consistency. Stir in the lemon juice, sugar or jaggery and fennel seeds and garnish with the chopped coriander.

Serve as a vegetarian main course with steamed rice or bread, or as an accompaniment.

SEAFOOD

56 SPICE-CRUSTED HALIBUT IN GREEN SPICED SAUCE
58 HALIBUT WRAPPED IN BANANA LEAF WITH COCONUT PASTE
59 FRESHWATER FISH COOKED WITH ONIONS
61 SEARED SEA BASS FILLET WITH FENUGREEK SAUCE AND POTATO AND BEAN STIR-FRY
64 BARRAMUNDI WITH KERALA CURRY SAUCE
65 BENGALI-STYLE FISH CURRY WITH MUSTARD PASTE
66 RAJASTHANI SPICE-CRUSTED MACKEREL WITH YOGHURT KADHI AND SPINACH PORIAL
68 ROAST SALMON WITH DILL AND MUSTARD, GREEN PEA RELISH
71 BENGALI-STYLE FISH COOKED WITH YOGHURT
73 ROAST COD FILLET WITH BENGALI-STYLE MUSTARD SAUCE AND RED ONIONS
74 POMFRET RECHEADO
76 SEARED BLACK BREAM WITH ROASTED AUBERGINE, TOMATO AND POTATO CRUSH AND KACHUMBER
79 TREASURE-OF-THE-EARTH WHOLE FISH COOKED IN A SEALED POT
80 STIR-FRIED SQUID WITH SWEET SPICES AND GREEN MOONG KEDGEREE
83 SEARED SCALLOPS WITH COCONUT AND GINGER SAUCE
84 KERALAN-STYLE MIXED SEAFOOD WITH COCONUT AND VINEGAR SAUCE
87 PRAWN BALCHAO
88 KING PRAWNS COOKED IN SAFFRON KORMA SAUCE
90 WILD PRAWNS BAKED WITH COCONUT AND MUSTARD
92 PRAWNS IN KERALA CURRY
93 KADHAI LOBSTER
96 BENGALI-STYLE GRILLED LOBSTER

SPICE-CRUSTED HALIBUT IN GREEN SPICED SAUCE

This is my take on a tandoori fish tikka, traditionally served with green chutney. The only difference is that I use a larger cut of fish and cook it in an ordinary oven rather than a tandoor, while the chutney is transformed into a hot sauce. Served with Lemon Rice (see page 181), it makes a stunning main course.

SERVES 4

4 x 200g (7oz) pieces of halibut fillet
1 tablespoon vegetable or corn oil

For the first marinade
1 teaspoon Ginger Paste (see page 202)
1 teaspoon Garlic Paste (see page 202)
$^{1}/_{2}$ teaspoon ground turmeric
1 teaspoon salt

For the second marinade
3 tablespoons Greek-style yoghurt
1 teaspoon yellow chilli powder
$^{1}/_{2}$ teaspoon salt
1 teaspoon coriander seeds, roasted in a dry frying pan and then crushed
1 teaspoon fennel seeds, roasted in a dry frying pan and then crushed
$^{1}/_{2}$ teaspoon cumin seeds, roasted in a dry frying pan and then crushed
$^{1}/_{2}$ teaspoon red chilli flakes

For the sauce
30g (1 cup) mint, roughly chopped
150g (3 cups) fresh coriander, roughly chopped
4 green chillies, finely chopped
250ml (1 cup) water
4 tablespoons vegetable or corn oil
4 garlic cloves, finely chopped
1 onion, finely chopped
5cm (2-inch) piece of fresh ginger, finely chopped
1 tablespoon gram (chickpea) flour
$1^{1}/_{2}$ teaspoons salt
1 teaspoon sugar
juice of $^{1}/_{2}$ lime

Pat the fish pieces dry on kitchen paper. Mix together all the ingredients for the first marinade, rub them over the fish and set aside for 10 minutes. Heat the oil in a large, non-stick frying pan, add the fish and sear for 1–2 minutes on each side, until lightly golden. Remove from the heat, drain on kitchen paper and keep warm.

Mix all the ingredients for the second marinade together and spread them over the fish. Place on a baking tray and bake in an oven preheated to 220°C/425°F/Gas Mark 7 for 8–10 minutes, turning once, until the fish is cooked through.

Meanwhile, prepare the sauce.
Mix the mint, coriander, green chillies, water and half the oil together and blend to a smooth paste in a food processor. Heat the remaining oil in a frying pan, add the garlic, onion and ginger and sauté till golden. Add the gram flour and stir for a few seconds, until the onion turns golden brown, with a sandy texture, and a nice roasted aroma begins to be released. Add the mint and coriander paste, plus the salt and sugar, and cook for about 2–3 minutes without allowing the sauce to discolour. Finish with the lime juice. Serve the fish with the sauce, accompanied by Lemon Rice (see page 181).

Cook's notes
You could apply both the marinades together without searing the fish if you are in a hurry.

To prepare this dish for a dinner party, the fish may be marinated a day before and simply cooked in the oven for 12–14 minutes before serving.

HALIBUT WRAPPED IN BANANA LEAF WITH COCONUT PASTE

This is quite similar to a Thai or Southeast Asian-style fish curry cooked in a banana leaf. Traditionally in India we steam these parcels but they would come out just as well from a low barbecue or an oven. If anything, I prefer them cooked on a barbecue as it adds a smoky element. If you can't get hold of banana leaf, wrap the fish in foil instead.

SERVES 4

4 x 150g (5oz) pieces of halibut fillet, skinned
1 banana leaf, cut into four 30cm (12-inch) squares
1/2 teaspoon red chilli flakes

For the coconut paste
1 tablespoon chopped fresh coriander
2 sprigs of mint, chopped
80g (scant 1 cup) fresh coconut, grated
2.5cm (1-inch) piece of fresh ginger, roughly chopped
4 garlic cloves, roughly chopped
6 green chillies, roughly chopped
125ml (1/2 cup) thick coconut cream
2 teaspoons cumin seeds, roasted in a dry frying pan
1/2 teaspoon ground turmeric
4 tablespoons vegetable or corn oil
juice of 1 lemon
2 teaspoons salt

Put all the ingredients for the coconut paste in a blender or food processor and mix to a smooth paste. Pat the halibut pieces dry and coat them thoroughly with the paste. Set aside for 30 minutes.

Place each piece of fish in a piece of banana leaf, sprinkle with the red chilli flakes and then wrap up the fish in the leaf, taking care to prevent any marinade and juices oozing out during cooking. Place the parcels in a steamer and steam for 10–15 minutes, until the fish is cooked through (or cook them on a low barbecue or in an oven preheated to 200°C/400°F/Gas Mark 6). Open up the parcels a little and serve immediately, with either Green Coconut Chutney (see page 197) or pickled onions.

Cook's note
This is an ideal dish for a dinner party, as you can simply wrap the fish beforehand and cook the parcels 15 minutes before you are ready to serve.

FRESHWATER FISH COOKED WITH ONIONS

BHEKTI DOPYAZA

This is a hugely popular traditional curry from West Bengal. The term *dopyaza* refers to the use of onions at 2 different stages of cooking. Traditionally bhekti fish would be used but tilapia and barramundi also work well.

SERVES 4

800g (1¾lb) tilapia, barramundi or similar fish fillets, skinned and cut into 5cm (2-inch) pieces
3 teaspoons salt
2 teaspoons ground turmeric
2 large onions
4 green chillies, deseeded and slit lengthwise in half
2 tablespoons chopped garlic
5cm (2-inch) piece of fresh ginger, finely grated
4 tablespoons ghee
3 tablespoons vegetable or corn oil
3 ripe tomatoes, skinned and chopped
250ml (1 cup) water
3 tablespoons chopped fresh coriander

For the ground spices
1 tablespoon coriander seeds
1 tablespoon cumin seeds
2.5cm (1-inch) piece of cinnamon stick
1 teaspoon green cardamom pods
5 cloves

Wash the fish and pat dry on kitchen paper. Mix with 1 teaspoon of the salt and 1 teaspoon of the turmeric and set aside.

Grind all the spices together using a spice grinder or coffee grinder, or a mortar and pestle.

Slice 1 onion into thick rounds and set aside. Finely chop the remaining onion and mix with the green chillies, garlic and ginger. Finally mix in the ground spices.

Heat the ghee and oil in a large saucepan, add the sliced onion and cook, stirring frequently, until light golden. Remove the onion from the pan with a slotted spoon, allowing the oil to drain back into the pan. Add the finely chopped onion mixture, the remaining turmeric and a teaspoon of the remaining salt to the pan and cook, stirring, for 15–18 minutes, until the colour darkens and the oil begins to separate from the mixture. Stir in the tomatoes and cook until the liquid from the tomatoes has almost evaporated. Add the fish pieces and stir carefully to avoid breaking them up. Add the water and remaining salt, then cover and cook for 12–15 minutes, until the fish is just done. Add the reserved fried onion, then cover and simmer for 3 minutes. Garnish with the chopped coriander and serve with steamed rice.

SEARED SEA BASS FILLET WITH FENUGREEK SAUCE AND POTATO AND BEAN STIR-FRY

This is one of those combinations that turn conventional wisdom about Indian food and wine pairings on its head. I find the herbaceous quality of fenugreek works very well with the Sauvignon Blancs of the New World, while their fresh, clean, mineral aspect is complemented by the mineral quality of the green beans. Try this for yourself!

SERVES 4

4 x 180g (6oz) sea bass fillets, scaled, trimmed and pin-boned
2 tablespoons vegetable or corn oil

For the fenugreek sauce
3 tablespoons vegetable or corn oil
1 onion, finely chopped
½ teaspoon ground turmeric
2.5cm (1-inch) piece of fresh ginger, finely chopped
2 green chillies, finely chopped
200g (scant 1 cup) Boiled Cashew Paste (see page 202)
200g (scant 1 cup) plain yoghurt
125ml (½ cup) fish stock
1 teaspoon salt
½ teaspoon sugar
juice of ½ lemon
2 tablespoons dried fenugreek leaves

For the marinade
1 teaspoon salt
½ teaspoon cumin seeds, crushed
½ teaspoon carom seeds
1 teaspoon finely chopped fresh ginger
juice of 1 lemon

For the potato and bean stir-fry
1 tablespoon vegetable or corn oil
½ teaspoon cumin seeds
1 large potato, peeled and cut into 5mm (¼-inch) dice
½ teaspoon salt
a pinch of ground turmeric
75g (3oz) fine green beans, cut into 5mm (¼-inch) dice

First make the fenugreek sauce. Heat the oil in a heavy-based pan, add the onion and sauté till golden brown. Add the turmeric, ginger and chillies, then stir in the cashew paste. Cook over a low heat, stirring constantly, for 4–5 minutes. Gradually add the yoghurt, stirring to prevent it splitting, then cook over a moderate heat for 2 minutes. Add the fish stock and cook for another 3 minutes. Now add the salt and sugar and adjust the seasoning if necessary. Stir in the lemon juice and fenugreek leaves, then remove from the heat and keep warm.

Pat the fish fillets dry on kitchen paper. Mix together all the ingredients for the marinade, rub them over the fish and set aside for 10 minutes.

Meanwhile, cook the stir-fry. Heat the oil in a large, heavy-based frying pan, add the cumin seeds and let them crackle. Add the potato, salt and turmeric and sprinkle with 1 tablespoon of water. Cover the pan and allow the potato to steam for 3–4 minutes. Remove the lid, stir the potatoes and add the beans. Cook, uncovered, for another 4–5 minutes, until the potatoes are tender but the beans do not discolour. Remove from the heat and keep warm.

To cook the sea bass, heat the oil in a large, non-stick frying pan, add the fish fillets, skin-side down, and cook over a medium heat for about 2 minutes on each side.

Divide the potato stir-fry between 4 plates and pour the sauce around it, then put the fish on top. Serve with steamed rice.

Cook's note
In order to get a crisp skin, don't move the fish around too much in the pan while it is cooking. You will see the belly side turning slightly opaque and that's a sign that the skin is nice and crisp. Simply turn the fillet over and then take the pan off the heat. The heat retained in the pan will complete the cooking perfectly.

‘THIS RATHER SIMPLE DISH, MADE WITH ROLLED-UP SPICED OMELETTE, IS QUICK AND EASY, YET IMPRESSIVE. YOU CAN BE REALLY IMAGINATIVE WITH THE FLAVOURINGS AND TRY WHATEVER IS IN SEASON.’

OMELETTE CURRY, PAGE 34

BARRAMUNDI WITH KERALA CURRY SAUCE

We use barramundi at The Cinnamon Club but in Kerala, where this dish originates, they use pearl spot, a local fish with a similar texture. If you prefer, you could try sea bass or black bream.

Traditionally this is made with fish and seafood cut into small pieces and simmered in the sauce. I prefer to cook whole fillets separately, as it enables you to appreciate the flavour and texture much better. It also makes for a more attractive presentation, particularly if you leave the skin on.

SERVES 4

4 x 200g (7oz) pieces of barramundi fillet
1 teaspoon salt
1/2 teaspoon black onion seeds
1/2 teaspoon red chilli flakes
1 tablespoon vegetable or corn oil
2 tablespoons pressed rice flakes (pawa), lightly roasted in a dry frying pan until golden

For the curry sauce
3 tablespoons vegetable or corn oil
1 teaspoon mustard seeds
1/2 teaspoon fenugreek seeds
10 fresh curry leaves
1 large onion, finely chopped
1/2 teaspoon ground turmeric
1 teaspoon ground coriander
1 1/2 teaspoons red chilli powder
3 tomatoes, finely chopped
2 kokum berries (or 2 tablespoons tamarind paste)
100ml (scant 1/2 cup) fish stock
125ml (1/2 cup) coconut milk
1 teaspoon salt
juice of 1/2 lemon

Pat the fish dry with kitchen paper, sprinkle with the salt, black onion seeds and red chilli flakes, then set aside for 30 minutes.

Meanwhile, make the sauce. Heat the oil in a heavy-based pan, add the mustard and fenugreek seeds and let them crackle for 30 seconds. Now add the curry leaves and onion and sauté for 6–8 minutes, until the onion is golden brown. Stir in the ground spices and tomatoes and cook over a high heat until the tomatoes are soft and completely disintegrated. Add the kokum berries and fish stock and simmer for 2–3 minutes. Stir in the coconut milk and salt and simmer for another couple of minutes or until the sauce has a creamy consistency. Squeeze in the lemon juice.

To cook the fish, heat the oil in a large, non-stick frying pan, add the fish fillets, skin-side down, and fry over a medium heat for 2–3 minutes on each side, until cooked through. Sprinkle the rice flakes evenly on top of the fish to form a crust. Pour the sauce on to 4 serving plates, place the fish on top and serve.

BENGALI-STYLE FISH CURRY WITH MUSTARD PASTE

SHORSHE BATA MAACH

This is a classic Bengali curry made using a fresh mustard-seed paste. Traditionally a freshwater fish called rohu is preferred here. It's ever so slightly oily and rich, which gives a unique taste to the dish, but it can be made just as well with any meaty white fish, such as perch, monkfish, cod or halibut.

SERVES 4

800g (1¾lb) meaty white fish fillets, skinned and cut into 4cm (1½-inch) dice
3 tablespoons mustard oil or vegetable oil
1 teaspoon black onion seeds
1 red onion, thinly sliced
2 green chillies, slit lengthwise into quarters
1 teaspoon salt
250ml (1 cup) water
4 tablespoons chopped fresh coriander

For the paste
1 tablespoon black mustard seeds
2 tablespoons yellow mustard seeds
6 green chillies, chopped

For the marinade
1 teaspoon salt
1 tablespoon Garlic Paste (see page 202)
1 tablespoon Ginger Paste (see page 202)
1 tablespoon mustard oil or vegetable oil
1 teaspoon ground turmeric

First make the paste. Put the black and yellow mustard seeds in a small bowl, add just enough water to cover and leave to soak for 3–4 hours. Put the mustard seeds in a small food processor with the green chillies and blitz to a paste, adding a little water. Set aside.

Pat the fish dry on kitchen paper. Mix together all the ingredients for the marinade, add the fish and coat well. Set aside for 10 minutes.

Heat 2 tablespoons of the mustard or vegetable oil in a heavy-based frying pan, add the fish and fry for 3–5 minutes, until just cooked. Remove the fish from the pan and set aside. Heat the remaining oil in the same pan, add the black onion seeds and let them crackle for 30 seconds. Add the red onion and stir for 2–3 minutes, until soft, then add the mustard paste, along with the slit green chillies. Fry the paste for 3–5 minutes, then add the salt, followed by the water. Bring to the boil, reduce the heat and add the fish pieces. Simmer for 2 minutes, then check the seasoning and stir in the chopped coriander. Cover with a lid, remove from the heat and leave to stand for 5–6 minutes. Serve with steamed rice.

Cook's notes

Take care not to make the mustard paste too fine or it will lose its grainy texture. Don't cook it for too long, as it can turn bitter.

Instead of making your own mustard paste, you could use 2 tablespoons of English mustard and 1 tablespoon of wholegrain Dijon mustard.

RAJASTHANI SPICE-CRUSTED MACKEREL WITH YOGHURT KADHI AND SPINACH PORIAL

This is not exactly the sort of dish Mum would cook! Mackerel is not to be found for hundreds of miles from Rajasthan but I find the play of spices with this fish very intriguing. A mixture of cloves, pepper, fennel and cinnamon – all in all quite strong, robust flavours – is more usually associated with the traditional game cooking of Rajasthan. Interestingly, British mackerel stands up really well to the spices and works like a dream.

SERVES 4

1 teaspoon cloves
1 teaspoon fennel seeds
1/2 teaspoon black peppercorns
5cm (2-inch) piece of cinnamon stick
1 teaspoon cumin seeds
1/2 teaspoon red chilli powder
4 large mackerel fillets, pin-boned and trimmed
1 tablespoon vegetable or corn oil
1 teaspoon salt
juice of 1/2 lemon

For the yoghurt kadhi
175g (3/4 cup) plain yoghurt
1 tablespoon gram (chickpea) flour
250ml (1 cup) water
1/2 teaspoon salt
a small pinch of ground turmeric
1 tablespoon ghee
1 dried red chilli
1/2 teaspoon cumin seeds
a sprig of fresh curry leaves
juice of 1/2 lemon

For the curry leaf spinach porial
2 tablespoons corn or vegetable oil
1 teaspoon mustard seeds
a sprig of fresh curry leaves
1 onion, finely chopped
1/2 teaspoon salt
1 green chilli, finely chopped
200g (7oz) spinach, including the stalks, finely shredded
100g (1 cup) fresh or frozen grated coconut

Start with the yoghurt kadhi. Whisk together the yoghurt, gram flour, water, salt and turmeric and pass through a fine sieve to get rid of any lumps. Place in a saucepan over a medium heat and bring to the boil, whisking constantly. Reduce the heat and simmer for 5–8 minutes, until the sauce turns glossy and thickens enough to coat the back of a wooden spoon lightly. Skim off any scum or impurities from the surface. In a small pan, heat the ghee to smoking point. Add the red chilli, cumin seeds and curry leaves and leave for a few seconds, until they splutter and crackle. Tip the contents of the pan over the sauce, squeeze in the lemon juice and set aside.

Prepare the fish next. Pound together all the spices to a coarse consistency, then mix them with the chilli powder. Sprinkle them over the mackerel on both sides. Mix together the oil, salt and lemon juice and drizzle them over the fish. Place the fillets under a hot grill, skin-side up, and cook for 8–10 minutes, until they are just done.

Meanwhile, for the porial, heat the oil in a frying pan, add the mustard seeds and curry leaves and cook for 10–15 seconds, until they start to crackle. Add the onion and sweat for about 5 minutes, until translucent. Now add the salt and chilli and stir for a minute. Add the spinach and cook, stirring, for 2–3 minutes. Finally stir in the coconut and heat through, then remove from the heat.

To assemble, pour the yoghurt kadhi into 4 deep bowls or plates and put the mackerel fillets on top. Place the porial over the fish as a garnish and serve immediately.

Cook's note
Using spinach stalks as well as leaves in the porial gives a much better flavour and texture.

ROAST SALMON WITH DILL AND MUSTARD, GREEN PEA RELISH

You could argue that, strictly speaking, this is not a curry, but by playing about with the proportions of a dish you can get many interesting results and that's precisely what we see here! It makes a fantastic light meal on a hot summer's day. The green pea relish has a kick reminiscent of Japanese wasabi.

SERVES 4

4 x 175g (6oz) pieces of wild salmon fillet
1 tablespoon vegetable or corn oil
1 quantity of Green Pea Relish (see page 188)

For the first marinade
1 teaspoon Ginger Paste (see page 202)
1 teaspoon Garlic Paste (see page 202)
1 teaspoon salt
1 teaspoon finely ground white pepper
1 teaspoon vegetable or corn oil

For the second marinade
2 tablespoons grated processed Cheddar cheese
2 tablespoons Greek-style yoghurt
1 tablespoon wholegrain mustard
2 green chillies, finely chopped
1 tablespoon single cream
1 teaspoon finely chopped dill

Pat the fish dry on kitchen paper. Mix together all the ingredients for the first marinade, rub them over the fish and set aside for 15 minutes.

Meanwhile, make the second marinade. Put the cheese in a small bowl and rub it to a paste with your fingers (a teaspoon of flour could be added to help prevent lumps forming). Add the yoghurt and mix to a smooth paste, then add the wholegrain mustard and chillies and finally mix in the cream and dill.

Heat the oil in a large ovenproof frying pan, add the fish and sear for about 1½ minutes on each side. Remove from the heat and spread the second marinade over the fish. Transfer to an oven preheated to 180°C/350°F/Gas Mark 4 and cook for 10–12 minutes, until the fish is just done. Drizzle with mustard oil and serve with a dollop of the Green Pea Relish, plus a green salad.

Cook's notes
Rather than marinating the fish when needed, you could keep it in the fridge overnight after applying the second marinade and cook it just before serving. Similarly the chutney can be prepared in advance and served either cold or warm, let down with a little water if it becomes too thick.

This recipes also works very well with swordfish.

BENGALI-STYLE FISH COOKED WITH YOGHURT

DOI MAACH

Doi maach literally translates as 'yoghurt fish'. In some communities, there is a myth that fish and milk should not be consumed at the same meal, as it is bad for the digestion, but this recipe from Bengal dispels the myth by combining the two in the same dish! An age-old favourite, it's an almost permanent fixture at Bengali banquets. It's easy to prepare and goes very well with plain rice.

You could use halibut or, if you want to try a freshwater fish, perch or carp.

SERVES 4

1kg ($2^1/_2$lb) firm white fish fillets, skinned and cut into 4cm ($1^1/_2$-inch) pieces
4 tablespoons mustard oil
3 cloves
2 green cardamom pods
2.5cm (1-inch) piece of cinnamon stick
1 teaspoon black peppercorns
1 dried bay leaf
1 teaspoon mustard seeds
2 onions, finely chopped
1 teaspoon salt
4 green chillies, slit open lengthwise
200g (scant 1 cup) plain yoghurt
1 tablespoon chopped fresh coriander

For the marinade
200g (scant 1 cup) plain yoghurt
1 teaspoon red chilli powder
1 teaspoon ground turmeric
1 tablespoon Ginger Paste (see page 202)
1 tablespoon Garlic Paste (see page 202)

Combine all the ingredients for the marinade, add the fish pieces and mix gently until they are well coated. Set aside to marinate for at least 30 minutes.

Heat 3 tablespoons of the mustard oil in a large, heavy-based pan over a medium heat. Add the cloves, cardamom, cinnamon, peppercorns and bay leaf and fry for 30 seconds, then add the mustard seeds and let them splutter. Add the onions and fry for 4–6 minutes, until translucent. Now add the fish and its marinade and mix gently but thoroughly. Add the salt and cook for 4 minutes, stirring occasionally. Add the slit green chillies, stir in the yoghurt and cook over a medium heat for 6–8 minutes, until the fish is done.

Garnish with the coriander and drizzle the remaining mustard oil over the top. Serve with steamed rice.

ROAST COD FILLET WITH BENGALI-STYLE MUSTARD SAUCE AND RED ONIONS

This is a deconstructed version of a *dopyaza* – a traditional Indian dish that derives its name from the addition of onions at two stages. In my version, the garnish of seared onions adds crunch and visual drama.

SERVES 4

4 x 180g (6oz) pieces of thick cod fillet (or pollack or any other firm white fish)
1 tablespoon vegetable or corn oil

For the mustard sauce
2 tablespoons mustard oil
1 bay leaf
1/2 teaspoon black onion seeds
1/2 teaspoon fennel seeds
1 onion, finely sliced
1 teaspoon Ginger Paste (see page 202)
1 teaspoon Garlic Paste (see page 202)
1/2 teaspoon red chilli powder
1/2 teaspoon ground turmeric
1 tomato, finely chopped
2 tablespoons wholegrain mustard
500ml (2 cups) fish stock or water
3 green chillies, slit lengthwise in half
1 teaspoon salt
1/2 teaspoon sugar
1/4 teaspoon garam masala
1 tablespoon chopped fresh coriander

For the marinade
1/2 teaspoon black onion seeds
1/2 teaspoon fennel seeds
1 dried red chilli, coarsely crushed
1 tablespoon vegetable or corn oil
1 teaspoon salt

To garnish
2 teaspoons ghee or butter
1 red onion, cut into rings
a pinch of black onion seeds
a pinch of salt
juice of 1/2 lemon

First make the sauce. Heat the oil in a heavy-based pan, add the bay leaf, onion seeds and fennel seeds, then quickly add the onion. Sauté until the onion is golden brown, then add the ginger and garlic pastes, chilli powder and turmeric. Stir-fry over a medium heat for 3–4 minutes, then add the tomato and cook for 4–5 minutes, stirring frequently so the mixture doesn't stick to the bottom of the pan. Add the mustard and cook over a medium heat for 3 minutes. Now pour in the stock or water and bring to a simmer.

Add the green chillies, salt, sugar, garam masala and coriander, then cover the pan and simmer for 2–3 minutes. Check the seasoning, remove from the heat and set aside.

Mix together all the ingredients for the marinade, rub them over the fish and set aside for 10–15 minutes. To cook the fish, heat the oil in a large, ovenproof frying pan, add the cod, skin-side down, and sear for 3 minutes. Turn and sear the other side for 2 minutes, then transfer the pan to an oven preheated to 200°C/400°F/Gas Mark 6 for 6–8 minutes, until the fish is just cooked.

Meanwhile, for the garnish, heat the ghee or butter in a frying pan, add the onion rings and cook, stirring constantly, until tender and well browned. Sprinkle with the black onion seeds and salt and drizzle with the lemon juice.

To serve, pour the sauce on to 4 deep plates, place the fish on top and garnish with the onion rings.

POMFRET RECHEADO

This Goan recipe is hardly a curry, in the sense that there is little or no sauce, but the spicing is very upfront and, cooked fresh, the fish doesn't really need a sauce. Although some people cook the fish entirely in a pan, you could finish it in the oven if you prefer. It also works well on a barbecue, as long as it's not too hot.

4 whole pomfret, cleaned
1 teaspoon salt
4 tablespoons vegetable or corn oil
juice of 1 lime

For the spice paste
5cm (2-inch) piece of cinnamon stick
8 green cardamom pods
1 tablespoon cloves
10 dried red chillies
2 tablespoons black peppercorns
2 teaspoons cumin seeds
2 tablespoons groundnut or vegetable oil
2 red onions, sliced
12 garlic cloves, chopped
5cm (2-inch) piece of fresh ginger, cut into fine strips
250ml (1 cup) dark malt vinegar
2 teaspoons salt
$^1/_2$ teaspoon sugar

To make the spice paste, roast all the whole spices together in a frying pan over a medium heat for a minute or so, then set aside.
Heat the oil in a frying pan, add the onions, garlic and ginger and sauté until golden brown. Remove from the heat and add to the whole spices. Add the vinegar and leave to soak for about 3 hours (or overnight). Grind the mixture to a coarse paste in a food processor and mix in the salt and sugar.

Slash the fish 2 or 3 times on each side, using a sharp knife. Season with the salt and set aside for 10 minutes. Rub the spice paste over the fish and stuff any excess inside the belly. Set aside for another 30 minutes.

Heat the oil in a large frying pan, add the pomfret and sear for a minute on each side. Transfer to a roasting tray and place in an oven preheated to 180°C/350°F/Gas Mark 4. Cook for 10–12 minutes. Remove from the oven, squeeze the lime juice over and serve with mashed potatoes and/or a green salad.

Cook's note
Feel free to use any white fish for this, such as black bream, sea bass or even Dover sole.

SEARED BLACK BREAM WITH ROASTED AUBERGINE, TOMATO AND POTATO CRUSH AND KACHUMBER

I love this dish for its simplicity. The aubergine crush and kachumber are probably two of the most familiar Indian accompaniments and might be considered mundane in some circumstances, but the combination with a simple fried fillet of bream is stunning. It's a great dish for entertaining, as much of it can be prepared in advance.

SERVES 4

4 black bream fillets (or any white fish), pin-boned
1 tablespoon vegetable or corn oil
1 quantity of Roasted Aubergine, Tomato and Potato Crush (see page 186)

For the kachumber
1/4 small cucumber, deseeded and cut into 3mm (1/8-inch) dice
1/2 carrot, cut into 3mm (1/8-inch) dice
1 tomato, deseeded and cut into 3mm (1/8-inch) dice
1/2 teaspoon salt
1 teaspoon sugar
juice of 1 lemon
2 tablespoons good olive oil
1 tablespoon finely chopped fresh coriander

For the marinade
1 teaspoon salt
1/2 teaspoon fennel seeds
1/2 teaspoon black onion seeds
1/2 teaspoon red chilli flakes

First make the kachumber. Place the diced cucumber, carrot and tomato in a mixing bowl. Whisk together the salt, sugar, lemon juice, olive oil and coriander to make a dressing and mix it with the diced vegetables. Check the seasoning.

Mix together all the ingredients for the marinade, rub them over the fish and set aside for 10 minutes.

Heat the oil in a large, non-stick frying pan, add the black bream fillets, skin-side down, and sear for 3–4 minutes, until well coloured underneath. Turn and cook for another 2 minutes or until just cooked through.

To serve, place the Roasted Aubergine, Tomato and Potato Crush in the centre of each plate and put the fish on top, then drizzle the kachumber around the plate.

TREASURE-OF-THE-EARTH WHOLE FISH COOKED IN A SEALED POT

ZAMEEN DOZ

This dish would originally have been cooked in an earthenware pot, using catfish or freshwater fish such as carp. Local potters would make beautiful fish-shaped pots in different sizes that would be just right for the fish being cooked. A pit would be dug in the ground, then the pot lowered into it, covered with burning cow-dung cakes and left to cook for hours. You can get more or less the same result by cooking the fish in a covered casserole in a very low oven.

Kingfish, pomfret, tilapia, sea bass, small barramundi, trout and black bream would all work well here.

SERVES 4

2 x 900g (2lb) whole fish, cleaned
1 teaspoon salt
juice of 2 limes
2 tablespoons ghee or clarified butter
2 tablespoons chopped coriander stalks
2 tablespoons Crisp Fried Onions (see page 203)

For the spice paste
2 blades of mace
6 black peppercorns
seeds from 4 black cardamom pods (discard the shells)
3 tablespoons fennel seeds
½ tablespoon royal (black) cumin seeds
1 tablespoon poppy seeds
1 tablespoon ground almonds
2 tablespoons desiccated coconut
300g (1¼ cups) Greek-style yoghurt
5cm (2-inch) piece of fresh ginger, roughly chopped
5 garlic cloves, roughly chopped
6 cloves, fried in 1 tablespoon ghee
2 teaspoons red chilli powder
4 green chillies, finely chopped
1 teaspoon ground turmeric
3 tablespoons gram (chickpea) flour
a pinch of saffron strands, infused in 2 tablespoons warm milk
1½ teaspoons salt
½ teaspoon sugar

To seal
250g (1⅔ cups) plain flour
125ml (½ cup) water

Slash the fish 3 or 4 times on each side with a sharp knife. Rub in the salt and lime juice and set aside for 15 minutes.

To make the spice paste, lightly roast all the dried whole spices (except the cloves) with the nuts in a dry frying pan, then blitz them to a smooth paste in a food processor with the yoghurt, ginger and garlic. Mix with all the remaining ingredients for the spice paste and smear the fish with the mixture inside and out. Set aside any excess.

Take an earthenware dish, with a tight-fitting lid, that is long enough to hold both fish side by side and grease it with the ghee or clarified butter (alternatively, you could line the dish with a banana leaf). Place the fish in it and cover with any excess spice paste. Mix together the flour and water to make a dough for sealing the lid and stretch it into a thin strip, long enough to cover the edge of the lid all the way round. Stick the dough on to the edge of the lid and place it on the dish, pressing lightly to make sure that it is completely sealed. Place in an oven preheated to 140°C/275°F/Gas Mark 1 and bake for 1 hour.

Remove the dish from the oven and carefully take the lid off. Sprinkle the chopped coriander stalks and fried onions on top of the fish and serve from the dish.

Cook's note
With a dish like this, don't worry about overcooking the fish. It's quite acceptable to cook it until the flesh is melting off the bone and has thoroughly absorbed the myriad flavours from the spices.

You could ask your fishmonger to butterfly the fish if you prefer to cook it without the bones.

STIR-FRIED SQUID WITH SWEET SPICES AND GREEN MOONG KEDGEREE

Kedgeree, or khichri as it is known in India, is a humble dish perfectly suited to cold, rainy days. When it is combined with smoky-sweet, spicy squid, there is a fascinating interaction of textures and flavours. You can replace the squid with octopus, prawns, shrimps or pretty much any shellfish you like.

SERVES 4

2 tablespoons vegetable or corn oil
500g (1lb 2oz) cleaned squid, cut into 1cm (1/2-inch) rings
50g (1 cup) fresh coriander, chopped
juice of 1 lemon

For the spice paste
10 cloves
1/2 teaspoon black peppercorns
1/2 teaspoon coriander seeds
1/2 teaspoon cumin seeds
2.5cm (1-inch) piece of cinnamon stick
1 tablespoon vegetable or corn oil
1 small onion, finely chopped
2 garlic cloves, finely chopped
1 1/2 teaspoons red chilli powder
1 tablespoon tomato purée
2 dried apricots, finely chopped
1 teaspoon salt
1/2 teaspoon sugar
100ml (scant 1/2 cup) water

For the kedgeree
100g (1/2 cup) split yellow moong lentils
400ml (1 2/3 cups) water
a pinch of ground turmeric
3 tablespoons ghee or clarified butter
1/2 teaspoon cumin seeds
4 garlic cloves, finely chopped
1 large onion, chopped
1cm (1/2-inch) piece of fresh ginger, finely chopped
2 green chillies, finely chopped
1 1/2 teaspoons salt
75g (1/3 cup) basmati rice, boiled
2 tablespoons sprouted green moong lentils
1 tomato, deseeded and cut into 1cm (1/2-inch) dice
2 tablespoons chopped fresh coriander
juice of 1 lemon

For the spice paste, roast the cloves, peppercorns, coriander seeds, cumin seeds and cinnamon stick on a baking sheet in a very low oven for a few minutes to remove any moisture. Grind them to a powder in a spice mill.

Heat the oil in a small pan, add the onion and sauté until golden brown. Add the garlic and sauté for a couple of minutes, then stir in the ground spices and chilli powder. Stir briskly for a few seconds, then add the tomato purée, dried apricots, salt and sugar. Add the water and cook over a medium heat for 4–6 minutes, until the mixture takes on a jammy consistency. Remove from the heat and set aside.

To make the kedgeree, wash the yellow moong lentils, put them in a pan with the water and turmeric and bring to the boil. Simmer for about 20 minutes, until the lentils are tender and all the water has evaporated. Remove from the heat and set aside.

Heat 2 tablespoons of the ghee or butter in a pan, add the cumin seeds and garlic and cook gently until golden. Add the onion and sauté until it begins to colour, then stir in the ginger and green chillies and cook for a minute. Stir in the yellow moong lentils and salt, then fold in the cooked rice. Add the sprouted green moong lentils, tomato and fresh coriander and stir over a low heat for 3–4 minutes. Finish with the remaining tablespoon of ghee or butter and the lemon juice. Remove from the heat and keep warm.

To cook the squid, heat the oil in a large, heavy-based frying pan until it starts to smoke. Add the squid rings and stir quickly until they begin to sear and colour in parts. Add the spice paste and stir-fry for a few seconds, until it coats the squid evenly. Sprinkle in the fresh coriander and squeeze over the lemon juice.

Divide the kedgeree between 4 plates and serve with the squid on top.

Cook's note
The secret to beautifully cooked, juicy squid is getting the pan very hot – i.e. to smoking point – then adding just enough squid to cover the pan in a single layer. If you add too much at once, or put it in an only moderately hot pan, all the juices will come out and the squid will bubble away to rubber. If you don't have a large enough pan to cook all the squid at once, do it in 2 batches.

SEARED SCALLOPS WITH COCONUT AND GINGER SAUCE

Inspired by the Keralan favourite, *moily* – a fish curry made with coconut milk, curry leaves, green chillies and ginger – this recipe highlights the beauty of simplicity. Probably one of the quickest and easiest dishes in the book, it always turns out a winner.

SERVES 4

1 tablespoon vegetable or corn oil
500g (1lb 2oz) fresh king scallops
1 teaspoon sea salt
1 teaspoon coriander seeds, roasted in a dry frying pan and then crushed
½ teaspoon cumin seeds, roasted in a dry frying pan and then crushed
½ teaspoon red chilli flakes

For the sauce
2 tablespoons coconut oil or vegetable oil
10 fresh curry leaves
1 onion, sliced
2.5cm (1-inch) piece of fresh ginger, cut into strips
4 green chillies, slit open lengthwise
½ teaspoon ground turmeric
500ml (2 cups) coconut milk
1 teaspoon salt

First make the sauce. Heat the oil in a large frying pan, add the curry leaves, onion, ginger and green chillies and cook, stirring, until the onion is soft. Add the turmeric, followed by the coconut milk and salt, and bring to a simmer. Cook for 3–5 minutes, until the sauce begins to turn glossy and thickens enough to coat the back of a spoon lightly.

To cook the scallops, heat the oil in a large, heavy-based frying pan, add the scallops and sear for about 1 minute per side, until golden brown. Sprinkle the salt on top and remove from the pan. Mix together the coriander and cumin seeds and chilli flakes and spread them on top of the scallops to give an even crust. Place them under a hot grill for 30 seconds. Serve with the sauce, and some steamed rice on the side.

Cook's note
Some people take the roe off scallops before cooking, but I like to leave it on; it tastes very good with the sauce. You could serve the scallops on wilted spinach or small rice pancakes, if you prefer.

KERALAN-STYLE MIXED SEAFOOD WITH COCONUT AND VINEGAR SAUCE

SEAFOOD MAPPAS

This recipe comes courtesy of Rakesh Nair, our sous-chef at The Cinnamon Club, who besides being a chef happens to have two Masters degrees – one in Mathematics and the other in Computer Sciences! When he introduced me to this recipe, it immediately stood out from typical southern Indian curries. The use of vinegar really lifts the spices and the fish. Easy to make, this one is a must try.

SERVES 4

200g (7oz) headless raw prawns, peeled and de-veined
200g (7oz) salmon fillet, skinned and cut into 2.5cm (1-inch) dice
200g (7oz) white fish fillet, such as halibut, cod or pollack, skinned and cut into 2.5cm (1-inch) dice
100g (3½oz) cleaned squid, cut into rings
200g (7oz) mussels, scrubbed and de-bearded

For the sauce
3 tablespoons vegetable or corn oil
4 garlic cloves, chopped
2.5cm (1-inch) piece of fresh ginger, cut into thin strips
2 red onions, finely sliced
4 green chillies, slit open lengthwise
2 tablespoons ground coriander
250ml (1 cup) seafood stock (or fish stock)
4 tablespoons toddy (palm) vinegar (replace with malt vinegar if necessary)
1 teaspoon salt
250ml (1 cup) coconut milk (if using canned milk, separate the thick milk from the thin part)
1 teaspoon garam masala

For tempering
1 tablespoon coconut oil or vegetable oil
½ teaspoon mustard seeds
10 fresh curry leaves
2 shallots, finely chopped

First make the sauce. Heat the oil in a pan, add the garlic, ginger and onions and sauté for 6–8 minutes, until the onions are really soft. Add the green chillies and ground coriander and cook, stirring, for a minute. Add the stock, vinegar and salt and simmer for 10 minutes.

Now add the prawns and cook over a medium heat for 2–3 minutes. As the sauce thickens, add about half the thin coconut milk, then add the salmon and white fish. Cover the pan and cook over a low heat for 2–3 minutes. Now add the remaining thin coconut milk, followed by the squid, and stir gently. Allow the liquid to come back to a simmer and then add the mussels. Simmer only until the mussels have opened up, then stir in the garam masala and thick coconut milk and remove from the heat.

To make the tempering, heat the oil in a small frying pan and add the mustard seeds, followed by the curry leaves and shallots. Sauté until the shallots have turned golden. Pour the tempering over the curry and cover with a lid. Leave for 5 minutes, to allow the flavours to permeate, then serve with steamed rice.

PRAWN BALCHAO

Although you could store this in the fridge for several days and serve it hot or cold as a pickle, it tastes just as delicious fresh and hot. You may find the portions slightly small for a main course but it works best combined with other dishes, and on its own may be a bit too spicy and full-on for a balanced meal. Try to combine it with a mild and saucy curry, such as Seafood Mappas (see page 84).

SERVES 4

4 tablespoons vegetable or corn oil
3 red onions, chopped
10 fresh curry leaves
1 tablespoon Ginger Paste (see page 202)
1 tablespoon Garlic Paste (see page 202)
4 green chillies, slit open lengthwise
$^1/_2$ teaspoon ground turmeric
600g (1lb 5oz) medium prawns, peeled
2 teaspoons salt
1 teaspoon sugar
3 tablespoons malt vinegar

For the spice mix
1 tablespoon cumin seeds
1 tablespoon black peppercorns
10 dried red chillies

For the spice mix, roast the ingredients separately in a dry frying pan over a medium heat for a minute or so, then grind together until fine.

Heat the oil in a large frying pan, add the onions and curry leaves and cook, stirring, until golden brown. Add the ginger and garlic pastes and green chillies and stir for a minute. Add the turmeric, followed by the spice mix and prawns, and sauté over a high heat for 4–5 minutes, until the prawns are cooked. Add the salt, sugar and malt vinegar and cook for another 4–5 minutes, until the oil separates from the mixture. Serve with steamed rice.

Cook's note
You could make the mixture as above, but omitting the prawns, then spread it over large butterflied prawns and grill them. Served with a salad of your choice, this makes an excellent summer lunch, washed down with a glass of fruity white wine.

KING PRAWNS COOKED IN SAFFRON KORMA SAUCE

JHINGA NISHA

This recipe from the courts of the Nawabs of Lucknow is a fine example of sophisticated Muslim cooking. Rich and regal, it is a true celebration dish. It may well have been the original korma that has been severely travestied many times over to end up in the ubiquitous British high-street curry house.

SERVES 4

1kg ($2^1/_4$lb) king prawns, peeled and de-veined (keep 200g (7oz) of the shells for the stock)
6 green cardamom pods
3 blades of mace
60g ($^2/_3$ cup) blanched almonds
60g ($^2/_3$ cup) unsalted cashew nuts
3 tablespoons ghee
2 large onions, finely chopped
4 green chillies, finely chopped
5cm (2-inch) piece of fresh ginger, finely chopped
a pinch of saffron strands, infused in 3 tablespoons warm milk
$1^1/_2$ teaspoons salt
100ml (scant $^1/_2$ cup) single cream
2 tablespoons finely chopped fresh coriander

For the stock
500ml (2 cups) water
$^1/_4$ teaspoon ground turmeric
2 green cardamom pods
2 blades of mace
1 bay leaf
$^1/_2$ carrot, thickly sliced
2 garlic cloves, crushed
2 black peppercorns

First make the stock. Wash the 200g reserved prawn shells in cold water and place them in a large pan with all the remaining stock ingredients. Bring to the boil, then reduce the heat and simmer for 15 minutes. Strain through a fine sieve and set aside.

Grind 3 of the cardamom pods and 1 blade of mace in a mortar and pestle, then set aside.

Add the almonds and cashew nuts to a pan of boiling water and simmer for 30–40 minutes, until softened. Drain well, reserving the liquid. Place the nuts in a food processor and blitz to a smooth paste, adding some of the reserved cooking liquid if required.

Heat the ghee in a wide, shallow pan over a medium heat. Add the remaining cardamom pods and mace blades and stir for 30 seconds. Now add the onions and sauté until golden. Add the chillies and ginger and sauté for 1 minute, then mix in the nut paste. Stir over a low to medium heat for 6–8 minutes, until the ghee separates out and the paste starts to leave the side of the pan.

Add the prawns and 4 tablespoons of the stock. Keep stirring, adding a further 2–4 tablespoons of stock 2 or 3 times, until the prawns begin to turn pink and the sauce is a coating consistency. Mix in the saffron milk and salt and simmer for a minute longer, until the prawns are cooked. Add the cream, heat through and transfer to a serving dish. Sprinkle with the ground mace and cardamom and the fresh coriander. Serve with steamed basmati rice or Layered Parathas (see page 196).

Cook's note
Take care while simmering the almond and cashew paste, as it may splutter and cause a nasty injury. The safest way is to cook it with the lid on, removing the lid every minute or so to stir with a long-handled spatula.

WILD PRAWNS BAKED WITH COCONUT AND MUSTARD

BHAPA BAGDA

This would make a great party dish, and it's certainly one that will impress. In India it is reserved for special occasions and intimate gatherings. The use of coconut, mustard, chilli and ginger creates an interesting play of flavours; the sweetness of the prawns and coconut is balanced by the heat from the chilli and ginger and the pungency of the mustard oil.

SERVES 4

8 large wild prawns (or ordinary large prawns if you can't get wild ones)
250ml (1 cup) thick coconut milk
100ml (scant ½ cup) Greek yoghurt
75g (3 oz) yellow mustard seeds, soaked overnight in just enough water to cover, then blended to a paste with 2 tablespoons white vinegar
6 green chillies, slit open lengthwise
5cm (2-inch) piece of fresh ginger, cut into thin strips
2 teaspoons salt
1½ teaspoons sugar
2 tablespoons Ginger-Garlic Paste (see page 202)
5 tablespoons mustard oil
1 teaspoon black mustard seeds
50g (1 cup) fresh coriander, finely chopped
1 teaspoon garam masala

Slice each prawn horizontally in half, with the head and shell still on. With the point of a sharp knife, remove the dark intestinal vein that runs down the back, then pat the prawns dry on kitchen paper.

Whisk together the coconut milk, yoghurt, mustard seed paste, chillies, ginger, salt, sugar, and ginger-garlic paste, then set aside.

In a frying pan, heat the mustard oil to smoking point and then let it cool. Reheat the oil and add the mustard seeds. Once they crackle, add the coconut and spice mixture and bring to the boil over a low heat, whisking constantly; be careful not to let the mixture separate. Simmer gently for 2–3 minutes, then remove from the heat.

Arrange the slit prawns on a baking tray, shell-side down. Pour the sauce over the tails and cover the tray with foil. Place in an oven preheated to 180°C/350°F/Gas Mark 4 and cook for 15–18 minutes, until the prawns are done. Remove from the oven, sprinkle with the chopped coriander and garam masala and serve immediately, with steamed rice.

Cook's note
You could simmer the prawns in a large, wide casserole dish instead of baking them; just take care not to move them around too much or they will break. They will still taste great, however!

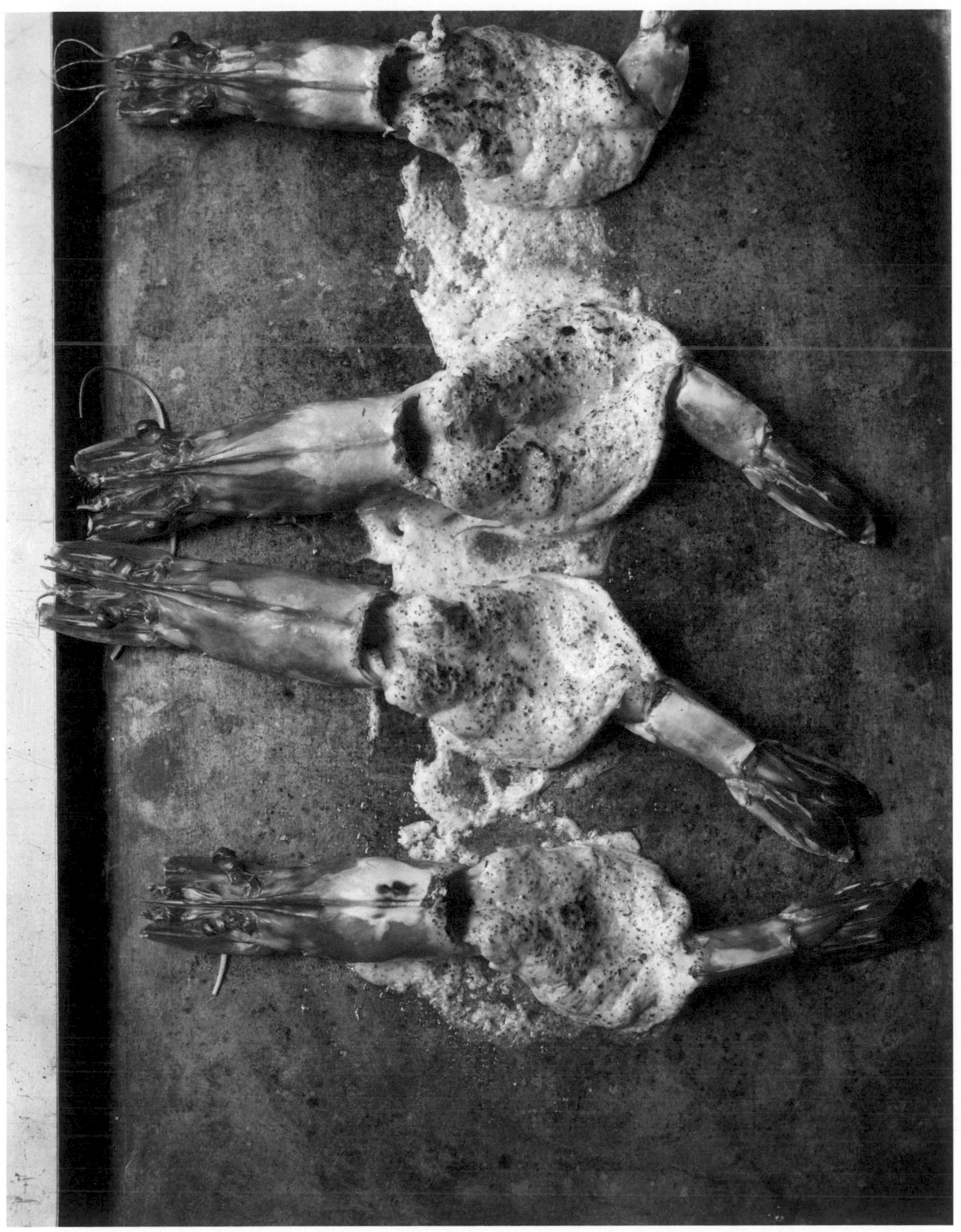

PRAWNS IN KERALA CURRY

This is one of my favourite curries. I still remember an outstanding version cooked for me on a boat in the backwaters of Kerala. It's hard to imagine something as simple as this could taste so delicious.

This is the complete opposite of what people tend to expect from Indian curries. Rather than being rich, heavy and thick, it has fresh flavours and a lightness of touch that quite simply make it one of the best curries of all time.

4 tablespoons vegetable or corn oil
1/2 teaspoon black peppercorns
1 teaspoon mustard seeds
1/2 teaspoon fenugreek seeds
10 fresh curry leaves
2 red onions, chopped
1/2 teaspoon ground turmeric
1 teaspoon ground coriander
2 teaspoons mild red chilli powder
2 tomatoes, finely chopped
1 teaspoon salt
20 king prawns, peeled and de-veined
4 kokum berries (or 2 tablespoons tamarind paste)
150ml (2/3 cup) seafood stock (or fish stock)
200ml (scant 1 cup) coconut milk

Heat the oil in a pan, add the peppercorns, mustard and fenugreek seeds, followed by the curry leaves and onions, and sauté until golden brown. Add the ground spices, tomatoes and salt and cook until the tomatoes are soft and completely disintegrated. Add the prawns and toss well for 3–5 minutes to coat them in the spice mixture. Stir in the kokum berries and stock and simmer for 2–3 minutes. Stir in the coconut milk and simmer for another 3–5 minutes, until the prawns are cooked and the sauce has a creamy consistency. Check the seasoning and adjust if necessary. Serve with steamed rice.

Cook's note

You could make this with a variety of seafood instead of simply prawns. Just be sure to work out a sequence in which to add them to the curry. It's best to start with firm fish, if using any, followed by prawns, then add mussels and squid at the end.

KADHAI LOBSTER

A kadhai is an Indian wok, usually made of iron, that differs from the Chinese wok in that it is much heavier and has 'ears' on the sides. Rather like Chinese stir-fries, Indian kadhai dishes are drier than traditional curries and use quick-cooking ingredients over a high heat, with the addition of crushed spices rather than finely ground ones.

Usually chicken, thin strips of lamb, pre-cooked kebabs or paneer are cooked using this method but I've taken it to another level by using lobster. It's a dish fit for a celebration!

SERVES 4

2 x 675g (1½lb) live lobsters
1 tablespoon butter
1 onion, diced
½ red pepper, deseeded and diced
½ yellow pepper, deseeded and diced
4 green chillies, slit open and cut into 8 pieces each
1 teaspoon red chilli flakes
½ teaspoon freshly cracked black peppercorns
1 tablespoon single cream
1 teaspoon dried fenugreek leaves, crushed with your fingertips
juice of ½ lemon
2 tablespoons chopped fresh coriander

For the kadhai masala
4 tablespoons vegetable oil
2 green cardamom pods
2.5cm (1-inch) piece of cinnamon stick
1 teaspoon cumin seeds, coarsely crushed
1 teaspoon coriander seeds, coarsely crushed
1 teaspoon fennel seeds, coarsely crushed
2 red onions, finely chopped
3 garlic cloves, chopped
2.5cm (1-inch) piece of fresh ginger, finely chopped
2 teaspoons red chilli powder
4 tomatoes, deseeded and finely chopped
1½ teaspoons salt
½ teaspoon garam masala

Put the lobsters in the freezer for about 2 hours, until comatose. Then plunge them into a large pan of boiling water and simmer for just 3 minutes. Remove from the pan and place them in a large bowl of ice for about 15 minutes, until chilled. Cut each lobster lengthwise in half and remove the flesh from the shell. Twist the claws off the body and crack them using the heel of a heavy knife. Remove the claw meat from the shells and set aside. Cut the body meat into 1cm (½-inch) dice and set aside.

For the kadhai masala, heat the oil in a kadhai or heavy-based pan, add the cardamom, cinnamon, cumin, coriander and fennel seeds and let them crackle. Add the chopped onions and sauté until golden brown, then add the garlic, ginger and red chilli powder and sauté for 1–2 minutes. Now add the chopped tomatoes and cook for 4–6 minutes, until the tomatoes are soft and the mix is homogenised. Stir in the salt and garam masala, remove from the heat and set aside.

In a separate pan, heat the butter and sear the lobster claw meat until lightly coloured all over. Add the onion, peppers and green chillies and sauté for about 3 minutes, until softened. Add the diced lobster meat and sauté over a high heat for 2 minutes. Add the chilli flakes and cracked pepper, then pour in the cooked masala and simmer for 2–3 minutes. Once the lobster meat is cooked through, check the seasoning. Stir in the cream and fenugreek, then finish with the lemon juice and chopped coriander. Serve with steamed rice.

Cook's notes
A fantastic way to present this dish is in the lobster shells. Simply dry the shells out first by putting them in a moderate oven for 5–6 minutes.

Although this is a kadhai dish, it works just as well in a tawa – i.e. a flat iron griddle. If using a griddle, just call your dish Tawa Lobster instead!

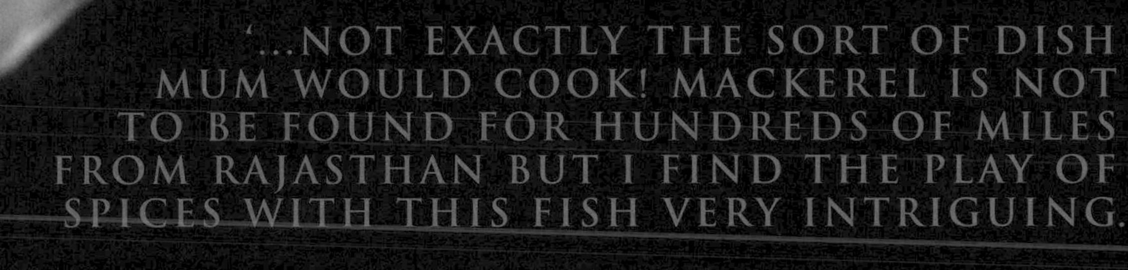
'...NOT EXACTLY THE SORT OF DISH MUM WOULD COOK! MACKEREL IS NOT TO BE FOUND FOR HUNDREDS OF MILES FROM RAJASTHAN BUT I FIND THE PLAY OF SPICES WITH THIS FISH VERY INTRIGUING.'

RAJASTHANI SPICE-CRUSTED MACKEREL WITH YOGHURT KADHI AND SPINACH PORIAL, PAGE 66

BENGALI-STYLE GRILLED LOBSTER

This is a very simple curry. The flavours are light and clean but it is the taste of the lobster that is most pronounced – as it should be! It makes an ideal light main course or a starter for an elaborate dinner party.

SERVES 4

2 x 675g ($1^1/_2$lb) live lobsters
2 tablespoons vegetable or corn oil
1 teaspoon salt
1 teaspoon ground cardamom
$^1/_2$ teaspoon sugar
2 tablespoons chopped fresh coriander
2 tablespoons thick coconut milk
juice of 1 lemon

For the claw meat
2 tablespoons vegetable or corn oil
1 large onion, finely chopped
2.5cm (1-inch) piece of fresh ginger, finely chopped
$^1/_2$ teaspoon red chilli powder
1 teaspoon red chilli flakes
1 teaspoon coriander seeds
1 teaspoon fennel seeds
1 tomato, finely chopped
1 teaspoon salt

Put the lobsters in the freezer for about 2 hours, until comatose. Then plunge them into a large pan of boiling water and simmer for just 3 minutes. Remove from the pan and place in a large bowl of ice for about 15 minutes, until chilled. Cut each lobster lengthwise in half. Twist the claws off the body and crack them open using the heel of a heavy knife, then remove the meat and set aside. Pat the lobster halves dry on kitchen paper.

Heat the oil in a large, heavy-based frying pan, add the lobster halves, flesh-side down, and sear for 1 minute, until the meat just starts to colour. Remove the lobsters from the pan and sprinkle with the salt, cardamom, sugar and coriander. Drizzle the coconut milk and lemon juice over and place under a hot grill for 8–10 minutes, until the lobster is cooked through and a light crust has formed.

Meanwhile, cook the claw meat. Heat the oil in a small frying pan, add the onion and sauté until golden brown. Add the claw meat and stir-fry over a high heat for 1–2 minutes. Add the ginger, chilli powder, chilli flakes, coriander and fennel seeds and sauté for a couple of minutes more. Now add the tomato and cook for about 3 minutes, until the tomatoes has blended in well and the mix is coating the claw meat. Season with the salt and remove from the heat.

Pile up the claw meat in the head cavity of the lobster halves and serve with a salad.

MEAT

100 RACK OF LAMB WITH SAFFRON SAUCE
102 RAAN
103 MODERN RAAN
106 SPICED MINCED LAMB WITH LIVER
107 LAMB NECK FILLET WITH MASALA MASH
108 HYDERABADI-STYLE LAMB BIRYANI
110 NARGISI KOFTA CURRY
113 LAMB COOKED WITH WINTER VEGETABLES AND SPINACH
114 FIERY RAJASTHANI LAMB CURRY
116 BRAISED SHOULDER OF YOUNG LAMB WITH MINT AND ONION
119 LAMB SHANKS WITH SAFFRON AND ROSEWATER
120 LAMB CURRY WITH WHITE SPICES
123 LAMB AND BEETROOT CURRY
124 LAMB CURRY WITH GREEN CHILLIES AND MINT
125 LAMB ROGAN JOSH
126 MEATBALL CURRY
128 MUGHAL-STYLE AROMATIC CURRY OF LAMB SHANKS
129 DECCAN LAMB COOKED WITH LENTILS
131 PUNJABI-SPICED MUTTON CHOPS AND MINCE
132 MUTTON COOKED WITH LENTILS, DRIED FRUIT AND NUTS
133 RAJASTHANI SEMI-DRY CURRY WITH MUTTON
136 MUTTON KOLHAPURI
137 BHOPAL-STYLE GOAT CURRY
138 BEEF BHUNA, BENGALI STYLE
141 SPICE-CRUSTED RIB EYE STEAK WITH MASALA SAUTÉED POTATOES
143 ROAST PORK CHOPS WITH SWEET SPICES, MUSTARD MASH AND DATE AND CHILLI SAUCE
144 COORG PORK STIR-FRY
146 PORK VINDALOO

RACK OF LAMB WITH SAFFRON SAUCE

This is the type of recipe that cries out to be modernised. It was one of the first to get me thinking about deconstructing traditional Indian dishes and creating contemporary versions. I've always maintained that simmering a fine rack of lamb in a sauce until it is cooked through is a waste of good meat. Instead, this method of roasting the meat separately and serving it with a sauce made according to the principles of French cuisine adds a different dimension to the concept of curry.

SERVES 4

2 racks of lamb, cut in half
1 tablespoon vegetable or corn oil

For the marinade
1 tablespoon Ginger Paste (see page 202)
1 tablespoon Garlic Paste (see page 202)
1 teaspoon red chilli powder
1 tablespoon vegetable or corn oil
1 teaspoon salt
juice of 1 lemon
2 tablespoons Greek-style yoghurt
1 tablespoon chopped fresh coriander
½ teaspoon garam masala

For the saffron sauce
1 tablespoon vegetable or corn oil
2 black cardamom pods
4 cloves
1 blade of mace
2 bay leaves
400g (14oz) tomatoes, roughly chopped
1 large onion, roughly chopped
2.5cm (1-inch) piece of fresh ginger, crushed
2 garlic cloves, crushed
2 teaspoons mild red chilli powder
500ml (2 cups) chicken stock or water
1 teaspoon salt
½ teaspoon sugar
¼ teaspoon garam masala
a small pinch of saffron strands
2 tablespoons single cream
1 tablespoon cold butter

If the racks haven't already been prepared, trim off the skin and fat, leaving just a thin layer of fat on the meat. Mix together all the ingredients for the marinade. Rub them over the lamb and set aside for 30 minutes.

To make the sauce, heat the oil in a large saucepan, add the whole spices and the bay leaves and let them crackle. Add the tomatoes, onion, ginger, garlic and chilli powder and cook for 4–5 minutes. Add the stock or water and simmer over a low heat for about 15 minutes, until the tomatoes have completely broken down and the onion is very soft. Purée in a blender or food processor, then strain through a fine sieve into a clean pan. Bring back to the boil and simmer until the sauce thickens enough to coat the back of a wooden spoon. Add the salt, sugar and garam masala, then sprinkle in the saffron and simmer for 2–3 minutes. Adjust the seasoning if necessary. Just before serving, stir in the cream and finally finish the sauce by stirring in the cold butter.

To cook the lamb, heat the oil in a large, heavy-based frying pan, then add the lamb racks and sear over a high heat until browned all over. Transfer to a roasting tray and place in an oven preheated to 200°C/400°F/Gas Mark 6. Roast for 10–15 minutes, depending on how well done you like your meat. Remove from the oven and leave to rest in a warm place for 5 minutes.

Divide the sauce between 4 serving plates, place the lamb on top and serve immediately.

Cook's note
The butter and cream emulsify the sauce, so it is best to add them at the very end after checking the seasoning. Don't let the sauce boil after adding the butter or it will separate and become thin.

RAAN

The grandest of Indian dishes, this is curry but not as we know it. It combines two cooking techniques, braising and roasting, and the result is highly impressive.

Although the recipe calls for lamb, feel free to use hogget, mutton or even goat.

SERVES 8–10

2 legs of lamb, weighing about 1.5kg each, trimmed of any surface fat
2 tablespoons red chilli powder
5 tablespoons Ginger Paste (see page 202)
6 tablespoons Garlic Paste (see page 202)
250ml (1 cup) malt vinegar
500g (2 cups) plain yoghurt
3 onions, sliced and fried until crisp (see page 203)
2 teaspoons royal (black) cumin seeds
1 tablespoon salt
6 bay leaves
3 cinnamon sticks, about 5cm (2 inches) each
5 green cardamom pods
2 tablespoons melted butter
2 teaspoons lemon juice
1 teaspoon chat masala
4 tablespoons single cream
1 teaspoon garam masala
1 tablespoon chopped fresh coriander

With the tip of a sharp knife, cut small incisions in the lamb legs at approximately 5cm (2-inch) intervals. Mix together the red chilli powder, ginger paste, garlic paste, vinegar, yoghurt, fried onions, royal cumin and salt, then massage them over the legs, rubbing and pressing the spices into the gashes created by the knife. Set aside for 15 minutes.

Put the legs, drained of all marinading liquid, on an oiled baking tray, add the bay leaves, cinnamon and green cardamom, then cover the tray with foil. Place in an oven preheated to 180°C/350°F/Gas Mark 4 and braise for 2½ hours, until the meat is very tender and ready to fall off the bone. Remove from the oven and leave to cool. Remove the legs from the liquid and allow them to dry. Pass the liquid through a fine sieve and reserve to make the sauce.

Take the meat off the bone and cut it into 5cm (2-inch cubes). Thread them on to 8–10 metal skewers and roast on a barbecue or under a very hot grill, basting frequently with the melted butter, until crisp and well browned. Finish with a drizzle of lemon juice, any leftover melted butter and the chat masala.

For the sauce, bring the cooking juices to the boil in a small pan and simmer until reduced to a coating consistency. Correct the seasoning and stir in the cream, garam masala and fresh coriander. Pour the sauce over the meat and serve with Naan Bread (see page 192).

Cook's note
It's important to drain all the liquid from the legs before roasting them, in order to get a crisp finish.

MODERN RAAN

Traditionally, raan is braised, as in the previous recipe, but I find that if the meat is good quality it can be roasted instead and works just as well, if not better. I've added a step of tunnel-boning the leg (you could ask your butcher to do this) to create a pocket, which can be filled with paneer cheese and dried fruits. This makes it truly special, just as a raan should be! Also, roasting this way keeps the meat moist compared to braising, where the meat is cooked through and therefore can be dry.

SERVES 4

1 leg of young lamb, weighing about 1.5 kg ($3^1/_4$lb)

For the marinade

250g (1 cup) Greek-style yoghurt
1 tablespoon Ginger Paste (see page 202)
1 tablespoon Garlic Paste (see page 202)
2 tablespoons Fried Onion Paste (see page 203)
1 teaspoon red chilli powder
$^1/_2$ teaspoon garam masala
1 tablespoon chopped fresh coriander
$1^1/_2$ teaspoons salt
2 tablespoons vegetable or corn oil

For the filling

60g ($^1/_2$ cup) khoya (reduced milk cakes, available in Indian stores), grated
75g ($^1/_2$ cup) paneer, grated
60g ($^1/_2$ cup) Cheddar cheese, grated
2 onions, sliced and fried until crisp (see page 203)
4 dried figs, cut into 5mm ($^1/_4$-inch) dice
4 dried apricots, cut into 5mm ($^1/_4$-inch) dice
1 tablespoon raisins
2 tablespoons cashew nuts, fried in a little oil until golden
5cm (2-inch) piece of fresh ginger, chopped
4 green chillies, chopped
$^1/_2$ teaspoon royal (black) cumin seeds
1 teaspoon salt
juice of 1 lime

For the onion salad

2 red onions, thinly sliced
$^1/_2$ cucumber, halved lengthwise and thinly sliced
1 carrot, cut into thin strips
1 tomato, deseeded and thinly sliced
$^1/_2$ teaspoon salt
$^1/_2$ teaspoon cumin seeds, roasted in a dry frying pan and then crushed
1 tablespoon chopped fresh coriander
juice of $^1/_2$ lime

Trim the excess fat off the lamb and, if your butcher hasn't tunnel-boned it for you, remove the thighbone by cutting around it carefully with a carving knife to leave a cavity. Prick the leg on the outside with a fork.

Combine all the ingredients for the marinade. Rub the marinade over the leg of lamb, both outside and inside the cavity, and leave for 15 minutes.

To make the filling, combine all the ingredients and then use to stuff the lamb leg. Truss the leg using a butcher's needle and twine to close the open part completely. Transfer to a roasting tray and place in an oven preheated to 220°C/425°F/Gas Mark 7. Roast for 10 minutes, then reduce the heat to 180°C/350°F/Gas Mark 4 and cook for a further 50 minutes. Remove from the oven and leave to rest for about 30 minutes.

Meanwhile, make the onion salad. Put all the cut vegetables except the tomato in a bowl of ice-cold water for 10 minutes to crisp them up. Strain and sprinkle with the salt, cumin and fresh coriander. Squeeze the lime juice over.

Cut the meat into slices 1cm ($^1/_2$ inch) thick and serve with the onion salad.

Cook's note
For something like this to be enjoyed at it's best, it is very important to rest the meat before serving. This makes it more tender and you won't lose the juices when you slice it.

SPICED MINCED LAMB WITH LIVER

KEEMA KALEJI

This rustic dish is one of the best examples of Punjabi *dhaba*-style cooking. You find these dishes featured in roadside cafés all over northern India. If you do get the chance to eat in these places, a word of caution: order this dish in a well-known and very busy place only, as it could be dodgy otherwise.

Although this is cooked in a saucepan here, it can be made just as well in a wok (kadhai) or even on a flat griddle (tawa).

SERVES 4

4 tablespoons vegetable oil or ghee
1 bay leaf
2.5cm (1-inch) piece of cinnamon stick
2 green cardamom pods
4 red onions, finely chopped
4 garlic cloves, finely chopped
2.5cm (1-inch) piece of fresh ginger, finely chopped
2 teaspoons red chilli powder
2 green chillies, finely chopped
1 teaspoon red chilli flakes
1 teaspoon ground turmeric
2 teaspoons ground cumin
1½ teaspoons salt
3 tomatoes, blended to a purée
500g (1lb 2oz) lean minced lamb
250g (1 cup) plain yoghurt
250g (9oz) lamb's liver, cut into 2cm (¾-inch) dice

To finish
¼ teaspoon garam masala
stalks from ½ bunch of coriander, finely chopped
juice of 1 lime or lemon

Heat 3 tablespoons of the oil or ghee in a heavy-based pan, add the bay leaf, cinnamon and cardamom pods and let them crackle. Add the chopped onions and fry over a moderate heat for 6–8 minutes, until they begin to turn golden brown. Add the garlic, ginger, chilli powder, green chillies, chilli flakes, turmeric, cumin and salt and stir-fry for about 6 minutes, until the mixture is cooked and brown. Add the puréed tomatoes and cook for 5 minutes. Raise the heat, add the mince and cook, stirring constantly to prevent lumps, for 5–6 minutes, until well browned all over.

Cover the pan, lower the heat and simmer for 10 minutes. When the moisture has evaporated and the mince is cooked, stir in the yoghurt. Cook for 3–4 minutes, until thoroughly blended.

Heat the remaining oil or ghee in a separate pan, add the diced liver and sear quickly for a minute or so, until browned on the outside. Tip it into the simmering mince. Stir in the garam masala, coriander stalks and lime or lemon juice. Serve hot, with chapattis or Layered Parathas (see page 196).

Cook's notes
If you want to add another texture to the mince, boil 2 eggs for 6–8 minutes, then peel them. Chop the whites and mix them into the mince, then grate the yolks on top as a garnish.

I have tried several variations, using sweetbreads, kidney and even brains instead of liver, and they all work very well.

LAMB NECK FILLET WITH MASALA MASH

Properly marinated lamb middle neck cooked in a slow tandoor is a thing of beauty, as I have found out over the years. Lamb neck is an unbelievably underrated cut. People seem to go crazy over best end of lamb but, besides being expensive, quite often it doesn't match up to the flavour and texture you can get from the neck. Here I roast the fillet with tandoori spicing and serve it with a creamy masala mash and herbaceous sauce.

SERVES 4

4 lamb neck fillets (about 750g (1lb 10oz) in total), trimmed
2 tablespoons vegetable or corn oil
Masala Mash (see page 181), to serve

For the marinade
1 tablespoon Ginger-Garlic Paste (see page 202)
1 teaspoon salt
$1/2$ teaspoon coarsely ground white pepper
2 tablespoons Greek-style yoghurt
1 tablespoon single cream
1 tablespoon cream cheese
2.5cm (1-inch) piece of fresh ginger, finely chopped
2 green chillies, finely chopped
1 tablespoon chopped fresh coriander
$1/2$ teaspoon Mace and Cardamom Powder (see page 204)
$1/2$ teaspoon salt

For the sauce
2 tablespoons ghee
3 green chillies, roughly chopped
100g (scant $1/2$ cup) Boiled Cashew Paste (see page 202)
4 tablespoons plain yoghurt
$1/2$ teaspoon ground turmeric
250ml (1 cup) lamb stock or water
1 red onion, cut into 1cm ($1/2$-inch) dice
1 tomato, deseeded and cut into 1cm ($1/2$-inch) dice
1 tablespoon single cream
juice of 1 lemon
1 teaspoon salt
1 tablespoon dried fenugreek leaves
4 tablespoons fresh coriander leaves

Mix all the ingredients for the marinade together, rub them over the lamb and set aside for 30 minutes.

Meanwhile, make the sauce. Heat the ghee in a pan, add the green chillies and cashew paste and cook over a medium heat for 5 minutes. Whisk in the yoghurt and cook for another 3–4 minutes. Stir in the turmeric, then the stock or water and simmer for about 5–6 minutes, until it is thick enough to coat the back of a spoon. Add the onion and tomato and cook for a minute longer. Stir in the cream, lemon juice and salt, sprinkle in the fenugreek and coriander, then remove from the heat and keep warm.

To cook the lamb, remove it from the marinade, reserving the leftover marinade. Heat the oil in a large, ovenproof frying pan, add the neck fillets and sear for about a minute on each side until lightly coloured. Transfer the pan to an oven preheated to 180°C/350°F/Gas Mark 4 and roast for 8 minutes.

Leave the meat to rest for 5 minutes, then spread the leftover marinade over it and flash it under a hot grill for 2 minutes or until it is lightly crisped up. Slice the fillets into 4 pieces each and serve with the sauce and Masala Mash.

Cook's note
You could cook the lamb fillets through completely on a barbecue rather than frying and roasting them.

HYDERABADI-STYLE LAMB BIRYANI

HYDERABADI KACCHI BIRYANI

This style of making biryani will always remain an enigma for anyone who has not seen it done. When I returned from a stint in Hyderabad in my training days and described the way it was made, everyone, including my tutors, thought I was pulling a fast one. No one would believe that you could start with raw meat and cooked rice in a pot and end up with the best biryani in the world. After all, the logical way of cooking this would be by starting with cooked meat and raw rice...but maybe that's why this example of black magic deserves its place in the book!

Before you start, you must make sure you have the right utensils for the job. You will need a heavy pot with a tight-fitting lid, large enough for the meat and rice to fill it by no more than two-thirds. This allows the steam to build up and assist the cooking, as well as helping to make the rice light and fluffy rather than stodgy and dense. At the same time, too large a pot will not work either.

If the pot you have is not the right size, just adjust the quantities and make the biryani in batches if need be. Traditionally it is a one-pot dish and well suited to feeding large numbers.

SERVES 4–6

1kg (2¼lb) boned leg of lamb, cut into 2.5cm (1-inch) dice (you could also use a few pieces on the bone)
5 tablespoons chopped fresh coriander
6 green chillies, slit open lengthwise
2 tablespoons ghee or vegetable oil
1g (about ¼ teaspoon) saffron strands, soaked in 125ml (½ cup) milk
4 tablespoons single cream

For the marinade
2 tablespoons Ginger-Garlic Paste (see page 202)
1 bay leaf
6 green cardamom pods
1 blade of mace
⅛ nutmeg, grated
½ teaspoon cloves
5cm (2-inch) piece of cinnamon stick
1 tablespoon red chilli powder
1 teaspoon ground turmeric
¼ small green papaya, peeled, deseeded and finely grated
500g (2 cups) plain yoghurt
2 teaspoons salt
1 teaspoon sugar
5 large onions, finely sliced and fried until crisp (see page 203)

For the rice
2.5 litres (2½ quarts) water
2 black cardamom pods
4 green cardamom pods
½ teaspoon cloves
75g (3½ cups) mint, chopped
1 tablespoon salt
600g (3 cups) basmati rice, washed and then soaked in cold water for 30 minutes
4 tablespoons ghee

To seal
250g (1 cup) plain flour
125ml (½ cup) water

Mix all the ingredients for the marinade together, setting aside half the fried onions for later use. Mix the lamb with the marinade and set aside for at least 3 hours.

Now cook the rice. Bring the water to the boil in a large pan, then add the whole spices, half the mint and the salt. Simmer for 5 minutes or so. Now add the soaked rice and simmer, uncovered, for 5–6 minutes, until the rice is half cooked. Drain through a colander and set aside. Melt the ghee in a small pan, then set aside.

Take a large, heavy-based casserole with a tight-fitting lid and put the marinated meat in it. Sprinkle with half the chopped coriander, the remaining mint and half the reserved fried onions. Spread the rice over the meat. Sprinkle with the remaining coriander and fried onions, plus the green chillies, melted ghee, saffron milk and cream.

Mix together the flour and water to make a dough for sealing the lid and stretch it into a thin strip, long enough to cover the edge of the lid all the way round. Stick the dough on to the edge of the lid and place it on the casserole, pressing lightly to make sure that it is well sealed. Place the sealed pot over a high heat for 10 minutes, allowing the steam to build up. As soon as steam starts escaping from the pot, reduce the heat to low and cook for another 12–15 minutes. Remove from the

heat and finish cooking in an oven preheated to 170°C/325°F/Gas Mark 3 for 30 minutes or so.

Remove the lid at the table for maximum impact. The beautiful aromas will waft through the room. Serve with Pomegranate Raita (see page 191) on the side, or as an accompaniment to another curry, such as Lamb Shanks with Saffron and Rosewater (see page 119).

Cook's note

If you're not sure about the thickness of your casserole, you'd be wise to place a heat diffusion mat under it to reduce the direct heat.

NARGISI KOFTA CURRY

This curry reminds me of a bygone era. It was a firm favourite on restaurant menus in India in the 1960s and 1970s but has since fallen out of favour, and you rarely see it now. Part of the reason is that it's a difficult dish to get right and can be tricky to put on a menu. However, it has a celebratory feel to it and used to be served quite frequently in the army officers' mess in India. Essentially the kofta are like Scotch eggs, simmered in a curry sauce. Instead of serving them in the sauce, you could serve them as a kebab on their own.

SERVES 4

For the koftas

6 small eggs
500g (1lb 2oz) lean minced lamb
1 onion, finely chopped
4 garlic cloves, finely chopped
1½ teaspoons salt
½ teaspoon garam masala
1½ teaspoons red chilli powder
2 tablespoons Crisp Fried Onions (see page 203)
6 cloves, roasted in a dry frying pan and then finely ground
1 tablespoon chopped mint
2 tablespoons ghee
3 tablespoons roasted chana dal, ground in a spice grinder
2 tablespoons coarse semolina
vegetable or corn oil for deep-frying

For the sauce

6 tablespoons vegetable or corn oil
2 bay leaves
4 cloves
3 onions, finely chopped
5cm (2-inch) piece of fresh ginger, grated
5 garlic cloves, chopped
1 teaspoon salt
2 tablespoons grated fresh coconut
6 large, ripe tomatoes, puréed
3 green chillies, finely chopped
½ teaspoon ground turmeric
1½ teaspoons red chilli powder
2 teaspoons ground cumin
1 teaspoon garam masala
350g (1½ cups) plain yoghurt
1 teaspoon rosewater or kewra (screw pine essence)
a pinch of saffron strands
2 tablespoons chopped fresh coriander

Boil the eggs until just over soft boiled – i.e. put them in a saucepan of cold water, bring to boiling point, then reduce the temperature to a simmer and time them for 4 minutes exactly. The white will be just set and the yolk creamy. Dip the eggs immediately in cold water, then peel and set aside.

To prepare the koftas, mix the mince with all the remaining ingredients except the semolina and oil. Chill for 15–20 minutes, then knead to form a smooth mix. Divide the mince into 6 equal portions. Encase each egg in the mixture, rather like Scotch eggs, making sure there are no holes in the coating. Place on a plate and sprinkle with the semolina.

In a large saucepan or a deep-fat fryer, heat the oil to 160°C/315°F. Add the eggs and cook until evenly coloured all over. Remove from the pan and drain on kitchen paper. (If you want to serve the koftas without the sauce, finish cooking them in an oven preheated to 180°C/350°F/Gas Mark 4 for 4–6 minutes.)

For the sauce, heat the oil in a heavy-based pan, add the bay leaves and cloves and let them crackle for 30 seconds or so. Add the chopped onions and sauté until golden. Add the ginger and garlic and sauté for 2–3 minutes, then add the salt and coconut and cook, stirring, for 2 minutes. Add the puréed tomatoes, green chillies and all the ground spices, including the garam masala. Simmer over a medium heat for 10–15 minutes until the oil begins to separate from the mixture. Stir in the yoghurt and ½ cup of water and cook for 2 minutes. Now add the prepared koftas, folding them in very gently to coat them with the sauce. Reduce the heat and simmer for 4–5 minutes. Finally stir in the rosewater or kewra and saffron and infuse for 2 minutes over a low heat.

Slice the eggs horizontally in half, then return them to the sauce. Garnish with the chopped coriander and serve with rice or chapattis.

Cook's note
Traditionally this dish is made with hard-boiled eggs but I much prefer it with soft-boiled ones. Depending upon availability, you could use duck's eggs or quail's eggs, and even serve these as snacks with the sauce on the side.

LAMB COOKED WITH WINTER VEGETABLES AND SPINACH

SAAG GOSHT

Although made in most of Punjab and northern India, this recipe has its origins in Kashmir, the northernmost state on the border of Pakistan, where the winters are severe. It is a simple yet warming everyday recipe using turnips, carrots and other familiar vegetables. It may well have been the starting point of what is usually known as saag gosht in the Western world, minus the root vegetables, but try it with the vegetables and see the difference for yourself.

SERVES 4

500g (1lb 2oz) spinach leaves
4 tablespoons ghee or vegetable oil
2 teaspoons cumin seeds
1 teaspoon cloves
2 large onions, finely chopped
4 tablespoons finely chopped garlic
4 tablespoons finely chopped fresh ginger
2 teaspoons red chilli powder
2 teaspoons salt
750g (1lb 10oz) boned leg of lamb, cut into 2.5cm (1-inch) cubes
4 green chillies, slit open lengthwise
½ turnip, cut into 1cm (½-inch) cubes
1 carrot, cut into 1cm (½-inch) cubes
300ml (1¼ cups) lamb stock or water
2 tomatoes, finely chopped
1 tablespoon gram (chickpea) flour
100g (3½oz) small pickling onions, peeled
1 tablespoon cold butter
juice of ½ lemon
1 teaspoon ground spice mix (equal parts of clove, nutmeg, mace and green cardamom, ground in a mortar and pestle)

Blanch the spinach in a large pan of boiling water until wilted, then refresh in cold water and drain. Squeeze out the excess liquid and blitz to a smooth purée in a blender or food processor. Set aside.

Heat the ghee or oil in a large, heavy-based pan and add the cumin and cloves. When they start to crackle, add the chopped onions and sauté until light golden. Add the garlic and ginger and sauté for 2–3 minutes, until the garlic begins to change colour, then add the chilli powder and salt and stir for another couple of minutes, until the spices begin to release their flavour and the fat starts to separate from the mixture.

Now add the lamb pieces and cook over a fairly high heat, stirring constantly, for 8–10 minutes, until the meat begins to brown at the edges. When most of the liquid has evaporated and the lamb is well coloured, stir in the green chillies, turnip and carrot. Add the lamb stock or water, then reduce the heat, cover the pan and cook gently for 30–40 minutes, until the lamb is almost cooked.

Remove the lid, add the tomatoes and cook for 10–12 minutes, until the lamb is cooked through and the tomatoes have been incorporated into the sauce. Add the gram flour and cook, stirring, for a minute, to eliminate any raw flavour. Add the small onions and cook for a minute or two, until glazed but still crunchy. Now add the puréed spinach, increase the heat and stir to mix thoroughly. Check the seasoning, then stir in the butter, lemon juice and spice mix. Serve immediately, with chapattis or other bread.

Cook's notes
Do not cook for too long after adding the spinach purée, or it will discolour and look horrible!

You could substitute diced paneer for the lamb. The cooking time will reduce drastically but the flavours are just as enjoyable.

FIERY RAJASTHANI LAMB CURRY

LAAL MAAS

The name of this dish means 'red meat' in Hindi, indicating the liberal use of dried red chillies that make this dish intensely hot, with robust, smoky flavours.
You could use either lamb or goat – they are interchangeable here. In Rajasthan they would invariably use goat.

This is one of those dishes that contains heat in every sense – it's both 'chilli hot' and 'spice hot'. Cloves and cardamom are effective heat-inducing spices, perfect for cold winter evenings. It's up to you how much heat you'd like in your finished dish. You may discard most of the chilli seeds if you want to reduce the heat, or keep them in if you like it really hot.

SERVES 4

5 tablespoons ghee or vegetable oil
1 teaspoon cloves
25 dried red chillies, stalks removed, broken into 2–3 pieces each and soaked in warm water for 30 minutes
2 bay leaves
6 green cardamom pods
4 black cardamom pods
6½ tablespoons finely chopped garlic
2 large onions, finely chopped
750g (1lb 10oz) lamb (or goat's) leg, cut on the bone into 4cm (1½-inch) dice
600ml (2 cups) water or lamb stock
30g (⅔ cup) fresh coriander, chopped
juice of 1 lemon

For the yoghurt mixture
250g (1 cup) plain yoghurt, whisked until smooth
2 teaspoons cumin seeds, roasted in a dry frying pan
4 teaspoons ground coriander
2 teaspoons red chilli powder
2 teaspoons salt

Mix the yoghurt with the cumin seeds, ground coriander, chilli powder and salt and set aside.
Heat 3 tablespoons of the ghee or oil in a large, heavy-based pan. Add the cloves, setting 4–6 aside for later, and 3–4 soaked red chillies, saving the rest for later. Add the bay leaves and the green and black cardamom. When they begin to crackle and change colour, add the garlic and sauté until it starts to turn golden. Add the onions and cook, stirring constantly, until light brown. Now add the meat and cook, stirring, over a high heat for 3–5 minutes. Again, save 3–4 red chillies for later and add the rest to the pan. Cook for 10–12 minutes, until the liquid has evaporated and the meat starts to brown. Add the yoghurt mixture and cook over a medium heat for 15–18 minutes, until the yoghurt has dried up. Pour in the water or lamb stock, then cover the pan, reduce to a simmer and cook for 30 minutes or until the meat is tender. Check the seasoning, remove from the heat and keep warm.

To finish, heat the remaining ghee or oil in a small pan, add the remaining cloves and red chillies and, as they change colour and release their flavours into the fat, pour the mixture over the lamb. Finish with the chopped coriander and lemon juice. This process is called a *tadka*, or tempering, and it boosts the flavours in the dish.

Cook's note
Mixing the ground spices with the yoghurt prevents them getting burnt in the fierce heat of the pan and also thickens the yoghurt, so it doesn't split.

BRAISED SHOULDER OF YOUNG LAMB WITH MINT AND ONION

Most Indian restaurants would use meat from the leg to make a curry but I feel that the shoulder is better suited to this, and it braises really well. This is a typical restaurant dish but I've adapted it so it is simple to do at home.

SERVES 4–6

2 x 1–1.5kg (2¼–3¼lb) shoulders of young lamb
10 green cardamom pods
2 blades of mace
8 cloves, roasted in a dry frying pan
2 x 5cm (2-inch) cinnamon sticks
1 teaspoon royal (black) cumin seeds
2 bay leaves
6 green chillies, slit open lengthwise
800ml water
1 tablespoon vegetable or corn oil
100g (3½oz) small red onions, Madras onions or shallots, peeled
4 tablespoons single cream
1 teaspoon dried fenugreek leaves, crushed between your fingertips
4 tablespoons chopped mint
juice of 1 lemon
½ teaspoon sugar (optional)

For the first marinade
1 tablespoon vegetable or corn oil
juice of 1 lemon
2 teaspoons ground white pepper
1 tablespoon salt
2 tablespoons Ginger-Garlic Paste (see page 202)

For the second marinade
¼ nutmeg, grated
75g (⅓ cup) Fried Cashew Paste (see page 202)
400g (1⅔ cups) Greek-style yoghurt, tied in a muslin cloth and left hanging up overnight to drain
½ teaspoon garam masala
2 tablespoons cream cheese

Trim any surface fat from the lamb shoulders, wash them under cold running water, then drain and pat dry on kitchen paper. Prick each shoulder 4–6 times with the tip of a sharp knife.

Mix together all the ingredients for the first marinade, rub them over the lamb and set aside for 15 minutes.

Mix together all the ingredients for the second marinade and apply them to the shoulders, rubbing and massaging the marinade into the gashes. Place the lamb shoulders in a roasting tray and add the whole spices, bay leaves and 2 of the green chillies. Now pour the water carefully into the tray. Cover with foil and place in an oven preheated to 200°C/400°F/Gas Mark 6. Roast for 30 minutes, then stir the juices and use to baste the meat. Reduce the heat to 170°C/325°F/Gas Mark 3 and cook for 1½ hours. Remove the tray from the oven, take out the meat and let it rest in a warm place for 20 minutes. Pass the cooking juices through a sieve to get rid of the whole spices and set aside.

Heat the oil in a saucepan, add the small onions and sauté for a minute or so, until shiny but still crunchy. Add the remaining green chillies, pour the strained cooking juices into the pan and bring to the boil. Stir in the cream, fenugreek and mint and finish with the lemon juice. Check the seasoning and add the sugar if necessary. Carve the lamb into 4 or 6 pieces, then pour the sauce on top. Serve with a bread of your choice.

LAMB SHANKS WITH SAFFRON AND ROSEWATER

This dish would be made with goat shanks in Lucknow, using the *dum* technique – i.e. cooking the meat in a pot sealed with dough over a very low heat for several hours, allowing the gelatine to be extracted from the bones. It results in a rich, flavourful, full-bodied, smooth sauce, perfumed with rosewater and fortified with saffron.

In India I used to serve 3 shanks per portion – something one can't imagine in the UK. Just one per person will more than suffice!

SERVES 4

4 medium lamb shanks
4 tablespoons vegetable or corn oil
2 black cardamom pods, crushed
2 cinnamon sticks
1 blade of mace
1/2 teaspoon cloves
2 onions, cut into quarters
4 tomatoes, cut into quarters
1 bay leaf
2 teaspoons red chilli powder
2 teaspoons Ginger-Garlic Paste (see page 202)
1 1/2 teaspoons salt
1/4 teaspoon garam masala

To finish
2 tablespoons single cream
1/2 teaspoon sugar
1 tablespoon rosewater
a pinch of saffron strands
1/2 teaspoon Mace and Cardamom Powder (see page 204)
1 tablespoon chopped fresh coriander

Put the shanks in a large saucepan, cover with cold water and bring to a simmer. Blanch for 5–6 minutes, then drain. Leave until cool enough to handle, then trim off the excess fat, leaving just a thin covering.

Heat a tablespoon of the oil in a heavy-based pan, add the whole spices and let them crackle. Add the onions, tomatoes, bay leaf and a teaspoon of the chilli powder and cook for 4–5 minutes. Pour in 750ml (3 cups) water, bring to a simmer and cook over a fairly high heat for about 20 minutes, till the tomatoes break down completely and the onions are soft. Remove from the heat, blend to a smooth purée in a food processor and then strain.

Heat the remaining oil in a large, heavy-based pan and add the lamb shanks. Cook until light brown all over, then add the ginger-garlic paste and cook for 2–3 minutes longer. Stir in the remaining red chilli powder, plus the salt and the cooked onion and tomato purée. Cook for 5–6 minutes over a moderate heat, then sprinkle in the garam masala. Add 1 litre (4 cups) of water, cover the pan and simmer over a low heat for about 50 minutes, stirring occasionally. Alternatively cover the pan with a tight-fitting lid and place in an oven preheated to 170°C/325°F/Gas Mark 3 for 1–1 1/2 hours.

When the meat is so tender that it is falling off the bone, remove the shanks from the sauce with a slotted spoon and keep warm. Pass the sauce through a fine sieve into a clean pan, stir in the cream and sugar and simmer until it is thick enough to coat the back of a spoon. Stir in the rosewater, saffron, mace and cardamom powder and chopped coriander. Check the seasoning and remove from the heat. Pour the sauce over the lamb shanks and serve with steamed rice or Pilau Rice (see page 180).

Cook's note
Although in India we cook the shanks on the hob, they come out much better if they are braised in the oven, and better still if you put the pot in the middle of the oven rather than at the bottom.

LAMB CURRY WITH WHITE SPICES

KALIA SAFED

The name of this recipe refers to a lamb dish cooked with white ingredients only or, if other ingredients are used, then they are added in whole form so they can be removed before serving. It used to be one of the many lamb or mutton dishes served as part of any ruler's repast – a white dish using meat was essentially devised to break the monotony of spiced and dark meat dishes. A version of this dish found in Rajasthan is also referred to as *safed maas* – literally meaning 'white meat'.

SERVES 4

800g (1¾lb) boned leg of lamb or mutton, cut into 4cm (1½ inch) cubes
50g (½ cup) broken cashew nuts
1 large onion, roughly chopped
4 tablespoons ghee
2 bay leaves
3 black cardamom pods
1½ teaspoons white peppercorns
5cm (2-inch) piece of fresh ginger, finely grated
1 tablespoon salt
450g (2 cups) Greek-style yoghurt
500ml (2 cups) water
1 teaspoon cloves
2 dried red chillies
1 teaspoon ground green cardamom
1 teaspoon lime juice

Put the meat in a large pan, cover with plenty of cold salted water and bring to the boil. Simmer for 2–3 minutes, then drain. Wash the meat twice in cold water to get rid of any blood.

Put the cashew nuts and onion in a small pan with enough water to cover, bring to the boil and simmer for 15–20 minutes, until tender, skimming any scum from the surface. Blend the mixture to a smooth paste in a food processor or blender, then set aside.

Heat 3 tablespoons of the ghee in a heavy-based pan, add the bay leaves and black cardamom pods and let them crackle. Add the meat, white peppercorns, ginger and salt and cook over a high heat for 5 minutes, stirring frequently. Reduce the heat, add the yoghurt and cook, stirring, until it begins to boil. Add the water, bring to the boil again, then reduce the heat, cover and cook for 30–40 minutes, until the meat is tender. Stir in the cashew and onion paste, cover the pan again and cook gently for 20 minutes.

Heat the remaining tablespoon of ghee in a small pan, add the cloves and red chillies and, as they change colour, tip them into the pan of simmering curry. Finally stir in the green cardamom and finish with the lime juice. Serve with bread or rice of your choice.

Cook's note
You may add various nuts, such as almonds and pistachios, and *khoya* (reduced milk cakes, available from some Indian shops) with the cashew paste if you want to make the curry richer. Some people like to finish it with cream for a smooth, rich sauce. The richer it gets, the closer it becomes to a korma.

LAMB AND BEETROOT CURRY

DO PEEAZA CHUKANDAR

This is a very unusual curry, found mostly in Muslim homes in eastern and central India. The use of beetroot imparts a lovely colour and rich, earthy flavour. It's particularly good for a winter's evening, with Naan Bread (see page 192) or Layered Parathas (see page 196).

SERVES 4

400g (14oz) raw beetroot
750g (1lb 10oz) boned leg of lamb, cut into 4cm ($1\frac{1}{2}$-inch) cubes
5 tablespoons ghee
1 teaspoon cloves
4 black cardamom pods
3 onions, thinly sliced
2 teaspoons red chilli flakes
500ml (2 cups) water
1 teaspoon garam masala
1 red onion, sliced into rounds
4 sprigs of fresh coriander
juice of $\frac{1}{2}$ lemon

For the marinade
150g ($\frac{2}{3}$ cup) plain yoghurt
1 tablespoon salt
$1\frac{1}{2}$ tablespoons red chilli powder
1 tablespoon ground coriander
2 tablespoons Ginger-Garlic Paste (see page 202)

Put the beetroot in a large pan, cover with plenty of water and bring to the boil. Reduce the heat, cover and simmer for about an hour, until the beetroot is tender and most of the water has evaporated. Whiz half the beetroot to a smooth paste in a food processor and cut the rest into 2.5cm (1-inch) cubes. Set aside.

Mix together all the ingredients for the marinade, add the meat and set aside for 20 minutes.

Heat 4 tablespoons of the ghee in a heavy-based pan, add the cloves and black cardamom pods and stir for 30 seconds. Add the sliced onions and fry until golden brown. Then add the marinated meat and cook over a high heat for 10 minutes, stirring constantly. Add the chilli flakes and cook for 2 minutes. Pour in the water, reduce the heat and simmer for 30–35 minutes. When the meat is almost cooked and little liquid remains, add the puréed and diced beetroot and cook for another 5 minutes or until the meat is tender. Stir in the garam masala and simmer over a low heat for a further 5 minutes.

Meanwhile, heat the remaining ghee in a frying pan, add the onion rings and sauté briefly for a minute or so. Remove from the heat and serve garnished with the coriander sprigs and onion rings and finished with a squeeze of lemon.

Cook's note
Adding 2 tablespoons of vinegar when boiling the beetroot gives a nice kick to the dish.

LAMB CURRY WITH GREEN CHILLIES AND MINT

KACCHI MIRCH KA GOSHT

I remember this from my time working at the Gharana restaurant at the Oberoi Grand Hotel in Calcutta. It is such a fine dish, rich and light, zingy and mild, soft and crunchy, fragrant and fresh – all the things one could possibly ask from a great curry. The ingredients are quite similar to a Rezala (see page 137). However, the addition of ingredients at different stages gives a sequence of textures and flavours that lifts a traditional curry.

SERVES 4

750g (1lb 10oz) boned leg of lamb, cut into 2.5cm (1-inch) cubes
1 litre (4 cups) water
2 bay leaves
5 black peppercorns
2 black cardamom pods

For the paste
2 large onions, diced
100g (1 cup) cashew nuts
2 blades of mace
3 green cardamom pods
300ml ($1^1/_4$ cups) water
200g (scant 1 cup) plain yoghurt

For the gravy
6 tablespoons ghee
2 cloves
3 green cardamom pods
2 tablespoons Ginger-Garlic Paste (see page 202)
$1^1/_2$ teaspoons salt
6–8 green chillies, cut in half
750ml (3 cups) water
4 tablespoons finely chopped mint
$^1/_4$ teaspoon Mace and Cardamom Powder (see page 204)
1 red onion, diced
1 tablespoon single cream
juice of 1 lemon

Wash the lamb in cold water, then set aside. Put the water, bay leaves, peppercorns and cardamom into a large pan and bring to the boil. Add the meat, bring the water back to the boil and skim off the scum from the surface. Drain through a colander and set the lamb aside. Blanching it in this way helps get rid of any blood in the meat, keeping it light in colour.

Next make the paste. Put the onions, cashew nuts, mace and cardamom in a pan, cover with the water and bring to the boil. Simmer until the onions and nuts are soft, then strain through a sieve. Add the yoghurt to the onion and cashew mixture and blitz in a food processor or blender until smooth.

For the gravy, heat half the ghee in a large, heavy-based pan, add the cloves and cardamom pods and let them crackle. Add the ginger-garlic paste and cook, stirring to prevent sticking, for 3–4 minutes. Add the lamb and sauté for 5 minutes over a high heat without letting it colour. Stir in the salt.

Pour in the cashew and onion paste and stir until the mixture comes to the boil. Add half the green chillies and the water, then cover the pan, reduce the heat and simmer for 35–40 minutes, until the meat is tender. Stir in the mint and mace and cardamom powder, followed by the diced onion and the remaining green chillies and ghee. Simmer for 3–4 minutes, until the onion is cooked but still crunchy. Stir in the cream and lemon juice and serve with steamed rice or Spring Onion Parathas (see page 195).

LAMB ROGAN JOSH

Most restaurants like to use meat from the leg to make a Rogan Josh but it comes out so much better if you use shanks, the sauce shiny and full of flavour from the gelatine. You could use whole shanks, as we do at The Cinnamon Club from time to time, but at home it's easier if the shanks are cut into 3 or 4 pieces, as you would for an *osso buco*. You can ask your butcher to cut them up for you. If you don't want to use lamb, the dish would be just as successful made with mutton or goat.

Not a lot of people know this, but *rogan josh* means 'red juice'. It's a Kashmiri dish, where the redness comes from the bark of a locally grown tree called *rattan jyoth*. It is more than likely that you will not be able to find this even in Asian shops, so I suggest you use crushed beetroot in the final tempering process instead.

SERVES 4

6 lamb shanks, cut into 3 or 4 pieces on the bone
4 tablespoons oil or ghee
2 black cardamom pods, lightly crushed
2 cinnamon sticks
$^1/_2$ teaspoon black peppercorns
2 large onions, finely chopped
$1^1/_2$ teaspoons salt
1 tablespoon Ginger Paste (see page 202)
1 tablespoon Garlic Paste (see page 202)
$1^1/_2$ tablespoons Kashmiri chilli powder
$^1/_2$ teaspoon ground coriander
200g (scant 1 cup) plain yoghurt
500ml (2 cups) lamb stock or water
1 teaspoon ground ginger
$^1/_2$ teaspoon ground fennel seeds
$^1/_4$ teaspoon garam masala
2 tablespoons single cream
1 tablespoon chopped fresh coriander

For tempering (optional)
1 tablespoon ghee
2 sticks of rattan jyoth (or $^1/_2$ raw beetroot, roughly crushed with a rolling pin or meat mallet)

Pat the cut lamb shanks dry on kitchen paper and set aside.

Heat the oil or ghee in a heavy-based casserole, add the crushed cardamom, cinnamon sticks and peppercorns and stir for 30 seconds or so, until they release their flavours into the oil. Add the onions and salt and cook for 10–12 minutes, until the onions are golden brown. Add the ginger and garlic pastes and cook for a couple of minutes, stirring constantly to prevent the pastes sticking to the pan. Now add the lamb and cook, stirring, for 10–12 minutes, until evenly coloured on all sides.

Add the chilli powder and ground coriander and cook for a further 2–3 minutes. Take care to handle the shanks carefully so the meat does not come off the bone at this stage. Gradually whisk in the yoghurt over a low heat until it has all been absorbed, stirring continuously. Add the lamb stock or water, bring to a simmer and cover with a tight-fitting lid. Cook over a low heat for 30–40 minutes, until the meat is tender enough to fall off the bone easily. You could add some more stock or water if the sauce is too thick or the mixture becomes too dry. Stir in the ground ginger, fennel and garam masala, then cover and set aside for 5 minutes.

For the tempering, heat the ghee in a small pan, tie up the rattan jyoth or beetroot in a square of muslin and add to the ghee. Leave it to infuse for 1 minute. Add the infused ghee and the muslin bag to the lamb shanks and simmer for 2 minutes, until the sauce turns dark red. Remove the meat from the sauce, then add the cream and chopped coriander to bring the sauce back together. Pour the sauce over the meat. Serve with steamed or boiled basmati rice or a bread of your choice.

Cook's notes
Take care not to add the yoghurt all at once, as this will lower the temperature of the sauce and the yoghurt will split.

Although it is not traditional to finish this dish off in the oven, I find the results are better if you do so. It improves the texture, the meat does not get broken up and, what's best if you're entertaining, it frees you up to get on with other things! After adding the water or stock, simply cover the casserole and braise in an oven preheated to 170°C/325°F/Gas Mark 3 for about 2 hours.

MEATBALL CURRY

KHOLA CURRY

This curry comes from the Chettinad region of Tamil Nadu, which is dominated by the Chettiar community, made up predominantly of bankers. The Chettiars made their fortune from labourers in Malaysia in the early nineteenth century and in the process amassed property all over Southeast Asia. They are mainly vegetarian, with meat and fish eaten as a special treat during big celebrations. As a wealthy community, it was the norm for them to hire help to assist *Archi* (the lady of the house) with cooking and cleaning. These cooks were not vegetarian, and Khola Curry was one of the many dishes they introduced into Chettiar homes.

SERVES 4

For the meatballs
500g (1lb 2oz) minced lamb
8 green chillies, roughly chopped
8 garlic cloves, roughly chopped
1/3 coconut, inner brown skin removed, flesh finely grated
80g (scant 1 cup) cashew nuts, lightly roasted in a dry frying pan
60g (1/3 cup) roasted chana dal
2 tablespoons each of poppy seeds and fennel seeds, roasted in a dry frying pan
5 shallots, roughly chopped
1 1/2 teaspoons ground turmeric
5cm (2-inch) piece of fresh ginger, roughly chopped
2 teaspoons salt

For the sauce
100ml (scant 1/2 cup) vegetable or corn oil
7.5cm (3-inch) piece of cinnamon stick
4 bay leaves
2 tablespoons fennel seeds
15 shallots, finely chopped
3 sprigs of fresh curry leaves
3 tablespoons Ginger-Garlic Paste (see page 202)
3 large tomatoes, diced
2 1/2 teaspoons red chilli powder
2 tablespoons ground coriander
1 teaspoon ground turmeric
500ml (2 cups) water or lamb stock
2 teaspoons salt

Blitz all the ingredients for the meatballs together in a food processor, or mince them in a mincer. Check the seasoning by frying a teaspoon or so of the mixture and tasting it. Divide into small balls (slightly smaller than golf balls) and leave in the fridge while you make the sauce.

Heat the oil in a heavy-based pan, add the cinnamon, bay leaves and fennel seeds and cook for about 30 seconds, until they crackle. Add the shallots and curry leaves and fry for 8–10 minutes, until the shallots are golden. Add the ginger-garlic paste and sauté for 2–3 minutes, then stir in the tomatoes and cook for 5 minutes. Stir in all the ground spices. Add the water or stock and salt, bring to the boil and simmer over a medium heat for 12–15 minutes, till the oil separates from the sauce. Add the meatballs to the sauce and simmer for 5–8 minutes, until just cooked through. Check the seasoning and serve immediately, with either Layered Parathas (see page 196) or Pilau Rice (see page 180).

Cook's notes
When you've removed the mince from the food processor, rinse out the processor with 500ml (2 cups) water and use this to cook the sauce rather than plain water; there's much more flavour.

You may need to oil the palms of your hands when shaping the meatballs, to prevent them sticking.

MUGHAL-STYLE AROMATIC CURRY OF LAMB SHANKS

NALLI KORMA

This recipe comes from the Awadh region of India. In the Mughal courts of Lucknow, such delicate dishes of slow-cooked meat with fragrant spicing were the norm. I find lamb shoulder shanks best for this dish, as the meat is lighter and less fibrous than leg shanks. In India, the shanks are smaller than the ones in the West and we use goat shanks instead of lamb.

SERVES 3

6 lamb shoulder shanks, French trimmed
1.5 litres (6 cups) water
5 tablespoons vegetable or corn oil
50g (1/2 cup) cashew nuts
4 onions, finely sliced
125ml (1/2 cup) water
2 bay leaves
3 green cardamom pods
2.5cm (1-inch) piece of cinnamon stick
1 tablespoon chopped fresh ginger
1 tablespoon chopped garlic
4 green chillies, chopped
2 teaspoons ground coriander
1 teaspoon red chilli powder
1 teaspoon salt
1 teaspoon garam masala
3 tablespoons plain yoghurt
1/2 teaspoon ground mace
1/3 teaspoon ground cardamom

For the marinade
1 tablespoon Ginger Paste (see page 202)
1 tablespoon Garlic Paste (see page 202)
1 teaspoon salt

To finish
a generous pinch of saffron strands

2 teaspoons kewra (screw pine essence) or rosewater
juice of 1 lime
3 tablespoons single cream

Put the shanks in a large pan, cover with the water and bring to the boil, then drain. Leave the shanks to cool, then trim off any surface fat.

Mix together the marinade ingredients, rub them over the lamb shanks and leave to marinate for 20 minutes. Infuse the saffron in the kewra or rosewater and set aside.

Heat half the oil in a heavy-based pan, add the cashew nuts and sauté until golden. Remove with a slotted spoon, allowing the oil to drain back into the pan, then set the nuts aside to cool. Fry the onions in the oil until golden brown, then remove with a slotted spoon and spread out on a tray to cool. Put the cashew nuts and onions in a blender and blitz to a paste, gradually adding the water.

Heat the remaining oil in a large, heavy-based pan, add the bay leaves, cardamom and cinnamon and let them crackle. Add the ginger, garlic and green chillies and sauté for 2 minutes. Now add the lamb, raise the heat and stir-fry until golden brown. Add the ground coriander, red chilli powder, salt and half the garam masala and cook, stirring, for 2 minutes. Add the yoghurt and cook over a high heat, stirring constantly, for 8–10 minutes, until it has been completely absorbed.

Now add the fried onion and cashew nut paste, the remaining garam masala and the ground mace and cardamom. Pour in enough water just to cover, bring to a simmer, then cover and cook for 40 minutes, until the meat is tender. Adjust the seasoning and finish with the lime juice, cream and the saffron mixture. Serve with Pilau Rice (see page 180) or Layered Parathas (see page 196).

Cook's note
You could braise the shanks in a sealed pot in a moderate oven for an hour or so after adding the water. This will ensure a slow release of gelatine. If the sauce is too thin, remove the shanks and simmer the sauce until it reduces and thickens enough to coat the back of a spoon. Finish with the lime juice, cream and saffron mixture.

DECCAN LAMB COOKED WITH LENTILS

DAL GOSHT

This is quite popular in the Deccan region, where it is thought to have originated from the kitchens of the Nizam, the rulers of Hyderabad. Also referred to as *dalcha*, it makes a great winter dish.

SERVES 4

750g (1lb 10oz) boned lamb, cut into 2.5cm (1-inch) cubes
200g (1 cup) chana dal (split yellow peas)
2 black cardamom pods
1 teaspoon ground turmeric
1 litre (4 cups) water
1½ teaspoons salt
4 tablespoons vegetable or corn oil
4 cloves
4 green cardamom pods
5cm (2-inch) piece of cinnamon stick
4 black peppercorns
1 bay leaf
4 onions, finely chopped
1 tablespoon Ginger-Garlic Paste (see page 202)
3 tomatoes, cut into quarters
10 fresh curry leaves
1 tablespoon tamarind paste
½ teaspoon garam masala
1 tablespoon chopped fresh coriander
2 teaspoons desiccated coconut
juice of ½ lime
a pinch of sugar

For the fresh spice mix
5 tablespoons coriander stalks
3 garlic cloves, roughly chopped
4 green chillies, roughly chopped
½ teaspoon coriander seeds, roasted in a dry frying pan
½ teaspoon cumin seeds, roasted in a dry frying pan
½ tablespoon vegetable or corn oil

Wash the lamb in cold running water, then drain and pat dry on kitchen paper. Set aside.

Blend all the ingredients for the fresh spice mix to a coarse paste in a small food processor and set aside.

Wash the chana dal and place in a heavy-based pan with the black cardamom pods, turmeric, water and ½ teaspoon of the salt. Bring to the boil and simmer for 30 minutes, until about three-quarters cooked. Remove from the heat and keep warm.

Meanwhile, heat the oil in another heavy-based pan, add the whole spices and the bay leaf and let them crackle for a minute or so. Add the onions and sauté for 8–10 minutes, until golden. Add the ginger-garlic paste and stir for a minute, then add the lamb, the remaining salt and 2 tablespoons of the fresh spice mix. Cook over a high heat, stirring constantly, for 6–8 minutes, until the lamb colours lightly. Drop the tomato quarters into the pan and cook for 3 minutes, until softened. Pour in 250ml (1 cup) water, reduce the heat and cover the pan. Simmer for 45 minutes, until the lamb is almost cooked.

Now pour in the chana dal and its cooking liquid and continue to cook for 6–8 minutes, until the lamb is tender. Stir in the fresh curry leaves, garam masala and tamarind paste, then reduce the heat and simmer for 2–3 minutes. Finish the dish with the chopped coriander, coconut, lime juice and sugar. Serve with steamed rice or Pilau Rice (see page 180).

PUNJABI-SPICED MUTTON CHOPS AND MINCE

RARHA MUTTON CHAAMP

This dish is typical of the rustic, Punjabi-style cooking that has been made popular by *dhabas*, or roadside cafés, which traditionally cater to the truck drivers who drive the length and breadth of the country, carrying goods of all types. The success of these *dhabas* is a testimony to the business acumen and adaptability of the Punjabis, who saw this opportunity as the majority of Indian truck drivers happen to be from Punjab.

SERVES 4

1 teaspoon Ginger Paste (see page 202)
1 teaspoon Garlic Paste (see page 202)
1 teaspoon ground cumin
2 teaspoons ground coriander
120g (1/2 cup) plain yoghurt
125ml (1/2 cup) water
3 tablespoons ghee
2 bay leaves
3 cloves
2 cardamom pods
2.5cm (1-inch) piece of cinnamon stick
5 black peppercorns
4 onions, finely sliced
8-bone mutton rack, French trimmed and cut into individual cutlets (ask your butcher to do this)
2 teaspoons salt
250g (9oz) minced mutton
2 teaspoons red chilli powder
3 ripe tomatoes, puréed
3 green chillies, finely chopped
5cm (2-inch) piece of fresh ginger, cut into thin strips
1/4 teaspoon garam masala
4 tablespoons chopped fresh coriander
juice of 1 lemon

In a bowl, mix the ginger and garlic pastes, cumin, coriander, yoghurt and water together and set aside. Heat the ghee in a large, heavy-based saucepan, add the bay leaves, cloves, cardamom, cinnamon and peppercorns and let them crackle. Add the onions and stir-fry until golden brown. Add the mutton cutlets and stir-fry over a high heat for 6–8 minutes, allowing them to turn an even brown. Add the salt and stir-fry for another 2 minutes, then reduce the heat and remove the cutlets from the pan.

Add the mince to the pan, raise the heat and cook, stirring, for 3–4 minutes. Pour in the yoghurt mixture and stir over a high heat for 8–10 minutes, until the mince is cooked and the yoghurt has dried out. Now add the chilli powder and puréed tomatoes and cook over a medium heat for 5 minutes, until the tomatoes are thoroughly incorporated.

Return the cutlets to the pan and cook for 6–8 minutes, until they are cooked through and coated in the mince mixture. Stir in the green chillies, ginger and garam masala and finish with the chopped coriander and lemon juice. Serve with Layered Parathas (see page 196) or Naan Bread (see page 192).

Cook's note
If the mince isn't cooked by the time the yoghurt has dried out, add about 250ml (1 cup) water and continue cooking.

MUTTON COOKED WITH LENTILS, DRIED FRUIT AND NUTS

HAREESA

This dish would originally have been made with camel meat and you could still use that if you are able to find any! The recipe comes from the Deccan region of India. The nomadic tribes that used to cook it would often serve it as a complete meal, containing rice, lentils and meat all in one. On cold winter nights, the savoury porridge would cook for hours over a slow-burning wood fire and its flavours would be rich and creamy.

SERVES 4

5 tablespoons ghee
1/2 teaspoon cloves
5cm (2-inch) piece of cinnamon stick
5 green cardamom pods
1/2 teaspoon black peppercorns
2 large onions, finely sliced
6 garlic cloves, finely chopped
1 teaspoon ground turmeric
1 tablespoon red chilli flakes
2 teaspoons salt
750g (1lb 10oz) lean mutton from the leg, cut into thin strips
2 litres (8 cups) water
150g (3/4 cup) masoor dal (red lentils)
50g (1/2 cup) basmati rice
125g plain yoghurt
5cm (2-inch) piece of fresh ginger, chopped
6 green chillies, slit open lengthwise
1 tablespoon coriander seeds, roasted in a dry frying pan and coarsely ground
1 tablespoon cumin seeds, roasted in a dry frying pan and coarsely ground
1 tablespoon fennel seeds, roasted in a dry frying pan and coarsely ground
125ml (1/2 cup) single cream
50g (1/2 cup) almonds and pistachios, chopped
1 tablespoon raisins
2 tablespoons chopped mint

Heat 4 tablespoons of the ghee in a large, heavy-based pan and add the cloves, cinnamon stick, cardamom pods and black peppercorns. Let them crackle, then add the onions and sauté until golden brown. Add the garlic and sauté for another couple of minutes, then stir in the turmeric, red chilli flakes and salt. Add the meat and cook, stirring, over a high heat for 15 minutes. Pour in the water, bring to the boil, then reduce the heat and simmer for 20–25 minutes, until the meat is nearly half cooked. Then add the lentils and rice and cook for another 20–25 minutes, until the meat, rice and lentils are all tender and most of the water has been absorbed.

Gradually stir in the yoghurt, then add the ginger, green chillies and ground roasted seeds. Cook over a medium heat for 10 minutes. Stir in the cream and cook for 3 minutes longer.

Heat the remaining tablespoon of ghee in a separate pan, add the almonds, pistachios and raisins and fry lightly for a couple of minutes. Stir in the mint and pour it all on to the porridge. Check the seasoning and serve immediately, with vegetables of your choice.

Cook's note
You could cook this dish with venison, water buffalo or any similar lean meat.

RAJASTHANI SEMI-DRY CURRY WITH MUTTON

HANDI BOOTHA

This Rajasthani speciality is often served as an appetiser, even though it's actually a curry. It's quite a dry dish, with rich, intense flavours, and is similar to a *kosha mangsho* (a rich but dry lamb curry from Bengal), and even the ever-popular *bhuna*, served in Indian restaurants across the UK. The inclusion of onions and tomatoes adds colour and texture to the dish and lightens it up.

SERVES 4

800g (1¾lb) boned leg of mutton, cut into 4cm (1½-inch) cubes
3 tablespoons vegetable or corn oil, or mustard oil
3 onions, finely chopped
4 tomatoes, puréed
500ml (2 cups) water

For the marinade
240g (1 cup) plain yoghurt
2 dried red chillies
5 cloves
3 green cardamom pods
½ teaspoon black peppercorns
2.5cm (1-inch) piece of cinnamon stick
2 bay leaves
5cm (2-inch) piece of fresh ginger, grated
3 garlic cloves, chopped
1 tablespoon red chilli powder
1 tablespoon ground cumin
1 tablespoon ground coriander
2 teaspoons salt

To finish the dish
1 tablespoon ghee
1 teaspoon cumin seeds
3 garlic cloves, chopped
2 onions, cut into 2.5cm (1-inch) dice
2 tomatoes, deseeded and diced
½ teaspoon garam masala
100g (2 cups) fresh coriander, chopped
½ teaspoon sugar
juice of ½ lemon

Wash the diced mutton under cold running water, then drain and pat dry on kitchen paper. Mix together all the ingredients for the marinade, add the meat and set aside for 15–20 minutes.

In the meantime, heat the oil in a large, heavy-based pan, add the chopped onions and sauté over a medium heat until brown. Add the marinated meat and stir over a high heat for 10–12 minutes, until the edges of the meat start to brown. Cook for a further 6 minutes or until the juices have dried up. Now add the tomatoes and cook over a high heat for 5–6 minutes. Add the water, cover the pan and simmer gently for 20–25 minutes, stirring occasionally, until the meat is tender. Remove from the heat and set aside.

In a separate large pan, heat the ghee, add the cumin seeds and garlic and sauté until golden. Add the diced onions and sauté until they are shiny but still crisp. Add the cooked mutton mixture and stir-fry over a high heat until the spices coat the pieces of meat and the moisture dries up. Add the tomatoes, garam masala and coriander and stir for a minute or two, taking care that the tomatoes and onions don't disintegrate. Check the seasoning, add the sugar and finish with the lemon juice. Serve with Layered Parathas (see page 196).

Cook's note
The initial cooking of the mutton can be done a day in advance. It is easier to stir-fry if it is cold.

'THIS CURRY REMINDS ME OF AN ERA GONE BY. IT WAS A FIRM FAVOURITE ON RESTAURANT MENUS IN INDIA IN THE 1960S AND 1970S BUT HAS SINCE FALLEN OUT OF FAVOUR, AND YOU RARELY SEE IT NOW.'

NARGISI KOFTA CURRY, PAGE 110

MUTTON KOLHAPURI

The cooking in Maharashtra can be broadly divided into two categories: Konkani, the food of the coastal region, and Malwani, the food of the landlocked interiors. Malwani cooking is earthy and rustic, based on fiery spices and coarse spice pastes. Kolhapur is a small town in Maharashtra, which has popularised this Malwani curry.

SERVES 4–6

2 tablespoons vegetable or corn oil
2 dried bay leaves
5 dried red chillies
8 cloves
4 x 2.5cm (1-inch) pieces of cinnamon stick
4 red onions, chopped
1kg ($2^1/_4$lb) boned leg of mutton (or lamb), cut into 2.5cm (1-inch) cubes
2 tablespoons red chilli powder
1 teaspoon ground turmeric
1 tablespoon salt
5 tomatoes, finely chopped
1 litre (4 cups) water
2 teaspoons garam masala
1 tablespoon chopped fresh coriander

For the roasted spice blend (Kolhapur masala)
1 teaspoon black peppercorns
2 blades of mace
2 teaspoons coriander seeds
2 teaspoons cumin seeds
2 tablespoons fennel seeds
2 tablespoons sesame seeds
1 tablespoon melon seeds (available in Asian stores)
2 teaspoons poppy seeds
2 tablespoons desiccated coconut
4 garlic cloves, chopped
7.5cm (3-inch) piece of fresh ginger, chopped

First prepare the spice blend. Roast the spices, seeds and coconut in a dry frying pan over a low heat for 4–5 minutes. Remove from the heat and grind to a paste with the garlic and ginger, adding a little water as needed.

Heat the oil in a large, heavy-based pan with a heavy lid, add the bay leaves, whole red chillies, cloves and cinnamon sticks and let them crackle for 30 seconds or so. Add the onions and sauté till golden brown.
Stir in the mutton and cook for 10–12 minutes, until browned, then mix in the chilli powder, turmeric, roasted spice blend and salt.
Cook for a good 5–8 minutes, stirring frequently to prevent the paste catching on the bottom of the pan.

Add the tomatoes and cook over a high heat for 10 minutes. Pour in the water, bring to a simmer, then reduce the heat and cover the pan. Simmer for 45 minutes–1 hour, until the mutton is tender. Add the garam masala and check the seasoning. Stir in the chopped coriander and serve with rice or bread of your choice.

BHOPAL-STYLE GOAT CURRY

REZALA

Many regions claim this dish originated in their area but it was the Begum of Bhopal who made it the most popular. I like it, as it's simple to make and very easy to remember. Strangely, it resembles a pound cake recipe, where you use equal quantities of everything and mix them up and bang them in the oven to get a cake! In this case, just mix together all the ingredients and seal the pot. Cook either on the hob over a very low heat or in the oven at 150°C/300°F/Gas Mark 2 for 2 hours. Beware though – the dish may have quite a kick, depending upon which type of green chilli you use.

SERVES 4

1kg (2¼lb) goat's meat from the leg, cut into 2.5cm (1-inch) cubes
200ml (scant 1 cup) vegetable oil or ghee
2 x quantity of Crisp Fried Onions (see page 203), coarsely crushed
200g (scant 1 cup) Greek-style yoghurt
200ml (scant 1 cup) water
25 green chillies, slit open lengthwise and deseeded
25g (1oz) piece of fresh pineapple, blended in a mini chopper or finely grated
4 tablespoons roasted gram (chickpea) flour
4 teaspoons salt
2 tablespoons finely chopped fresh ginger
1 tablespoon Garlic Paste (see page 202)
1 teaspoon allspice
2 teaspoons cumin seeds
4 black cardamom pods
2 teaspoons garam masala

To seal
250g (1⅔ cup) plain flour
125ml (½ cup) water

To finish
100ml (scant ½ cup) single cream
1 tablespoon cashew nuts, fried in a little oil until golden
100g (2 cups) fresh coriander, chopped
juice of 1 lemon
1 tablespoon chopped mint

Mix the meat with all the other ingredients and set aside for 10–15 minutes.

Choose an earthenware casserole or a heavy-based pan with a tight-fitting lid. Place the marinated meat in the pot. Mix together the flour and water to make a dough for sealing the lid and stretch it into a thin strip, long enough to cover the edge of the lid all the way round. Stick the dough on to the edge of the lid and place it on the casserole, pressing lightly to make sure that it is completely sealed. Place the pan over a low heat and cook for 2 hours. Remove the lid and check to see if the meat is done; if not, simply cover again and cook until it is tender. Stir the sauce and finish by adding the cream, plus another couple of tablespoons of water if necessary to loosen it. Bring to the boil, check the seasoning and correct if required. Sprinkle with the fried cashew nuts, chopped coriander, lemon juice and mint and serve immediately.

Cook's note
You could substitute mutton or hogget for the goat and, if your butcher cuts the meat into escalopes, you could try using these rather than diced meat. It will reduce the cooking time by almost half and taste just as good. Cuts from the neck or shoulder also work well in this kind of dish.

BEEF BHUNA, BENGALI STYLE

Bhuna is a term you commonly find on restaurant menus. It refers to cooking meat with spices with little or no water added. This requires constant stirring to prevent the spices sticking to the bottom of the pan but the resulting dish is rich and intense in flavour from the caramelisation of the onions and the frying of the spices. I've made things easier here by adding a little water but do make sure that all or most of it dries up so there is no loss of flavour.

SERVES 4–6

750g (1lb 10oz) boneless beef chuck steak, cut into 4cm (1½-inch) cubes
3 tablespoons ghee
½ teaspoon cloves
2 green cardamom pods
1 black cardamom pod
½ teaspoon black peppercorns
2 bay leaves
3 green chillies, slit lengthwise in half
250ml (1 cup) water
2 tomatoes, finely chopped
2.5cm (1-inch) piece of fresh ginger, finely chopped
3 tablespoons tamarind paste
juice of ½ lemon
2 tablespoons chopped fresh coriander
a pinch of sugar

For the marinade
2 onions, finely chopped
3 tablespoons Ginger-Garlic Paste (see page 202)
2 teaspoons salt
2 teaspoons red chilli powder
2 teaspoons cumin seeds, roasted in a dry frying pan and then ground
2 teaspoons ground coriander
½ teaspoon ground turmeric

Mix together all the ingredients for the marinade. Add the beef, turning to coat it well, and set aside for 30 minutes.

Heat the ghee in a large, heavy-based pan, add the whole spices and bay leaves and let them splutter. Add the marinated meat and stir well over a high heat, until the juices are absorbed and the meat begins to brown. Add the green chillies and water, then reduce the heat, cover and cook gently for 25–30 minutes, until the beef is about two-thirds done. Add the tomatoes and ginger and cook for 8–10 minutes over a high heat, stirring all the time to mash up the tomatoes. You may have to add a couple of tablespoons of water to prevent the sauce sticking to the bottom of the pan.

When fat begins to leave the side of the pan, the meat has reached the bhuna stage. Now stir in the tamarind paste and lemon juice, followed by the chopped coriander. Finally add the pinch of sugar, then cover the pan and switch off the heat. Leave for about 5 minutes so the meat can complete the cooking in its own heat. Serve with Layered Parathas (see page 196).

SPICE-CRUSTED RIB EYE STEAK WITH MASALA SAUTÉED POTATOES

Steak and chips, I suppose! This is, of course, a purely concocted dish, drawing inspiration from the all-time favourite way of enjoying good meat. All I have done is spice things up a little, being careful not to let the spices overpower the main element and detract from the enjoyment of the meat. The semi-dry spice crust on the steak provides a balance of textures and serves as both crust and sauce.

SERVES 4

4 x 200g (7oz) rib eye steaks
1 tablespoon vegetable or corn oil
chopped chives, to garnish

For the marinade
1 teaspoon red chilli powder
½ teaspoon salt
1 tablespoon vegetable or corn oil

For the spice crust
2 tablespoons vegetable or corn oil
1 large onion, finely chopped
1 teaspoon salt
2.5cm (1-inch) piece of fresh ginger, finely chopped
1 teaspoon red chilli powder
3 tomatoes, finely chopped
1 teaspoon red chilli flakes
1 teaspoon coriander seeds, crushed
1 teaspoon fennel seeds, crushed

For the masala sautéed potatoes
4 medium-sized starchy potatoes, such as Maris Piper, peeled and cut into slices about 5mm (¼ inch) thick
2 teaspoons salt
1 teaspoon ground turmeric
2 tablespoons vegetable or corn oil
1 teaspoon cumin seeds
1 large onion, finely chopped
½ teaspoon red chilli powder
1 teaspoon ground cumin
1 teaspoon salt
1 red onion, sliced into rings
1 tomato, deseeded and diced
1cm (½-inch) piece of fresh ginger, finely chopped
1 tablespoon chopped fresh coriander
2 green chillies, finely chopped

Mix together the ingredients for the marinade, rub them over the steaks and set aside.

To make the spice crust, heat the oil in a heavy-based pan, add the onion and sauté over a high heat for 2–3 minutes. Add the salt, reduce the heat, then cover and cook for 15–20 minutes, until the onion is soft and disintegrated. Add the ginger, chilli powder and tomatoes and cook, stirring, for 3–5 minutes, until the tomatoes have reduced and the mixture becomes quite dry. Stir in the chilli flakes, coriander seeds and fennel seeds, then remove from the heat and set aside.

For the masala sautéed potatoes, blanch the potato slices by simmering them in a pan of boiling water with the salt and half the turmeric for 2–3 minutes, then drain well. Heat the oil in a large, heavy-based frying pan and add the cumin seeds. When they start to crackle, add the chopped onion and sauté until golden brown. Add the remaining turmeric and the blanched potatoes to the pan and sauté over a medium heat until the potatoes start to crisp up around the edges. Now stir in the chilli powder, cumin and salt, add the onion rings and diced tomato and cook, stirring, for 2 minutes. Sprinkle in the ginger, coriander and green chillies and cook for 2–3 minutes, until the onion rings start to wilt and the potatoes are crisp.

To cook the steaks, heat the oil in a large, heavy-based frying pan, add the steaks and sear them for 2–3 minutes on each side for medium rare (if you prefer your meat more cooked, place it in an oven preheated to 180°C/350°F/Gas Mark 4 to obtain the desired degree of doneness). Leave to rest for 2–3 minutes. Spoon the spice crust over the steaks and place under a hot grill for a minute or two, until it begins to colour.

Divide the potatoes between 4 plates, put the steak on top, garnish with chives and serve immediately.

Cook's note
The spice crust for the steak can be made well in advance.

The method for the sautéed potatoes is quite similar to the French one, where the potatoes are cut thick and fried over a fairly slow heat for even cooking and a crisp texture. You may also add a pinch of dried thyme for extra depth of flavour, if you like.

ROAST PORK CHOPS WITH SWEET SPICES, MUSTARD MASH AND DATE AND CHILLI SAUCE

This may seem an unusual combination but the flavours and textures complement each other brilliantly. I consider this to be one of the joys of modern cooking – the sense of liberation you get from combining a Bengali-style mustard mash with sweet spiced pork plus a date and chilli sauce inspired by an Indian chutney. Enjoy the freedom!

SERVES 4

4 pork chops, trimmed
2 tablespoons vegetable or corn oil

For the date and chilli sauce
100g (3/4 cup) dried dates
4 garlic cloves, chopped
5 dried red chillies, broken into 2–3 pieces each
2.5cm (1-inch) piece of fresh ginger, chopped
1.5 litres (6 cups) chicken stock or water
2 tablespoons soy sauce
2 tablespoons balsamic vinegar
1/2 teaspoon salt
1 teaspoon sugar

For the spice rub
1 teaspoon black peppercorns
1/4 nutmeg
1/2 teaspoon cloves
2 blades of mace
1 teaspoon green cardamom pods
2.5cm (1-inch) piece of fresh galangal, chopped
1/2 teaspoon allspice berries
2.5cm (1-inch) piece of fresh ginger, chopped
1/2 teaspoon ground turmeric
2 teaspoons fennel seeds
1/4 teaspoon dried lavender
5cm (2-inch) piece of cinnamon stick
1 teaspoon salt
1 teaspoon red chilli flakes

For the mustard mash
500g (1lb 2oz) floury potatoes such as Desiree, peeled and cut into chunks
1/2 teaspoon ground turmeric
1 teaspoon salt
100g (scant 1/2 cup) butter
1 tablespoon vegetable or corn oil
1/2 teaspoon mustard seeds
2 green chillies, chopped
2 tablespoons Dijon or English mustard
2 tablespoons single cream
1 tablespoon chopped fresh coriander

For the sauce, put the dates, garlic, chillies, ginger and stock or water in a saucepan along with any pork trimmings and bring to a simmer. Reduce the heat and cook for 15–20 minutes, until the dates are tender. Remove from the heat and blend with a hand-held blender to give a smooth sauce. Strain through a fine sieve into a clean pan and return to the heat. Bring to a simmer, add the soy sauce, balsamic vinegar, salt and sugar and simmer until it has reduced and thickened enough to coat the back of a spoon and gets a glaze. Remove from the heat and set aside.

To make the spice rub, spread all the ingredients out on a baking tray and place in a very low oven for about 15 minutes, until completely dried out but not burned. Pound them to a coarse powder in a mortar and pestle and rub the mixture over the pork chops. Set aside for 10 minutes.

For the mash, boil the potatoes with the turmeric and salt until tender. Drain and push through a fine sieve, then mix with the butter. Heat the oil in a heavy-based frying pan, add the mustard seeds and let them crackle. Add the green chillies, then stir in the mashed potatoes, add the mustard and cream and cook until the mixture leaves the side of the pan. Stir in the coriander and remove from the heat.

To cook the pork chops, heat the 2 tablespoons of oil in a large, ovenproof frying pan and sear the chops for 3–4 minutes on each side, until they have a crisp skin and a good brown colour. Transfer the pan to an oven preheated to 200°C/400°F/Gas Mark 6 for 4–5 minutes or so to cook through.

To serve, divide the mash between 4 plates, sit the chops on top and pour the sauce around.

Cook's note
If you can obtain the Moroccan spice mix, *ras-el-hanout*, you could use that for the spice rub instead of roasting and grinding your own – just add a few coarsely crushed spices to it, such as fennel, cumin and coriander, and some chilli flakes.

COORG PORK STIR-FRY

PANDHI CURRY

This dish comes from the Coorg region of Karnataka. A pleasant hill station perched in the Western Ghats, Coorg is often referred to as the Scotland of India and is rich in wildlife. The Kodava people were avid hunters in years gone by. The local wild boar provided them with easy pickings and became a staple food, marking the beginnings of the famous Pandhi Curry. Today, many Kodava families have their own pigs and this remains one of their favourite dishes. The meat is cooked twice – first braised slowly until tender, then stir-fried to finish the dish. The high heat during the second cooking caramelises the onions and meat, adding a depth of flavour. This double-cooking technique is also found in certain Bengali-style *bhunas*.

SERVES 4

750g (1lb 10oz) pork loin, cut into 4cm (1½-inch) cubes

For the marinade

2 tablespoons Ginger-Garlic Paste (see page 202)
1 teaspoon ground turmeric
2 teaspoons salt
8–10 black peppercorns
3 bay leaves
4 tablespoons honey
3 tablespoons soy sauce
10 kokum berries, soaked in 100ml (scant ½ cup) hot water for 30 minutes

For the stir-fry

2 tablespoons vegetable or corn oil
4 dried red chillies
10 fresh curry leaves
4 red onions, sliced

Mix together all the ingredients for the marinade, including the soaking water from the kokum berries. Add the pork and leave to marinate in the fridge overnight.

The next day, transfer the pork to a heavy-based saucepan and add just enough water to cover. Bring to a simmer and cook, covered, for 1 hour or until the pork is very tender. Drain the meat, reserving the liquid.

Heat the oil for the stir-fry in a large frying pan or wok and add the dried red chillies. Let them darken, then add the curry leaves and fry for 30 seconds or so, until they start to crisp up. Now add the sliced red onions and sauté until translucent. Add the drained pork and cook, stirring constantly, for 6–8 minutes, until caramelised. Add a tablespoon or two of the reserved cooking liquid and continue to cook until it has evaporated. The meat will acquire a shiny glaze. Correct the seasoning and serve with steamed rice.

Cook's notes
Use as little water as possible to cook the pork first time around. The liquid will have stronger flavours when you can add it to the stir-fry later.

Keep the seasoning slightly milder than you'd like to end up with, as the prolonged cooking makes the final flavour very intense.

Th
In
on
pe
wit
rest
con
vine
wid
colo
beca
noto
with
to an
comes
other
dimen

SER

4 tables
1 tables
800g (1
(1-inc
on the
4 tablesp
2 onions
10 garlic
5cm (2-in
into thi
3 ripe tom
1 teaspoon
4 green ch
1 teaspoon
250ml (1 c
1 teaspoon

For the mas
seeds from 6
1 teaspoon b
4 dried chilli
6 cloves

POULTRY AND GAME

150 SYRIAN-CHRISTIAN CHICKEN STEW
151 CHICKEN DRUMSTICKS COOKED IN A SEALED POT
152 JUNGLE CURRY OF COUNTRY CHICKEN WITH FRESH FENUGREEK
155 BARBECUED HALF CHICKEN WITH TOMATO AND FENUGREEK SAUCE
156 CHARGRILLED MUSTARD CHICKEN WITH GREEN FENUGREEK SAUCE
158 CHICKEN CAFREAL
159 PARSEE-STYLE HOT AND SWEET CHICKEN CURRY WITH APRICOTS
160 OLD DELHI-STYLE CHICKEN CURRY
163 SPICE-ROASTED WHOLE CHICKEN
164 TANJORE-STYLE CHICKEN CURRY
165 DUCK CURRY WITH PEANUTS, SESAME AND TAMARIND
166 HALF A DOZEN QUAILS IN SPICY CURRY
168 DRY-SPICE-CRUSTED GUINEA FOWL WITH YELLOW LENTIL SAUCE
171 MIXED GAME COOKED IN AN INDIAN WOK
172 ROAST GROUSE WITH BLACK LENTILS
174 SPICED ROAST PARTRIDGE BREASTS WITH CURRIED PEARS
175 ROAST SADDLE OF RED DEER WITH PICKLING SAUCE
176 RABBIT COOKED IN A PIT

SYRIAN-CHRISTIAN CHICKEN STEW

KOZHI CURRY

This stew is made for breakfast in Syrian-Christian households in Kerala and is traditionally served with *appams* – fermented rice batter pancakes cooked in a heavy iron wok. They have thin, crisp sides and a soft, fluffy centre and look beautiful, as they take the shape of the pan they are cooked in. Lovely as they are, they are also incredibly difficult to make unless you are very experienced and I have seen many a chef struggle with them. I've devised a special recipe for sweet and sour rice that uses the same flavours and therefore tastes just as good but takes away the element of uncertainty!

SERVES 4

3 tablespoons coconut oil or vegetable oil
5cm (2-inch) piece of cinnamon stick
6 cloves
4 green cardamom pods
4 garlic cloves, thinly sliced
5cm (2-inch) piece of fresh ginger, cut into thin strips
2 red onions, thinly sliced
8 green chillies, slit open lengthwise
10 fresh curry leaves
1 x 1.5kg (3¼lb) free-range chicken, cut into 8 pieces
1 teaspoon salt
1 tablespoon black peppercorns, coarsely crushed
500ml (2 cups) coconut milk
3 tablespoons toddy (palm) vinegar (you could substitute sherry vinegar or white wine vinegar)
½ teaspoon garam masala

For the sweet and sour rice
2 tablespoons vegetable oil
2 star anise
4 green cardamom pods
2 bay leaves
1 onion, chopped
10 fresh curry leaves
1 teaspoon salt
1 teaspoon sugar
3 tablespoons white vinegar
220ml (scant 1 cup) water
5 tablespoons coconut milk
150g (¾ cup) basmati rice, washed under cold running water, then soaked for 20 minutes

Heat the coconut or vegetable oil in a large saucepan and add the whole spices, followed by the garlic, ginger, onions, green chillies and curry leaves. Cook over a medium heat until the onions are soft. Add the chicken, salt and pepper and stir for a minute. Stir in the coconut milk, bring to the boil, then reduce the heat and simmer, covered, for about 45 minutes, until the chicken is cooked through.

Meanwhile, for the sweet and sour rice, heat the oil in a pan, add the star anise, cardamom and bay leaves and stir for 30 seconds or so, until they release their flavours into the oil. Add the onion, curry leaves, salt and sugar and cook gently until the onion is translucent. Pour in the vinegar, water and coconut milk, bring to the boil, then add the soaked rice. Mix well, stirring for 5 minutes or so, then lower the heat, cover the pan with a tight-fitting lid and cook for another 7–8 minutes. All the liquid should be absorbed by now. Remove the lid, stir the rice to open up the grains, then cover with the lid again and set aside, off the heat, for 10 minutes to cook in its own steam.

When the chicken is done, add the vinegar, sprinkle in the garam masala and mix well. Remove from the heat and serve with the sweet and sour rice.

Cook's note
You could cook this dish with boneless chicken meat if you prefer, though with chicken on the bone there is more flavour. If using boned chicken, choose just the thighs, cut in half, and cook them slowly until tender. Chicken breasts will cook much faster but tend to become dry and the dish will lack depth of flavour.

CHICKEN DRUMSTICKS COOKED IN A SEALED POT

DUM KA MURGH

This Hyderabadi speciality comes from the royal courts of Lucknow, where the techniques of smoking and cooking in a sealed pot over a low heat were perfected. The smokiness of the cloves and the richness of the nuts make this dish truly unique. It's one of my favourite recipes in the entire book.

It used to be quite common for marriages to take place between the royal families of the various courts in India, and each time the bride would bring an entourage of cooks, maids and other servants. This explains how some recipes made their way into different regions.

SERVES 4

3 tablespoons ghee or vegetable oil
2 bay leaves
3 green cardamom pods
1 teaspoon black peppercorns
2 x 2.5cm (1-inch) cinnamon sticks
3 blades of mace
½ teaspoon royal (black) cumin seeds
3 tablespoons Ginger-Garlic Paste (see page 202)
12 free-range chicken drumsticks, skinned
2 teaspoons salt
6 green chillies, slit lengthwise in half
500g (2 cups) plain yoghurt
½ teaspoon garam masala
2 tablespoons Crisp Fried Onions (see page 203)
a small bunch of mint leaves
a small pinch of saffron strands

For the pastes
120g (½ cup) broken cashew nuts, soaked in 750ml (3 cups) water for 30 minutes
2 teaspoons white poppy seeds, soaked in 120ml (½ cup) water for 30 minutes
3 onions, roughly chopped

To finish
4–6 cloves
1 teaspoon ghee
2 tablespoons single cream (optional)

First make the pastes. Place the cashew nuts and poppy seeds, along with their soaking water, in a blender or food processor and blitz to a smooth paste. Boil the onions in 500ml (2 cups) water until they are soft and most of the water has been absorbed, then blend to a smooth paste. Set the pastes aside.

Heat the ghee or oil in a large, heavy-based pan, add the bay leaves and whole spices and let them splutter. Now add the boiled onion paste and stir-fry for 8–10 minutes, until golden. Stir in the ginger-garlic paste and sauté for 3–4 minutes. Add the chicken drumsticks, salt and green chillies and stir-fry over a high heat for 6–8 minutes.
Pour in the cashew nut and poppy seed paste and cook for another 5–6 minutes, stirring frequently to ensure that the paste does not stick to the bottom of the pan. Reduce the heat, pour in the yoghurt and bring to the boil, stirring continuously. Cover the pan with a tight-fitting lid and cook gently for 20 minutes. Stir in the garam masala and simmer for 8–10 minutes, until the ghee begins to separate from the mixture. Now sprinkle in the fried onion, mint leaves and saffron.

To finish, place a small metal bowl containing 1–2 pieces of smouldering charcoal in the centre of the pan, put the cloves on the charcoal and drizzle with the teaspoon of ghee. Immediately cover the pan with a tight-fitting lid, making sure the emerging smoke does not escape.

Place the entire pot in an oven preheated to 180°C/350°F/Gas Mark 4 for 10 minutes. Remove from the oven, set aside for 5 minutes and then take the lid off. Remove the metal bowl. Check the seasoning and add the single cream to bring the sauce back together if the fat has separated out from it. Serve with pilau rice or a bread of your choice.

Cook's notes
If you don't want to try the charcoal method of smoking the dish, simply heat a tablespoon of ghee to smoking point in a small pan, add the cloves and let them splutter. Immediately tip the cloves over the curry and cover with the lid for 5 minutes or so, until the dish acquires a smoky flavour from the cloves.

The same dish garnished with halved or quartered soft-boiled eggs is known as Dum ka Murgh 'Asifi' in Hyderabad, probably paying respects to a Mr Asif who came up with this novel garnish!

JUNGLE CURRY OF COUNTRY CHICKEN WITH FRESH FENUGREEK

METHI WALA JUNGLEE MURGH

This is a very basic, rustic curry that could be made with any kind of chicken but works particularly well with free-roaming, older birds. Their meat is slightly tougher than that of young birds but there is so much more flavour. In the past, when people cooked this outdoors over a wood fire with very basic implements, the spices would often be added whole and the vegetables roughly cut, hence the name jungle curry

SERVES 4

5 tablespoons vegetable or corn oil
5 cloves
2.5cm (1-inch) piece of cinnamon stick, broken in half
2 black cardamom pods
$^1/_2$ teaspoon black peppercorns
$^1/_4$ teaspoon fenugreek seeds
1 bay leaf
4 onions, finely chopped
1 tablespoon chopped garlic
1 x 1.2–1.5kg ($2^3/_4$–$3^1/_4$lb) free-range chicken, skinned and cut into 8 pieces
1 tablespoon Ginger Paste (see page 202)
2 teaspoons salt
$1^1/_2$ teaspoons red chilli powder
1 teaspoon red chilli flakes
1 teaspoon ground cumin
1 teaspoon ground coriander
4 tomatoes, chopped
120g ($^1/_2$ cup) plain yoghurt
2 green chillies, chopped
500ml (2 cups) water
5 tablespoons fresh fenugreek leaves, blanched in boiling water for 1 minute, then drained and chopped
$^1/_4$ teaspoon garam masala
$^1/_2$ teaspoon dried fenugreek leaves, crumbled between your fingers
juice of $^1/_2$ lemon

Heat the oil in a large, heavy-based pan, add the whole spices and bay leaf and let them splutter. Once the spices change colour, add the onions and garlic and sauté until golden brown. Add the chicken pieces and stir-fry for 6–8 minutes over a high heat, until browned at the edges. Add the ginger paste, salt, chilli powder, chilli flakes, cumin and coriander and cook, stirring, over a high heat for 2–4 minutes. Add the tomatoes and cook for 8–10 minutes, stirring constantly to ensure that the spices do not stick to the bottom of the pan.

Once the oil starts to separate out from the masala round the edges of the pan, add the yoghurt and green chillies, reduce the heat and cook, stirring frequently, till the liquid comes to the boil again. Add the water, bring to the boil, then simmer over a low heat for 10 minutes or until the chicken is fully cooked. Stir in the blanched fenugreek leaves, followed by the garam masala, dried fenugreek and lemon juice. Serve with rice or chapattis.

Cook's note
To make this dish dairy free, you could replace the yoghurt with water.

BARBECUED HALF CHICKEN WITH TOMATO AND FENUGREEK SAUCE

This is the sort of dish where barbecue meets curry and has a lot of fun. The smokiness of barbecue cooking is reminiscent of the tandoor. Poussins are ideal here, cut in half lengthways and cooked on bamboo or metal skewers. I find this dish goes down particularly well at the end of a barbecue, when you want to settle down to something with a bit of sauce and a bit more substance.

SERVES 4

2 x 750–800g (1lb 10oz–1¾lb) poussins, skinned and cut lengthwise in half

For the marinade

2 tablespoons vegetable or corn oil
2 tablespoons red chilli powder
2 tablespoons Ginger-Garlic Paste (see page 202)
1 tablespoon ground cumin
1½ teaspoons ground coriander
250g (1 cup) plain yoghurt
1½ teaspoons salt
juice of 1 lemon

For the tomato and fenugreek sauce

12 very ripe tomatoes, roughly chopped
2 bay leaves
3 garlic cloves, peeled
2.5cm (1-inch) piece of fresh ginger, crushed
3 cloves
3 green cardamom pods
250ml (1 cup) water
2 teaspoons red chilli powder
60g (¼ cup) unsalted butter
¼ teaspoon garam masala
1 teaspoon dried fenugreek leaves, crushed between your fingertips
4 tablespoons single cream
1½ teaspoons salt
2 teaspoons sugar
1 tablespoon finely chopped coriander stalks

Wash the poussins, dry them on kitchen paper, then make incisions in the breast and legs at approximately 5cm (2-inch) intervals with the tip of a sharp knife. These incisions help the birds retain the flavours of the marinade and cook evenly.

Combine all the ingredients for the marinade in a large bowl, add the chicken pieces and mix well, Thread the chicken on to bamboo or metal skewers and place in the fridge for at least 30 minutes.

Meanwhile, make the sauce. Put the tomatoes, bay leaves, garlic, ginger, cloves, cardamom pods and water in a pan and bring to the boil. Simmer until the tomatoes have disintegrated, then remove the bay leaves and leave to cool. Purée the mixture in a blender and then pass it through a sieve to get rid of the tomato seeds and skin. Bring to the boil in a clean pan, add the red chilli powder and simmer for 5–8 minutes. Now add the butter and cook for 6–7 minutes over a low heat, stirring constantly so the butter does not split. Add the garam masala and crushed dried fenugreek and cook for 2–3 minutes. Pour in the cream and simmer until the sauce becomes thick and glossy. Adjust the seasoning by adding the salt and sugar, then finish with the coriander stalks. Remove from the heat and keep warm.

Place the poussin skewers on a medium-hot barbecue and cook for 10–12 minutes on each side, until the birds are cooked through (or you could cook them under a hot grill). Pour the sauce over the barbecued poussins and serve with Naan Bread (see page 192).

Cook's note

If you have some of these cooked chickens left over, you could prepare the sauce without butter, pour it into a baking tray and place the chickens on top. Heat through in the oven at 180°C/350°F/Gas Mark 4 and serve dotted with knobs of butter and drizzled with cream.

CHARGRILLED MUSTARD CHICKEN WITH GREEN FENUGREEK SAUCE

This is a deconstructed *methi* chicken, where the legs and breasts are cooked separately and then put together on the plate to create layers of flavour and texture.

The recipe is actually easier than it looks, and I have found that by cooking the parts separately you create a delightful lightness of touch.

SERVES 4

4 chicken breasts, skin removed but wing bone attached
2 tablespoons vegetable or corn oil

For the marinade
1 tablespoon Ginger-Garlic Paste (see page 202)
1 teaspoon salt
½ teaspoon ground turmeric
1 teaspoon Dijon mustard
1 tablespoon plain yoghurt
1 tablespoon mustard oil
juice of ½ lemon

For the green fenugreek sauce
3 tablespoons vegetable or corn oil
1 bay leaf
2 green cardamom pods
1 teaspoon cumin seeds
3 onions, finely chopped
2 green chillies, slit lengthwise in half
½ teaspoon ground turmeric
1 teaspoon red chilli powder
2 chicken thighs, boned and cut into 1cm (½-inch) dice
2 tomatoes, finely chopped
120g (½ cup) plain yoghurt
250ml (1 cup) chicken stock or water
1 teaspoon salt
5 tablespoons chopped fresh fenugreek leaves
½ teaspoon garam masala
1 teaspoon dried fenugreek leaves
½ teaspoon sugar

Mix together all the ingredients for the marinade, add the chicken breasts and coat well. Leave in the fridge for 20 minutes.

Meanwhile, make the sauce. Heat the oil in a heavy-based pan and add the bay leaf, cardamom and cumin seeds. When they crackle, add the onions and sauté over a moderate heat until golden. Add the green chillies, turmeric and chilli powder and sauté for 2 minutes. Now add the diced chicken thighs and cook for 8–10 minutes over a medium heat. Stir in the tomatoes and cook for 5–8 minutes, until the oil separates from the mixture. Add the yoghurt and cook, stirring continuously, for 3–4 minutes over a medium heat. Add the chicken stock or water and salt, cover the pan and simmer for 5–6 minutes. Stir in the fenugreek leaves, garam masala, dried fenugreek and sugar and simmer for 2 minutes. Remove from the heat and keep warm.

To cook the chicken, heat the oil in an ovenproof frying pan, add the chicken breasts and sear for 2 minutes on each side. Transfer the pan to an oven preheated to 200°C/400°F/Gas Mark 6 and cook for 6–8 minutes, until the chicken is done. Serve the chicken on the sauce, with Masala Mash (see page 181) or steamed rice.

CHICKEN CAFREAL

This is the type of dish where anything goes. I've seen people cook it as a curry, grill it on a barbecue, serve it fried and even roast it in the oven. My favourite version is the roasted one, as it makes great gravy for dunking bread into. Carve the chicken at the table and don't bother with cutlery – go at it with your fingers and tear into it.

SERVES 4

1 x 1.2–1.5kg ($2^3/_4$–$3^1/_4$lb) free-range chicken
juice of 1 lime
1 tablespoon chopped fresh coriander

For the spice paste
4 tablespoons vegetable or corn oil
5cm (2-inch) piece of cinnamon stick
6 cloves
4 green cardamom pods
4 star anise
4 garlic cloves, chopped
5cm (2-inch) piece of fresh ginger, chopped
5 green chillies, chopped
$1^1/_2$ teaspoons salt
1 teaspoon sugar
1 tablespoon ground coriander
1 teaspoon red chilli powder
1 teaspoon ground cumin
$^1/_2$ teaspoon ground turmeric
120g ($1^1/_2$ cups) coriander stalks, chopped
5 tablespoons grated fresh coconut
1 tablespoon Worcestershire sauce

To make the spice paste, put all the ingredients in a food processor and blitz to a paste. Rub the paste over the chicken, inside and out. Push some of the mixture between the skin and the flesh, taking care not to rip the skin. Set aside for 30 minutes.

Place the chicken in an oven preheated to 200°C/400°F/Gas Mark 6 and roast for about 40–45 minutes, until cooked through.Remove from the oven and leave to rest for 15–20 minutes. Reserve the juices.

To make the gravy, pour the reserved juices into a pan and simmer until slightly reduced. Adjust the seasoning, if necessary, and stir in the lime juice. Sprinkle the fresh coriander on top of the chicken, then serve with the gravy and hunks of baguette or similar bread.

Cook's note
If you want to reduce the cooking time, cut the chicken in half lengthwise, then marinate as above. Cook under a medium-hot grill for 15–18 minutes on each side. This not only reduces the cooking time but also gives a much crisper skin.

PARSEE-STYLE HOT AND SWEET CHICKEN CURRY WITH APRICOTS

SALLI MURGHI

This quintessential Parsee favourite is quite a big boy in terms of flavours and textures: dark, rich, sweet and spicy, crisp and soft all at the same time. It is one of the trademark dishes of the wealthy Zoroastrian community in Mumbai and one of the very few Indian curries to combine meat and fruit so successfully.

SERVES 4

4 tablespoons vegetable or corn oil
1 teaspoon cumin seeds
5cm (2-inch) piece of cinnamon stick
3 black cardamom pods
1/2 teaspoon cloves
3 onions, finely chopped
1 tablespoon Ginger Paste (see page 202)
1 tablespoon Garlic Paste (see page 202)
1 free-range chicken, cut into 8–10 pieces
2 teaspoons salt
3 tomatoes, puréed
4 tablespoons white vinegar
8 dried apricots, sliced
1/2 teaspoon sugar
1 tablespoon dark soy sauce (optional)
2 tablespoons chopped fresh coriander

For the spice mix
5 dried red chillies
5cm (2-inch) piece of cinnamon stick
1 teaspoon cumin seeds
2 black cardamom pods
5 cloves

For the potato straws
1 large potato (such as Desiree), peeled and cut into matchsticks
vegetable or corn oil for frying
1/2 teaspoon salt
1/2 teaspoon red chilli powder

For the spice mix, roast all the spices in a dry frying pan over a medium heat for a minute or so and then grind them to a fine powder in a spice grinder or coffee grinder. Set aside.

To make the potato straws, wash the potato matchsticks in cold water, then drain and pat dry on kitchen paper. Pour about 5cm (2 inches) of oil into a saucepan or a deep frying pan and heat to 180°C/350°F. Add the potato strips and fry for about 2 minutes, until crisp and golden. Remove and spread out on kitchen paper to drain. Sprinkle with the salt and chilli powder, mix well and set aside.

To make the chicken curry, heat the oil in a saucepan, add the whole spices and let them crackle. Add the onions, and cook, stirring, over a high heat until golden brown. Add the ginger and garlic pastes, followed by the chicken, and stir for 2–3 minutes, until the chicken begins to colour. Add the salt and puréed tomatoes and cook, stirring, for 6–8 minutes, until the liquid from the tomatoes has evaporated. Reduce the heat, cover the pan and cook gently for about 25 minutes, until the chicken is almost done. Add the ground spice mix, stir in the vinegar, apricots and sugar and cook for another 5 minutes. If the chicken doesn't have a rich glaze, add the soy sauce. Sprinkle in the coriander and remove from the heat. Serve the chicken curry garnished with the potato straws and accompanied by Brown Basmati Pilau (see page 180).

OLD DELHI-STYLE CHICKEN CURRY

MURGH MAKHANWALA

In the 1950s, the legendary Moti Mahal restaurant in Old Delhi created the dish that symbolises Indian food for millions of people all over the world. Also known as butter chicken, it's the dish to sell your soul for!

This happens to be the first curry ever to appear on the menu at The Cinnamon Club and, although it features in the original *Cinnamon Club Cookbook* (2003, Absolute Press) the recipe has evolved, so I'm including it here too. Besides, I can't imagine a curry book without butter chicken. Ideally it would be cooked in a tandoor oven to give a smoky flavour, but an ordinary oven or barbecue is a good enough alternative.

SERVES 4

1 x 1.2kg free-range chicken, skinned and cut into 4 pieces on the bone

For the marinade
2 tablespoons Ginger-Garlic Paste (see page 202)
1 tablespoon vegetable or corn oil
1½ teaspoons salt
juice of 1 lemon
2 teaspoons red chilli powder
120g (½ cup) Greek-style yoghurt
¼ teaspoon garam masala

For the sauce
1.2kg (2¾lb) tomatoes, cut in half
125ml (½ cup) water
5cm (2-inch) piece of fresh ginger, half crushed and half finely chopped
4 garlic cloves, peeled
4 green cardamom pods
2 cloves
1 bay leaf
1 tablespoon red chilli powder
80g (⅓ cup) butter, diced
2 green chillies, slit into quarters
5 tablespoons single cream
1½ teaspoons salt
2 teaspoons dried fenugreek leaves, crushed between your fingertips
¼ teaspoon garam masala
1½ tablespoons sugar

Make small cuts all over the chicken pieces with a sharp knife to help the marinade penetrate. To marinate the chicken, mix it with the ginger-garlic paste, oil, salt, lemon juice and chilli powder and leave for 10 minutes. Then mix the yoghurt and garam masala together and apply to the chicken. Set aside for another 10 minutes, if you have time, or proceed to cook either on a barbecue on skewers or in an oven preheated to 220°C/425°F/Gas Mark 7 for 15–18 minutes. You may need to turn the pieces after 10 minutes or so to ensure they colour evenly on both sides. The chicken should be not quite cooked through. Strain off the juices through a fine sieve and set aside.

For the sauce, put the tomatoes in a pan with the water, crushed ginger, garlic, cardamom, cloves and bay leaf and bring to the boil. Simmer until the tomatoes have completely disintegrated. Now blend this tomato broth with a hand-held blender and pass it through a sieve to obtain a smooth purée. Return to a clean pan, add the chilli powder and simmer for 12–15 minutes. It should slowly begin to thicken. When the sauce turns glossy, add the chicken pieces and the reserved roasting juices. Then add a cup of water and simmer for about 5 minutes.

Slowly whisk in the butter a couple of pieces at a time and simmer for 8–10 minutes, until the chicken is cooked through and the sauce is beginning to acquire a glaze. Add the chopped ginger, slit green chillies and cream and simmer for a minute or two longer, taking care that the sauce does not split. Stir in the salt, crushed fenugreek leaves and garam masala, then check the seasoning and add the sugar. Serve with Naan Bread (see page 192) or Pilau Rice (see page 180).

Cook's note
The beauty of this dish is that it is quite similar to French cooking, since the butter is added at the end to emulsify and enrich the tomato sauce. Not many people realise this, and cook it for too long after adding the butter, which can cause the sauce to separate and lose its richness. If this does happen, simply whisk in a couple of tablespoons of water and a tablespoon of cream to bring the emulsion back.

SPICE-ROASTED WHOLE CHICKEN

MURGH MUSSALAM

A grand celebration dish, this is one you will struggle to find on restaurant menus anywhere. It has long been considered the king of Indian dishes and this version makes it even more special by adding raw rice to the cavity of the chicken, which is cooked by the time the bird is ready.

SERVES 4

1 x 1.2–1.5kg (2¾–3¼lb) free-range chicken
1 medium egg

For the marinade
2 tablespoons Ginger-Garlic Paste (see page 202)
1 tablespoon vegetable or corn oil
2 teaspoons salt
2 teaspoons red chilli powder
juice of 1 lemon
½ teaspoon garam masala
1 teaspoon dried fenugreek leaves
400g (1⅔ cups) plain yoghurt
5 tablespoons Crisp Fried Onions (see page 203)
3 tablespoons Fried Cashew Paste (see page 202)
1 tablespoon chopped mint

For the filling
50g (¼ cup) basmati rice, soaked in lukewarm water for 20 minutes
½ teaspoon royal (black) cumin seeds
1 tablespoon Crisp Fried Onions (see page 203)
½ teaspoon salt
a pinch of saffron strands

To finish
2 tablespoons single cream
1 tablespoon finely chopped coriander stalks
chat masala, for sprinkling

Mix together all the ingredients for the marinade and insert them carefully between the skin and the flesh of the chicken to spread the spices as much as possible, putting some inside the cavity as well. Set aside to marinate for 30 minutes. Reserve the excess marinade. Meanwhile, boil the egg for exactly 4 minutes, starting in cold water, then chill it in iced water. Peel and set aside.

Mix together all the ingredients for the filling and stir in just enough of the reserved marinade to bind the rice together. Now fill about a third of the chicken cavity with the spiced rice, place the egg in the centre of the cavity and then fill up with the remaining rice. Put the chicken in a roasting tin; you can use strips of foil to keep the legs crossed – this is important, as they cover the cavity, helping the rice to cook. Cover the tin with foil, place in the centre of an oven preheated to 200°C/400°F/Gas Mark 6 and roast for 40–45 minutes, basting half way through. Then remove the foil and cook for another 15–20 minutes. The skin should be golden and crisp; if you think it needs some more colour, place the bird under the grill for 2–3 minutes. The rice should be cooked by the time the chicken is ready. Remove from the oven and leave to rest for 20 minutes.

Strain off the juices into a small pan, add any remaining marinade and bring to the boil. Stir in the cream, correct the seasoning and finally stir in the fresh coriander. Sprinkle with chat masala and serve the whole bird at the table with the sauce on the side. Accompany with Pilau Rice (see page 180).

Cook's note
You could marinate the bird and stuff the cavity the night before and simply place it in the oven roughly an hour and a half before you need it. It's an ideal dish for preparing in advance and lets you get on with entertaining your guests while it's cooking.

TANJORE-STYLE CHICKEN CURRY

I consider this South Indian curry to be quite special, as its flavours are uncharacteristically clean and fresh compared to others from the south, which can be quite heavy on spicing. Tanjore, or Thanjavur as some call it, is certainly not known for its meat dishes but this one is a real winner.

SERVES 4

800g (1¾lb) chicken thighs, skinned, boned and cut in half

For the marinade
1 teaspoon Ginger Paste (see page 202)
1 teaspoon Garlic Paste (see page 202)
1½ teaspoons salt
½ teaspoon ground turmeric
4 green chillies, chopped
2 tablespoons vegetable or corn oil
juice of ½ lemon

For the green spice paste
100g (2 cups) fresh coriander, roughly chopped
25g (¾ cup) mint, roughly chopped
25g (2½ cups) fresh curry leaves
5 garlic cloves, roughly chopped
5cm (2-inch) piece of fresh ginger, roughly chopped
4 green chillies, roughly chopped

For the sauce
3 tablespoons vegetable or corn oil
30 fresh curry leaves
½ teaspoon mustard seeds
4 dried red chillies
1 onion, chopped
½ teaspoon ground turmeric
1 teaspoon red chilli powder
1 teaspoon ground coriander
2 tomatoes, chopped
100g (scant ½ cup) Boiled Cashew Paste (see page 202)
1 teaspoon salt
3 tablespoons single cream

Mix together all the ingredients for the marinade and rub them on to the chicken thighs. Set aside for 20 minutes.

To make the green spice paste, blend all the ingredients together in a food processor, adding a little water or oil if necessary.

Spread the chicken pieces out on a roasting tray and place in an oven preheated to 220°C/425°F/Gas Mark 7. Roast for 15 minutes, until about two-thirds cooked through, then remove from the oven and set aside.

For the sauce, heat the oil in a frying pan, add the curry leaves and fry over a high heat until crisp. Remove with a slotted spoon, drain on kitchen paper and set aside. Add the mustard seeds and red chillies to the oil in the pan. When they begin to crackle, add the onion and sauté until golden brown. Stir in the ground spices, followed by the tomatoes, and cook over a medium heat until the tomatoes have completely broken down and reduced by about half.

Add the cashew paste and salt and cook over a low heat, stirring constantly, until the oil begins to separate from the mixture. Add the chicken, along with any juices from the tray, and simmer for 5 minutes. Stir in the green spice paste and cook for another 5 minutes. Crush the fried curry leaves and add them to the pan. Stir in the cream, then remove from the heat and serve with steamed rice or Layered Parathas (see page 196).

DUCK CURRY WITH PEANUTS, SESAME AND TAMARIND

HYDERABADI BUTTAKH KA SALAN

The original version of the Hyderabadi favourite, *salan*, this is a beautiful dish with fragrant spices, complex flavours and a nutty richness.

SERVES 4

1 duck, cut into 10 pieces on the bone
1/2 teaspoon salt

For the sauce
2 tablespoons coriander seeds
1 tablespoon sesame seeds
1 teaspoon cumin seeds
100g (1 cup) desiccated coconut
4 tablespoons vegetable or corn oil
50g (1/2 cup) peanuts
4 dried red chillies
1/2 teaspoon mustard seeds
1/2 teaspoon black onion seeds
2 sprigs of fresh curry leaves
2 quantities of Boiled Onion Paste (see page 203)
1 teaspoon red chilli powder
1/2 teaspoon ground turmeric
1 litre (4 cups) water
1 1/2 teaspoons salt
1/2 teaspoon sugar
2 tablespoons tamarind paste
25g (1/2 cup) fresh coriander, chopped

Place the duck pieces in a roasting tin, sprinkle with the salt and roast in an oven preheated to 200°C/400°F/Gas Mark 6 for 20–25 minutes.

Meanwhile, make the sauce. Mix together the coriander, sesame and cumin seeds and roast them in a dry frying pan over a moderate heat for a minute or so. Tip them out on to a plate and set aside. Roast the coconut in the same pan until golden and add to the seeds. Heat a tablespoon of the oil in the pan, add the peanuts and fry until golden. Remove and combine with the seeds and coconut. Blend to a smooth paste in a food processor, adding as little water as possible.

Heat the remaining oil in a pan and add the red chillies and mustard seeds. When they crackle, add the onion seeds and curry leaves, followed by the onion paste, and cook for 8–10 minutes. Now add the nut and seed paste and stir over a low heat for a couple of minutes. Add the chilli powder and turmeric, followed by the roast duck pieces, and cook over a high heat for 2–3 minutes, stirring constantly. Pour in the water, reduce the heat and simmer for 30 minutes, until the duck is almost tender. Stir in the salt, sugar and tamarind paste and cook for 5–6 more minutes. Sprinkle in the coriander and serve with Pilau Rice (see page 180).

Cook's note
You could make the sauce separately and serve with seared duck breasts if you do not like bones.

HALF A DOZEN QUAILS IN SPICY CURRY

BATEYR MASALA

When the reign of the Nawabs was at its peak in Lucknow, *bawarchis*, or cooks, supplied a variety of foods to the *dyodhi* (literally, threshold of the door) of their patrons. The food came in trays covered with a dome-shaped frame draped in muslin, which was secured with a tape and sealed with *lac* (a kind of resin) in order to prevent anyone tampering with it. Come to think of it, in the 1750s this must have been quite an advanced system of home deliveries and take-outs!

A dish such as this one was for special occasions; or if a cook managed to lay his hands on some sand grouse or other exotic game, he would simply prepare the dish for a client that he knew would love it and take it along. Quite often he'd arrive unannounced and uninvited, and almost always his dish would be accepted and he would be rewarded for his efforts.

SERVES 6

6 large quails, weighing 250–300g (9–10oz) each, skinned
2 tablespoons Ginger Paste (see page 202)
2 tablespoons Garlic Paste (see page 202)
1 teaspoon ground turmeric
2½ teaspoons salt
100ml (scant ½ cup) vegetable oil or ghee
2.5cm (1-inch) piece of cinnamon stick
a blade of mace
2 black cardamom pods
1 tablespoon black peppercorns
½ teaspoon cloves
5 green cardamom pods
1½ x quantity of Fried Onion Paste (see page 203)
2 tablespoons ground coriander
450g (2 cups) plain yoghurt, whisked with ½ tablespoon roasted gram (chickpea) flour until smooth
1 teaspoon garam masala
2 tablespoons finely chopped fresh coriander
a few drops of rosewater
a pinch of saffron strands

Wash the quails inside and out under cold running water, drain on a wire rack and then pat dry on kitchen paper. Mix together 1 tablespoon of ginger paste, 1 tablespoon of garlic paste, ½ teaspoon of turmeric and 1 teaspoon of salt and rub them over the birds. Set aside for 10–15 minutes.

Choose a wide, shallow pan, preferably one that can hold all 6 quails comfortably and has a well-fitting lid. Heat the oil or ghee in it, then carefully place the quails in the hot oil, taking care not to crowd the pan. Cook over a high heat until evenly coloured on all sides, then remove the birds from the pan and set aside.

Reheat the oil, add the whole spices and stir for a minute to release their flavours. Add the onion paste and the remaining ginger and garlic pastes and cook over a medium heat for 5–6 minutes, stirring to prevent the pastes sticking to the bottom of the pan. Add the coriander and the remaining turmeric and salt and cook for 6–7 minutes, until the fat begins to separate from the pastes.

Return the seared quails to the pan and mix carefully, taking care not to break the birds. Now pour over the whisked yoghurt, cover the pan, reduce the heat and simmer for 12–15 minutes, until the birds are cooked through. Remove the lid, stir the sauce to check the consistency and add a little water if necessary; the sauce should coat the birds lightly. Correct the seasoning if required. Stir in the garam masala and fresh coriander, then sprinkle in the rosewater and saffron. Put the lid back on and remove from the heat.

Serve with a pilau of your choice (see page 180).

Cook's note
This could also be made with other game birds, such as partridge, pheasant and grouse, so feel free and go game!

DRY-SPICE-CRUSTED GUINEA FOWL WITH YELLOW LENTIL SAUCE

This is a modern interpretation of a typical, everyday, middle-class Indian dish of *dal-roti* and *kukkad* – i.e. lentils, bread and country chicken.

SERVES 4

4 guinea fowl breasts, boned, skinned and each cut into 3–4 pieces
1 tablespoon vegetable or corn oil
4 wooden skewers, soaked in water for 30 minutes

For the marinade
1 tablespoon Ginger-Garlic Paste (see page 202)
1½ teaspoons salt
1 teaspoon red chilli flakes
1 teaspoon red chilli powder
½ teaspoon ground allspice
juice of 1 lemon
2 tablespoons plain yoghurt
1 tablespoon finely chopped coriander stalks

For the coarsely ground spice crust
2 teaspoons cracked black peppercorns
6 cloves, coarsely ground
2 teaspoons fennel seeds, coarsely ground

For the yellow lentil sauce
120g (⅔ cup) yellow moong lentils (split yellow mung beans)
750ml (3 cups) water
1 teaspoon ground turmeric
1½ teaspoons salt
1 tablespoon ghee
1 dried red chilli
a pinch of asafoetida
1 teaspoon cumin seeds
2 garlic cloves, finely chopped
1 onion, finely chopped
1 tomato, finely chopped
1cm (½-inch) piece of fresh ginger, chopped
1 tablespoon chopped fresh coriander
juice of ½ lemon

For the marinade, mix together the ginger-garlic paste, salt, chilli flakes, chilli powder, allspice and lemon juice, then rub them over the guinea fowl breast pieces and set aside. In the meantime, mix half the coarsely ground spices with the yoghurt and coriander stalks. Apply this mixture to the breast pieces to complete the marinade, thread the guinea fowl onto the wooden skewers and set aside while you prepare the sauce.

To make the lentil sauce, rinse the lentils under cold running water, then place in a pan with the water, turmeric and salt. Bring to the boil, then reduce the heat and simmer for about 25 minutes, until the lentils have thoroughly disintegrated. Blend the mixture to a purée with a hand-held blender.

Heat the ghee in a heavy-based pan, add the whole dried chilli, asafoetida, and cumin seeds and let them crackle. Add the garlic, wait for it to turn golden brown, then add the onion. Sauté over a moderate heat until golden. Add the tomato and cook for 3 minutes, then pour in the puréed lentils. Stir in the ginger and coriander and bring to the boil. Adjust the seasoning and finish with the lemon juice.

To cook the guinea fowl, heat the oil in a large, ovenproof frying pan (big enough to accommodate the skewers) and sear the guinea fowl skewers for 2 minutes on each side. Sprinkle the rest of the coarsely ground spices over the guinea fowl, then transfer the pan to an oven preheated to 200°C/400°F/Gas Mark 6 and cook for 6–8 minutes. Serve on the lentil sauce, accompanied by bread or rice.

Cook's note
The guinea fowl could be replaced with chicken breasts or thighs and the skewers will cook every bit as well under a grill or on a barbecue.

MIXED GAME COOKED IN AN INDIAN WOK

KADHAI KA SHIKAR

Shikar is a Hindi term for hunted meat, and this kadhai-style preparation is a quick and easy way to enjoy whatever you may be able to lay your hands upon.

SERVES 4

1 grouse
1 partridge
1 quail
1 pheasant
3 tablespoons vegetable or corn oil
2 dried red chillies
1 teaspoon coriander seeds, crushed
1/2 teaspoon cumin seeds
1/2 teaspoon fennel seeds
2 bay leaves
2 onions, 1 1/2 finely chopped and 1/2 cut into strips 1cm (1/2 inch) thick
4 garlic cloves, chopped
5cm (2-inch) piece of fresh ginger, chopped
2 green chillies, chopped
1 teaspoon red chilli powder
1 teaspoon ground coriander
1/2 teaspoon ground cumin
5 tomatoes, 4 puréed and 1 deseeded and cut into strips 1cm (1/2 inch) thick
1 1/2 teaspoons salt
1/2 teaspoon sugar
1 tablespoon chopped fresh coriander
juice of 1 lime

For the spice mix
3 dried red chillies
1 tablespoon coriander seeds
2 teaspoons fennel seeds
1 teaspoon cumin seeds
1 teaspoon black peppercorns
2.5cm (1-inch) piece of cinnamon stick
1/2 teaspoon carom seeds

Skin the birds, then cut the breasts off the bone. You won't need the legs but you could keep them to use for another dish. Cut the breasts into strips about 1cm (1/2 inch) thick and set aside.

To make the spice mix, roast all the ingredients in a dry frying pan over a moderate heat for a couple of minutes and then pound them to a coarse powder using a mortar and pestle. Set aside.

Heat the oil in a wok or a large frying pan, add the whole spices and bay leaves and let them crackle. Add the finely chopped onions and sauté until golden. Add the garlic, ginger and green chillies and sauté for a minute. Stir in the chilli powder, ground coriander and cumin and cook for another minute. Add the puréed tomatoes and continue cooking until they are reduced by half. Add the meat and sauté over a high heat for 2 minutes to sear it quickly. Add the onion strips, reduce the heat, stir in the spice mix, salt and sugar and cook for another minute or so. Add the tomato strips and mix well. Sprinkle in the fresh coriander, squeeze in the lime juice and remove from the heat. Serve with Naan Bread (see page 192) and a light salad.

Cook's notes
The leg meat from the birds could be minced and prepared in the same spices as above to make a game *keema*, or game curry.

You could also use hare or venison in this dish.

ROAST GROUSE WITH BLACK LENTILS

This sort of dish makes me feel fortunate to be cooking in Britain. Although India has a rich tradition of game cooking, it has now disappeared, due to a complete ban on hunting for the last 60 years, and an entire generation of chefs has never cooked any kind of game whatsoever. This is my effort to reclaim and preserve the lost art of Indian game cooking.

The grouse need to be skinned, the breasts and legs removed, boned and trimmed, then the meat from the legs, plus any trimmings, minced. Your butcher should be able to do this for you, given a little notice.

SERVES 4

4 grouse, prepared as described above
1 tablespoon vegetable or corn oil
Black Lentils (see page 184), to serve

For the marinade

1 tablespoon vegetable or corn oil
1½ teaspoons salt
1 tablespoon Ginger-Garlic Paste (see page 202)
1 teaspoon cumin seeds, roasted in a dry frying pan and then coarsely ground
8 cloves, roasted in a dry frying pan and then coarsely ground
1 teaspoon red chilli powder

For the mince

3 tablespoons vegetable or corn oil
1 bay leaf
2 dried red chillies
1 teaspoon coriander seeds, crushed
1 onion, finely chopped
1 tablespoon Ginger-Garlic Paste (see page 202)
1 teaspoon red chilli powder
1 teaspoon ground coriander
½ teaspoon ground cumin
1 tomato, chopped
1 teaspoon salt
1 tablespoon chopped fresh coriander

Mix all the ingredients for the marinade together in a large bowl and gently fold the grouse breasts into it. Leave to marinate in the fridge for 30 minutes.

Meanwhile, for the mince, heat the oil in a pan and add the bay leaf and whole dried chillies, then the coriander seeds. Sauté for a minute or so, until they release their flavours. Add the onion and sauté until golden. Add the ginger-garlic paste and stir for a minute, then sprinkle in the chilli powder, coriander and cumin and stir for another minute. Now add the tomato and salt and cook for about 5 minutes, until the oil starts separating from the mixture. Stir in the minced leg meat and cook for 6–8 minutes over a medium heat, until the mince is done. Stir in the chopped fresh coriander.

To cook the grouse breasts, heat the oil in a frying pan, add the marinated grouse breasts and sear for 30 seconds on each side. Place the pan under a hot grill and cook for 1 minute. Remove from the heat, leave to rest for 5 minutes, then serve with the mince and Black Lentils.

Cook's notes

If you don't like your game too strong, then it is advisable to bulk the minced leg meat up with about 100g (4oz) lean minced lamb or beef. Alternatively, you could boil the mince in salted water with a pinch of turmeric for 5–6 minutes to make it milder, then drain well.

The grouse goes equally well with Pumpkin Pickle (see page 190). The rich, sweet flavours of the pickle work very well with the earthy, musky flavour of grouse.

Take care not to over cook the breasts, as they dry up very quickly. Since it is a very lean meat, grouse is best cooked fast and served medium.

SPICED ROAST PARTRIDGE BREASTS WITH CURRIED PEARS

Mention this dish and it always reminds people of Christmas. It's quite appropriate, as both partridges and pears are at their best at that time of year. The combination of flavours is rather unusual but it felt right when I thought of it and it tastes fantastic.

SERVES 4

8 partridge breasts

For the first marinade
1 teaspoon salt
1 tablespoon Ginger Paste (see page 202)
1 tablespoon Garlic Paste (see page 202)

For the second marinade
2 teaspoons dried mango powder
2 tablespoons white vinegar
250g (1 cup) plain yoghurt
4 green chillies, finely chopped
1 teaspoon salt
2 tablespoons chopped coriander stalks
1 teaspoon garam masala
1 teaspoon sugar
3 tablespoons peanuts, roasted in a dry frying pan and then coarsely crushed

For the curried pears
2 tablespoons vegetable or corn oil
a pinch of asafoetida
1 teaspoon cumin seeds
1 teaspoon chopped fresh ginger
1 green chilli, chopped
2 pears, quartered and cored
150g ($^2/_3$ cup) plain yoghurt
1 teaspoon ground turmeric

Mix together all the ingredients for the first marinade, rub them over the partridge breasts and set aside for 10 minutes.

Mix all the ingredients for the second marinade with the partridge breasts, adding the peanuts last. Leave to marinate for 30 minutes or so.

Meanwhile, prepare the curried pears. Heat the oil in a large frying pan and fry the asafoetida, cumin seeds, ginger and green chilli for about 30 seconds over a high heat. Add the pears and toss for a minute. Add the yoghurt and turmeric and cook over a low heat for a minute or so, stirring constantly, until the pears are glazed and evenly coated with the sauce. Remove from the heat and keep warm.

Thread the partridge breasts on skewers and cook in an oven preheated to 200°C/400°F/ Gas Mark 6 for 6–8 minutes. Alternate the partridge with the pears on a platter and serve.

Cook's note
When you come to serving, if you feel the pears have soaked up all the sauce, just add half a cup of water and reheat to bring the sauce back. Serve immediately.

ROAST SADDLE OF RED DEER WITH PICKLING SAUCE

This is one of the dishes I am immensely proud of, and I believe it embodies what contemporary curry is all about. Game cooking is fast becoming a lost art in Indian cuisine and I feel passionately about preserving it. This recipe is a perfect example of combining old and new, East and West – the best of both worlds.

It first appeared on the menu at The Cinnamon Club in 2003, when it was probably the first dish to cross the £30 mark in an Indian restaurant anywhere in the world! Although it was well received, it was not perceived as a curry until 2006, when it won the UK Best Dishes Award for Best Curry. It goes to show how much curries have changed all around the world over the last few years.

SERVES 4

1kg (2¼lb) venison from the saddle, trimmed and cut into 4 steaks
1 tablespoon Rajasthani Spice Paste (see page 203)
1 tablespoon Greek-style yoghurt
3 tablespoons vegetable or corn oil

For the marinade
½ teaspoon salt
½ teaspoon red chilli powder
1 tablespoon vegetable or corn oil

For the pickling sauce
3 tablespoons oil, preferably mustard oil
1 teaspoon pickling spice mix (1 part mustard seeds, 1 part black onion seeds, 1 part cumin seeds, ½ part fenugreek seeds, 2 parts fennel seeds)
1 onion, finely chopped
½ teaspoon ground turmeric
200g (scant 1 cup) Boiled Cashew Paste (see page 202)
3 tablespoons Greek-style yoghurt
250ml (1 cup) lamb stock or water
4 green chillies, slit open lengthwise
1 teaspoon salt
1 tablespoon jaggery or molasses sugar
1 tablespoon chopped fresh coriander

Mix together all the ingredients for the marinade, rub them over the steaks and set aside for 30 minutes. Mix the Rajasthani spice paste and yoghurt together and set aside.

Meanwhile, prepare the sauce. Heat the oil in a heavy-based frying pan and add the pickling spice mix. When the seeds begin to crackle, add the onion and sauté until golden brown. Add the turmeric, followed by the cashew paste, and cook, stirring, over a medium heat for 5 minutes. Now whisk in the yoghurt and stir over a low heat for 5 minutes, taking care that it does not split. Add the stock or water, green chillies and salt and simmer for about 10 minutes, until the sauce thickens and gets a glaze. Stir in the jaggery or molasses and chopped coriander and mix well. Remove from the heat, cover and keep warm while you cook the steaks.

Heat the oil in a large, ovenproof frying pan, add the meat and sear over a medium heat for 5–6 minutes on each side, until browned all over. Transfer to an oven preheated to 200°C/400°F/Gas Mark 6 and roast for 6–8 minutes if you like your meat pink, longer if you like it cooked more. Remove the steaks from the oven and spread the Rajasthani spice paste and yoghurt mixture over the top. Place under a hot grill (or return to the oven) for 1–2 minutes, until the top is lightly browned.

Divide the sauce between 4 serving plates and place the steaks on top – you can slice them or serve them whole, as you prefer. Serve with Pilau Rice (see page 180) or Masala Mash (page 181) on the side.

Cook's note
If you want to prepare this for a dinner party or for more people, ask your butcher to bone and roll an entire saddle for you, then double the quantities of the other ingredients and simply marinate the saddle with all the spices, including the Rajasthani spice mix and yoghurt. Roast it in the oven at 200°C/400°F/Gas Mark 6 for about 15 minutes. Remove from the oven and let it rest for 15 minutes, then carve and serve. Nice and easy! Remember, since venison is so lean, it can dry out very quickly, so it is always best to cook it fairly rare and let it rest for long enough.

RABBIT COOKED IN A PIT

KHAD KHARGOSH

This typical hunter's dish makes a complete meal on its own. In the days of the princes and Rajput kings, it would have been cooked on hunting expeditions, the rabbit wrapped in leaves and baked in a pit dug in the ground. I have replaced the leaves with foil (and the pit with an oven!).

SERVES 4

4 rabbit legs
4 white tortillas or chapattis
2 tablespoons butter or ghee, melted

For the marinade
4 tablespoons Greek-style yoghurt
1 tablespoon Ginger Paste (see page 202)
1 tablespoon Garlic Paste (see page 202)
1 teaspoon red chilli flakes
2 tablespoons Crisp Fried Onions (see page 203)
1 teaspoon cloves, lightly roasted in a dry frying pan and then ground to a powder
1 teaspoon ground turmeric
2 teaspoons red chilli powder
2 tablespoons Fried Cashew Paste (see page 202)
5cm (2-inch) piece of fresh papaya or pineapple, blended to a paste in a mini-chopper
6 green chillies, finely chopped
6 tablespoons mustard oil
2 tablespoons chopped fresh coriander
1½ teaspoons salt
½ teaspoon sugar

For the garlic chutney
20 dried red chillies
250ml (1 cup) malt vinegar
5 tablespoons vegetable or corn oil
½ teaspoon cumin seeds
2 heads of garlic, peeled and chopped
2 tablespoons tomato paste
1 teaspoon salt
2 teaspoons sugar
1 tablespoon chopped coriander roots
juice of ½ lime

First make the garlic chutney. Soak the dried chillies in the vinegar overnight, then blitz to a smooth paste in a food processor or blender. Heat the oil in a frying pan and add the cumin seeds, followed by the garlic and the chilli paste. Cook over a low heat for 20 minutes, stirring occasionally. Stir in the tomato paste, salt and sugar and continue to cook for about 10 minutes, until the mixture has reduced and thickened and the oil begins to separate from it. Sprinkle in the chopped coriander roots and squeeze in the lime juice. Mix well, remove from the heat and leave to cool. Store in the fridge.

To make the marinade, combine all the ingredients and mix well. Put the rabbit legs in a roasting tray, mix with the marinade and set aside for 15 minutes. Cover the tray tightly with foil, transfer it to an oven preheated to 180°C/350°F/Gas Mark 4 and braise for about an hour, until the meat is very tender. Remove the legs carefully and leave to cool.

Put the braising liquid in a pan and simmer until reduced to a thick, sauce-like consistency. Leave it to cool, then smear the legs with this sauce, coating them evenly on all sides.

Brush the tortillas or chapattis with the melted butter or ghee and wrap each one tightly around a rabbit leg. Trim off any excess, then wrap in foil, sealing it completely. Place in an oven preheated to 180°C/350°F/Gas Mark 4 and bake for 20–30 minutes, until the bread is crisp. Remove from the oven, carefully tear off the foil and serve with the garlic chutney.

ACCOMPANIMENTS

180 PILAU RICE
180 BROWN BASMATI PILAU
181 LEMON RICE
181 MASALA MASH
182 YELLOW LENTILS
184 BLACK LENTILS
186 CURRY LEAF AND TOMATO QUINOA
186 ROASTED AUBERGINE, TOMATO AND POTATO CRUSH
188 GREEN PEA RELISH
188 ROASTED YELLOW LENTIL RELISH
190 TAPIOCA CHIPS
190 PUMPKIN PICKLE
191 POMEGRANATE RAITA
191 CARROT AND PEANUT SALAD
192 NAAN BREAD
195 SPRING ONION PARATHAS
196 LAYERED PARATHAS
197 PEANUT CHUTNEY
197 GREEN COCONUT CHUTNEY
198 LASSI/CHAAS
198 LASSI
198 CHAAS
198 CUMIN COOLER

PILAU RICE

Broadly speaking, there are two ways of cooking rice: the boiling method and the absorption method. Plain boiled rice is the most commonly served in Indian households but pilaus, which are cooked by the absorption method, are much better as they retain more flavour and nutrients. They do rely on precise ratios and cooking times but the results are worth the effort.

SERVES 4–6

500g ($2^1/_2$ cups) basmati rice
3 tablespoons ghee
1 teaspoon cumin seeds
3 cloves
2 green cardamom pods
1 cinnamon stick
1 bay leaf
1 red onion, sliced
1 litre (4 cups) water
1 teaspoon salt
1 teaspoon chopped fresh mint
1 teaspoon chopped fresh coriander

Wash the rice under cold running water once or twice, then place in a bowl of cold water and leave to soak for 25 minutes (this reduces the cooking time and prevents the grains breaking during cooking).

Heat the ghee in a large, heavy-based casserole and add the whole spices and the bay leaf. When they crackle, add the sliced onion and sauté until golden brown. Now add the water and salt and bring to the boil. Drain the rice and add to the pan. Cover until it returns to the boil, then remove the lid and cook over a medium-high heat for about 6 minutes, stirring occasionally but keeping in mind that too much handling can break the rice grains.

When the water has nearly all been absorbed and you can see small holes on the surface of rice, sprinkle over the mint and coriander. Cover the casserole with a tight-fitting lid, reduce the heat to minimum and cook for 10 minutes (or cook in a very low oven for 10 minutes).

BROWN BASMATI PILAU

This is a healthier version of the traditional white rice pilau. Don't expect brown rice to be as light and fluffy but enjoy its interesting, nutty flavour.

SERVES 4-6

500g ($2^1/_2$ cups) brown basmati rice
3 tablespoons ghee or vegetable oil
1 teaspoon cumin seeds
4 cloves
1 bay leaf
1 small cinnamon stick
4 green cardamom pods
1 onion, thinly sliced
1.25 litres (5 cups) water
a few mint leaves, shredded
1 teaspoon salt

Wash the rice under cold running water once or twice, then leave it to soak in a bowl of cold water for 25 minutes.

Heat the ghee or oil in a heavy-based pan and add the cumin seeds, cloves, bay leaf, cinnamon and cardamom pods. When they crackle, add the sliced onion and sauté until light golden. Drain the rice, add to the pan and sauté for 2–3 minutes, taking care that the rice does not break. Now add the water, mint and salt and bring to the boil. Reduce the heat to low, cover and cook for about 20 minutes, until the rice is tender and the water has all been absorbed. Remove from the heat and stir the rice gently to mix. Cover the pan and leave to rest for 15 minutes or so.

Cook's note
Stirring the rice and turning it over gently after the water has been absorbed ensures that the grains are evenly cooked. By resting it for 15 minutes, you give the grains ample time to gain volume so that they don't stick to each other.

LEMON RICE

This is one of several types of dishes made from humble boiled rice in southern India and it makes you realise just how versatile rice can be. It adds colour, flavour and vibrancy to any dish it accompanies.

SERVES 4–6

400g (2 cups) basmati rice
3 tablespoons vegetable or corn oil
1 tablespoon mustard seeds
1 tablespoon chana dal (yellow split peas)
1 teaspoon urad dal (white urid lentils) – optional
20 fresh curry leaves
1 teaspoon ground turmeric
1½ teaspoons salt
juice of 3 lemons

Wash the rice under cold running water once or twice, then place in a bowl of cold water and leave to soak for 25 minutes. Drain well. Bring 1 litre (4 cups) of water to the boil in a saucepan and add the rice. Simmer, uncovered, for 8–10 minutes, until the grains are tender but not mushy. Drain through a sieve and set aside.

Heat the oil in a large pan, add the mustard seeds, chana dal and urid lentils, if using, and let them crackle. When they start to turn almost golden, add the curry leaves, then the turmeric, and stir for a minute (you may need to sprinkle in some water to prevent the turmeric burning). Add the cooked rice, salt and lemon juice and toss gently to mix well without breaking the rice grains.

MASALA MASH

Although masala mash is a term that's appeared on a lot of restaurant menus in the last few years, it was The Cinnamon Club that first started using it. Originally it was more of a spiced potato crush than a mash but it has evolved over the years to get closer to mash as we know it in the West.

SERVES 4

500g (1lb 2oz) floury potatoes such as Desiree, peeled and cut into chunks
4 tablespoons ghee
½ teaspoon cumin seeds
1 onion, finely chopped
¼ teaspoon ground turmeric
1cm (½-inch) piece of fresh ginger, finely chopped
2 green chillies, finely chopped
1 teaspoon salt
2 tablespoons single cream
1 tablespoon chopped fresh coriander

Cook the potatoes in boiling salted water until tender. Drain, mash thoroughly and set aside. Heat the ghee in a saucepan, add the cumin seeds, followed by the onion, and cook until the onion is tender. Add the turmeric, ginger and green chillies and stir for 30 seconds. Add the potatoes and salt and mix well over a low heat until the potatoes are heated thoroughly and coloured evenly by the turmeric. Add the cream, sprinkle in the coriander leaves and remove from the heat.

YELLOW LENTILS

TADKA DAL

This is India's everyday dal, compared to Black Lentils (see page 184), which is more for special occasions and tends to be cooked in restaurants rather than at home.

In most households the lentils would be served quite thin and watery, simply boiled and tempered with spices. The process of adding spices crackling in hot fat to cooked dal is commonly known as *tadka*, hence the name of this dish.

The flavours and spices vary from region to region. In Rajasthan they would simply use asafoetida, cumin and chilli, in the Punjab garlic, onion and tomatoes are added, while in southern India it's common to see lentils tempered with curry leaves, chillies and mustard seeds. The options and flavour combinations are endless.

SERVES 4–6

100g (1/2 cup) masoor dal (red lentils)
100g (1/2 cup) moong dal (split yellow mung beans)
1.2 litres (5 cups) water
1/2 teaspoon ground turmeric
2 teaspoons salt
2 tablespoons ghee
2 dried red chillies
a pinch of asafoetida
1 teaspoon cumin seeds
4 garlic cloves, finely chopped
1 onion, finely chopped
1 teaspoon red chilli powder
1 tomato, finely chopped
2.5cm (1-inch) piece of fresh ginger, chopped
2 green chillies, chopped
1 tablespoon chopped fresh coriander
juice of 1/2 lemon

Wash the red and yellow lentils under cold running water, then drain well. Put them in a pan with the water, turmeric and salt, bring to the boil, then reduce the heat and simmer for 30–40 minutes, until they are so thoroughly disintegrated that you cannot tell the different lentils apart. Remove from the heat and keep warm.

Heat the ghee in a heavy-based pan, add the whole red chillies, asafoetida, and cumin seeds and allow them to crackle. Add the garlic, wait for it to turn golden, then add the onion and sauté over a moderate heat until golden brown. Add the chilli powder and sauté for a minute or two. Add the tomato and cook for 5–6 minutes over a moderate heat. Throw in the ginger, green chillies and coriander, then pour the mixture over the lentils. Adjust the seasoning and finish with the lemon juice.

Cook's note

In some parts of the country, as many as five different types of lentils are used. You could include as many types as you can find; just make sure that most of them have had their husk removed, otherwise it changes the colour of the final dish.

Left to right
Yellow Lentils (this page);
Pumpkin Pickle (page 192);
Carrot and Peanut Salad (page 193).

BLACK LENTILS

Probably India's favourite lentil recipe, this northern speciality features in all Indian restaurants of any standing. Rich, creamy, earthy, musky and fragrant all at the same time, it is one of the most wonderful dishes you could ever come across. Bukhara in Delhi, which always features in the world's top 50 restaurants (the only restaurant in India to appear on this elite list), has had this dish on its menu since 1978 and sells over 60 litres of it every day!

SERVES 4–6

- 250g (1 1/4 cups) black urid lentils, soaked in lukewarm water overnight and then drained
- 2.5 litres (2 1/2 quarts) water
- 4 tablespoons vegetable or corn oil
- 2 black cardamom pods
- 1 green cardamom pod
- 1 bay leaf
- 1 tablespoon chopped garlic
- 1 1/2 tablespoons Ginger-Garlic Paste (see page 202)
- 1 tablespoon red chilli powder
- 1 1/2 teaspoons salt
- 6 tablespoons thick tomato purée, or 6 large ripe tomatoes, puréed
- 100g (scant 1/2 cup) salted butter, diced
- 1 teaspoon dried fenugreek leaves, crushed between your fingertips
- 1 teaspoon garam masala
- 1 teaspoon sugar
- 4 tablespoons single cream

Place the drained lentils in a large pan with the water, bring to the boil and simmer for 1 hour or until they are thoroughly tender but not mushy.

Heat the oil in a large, heavy-based pan, add the cardamoms and bay leaf and let them crackle. Add the chopped garlic and stir until golden, then add the ginger-garlic paste and sauté for 3–4 minutes. Add the chilli powder, salt and tomato purée and cook for 5 minutes.

Pour the lentils and their cooking liquid into the pan and cook over a medium heat, stirring constantly, until they are mashed and thoroughly incorporated into the mixture. Add the butter a little at a time and keep stirring to prevent it separating. Stir in the fenugreek leaves, garam masala, sugar and cream and cook for 3–4 minutes, then remove from the heat. Serve as an accompaniment to another dish or with bread.

Cook's notes
Wash the lentils in 3–5 changes of water before you soak them; this will prevent them going murky during cooking.

Clockwise from top
Peanut Chutney (page 197);
Black Lentils (this page);
Kachumber (page 76).

CURRY LEAF AND TOMATO QUINOA

We've only had quinoa on the menu at The Cinnamon Club for a few weeks, so it's relatively new and we're quite excited about it. For people with a gluten intolerance, it's an absolute godsend. I've discovered that it cooks beautifully as a southern Indian *upma*, which is normally made with semolina, and it can even be substituted for rice in some recipes.

SERVES 4 (OR 2 AS A MAIN COURSE)

100g (2/3 cup) quinoa
2 tablespoons vegetable or corn oil
1 dried red chilli, broken into 3 pieces
1 teaspoon mustard seeds
20 fresh curry leaves
1 large onion, finely chopped
1 green chilli, finely chopped
1cm (1/2-inch) piece of fresh ginger, finely chopped
1 tomato, coarsely chopped
1 1/2 teaspoons salt
1/4 teaspoon red chilli powder
1/2 teaspoon sugar
1 tablespoon finely chopped fresh coriander or basil
juice of 1/2 lemon

Soak the quinoa in cold water for 15 minutes, then drain and rinse. Put it in a pan with 300ml (1 1/4 cups) salted water, bring to the boil and simmer for about 15 minutes, until the grains are cooked but still retain some bite (quinoa develops a white ring round the circumference of each grain when it is about ready). Drain off any excess water.

While the quinoa is cooking, start preparing the tempering. Heat the oil in a heavy-based pan and add the red chilli and mustard seeds. Let them crackle and splutter for about 30 seconds, then add the curry leaves. As soon as they are crisp, add the onion and cook for 6–8 minutes, until starting to turn golden. Now add the green chilli and ginger and stir for a minute. Add the chopped tomato, salt and chilli powder and cook over a medium heat for 8–10 minutes, until most of the moisture from the tomato has evaporated and the mixture begins to come together.

Add the cooked quinoa and mix for a minute or two, until heated through. Finish with the sugar, coriander or basil and lemon juice. Mix thoroughly and serve hot.

ROASTED AUBERGINE, TOMATO AND POTATO CRUSH

This rustic, earthy accompaniment is quite versatile and goes with lots of things. In the summer I like to serve it with grilled fish dishes, while in the autumn it's good with stuffed breads. It also makes a great accompaniment to kedgeree.

SERVES 4

1 large aubergine
2 tomatoes
1 medium potato, boiled, peeled and mashed
2 green chillies, finely chopped
1cm (1/2-inch) piece of fresh ginger, finely chopped
1 tablespoon chopped fresh coriander
1 teaspoon salt
1/2 teaspoon sugar
juice of 1 lemon
1 tablespoon mustard oil

Prick the aubergine all over with a knife, then place in an oven preheated to 180°C/350°F/Gas Mark 4 and roast for 20–30 minutes, until soft. Roast the whole tomatoes in the oven for 15 minutes. Remove them both from the oven and leave until cool enough to handle, then peel. Place the aubergine and tomato flesh in a mixing bowl, add all the remaining ingredients and mash together well. Check the seasoning and serve warm.

Cook's note
You could make this with just aubergines or potatoes as well.

Opposite
Curry Leaf and Tomato Quinoa

GREEN PEA RELISH

I discovered this recipe only very recently, even though I grew up in the region that it comes from – the border of Bengal and Bihar, in eastern India – and I was totally taken aback by it. The sweetness of the peas is beautifully balanced by the kick from the garlic and mustard oil, and it is reminiscent of Japanese wasabi in both appearance and taste.

SERVES 4

300g (2 cups) fresh or frozen peas
2.5cm (1-inch) piece of fresh ginger, chopped
3 garlic cloves, chopped
3 green chillies, chopped
1/2 teaspoon salt
1/2 teaspoon sugar
1 1/2 tablespoons mustard oil
1/2 teaspoon mustard seeds
10 fresh curry leaves
juice of 1/2 lime

Place the peas, ginger, garlic, green chillies, salt, sugar, and 1 tablespoon of the mustard oil in a food processor and blitz to a smooth purée. Transfer to a bowl. Heat the remaining mustard oil in a small pan, add the mustard seeds and curry leaves and let them crackle. Remove from the heat and pour the mixture over the pea purée. Check the seasoning and finish with the lime juice.

ROASTED YELLOW LENTIL RELISH

SATTU KA MASALA

This rather spicy relish is extremely versatile and can be used as an accompaniment to a simple meal of steamed rice and vegetables or as a filling for bread. It's quite common in parts of eastern Uttar Pradesh, Rajasthan and Bihar and is particularly suitable for areas of dry, arid heat, as it helps water retention in the body.

SERVES 8–10

400g (14oz) roasted gram (chickpea) flour
about 5 tablespoons mustard oil, or the oil from hot mango pickle
2 red onions, finely chopped
4 garlic cloves, finely chopped
4 green chillies, finely chopped
2.5cm (1-inch) piece of fresh ginger, finely chopped
1/2 teaspoon carom seeds
1 1/2 teaspoons black onion seeds
3 teaspoons salt
1 tablespoon sugar
3 tablespoons chopped fresh coriander
4 tablespoons raisins
juice of 1 lemon

Mix together all the ingredients, adding more oil if necessary to help them hold together, and serve straight up. Alternatively you can use this relish to fill paratha dough (see page 196) and make stuffed parathas. They go really well with yoghurt and are great as a vegetarian main course.

Cook's note
The relish will keep in an airtight container in the fridge for up to a week.

Clockwise from top
Green Pea Relish (this page); Pomegranate Raita (page 193); Roasted Yellow Lentil Relish (this page).

TAPIOCA CHIPS

These make a great alternative to potato crisps, and add texture to any dish. They can be served with pretty much anything: to perk up a simple vegetarian or seafood dish or as a snack with a chutney or dip of your choice.

SERVES 4

vegetable or corn oil for deep-frying
1 medium-sized tapioca (cassava)
1 teaspoon salt
½ teaspoon red chilli powder
a pinch of sugar
a pinch of asafoetida

Heat the oil to 180°C/350°F in a deep-fat fryer or a deep saucepan. Peel the tapioca and slice it into thin rounds using a mandoline or a vegetable slicer. Quickly drop them one by one into the hot oil and stir with a slotted spoon to prevent them sticking together. Cook for 3–4 minutes, until golden and crisp. Remove and spread them out on kitchen paper to drain. Transfer to a mixing bowl while still warm, sprinkle with the seasonings and mix well.

PUMPKIN PICKLE

This is my mother's recipe for a sweet pumpkin pickle. I am a great fan of its rich, spicy flavours. It makes an excellent accompaniment to game dishes such as grouse or venison, it's fantastic with parathas and may even be used as a spread in sandwiches or to perk up wraps.

SERVES 4

4 tablespoons vegetable or corn oil
½ teaspoon fenugreek seeds
4 dried red chillies, broken into 2–3 pieces each
700g (1lb 9oz) peeled pumpkin flesh, cut into 1cm (½-inch) dice
2 teaspoons salt
1 tablespoon red chilli powder
1 teaspoon ground turmeric
5 tablespoons sugar
2 teaspoons dried mango powder (or mango pickle from a jar)

Heat the oil in a pan, add the fenugreek seeds and dried red chillies and let them pop. Add the pumpkin and stir over a high heat for 3–4 minutes. Stir in the salt, chilli powder and turmeric, then reduce the heat, cover and cook until the pumpkin is soft and begins to break down. Stir in the sugar – the sweetness balances the heat and spice and also makes the pickle glossy. Finish with the dried mango powder or mango pickle.

POMEGRANATE RAITA

Raita is a common accompaniment to Indian meals. It helps take the heat off certain dishes, keeps the body cool in hot months and aids digestion.

SERVES 4

1 pomegranate
500g (2 cups) Greek-style yoghurt
1 spring onion, finely chopped
2.5cm (1 inch) piece of fresh ginger, finely chopped
2 green chillies, finely chopped
1 teaspoon cumin seeds, roasted in a dry frying pan and then ground
1 teaspoon salt
1/2 teaspoon sugar
1 tablespoon chopped fresh coriander

Cut the pomegranate in half and remove the seeds, gently tapping the halves with a rolling pin or the back of a heavy knife to loosen them. Reserve a few seeds for garnish. Combine the rest with all the other ingredients except the coriander leaves and mix well. Transfer the raita to 4 bowls, sprinkle the coriander and reserved pomegranate seeds on top and chill until ready to serve.

CARROT AND PEANUT SALAD

Known in India as a *koshimbir*, this is one of the few bona fide salads served there. The combination of carrots and peanuts is unique and works very well with the fresh flavours, especially when carrots are in season and taste sweet.

SERVES 4

50g (1/2 cup) roasted peanuts
3 large carrots, grated
1 1/2 teaspoons salt
1 teaspoon sugar
juice of 1 lemon
1 tablespoon chopped fresh coriander

For tempering
1 tablespoon vegetable or corn oil
1/2 teaspoon mustard seeds
2 dried red chillies, broken into quarters
a sprig of fresh curry leaves

Crush the peanuts lightly in a pestle and mortar and mix with the rest of the ingredients.

To make the tempering, heat the oil in a small frying pan and add the mustard seeds and red chillies. When they begin to crackle and change colour, add the curry leaves, then pour the mixture over the salad. Mix well and serve.

Cook's notes
You can have all the ingredients prepared beforehand and assemble just before serving.

If you keep the salad for too long after mixing, the carrots and peanuts lose their crunch and it's not half as much fun.

NAAN BREAD

This humble bread from Delhi and Punjab is probably one of the tandoor's finest gifts to mankind. It is popular the world over and makes an excellent accompaniment to any curry. Try using it for sandwiches, rolls or even as a base for canapés, too.

MAKES 16

3 tablespoons caster sugar
2 eggs
400ml ($1^{2}/_{3}$ cups) whole milk
750g (5 cups) plain white flour
$1^{1}/_{2}$ teaspoons baking powder
1 tablespoon salt
3 tablespoons vegetable oil

Mix the sugar, eggs and milk together until the sugar has dissolved. Sift the flour into a bowl and stir in the baking powder and salt. Add the milk mixture to the flour, stir to combine, then turn out on to a floured work surface and knead lightly to make a soft dough. Take care not to work the gluten too much, or the dough will become too stretchy. Cover with a damp cloth and leave to rest for 15 minutes.

Lightly knead the oil into the dough until thoroughly incorporated. Divide the dough into 16 pieces and roll each one out on a lightly floured surface into a circle about 10cm (4 inches) in diameter.

Traditionally naan bread is cooked in a charcoal-fired clay oven but instead you can preheat your oven, with some baking sheets in it, to 220°C/425°F/Gas Mark 7, then put the breads on the hot baking sheets and cook for 4–5 minutes. You might need to turn the bread over if the underneath starts to colour but the top is still pale.

Alternatively, crank up your grill to maximum power and keep it ready. Place a few large, heavy-based frying pans on the hob and, when they're good and hot, place two naan breads in each one and cook for a couple of minutes until they start to colour lightly underneath. Remove the pan from the hob and place directly under the grill for a minute or so, until the bread puffs up and colours a little. *Voilà*! Your naan bread is ready and you did not even need a tandoor oven.

Cook's note
You can get as creative as you like with toppings for naan: before baking, try sprinkling them with turmeric, crushed chilli, fresh coriander, garlic, grated cheese, pesto, sun-dried tomatoes, olives – quite simply anything you fancy!

SPRING ONION PARATHAS

These are one of my childhood favourites. Normally these triangular breads are quite plain but my mother used to spice them up with onions, ginger, chillies etc. They also include some ghee to act as a shortening, which makes them really crisp. Serve with a simple chutney or dip, or cut them into small pieces to serve as canapés.

MAKES 8

500g (3 1/3 cups) plain white flour
2 tablespoons ghee
1/2 teaspoon carom seeds
1/2 teaspoon black onion seeds
3 green chillies, deseeded and finely chopped
1 red onion, finely chopped
2.5cm (1-inch) piece of fresh ginger, finely chopped
the green parts of 2 spring onions, finely chopped
1 1/2 teaspoons salt
1 tablespoon chopped fresh coriander, preferably the stalks
180ml (3/4 cup) water
4 tablespoons vegetable or corn oil

Put 400g (2 2/3 cups) of the flour into a bowl and rub in the ghee with your fingertips until it is evenly incorporated. Add all the remaining ingredients except the water and oil and mix well. Gradually add the water, little by little, and knead until it comes together into a very stiff dough. If necessary, sprinkle in an extra tablespoon or so of water. Cover with a damp cloth and leave to rest for 10 minutes.

Divide the dough into 8 pieces and shape each one into a smooth, round ball. Flatten each ball lightly with the palm of your hand. Roll out into a circle about 15cm (6 inches) in diameter, dusting with some of the reserved flour. Brush some of the oil over the top and dust with more flour. Fold the dough in half to make a semi-circle, then brush with more oil and sprinkle with flour. Fold again to get a small triangle. Roll out carefully to make a larger triangle about 3mm (1/8-inch) thick.

Place the paratha on a hot tawa or in a heavy-based frying pan and cook over a medium heat for 2–3 minutes, until the dough begins to dry out and get specks of brown underneath. Turn and cook the other side. While the second side is cooking, brush the first side lightly with oil. Turn again and cook until the colour deepens underneath, brushing the top with oil again. Turn once more. You should see the layers open up as the bread cooks. Remove from the heat once both sides are golden and crisp. Wrap loosely in foil to keep warm while you cook the remaining breads in the same way.

Cook's note

Take care not to add too much water to the dough, as the vegetables give out moisture and will eventually soften the dough, making it difficult to achieve a crisp, layered texture.

LAYERED PARATHAS

This is probably the most frequently cooked bread in Indian homes. Naan is usually eaten only in hotels and restaurants. Made with wholemeal flour, parathas are very versatile and can be served for breakfast, lunch or dinner.

MAKES 8

- 400g (2²/₃ cups) wholemeal flour
- 2 teaspoons salt
- 1 teaspoon carom seeds and/or ½ teaspoon black onion seeds
- 200ml (scant 1 cup) water
- 2 tablespoons vegetable or corn oil
- 5 tablespoons ghee

Set aside about 4 tablespoons of the flour and put the rest in a bowl. Add the salt, carom and/or black onion seeds, water and oil and knead until everything comes together into a smooth, stiff dough. Cover with a damp cloth and leave to rest for 20 minutes. Divide the dough into 8 portions, shape them into balls and leave to rest for another 15 minutes.

Flatten each ball lightly with the palm of your hand. Sprinkle some of the reserved flour on it and roll out into a circle about 20cm (8 inches) in diameter. Brush the top with ghee and sprinkle with a little more flour. Fold the dough in half to make a semi-circle, then brush with more ghee and sprinkle with flour. Fold again to give a small layered triangle.

Roll out each triangle to make a large triangle, taking care not to roll the dough too thin or you will lose the layers in the bread – roughly 3mm (⅛ inch) thickness is fine.

Heat a heavy-based frying pan or a flat griddle over a high heat, place one of the triangles in it and cook for 2–3 minutes, until the dough begins to dry out and colours underneath. Turn and cook the other side, then reduce the heat to medium. Brush the top of the bread with ghee and turn it over again until it develops a deeper colour. Brush the top and turn again. You will notice that as the bread cooks it puffs up, opening out the layers. The application of ghee and flour between the layers facilitates this. Cook the remaining breads in the same way, wrapping them loosely in foil to keep warm while you wait for the rest to be done.

PEANUT CHUTNEY

This simple and delicious chutney goes well with South Indian curries and Oriental-style dishes.

SERVES 4

2 tablespoons vegetable or corn oil
180g ($1^3/_4$ cups) skinned peanuts
$^1/_2$ teaspoon red chilli powder
3 garlic cloves, roughly chopped
1cm ($^1/_2$-inch) piece of fresh ginger, roughly chopped
2 red chillies, roughly chopped
1 teaspoon salt
1 teaspoon sugar
4 tablespoons coconut milk
juice of 1 lemon

Heat the oil in a frying pan, add the peanuts and fry until golden. Remove from the heat and leave to cool.

Put all the ingredients in a food processor and blend to a paste. Check the seasoning and serve at room temperature.

Cook's note
You could replace the peanuts with cashew nuts if you wished. You could also thin the chutney with additional coconut milk and a little water to make a peanut sauce.

GREEN COCONUT CHUTNEY

Serve this simple yet versatile chutney to accompany any southern Indian dish. Mint is my little addition; you could also use tomatoes and red chillies for a red chutney, or even green mangoes for a fresh, sharp chutney.

SERVES 4

1 coconut, grated
50g (1 cup) fresh coriander leaves
20g ($^1/_2$ cup) fresh mint leaves
4 green chillies, chopped
2 tablespoons roasted chana dal
1 teaspoon salt

For tempering
1 tablespoon vegetable or corn oil
10 fresh curry leaves
$^1/_4$ teaspoon mustard seeds

Put the coconut, coriander, mint, chillies, chana dal and salt in a blender or food processor and blend to a soft, spoonable consistency. To temper the chutney, heat the oil to smoking point in a small pan and add the curry leaves and mustard seeds. As soon as they start to crackle, add the chutney and remove the pan from the heat.

LASSI

This popular Punjabi drink is often served as an aperitif in Indian restaurants and comes in various guises. It can be served sweet or salted (see Chaas, below), thick (to be enjoyed as a nourishing drink) or thin (as a summer cooler). You can flavour lassis with rosewater, ripe mango or dried fruits. You will find it served in tall, stainless steel glasses and it is almost a meal on its own. In India, it is common to serve lassi with curries, as you would wine with food in the West; there is no tradition of drinking alcohol with a meal there.

MAKES 1 LITRE (4 CUPS)

700g (2¾ cups) plain yoghurt
300ml (1¼ cups) iced water
4 tablespoons sugar
a few drops of rosewater

Blend everything together in a blender or food processor and serve in tall glasses.

CHAAS

The Rajasthani version of the lassi. Chaas is served really thin, salted and spiced with cumin, ginger and chillies. It's known to be a digestive aid, as well as an effective thirst quencher.

MAKES 1 LITRE (4 CUPS)

500g (2 cups) plain yoghurt
500ml (2 cups) iced water
2 green chillies, deseeded, finely chopped
1cm (½-inch) piece of fresh ginger, finely chopped
½ tablespoon finely chopped fresh coriander
2 teaspoons salt
1 teaspoon cumin seeds, roasted in a dry frying pan and then crushed
1 tablespoon vegetable oil
¼ teaspoon asafoetida

Whisk together the yoghurt, water, chillies, ginger, coriander, salt and cumin seeds. In a small pan, heat the oil and add the asafoetida. Stir for 20 seconds or so, until the flavours are released, then pour it over the yoghurt and mix thoroughly. Serve chilled.

CUMIN COOLER

JAL JEERA

A wonderfully refreshing drink, especially on a hot day.

MAKES 1 LITRE (4 CUPS)

50g (2½ cups) mint leaves
1 litre (4 cups) water
1 tablespoon cumin seeds, roasted in a dry frying pan and then crushed
1½ tablespoons fennel seeds, roasted in a dry frying pan and then crushed
juice of 4 lemons
1 teaspoon ground black pepper
2 tablespoons salt
6 tablespoons sugar

Add the mint leaves to the water and chill for 30 minutes. Remove the mint, reserve 15–20 small leaves for garnish and muddle the rest to a fine paste using a mortar and pestle. Return them to the water, then strain through a sieve to remove any coarse bits. Add the rest of the ingredients to the water and stir well. Check the seasoning; the flavours should be quite intense from the mint, cumin, salt and sugar.

Take 6 chilled glasses and fill them about a third full with crushed ice. Pour over the cumin drink, garnish with the reserved mint leaves and serve immediately.

Left to right
Cumin Cooler; Lassi.

202 BASICS
205 GLOSSARY
208 INDEX

214 A NOTE FOR AMERICAN READERS
215 ACKNOWLEDGEMENTS

BASICS

GINGER PASTE

MAKES ABOUT 6 TABLESPOONS

175g (6oz) fresh ginger, peeled
5 tablespoons water

Chop up the ginger and process it to a paste with the water in a food processor or blender. The paste will keep for 1 week in the fridge.

GARLIC PASTE

MAKES 6–8 TABLESPOONS

175g (6oz) garlic, peeled
5 tablespoons water

Chop up the garlic and process it to a paste with the water in a food processor or blender. The paste will keep for 1 week in the fridge, but if you substitute oil for water it should keep for 2 weeks.

GINGER-GARLIC PASTE

MAKES ABOUT 10 TABLESPOONS

100g (3½oz) fresh ginger, peeled
100g (3½oz) garlic, peeled
175ml (¾ cup) water

Chop up the ginger and garlic and process them to a paste with the water in a food processor or blender. The paste will keep for 1 week in the fridge.

FRIED CASHEW PASTE

MAKES ABOUT 300G (11OZ)

200g (2 cups) cashew nuts
2 tablespoons vegetable or corn oil
200ml (scant 1 cup) water

Fry the cashew nuts in the oil until golden, then remove from the pan with a slotted spoon. Soak them in the water for 20 minutes, then drain. Blend to a smooth paste in a food processor or blender with 5 tablespoons of water. The paste will keep for 4 days in the fridge.

BOILED CASHEW PASTE

MAKES ABOUT 400G (14OZ)

200g (2 cups) cashew nuts
1 blade of mace
1 green cardamom pod
300ml (1¼ cups) water

Soak the cashew nuts in enough water to cover for 10 minutes, then drain. Put them in a pan with the mace, cardamom and water, bring to the boil and simmer for 25 minutes. Remove from the heat and leave to cool. Blend to a smooth paste in a food processor or blender with 100ml (scant ½ cup) water. The paste will keep for 4 days in the fridge.

CRISP FRIED ONIONS

MAKES ABOUT 110G (4OZ)

600g (1lb 5oz) onions, sliced
at least 600ml (2½ cups) vegetable or corn oil for deep-frying

Deep-fry the onions in medium-hot oil until golden brown, then remove and drain on kitchen paper. Store in an airtight container for up to a week.

FRIED ONION PASTE

MAKES ABOUT 150G (5OZ)

Prepare Crisp Fried Onions as above, then put them in a food processor or blender with 200ml (scant 1 cup) water and process until smooth. The paste will keep for 1 week in the fridge.

BOILED ONION PASTE

MAKES ABOUT 300G (11OZ)

1 large onion, cut into 2.5cm (1-inch) dice
250ml (1 cup) water

Put the onion and water in a small pan and simmer for 15–20 minutes, until the onion is soft. Purée in a food processor or blender until smooth. The paste will keep for 3 days in the fridge.

RAJASTHANI SPICE PASTE

This can be used with game, chicken or any other kind of meat, and even some types of fish – red snapper is particularly good.

2 tablespoons mustard oil or sunflower oil
2 tablespoons ghee
1 large onion, sliced
6 garlic cloves, chopped
20 cloves
10 green cardamom pods
1 tablespoon coriander seeds
1 teaspoon black peppercorns
1 tablespoon fennel seeds
150g (3 cups) fresh coriander leaves, chopped
1 teaspoon salt
150g (⅔ cup) plain yoghurt

Heat the mustard or sunflower oil in a heavy-based frying pan until smoking, then add the ghee. Add the sliced onion and cook until softened but not coloured. Add the garlic and cook for a few minutes, until it starts to brown. Add the cloves, cardamom, coriander seeds, peppercorns and fennel seeds in that order and stir quickly over a high heat for a couple of minutes, taking care that the spices do not burn. Stir in the coriander and salt, then remove from the heat and leave to cool. Transfer the mixture to a food processor or blender, add the yoghurt and blend to a paste.

MACE AND CARDAMOM POWDER

MAKES ABOUT 10 TEASPOONS

$^1/_4$ nutmeg
40g ($1^1/_2$oz) blades of mace
50g ($1^3/_4$oz) green cardamom pods

Grate the nutmeg or pound it with a mortar and pestle to break it up. Dry all the spices in a microwave for 30 seconds, then grind them to a fine powder, using a spice grinder. Store in an airtight container and use within a week.

GARAM MASALA

There are many versions of garam masala; this is a good basic one. It is generally added to dishes towards the end of cooking to impart flavour, not to add heat as its name might suggest (*garam* means hot and *masala* means mix).

I would always recommend making your own garam masala if possible. Commercial blends use a larger proportion of the cheaper spices and less of the more expensive aromatic ones, such as cardamom and cinnamon.

50g ($1^3/_4$oz) coriander seeds
50g ($1^3/_4$oz) cumin seeds
20 green cardamom pods
10 cinnamon sticks, about 2.5cm (1 inch) long
2 tablespoons cloves
10 blades of mace
10 black cardamom pods
$^1/_2$ nutmeg
1 tablespoon black peppercorns
4 bay leaves

Put all the ingredients on a baking tray and place in a low oven (about 110°C/225°F/Gas Mark $^1/_4$) for 3–5 minutes; this intensifies the flavours. You could even dry the spices in a microwave for 20 seconds or so.

Grind everything to a fine powder in a spice grinder, then sieve the mixture to remove any husks or large particles. Store in an airtight container and use within 2 weeks.

ROASTING (AND CRUSHING) SEEDS

Put the seeds in a moderately hot frying pan or under the grill and roast for a minute or two, until they are just dried but not coloured. Remove from the heat and allow to cool to room temperature, then pound in a mortar and pestle until the seeds are crushed but still coarse enough to be identified separately. If you want to grind the seeds to a powder, the best way to do this is in a spice grinder.

GLOSSARY

ASAFOETIDA
This essential Indian flavouring has a very unpleasant smell and taste, so is never used alone, but when added to a dish it somehow rounds off the flavours. It is sold as a powder or granules and will keep well for up to a year. In addition to its culinary uses, asafoetida is reputed to be a cure for flatulence and helpful for respiratory problems such as asthma.

CAROM SEEDS (AJOWAN)
Closely related to cumin, which it resembles in appearance and fragrance, carom has a hot, bitter taste. When it is cooked with other ingredients, however, the flavour mellows. It is particularly good in fish and seafood dishes and with root vegetables.

CHANA DAL
This is essentially split yellow peas from which the husk has been removed. A very versatile ingredient, it is used in many different forms in various parts of the country and is cooked as a pulse on its own in Bengal and eastern India. Chana dal is also used to make gram flour (see page 206).

CHAT MASALA
This spice mix typically consists of dried mango powder, cumin, black salt, dried ginger, coriander seeds, black pepper and sugar. It is used as a seasoning to perk up street snacks (known as chaats in Hindi) and various tandoori kebabs. On its own, it is rather an acquired taste, although it can be added to all sorts of everyday items. Ready-prepared chat masala is available in Indian and Asian grocery shops.

CURRY LEAVES
Curry leaves can be found pretty much all over India, right from the Himalayan foothills in the north to the southern coast and Sri Lanka. Curry leaves are to southern Indian cuisine what coriander leaves are to the north. Although readily available dried in the UK, they are much better bought fresh from Indian stores, where they may be labelled meetha neem or *kari* (sometime kadhi) patta. They will keep in an airtight bag in the fridge for at least a week and can also be frozen. Although dried curry leaves have little flavour, fresh leaves, when bruised, are very aromatic. They give off an intense, spicy aroma with a citrus note and have a warm, lemony, slightly bitter taste.

DRIED MANGO POWDER
Also known as amchoor, this is made by drying unripe green mangoes and grinding them to a tart powder. Pale beige to brownish in colour, with a sour, tangy, fruit flavour, it is used to add acidity to dishes, especially in northern India. It is popular in vegetable stir-fries, soups, curries, and for tenderising meat and poultry.

DRIED POMEGRANATE SEEDS (ANARDANA)
Sun-dried pomegranate seeds are used in both Indian and Iranian cooking and impart a sweet-sour flavour to various curries. Pomegranate has recently acquired the status of 'superfood' and the seeds are thought to have beneficial health properties. On another note, this is one of the very few ingredients that are used in Indian cooking to add texture.

FENUGREEK

The fresh leaves of this aromatic plant are eaten as a vegetable; dried fenugreek leaves (kasoori methi) are used to flavour all sorts of Indian savouries and curries. The best-quality kasoori methi comes from Qasoor in Pakistan.

Fenugreek seeds are used as a spice. Ancient herbalists prescribed them to aid digestion, a remedy that continues to be used today.

GHEE

This is clarified butter, the pure butterfat, clear and golden in colour. Traditionally in India, ghee is made from buffalo milk, which is higher in fat than cow's milk. The process involves souring the milk to make yoghurt and then churning this to yield butter. Unsalted butter made from cow's milk can also be clarified to make ghee.

GRAM FLOUR/ROASTED GRAM FLOUR

Also known as besan, gram (chickpea) flour is obtained by husking split yellow peas (chana dal) and then grinding them into a powder. It is a very versatile flour, commonly used in fritter batters, dumplings and to make bread. Gram flour can be stored in an airtight jar for up to 6 months.

Roasted gram flour (daria dal) is another form in which chickpeas are available in India. The split peas are roasted first and then ground to make flour. Roasting takes away the raw taste of the flour and increases its ability to retain water; it is often used as a thickening agent.

JAGGERY

Jaggery is a term used loosely to refer to unrefined sugar from both sugar cane and palm. If you cannot find it, dark molasses sugar can be substituted. Jaggery is considered by some to be particularly wholesome since, unlike refined sugar, it retains some minerals and there are no chemicals involved in its processing; it also enters the bloodstream more slowly than refined sugar. Indian Ayurvedic medicine considers jaggery to be beneficial in treating various lung and throat ailments.

KEWRA (SCREWPINE ESSENCE) AND ROSEWATER

Essences have been an important part of Indian cookery since antiquity. During the time of the Mughal emperors, rare flowers were grown in the royal greenhouses to make attars, or fragrant essential oils, and some of these turned up in the kitchen. Floral essences such as rosewater and kewra are the most popular today, used to flavour biryanis, pulaos, kebabs, desserts and treats.

Kewra is available from most Asian stores, though rosewater can be substituted if necessary. It's never a problem to omit it from a recipe if you find it hard to get.

KOKUM BERRIES

Kokum is a dried fruit from the mangosteen family, sold either whole, as berries, or deseeded. Tart and astringent, it is often used in South Indian and Goan cooking instead of tamarind, vinegar or lemon juice to impart colour and sourness.

MUSTARD OIL

As the name suggests, this oil is extracted from mustard seeds. It is pungent in taste and smell and deep gold in colour. Mustard oil is greatly favoured in Bengal and eastern India, and certain Rajasthani dishes get their flavour from it. When used, the oil is usually heated almost to smoking point first, then cooled down and reheated again, to tone down its aroma.

PANEER

An Indian version of cottage cheese, paneer is made by curdling milk with lemon juice to separate the curds from the whey. The solids are then collected in a piece of muslin, tied and pressed under a heavy weight for a few hours to set. On its own, paneer tastes quite bland but it is widely used in vegetarian dishes.

TAMARIND PASTE

The pulp from tamarind is sold in most Asian shops in the UK and needs to be soaked in water and then strained before use. Ready-prepared tamarind paste is available too, in supermarkets and Asian shops. It can be used to flavour sauces, impart acidity to dishes and even as a thickening agent.

Tamarind comes from a tropical tree native to Africa, but it was introduced into India so long ago that it has often been reported as indigenous there. It was from India that it reached the Persians and Arabs, who called it tamar hindi, or Indian date. In Thailand, there is a carefully cultivated sweet variety with little or no tartness, grown specifically to be eaten as a fresh fruit.

INDEX

A

Almonds
Mutton cooked with lentils, dried fruit and nuts *132*

Asafoetida *205*

Aubergine
Baby aubergines with sesame and tamarind sauce *16*
Roasted aubergine, tomato and potato crush *188*
Seared aubergine steaks with sesame and tamarind sauce *18*
Seared black bream with roasted aubergine, tomato and potato crush and kachumber *76*

B

Baby aubergines with sesame and tamarind sauce *16*

Banana leaf
Halibut wrapped in banana leaf with coconut paste *58*

Barbecued half chicken with tomato and fenugreek sauce *155*

Barramundi
Barramundi with kerala curry sauce *64*
Freshwater fish cooked with onions *59*
See also Treasure-of-the-earth whole fish cooked in a sealed pot *79*

Beans
Green moong tadka with scrambled egg *36*
Seared sea bass fillet with fenugreek sauce and potato and bean stir-fry *61*
Stir-fried squid with sweet spices and green moong kedgeree *80*

Beef
Beef bhuna, Bengali-style *138*
Spice-crusted rib eye steak with masala sautéed potatoes *141*

Beetroot
Lamb and beetroot curry *123*

Bengali-style fish cooked with yoghurt *71*
Bengali-style fish curry with mustard paste *65*
Bengali-style grilled lobster *96*
Bhopal-style goat curry *137*
Black lentils *186*
Braised shoulder of young lamb with mint and onion *116*

Bread
Naan bread *194*
Layered parathas *198*
Seared bottle gourd with chickpea bread and bottle gourd cooked in milk *20*
Spring onion parathas *197*

Bream
Seared black bream with roasted aubergine, tomato and potato crush and kachumber *76*
See also Barramundi with Kerala curry sauce *64*
See also Pomfret Recheado *74*
See also Treasure-of-the-earth whole fish cooked in a sealed pot *79*

Boiled cashew paste *202*
Boiled onion paste *203*

Bottle Gourd
Bottle gourd and yellow split pea curry *52*
Seared bottle gourd with chickpea bread and bottle gourd cooked in milk *20*

Brown basmati pilau *182*

Butter
Paneer butter masala *45*

C

Cardamom
Braised shoulder of young lamb with mint and onion *116*
Garam masala *204*
Mace and cardamom powder *204*
Pilau rice *182*
Rajasthani spice paste *203*

Carom seeds (ajowan) *205*

Carp
See Bengali-style fish cooked with yoghurt *71*

Carrot
Carrot and peanut salad *193*
Winter vegetable curry with carrots, peas and tomatoes *28*

Cashews
Boiled cashew paste *202*
Chicken drumsticks cooked in a sealed pot *151*
Fried cashew paste *202*
Lamb curry with white spices *120*
Mughal-style aromatic curry of lamb shanks *128*
Spiced grated paneer with peppers *42*

Cauliflower
Home-style curry of potatoes and cauliflower *30*

Chaas *200*

Chana dal *205*

Chargrilled mustard chicken with green fenugreek sauce *156*

Chat masala *205*

Cheese
Paneer butter masala *45*
Paneer cheese in a creamy fenugreek sauce *41*
Potatoes filled with paneer and dried fruit *51*
Spiced grated paneer with peppers *42*

Chicken
Barbecued half chicken with tomato and fenugreek sauce *155*
Chargrilled mustard chicken with green fenugreek sauce *156*
Chicken cafreal *158*
Chicken drumsticks cooked in a sealed pot *151*
Jungle curry of country chicken with fresh fenugreek *152*
Old Delhi-style chicken curry *160*
Parsee-style hot and sweet chicken curry with apricots *159*
Spice-roasted whole chicken *163*
Syrian-Christian chicken stew *150*
Tanjore-style chicken curry *164*
See also Dry-spice-crusted guinea fowl with yellow lentil sauce *168*

Chickpeas
Chickpea dumplings in yoghurt sauce *25*
Chickpea polenta in yoghurt sauce *24*
Seared bottle gourd with chickpea bread and bottle gourd cooked in milk *20*
Punjabi chickpea fritters in yoghurt curry *23*
Punjabi spiced chickpeas *39*

Chillies
Bhopal-style goat curry *137*
Chaas *200*
Fiery Rajasthani lamb curry *114*
Lamb curry with green chillies and mint *124*
Meatball curry *126*
Roast pork chops with sweet spices, mustard mash and date and chilli sauce *143*

Chutneys
Garlic chutney *176*
Green coconut chutney *199*
Peanut chutney *199*

Cinnamon
Garam masala *204*
Rajasthani spice-crusted Mackerel, yoghurt kadhi and spinach porial *66*

Cloves
Garam masala *204*
Rajasthani spice-crusted Mackerel, yoghurt kadhi and spinach porial *66*
Rajasthani spice paste *203*

Coconut
Duck curry with peanuts, sesame and tamarind *165*
Green coconut chutney *199*
Halibut wrapped in banana leaf with coconut paste *58*
Keralan-style mixed seafood with coconut and vinegar sauce *84*
Meatball curry *126*
Seared scallops with coconut and ginger sauce *83*
Wild prawns baked with coconut and mustard *90*

Cod
Bengali-style fish curry with mustard paste *65*
Keralan-style mixed seafood with coconut and vinegar sauce *84*
Roast cod fillet with Bengali-style mustard sauce and red onions *73*

Coriander
Chicken cafreal *158*
Rajasthani spice paste *203*
Spice-crusted halibut in green spiced sauce *56*
Tanjore-style chicken curry *164*
Garam masala *204*

Coorg pork stir-fry *144*

Corn
Tawa palak methi mushroom *48*

Crisp fried onions *203*

Cucumber
Seared black bream with roasted aubergine, tomato and potato crush and kachumber *76*

Cumin
Cumin cooler *200*
Garam masala *204*

Curry leaf and tomato quinoa *188*

Curry leaves *205*
Curry leaf and tomato quinoa *188*
Lemon rice *183*
Rajasthani spice-crusted Mackerel, yoghurt kadhi and spinach porial *66*
Tanjore-style chicken curry *164*

D

Dal
Bottle gourd and yellow split pea curry *52*

Date
Roast pork chops with sweet spices, mustard mash and date and chilli sauce *143*

Deccan lamb cooked with lentils *129*

Dill
Roast salmon with dill and mustard, green pea relish *68*

Dover sole
See Pomfret Recheado *74*

Dried mango powder *205*
Dried pomegranate seeds (anardana) *205*
Dry-spice-crusted guinea fowl with yellow lentil sauce *168*

Duck
Duck curry with peanuts, sesame and tamarind *165*

Dumplings
Chickpea dumplings in yoghurt sauce *25*

E

Eggs
Green moong tadka with scrambled egg *36*
Nargisi kofta curry *110*
Omelette curry *34*

F

Fennel
Cumin cooler *200*
Rajasthani spice-crusted mackerel, yoghurt kadhi and spinach porial *66*

Fenugreek *206*
Barbecued half chicken with tomato and fenugreek sauce *155*
Chargrilled mustard chicken with green fenugreek sauce *156*
Gujarati-style sweet and sour mixed vegetables *47*
Jungle curry of country chicken with fresh fenugreek *152*
Paneer cheese in a creamy fenugreek sauce *41*
Seared sea bass fillet with fenugreek sauce and potato and bean stir-fry *61*
Tawa palak methi mushroom *48*

Fiery Rajasthani lamb curry *114*

Fish
Barramundi with kerala curry sauce *64*
Bengali-style fish cooked with yoghurt *71*
Bengali-style fish curry with mustard paste *65*
Freshwater fish cooked with onions *59*
Halibut wrapped in banana leaf with coconut paste *58*
Keralan-style mixed seafood with coconut and vinegar sauce *84*
Pomfret recheado *74*
Prawns in Kerala curry *92*
Rajasthani spice-crusted mackerel, yoghurt kadhi and spinach porial *66*
Roast cod fillet with Bengali-style mustard sauce and red onions *73*
Roast salmon with dill and mustard, green pea relish *68*
Seared black bream with roasted aubergine, tomato and potato crush and kachumber *76*
Seared sea bass fillet with fenugreek sauce and potato and bean stir-fry *61*
Stir-fried squid with sweet spices and green moong kedgeree *80*
Spice-crusted halibut in green spiced sauce *56*
Treasure-of-the-earth whole fish cooked in a sealed pot *79*

Freshwater fish cooked with onions *59*
Fried cashew paste *202*
Fried onion paste *203*

Fritters
Punjabi chickpea fritters in yoghurt curry *23*

Fruit
Lemon rice *183*
Mutton cooked with lentils, dried fruit and nuts *132*
Parsee-style hot and sweet chicken curry with apricots *159*
Pomegranate raita *193*
Potatoes filled with paneer and dried fruit *51*
Seared bottle gourd with chickpea bread and bottle gourd cooked in milk *20*
Spiced roast partridge breasts with curried pears *174*

G

Game
Dry-spice-crusted guinea fowl with yellow lentil sauce *168*
Half a dozen quails in spicy curry *166*
Mixed game cooked in an Indian wok *171*
Rabbit cooked in a pit *176*
Roast grouse with black lentils *172*
Roast saddle of red deer with pickling sauce *175*
Spiced roast partridge breasts with curried pears *174*

Garam masala *204*

Garlic
Garlic chutney *176*
Garlic paste *202*
Ginger-garlic paste *202*
Rajasthani spice paste *203*

Ghee *206*

Ginger
Ginger paste *202*
Ginger-garlic paste *202*
Seared scallops with coconut and ginger sauce *83*

Goat
Bhopal-style goat curry *137*
Raan *102*
See also Fiery Rajasthani lamb curry *114*

Gram flour/roasted gram flour *206*
Green coconut chutney *199*
Green moong tadka with scrambled egg *36*
Green pea relish *191*

Grouse
Mixed game cooked in an Indian wok *171*
Roast grouse with black lentils *172*
See also Half a dozen quails in spicy curry *166*

Guinea Fowl
Dry-spice-crusted guinea fowl with yellow lentil sauce *168*

Gujarati-style sweet and sour mixed vegetables *47*

H

Half a dozen quails in spicy curry *166*

Halibut
Bengali-style fish curry with mustard paste *65*
Keralan-style mixed seafood with coconut and vinegar sauce *84*
Halibut wrapped in banana leaf with coconut paste *58*
Spice-crusted halibut in green spiced sauce *56*
Halibut wrapped in banana leaf with coconut paste *58*
See also Bengali-style fish cooked with yoghurt *71*

Hare
See Mixed game cooked in an Indian wok *171*

Home-style curry of potatoes and cauliflower *30*
Hyderabadi-style lamb biryani *108*

J

Jaggery *206*

Jungle curry of country chicken with fresh fenugreek *152*

K

Kadhai lobster *93*

Kedgeree
Stir-fried squid with sweet spices and green moong kedgeree *80*

Keralan-style mixed seafood with coconut and vinegar sauce *84*

Kewra (screwpine essence) *206*

Kidney
See Spiced miced lamb with liver *106*

King prawns cooked in saffron korma sauce *88*

Kingfish
See Treasure-of-the-earth whole fish cooked in a sealed pot *79*

Kokum berries *206*

Korma
King prawns cooked in saffron korma sauce *88*

L

Lamb
Braised shoulder of young lamb with mint and onion *116*
Deccan lamb cooked with lentils *129*
Fiery Rajasthani lamb curry *114*
Hyderabadi-style lamb biryani *108*
Lamb and beetroot curry *123*
Lamb cooked with winter vegetables and spinach *113*
Lamb curry with green chillies and mint *124*
Lamb curry with white spices *120*
Lamb neck fillet with masala mash *107*
Lamb rogan josh *125*
Lamb shanks with saffron and rosewater *119*
Meatball curry *126*
Modern raan *105*
Mughal-style aromatic curry of lamb shanks *128*
Nargisi kofta curry *110*
Raan *102*
Rack of lamb with saffron sauce *100*
Spiced minced lamb with liver *106*

Lassi *200*
Layered parathas *198*

Lemon
Lemon Rice *183*

Lentils
Black lentils *186*
Bottle gourd and yellow split pea curry *52*
Deccan lamb cooked with lentils *129*
Dry-spice-crusted guinea fowl with yellow lentil sauce *168*
Green moong tadka with scrambled egg *36*
Gujarati-style sweet and sour mixed vegetables *47*
Mutton cooked with lentils, dried fruit and nuts *132*
Roasted yellow lentil relish *191*
Roast grouse with black lentils *172*
Yellow lentils *184*

Lobster
Bengali-style grilled lobster *96*
Kadhai lobster *93*

M

Mace
Mace and cardamom powder *204*

Mackerel
Rajasthani spice-crusted Mackerel, yoghurt kadhi and spinach porial *66*

Mango
Dried mango powder

Masala
Lamb neck fillet with masala mash *107*
Masala mash *183*
Paneer butter masala *45*
Spice-crusted rib eye steak with masala sautéed potatoes *141*

Masala mash *183*

Meat
Barbecued half chicken with tomato and fenugreek sauce *155*
Beef bhuna, Bengali-style *138*
Bhopal-style goat curry *137*
Braised shoulder of young lamb with mint and onion *116*
Chargrilled mustard chicken with green fenugreek sauce *156*
Chicken cafreal *158*
Chicken drumsticks cooked in a sealed pot *151*
Coorg pork stir-fry *144*
Fiery Rajasthani lamb curry *114*
Hyderabadi-style lamb biryani *108*
Jungle curry of country chicken with fresh fenugreek *152*
Lamb and beetroot curry *123*
Lamb cooked with winter vegetables and spinach *113*
Lamb curry with green chillies and mint *124*
Lamb curry with white spices *120*
Lamb neck fillet with masala mash *107*
Lamb rogan josh *125*
Lamb shanks with saffron and rosewater *119*
Meatball curry *126*
Modern raan *105*
Mughal-style aromatic curry of lamb shanks *128*
Mutton cooked with lentils, dried fruit and nuts *132*
Mutton kolhapuri *136*
Nargisi kofta curry *110*
Old Delhi-style chicken curry *160*
Parsee-style hot and sweet chicken curry with apricots *159*
Pork vindaloo *146*
Punjabi-spiced mutton chops and mince *131*
Raan *102*
Rack of lamb with saffron sauce *100*
Rajasthani semi-dry curry with mutton *133*
Roast pork chops with sweet spices, mustard mash and date and chilli sauce *143*
Spice-crusted rib eye steak with masala sautéed potatoes *141*
Spiced minced lamb with liver *106*
Spice-roasted whole chicken *163*
Syrian-Christian chicken stew *150*
Tanjore-style chicken curry *164*

Meatball curry *126*

Milk
Seared bottle gourd with chickpea bread and bottle gourd cooked in milk *20*

Mint
Braised shoulder of young lamb with mint and onion *116*
Cumin cooler *200*
Green coconut chutney *199*
Lamb curry with green chillies and mint *124*
Spice-crusted halibut in green spiced sauce *56*
Tanjore-style chicken curry *164*

Mixed game cooked in an Indian wok *171*
Modern raan *105*

Monkfish
See Bengali-style fish curry with mustard paste *65*

Mughal-style aromatic curry of lamb shanks *128*

Mushrooms
Morel mushroom and green pea curry *40*

Mussels
Keralan-style mixed seafood with coconut and vinegar sauce *84*

Mustard
Bengali-style fish curry with mustard paste *65*

Chargrilled mustard chicken with green fenugreek sauce *156*
Mustard oil *207*
Punjabi-style mustard greens *46*
Roast cod fillet with Bengali-style mustard sauce and red onions *73*
Roast pork chops with sweet spices, mustard mash and date and chilli sauce *143*
Roast salmon with dill and mustard, green pea relish *68*
Tawa palak methi mushroom *48*
Wild prawns baked with coconut and mustard *90*

Mutton
Mutton cooked with lentils, dried fruit and nuts *132*
Mutton kolhapuri *136*
Punjabi-spiced mutton chops and mince *131*
Raan *102*
Rajasthani semi-dry curry with mutton *133*
See also Bhopal-style goat curry *137*

N

Naan
Naan bread *194*

Nargisi kofta curry *110*

O

Octopus
See Stir-fried squid with sweet spices and green moong kedgeree *80*

Offal
Spiced minced lamb with liver *106*

Okra
Stir-fried okra *33*

Old Delhi-style chicken curry *160*
Omelette curry *34*

Onions
Boiled onion paste *203*
Braised shoulder of young lamb with mint and onion *116*
Crisp fried onions *203*
Freshwater fish cooked with onions *59*
Fried onion paste *203*
Spring onion parathas *197*
Roast cod fillet with Bengali-style mustard sauce and red onions *73*

P

Paneer *207*
Paneer butter masala *45*
Paneer cheese in a creamy fenugreek sauce *41*
Modern raan *105*
Spiced grated paneer with peppers *42*
See also Lamb cooked with winter vegetables and spinach *113*

Parathas
Layered parathas *198*
Spring onion parathas *197*

Parsee-style hot and sweet chicken curry with apricots *159*

Partridge
Mixed game cooked in an Indian wok *171*
Spiced roast partridge breasts with curried pears *174*
See also Lamb cooked with winter vegetables and spinach *113*

Pastes
Baby aubergines with sesame and tamarind sauce *16*
Bengali-style fish curry with mustard paste *65*
Boiled cashew paste *202*
Boiled onion paste *203*
Fried cashew paste *202*
Fried onion paste *203*
Garlic paste *202*
Ginger paste *202*
Ginger-garlic paste *202*
Halibut wrapped in banana leaf with coconut paste *58*
Tamarind paste *207*

Peanuts
Carrot and peanut salad *193*
Duck curry with peanuts, sesame and tamarind *165*
Peanut chutney *199*

Peas
Bottle gourd and yellow split pea curry *52*
Green pea relish *191*
Morel mushroom and green pea curry *40*
Roast salmon with dill and mustard, green pea relish *68*
Winter vegetable curry with carrots, peas and tomatoes *28*

Peppers
Spiced grated paneer with peppers *42*

Perch
See also Bengali-style fish cooked with yoghurt *71*
See also Bengali-style fish curry with mustard paste *65*

Pheasant
Mixed game cooked in an Indian wok *171*
See also Half a dozen quails in spicy curry *166*

Pickle
Pumpkin pickle *192*

Pilau
Brown basmati pilau *182*
Pilau rice *182*

Pistachios
Mutton cooked with lentils, dried fruit and nuts *132*

Polenta
Chickpea polenta in yoghurt sauce *24*

Pomegranate
Dried pomegranate seeds (anardana) *205*
Pomegranate raita *193*

Pomfret
Pomfret recheado *74*
See also Treasure-of-the-earth whole fish cooked in a sealed pot *79*

Poppadom curry *24*

Pork
Coorg pork stir-fry *144*
Pork vindaloo *146*
Roast pork chops with sweet spices, mustard mash and date and chilli sauce *143*

Potato
Home-style curry of potatoes and cauliflower *30*
Lamb neck fillet with masala mash *107*
Masala mash *183*
Potatoes filled with paneer and dried fruit *51*
Roasted aubergine, tomato and potato crush *188*
Roast pork chops with sweet spices, mustard mash and date and chilli sauce *143*
Seared black bream with roasted aubergine, tomato and potato crush and kachumber *76*
Seared sea bass fillet with fenugreek sauce and potato and bean stir-fry *61*
Spice-crusted rib eye steak with masala sautéed potatoes *141*

Prawns
Keralan-style mixed seafood with coconut and vinegar sauce *84*
King prawns cooked in saffron korma sauce *88*
Prawn balchao *87*
Prawns in Kerala curry *92*
Wild prawns baked with coconut and mustard *90*
See also Stir-fried squid with sweet spices and green moong kedgeree *80*

Pumpkin
Pumpkin pickle *192*

Punjabi chickpea fritters in yoghurt curry *23*
Punjabi spiced chickpeas *39*
Punjabi-spiced mutton chops and mince *131*
Punjabi-style mustard greens *46*

Q

Quail
Half a dozen quails in spicy curry *166*
Mixed game cooked in an Indian wok *171*

Quinoa
Curry leaf and tomato quinoa *188*

R

Raan *102*

Rabbit
Rabbit cooked in a pit *176*

Rack of lamb with saffron sauce *100*

Raita
Pomegranate raita *193*

Rajasthani semi-dry curry with mutton *133*
Rajasthani spice paste *203*

Relishes
Green pea relish *191*
Roasted yellow lentil relish *191*
Roast salmon with dill and mustard, green pea relish *68*

Rice
Brown basmati pilau *182*
Lemon Rice *183*
Pilau rice *182*

Roast cod fillet with Bengali-style mustard sauce and red onions *73*
Roast grouse with black lentils *172*
Roast pork chops with sweet spices, mustard mash and date and chilli sauce *143*
Roast saddle of red deer with pickling sauce *175*
Roast salmon with dill and mustard, green pea relish *68*
Roasted aubergine, tomato and potato crush *188*
Roasted yellow lentil relish *191*

Rose
Lamb shanks with saffron and rosewater *119*
Lassi *200*

S

Saffron
King prawns cooked in saffron korma sauce *88*
Lamb shanks with saffron and rosewater *119*
Rack of lamb with saffron sauce *100*

Salads
Carrot and peanut salad *193*

Salmon
Keralan-style mixed seafood with coconut and vinegar sauce *84*
Roast salmon with dill and mustard, green pea relish *68*

Sauces
Baby aubergines with sesame and tamarind sauce *16*
Barbecued half chicken with tomato and fenugreek sauce *155*
Barramundi with kerala curry sauce *64*
Chargrilled mustard chicken with green fenugreek sauce *156*
Chickpea dumplings in yoghurt sauce *25*
Chickpea polenta in yoghurt sauce *24*
Dry-spice-crusted guinea fowl with yellow lentil sauce *168*
Keralan-style mixed seafood with coconut and vinegar sauce *84*
King prawns cooked in saffron korma sauce *88*
Paneer cheese in a creamy fenugreek sauce *41*
Rack of lamb with saffron sauce *100*
Roast cod fillet with Bengali-style mustard sauce and red onions *73*
Roast pork chops with sweet spices, mustard mash and date and chilli sauce *143*
Roast saddle of red deer with pickling sauce *175*
Seared aubergine steaks with sesame and tamarind sauce *18*
Seared scallops with coconut and ginger sauce *83*
Seared sea bass fillet with fenugreek sauce and potato and bean stir-fry *61*
Spice-crusted halibut in green spiced sauce *56*

Scallops
Seared scallops with coconut and ginger sauce *83*

Sea bass
Seared sea bass fillet with fenugreek sauce and potato and bean stir-fry *61*
See also Barramundi with Kerala curry sauce *64*
See also Pomfret Recheado *74*
See also Treasure-of-the-earth whole fish cooked in a sealed pot *79*

Seared aubergine steaks with sesame tamarind sauce *18*
Seared black bream with roasted aubergine, tomato and potato crush and kachumber *76*
Seared bottle gourd with chickpea bread and bottle gourd cooked in milk *20*
Seared scallops with coconut and ginger sauce *83*
Seared sea bass fillet with fenugreek sauce and potato and bean stir-fry *61*

Sesame
Baby aubergines with sesame and tamarind sauce *16*
Duck curry with peanuts, sesame and tamarind *165*
Seared aubergine steaks with sesame and tamarind sauce *18*

Shellfish
Bengali-style grilled lobster *96*
Kadhai lobster *93*
Keralan-style mixed seafood with coconut and vinegar sauce *84*
King prawns cooked in saffron korma sauce *88*
Prawn balchao *87*
Prawns in Kerala curry *92*
Seared scallops with coconut and ginger sauce *83*
Wild prawns baked with coconut and mustard *90*

Shrimp
See also Stir-fried squid with sweet spices and green moong kedgeree *80*

Spice-crusted halibut in green spiced sauce *56*
Spice-crusted rib eye steak with masala sautéed potatoes *141*
Spiced roast partridge breasts with curried pears *174*
Spice-roasted whole chicken *163*
Spiced grated paneer with peppers *42*
Spiced minced lamb with liver *106*

Spinach
Gujarati-style sweet and sour mixed vegetables *47*
Lamb cooked with winter vegetables and spinach *113*
Punjabi-style mustard greens *46*
Rajasthani spice-crusted mackerel, yoghurt kadhi and spinach porial *66*
Tawa palak methi mushroom *48*

Spring onion parathas *197*
Stir-fried okra *33*
Stir-fried squid with sweet spices and green moong kedgeree *80*

Stir-fries
Coorg pork stir-fry *144*
Seared sea bass fillet with fenugreek sauce and potato and bean stir-fry *61*
Stir-fried okra *33*
Stir-fried squid with sweet spices and green moong kedgeree *80*

Squid
Keralan-style mixed seafood with coconut and vinegar sauce *84*
Stir-fried squid with sweet spices and green moong kedgeree *80*

Swordfish
See also Roast salmon with dill and mustard, green pea relish *68*

Syrian-Christian chicken stew *150*

T

Tamarind
Baby aubergines with sesame and tamarind sauce *16*
Duck curry with peanuts, sesame and tamarind *165*
Seared aubergine steaks with sesame and tamarind sauce *18*
Tamarind paste *207*

Tanjore-style chicken curry *164*
Tapioca chips *192*
Tawa palak methi mushrooms *48*

Tilapia
Freshwater fish cooked with onions *59*
See also Treasure-of-the-earth whole fish cooked in a sealed pot *79*

Tomatoes
Barbecued half chicken with tomato and fenugreek sauce *155*
Curry leaf and tomato quinoa *188*
Old Delhi-style chicken curry *160*
Roasted aubergine, tomato and potato crush *188*
Seared black bream with roasted aubergine, tomato and potato crush and kachumber *76*
Winter vegetable curry with carrots, peas and tomatoes *28*

Trout
See also Treasure-of-the-earth whole fish cooked in a sealed pot *79*

V

Vegetarian
Baby aubergines with sesame and tamarind sauce *16*
Black lentils *186*
Brown basmati pilau *182*
Carrot and peanut salad *193*
Chickpea dumplings in yoghurt sauce *25*
Cumin cooler *200*
Curry leaf and tomato quinoa *188*
Green coconut chutney *199*
Green moong tadka with scrambled egg *36*
Green pea relish *191*

Gujarati-style sweet and sour mixed vegetables *47*
Home-style curry of potatoes and cauliflower *30*
Layered parathas *198*
Lassi *200*
Lemon rice *183*
Masala mash *183*
Morel mushroom and green pea curry *40*
Naan bread *194*
Omelette curry *34*
Paneer butter masala *45*
Paneer cheese in a creamy fenugreek sauce *41*
Peanut chutney *199*
Pilau rice *182*
Pomegranate raita *193*
Poppadom curry *24*
Potatoes filled with paneer and dried fruit *51*
Pumpkin pickle *192*
Punjabi chickpea fritters in yoghurt curry *23*
Punjabi spiced chickpeas *39*
Punjabi-style mustard greens *46*
Roasted aubergine, tomato and potato crush *188*
Roasted yellow lentil relish *191*
Seared aubergine steaks with sesame and tamarind sauce *18*
Seared bottle gourd with chickpea bread and bottle gourd cooked in milk *20*
Spiced grated paneer with peppers *42*
Spring onion parathas *197*
Tawa palak methi mushroom *48*
Winter vegetable curry with carrots, peas and tomatoes *28*
Yellow lentils *184*

Venison
Roast saddle of red deer with pickling sauce *175*
See also Mixed game cooked in an Indian wok *171*

W

Winter vegetable curry with carrots, peas and tomatoes *28*

Y

Yellow lentils *184*

Yoghurt
Bengali-style fish cooked with yoghurt *71*
Chaas *200*
Chickpea dumplings in yoghurt sauce *25*
Chickpea polenta in yoghurt sauce *24*
Fiery Rajasthani lamb curry *114*
Half a dozen quails in spicy curry *166*
Jungle curry of country chicken with fresh fenugreek *152*
Lamb curry with white spices *120*
Lassi *200*
Modern raan *105*
Old Delhi-style chicken curry *160*
Poppadom curry *24*
Punjabi chickpea fritters in yoghurt curry *23*
Punjabi-spiced mutton chops and mince *131*
Raan *102*
Rajasthani semi-dry curry with mutton *133*
Rajasthani spice-crusted mackerel, yoghurt kadhi and spinach porial *66*
Rajasthani spice paste *203*
Spiced minced lamb with liver *106*
Spice-roasted whole chicken *163*

A NOTE FOR AMERICAN READERS

In the recipes, American measures are given in brackets after the metric measures. Below are the American terms for some of the ingredients and equipment used in this book.

Aubergine eggplant
Beetroot beets
Bicarbonate of soda baking soda
Caster sugar superfine sugar
Coriander cilantro (when referring to the green, leafy herb rather than the seeds)
Frying pan skillet
Greek yoghurt thick plain yoghurt
Grill broiler
Grilled broiled
Hard-boiled egg hard-cooked egg
Kitchen paper paper towels
Minced meat ground meat
Muslin cheesecloth
Pepper, red or green bell pepper, red or green
Plain flour all-purpose flour
Prawns shrimp
Sieve strainer
Single cream light cream
Spring onion scallion
Tomato purée tomato paste
Wholemeal flour whole wheat flour

ACKNOWLEDGEMENTS

Firstly to my mother, who has been cooking curry for over 40 years now. At an average of five dishes a day, six days a week, she has cooked close to 50,000 curries! Roughly a quarter of a million meals!

Jon Croft, for coming up with the idea of a curry book. It made me realise how little I knew of the subject and how much I'd forgotten.

Abdul Yaseen, Hari Nagaraj, Rakesh Nair, James Mossman, Imamuddin Khan and the rest of the team at The Cinnamon Club, who were all so excited and have contributed in their own ways. I could never have imagined a book on curry would inspire so much enthusiasm! They are the best team one could ask for.

Cristian Barnett, for making it fun to photograph curry. It was the most daunting aspect of the book and he made it seem effortless. Cristian, you have made curry look good!

Matt Inwood at Absolute Press, for his art direction; he gives the book its edge.

Jane Middleton, for her patience, being so fabulous yet firm, and for making sure the recipes work. I don't know a better person to edit this book and I can't possibly thank her enough.

Finally Archana, my wife, for putting things in perspective. It was so easy to get carried away one way or the other with a book like this.

our Work

Enter to see some examples of work we have

Welcome to Ins

ork

examples of work we have prepared:

KEN MILBURN and JANINE WARNER

Flash 3 Web Animation f/x and design

The Coriolis Group, Inc.
An International Thomson Publishing Company
14455 N. Hayden Road, Suite 220
Scottsdale, Arizona 85260

602/483-0192
FAX 602/483-0193
http://www.coriolis.com

Library of Congress Cataloging-In-Publication Data
Milburn, Ken, 1935-
Flash 3 Web animation f/x and design / by Ken Milburn and Janine Warner.
p. cm.
Includes index.
ISBN 1-57610-382-X
1. Computer animation. 2. Flash (Computer file) 3. Multimedia systems. 4. Web sites--Design. I. Warner, Janine, 1967- . II. Title.
TR897.7.M56 1999
006.6'96--dc21 98-41455
CIP

Printed in the United States of America
10 9 8 7 6 5 4 3 2

Publisher
Keith Weiskamp

Acquisitions Editor
Stephanie Wall

Marketing Specialist
Dylan Zoller

Project Editor
Melissa D. Olson

Technical Reviewer
Gary Kubicek

Production Coordinator
Jon Gabriel

Cover Design
Anthony Stock
Additional art provided by Brandon Riza

Layout Design
April Nielsen

CD-ROM Developer
Robert Clarfield

an International Thomson Publishing company

Albany, NY • Belmont, CA • Bonn • Boston • Cincinnati • Detroit • Johannesburg
London • Madrid • Melbourne • Mexico City • New York • Paris • Singapore
Tokyo • Toronto • Washington

Other Titles For The Creative Professional

3D Studio MAX R2.5 f/x and design
by Jon A. Bell

Adobe PageMill 3 f/x and design
by Daniel Gray

Character Animation In Depth
by Doug Kelly

Photoshop 5 In Depth
by David Xenakis & Sherry London

QuarkXPress 4 In Depth
by William Harrel & Elaine Betts

FLASH 3
WEB ANIMATION
FX AND DESIGN

I would have to dedicate any book I wrote to my friends and family. All of you have supported me spiritually, emotionally, and intellectually, and I will never stop being grateful. Because I mean to include everyone, I'm not going to name anyone—for fear of leaving out someone truly important.

—Ken Milburn

❧

About The Author

Ken Milburn is a freelance writer who specializes in computer books and magazine articles related to graphics and Web design. More than 250 of his articles and reviews on computer graphics and multimedia have appeared in such national publications as *InfoWorld, PC World, MacWeek, MacUser, Popular Computing, PC Computing, Computer Graphics World, Publish Magazine,* and *Windows Magazine*.

Ken is the author of *Photoshop 4 f/x* and *The Flash 2 Web Animation Book*. His other books include *Conversion Techniques for Web Publishing, Designing Web Pages with FrontPage 97*, and *Designing Web Pages with PageMill 2*. In addition to *Flash 3 Web Animation f/x and design,* his current projects are *Master Photoshop 5 Visually* and *Fundamental Painter 6*.

Ken is also widely recognized for his illustration work. He has sold images to Multimedia Live!, *Computer Artist* magazine, *Me!dia* magazine, and other clients. *Design Graphics Magazine* has featured a 10-page, color portfolio of his landscape paintings. Ken's work has appeared on the CD-ROMs for Fractal Design Painter 4 and Movie Works 2. Samples of Ken's illustrations can be found at **www.kenmilburn.com**. He can be contacted at **kmilburn@pacbell.net**.

Janine Warner is the author of six books on Web design, including *Dreamweaver for Dummies, The Flash 2 Web Animation Book,* and *Conversion Techniques for Web Publishing*. She is also a freelance writer who specializes in reviewing Web design programs and is a frequent contributor to *Publish Magazine*.

In September, she joined *The Miami Herald* as managing editor of online services, where she heads a team of developers responsible for publishing both the Spanish and English newspapers on the Internet. From 1994 to 1998, she ran Visiontec Communications, a Web design company that served such diverse clients as Levi Strauss & Co., AirTouch International, and the Pulitzer prize-winning newspaper, the *Point Reyes Light*.

An award-winning former reporter, Janine earned a degree in journalism and Spanish from the University of Massachusetts in Amherst. To learn more about her work, visit **www.visiontec.com**, or email **janine@visiontec.com**.

ACKNOWLEDGMENTS

I have led off the acknowledgements of so many books by mentioning my best friend and coauthor, Janine Warner, that I'm afraid it will be seen as obligatory. In one acknowledgment, I called her a Web goddess. Now, she's the managing editor of online services for *The Miami Herald.* Just so you know she truly is a Web goddess. She's also an inspiration for her soul, humanity, and generosity.

I'm nearly as crazy about my editors at The Coriolis Group, although I haven't had as many years to get to know them. The genius of Stephanie Wall and Mariann Barsolo is made apparent by the fact that, as acquisitions editors, they hired Janine and me to write this book. Melissa Olson, the developmental editor is a thorough professional with a terrific sense of humor. Also, thanks to Jon Gabriel, April Nielsen, and Anthony Stock for making this book look so good, Robert Clarfield for his work on the CD-ROM, and Dylan Zoller for her marketing expertise.

I especially want to thank Macromedia and its public relations and technical staff for supplying me with all the needed materials and technical information.

Finally, I must thank the Fairfix Café in Fairfax, California, for providing me the "desk space."

—Ken Milburn

More than anyone, I have to thank Ken Milburn for his vision, creative talent, and consistent friendship. Before Macromedia even purchased Future Splash (the predecessor to Flash), Ken realized that vector graphics on the Web would solve many problems, from limited bandwidth to the low resolution of a computer screen. His appreciation for this powerful technology helped convince me of its potential, and I was delighted when he asked me to help write this book. Thanks also to Ken for the beautiful artwork that adorns the walls of my home, the late-night phone calls, and the warm hugs.

Thanks to my loving and supportive family, my parents (Malinda, Robin, Janice, and Helen), and my big brothers (Kevin and Brian). Thanks also to my cool, and still newlywed, uncle Tom and aunt Mindy.

Thanks to the brilliant and caring Robert "Bobbins" Cowart for all the love and support, to Adriene Josephs for being there whenever I need to talk, and to Kare Anderson for her ideas and her grace. Thanks to

Terri Parker and Yolanda Burrell for making me laugh, and to Francisco Rivera and Teresa Laddish for their friendship and for serving so many clients so well.

Last, but by no means least, thanks to the multitalented staff at The Miami Herald Online, who have welcomed me with their unfailing energy, humor, and patience, and whose continued efforts make **www.herald.com** and **www.elherald.com** the best news sites on the Web in English or Spanish.

—Janine Warner

Contents At A Glance

Chapter 1 The Many Faces Of Flash

Chapter 2 The Anatomy Of Flash

Chapter 3 Flash From Here To There (And Back)

Chapter 4 Drawing With Flash

Chapter 5 The Essentials Of Making A Flash Animation

Chapter 6 The Symbols Of Power

Chapter 7 Advanced Techniques

Chapter 8 Buttoning Up Flash And Interactivity

Chapter 9 Using The Design In Motion Suite (And Other Macromedia Software)

Chapter 10 Placing Flash On An HTML Page

Chapter 11 Expanding Flash And Your Audience

Chapter 12 Case Studies

Appendix Using Tell Target

Flash 3 Web Animation F/X and Design

Table Of Contents

Introduction xvii

Chapter 1
The Many Faces Of Flash 1

Why Flash Is The Answer To A Web Author's Prayers 2
New Features In Flash 3 6
Flash 2 Features Revisited 11
Flash As A Visualization Tool 18
Flash As A Graphics And Animation Utility 20
Flash As An Illustration And Presentation Program 22
Teaming Flash With Other Multimedia Web Tools 25

Chapter 2
The Anatomy Of Flash 29

Flash's Interface Components 30

Chapter 3
Flash From Here To There (And Back) 61

Whether To Design Specifically For Browser Or Offline 63
A Precision Placement Tool 64
Perfect Type 65
Easy Shapes 66
Export To Bitmapped File Formats 69
Export To Insta.HTML 70
Using Aftershock 70

Integration With Other Macromedia Products 73

Creating Templates For Flash Generator 73

Chapter 4 Drawing With Flash 75

You Don't Need Drawing Talent 76

Before Doing The Exercises 77

Learning To Draw Freehand With Flash 92

Drawing With Animation In Mind 105

The Drawing Tools And Their Modifiers 113

Flash's Drawing Aids 130

Commands And Tools For Refining Drawing Elements 133

Assembling And Disassembling Groups And Symbols 136

Inserting Objects Created In Other Applications 136

What You Shouldn't Expect From Flash As A Drawing Program 137

Chapter 5 The Essentials Of Making A Flash Animation 139

The Basics Of Animation 140

Easy Animation Techniques 150

Animation Fundamentals 165

The Power Of Layers 173

The Symbols Of Power 176

Makin' The Scene 180

Onion-Skinning 182

Chapter 6
The Symbols Of Power 187

Graphic Symbols 188
Buttons 190
Movie Clips 192
Bitmaps 193
Sounds 193
Using The Library Window And Menu 195
Editing Symbols 197
Making Animated Symbols 197
Instances And Instance Modifications 197

Chapter 7
Advanced Techniques 207

Combining Symbols 208
Creating Multilayer Animation 213
Combining Interactivity And Multiple Scenes 227
Creating Transparency Effects 229
More About Sound And Flash Animation 237
Finalizing And Publishing The Movie 245
Playing Flash Movies 248
Exporting To Other File Formats 250

Chapter 8
Buttoning Up Flash And Interactivity 253

Creating Buttons 254
Interactivity And Assigning Actions 263
Cool Button Tricks 271

Chapter 9
Using The Design In Motion Suite (And Other Macromedia Software) 275

Using FreeHand 8.01 With Flash 276

Using Insta.HTML 295

Using Fireworks With Flash 297

Using Dreamweaver With Flash 300

3D Tools And Flash 303

Chapter 10
Placing Flash On An HTML Page 305

Aftershock 306

Macromedia Dreamweaver: The Ultimate WYSIWYG HTML Editor 311

Basic HTML 315

HTML And Multimedia 315

Chapter 11
Expanding Flash And Your Audience 327

Making Sure You Have The Biggest Possible Audience 328

Expanding Flash To New Horizons 331

Chapter 12
Case Studies 335

Interview With Josh Ulm, Quokka Sports (www.quokka.com) 336

Interview With Elmer Erana, Fusion Media Group, Inc. (www.fusionmediagroup.com) 342

Interview With Christopher Colshorn, I-D Gruppe (www.idgruppe.com) 349

Appendix
Using Tell Target 353

Tell Target Tutorial 354

Things You Should Remember About Tell Target 358

Some Suggestions On Ways To Use Tell Target 359

Index 361

FLASH 3 WEB ANIMATION F/X AND DESIGN

INTRODUCTION

In the time since Janine Warner and I wrote the original book on Macromedia's Flash, *The Flash 2 Web Animation Book*, both the program and its user base have grown and matured enormously. Needed features, such as transparent objects and animated buttons, have been added. The already superfriendly user interface has become even more so. The requirement that viewers must install a plug-in before viewing Flash content on the Web is on its way to oblivion. The Flash player is built into all current versions of Netscape Navigator and Microsoft Internet Explorer, the AOL browser, and the Web TV browser. Flash authors can now distribute their productions freely for offline use as well.

You should find this book useful whether you're an advanced multimedia author or a beginner in interactive computer graphics. The nature of Flash 3 is part of the reason for this. Everything you need is built into the program: drawing tools, artificial intelligence to help you draw, an animation studio, and a hearty (if not ultimately sophisticated) set of interactive capabilities.

You'll realize quickly that Flash is equally useful for still graphics, offline presentations, and multimedia titles, as well as for its strong reputation as a Web animation tool.

Look, Ma, No More World Wide Wait

If you're not familiar with Flash or why it's generated so much industry buzz, it's because the program has revolutionized the method and speed of graphics delivery on the Web. It accomplishes this through two well-established technologies: vector graphics and streaming media.

Until Flash came along, the standards for Web graphics (whether static or animated) were based on bitmapped formats. Bitmaps are rows and columns (called rasters) of individually colored dots, and computers must store and interpret data for each of these dots (called pixels). Vector graphics store formulas for creating geometric shapes. Computers interpret these formulas, which allow graphics to be drawn at any size and resolution. Because less data is required to store the formula information, pictures can race across the Web at much higher speeds.

Streaming technology causes animation frames to begin playing as soon as enough frames have been received to allow the animation to play smoothly while the rest of the frames arrive.

What This Book Covers

This book teaches you how to use Flash 3's new features, as well as the program's basics. I've included late-breaking information about how to use the Tell Target feature. I'll also introduce you to working with some of the Macromedia programs that supplement Flash: FreeHand (an advanced vector-illustration program), InstaHTML (which converts FreeHand vector drawings and text into HTML), Fireworks (a program for preparing bitmapped graphics for the Web and Flash), and Dreamweaver (a Web-authoring program). Janine Warner tells you how to use the HTML tags needed to place Flash content on Web pages, as well as how to avoid having to write HTML code. She also presents case studies of three sites that use Flash technology to reach diverse goals.

There are some things this book doesn't cover. This isn't a book for programmers, so there's no in-depth discussion about how to write Java, JavaScript, or ActiveX code, which can interface with Flash. Also, we don't cover the nitty-gritty of creating code for Flash Generator.

Conventions Used In This Book

We deferred to the conventions used in Macromedia's documentation when deciding what terminology to use to describe Flash's features.

Though the terms sound synonymous, we make a distinction between telling you to *choose* something and telling you to *select* something. The word *choose* is always associated with a tool or a menu command; in other words, you are choosing to make a specific thing happen. The word *select* is always associated with designating the object of your choice. So, for instance, you select a line, shape, layer, or frame.

Flash 3 is full of menus, some of which are found on the menu bar. Others are located on layer bars, attached to frames, and so forth. We preface a menu command with its location. For instance, "from the Frames menu, choose..." Commands that are on cascading or hierarchical menus are given in the sequence in which they are encountered, and they are separated by pipe characters (vertical bars). For example, Modify|Style|Plain.

Both Flash 3 and this book are meant to be accessible to Macintosh and Windows users. For that reason, all keyboard shortcuts are given with the Mac key name first, followed by the Windows key name. The two are divided by a slash (/). The equivalent keys are Cmd/Ctrl, Opt/Alt, and Delete/Backspace. Keys that are identical to both systems (such as Shift, space, or any of the alphanumeric keys) are given only once.

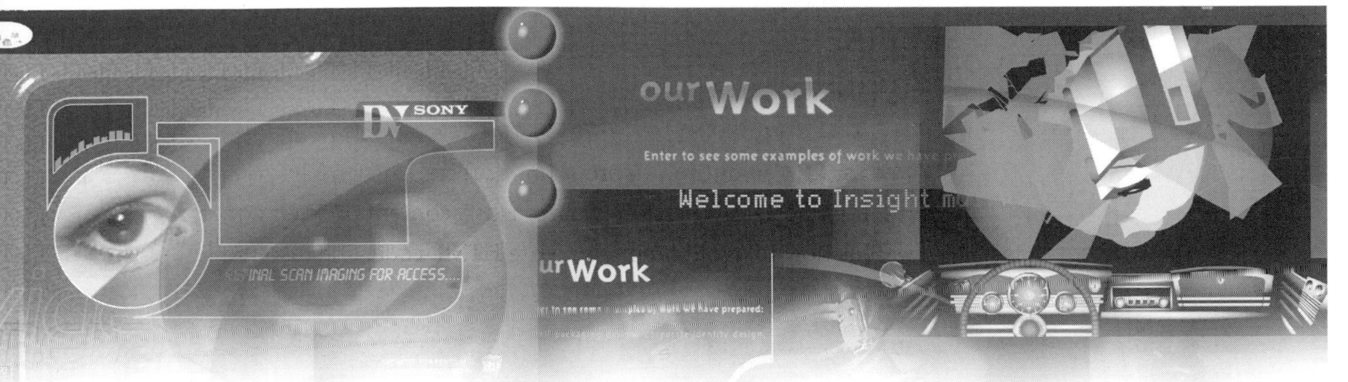

1 The Many Faces Of Flash

Ken Milburn

Flash is much more than a program for making quick-performing Web animations. This chapter introduces you to the ways Flash can contribute to your workflow—both on and off the Web.

The Web has been abuzz for months about the hot look and performance of Web pages made with Flash. The accolades are well deserved. No other product can produce a high-performance, full-screen, animated, interactive Web page nearly as well or as easily (see Figure 1.1). But, if that's all you know about Flash, you've only scratched the surface.

Why Flash Is The Answer To A Web Author's Prayers

If you're a Web author and you design graphics or illustrations for print, Flash is easily the best bargain in computer graphics. The characteristics that make this so are:

- A (nearly) universal playback standard
- Speed
- Image and text quality
- Scalability

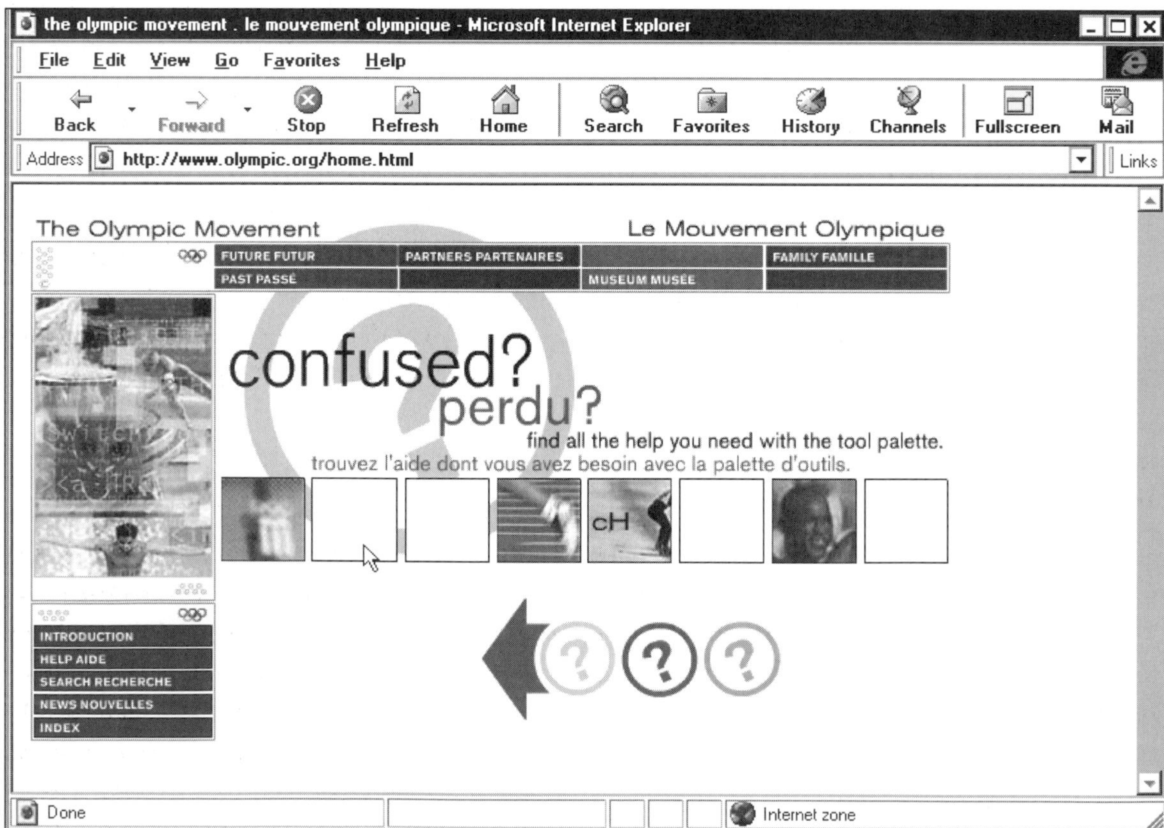

Figure 1.1 A Flash Web site for the Olympic Movement (**www.olympic.org/home.html**). Notice the smooth-edged graphics in the large window. Text and buttons are animated.

- Ease of use
- Versatility

A (Nearly) Universal Playback Standard

Several factors place Flash 3 squarely on the path to becoming a universal standard for authoring and playing vector graphics on the Web.

Macromedia has made the source code for creating Flash content available to anyone who wants it. As a result, you can expect to see Flash technology built into many new Web-authoring products, including Netscape Communicator.

As of summer '98, the Flash plug-in is built into the two browsers that command more than 90 percent of the current browser market: Netscape Navigator and Microsoft Internet Explorer. This includes all version 4 browsers that were shipped after July '98 (and a few that shipped a little earlier, including all versions of Internet Explorer that were bundled with Windows 98). Of course, Flash will be built into future versions of browsers from Netscape and Microsoft.

What if you have an older browser? If you have anything newer than version 3 that's compatible with Netscape plug-ins, you can download and install the Flash 3 plug-in in less than five minutes—and at no cost. The entire code is under 200K. More than 40 million of these plug-ins for legacy browsers have been downloaded from the Macromedia site.

Of course, these provisions don't include absolutely everybody. However, this book will show you how to place code on your Flash site that can detect the type of browser that is viewing the site and then do one of three things:

- Play the Flash site if the browser is already Flash compatible (has the plug-in installed or built-in).
- Automatically install the plug-in (browser and version permitting).
- Play a Java or conventional version of the Flash site if nothing else works.

So, create a site in Flash, and you can set it up so that no viewer gets shut out. Furthermore, in the not-too-distant future, everyone will have the plug-in anyway. Oh, yeah, did I mention Web TV? The Flash player is already built into it, as well.

Speed

A full-screen Flash animation consisting of several scenes can load into a viewer's browser and begin playing in less than 10 seconds. It would typically take more than a minute (and potentially many minutes) to load and play a traditional Web movie of comparable size and complexity.

This enormous performance gain is due to the fact that Flash describes images by using vector graphics, rather than the bitmaps used in more traditional Web animation techniques. If you aren't yet familiar with the terms *vector* and *bitmap*, here's an explanation.

The content of a Flash Web page consists of mathematical formulas (vectors) that describe the geometry of shapes and the characteristics of colors. Because these instructions are stored as plain text, very little data is needed to describe an entire screen of moving graphics. Such image geometry is known in the trade as *vector graphics*.

Traditional Web animation techniques, on the other hand, describe images as a matrix (raster) of colored pixels. The size of individual pixels (as well as their total number in a given image) is fixed. In addition, it takes several bits of data to describe each pixel. So, a small image of 360 by 240 pixels typically requires 74,000 bytes of data. Remember, this is for a single frame and that, typically, Web animations need to run at several frames *per second* (8 to 15 is typical). As a result, you could have several frames of a Flash movie stored in a file that is only one-third the size of the single, bitmapped frame.

The image sizes used in the preceding examples are typical, but you should be aware that many variables can affect the size of a given image. Some of these are the number of colors (bitmaps) or geometrical shapes (vector drawings), the file format, and the method of compression used to store the file. Even so, a Flash file will almost always load and play at several times the speed of a bitmapped animation.

Image And Text Quality

The elements of a Flash page are so clean and professional that viewing a Flash page for the first time can be startling (especially if it contains lots of hard-edged graphics such as buttons, text, and logos). Another Flash benefit is that you'll never see any stray or mushy pixels in areas of solid color or gradients. (We geeks call those things *artifacts*.)

Because vector graphics *tell* the target computer how to draw the image, the image always looks as good as it possibly could on that computer. In contrast, bitmapped animations are often made by resizing and distorting a matrix of pixels of a fixed size. In this process, some needed pixels are lost or exaggerated, and image quality suffers significantly.

Flash also gives authors the option of displaying graphics as fully antialiased. *Antialiasing* is a process that smoothes hard edges by blending the edge pixels with pixels of the background color, thus softening the edge. Since no pixels are contained in the file itself, Flash accomplishes this antialiasing using the pixels on the viewer's screen.

Scalability

Although this characteristic of vector graphics is a bonus in almost any instance, scalability is a major boon for displaying road maps (say, for giving directions to your business) and detailed technical drawings (such as those you might want to include on an instructional site).

Do you ever wish you could make a browser window smaller without cutting off part of the site's content? Do you ever wish you could zoom in to see details in a map or technical drawing you've found on the Web? Well, with Flash you can. Flash can be told to automatically adjust the size of a window's content whenever the viewer changes the size of the window.

It just so happens that scalability is another advantage of vector graphics. The formula for describing the shapes in any given image stays the same regardless of the size or resolution at which those shapes are shown or printed. When you zoom in on one of these images, all you are doing is instructing the computer to multiply or divide the formula. As long as the detail is in the original drawing, a viewer can see it clearly at any size.

Ease Of Use

My kids are grown up and bright, so of course even they could learn to use Flash 3 over a couple of evenings. Better yet, they could have done so when they were in grade school, and so could your kids—and even you.

That is not to say that you'll learn and make immediate use of all of the program's potential with no effort. As is the case with any other powerful and versatile tool, practice makes perfect (or at least it brings you *closer* to perfection and makes it harder for the competition).

This is also the point at which I should warn you that no program can make you an artist. Flash, however, can turn nervous lines into straight ones or squiggly shapes into smooth curves. The program has built-in shape recognition, and the use of its drawing tools is more natural and intuitive than is the case with such illustration programs as Adobe Illustrator or Macromedia FreeHand. See Figure 1.2.

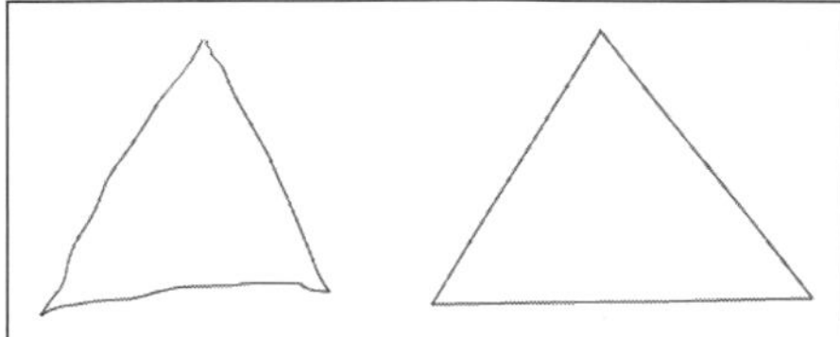

Figure 1.2 Flash automatically recognizes the shape on the left as a triangle.

Versatility

Some advantages of Flash that contribute to its versatility are:

- Flash makes the cleanest, highest performing, and most graphically rich Web pages of any single tool currently available, even if you don't use the plug-in.
- Flash is the best tool available for "quick sketching" ideas for Web pages, presentations, graphic design, and illustration. Many commercial illustrators conceptualize or prepare graphics in Flash and then export their sketches to FreeHand or Illustrator for fine-tuning.
- Flash is a powerful illustration and presentation program that can be put to good use (with great results) even if you don't know how to draw.
- Flash allows you to create animations of all kinds without prior training or experience as an animator.
- Flash can prepare content for virtually all Web, multimedia, presentation, and graphics programs running under Macintosh and Windows.

In all the Web hoopla, you might have missed the fact that Flash is every bit as capable of creating content for conventional multimedia and print. Although in this book I will tell you everything I think you would care to know about using Flash to prepare Web content, I intend to be equally zealous in talking about its considerable abilities in preparing content for the other media as well.

Just to tease you a bit more, did you know that Flash will let you import a scan and instantly turn it into a fully scalable drawing that uses a fraction of the file space required by the original? Or that Flash's powerful animation tools can be used to create animated graphics

> **Note:** *Many illustrators have found that Flash is a marvelous tool for optimizing the complex drawings they create in advanced vector programs such as FreeHand, Illustrator, or CorelDRAW. They simply import a drawing into Flash and then break apart and ungroup all the elements of the drawing. This drops the elements onto the canvas, where overlapping shapes auto-edit themselves into individual shapes. The resultant file is often significantly smaller, so it will print much faster when placed into documents.*

interchange format (GIF) files that can be used on any Web page? Or that you can import graphics into Flash from just about any source and modify them to your heart's content without having the slightest iota of drawing talent?

This is only the beginning of all the wonders that this easy-to-use and inexpensive program has to offer. The next section in this chapter examines the new features in Flash 3 and recaps the features that were new in Flash 2. Then, I will detail what Flash can do for you on the Web, as a visualization and storyboarding tool, as a graphics and animation utility, and as an illustration and multimedia presentation program. Finally, the last section discusses the ease and benefits of teaming Flash with other applications, such as Macromedia's Director, Authorware, and FreeHand, and Adobe's Photoshop, Illustrator, and Premier.

New Features In Flash 3

With more than 40 million Flash plug-ins downloaded from the Macromedia site (**www.macromedia.com**), it is obvious to Macromedia that it's worthwhile to continue to develop this product. The new features in version 3 aren't nearly as noticeable for their number as they are for their usefulness. The short list follows, after which you'll find a more detailed description of each feature:

- Transparent graphics
- Shape morphing
- Multidirectional rotations tweened from only two keyframes (drawing the transitional frames between the first and last frames of a motion transition)
- Layer masks
- More-versatile symbols
- Expanded actions
- Ability to add labels and comments to frames
- Clearer and more informative interface (most frequently used commands are now on main menu)
- Inspector window that shows properties of shapes
- Optional standard multiple selection
- Improved frame selection
- Improved cornerpoint creation

- Ability to create templates for interactive site content
- Automated creation of HTML code
- Instant performance reporting
- Support for PNG (portable network graphics)
- Improved support and interfacing with FreeHand
- New standalone projector requires no browser or ActiveX control

Transparent Graphics

You can now specify that any color gradient be as transparent or as opaque as you like. You can also apply transparency to symbols and groups. You can even make the transparency of a fill or outline fade over time.

For the first time, it is also possible to import transparency in bitmaps, thanks to the support for the PNG format, which features Alpha channels. (You'll find more information about PNG in Chapter 7.)

Shape Morphing

You can now make one shape change into another over time, simply by defining start and stop keyframes in Flash's Timeline and then placing the start and finish shapes in the appropriate frames. You can then tell Flash to automatically tween the progression of shape-shifting frames. This process also results in significantly smaller file sizes than was the case when each change needed to be drawn in an individual keyframe. This is because you need to download only two images instead of several.

Multidirectional Rotations Tweened From Only Two Keyframes

This feature is amazing. You can place an element (object, symbol, or group) in a start keyframe and then in an end keyframe. You can transform that element in as many directions as you like by telling Flash to tween the transformations. In between, the object will rotate and transform in the same sequence you used in the end keyframe. It's powerful stuff.

Layer Masks

If you've worked in Photoshop, you know that you can use a layer mask to keep certain areas of a given layer from being visible to the other layers. Now, you can do the same in Flash 3. You could, for instance, use a layer mask to simulate the point of view of someone who's trying to peek through a hole in a wall.

More-Versatile Symbols

It's now possible to assign three different types of behaviors to symbols: movie clip, button, and graphic. You can have animated buttons because movie clips can have all the interactive properties of a Flash 3 movie. Thus, you can have interactive movies within movies.

Movie-clip animations aren't Timeline dependent, and they can play in a single frame (such as a button frame).

Graphics are the equivalent of the symbols in Flash 2 and are controlled by the Timeline.

Buttons are nearly the same as in Flash 2, except that (as already noted) they can include movie clips.

Expanded Actions

The actions in Flash 3 are much more powerful than in Flash 2. Actions cause Flash to do something when cued by the clicking of a button or the playing of a specific frame. Now, you can attach multiple actions to a single *event* (button or frame). You can also attach different actions to each *instance* (appearance) of any given symbol.

A dialog box has been added to help you assign actions to events.

Ability To Add Labels And Comments To Frames

You can add labels and comments to individual frames. These stay with the frames even if their position is changed, because you added or deleted frames from the movie.

Clearer And More Informative Interface

Several new features, some of which are covered in this chapter, have been added to make working in Flash easier and more intuitive. Among these new features is the presence on the main menu of many important commands that were formerly hidden in specialized menus (such as the Timeline menu).

Inspector Window That Shows Properties Of Shapes

When you want to know what the properties of an item are, you can choose Window|Inspector. A dialog box pops up to show you the dimensions and type (for example, Shape, Group, Symbol) of the item. See Figure 1.3.

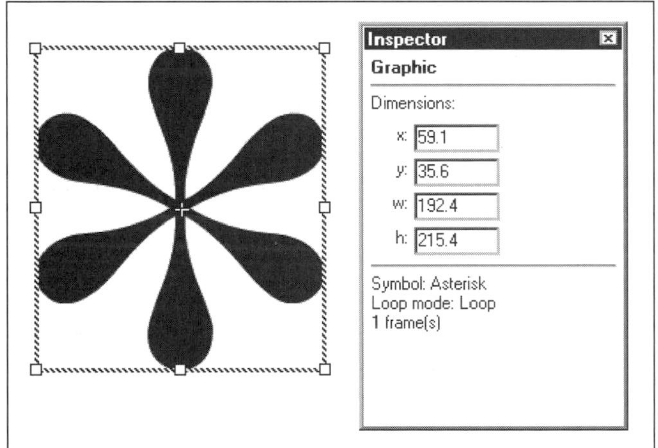

Figure 1.3 The new Inspector window.

Optional Standard Multiple Selection

Earlier versions of Flash kept selecting items as you clicked them. This made many users nuts because it was too easy to forget that you had already selected an item when you clicked to select another. After all, ingrained habits are hard to break. Every other application that runs in either Mac or Windows drops any previously selected item when you select a new item (unless you press Shift as you click additional items to be selected).

Flash 3 still uses the old maddening selection method as the default, but you can choose to use the standard Shift Select method by checking it in the program's Preferences dialog box. See Figure 1.4.

Preferences
Bitmaps on Clipboard
Color depth: Match screen
Resolution: Screen dpi
Size limit: 250 Kb Smooth
Gradients on Clipboard
Quality: Normal
Undo Levels: 20
Printing Options: Disable PostScript
Selection Options: Shift Select
Timeline Options: Show frame popup menu
OK
Cancel
Help

Figure 1.4 Check the Shift Select option in the Preferences dialog box to employ this usual selection method.

Improved Frame Selection

This feature is another in the "why didn't they think of that sooner" category. Now, when you select (by clicking) a frame in the Timeline, it immediately appears on the stage, and the current frame pointer immediately moves to that frame.

Improved Cornerpoint Creation

You can now insert a cornerpoint into a curved section of a shape. You do this simply by pressing Opt/Alt (Option on the Mac and Alt in Windows) while dragging with the selection arrow to reshape the curve. See Figure 1.5. (For a better understanding of how Flash reshapes your drawings, see Chapter 4.)

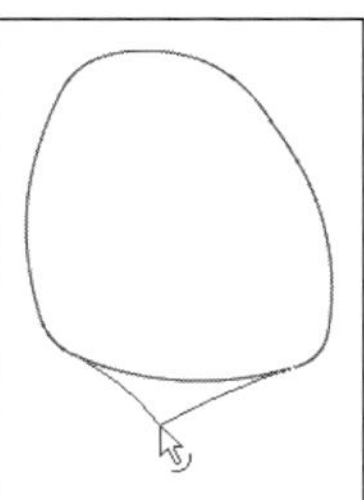

Figure 1.5 Dragging a corner from a curve after pressing Opt/Alt.

Ability To Create Templates For Interactive Site Content

A new Macromedia program, Flash Generator, creates server-based, interactive Web animations. In layperson's terms, this means that the animations change according to the data (which can be as simple as a yes/no button click) input by the viewer. Although authoring with Generator is a topic for advanced users, you can create templates to use with Generator directly in Flash. All this will be detailed further in Chapter 7.

Automated Creation Of HTML Code

Flash 3 ships with a new Macromedia utility called Aftershock. Aftershock automatically creates the **<EMBED>** and **<OBJECT>** tags needed to insert a Flash movie into an HTML (Hypertext Markup Language) document. This utility is a separate application, and it will be covered in Chapter 10.

Instant Performance Reporting

You'll love this feature if you've spent time optimizing Flash files after discovering the hard way that some download times were unexpectedly long. You can test the movie, then call up the bandwidth profiler to see what the performance of the movie will be (given a specific modem speed). The default speed is 28.8Kbps for testing, but Flash 3 reports a transfer speed of 2.3Kbps, which is more realistic and typical of actual Web performance over 28.8 modems. The bandwidth profiler is shown in Figure 1.6.

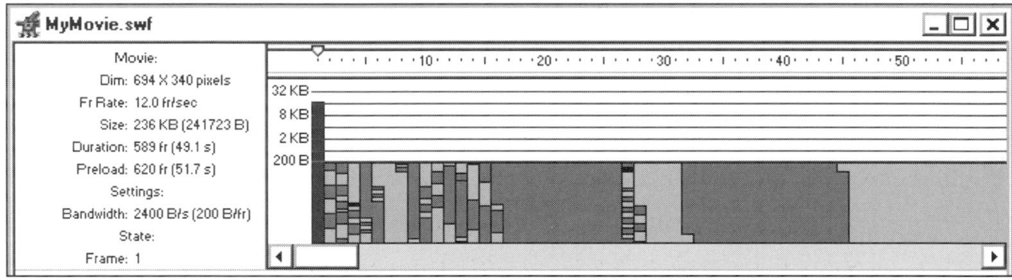

Figure 1.6 Instant performance graphing with the bandwidth profiler.

PNG Graphics Support

Although GIF and JPEG have been the standard formats for bitmapped Web graphics, a new format has been incorporated into the version 4 browsers. This format, portable network graphics (PNG), supports Alpha channel transparency and both true-color (millions of colors) and indexed-color (256 or fewer colors) as well as compressed and uncompressed file formats.

The most significant aspect of Flash 3's support of the PNG format is that it allows you to specify transparent areas (such as the background) of images.

Improved Support And Interfacing With FreeHand

FreeHand is Macromedia's professional-level, vector-based illustration tool, competing directly with Adobe Illustrator and CorelDRAW. FreeHand is arguably the most versatile of the three. It is now possible to convert FreeHand CMYK files to RGB for use in Flash. (The Web is an RGB medium.) Perhaps more importantly, you can preserve layers when transferring files between FreeHand and Flash. Finally, you can cut a selected FreeHand graphic to the clipboard and then paste it into a Flash 3 frame without losing any information regarding curves, gradients, or RGB color information.

It's worth noting that FreeHand 8 is capable of importing graphics from most of the popular vector graphics formats (most notably Illustrator, Corel, and AutoCAD), thus providing a bridge for bringing all sorts of graphics into Flash, including maps and technical drawings.

New Standalone Projector Requires No Browser Or ActiveX Control

The new player makes Flash 3 an excellent choice for creating offline (that is, disk-based) interactive content. If you double-click the file name or icon of a movie exported as a Shockwave Flash movie, it will automatically open in the standalone player application.

At that point you can choose File|Create Projector. The movie is then exported in a standalone version that can be distributed on anything from floppies to CD-ROMs. All it takes to play that movie is to double-click it. No other software is required on the viewer's computer.

Flash 2 Features Revisited

If you're already familiar with FutureWave, FutureSplash, or with Macromedia's initial release of Flash, you'll want to know what Flash 2 added. Well, there weren't a lot of new features, but they made a big difference. The features include synchronized sound, greatly enhanced bitmap image support, tweening of color changes, expansion of the symbol palette into something called the Library (which also catalogs bitmaps and sounds), and the ability to make buttons of anything in a Flash scene and to do it more easily.

Synchronized Sound

Alas, you still can't use MIDI files, but you can import digitized analog sound in the form of either AIFF (Macintosh's audio interchange format) or WAV (Windows audio/video) files. (MIDI files are analogous to vector graphics and are more compact than the digitized analog sound files.) The advantages of AIFF or WAV files are the ease with which sounds can be digitized from almost any source, and the abundance of commercial "clip sounds" (in AIFF or WAV formats) that are available at reasonable costs.

Flash lets you cut a sound file to include only the segment you absolutely need. This means that, if you want only the "Ta ta ta ta" of the William Tell Overture (the theme song of *The Lone Ranger*), you don't have to store the file for the entire work. Once you have edited the sound segment, you can synchronize it to any keyframe in an animation, or you can have it start at the click of a button. Another nice feature of the new sound support is that, once you've cataloged a sound in the Library, any edits you make to that file are reflected automatically whether or not that sound is used in any Flash movie. You'll find everything you need to know about adding sound to Flash in Chapter 7.

Animated Color Change

Flash automatically draws the frames for objects that change shape, orientation, or position in between keyframes (the first and last frames of a motion transition), just as its predecessor, FutureSplash, did. Flash 2 also made it possible to make transitions in the color between one keyframe and another. You don't do this, as you would in some other programs, by simply specifying that the program tween two differently colored objects. Instead, you must use a specialized dialog box. These steps are detailed in Chapter 7.

The Library

In Flash 2, the Library took the place of the symbol palette that existed in earlier versions of Flash/Splash. The big difference is that the Library holds bitmap graphics and sounds, in addition to symbols. The advantage here is that you store these elements once and then use them many times in a Flash movie. This is especially important if those movies are destined for use in a Web site (because the overall file size is reduced considerably).

The Library in Flash 3 has a slightly different menu interface than in Flash 2 (which, in turn, differed somewhat from the original). See the

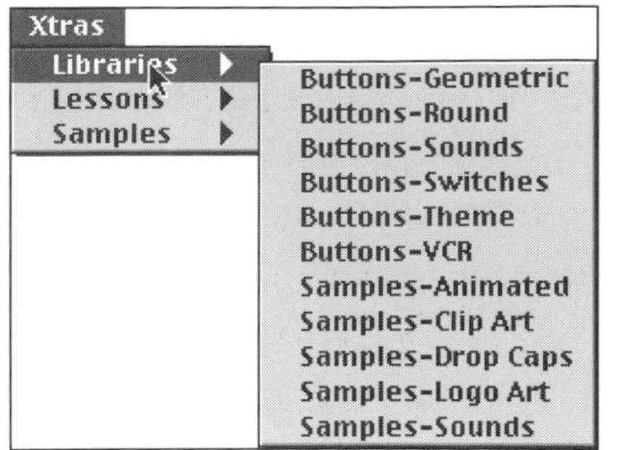

Figure 1.7 Flash 2's Libraries menu.

Figure 1.8 Flash 3's Libraries menu.

Flash 2 Libraries menu in Figure 1.7 and the Flash 3 Libraries menu in Figure 1.8. In Flash 3, you access the Libraries by choosing Libraries, rather than Xtras|Libraries.

The Flash 2 Library window is in Figure 1.9; Flash 3's Library window is in Figure 1.10. The three status buttons control whether to display symbols (movies and buttons), graphics (bitmaps), or sounds. The right-arrow button plays animated symbols and sounds, while the down-arrow button pops up the Symbols Palette menu. In Flash 3, the Symbols Palette menu has a new command, Select Unused Media.

Figure 1.9 Flash 2's Library window.

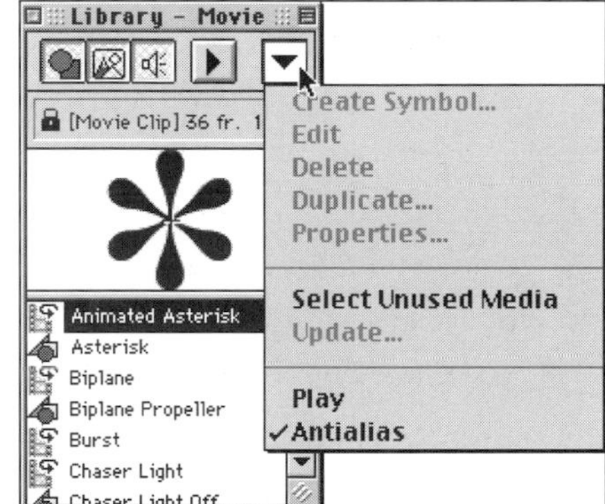

Figure 1.10 Flash 3's Library window.

Easy Button Making

Because Flash 3 makes it possible to use movies as Library symbols, now you can have animated buttons. And they're just as easy to make as ever. To make a button, simply turn anything selected on screen into a symbol and check the Button Behavior box. Then, you can directly edit any of the button's four frames (Up, Over, Down, and Hit). Because Flash's buttons are so powerful and versatile, an entire chapter of this book, Chapter 6, is devoted to the subject. It includes lots of tips, tricks, and examples.

Flash And The Web

All the raving you may have heard about the prowess of Flash on the Web is well warranted. If you don't believe that and have ready access to the Web, check out the sites for any of the case study examples in this book. If you're just thinking about using Flash, don't have the program and, therefore, don't have the plug-in, don't worry. Any of these sites will give you the option of installing the plug-in. It uses less than 150K of your system's memory, won't cause any conflicts that I've been able to find, and downloads and installs in less than two minutes. If you have Netscape Navigator 4 or Microsoft Internet Explorer 3 (or later), the plug-in will even autoload.

Chapter 12 features three new case studies, each of a different Web design firm that relies heavily on Flash technology to maximize impact with their viewers: Quokka Sports (**www.quokka.com**), The Fusion Media Group, Inc. (**www.fusionmedia.com**), and I-D Gruppe (**www.idgruppe.de**). See Fusion Media's Web site in Figure 1.11.

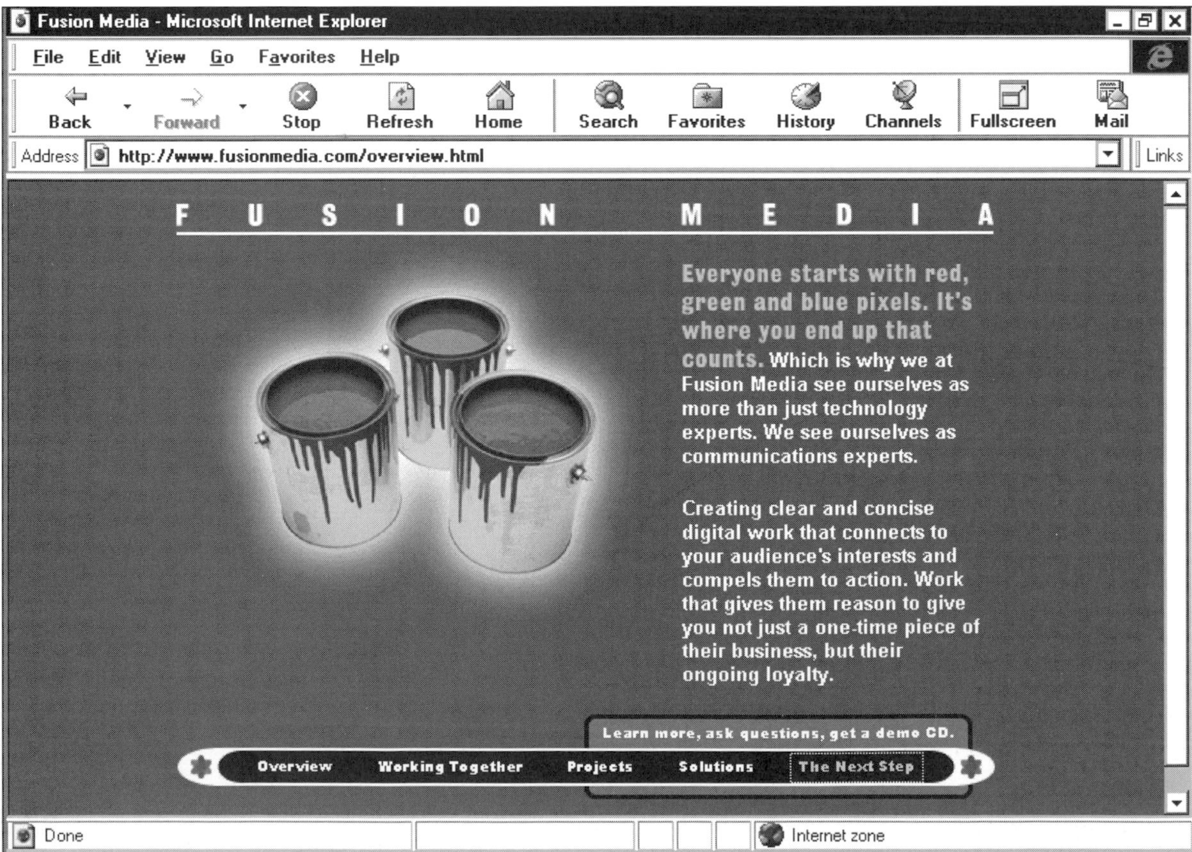

Figure 1.11 In Fusion Media's Wired Realm, the photos and type animate at high speed over a 28.8Kbps connection.

While Flash can create Web content that doesn't require any plug-ins, a full-on Flash site is a revelation as to how a Web site should look and work. It's far superior to ordinary HTML pages. The reasons for this are detailed in the following sections, but here's the short list:

- You can use much smaller—and therefore faster and more efficient—page and graphics files.
- Graphics and animations can be of any dimension without speed penalties.
- Page contents scale automatically to fit the user's window.
- Any object or any area on the screen can be a button.
- Buttons can change to any static image on mouse-over and can link to animations, new scenes, or URLs by clicking.
- Graphics and text are always antialiased, so edges are always smooth, clean, and professional looking.
- You can have any mixture of Flash and HTML on a page.
- The plug-in automatically downloads for the most recent versions of the most popular browsers.

One Of The Most Widely Distributed Plug-Ins

I can't emphasize strongly enough that Flash is useful for creating all sorts of Web and print content that requires no plug-ins at all. However, there's no doubt that the most revolutionarily Web pages are created to take advantage of Flash's vector graphics. For that reason, Flash is much more powerful when used to create Web pages and elements that will be viewed with a plug-in—or in later fourth-generation and all fifth-generation browsers that have the plug-in incorporated.

Oddly, the Flash plug-in is installed in more early-generation browsers than you might think. The reason is simple: The most visited site on the Net, MSN (Microsoft Network), uses Flash for many of its primary interface elements. So, virtually everyone who has visited the site has downloaded the plug-in, often without even realizing it. That is because the plug-in downloads automatically if your browser is (at least) Microsoft Internet Explorer 3 or Netscape Navigator 4. If your browser is an earlier version of one of these, you can still download and install the plug-in in less than two minutes. After all, its file size is well under 200K.

Automatic Antialiasing Of Animations And Graphics

Flash's Web output is automatically antialiased (unless you elect to turn it off). So the edges of graphic elements are never jagged or pixelated, as they often are with the bitmapped graphics commonly found on the Internet.

Animations And Graphics Of Any Dimension

Because vector graphics are drawn according to coded instructions rather than using a fixed-size pixel mosaic, the resolution speed and definition of graphics do not depend on file size. It is nothing short of astonishing to see a full-screen animation load and play *instantly* over a 14.4Kbps connection. Remember, however, that the secret to speed and performance is still the size of the files. If you make drawings that consist of hundreds of elements and use few symbols in those drawings, you can expect much poorer performance than for drawings and animations consisting of fewer shapes, simpler shapes, and symbols in less complex shapes.

Fast Animations, Even Over 14.4Kbps Connections

As I've seen, vector graphics provide a great speed advantage. The other reason Flash animations are so quick is a technology called data streaming. This means that the information in the file is organized *top down*, so that what's needed first arrives first on your computer. Thus, the animation can start playing the moment anything gets to your computer; you don't have to wait for an entire file to load before it can play.

If you are using a browser with the Flash plug-in installed and you visit a Flash site, any delay in viewing the Flash graphics will be due to factors beyond the control of Flash, such as heavy Web traffic or the presence of many non-Flash graphic elements on the same page as the Flash elements.

Automatically Scales To Fit The Window

You can specify that the content of a Flash *scene* (which can be a static collection of graphics or an animation) either displays at a fixed size or scales to fit the window in which it is being viewed. This capability is a great advantage in designing Web pages that will look the same on anyone's browser. Figure 1.12 shows you the same page in browser windows of two different sizes.

Automatic Antialiasing Of Shape Edges And Type

Above-average antialiasing creates uniquely smooth edges and readable type. Flash allows you to specify whether you want your Flash movies shown or viewed in Rough or High Quality mode (which is the default). If High Quality is turned off, antialiasing is turned off.

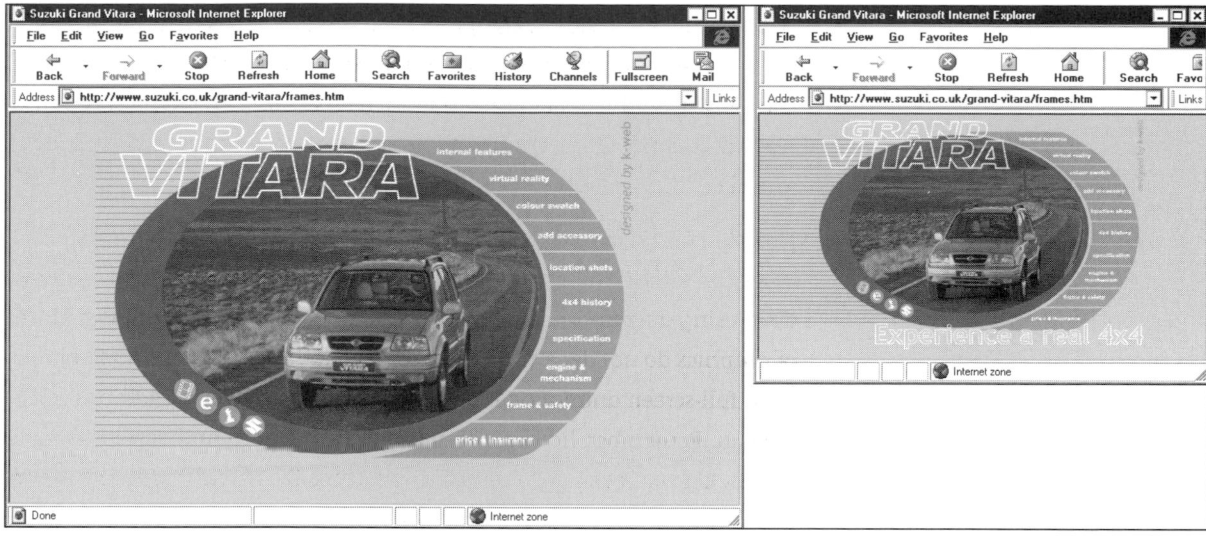

Figure 1.12 The same Flash page in browser windows of two different sizes.

Normally, however, antialiasing is calculated by the player each time the screen or the graphic is rescaled. The result is that the contents of your screens always look sharp and professional. Figure 1.13 shows the same image in both High Quality and Rough modes.

Entire Web sites can be designed using nothing but Flash and a rudimentary knowledge of a few HTML tags (which I will include for you).

Chapter 10 will provide complete instructions for using Flash within HTML pages. For now, just know that Flash "movies" (whether these are simply buttons, small still frames, or full-screen animations) are simply put onto the Web with the addition of simple instructions in the

Figure 1.13 The enlarged edge of an S, at left, is antialiased in High Quality mode. At right, it is seen with antialiasing turned off in Rough mode.

HTML code that describe the page (either an **<EMBED>** tag or an **<OB-JECT>** tag). The **<EMBED>** tag works with Netscape Navigator 2 or later and all other browsers that support Netscape Navigator 2 compatible plug-ins. The **<OBJECT>** tag will be recognized by Netscape Navigator 4 or Microsoft Internet Explorer 3 (or later versions).

The use of **<OBJECT>** tags allows the use of a CODEBASE parameter that causes the Flash plug-in to download and install automatically. This is such a great advantage that it makes sense to nest the **<EMBED>** tag inside the **<OBJECT>** tag. When you do so, all browsers equipped with a Flash plug-in can use the Flash movie, and all the latest Netscape and Microsoft browsers will download the plug-in automatically, if required. Users of browsers not so equipped can be given the option to download and install Flash in an HTML message and link on the page.

In addition to Chapter 10's instructions for coding HTML pages for use with Flash, you will find "cut-and-paste" HTML code on this book's companion CD-ROM.

You can also use most of the WYSIWYG (What You See Is What You Get) Web-authoring programs to place Flash 2 or 3 content into Web pages, but you will want to edit the HTML code to include both the **<EMBED>** and **<OBJECT>** tags. (Macromedia's Dreamweaver is one such tool that will do that for you.)

JavaScripts can also be placed in your HTML documents to detect the presence of a Flash plug-in in a visitor's browser and then play either a Flash or non-Flash version of the site, accordingly. You will find out how to do this in Chapter 10. There's even a JavaScript-detection script on the companion CD-ROM that you can cut, paste, and modify.

Zoom-In Increases Detail

You can put highly detailed graphics and text (that otherwise would be too small to see or read) on a Flash page, and viewers then can zoom in to see or read the detail up close. This is a real boon in applications in which you want to present detail to those who are interested enough to look for it. An example might be a page featuring a city map or a hidden clue in an interactive training demo or adventure game.

Flash As A Visualization Tool

Flash is, in my opinion, the best "sketchpad" I've come across for visualizing graphic designs, presentations, Web pages, or animations. Why? First, it makes the process of sketching and putting your ideas in sequence as easy and intuitive as doodling on a napkin over a business lunch. It's even intelligent enough to straighten your squiggles into straighter lines and geometric shapes. See Figure 1.14 for a before-and-after look at how Flash can clean up a simple drawing for you.

Figure 1.14 The sketch on the left was drawn freehand with Flash's shape recognition turned off, the sketch on the right with it turned on.

The ease with which you can sketch is, by no means, the end of the story. Flash is rich with graphics and animation tools that let you take those very sketches and turn them into comprehensives (a trade term for a highly polished preview) for client approval, and then on to finished work. Even if Flash 2 doesn't have all the tools you might want from Illustrator or Photoshop, you can export to those programs and use their tools. You also can use all the fancy font techniques that Illustrator or FreeHand can produce and just drop them into Flash. Want more? You can also use virtually all the clip art on the planet—even bitmapped clip art. Just import the file and choose Modify|Trace Bitmap to quickly manufacture an editable vector drawing of the image.

Flash is also a great tool for quickly drawing storyboards. You can sketch a different scene in each frame of the movie. You can use the onion-skinning feature that lets you see through one or more frames as though they were sheets of celluloid lying atop one another. (This feature will figure more prominently in the chapter on animation.) So you can even register the elements on one page over any elements to be repeated on the next page, making it very easy to keep layouts consistent from page to page.

If you want to distribute hand-printed, comic-strip storyboards to colleagues and clients for approval, it's no problem. You can set the Page Setup options to print storyboards with any number of frames across the page (in either landscape or portrait orientation). You can have these thumbnails framed in a box, squared off in a grid, or simply printed side by side on a blank page. The Page Setup dialog box to configure storyboard printing is shown in Figure 1.15.

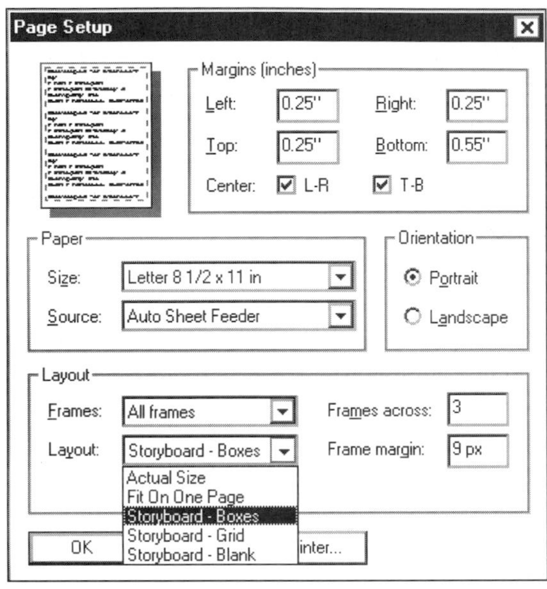

Figure 1.15 The Page Setup settings for printing storyboards.

Once your storyboard has been approved, you can polish the frames into finished Web content, offline presentations, animations (no problem to insert frames), or illustrations—whatever the job calls for.

Flash As A Graphics And Animation Utility

Flash is so capable at creating Flash movies that people tend to forget that it's a great tool for creating graphics and animations to be used in other forms and formats. It is fully capable of exporting animations as GIFs, QuickTime or AVI movies—even frames to be inserted in Director or Authorware (to be viewed with an ActiveX control). All you have to do is choose File|Export Movie, and then pick the desired destination format from the pull-down menu in the resultant dialog box. File types to which you can export motion sequences from Flash are shown in Table 1.1. Of course, if you export to a non-Flash movie format, you will lose sound and interactivity.

Table 1.1 Export movie file types.

Extension	File Type	Platform
.AI	Adobe Illustrator sequence	Windows, Macintosh
.GIF	Animated GIF	Windows, Macintosh
.BMP	Bitmapped sequence	Windows
.DXF	Autodesk DXF (data exchange format) sequence	Windows, Macintosh
.EMF	Enhanced metafile sequence	Windows
.EPS	Encapsulated postscript sequence	Windows, Macintosh
.SPL	FutureSplash player	Windows, Macintosh
.JPG	JPEG sequence	Windows, Macintosh
.PCT	PICT sequence	Macintosh
.SWF	Shockwave Flash movie	Windows, Macintosh
.MOV	QuickTime movie	Macintosh
.AVI	Windows AVI movie	Windows
.WMF	Windows Metafile sequence	Windows

Flash also can import and export static images to many common file formats. Simply choose File|Export Image from the menu bar, and choose the desired format from among those listed in Table 1.2.

Table 1.2 Import/export static image file types.

Extension	Program Compatibility	Platform
.AI, .EPS	Adobe Illustrator 6 or earlier	Windows, Macintosh
.GIF	GIF 89a	Windows, Macintosh
.BMP	Windows bitmap	Windows
.DXF	Autodesk DXF (data exchange format)	Windows, Macintosh
.EMF	Enhanced metafile	Windows
.JPG	JPEG	Windows, Macintosh
.PCT	Many Macintosh paint and draw programs	Macintosh
.SWF	Shockwave Flash Frame	Windows, Macintosh
.WMF	Windows metafile	Windows

Another way that Flash is useful as a graphics utility is in converting digitized photos and scans (bitmaps) into drawings (vectors). Flash will do this automatically at your request. Simply use File|Import to place the bitmap in the active layer and frame, then choose Modify|Trace Bitmap from the menu bar. Figures 1.16 and 1.17 show the Trace Bitmap process.

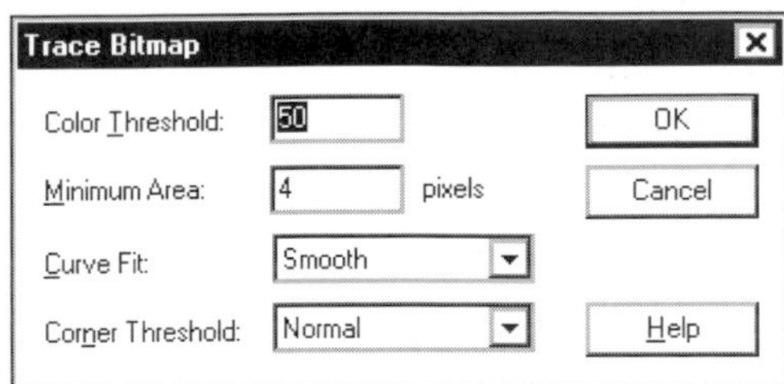

Figure 1.16 The Trace Bitmap options dialog box.

Figure 1.17 A rose photo traced with the settings in Figure 1.16.

There's another facet of using Flash as a graphics utility. You can minimize the file size of many bitmapped illustrations to be used as elements in HTML Web pages by autotracing them. The result looks just like the autotraced drawing in Figure 1.17. If you export the file as a GIF bitmap, the resultant file is even smaller than a JPEG of the same dimensions. For instance, the JPEG version of this image is 50K, while the GIF image exported from the drawing is only 17K. This is because autotracing averages the color within any of the traced subshapes to a single color. The result is that there is more information in the file that can be repeated with a single instruction. For information about how to export a drawing as a GIF, see the "Exporting to GIF" section later in this chapter.

Flash As An Illustration And Presentation Program

Flash is useful both as an illustration program and as a program for making offline presentations. As an illustration program, it is especially useful for businesspeople whose primary job isn't illustration. This is true because of its easy interface, its built-in lessons and help, its ability to automate the straightening and smoothing of lines, and its recognition of primitive shapes. In addition, editing shapes is much easier than in traditional types of drawing programs. The series of figures that follows will illustrate some of these differences.

Flash is a reasonably capable, all-purpose illustration program for several reasons. First, it uses the same type of Bezier curve vector graphics as the "professional" illustration and presentation programs. Second, Flash can import and export files to vector formats that can be exchanged with other programs. Third, the graphics that it produces, like its illustration program colleagues, are resolution-independent. Finally, Flash offers a wealth of drawing, animation, and interactivity features that can't be found in its competitors.

Flash doesn't do everything that illustration programs do (for instance, no blends, no plug-ins, no control points). Even if you're enough of a pro to use the more sophisticated features of FreeHand, Illustrator, or CorelDRAW, Flash provides a faster and more intuitive starting point. If you really need more features, you can simply export to Illustrator format and import into any of the previously mentioned programs.

Drawing procedures are essentially the same whether you're making drawings for a static illustration or an animated Flash movie. These procedures are explained thoroughly in Chapter 4. However, to give you a quick look at the difference between drawing in Flash and drawing in an illustration program (FreeHand, in this instance), take a look at Figures 1.18 and 1.19.

Here's another thing to consider: If you're new at illustration but need to create flyers or brochures with images, simply import vector clip art from any of dozens of CD-ROM or Internet libraries available. Then it's easy to modify and enhance with text, gradient backgrounds, and additional shapes. To import or export graphics into Flash, choose File|Import or File|Export from the menu bar. You can choose any of the formats from Table 1.1.

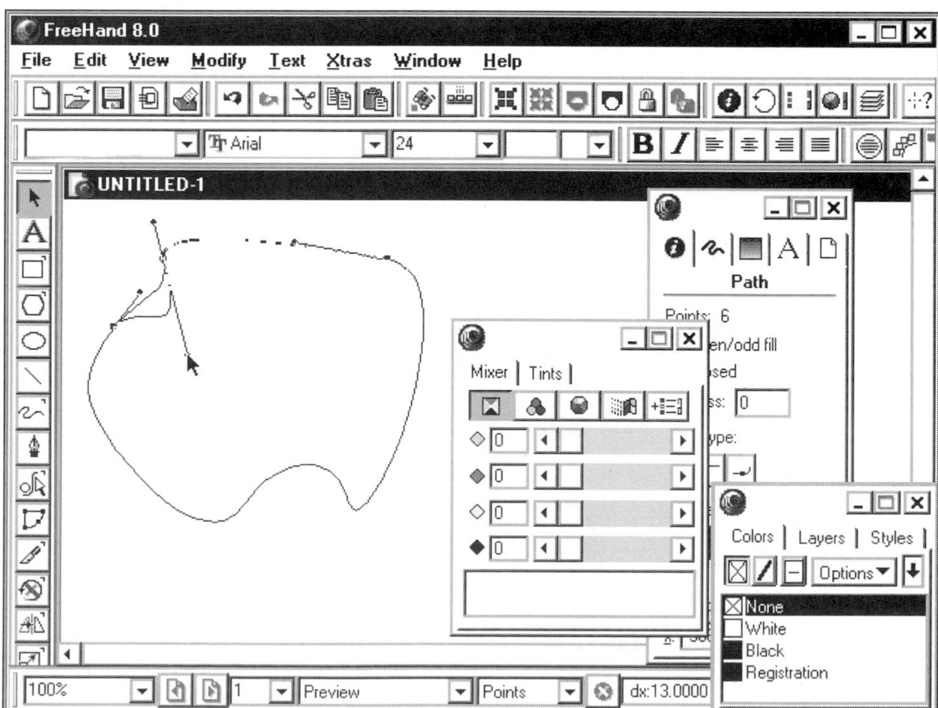

Figure 1.18 Editing a shape in FreeHand involves manipulating anchor points and control points (the dots and the ends of the levers). This method is extremely accurate and, with practice, even more efficient than drawing in Flash—but it isn't very much like drawing on paper.

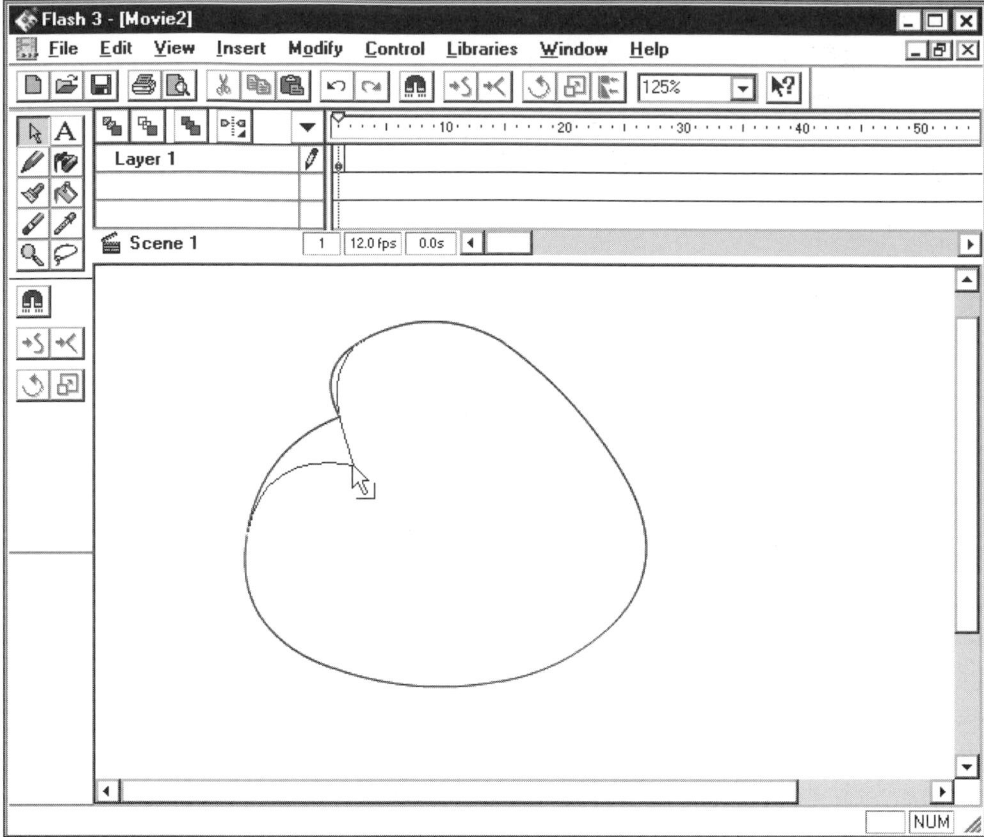

Figure 1.19 Editing a shape in Flash is done by dragging lines into curves or moving the point at which two lines connect. The symbol under the arrow tells you which is which. Another method for editing in Flash is to simply erase the shape you want to change and then draw a new one with the Pencil. This method is intuitive, but not as accurate.

Another way to draw graphics without knowing how is to simply trace photographs. Flash will autotrace them for you, though this isn't ideal if you want to control the smoothness and the exact shape of curves or the order in which groups of colors overlay one another. The alternative is to simply place the photograph in a cell, then create a new cell and use the onion-skinning feature to trace the original image.

If you are going to use Flash to create page graphics, be sure to set up the work area to match the dimensions and proportions of your desired output page. Otherwise, you'll get the default Web screen size work area of 550 by 400 pixels. To change this, choose Modify|Movie from the menu bar. You'll see the dialog box shown in Figure 1.20. The only settings you need change are the width and height dimensions. Be sure to type the abbreviation for the type of measurement unit you want to use.

***Note:** Don't use other people's art unless you've been given permission or are otherwise licensed to do so. Doing so is bad public relations at best and immoral and illegal at worst.*

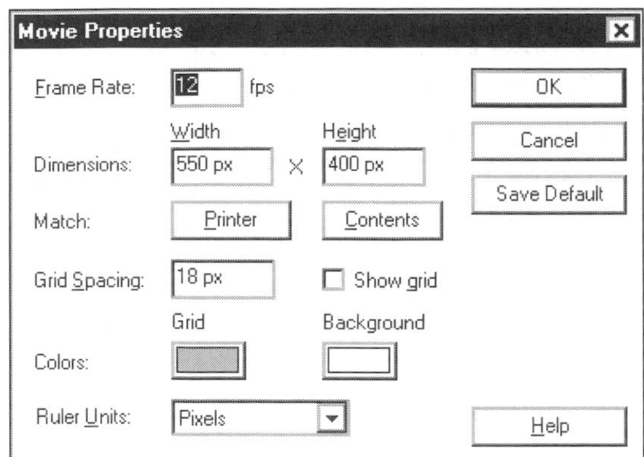

Figure 1.20 The Movie Properties dialog box for setting up workspace (page) size.

Teaming Flash With Other Multimedia Web Tools

You also can use Flash as a sketchpad and animation utility in conjunction with other multimedia and Web tools. For openers (well, actually I've already said this several times in this chapter), it's an easy way to combine smooth antialiased drawing, text, and bitmapped graphics into a GIF or JPEG file to be placed in any standard Web page. There's no big trick to doing this: Simply export the current frame as an image (choose File|Export|Image), and then choose either GIF or JPEG as the file format.

Which one should you choose? That's pretty easy: If you want the graphic to have a transparent background (so it floats on a Web page) or if the image is composed of relatively flat colors, hard-edged (but antialiased) graphics, as well as text, you'll get the smallest file and therefore the highest performance from exporting to GIF format. If the image is a photograph significantly larger than 72 by 108 pixels, save as JPEG. If your image contains some photographic material and lots of text or is a small photograph, export to GIF, but be sure to check the Smooth box and the Dither Solid Colors box.

Exporting To GIF

Figure 1.21 shows the options in the Export GIF dialog box. The following sections explain the settings available in this dialog box.

Height And Width

These settings default to the actual size of the current image or full document size in pixels, depending on your choice in the Include pull-down menu.

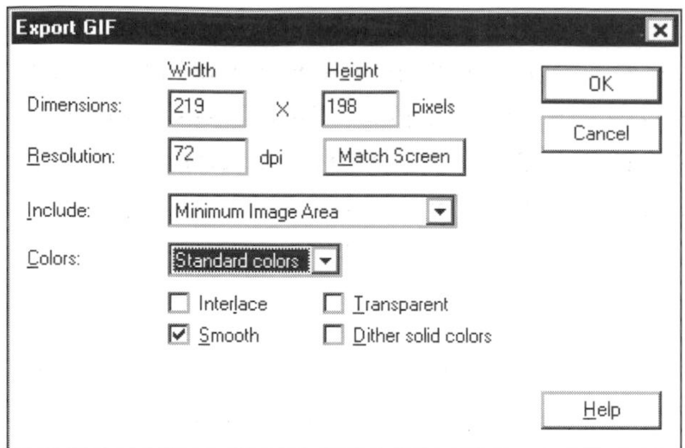

Figure 1.21 The Export GIF dialog box settings.

Resolution

You can enter any dpi (dots per inch) setting. If you click on the Match Screen button, the resolution is set to 72 dpi.

Include

This is a pull-down menu. The choices are Full Document Size (which saves a file as large as the entire workspace specified for the current movie) and Minimum Image Area (which crops the image to include only that rectangular portion of the workspace that actually includes a picture).

Colors

Your options are Black and White, 4, 8, 16, 32, 64, 128, and 256 colors. Pick the smallest number that will give you an acceptable representation of your image while also maintaining the smallest possible file size. There's also an option for standard colors, a cryptic name for the 216-color palette used by Netscape Navigator and Microsoft Internet Explorer.

Interlace

If checked, this box saves the file to a format that will load quickly on a Web page, at first at low resolution, then graduating to full resolution. This is an invaluable option for larger GIFs that may take some time to load.

Smooth

If checked, this feature enables Flash's antialiasing, thus dithering abrupt transitions between colors. Dithering makes for smoother text edges and minimizes banding in gradient colors.

Transparent

A check makes the background color of your movie the transparent color for your GIF file. In other words, any portion of the workspace that is not actually covered by a drawing will be transparent.

Dither Solid Colors

This dithers all colors that don't exactly match the colors in the palette with which you are working. Dithering places the palette's colors side by side in the pixel mosaic so that, if viewed from a distance, they appear to create colors more closely matching those in the original. Warning: Dithering significantly increases file size.

Exporting To JPEG

Flash also gives you sophisticated options for exporting to JPEG format. You see the dialog box in Figure 1.22. There aren't as many options as for GIF, and the first three (Dimensions, Resolution, and Include) are the same. In addition, however, there's a Quality slider and a Progressive Display check box. The Quality slider produces the smallest files at the lowest-quality setting and the largest at the highest-quality setting. If you plan to export a Flash file for use in a photographic application such as Photoshop, be sure to save the file at the highest setting. Also, remember that each save-reload-edit cycle deteriorates the quality of a JPEG image.

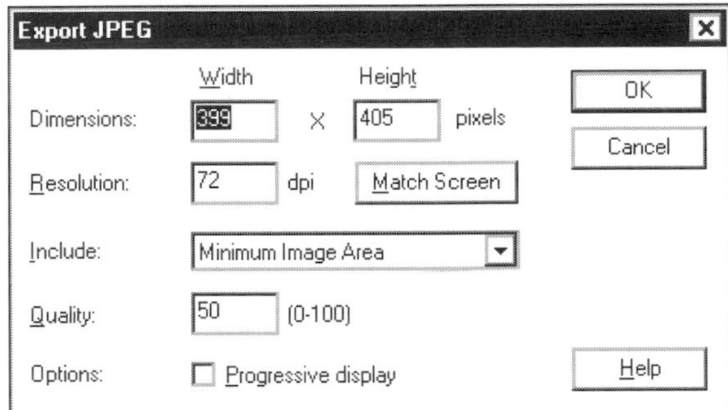

Figure 1.22 The Export JPEG dialog box.

Using Flash With Director And Authorware

Macromedia, as you're probably aware, also makes other highly regarded multimedia authoring programs, namely, Director and Authorware. Flash's Shockwave Flash files (an export format) can be viewed directly in both of these programs. You do this with an ActiveX control.

You also can place the content you create in Flash into Director or Authorware by exporting either images or movies as still motion sequences and then importing them into the target application. Depending on which platform you're working on, you can save images and motion sequences as BMP (Windows 95/NT) or PICT (Macintosh) files or file sequences. You also can export Flash animation sequences (movies) as either AVI (Windows 95/NT) or QuickTime files that can be imported directly into Director's Cast or Authorware's Timeline.

Using Flash With Video Editing Programs

Any of the graphics file types listed in Table 1.1 can be used in Adobe Premiere, and at least some of them can be read into other video editing and effects programs. You've probably already caught on to this by now, but all you have to do to export a Flash movie as an animation sequence is choose File|Export|Movie, and then pick your chosen format from the dialog box's pull-down menu.

Moving On

I hope this chapter has given you an overview of the many ways in which you might find Flash useful, whether your goal is to create content for the Web or for more traditional, offline media.

The next chapter will show you how Flash is structured. Its purpose is to orient your thoughts toward the most productive procedure for producing content in Flash (according to your specific needs). Then, you will be best prepared for the details of how to draw, build animations, make buttons, and incorporate sound into your productions. The adventure begins now!

2

The Anatomy of Flash

Ken Milburn

This chapter provides a quick reference to the essential features in Flash 3. If you need to find out how to use a particular feature in a hurry, this is a good place to start.

Flash calls everything it does a movie, even if there's only one frame in the shape of an 8.5"×11" page. Actually, movies can be as large as 40 by 40 inches. You can have as many frames in a movie as you like, and you can vary the rate at which they play (within limits, which we'll get to later). Within a movie, you also can have as many *scenes* (movies within a movie) as you like. All these frames and scenes are placed in the proper sequence along a *timeline*. Not only can the structure of a movie's frames be complex, the structure of individual frames has quite a few components: *objects*, *groups*, *text*, *overlays*, *symbols*, and *backgrounds*.

This chapter will show you how all these pieces function together to help make your work in Flash more efficient and professional.

Flash's Interface Components

When you first open Flash, you're confronted with a fairly complex screen layout. In actuality, this layout is dead simple compared to the interface for most animation programs (few of which have near the range or functionality of Flash). Besides, once you get the idea of what each of the functional areas does, you'll start to feel right at home. Figure 2.1 shows the Flash screen as you see it when you first start using the program.

The following sections describe the function of each of the main areas of the Flash 3 interface.

Menu Bar

The menu bar is the row of menu titles that appears at the top of almost every window in programs for Windows or the Mac. Figure 2.2 shows the Flash menu bar and a pull-down menu.

In this book, an instruction that reads "choose Command|Subcommand|Subcommand" means that those commands can be found on the menu bar unless otherwise noted.

Each of the menu titles and their functions is discussed in the following sections.

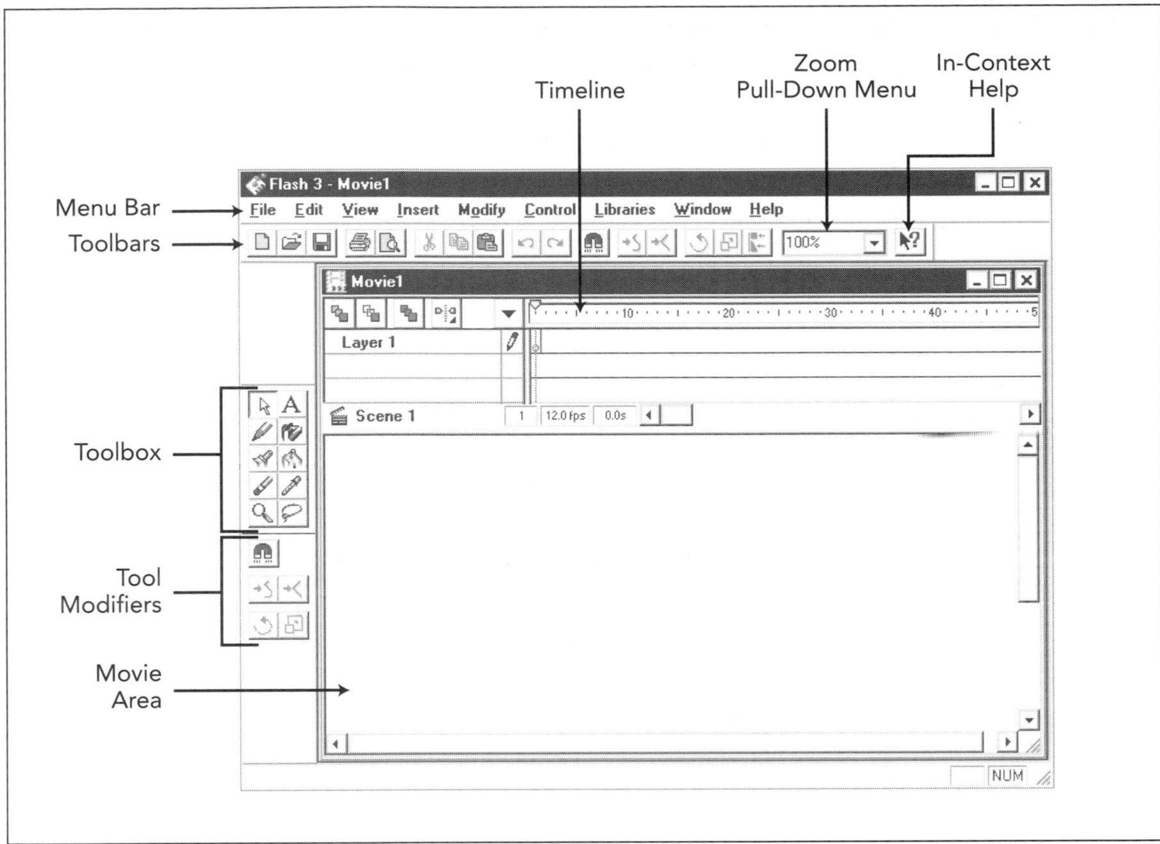

Figure 2.1 Your first look at the Flash interface. Labels indicate the major functional areas.

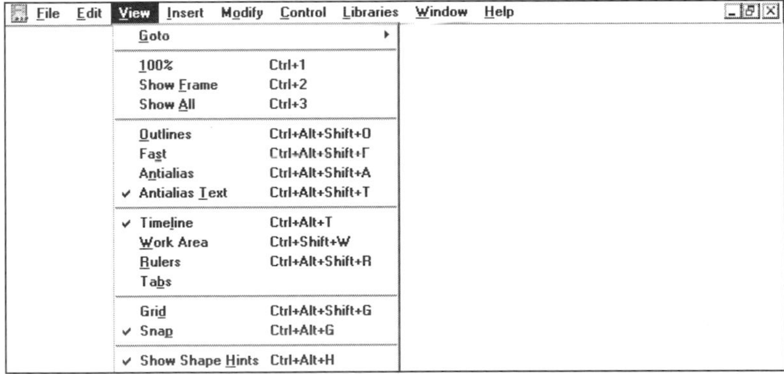

Figure 2.2 The menu bar with the View pull-down menu displayed.

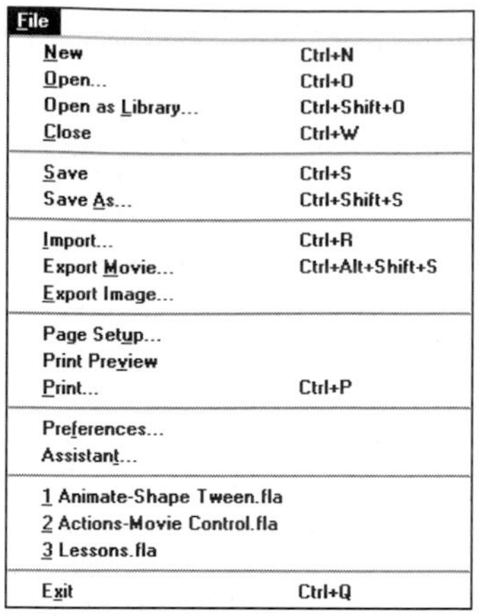

File	
New	Ctrl+N
Open...	Ctrl+O
Open as Library...	Ctrl+Shift+O
Close	Ctrl+W
Save	Ctrl+S
Save As...	Ctrl+Shift+S
Import...	Ctrl+R
Export Movie...	Ctrl+Alt+Shift+S
Export Image...	
Page Setup...	
Print Preview	
Print...	Ctrl+P
Preferences...	
Assistant...	
1 Animate-Shape Tween.fla	
2 Actions-Movie Control.fla	
3 Lessons.fla	
Exit	Ctrl+Q

Figure 2.3 The Flash 3 File menu.

File Menu

The File menu appears on every Windows and Mac menu bar. See Figure 2.3.The Flash 3 File menu has some unique commands worth noting, as detailed in Table 2.1.

Table 2.1 File menu commands and keyboard shortcuts.

Command Name	Shortcut Key(s)	Description
New	Cmd/Ctrl+N	Opens a new file. There is no dialog box for setting page size, background color, and so on. Do that by choosing Modify|Movie.
Open	Cmd/Ctrl+O	Opens the standard dialog box to open files.
Open as Library	Cmd/Ctrl+Shift+O	Opens the library of symbols, sounds, and bitmaps from any Flash movie so that you can use the library in conjunction with a new file. You can also open the libraries that come with Flash by choosing Xtras|Library.
Close	Cmd/Ctrl+W	Closes the currently active movie.
Save	Cmd/Ctrl+S	Saves the currently active movie to the same file name and disk location.
Save As	Cmd/Ctrl+Shift+S	Gives you the opportunity to save the currently active movie to a new file name and/or disk location. This command is your best way to create a new movie from elements of an old one without destroying the old one.
Import	Cmd/Ctrl+R	Imports either single-frame graphics or sequences of graphics into the current layer of the current frames according to the file number. For instance, BALL1.GIF would be entered into the current frame, BALL2.GIF into the next frame, and so on. This command is inoperable (the text appears grayed out) if there is no current layer.
Export Movie	Cmd/Ctrl+Opt/Alt +Shift+R	Exports the current movie either to a movie format or to a numbered sequence of still files. Movie formats are Shockwave Flash, Animated GIF, QuickTime movie (Mac only) or AVI (Windows only). Almost all the still-image formats can be saved as a sequence. (Export movie file types were covered in Chapter 1.)
Export Image	None	Exports the contents of the current frame to a still-image format. (Export image file types were covered in Chapter 1.)
Page Setup	None	This is the command that lets you specify storyboard output, in addition to letting you set the typical page size, orientation, and margins for your printer. See Figure 2.4.
Print Preview	None	Lets you preview on screen the output of a page as it comes from your currently selected printer. Buttons at the top of the screen let you print, move to the next or previous page, see two pages at a time, zoom in or out, and close the preview window. See Figure 2.5.

(continued)

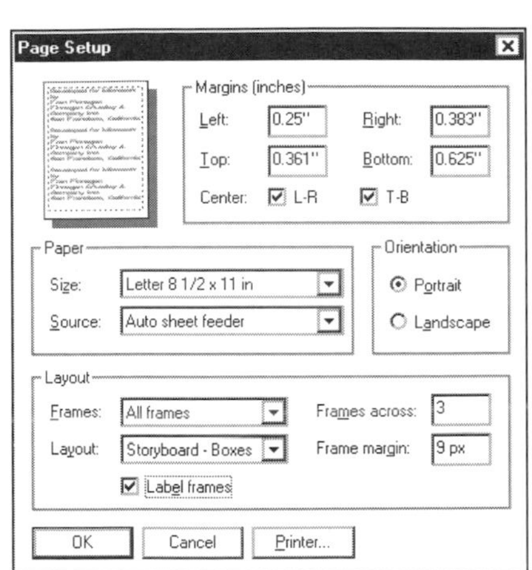

Figure 2.4 The Page Setup dialog box with storyboard settings.

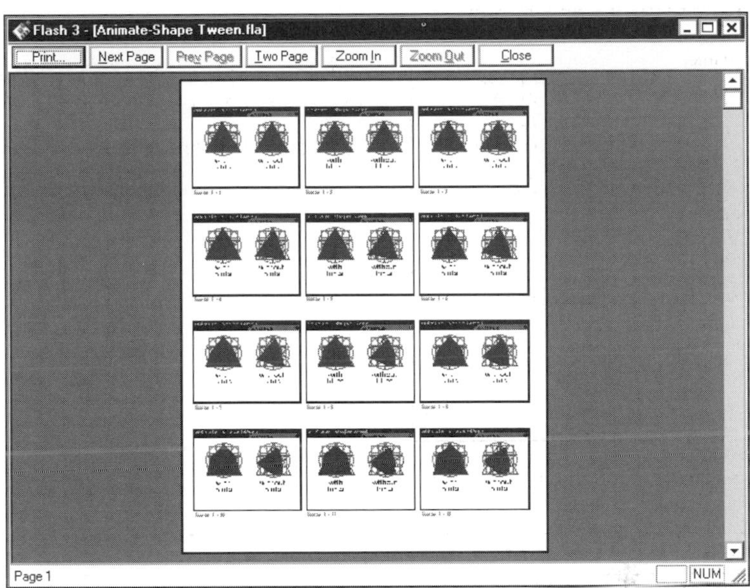

Figure 2.5 The Print Preview screen showing the result of the storyboard settings in Figure 2.4.

Table 2.1 File menu commands and keyboard shortcuts *(continued)*.

Command Name	Shortcut Key(s)	Description
Print	Cmd/Ctrl+P	Produces the standard print dialog box.
Preferences	None	Lets you set the parameters for all the movies you create in Flash until you next reset the parameters. The dialog box (see Figure 2.6) is self-explanatory.
Assistant	None	Short for Drawing Assistant. This is where you "tune" Flash's shape recognition and other AI (artificial intelligence) components that "steady" your drawing ability. (See Figure 2.7.) This option's functions are detailed in Chapter 4.
Exit	None	Quits the program and asks if you want to save any unsaved files.

Figure 2.6 The Preferences dialog box, showing the default settings for Windows.

Figure 2.7 The (Drawing) Assistant dialog box, showing the contents of one of the pull-down menus.

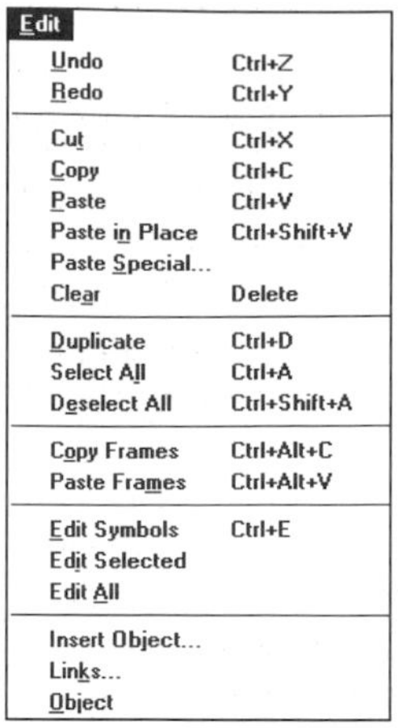

Edit
Undo Ctrl+Z
Redo Ctrl+Y
Cut Ctrl+X
Copy Ctrl+C
Paste Ctrl+V
Paste in Place Ctrl+Shift+V
Paste Special...
Clear Delete
Duplicate Ctrl+D
Select All Ctrl+A
Deselect All Ctrl+Shift+A
Copy Frames Ctrl+Alt+C
Paste Frames Ctrl+Alt+V
Edit Symbols Ctrl+E
Edit Selected
Edit All
Insert Object...
Links...
Object

Figure 2.8 The Flash 3 Edit Menu.

Edit Menu

This is the second menu that appears in nearly all Mac and Windows applications. See Figure 2.8. The commands on the Edit menu in Flash 3 aren't quite the same as those on the Edit menu in your word processor, though. First of all, you can allow multiple (up to 200 levels) Undo and Redo operations. There are also such unique commands as Paste in Place, Paste Special, Edit Symbols, Insert Object, and others. Table 2.2 describes the options available on the Edit menu.

Table 2.2 Edit menu commands.

Command Name	Shortcut Key(s)	Description
Undo	Cmd/Ctrl+Z	You can have as many as 200 levels of Undo (provided your RAM capacity permits). To set the number of Undo levels, choose File|Preferences.
Redo	Cmd/Ctrl+Y	Redo undoes the last Undo (thus restoring your work to its previous state). The command is ghosted if you have changed the drawing since the last Undo.
Cut	Cmd/Ctrl+X	Removes the current selection and places it on the clipboard until the next Cut or Copy command is issued from Flash (or any other program).
Copy	Cmd/Ctrl+C	Copies the current selection to the clipboard. See also Cut.
Paste	Cmd/Ctrl+V	Pastes the contents of the clipboard onto the current layer of the current frame. The contents will be centered in the window and will appear as a selection that can be moved until you make another selection. At that point, the pasted content becomes part of the underlying image. If you want to prevent this, you group the clipboard contents while they're still selected. To do this, choose Modify|Group. The group then becomes an overlay which floats above the other contents of the current layer.
Paste in Place	Cmd/Ctrl+Shift+V	Pastes the contents of the clipboard into their original location within the frame. Use this command when you want to move an element from one layer to another without changing its position in the movie.
Paste Special	None	Lets you paste the clipboard contents as a Flash movie, drawing, or a device-independent bitmap (DIB). You can paste the content but have it represented by an option, so all that appears at the current location is an icon, which can be clicked to activate the designated content. See Figure 2.9.
Clear	Delete/Backspace	Erases the current selection. It is not placed on the clipboard (although you can use the Undo feature).
Duplicate	Cmd/Ctrl+D	Duplicates the current selection within the current frame and layer.
Select All	Cmd/Ctrl+A	Selects everything in the active workspace—not the entire movie.

(continued)

Table 2.2 Edit menu commands *(continued)*.

Command Name	Shortcut Key(s)	Description
Deselect All	Cmd/Ctrl+Shift+A	Drops any current selections. More useful than at first might be apparent, since you may inadvertently make multiple selections by clicking multiple times.
Copy Frames	Cmd/Ctrl+Opt/Alt+C	Copies all selected frames to the clipboard.
Paste Frames	Cmd/Ctrl+Opt/Alt+V	Inserts all clipboard frames at the current frame. If several frames are highlighted before the Paste Frames command is issued, the clipboard frames will replace the selected frames. The number of clipboard frames and selected frames doesn't need to match.
Edit Symbols	Cmd/Ctrl+E	This is a very cool and useful command. It lets you modify Symbols without taking them apart. And, it then automatically modifies all occurrences of that symbol throughout your movie. The symbol to be edited will appear in its own frame. (This is called switching into Edit Symbol mode.) You can switch to any symbol in the movie by clicking on its tab, which will appear on the right side of the workspace. This command is grayed out if there are no symbols in the current movie. To revert to Edit Movie mode, click on the blue-circled arrow at the top of the symbols tabs.
Edit Selected	None	Automatically switches modes to let you edit any selected symbol in an environment that's independent of other information in the movie, drawing, or layer. This feature also lets you edit any selected group (object) but doesn't put that selection on a clean screen (although the other contents of the movie can't be edited until you switch back to the Edit All mode). See Edit All.
Edit All	None	Switches you back from Edit Group mode to normal editing mode. You also can do this by double-clicking outside the selected group (object).
Insert Object	None	Inserts something from another application as an object in the current movie. (See Figure 2.10.) Objects can be linked to keyframes and buttons.
Links	None	Lets you edit the properties of links between the current movie and other Flash movies, objects, or Web URLs. The command is grayed out if no links are embedded in the current movie.
Object	None	Lets you edit objects that have been created in other applications.

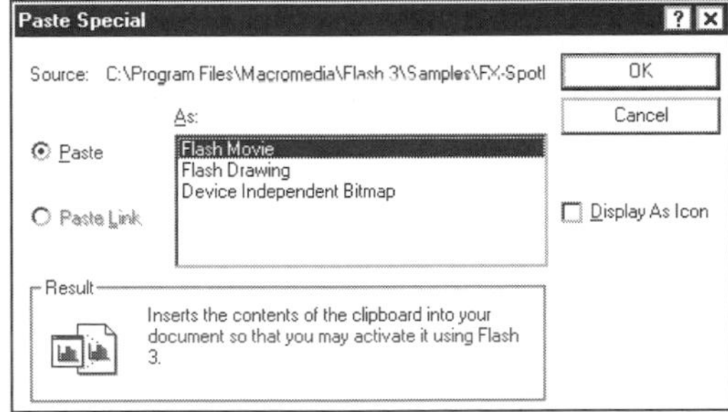

Figure 2.9 The Paste Special dialog box.

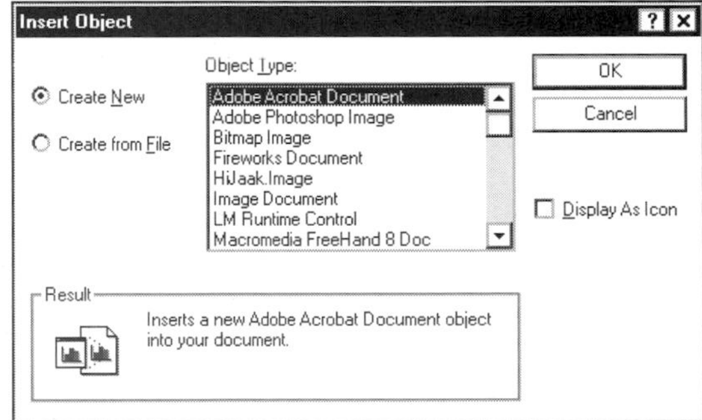

Figure 2.10 The Insert Object dialog box, showing some of the applications that can be used to create content for Flash 3.

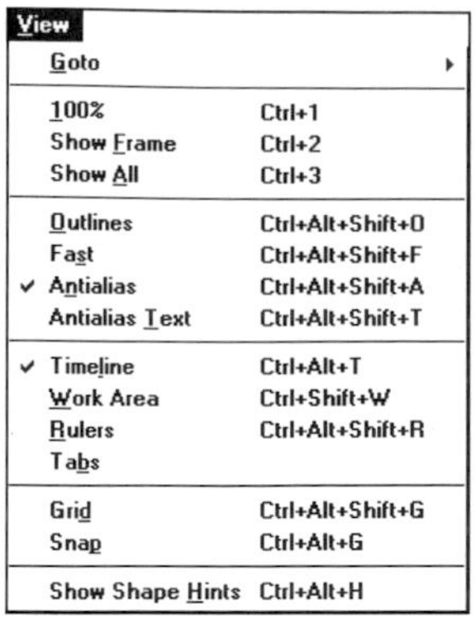

View
Goto
100% Ctrl+1
Show Frame Ctrl+2
Show All Ctrl+3
Outlines Ctrl+Alt+Shift+O
Fast Ctrl+Alt+Shift+F
✓ Antialias Ctrl+Alt+Shift+A
Antialias Text Ctrl+Alt+Shift+T
✓ Timeline Ctrl+Alt+T
Work Area Ctrl+Shift+W
Rulers Ctrl+Alt+Shift+R
Tabs
Grid Ctrl+Alt+Shift+G
Snap Ctrl+Alt+G
Show Shape Hints Ctrl+Alt+H

Figure 2.11 The View menu.

View Menu

The View menu controls how you see your workspace, the quality of the graphics display, and which interface elements will be visible. See Figure 2.11. Table 2.3 details the View menu commands.

Table 2.3 View menu commands.

Command Name	Shortcut Key(s)	Description
Goto	None	Lets you move up or down a page. Also lists all the pages that are currently open and lets you jump directly to any of them.
100%	Cmd/Ctrl+1	Changes the window to show the current page at full size (according to the dimensions set in the Movie Properties dialog box).
Show Frame	Cmd/Ctrl+2	Shows the entire current frame.
Show All	Cmd/Ctrl+3	Sets the zoom level to display the entire scene.
Outlines	Cmd/Ctrl+Opt/Alt +Shift+O	Removes fills and line thicknesses from drawings. This can make it easier to edit shapes since their outlines aren't hidden by fills and overlays. See Figure 2.12.
Fast	Cmd/Ctrl+Opt/Alt +Shift+F	Antialiasing is off. Displays all the colors and lines of the drawing.
Antialias	Cmd/Ctrl+Opt/Alt +Shift+A	This was formerly called Smooth, but it was too easily confused with the smooth tool modifier. Antialiases the edges of drawings. Has little effect on monitors with fewer than 256 colors and no effect on black-and-white monochrome displays. Text and bitmaps are not antialiased by this command. Displays slower than Fast mode, and faster than Antialias Text.
Antialias Text	Cmd/Ctrl+Opt/Alt +Shift+T	Same as Antialias but adds antialiased text and bitmaps. Draws even slower. Best mode for offline graphics, slowest for modem-connected online animations. Again, has little effect on monitors with fewer than 256 colors and no effect on black-and-white monochrome displays.
Timeline	Cmd/Ctrl+Opt/Alt+T	Toggles the presence of the Timeline. When selected, a check mark appears next to this item, and the Timeline is on. Turning Timeline off makes it easier to view a larger area of the screen.
Work Area	Cmd/Ctrl+Shift+W	Fills the active window with the work area.
Rulers	Cmd/Ctrl+Opt/Alt +Shift+R	Places rulers along the top and left sides of the work area. Increments are those specified in the Modify|Movie command.
Tabs	None	Shows tabs, on the right side of the screen, for all the pages in the active movie.
Grid	Cmd/Ctrl+Opt/Alt +Shift+G	Shows a positioning grid, at whatever increments you specify in the Modify|Movie command.
Snap	Cmd/Ctrl+Opt/Alt+G	Automatically aligns line ends, corners, lines, or elements to one another or to grid intersections (whether or not the grid is visible). You can temporarily toggle snapping by pressing the Shift key as you draw. You also can toggle snapping by clicking on the magnet modifier in the Drawing toolbox.
Show Shape Hints	Cmd/Ctrl+Opt/Alt+H	Shape Hints are new to Flash 3. When turned on, they show points that correspond to starting and ending shapes of objects that will be morphed. This makes it easier to avoid unintentional distortion effects in tweened frames.

Figure 2.12 The same Flash frame in Show Outlines mode (left) and Antialiased mode.

Insert Menu

The Insert menu (See Figure 2.13) contains the commands that are used to insert new elements—such as symbols, layers, frames, and scenes—in a Flash movie. Table 2.4 is meant to be a quick reference. If some of these terms are new to you, you'll find more complete discussions of them in Chapter 5.

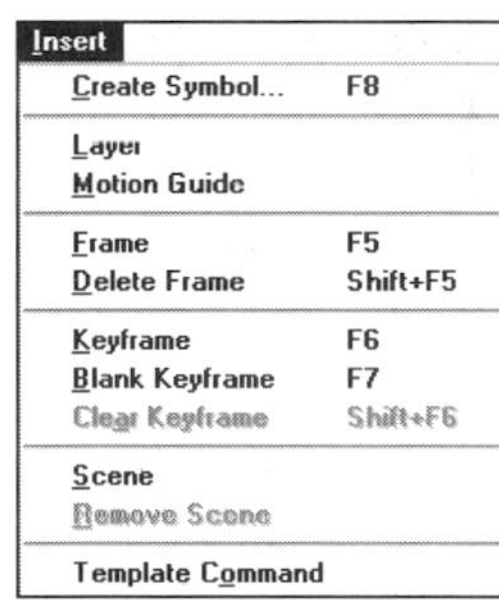

Figure 2.13 The Insert menu.

Table 2.4 Insert menu commands.

Command Name	Shortcut Key(s)	Description
Create Symbol	F8	Either creates a symbol from the active selection or (if nothing is selected) creates an empty symbol. All symbols must be given a name. If an empty symbol is created, a new master scene (clean drawing area) is displayed so you can draw the symbol without affecting other elements in the movie. This command can be an excellent way to quickly create a floating item in a scene.
Layer	None	Adds a new layer to the scene and automatically makes it the current layer.
Motion Guide	None	Creates a motion path layer so you can draw a path for a tweened overlay.
Frame	F5	Adds frames to one or more layers. To add a specific number of frames, highlight as many as you want to add following the I-beam in the Timeline.
Delete Frame	Shift+F5	Deletes any and all frames currently selected in the Timeline.
Keyframe	F6	Makes the currently highlighted frame(s) keyframe(s). The contents of the first keyframe are automatically copied through all keyframes.
Blank Keyframe	F7	Same as Keyframe but does not copy the first keyframe into the new keyframes.
Clear Keyframe	Shift+F6	Deletes the keyframe characteristic from the frame, making it a regular frame.
Scene	None	Inserts a new scene (page) into the current movie. Automatically makes page tabs visible (until you turn them off). The workspace will be blank, so that you have, essentially, started a new movie within the current movie.
Remove Scene	None	Deletes the current scene (page) from the current movie.
Template Command	None	Allows you to insert Generator Template commands by choosing them from a list, rather than typing in code. You need to have Flash Generator extension files installed. (You will need to have a copy of Generator to install these.)

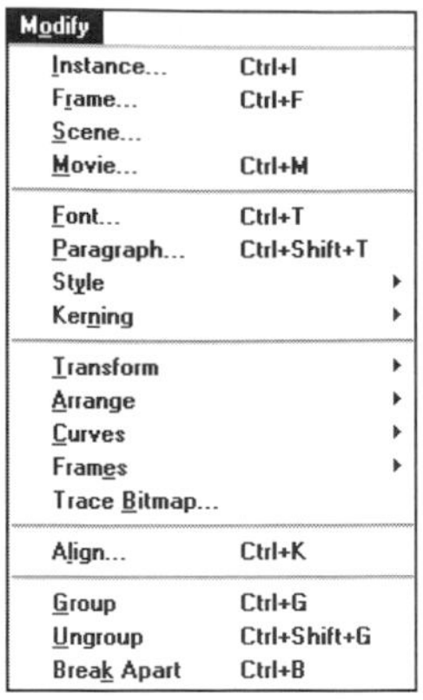

Modify	
Instance...	Ctrl+I
Frame...	Ctrl+F
Scene...	
Movie...	Ctrl+M
Font...	Ctrl+T
Paragraph...	Ctrl+Shift+T
Style	▸
Kerning	▸
Transform	▸
Arrange	▸
Curves	▸
Frames	▸
Trace Bitmap...	
Align...	Ctrl+K
Group	Ctrl+G
Ungroup	Ctrl+Shift+G
Break Apart	Ctrl+B

Figure 2.14 The Modify menu.

Modify Menu

This is the menu to memorize. The Modify menu commands (see Figure 2.14) help you tweak your creative efforts into a state of brilliance, or at least to look more like what you had in mind. See Table 2.5 for descriptions of the Modify menu commands.

Figures 2.15 through 2.29 show the dialog boxes associated with the Modify commands.

Table 2.5 Modify menu commands.

Command Name	Shortcut Key(s)	Description
Instance	Cmd/Ctrl+I	Brings up the Instance Properties dialog box. (See Figures 2.15 through 2.17.) Allows you to change the characteristics (such as alpha transparency and color) of a particular instance of a symbol. Also used to enter a name for an instance so that it can be used as the object of a Tell Target action.
Frame	Cmd/Ctrl+F	Brings up the Frame Properties dialog box. (See Figures 2.18 through 2.22.) Allows you to name a Frame so that it can be used as the target of an action and to change the properties of an individual frame.
Scene	None	Opens the Scene Properties dialog box. (See Figure 2.23.) All you can do, however, is change the name of the current scene.
Movie	Cmd/Ctrl+M	Changes the parameters for the current movie. See the dialog box in Figure 2.24. Any modifications you make here will affect the entire movie uniformly. The effects of most of the commands in the dialog box are obvious from their names, with the exception of the Match buttons. Match Printer sizes the movie to the page setup. Match Contents makes the entire movie as large as the largest drawing in the movie. (Use this to quickly adjust the movie to be the same size as something you just imported.)
Font	Cmd/Ctrl+T	Brings up the Font dialog box. (See Figure 2.25.) There's nothing mysterious or magical about this one. Style settings are limited to bold and italic.
Paragraph	Cmd/Ctrl+Shift+T	Brings up a dialog box to let you set paragraph properties. See Figure 2.26.
Style	None	Brings up the Modify|Style submenu. Allows you to change text to plain, bold, or italic and to align text as left, right, center, or justified.
Kerning	None	Brings up the Kerning submenu. Manually controls the spacing between letters. The Narrower or Wider options adjust the space between letters by a single pixel. Repeat this command to increase or decrease the space between letters. The Reset option returns all selected text to the default spacing. Windows users can control kerning by pressing Control+Alt and the arrow keys.
Transform	None	Your options are Scale (freehand scale by dragging bounding boxes), Rotate (freehand), Scale and Rotate (numeric entry for each), Rotate Left (90 degrees), Rotate Right (90 degrees), Flip Vertical, Flip Horizontal, Remove Transform, and Edit Center (lets you move the snap center).
Arrange	None	Changes the stacking order of overlays in the overlay level: Bring To Front, Move Ahead (up one level), Move Behind (down one level), Send to Back.

(continued on page 41)

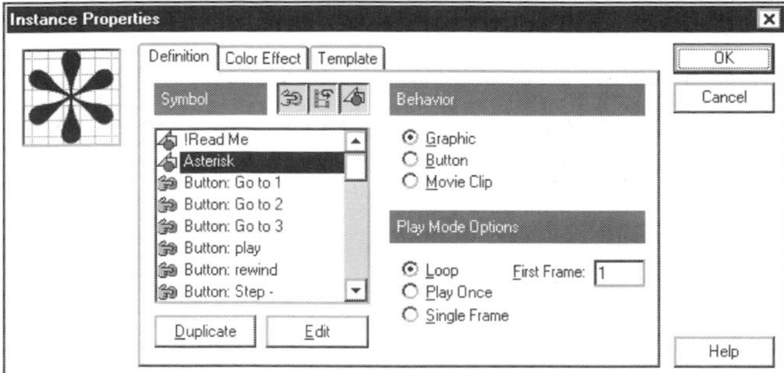

Figure 2.15 The Instance Properties dialog box Definition tab.

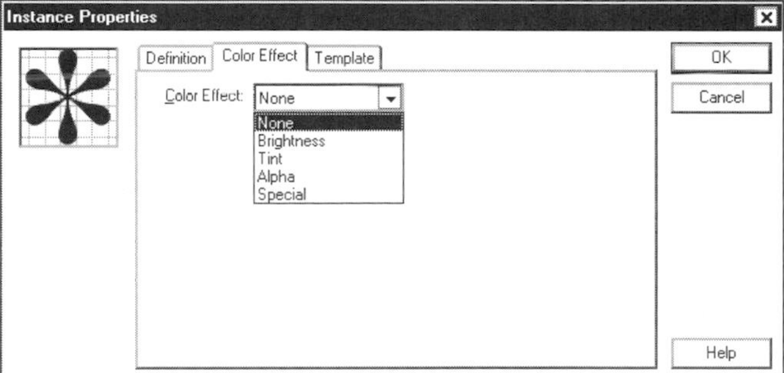

Figure 2.16 The Instance Properties dialog box Color Effect tab.

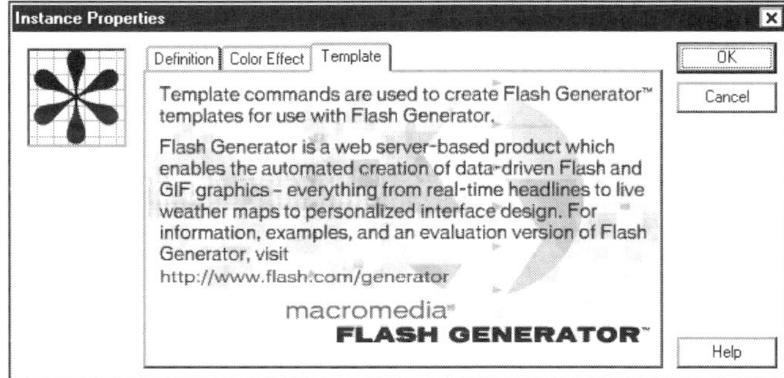

Figure 2.17 The Instance Properties dialog box Template tab.

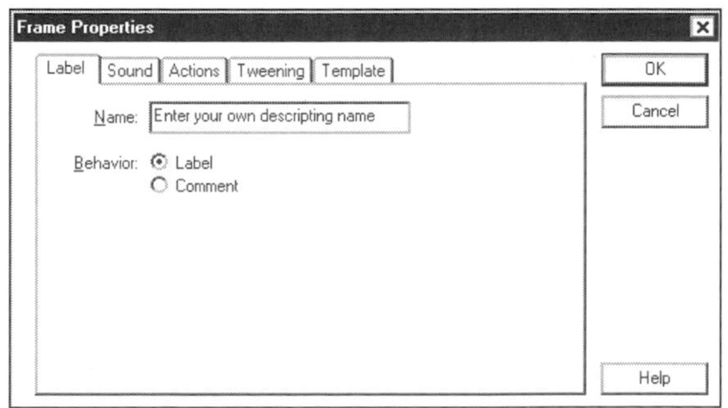

Figure 2.18 The Frame Properties dialog box Label tab.

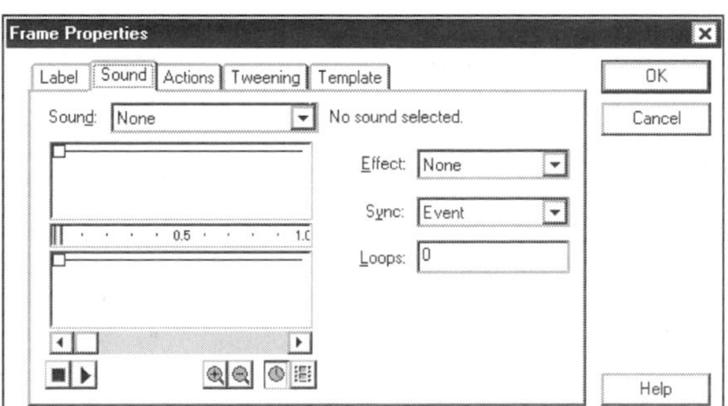

Figure 2.19 The Frame Properties dialog box Sound tab.

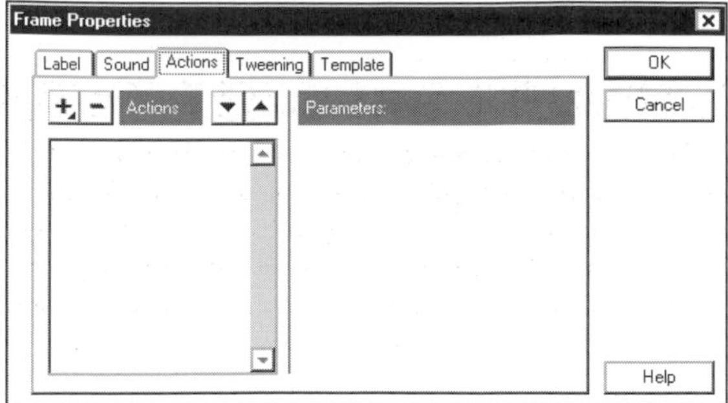

Figure 2.20 The Frame Properties dialog box Actions tab.

Figure 2.21 The Frame Properties dialog box Tweening tab.

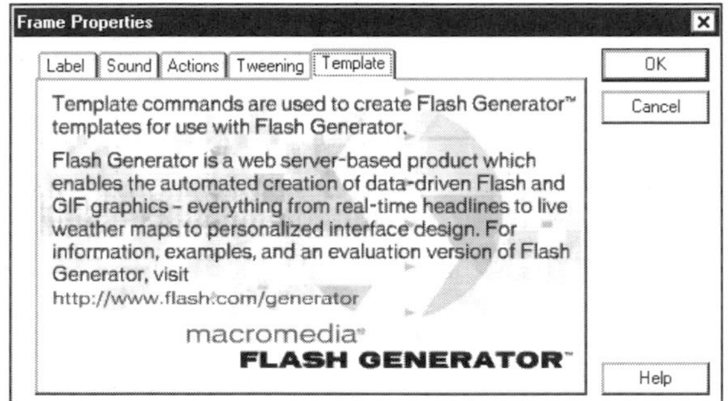

Figure 2.22 The Frame Properties dialog box Template tab.

Figure 2.23 The Scene Properties dialog box.

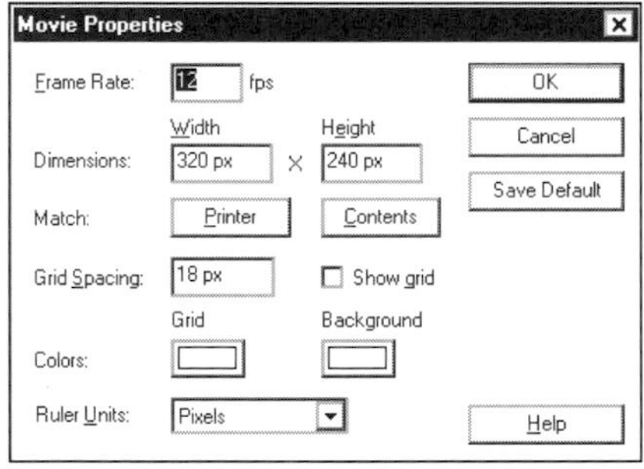

Figure 2.24 The Movie Properties dialog box.

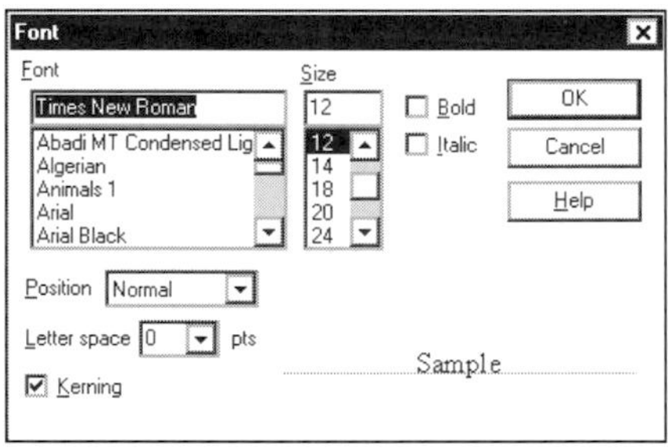

Figure 2.25 The Font dialog box.

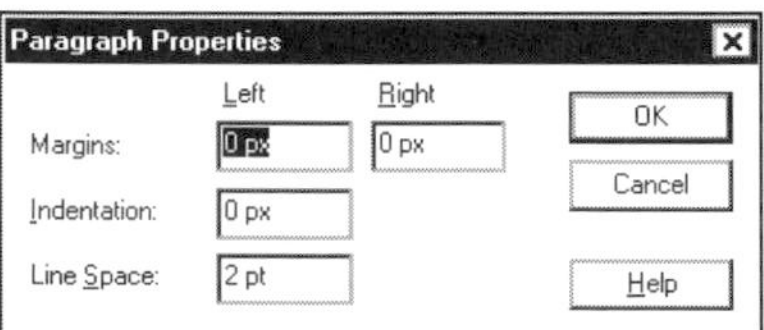

Figure 2.26 The Paragraph Properties dialog box.

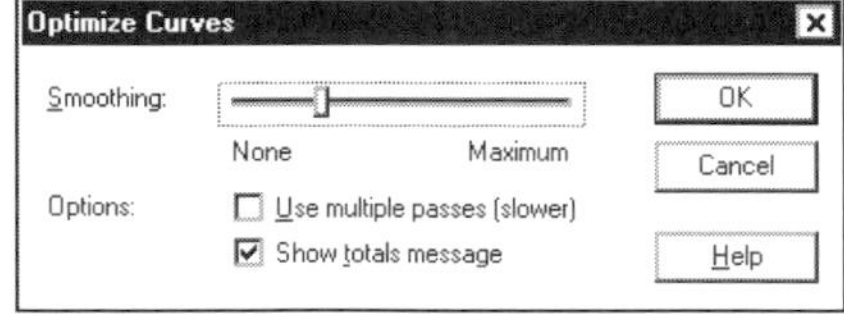

Figure 2.27 The Optimize Curves dialog box.

Table 2.5 Modify menu commands *(continued from page 38).*

Command Name	Shortcut Key(s)	Description
Curves	None	Dictates how the Pencil tool or the selected line behaves. Submenu choices are Smooth (makes curves progressively smoother and joins short curve line segments; has no effect on straight lines); Straighten (makes line segments straighter and eventually will shorten them; also turns shapes into geometrics: circles, ovals, rectangles, squares, triangles, and arcs); Optimize (works with the dialog box settings shown in Figure 2.27).
Frames	None	Allows you to either Reverse the order in which the selected Frames appear or Synchronize Symbols with the number of frames available after the keyframe by inserting any needed additional frames.
Trace Bitmap	None	Traces a scanned image, digitized photo, or other bitmap into vector shapes according to changes in color in the original image and the settings you use. (See Figure 2.28.) For details on the Trace Bitmap dialog box, see Chapter 3.
Align	Cmd/Ctrl+K	Aligns the selected shapes either horizontally or vertically, along a side or center. You also can elect to have shapes evenly spaced between the first and last objects you selected. You can also make the height and/or width of all the selected shapes match the first shape you selected in size by height, width, or both. See Figure 2.29.
Group	Cmd/Ctrl+G	Combines all selected lines into a single selection and turns that selection into an overlay. If nothing is selected, anything you draw will be grouped into an overlay.
Ungroup	Cmd/Ctrl+Shift + G	Ungroups everything in the current selection. Also removes overlay characteristics.
Break Apart	Cmd/Ctrl+B	Breaks any selected overlays or symbols into their components. If you break apart a symbol, the components are actually copied to the canvas, and the link to the symbol library is broken.

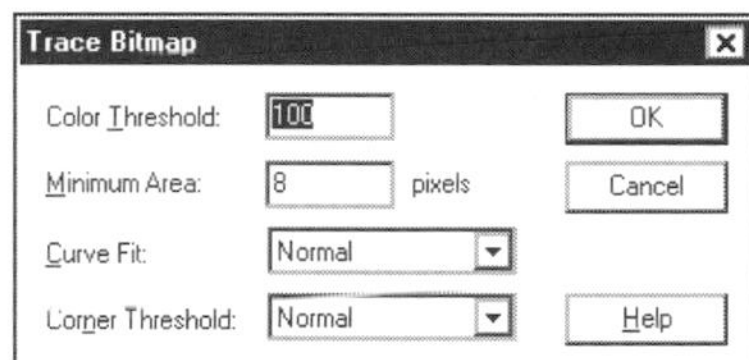

Figure 2.28 The Trace Bitmap dialog box.

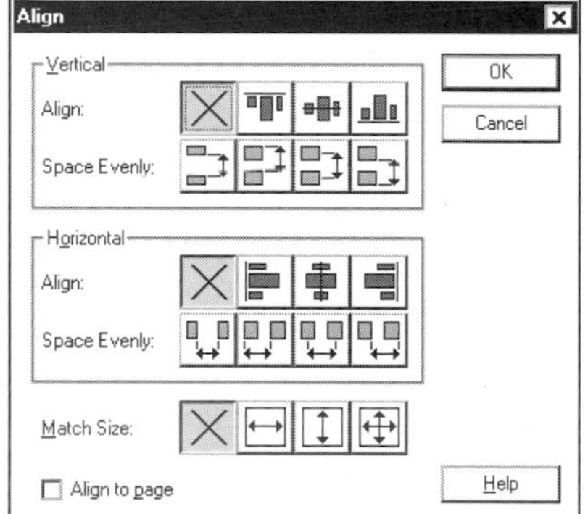

Figure 2.29 The Align dialog box.

Control	
Play	Enter
Rewind	Ctrl+Alt+R
Step Forward	>
Step Backward	<
Test Movie	Ctrl+Enter
Test Scene	Ctrl+Alt+Enter
Settings...	
✔ Loop Playback	
Play All Scenes	
✔ Enable Frame Actions	Ctrl+Alt+A
✔ Enable Buttons	Ctrl+Alt+B
Mute Sounds	Ctrl+Alt+M

Figure 2.30 The Control menu.

Control Menu

This menu doesn't control your work situation or the level of your temper. This is the menu (see Figure 2.30) for controlling how animations play. Its commands are discussed in Table 2.6.

Table 2.6 Control menu commands.

Command Name	Shortcut Key(s)	Description
Play	Enter/Return	Toggles (turns on and off) the movie playing in the current work window.
Rewind	Cmd/Ctrl+Opt/Alt+R	Displays the first frame of the current scene.
Step Forward	>	Moves forward one frame at a time. You can also move forward a frame by simply pressing > or the period key (.).
Step Backward	<	Moves backward one frame at a time. You can also move backward a frame by simply pressing < or the comma key (,).
Test Movie	Cmd/Ctrl +Return/Enter	Exports the selected (current) movies as an SWF file, which automatically opens in a new window, where it will appear exactly as it would on the Web. This command can be used to test all interactive functions and can be used instead of the Export Movie command.
Test Scene	Cmd/Ctrl+Opt/Alt +Return/Enter	Exports the selected scene to an SWF file and then lets you test as above.
Settings	None	Lets you specify the export settings (see Figure 2.31) that will be applied when you choose Test Scene or Test Movie.
Loop Playback	None	Causes the movie to automatically restart at the first frame after playing the last frame. This setting remains with the movie if the movie is compressed and exported.
Play All Scenes	None	Plays the whole movie, including all noncurrent scenes, in sequence. Movies are automatically exported in this mode.
Enable Frame Actions	Cmd/Ctrl+Opt/Alt+A	Turns on any actions you've assigned to a frame. Actions are events that can occur at the instant a keyframe plays: Play, Stop, Goto, Get URL, Goto and Play, Get URL and Goto, Get URL Goto and Play, and Stop All Sounds. A different list of actions can be assigned to buttons.
Enable Buttons	Cmd/Ctrl+Opt/Alt+B	Lets all the buttons in the scene behave as buttons rather than as overlays. Active buttons can be difficult to edit, but be sure to turn this option on before exporting a movie (or the buttons won't function).
Mute Sounds	Cmd/Ctrl+Opt/Alt+M	Replaces Play Sounds in the Flash 2 menu. Lets you turn off sounds while you're editing. When you choose this command and then choose Control| Play Movie, the movie will play silently. This speeds editing, and you won't have to listen to constantly repeated sound snippets when tweaking transitions between short scenes.

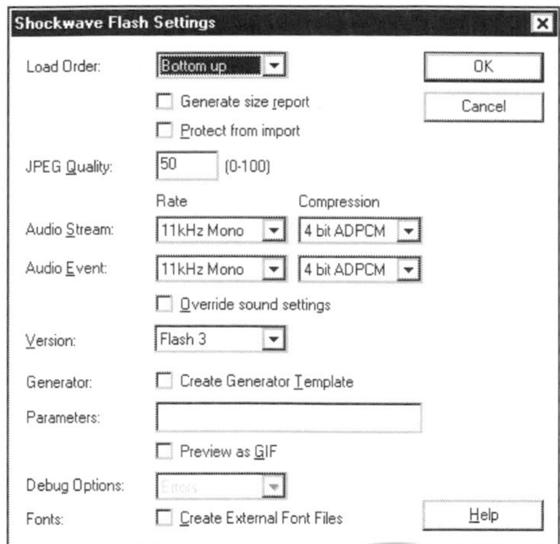

Figure 2.31 The Settings dialog box.

Libraries Menu

Figure 2.32 The Libraries menu.

The Libraries menu in Flash 3 replaces the Xtras Menu in Flash 2. This menu (see Figure 2.32) simply calls up each of the four library types: Buttons, Graphics, Movie Clips, and Sounds. Table 2.7 describes the Libraries menu commands.

For more information on the default libraries for Buttons, Graphics, Movie Clips and Sounds, see Figure 2.33.

Table 2.7 Libraries menu commands.

Command Name	Shortcut Key(s)	Description
Buttons	None	Buttons are four-frame movies that consist of Up, Over, Down, and Hit states. In Flash 3, any of these frames can contain either a graphic or movie symbol, so buttons can be animated.
Graphics	None	Graphics are static (single-frame) symbols that can contain any number of line segments, layers, other graphic symbols, and instance properties.
Movie Clips	None	Movie Clips consists of multiple-frame movies. Movie Clips can contain all the characteristics of any Flash 3 movie, including all interactive controls and sounds.
Sounds	None	All sounds are stored in the Library, and can be used as if they were Symbols (which technically, they aren't).

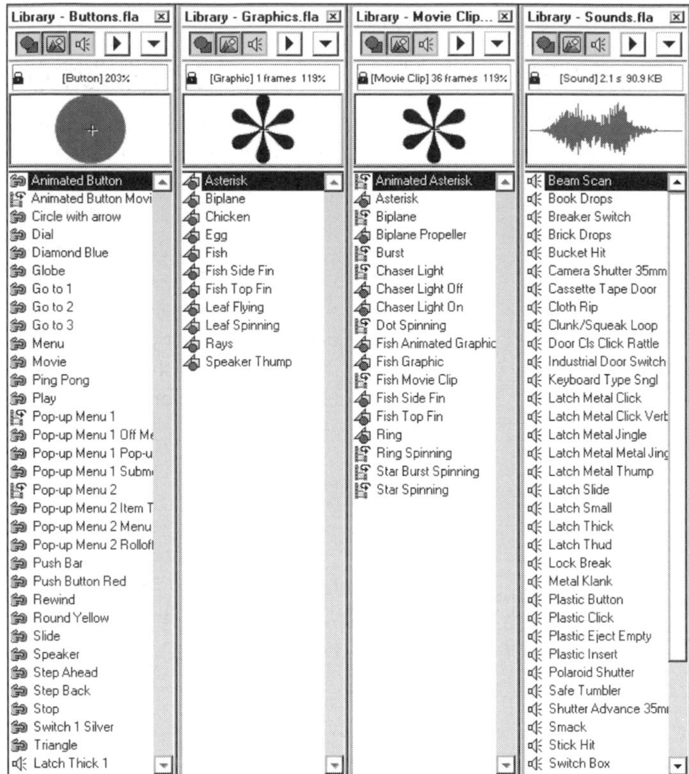

Figure 2.33 The default Buttons, Graphics, Movie Clips, and Sounds libraries.

Window Help
New Window Ctrl+Alt+N
Arrange All
Cascade
Toolbar...
Controller
Colors
Inspector Ctrl+Alt+I
Output
Library Ctrl+L
✓ 1 Movie1

Figure 2.34 The Window menu.

Window Menu

With Flash, you can open several movies at the same time, with each appearing in its own window. The Window menu (see Figure 2.34) controls how these windows appear, both in relationship to one another and to individual user-interface content. Following Table 2.8, three figures (Figures 2.35, 2.36, and 2.37) illustrate the results of the Arrange All and Cascade commands and show Flash's Toolbars dialog box.

Table 2.8 Window menu commands.

Command Name	Shortcut Key(s)	Description
New Window	Cmd/Ctrl+Opt/Alt+N	Opens another window displaying the active movie. This allows you to view a different part of the movie or different sets of layers. This is particularly useful for editing two different scenes or frames in the same movie. Any edits made in one window are automatically made in all other windows.
Arrange All	None	Puts all the open windows in columns and rows (tiles), so that they all become visible. You can see the result of the Arrange All command in Figure 2.35.

(continued)

Table 2.8 Window menu commands *(continued)*.

Command Name	Shortcut Key(s)	Description
Cascade	None	Arranges windows so you can see the title bar of each. See Figure 2.36.
Toolbar	None	Opens the Toolbars dialog (see Figure 2.37). This dialog box gives you options for showing or hiding various toolbars and for assigning such properties as size and color to them.
Controller	None	Remember this one. It lets you put a VCR control window on screen in order to play, stop, step, or rewind your movie at the click of a button.
Colors	None	It's in a strange place, but this is the command to open the Color Picker dialog box so that you can choose colors for your graphics and text lines and fills. You can choose either gradient or solid colors for both lines and fills. Text can use only solid colors (unless you ungroup it so that it becomes simply shapes).
Inspector	Cmd/Ctrl+Opt/Alt+I	Activates the Inspector window, which contains the type of symbol; the location of the top-left corner of the symbol; the symbol's width and height; and the symbol's name, settings, and any applicable actions.
Output	None	Brings up a window that shows any calls made to another device or browser window. Unless this window is open, there is no way to tell when action calls are being made because there is no Internet connection.
Library	Cmd/Ctrl+L	Brings up the Library window for the current movie. This library lists all symbols, bitmaps, and sounds currently used in the movie, whether they were opened from another library (such as one of those that ships with Flash) or created on the fly.
List of open windows	None	At the bottom of the menu is a list of open windows. This list lets you choose which window the program will place in the foreground.

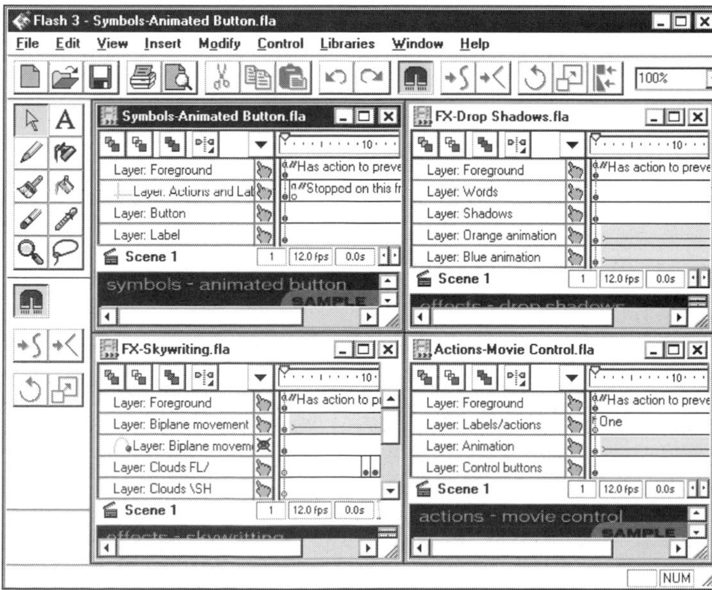

Figure 2.35 Four Flash movie windows after Arrange All was selected.

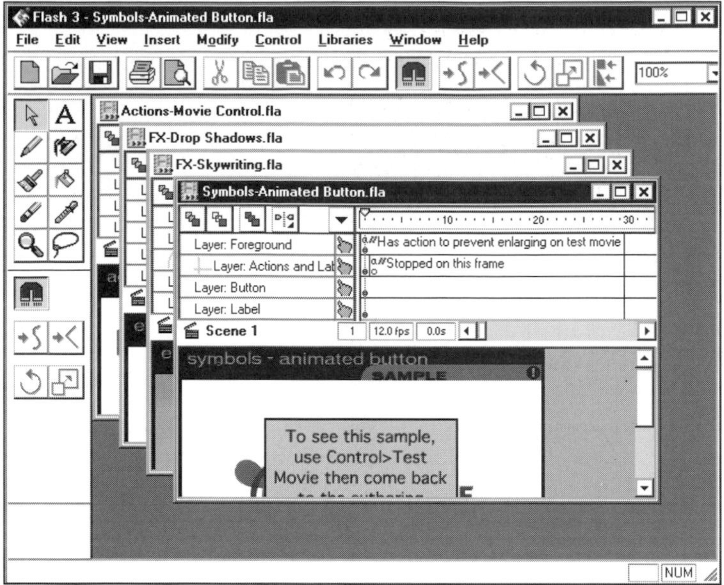

Figure 2.36 The result of using the Cascade command with the same four windows open.

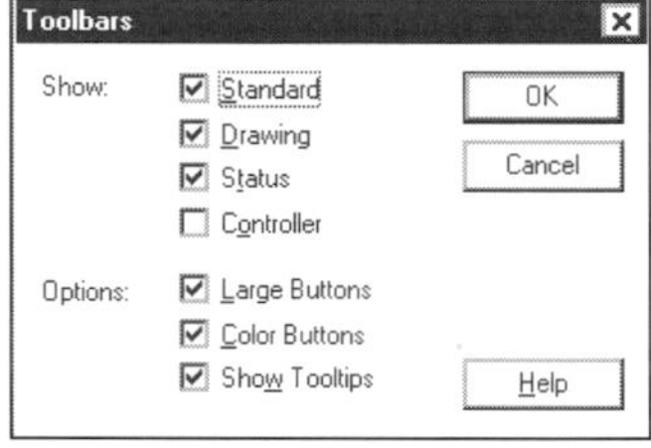

Figure 2.37 The Toolbars dialog box.

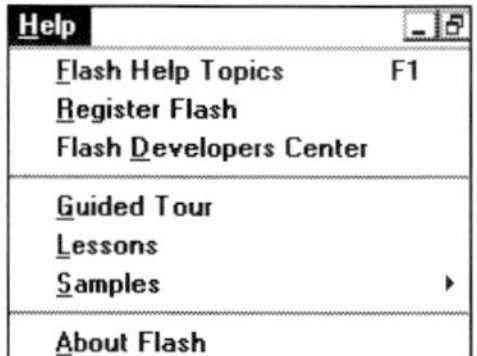

Figure 2.38 The Help menu.

Help Menu

Flash is one of the few cross-platform programs for which the online help is as complete on the Macintosh as in Windows. See Figure 2.38. On the Macintosh, however, online help is accessed under the Help icon. Table 2.9 details the Windows Help menu, but Mac users will find their content is the same (although with slight differences in organization).

You can get additional, updated help online at the Macromedia site (**www.macromedia.com/support/flash**). See Figure 2.40.

Table 2.9 Help menu commands.

Command Name	Shortcut Key(s)	Description
Flash Help Topics	F1	Presents the main contents page for Flash in your default browser. (See Figure 2.39.) Clicking on any of the buttons takes you directly to that section.
Register Flash	None	Lets you register Flash online.
Flash Developer's	None	Takes you to the Flash Support Overview page of the Macromedia Center site. You can click a button to go to the Developer's Center, What's New, Tech Notes, Get Updates and Downloads, access Support Programs, and get Tips on Flash from the ZDNet site.
Guided Tour	None	Takes you on an interactive guided tour within your browser.
Lessons	None	Takes you through an entirely new and more businesslike (some would say more practical) set of lessons that teach you the basics of Flash. These lessons happen within a Flash movie, not in a browser window.
Samples	None	Shows you several instructional samples within the Test Movie context.
About Flash	None	Brings up the Flash 3 splash screen. This is where you'll find your registration information (such as your serial number).

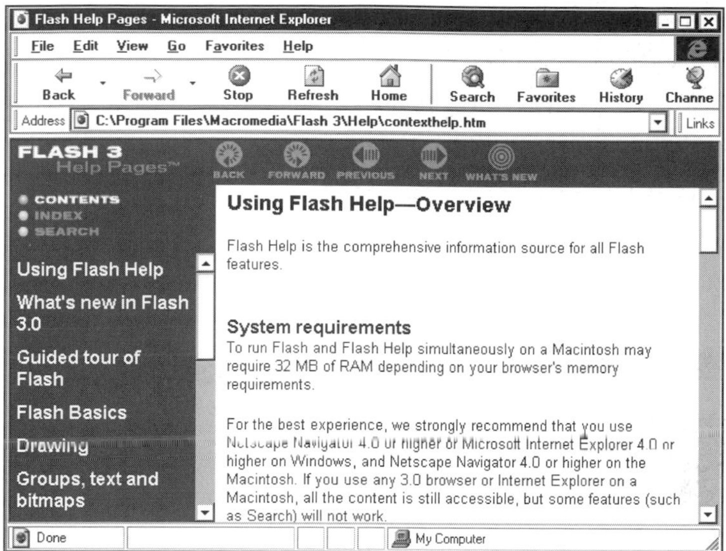

Figure 2.39 The opening screen for Flash Help.

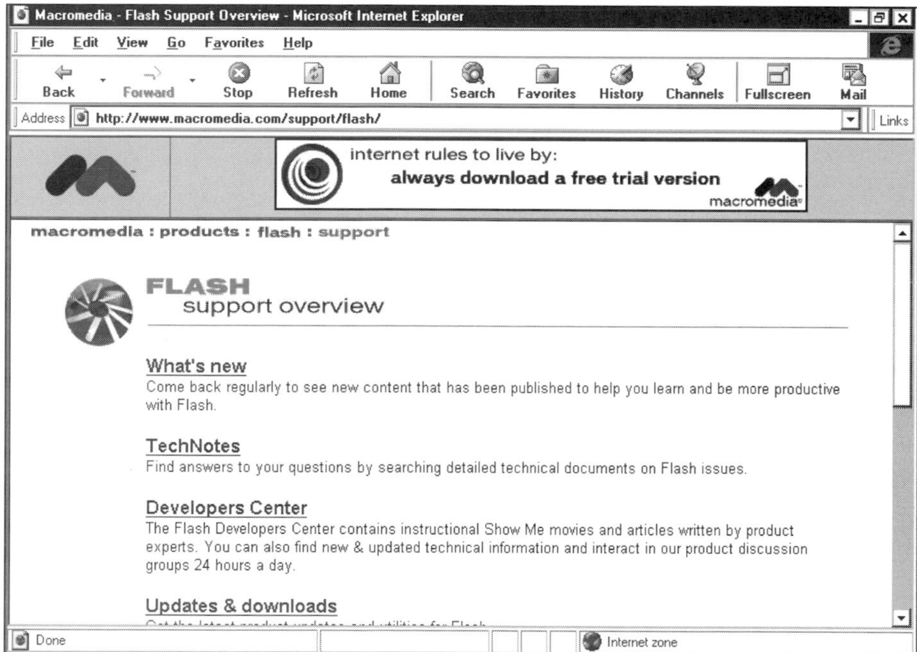

Figure 2.40 The Flash support site at Macromedia. The contents of the main window were all created in Flash.

Toolbar

The Flash toolbar sits just below the menu bar and spans the window. This toolbar is a shortcut to many of the functions and commands that are available—but perhaps not as readily visible—within other Flash interface components. You can see the Flash toolbar in Figure 2.41. It hasn't changed at all since Flash 2. Table 2.10 describes the buttons on the Flash 3 toolbar.

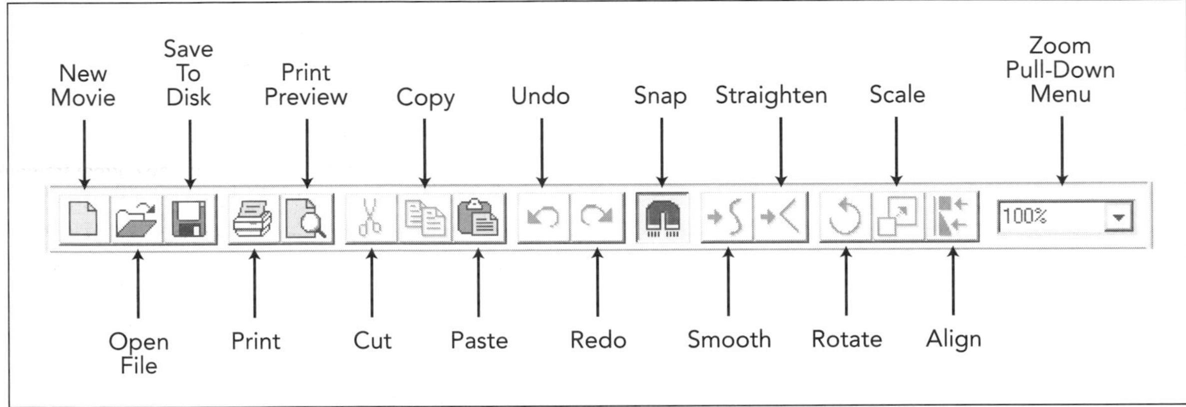

Figure 2.41 The Flash toolbar.

Table 2.10 The Flash toolbar buttons.

Button Name	Description
New Movie	Opens a new, empty Flash movie.
Open File	Opens a Flash movie previously stored on a drive attached to your computer. The standard File Open dialog box appears.
Save To Disk	Saves the current file. Opens the standard File Save dialog box.
Print	Brings up the standard printer dialog box for the installed default printer.
Print Preview	Previews on screen the way the full page will look when the first frame of the movie is printed.
Cut	Deletes the current selection from the canvas and places it on the clipboard.
Copy	Copies the current selection from the canvas and places it on the clipboard.
Paste	Places the contents of the clipboard onto the canvas.

(continued)

Table 2.10 The Flash toolbar buttons *(continued)*.

Button Name	Description
Undo	Returns the movie to its state previous to the last-issued command or the last-used tool. Repeated clicking on this button will move you back through commands issued, one step at a time, up to 200 levels.
Redo	Undoes the Undo. Also works at up to 200 levels.
Snap	Turns on Snap, which causes the mouse cursor to snap to the nearest grid point or drawing entity.
Smooth	Smooths the currently selected line(s), regardless of which tool is in use.
Straighten	Straightens the currently selected line(s), regardless of which tool is in use.
Rotate	Rotates the currently selected line(s), regardless of which tool is in use.
Scale	Resizes the currently selected line(s), regardless of which tool is in use.
Align	Brings up the Align dialog box. (The Align dialog box was shown in Figure 2.29.)
Zoom Pull-Down Menu	This zoom pull-down menu is the quick and easy way to zoom your view of the current frame to a specific percentage of magnification. The menu is actually part of the toolbar. See Figure 2.42.
In-Context Help	The in-context help button is at the right end of the toolbar. Click on this button—then on the tool or menu item you want to learn about—and you will find yourself in your default Web browser, surfing the online (or, if you're not connected, on-disk) Flash Help site. The Help button automatically links you to information on the tool or command you chose. See Figure 2.43.

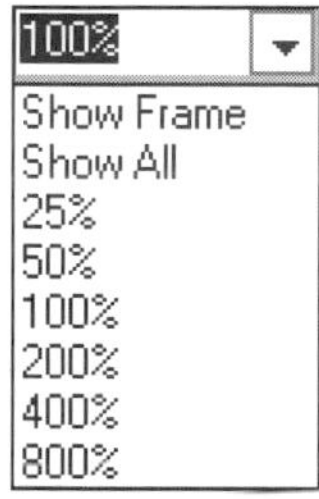

Figure 2.42 The zoom pull-down menu.

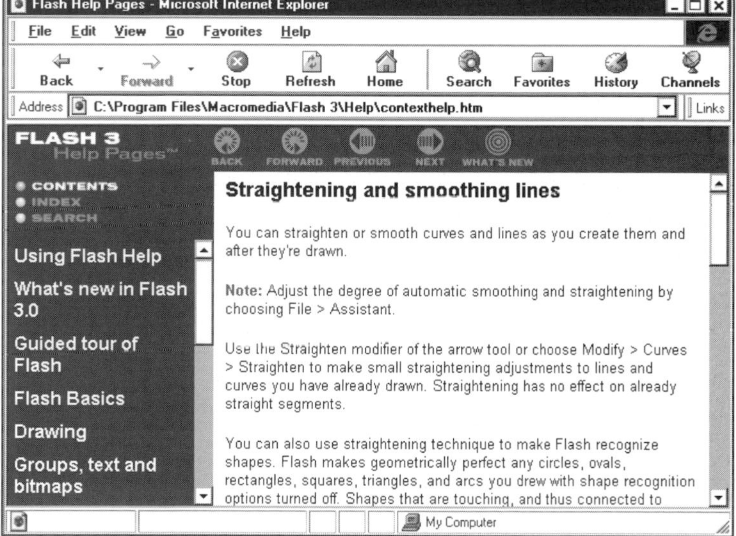

Figure 2.43 The online in-context help for the straighten modifier.

Toolbox

The toolbox contains the instruments for creating drawings. It's also been left undisturbed in Flash 3. These tools will be explained more fully in Chapter 4. The toolbox can be seen in Figure 2.44.

The functions of each of these tools is briefly described in Table 2.11.

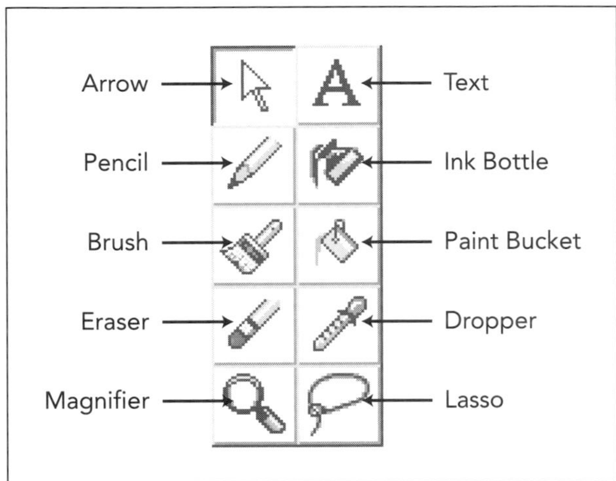

Figure 2.44 The Flash toolbox.

Table 2.11 Flash toolbox tools.

Tool Name	Shortcut Key(s)	Description
Arrow	A	Selects individual graphic elements, such as lines and fills. Double-clicking on an object or symbol lets you edit it. The Arrow also is used for editing shapes.
Text	T	Lets you type and edit text directly on the image. Text is entered as an overlay.
Pencil	P	Draws lines of any color, thickness, or style.
Ink Bottle	I	Places a pencil line around any solid colors, or changes the color and style of existing pencil lines that have been selected.
Brush	B	Paints solid colors that are shapes. In other words, you can edit the outline of the shape.
Paint Bucket	U	Fills any area enclosed or semi-enclosed by shape outlines.
Eraser	E	Alters any shape on the canvas by removing any areas that are brushed with this tool. Will not erase objects, symbols, or the contents of locked layers.
Dropper	D	Picks up the properties of a shape or line and imposes them on any other selected item of the same type.
Magnifier	M	Zooms in by 100 percent at each click or to the area of the marquee, if you drag a rectangle. Zooms out in 50 percent increments if you select the minus zoom modifier.
Lasso	L	Selects irregularly shaped portions of the active layer(s). Moving or cutting the selection creates an entirely new shape.

Tool Modifiers

Tool modifiers are the group of icons that dictate the specific behavior of the chosen tool. The sets of modifiers are specific to each tool and will be described in detail in Chapter 4. Figure 2.45 shows the modifiers for the Arrow tool.

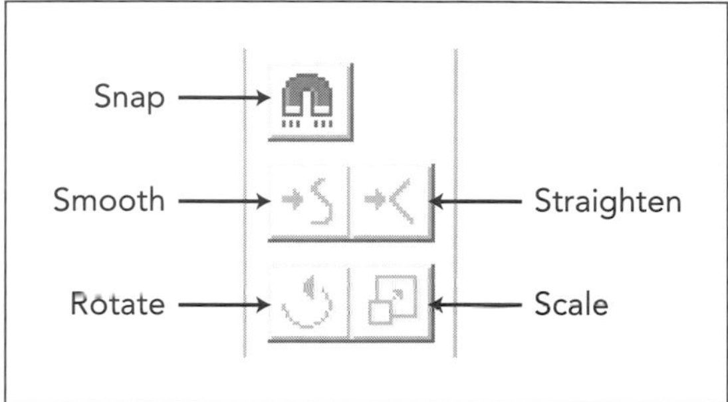

Figure 2.45 The tool modifiers.

Timeline

The Timeline is the main repository of tools and commands for creating and editing animations. It is also the basic mechanism for controlling where various scenes start, stop, and overlap one another. Quite a few Flash commands are hidden within various elements of the Timeline: the Onion Skin menu, the Frame View menu, the Layer menu, and the Frame menu. The functions of this menu are the subject of Chapter 5, so I won't detail them here. In the meantime, you can see what the Timeline looks like and what its various subfunction groups are called in Figure 2.46.

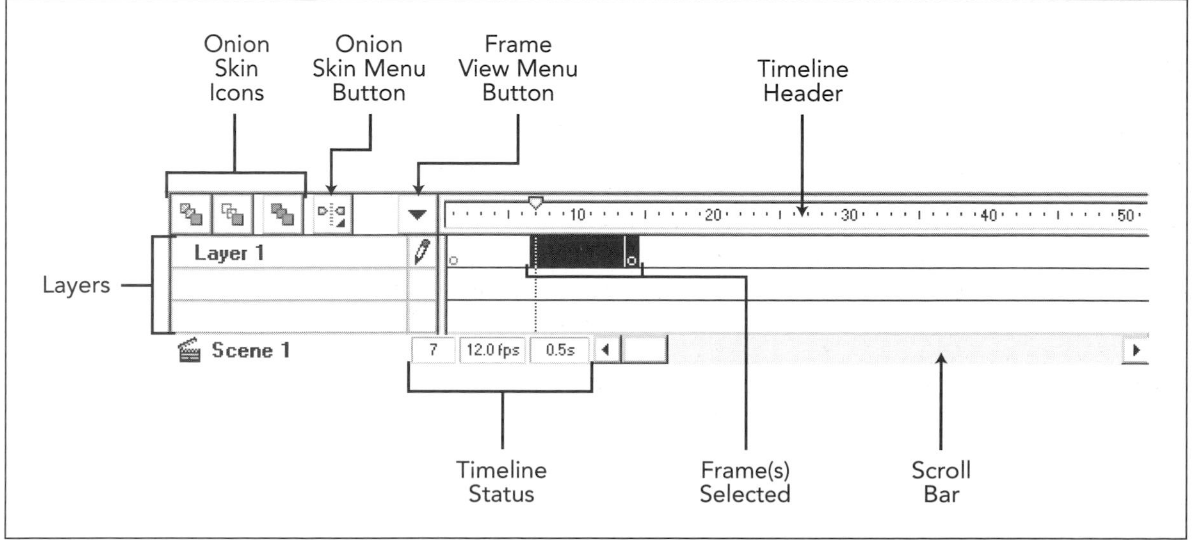

Figure 2.46 The Flash Timeline.

Movie Area

This is the area that displays the visible contents of the active frame of your Flash movie. All drawing and editing are done within the confines of this area.

Rulers, Grids, And Tabs

These are aids to help you organize and place elements in your movie. The screen shot in Figure 2.47 shows rulers bordering the edges of the movie area, a grid superimposed over the scene, and a scene tab in the upper-right margin of the working window (currently labeled Scene 1).

Rulers can be set in increments of whatever unit you have specified in the Modify|Movie box of the Movie Properties dialog box: pixels, inches, decimal inches, points, centimeters, or millimeters.

Grid spacing is set by whatever unit number and type you specify in the Grid Spacing box in the Movie Properties dialog box. Grids are always evenly spaced horizontally and vertically. The snap points of objects will snap to grid intersections when they are within a three-pixel radius of one another.

Tabs allow you to see the location and order of all the scenes in your movie. Scenes are automatically named Scene 1, Scene 2, and so on—unless you change them. Double-clicking on a scene tab brings up a dialog box that allows you to enter any name you wish. Just remember that longer names make longer tabs.

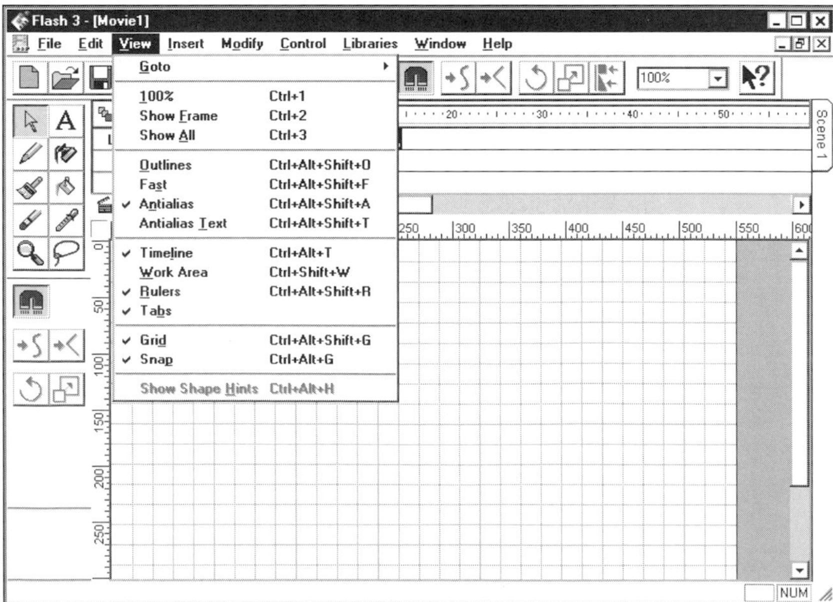

Figure 2.47 The Flash window, showing rulers, a grid, and a scene tab.

The Canvas (A.K.A. The Stage)

The canvas is Flash's basic creative environment. Each frame of each layer in a movie has a canvas. Canvases are always transparent except for what you paint, draw, or type on them. Painting or drawing on the canvas—although it results in vector-defined shapes—has more in common operationally with bitmap paint programs such as Photoshop or Windows Paint than with most other vector programs such as FreeHand, CorelDRAW, or Illustrator. In Flash, anything you create on the canvas sticks to it and also overlays and alters any previously made shapes that you've painted over. So if I first paint a blob like this:

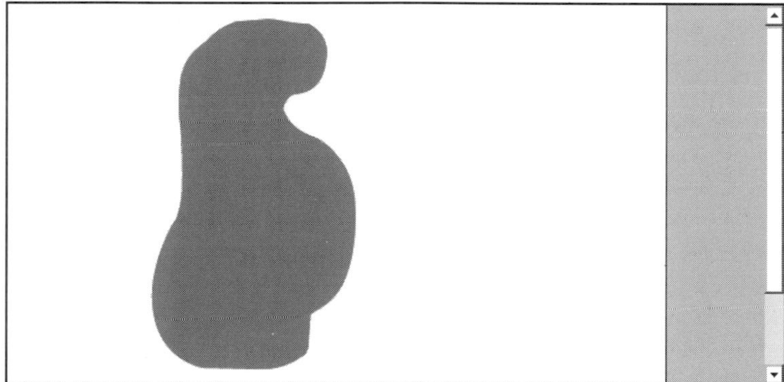

and then I draw some circles and a dotted line on top of it, like this:

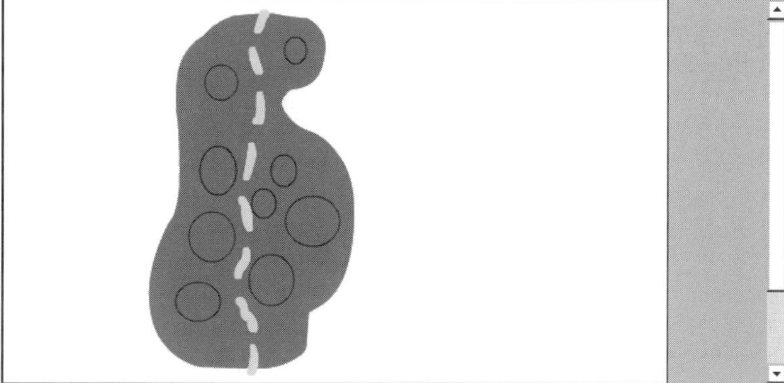

I can select, move, and fill any of the dissected parts, because each has become a separate vector element, like this:

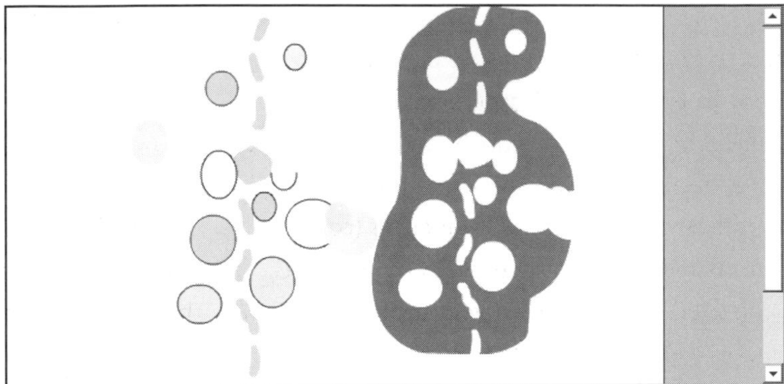

Notice that drawing new elements atop existing elements breaks all the elements into separate components. This makes it very easy to edit parts of shapes in Flash, but it has the disadvantage of breaking up shapes that you wanted to keep together. That's okay, though. If you want to make sure a shape stays whole before you draw on top of it, select and group it. The group then becomes an overlay that floats in its own, independent space. (For more information, see the "Overlays And Groups" section later in this chapter.)

Scenes (Pages)

Flash movies can contain any number of scenes, and a scene can contain any number of frames and layers. In other words, a scene is a movie within the movie.

Macromedia uses the terms *page* and *scene* interchangeably, but I'll try to be consistent in calling them *scenes*. Sometimes, however, you will find it handier to call scenes *pages*, especially if you are working with an offline linear application that is organized more like a book than a movie, where each scene may be a single frame. Examples that lend themselves to that approach would be a catalog or a training tutorial.

Scenes serve two purposes: to make it easier to organize and edit your movie, and to make it easy to navigate directly to a particular scene.

To navigate directly to a scene, choose View|Tabs (unless, of course, they're already visible). Then, just click on the tab that shows the name or number of the scene you want to see.

When you open a new movie file in Flash, you have automatically opened Scene 1. (In other words, all Flash movies have at least one scene.) Because a scene can be of any length, you can make very complex movies that consist of only one scene. You also can import Shockwave Flash movies into a new scene. Just remember that the imported frames will inherit the properties of the current movie, so you'll probably want to make sure that both movies have at least the same horizontal and vertical dimensions. You also could import frames from animation sequences (consecutively numbered still files, such as FLOWER01.JPG, FLOWER02.JPG, and so on). However, those movies won't be able to take advantage of all Flash features (most notably sound), may require some editing of shapes and colors (if they are from vector formats, such as WMF or AI), and may create much larger files if their graphics are bitmapped rather than vector (for example, animated GIFs or sequentially numbered JPEG/JPGs).

You can easily add and delete scenes and change their order. To add a scene, choose Insert|Scene. The new scene will have the same movie properties as the last scene, since movie properties must be the same for an entire movie. By the same token, if you change the properties for the new scene, they will be applied to all the scenes in that movie.

Symbols

Symbols is a strange name for what other programs call actors (Director), characters, or sprites. The latter are all far more descriptive (although in Flash, symbols can be buttons as well as actors). A symbol is a self-contained drawing or movie with a transparent background that allows it to be "suspended" within a movie scene. You can have as many symbols within a scene (page) as you like (give or take the limitations of your computer's installed random access memory (RAM).

The real miracle of symbols is that they can be fully animated within themselves and can then be animated in a different way within your scene. For instance, you can animate a person's stride, save the animation as a symbol, and then animate the movement of the symbol along a path. The result is that arms, legs, and body make all the moves necessary to imitate the natural body movements that occur during walking, while the body itself (the symbol) moves across the frame. Remember, you can apply this technique to anything that moves: a bird, a plane, or a speeding bullet...even Superman himself.

Creating Symbols

It's usually easier to create symbols in a blank scene, so that you don't have to worry about isolating the symbol from its surroundings. One way to do this is to create all the symbols first, then delete the scenes in which they occur after they've been saved to a library. You then can reintroduce them into the movie as many times and in as many different frames or scenes within the movie as you like.

You certainly aren't limited to creating symbols as I've just suggested. Anything you've selected can be turned into a symbol. Just choose Insert|Create Symbol. When you do this, a symbol scene (that can, later, be made to have multiple frames) is created automatically as soon as you name the symbol in the Symbol Properties dialog box. (See Figure 2.48.) You have to give a symbol a name before it can become a symbol. If you click the Button Behavior radio button, the symbol will automatically have the four frames required of a button.

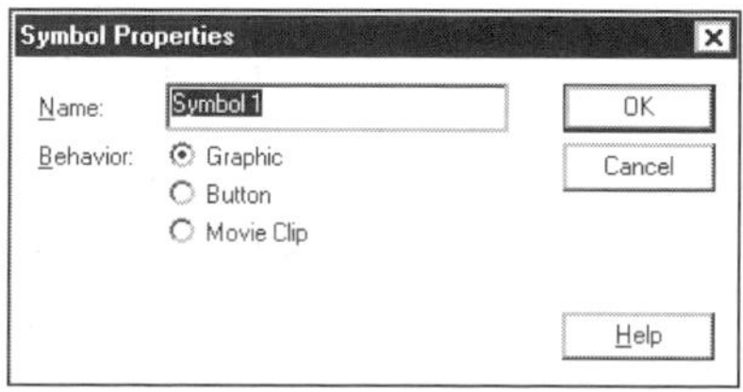

Figure 2.48 The Symbol Properties dialog box.

The third approach to creating a symbol is to choose Insert|Create Symbol when nothing has been selected previously. This method has the advantage of letting you create symbols in a blank movie, because the workspace automatically becomes a blank symbol scene. You then can draw and animate anything you like, over as many frames as you like—all independent of the rest of the movie. Anything you create, including adding text and other symbols, can use as many layers as you like, and can all become a part of the new symbol.

To terminate the creation of a new symbol, either choose Edit|Movie from the menu bar or click on the Edit Movie button in the tab bar. (The button is at the top of the bar and features an arrow in a blue circle.)

Editing Symbols

You can change the elements, shapes, or behavior in a symbol by entering Edit Symbol mode. This lets you work on a symbol as if it were an independent movie, just as when you created a new symbol in the previous section. There are three ways to enter the Edit Symbol mode:

- Use the Arrow tool and click on the symbol in the current scene that you want to edit. Then, choose Edit|Edit Symbols from the menu bar.
- Use the Arrow tool and double-click on the symbol in the scene. (This is actually called the symbol's link, because the symbol itself resides in the library.)
- Open the library (choose Window|Library) and scroll to the symbol you want to edit, then double-click in its image window. This method also lets you edit sounds and bitmaps.

Using Symbols

It's a good idea to create symbols and then use the symbols to create the graphic elements in scenes. Thus, symbols of only two or three people could be used to make a crowd, or a symbol of a flower could be used to plant a garden. Because the symbol actually is stored only once, repeated use of the same symbol saves huge amounts of file space and greatly speeds the playing of your movie. Use your imagination to find ways of maximizing this technique. For instance, all the tiles on a roof could be the same symbol, as could all the chairs in a theater, not to mention all the navigational buttons in a Web site.

Overlays And Groups

Overlays are permanently combined elements that float above the canvas. Groups, text, symbols, and (usually) bitmaps are all overlays as soon as they are created.

The most versatile type of overlay is a group, because groups (like symbols) can contain any combination of other types of elements. You can draw and paint anything you like on the canvas, then select any or all of those elements and put them into a group. You can make compound groups by selecting multiple groups, symbols, and text, and then combining them into a "supergroup." Suppose you select the Pencil tool and sketch a simple shape, like this:

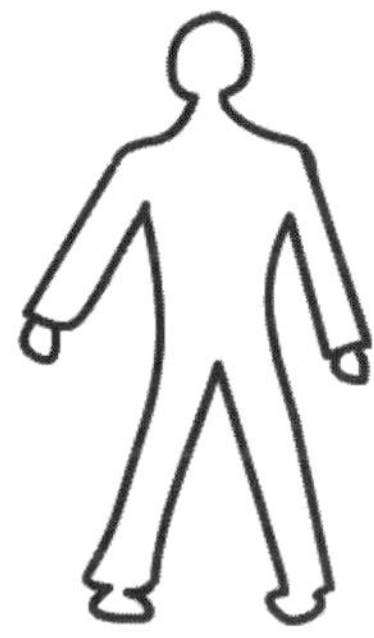

Several of the lines that make up this shape are separate elements. You can see in the next sketch that I have selected every other connected line in this profile and moved them individually, like this:

But, if I select all the elements (line segments, in this case) and then group them, when I select anything in this group, the whole group is selected, see?

I can then add a symbol from the library, select both items, and group them. If I ungroup the resulting group, the original groups will still be intact, as in the next sketch:

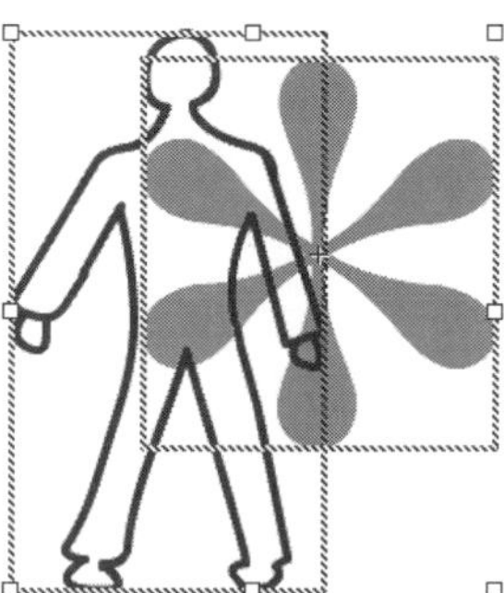

Creating A Group

Creating a group is dead easy. Select the elements you want to group and press Cmd/Ctrl+G. If you insist on making life harder than it is, you can create a group in these other ways:

- After selecting all the existing elements that you want to group, choose Modify|Group from the menu bar.
- Create an empty group by selecting nothing (you can ensure that this is the case by pressing Cmd/Ctrl+Shift+A), then choosing Modify|Group from the menu bar. This method has the big advantage of letting you create your group in a clean, uncluttered, fresh workspace. When you terminate group creation, any elements that you have introduced are automatically placed in a single group that overlays the canvas in which you were previously working.

Editing A Group

The procedure for editing a group is almost the same as for editing a symbol. Select the group, then either choose Edit|Select from the menu bar or double-click on the Arrow tool on the selection. Everything in the current frame that is not part of the group will fade to about 50 percent of normal intensity. All the faded elements are now locked, so there's no danger of affecting them when you edit the elements in your group.

Leaving Group Edit Mode

There are two ways to get back to normal Movie Edit mode: You can choose Edit|Movie from the menu bar. Alternatively, you can double-click on any of the ghosted elements. When you see the ghosted elements return to normal intensity, you will know that you're back to normal.

Layers

In a sense, layers are another kind of overlay. Because they can each hold any of the other types of overlays described earlier, we can think of them as superlayers. Each layer has its own transparent canvas, so you can always create an independent drawing simply by creating a new layer and then drawing on it. Since layers are transparent (except, of course, for the drawings and overlays they contain), you can stack as many as you like. (You can also have transparency in the drawings and overlays.) All elements (drawings, text, symbols, etc.) on a given layer are separate from the elements on any other layer. You can change the stacking order of layers anytime you like.

Layer Menu

The Layer menu hides quite a few of Flash's commands behind the layer status icons at the right side of each layer name bar. These are the commands that let you create, delete, show, hide, and otherwise control layers. The Layer menu is shown in Figure 2.49, and its commands are detailed in Table 2.12.

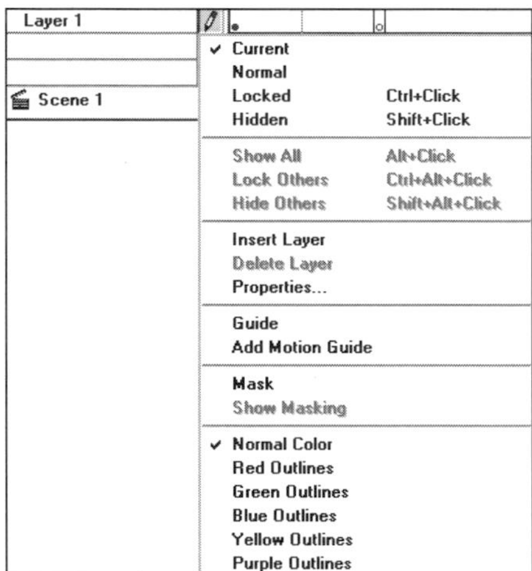

Figure 2.49 The Layer menu.

Table 2.12 Layer menu commands.

Command Name	Shortcut Key(s)	Description
Current	None	This is the layer that will be affected by any new drawing, pasting, or animation.
Normal	None	You can see the layer and can edit its elements.
Locked	Cmd/Ctrl+Click	You can see the layer, but it won't be affected by any editing, drawing, pasting, or animation.
Hidden	Shift+Click	Makes the layer invisible.
Show All	Opt/Alt +Click	Makes all layers visible.
Lock Others	None	Locks all but the menu layer.
Hide Others	Shift+Opt/Alt+Click	Hides all but the menu layer.
Insert Layer	None	Adds a new layer just above the menu layer.
Delete Layer	None	Deletes the menu layer (and everything on it).
Properties	None	Brings up a dialog box that lets you rename the layer.
Guide	None	Designates the menu layer as a guide layer. The images placed on guide layers are used as aids for positioning elements in other layers. Any layer can be a guide layer, but they work best if there's nothing else on that layer. You may want to create a new layer, and then use this command. The contents of guide layers don't print or stay with exported movies.
Add Motion Guide	None	Creates a layer that is always attached to the layer that you used to create it. Once you've added a motion guide layer, draw the motion path with the Pencil tool. Chapter 5 will explain how to employ motion paths.
Mask	None	Creates a new mask layer. Any filled shapes you make on this layer will appear as holes in the layer, making it possible to see the content of the layer immediately below.
Show Masking	None	Unless this command is chosen, the contents of a mask layer will appear as the contents of a regular layer.
Normal Color	None	Shows colors as you created them.
Red Outlines	None	Shows only the outlines for the menu layer and shows them in red.
Green Outlines	None	Shows only the outlines for the menu layer and shows them in green.
Blue Outlines	None	Shows only the outlines for the menu layer and shows them in blue.
Yellow Outlines	None	Shows only the outlines for the menu layer and shows them in yellow.
Purple Outlines	None	Shows only the outlines for the menu layer and shows them in purple.

Moving On

Now that you understand how Flash structures a movie and how many ways you can put the program to productive use, it's time to get to work.

In the next chapter, you'll learn more of the specifics regarding what makes Flash so useful in designing Web sites and interactive offline titles, such as training materials and on floppy portfolios.

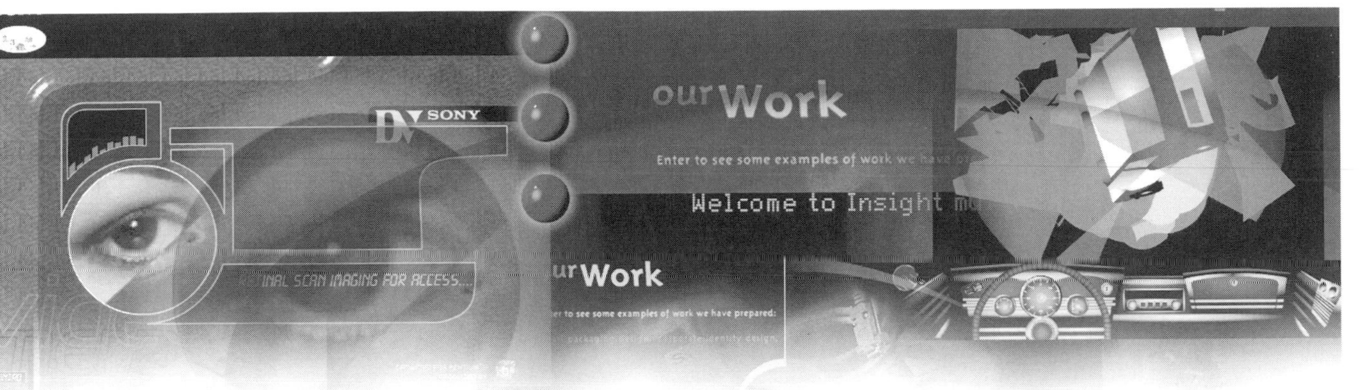

3

Flash From Here To There (And Back)

Ken Milburn

This chapter introduces you to the synergy that exists between Flash and other Macromedia products, especially Dreamweaver, Fireworks, FreeHand, and Insta.HTML. Most of the techniques discussed here are covered in greater depth in later chapters. They are introduced here only to help you plan ahead as you design your projects.

Flash doesn't fit the usual category of a what-you-see-is-what-you-get (WYSIWYG) Web authoring tool, yet you can use it to author entire Web sites. Why would you want to? Because the results would look better and reduce the viewer's waiting time. Also, those characteristics of HTML that make precision placement of design elements such a pain are not a factor when designing in Flash. Furthermore, when you want to add animation or event-triggered actions, you don't have to use another type of software (such as a GIF animator, Java, or JavaScript). Even if your Web sites contain elements that you can't author in Flash (such as QuickTime movies, GIF or Java animations, Cascading Style Sheets, or database-linked forms) you can design everything else in Flash and then use another authoring tool to create the few pages needed to contain those elements.

Another huge advantage of Flash is that you can design once and then deliver either online or offline (and also either with or without a browser). This chapter will help you decide whether you want to plan carefully—so that your creations will be optimized for the Web—or to simply design without restrictions for offline playback from CD-ROM, floppy disk, hard drive, or a local area network (LAN). Figure 3.1 shows a Flash movie playing in a browser; Figure 3.2 shows the same movie playing offline as a projector.

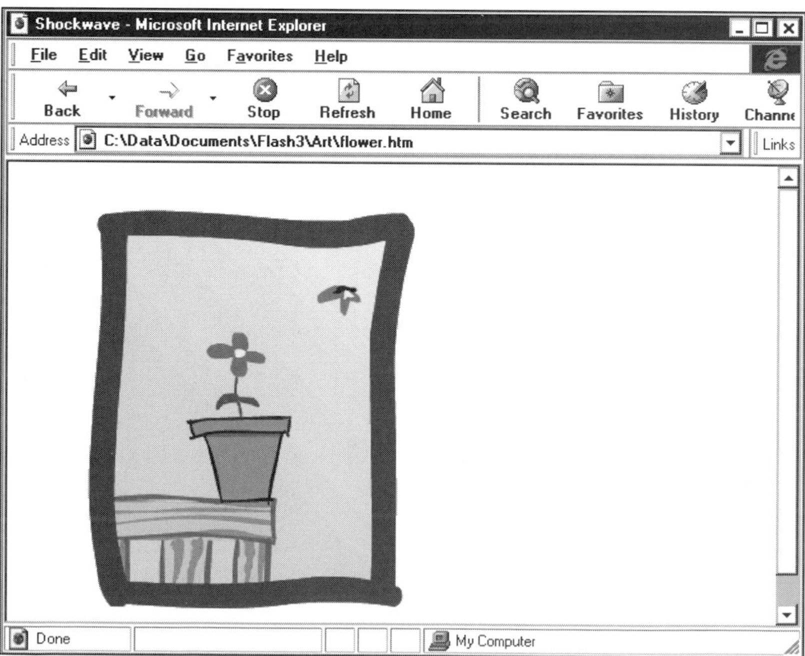

Figure 3.1 A Flash 3 movie playing in Internet Explorer 4.

To play a Flash movie without a browser, first choose File|Export Movie from the main menu, and export to the SWF Flash file format. Now, as long as you have Flash installed, simply double-click on the file name of that movie in your computer's directory (an open folder on the Macintosh or in the Explorer in Windows). The movie will appear in the standalone player window. See Figure 3.3.

If you want to distribute your Flash 3 file to anyone who has a compatible computer, simply play the file outside the browser, as described previously. From the standalone player's menu bar, choose File| Create Projector. (See Figure 3.3.) A standard Save As dialog box appears. Give your file a descriptive name and navigate to the drive and directory where you want to save it. The standalone player will automatically make the file an executable application and, in the case of Windows, add the necessary .EXE extension.

Once you have saved any Flash 3 movie as a projector, you can play it on any other computer that uses the same operating system as the computer on which the movie was created.

Creating Both Macintosh And Windows Projectors

If you want to create both Macintosh and Windows projectors, simply transfer your original SWF file to a computer that uses a different operating system but has Flash 3 installed. In the new computer's directory, double-click on the file name to start the standalone player and then create a projector (as described previously).

Whether To Design Specifically For Browser Or Offline

Since anything you create in Flash 3 can be distributed either on or off the Web, it is tempting to think that you can create your projects once, and they will fit either distribution. That's a good idea most of the time, although there is a catch: If you're designing for the Web, you

Figure 3.2 The Flash 3 movie playing offline with no browser.

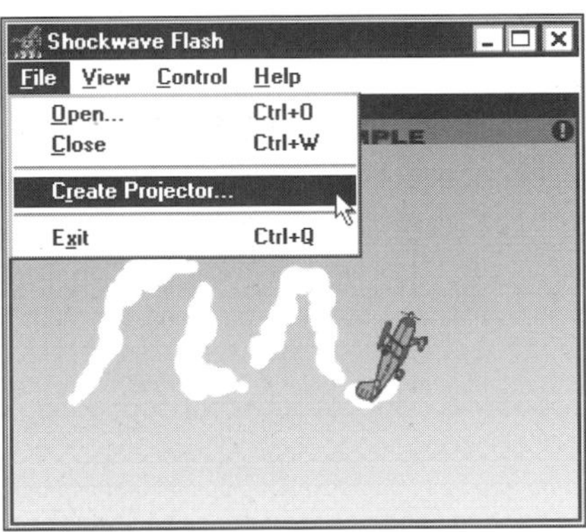

Figure 3.3 Creating a projector from the standalone player.

must constantly compromise your design in the interest of minimizing file size in order to maximize online performance.

However, if your project can be kept simple, you can design once for both online and offline delivery.

You should design a movie specifically for offline media if the presentation or interactive title would benefit significantly from:

- Gradient morphs
- Higher frame rates
- Detailed drawings (such as maps and scientific illustrations)
- Many animated layers
- Heavy use of imported bitmapped graphics
- High-fidelity stereo sound or extensive voice narration

A Precision Placement Tool

You can place drawing elements and text in a Flash movie with the same precision and just as intuitively as in traditional programs for page design (Quark and PageMaker) or illustration (FreeHand, Illustrator, and CorelDRAW).

Flash lets you choose ruler units (pixels, inches, decimal inches, centimeters, millimeters, and points). If you are designing for the screen, you will want to choose pixels as your unit of measurement. If you are designing for the printed page, you will want to use one of the other units. Flash does not let you choose picas for setting ruler or grid spacing. However, if you have an illustration program, you could export to Adobe Illustrator format, open the file in your illustration program, and tweak your placement there, then export the result in the same illustration format and import it back into Flash. For more details on importing to and from illustration programs, see Chapters 7 and 9.

Flash 3 also doesn't directly support guidelines such as those found in most illustration programs. You can, however, use a guide layer. (A guide layer is simply a layer that doesn't show up on playback.) You can use any of the Flash drawing tools on a guide layer to make guidelines, motion paths, and text annotations or to hold any sort of visually helpful hint (such as a starburst or exclamation point to attract attention).

Perfect Type

No longer do you need to limit your Web pages and interactive titles to only those fonts supported by the majority of browsers. Nor do you need to depend on using nested tables in order to place type where you would like it.

Flash provides you with a way to lay out and design interactive Web content that features fully antialiased (edge-smoothed) type in any outline font that's installed in your operating system. The result will appear correctly on any Web or offline viewer's computer, regardless of whether the fonts you used are installed on that computer.

Flash 3 provides text modifiers for font, type size (in points), text color, bold, italic, paragraph alignment, and paragraph properties. See Figure 3.4.

You can modify text at any time by reselecting it and then dragging the text cursor over any range of letters to change their properties. No restrictions prevent you from changing the text properties for part of a paragraph. However, the paragraph properties always apply to the entire paragraph.

Text properties allow you to control the left and right margins, paragraph indentation, and line spacing. There is no provision for kerning or leading. (If you own the Design in Motion suite or another illustration program, you could set your type more precisely using the leading

Creating Text Effects

Although there are no type styles for underlines, outlines, or shadows, Flash lets you create these effects with ease.

To create underlines, use the Pencil tool with the line modifier.

To create outlines, select the text and choose Modify|Break Apart from the menu bar, then use the Ink Bottle tool to make the outline in any color and thickness.

To create drop shadows, select the text and press Cmd/Ctrl+D to duplicate it. Change the text color to the appropriate gray, make both groups of text into Symbols, move the shadow into position, and then (if necessary) choose Modify|Arrange|Bring To Front to place the main set of letters over the shadow.

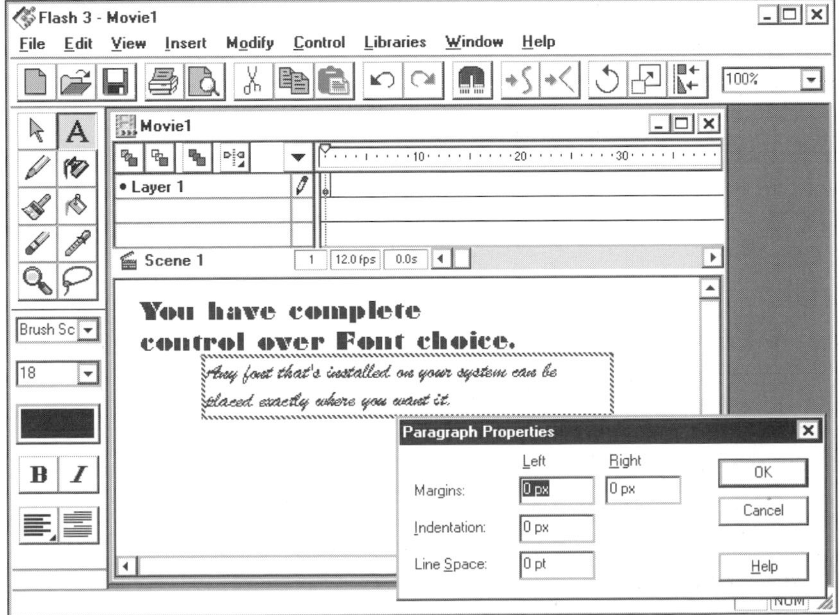

Figure 3.4 Flash 3's text modifiers and Paragraph Properties dialog box.

and kerning controls in those programs and then importing the result into Flash.)

Easy Shapes

It seems like every art director I run into lately admits to doing his or her concept sketches in Flash and then exporting the result to an illustration program for tweaking. The principal reason for doing this is that Flash provides a way to let you draw as naturally as if you were sketching on paper. At the same time, it produces precision geometry that can be easily read and tweaked by even the most sophisticated illustration software, which is the software usually used to specify graphic design for single-page print projects. Examples of single-page projects include book and album covers, all sorts of advertisements, and package design.

You can sketch intuitively in Flash, using the Pencil tool and the shape-recognition modifiers, which ensures that you'll have smoother lines and fewer control points than if you used only the freehand tool in your illustration program. Making rough shape adjustments is also quicker and easier in Flash, because you can do so by simply dragging the outlines. See Figure 3.5.

Then, you can export to Adobe Illustrator by choosing File|Export and then Adobe Illustrator (the .AI file extension) in the resulting Save As dialog box. Import the Illustrator file into your illustration program and use all the power of that program to precisely control Bezier curve

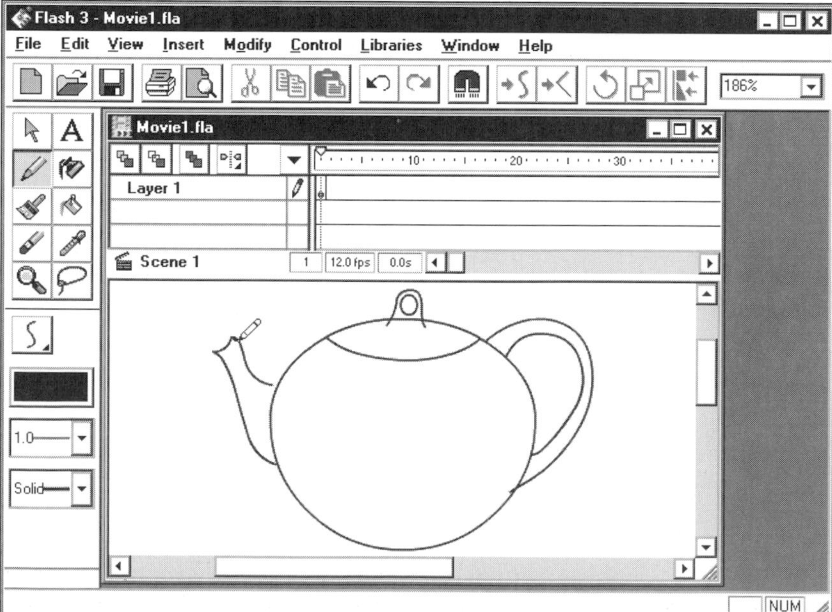

Figure 3.5 A quick sketch of a teakettle, made freehand in Flash.

control points and to make radical drawing commands, such as blends. See Figure 3.6.

Flash 3 is also a great tool for simplifying drawings made in more complex illustration programs. If you export the file from the originating illustration program and then import it into Flash, all the layers will be shown as groups. See Figure 3.7.

If you import a drawing made of overlapping shapes, there will be many grouped objects. You can see these groups if you press Cmd/Ctrl+A or choose Edit|Select All from the main menu. The objects that are grouped will be enclosed in selection rectangles, as in Figure 3.8.

If you ungroup all the subgroups, all of the shapes will be dropped onto the canvas and will, at that point, autoedit one another so that each line and color becomes its own independent shape. Because there are no longer any underlying shapes, the file size will be a fraction of the original, and you'll still retain all the visible information in the file.

This is a terrific way to store clip art or art for your own library that you may want to use later without modification. It's also a terrific way to simplify a drawing so that you can add even more layers and details in your illustration program. If you group everything in the re-imported program after using the technique described previously, all the new elements will remain independent, making them much easier to select and adjust.

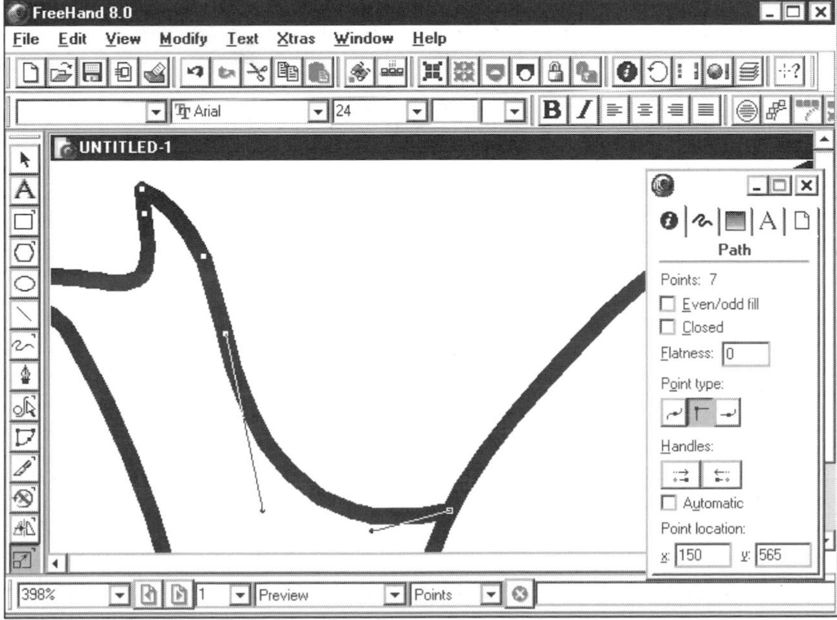

Figure 3.6 Tweaking the teakettle's control points in Macromedia FreeHand.

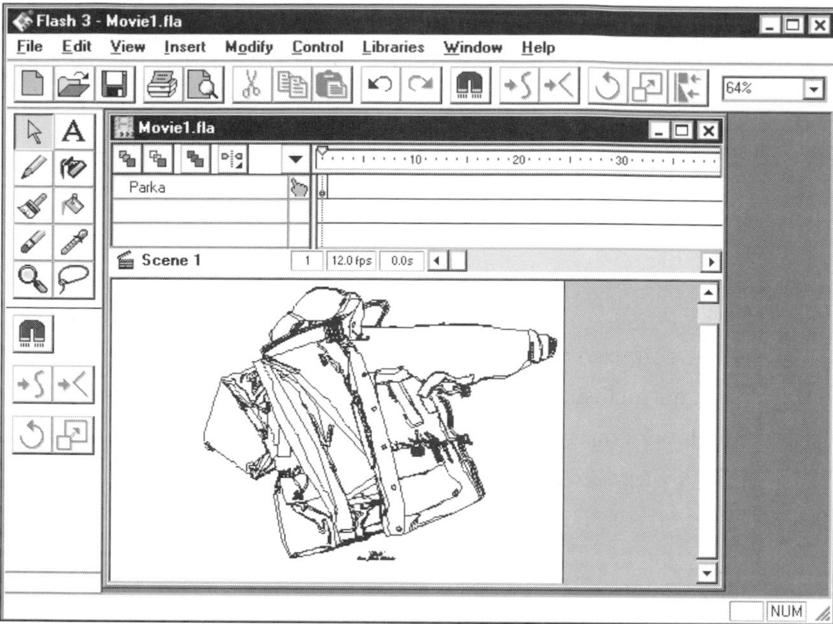

Figure 3.7 A multilayered FreeHand drawing imported into Flash, showing only the outlines.

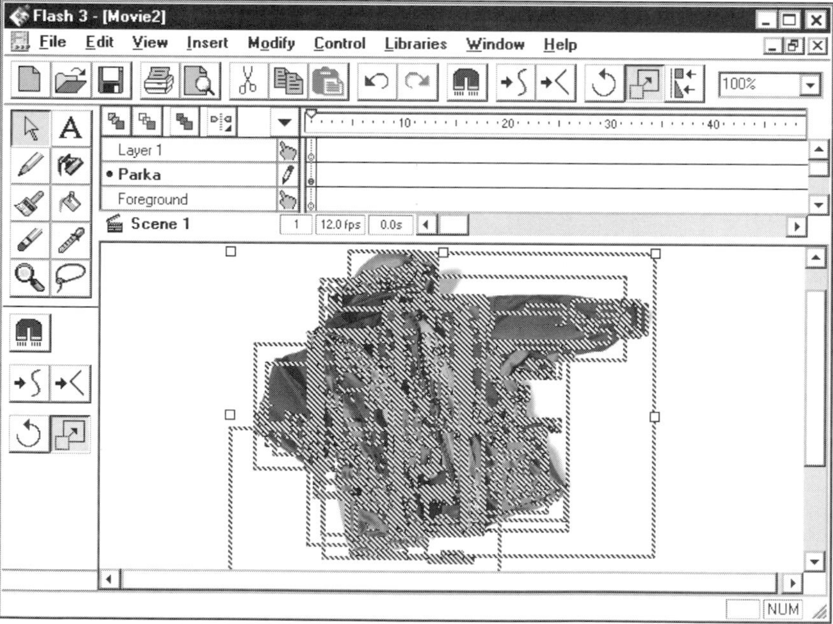

Figure 3.8 The jacket drawing after ungrouping the overall group. Each selection square represents a subgroup.

Finally, if you plan to use a drawing made in an illustration program inside a Flash movie destined for the Web, the kind of optimization described previously is a must.

You will find detailed instructions for optimizing imported illustration files in Chapter 9.

Export To Bitmapped File Formats

You may also be surprised to discover that you can use Flash 3 to create graphics and animations for conventional Web content. You can also use the same features to create bitmapped (pixel-based) images to use in photo-editing programs such as Photoshop, Macromedia xRes, and MetaCreation's Painter.

There are many reasons why you might want to use Flash 3 for these more conventional tasks. Animated GIFs have become the ubiquitous form of animation used on the Web, and they can be a simple and efficient element for inclusion in complex interactive projects (such as Director movies or PowerPoint presentations). You can export any or all of a Flash 3 movie as an animated GIF, Windows AVI (the Windows movie file format), or as a sequence of still images in all of the still-image formats supported by Flash 3. (This last option may be a good way to import animations into programs that can't import animated GIF or AVI movies.) To export a movie, just choose File|Export Movie. A standard Save As dialog box will appear. Choose a file format from the Save As Type pulldown menu, enter a file name, and click OK. See Figure 3.9.

You can also export any individual frame to GIF, JPEG, or PNG format. The result can then be either enhanced in another program or used on a standard HTML Web page.

Use the information in Table 3.1 as a quick reference when you are choosing which file format is best suited for your needs.

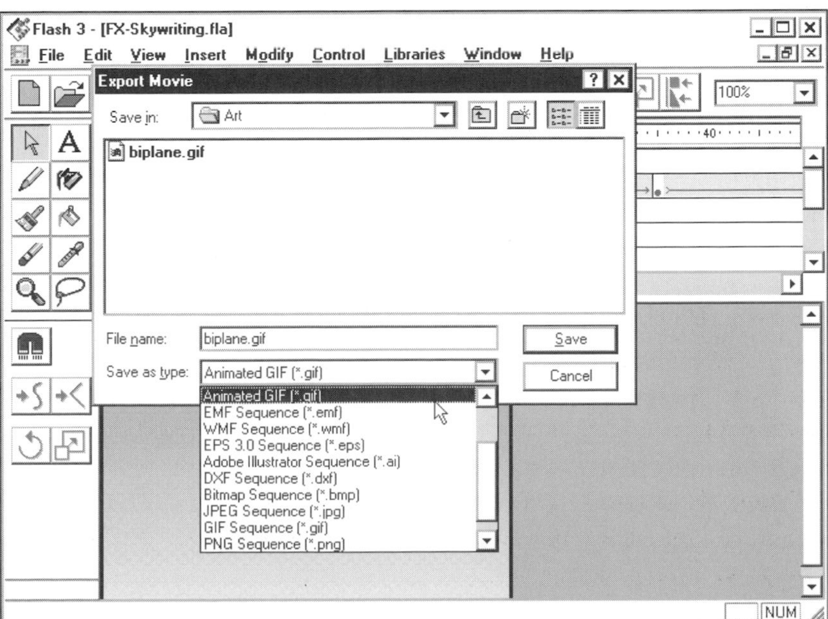

Figure 3.9 The Export Movie Save As dialog box with the Save As Type menu.

Table 3.1 Flash 3 file export formats.

File Format	Best Use(s)
GIF	Very small (thumbnail) photos or flat-colored, hard-edged text and graphics. GIF is the most commonly used format for Web graphics. Compression is lossless (no changes are made to the pixel structure of the image) and is most efficient when the subject is composed of defined edges and solid colors.
JPEG	The Web format most commonly used for photographs and other images that feature continuous tone-shaded colors and soft edges. Since browsers must decompress the image before it can be viewed, larger images are more appropriate and more efficient than smaller ones—especially since smaller images contain fewer pixels and are therefore less likely to contain more than 216 colors (the maximum number in a Web-safe palette). JPEG compression is highly efficient, but it can cause the loss of detail or the introduction of image artifacts (minute blotches), especially at higher compression ratios.
PNG	PNG is a new cross-platform file format invented for the Web. It is the only Web format that can contain alpha channel masks. (Alpha channel masks make it possible to have graduated or partial transparency in an image.) However, only version 4 and later Netscape and Microsoft browsers will recognize the PNG format files unless they use a special plug-in. Use the PNG format when higher-fidelity or graduated transparency is a must. Also use this format when you want to export the highest-quality bitmap for further editing in an image editor such as Photoshop 5, Fireworks, Image Ready, or Photo Paint. *Caution*: Older versions of such programs may not recognize this format. If you have an older image-editing program that accepts Photoshop-compatible plug-in modules, you can download a plug-in from **www.adobe.com**.

Export To Insta.HTML

Actually, I didn't know how to get the idea across in the headline efficiently, but strictly speaking, you can't export a file directly from Flash 3 to Insta.HTML. You can, however, export a frame as a vector-format still to FreeHand 8, add to or modify that image, then export the result through Insta.HTML.

Oops. There I go, getting ahead of myself again. You may not know what Insta.HTML is. It is a FreeHand Xtra (plug-in) that turns the content of a FreeHand page into an HTML document. Text is converted to its closest HTML equivalent, and graphics are automatically converted to (it is hoped) the most appropriate bitmapped format. At the same time, tables are automatically created in the HTML document to keep the text and graphic elements as correctly positioned as possible in HTML. Figure 3.10 gives you an idea of what it's like to export a FreeHand page to Insta.HTML.

Insta.HTML is part of the Macromedia Design in Motion suite and is discussed in greater detail in Chapter 9.

Using Aftershock

Aftershock is a standalone program that ships with both Flash 3 and the Design in Motion suite. Aftershock makes it incredibly easy to ensure that your Flash movies are properly embedded in HTML in such a way that they can be seen by the largest number of browsers.

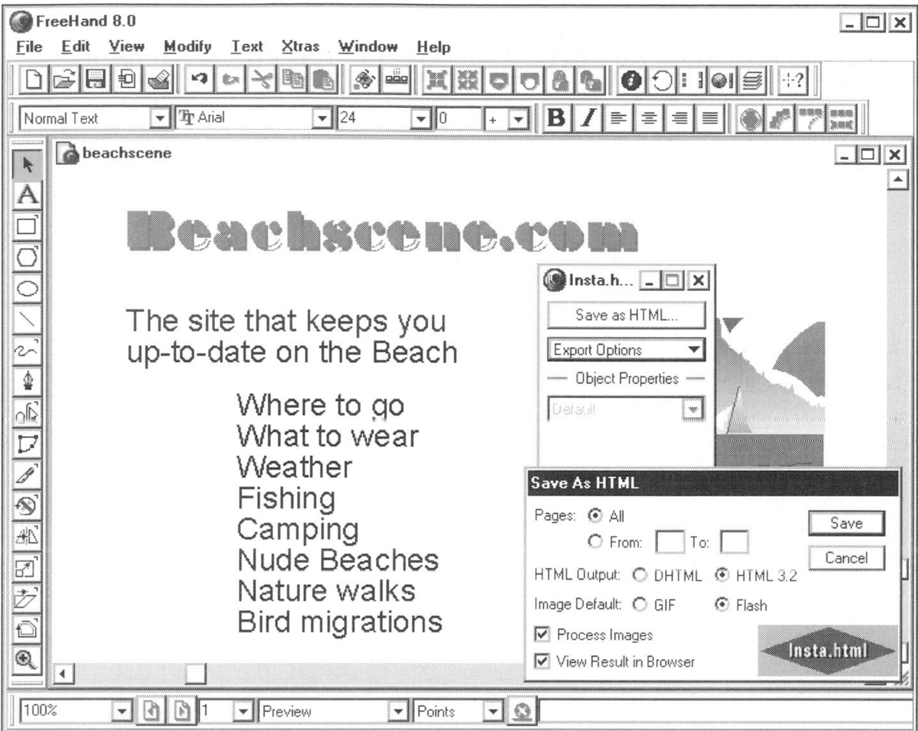

Figure 3.10 The Insta.HTML interface.

Aftershock's interface lets you choose any and every possible parameter setting for the **<EMBED>** and **<OBJECT>** tags.

You can also use Aftershock in many other ways to ensure that your Flash-designed Web site will be accessible, at least in some way, by almost anyone with a browser. Aftershock gives you the options to do any or all of the following:

- Create a detection script in JavaScript that can recognize whether a viewer's browser is equipped to play your Flash movies and, if not:
    - Download and install the appropriate plug-in or ActiveX control.
    - Display your movie as a static or animated GIF.
- Create a cookie that gives viewers a choice as to how they would like to view your Flash movies.
- Deliver your Flash movie as a Java applet.
- Represent your movie as a static GIF.
- Represent your movie as an animated GIF.
- Aid search-engine indexing and link-verification tools by generating lists of links and text contained in a Flash movie.

You will learn a great deal more about Aftershock and the specifics of using it in Chapter 10. Meanwhile, here's a screenshot of the user interface (Figure 3.11) and a quick run-through of the basic steps for using Aftershock.

You will be using a Flash movie in a Web site in one of two scenarios:

- You have created your entire site in one movie and need only to surround it with an HTML document.
- Your Flash movies are part(s) of an otherwise conventional site, in which case, you want to place the movies into existing HTML documents.

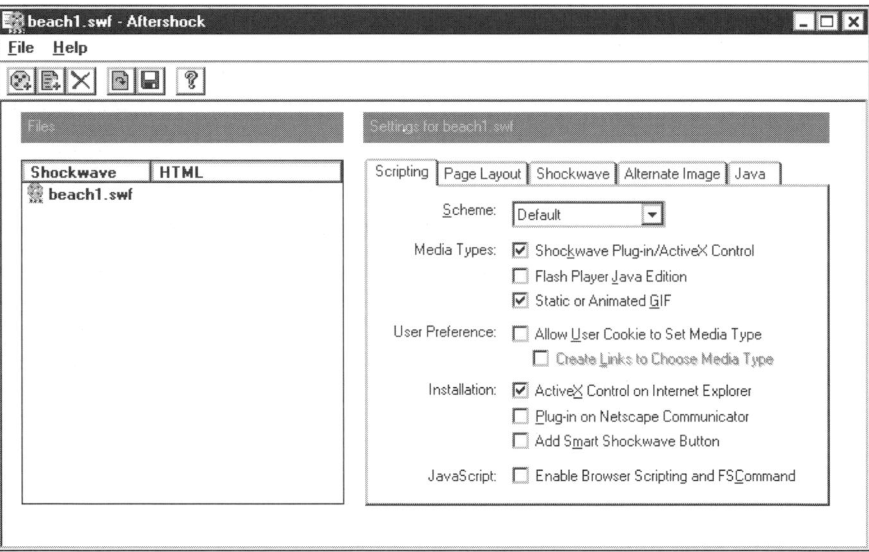

Figure 3.11 The Aftershock interface.

Placing A Flash Movie Into A New HTML Document

To place a Flash movie into a new HTML document, follow these steps:

1. Double-click on the Aftershock icon on your desktop (or, if in Windows, choose Macromedia|Flash 3|Aftershock from the Start menu).
2. Choose File|Add|Shockwave.
3. Select your movie from the Open dialog box.
4. Accept the defaults for all the tabs. (These choices—and there are many—are explained in Chapter 10.)
5. Choose File|Save and name the new HTML document.

Updating An Existing HTML Document That Contains Flash

To update an existing HTML document that already contains Flash, follow these steps:

1. Start Aftershock. (See Step 1 in the "Placing A Flash Movie Into A New HTML Document" section.)
2. Choose File|Add|HTML.
3. Use the resulting Open dialog box to locate and open the file to which you want to add a movie.
4. Make any needed changes in the tab settings.
5. Choose File|Save.

Because Insta.HTML can save a FreeHand vector drawing as either a Flash graphic or a bitmap (GIF, JPEG, or PNG), you can create precisely designed layouts in FreeHand and then export them to either type of site.

Integration With Other Macromedia Products

Macromedia has been working on integrating its applications so that they not only serve their intended purpose, but serve one another as well. I've already mentioned how useful FreeHand and the Insta.HTML Xtra can be. The other two products that should be of interest to you are Dreamweaver (Macromedia's WYSIWYG Web-authoring tool) and Director (Macromedia's hyperpowerful, industry-standard multimedia authoring tool).

Dreamweaver will let you insert a Flash movie precisely where you want in any existing HTML document. All you have to do is open your target document in Dreamweaver, choose Insert|Flash Movie, and navigate to the movie you want to insert. (See Figure 3.12.) Furthermore, you can then simply drag the corner of a bounding box to scale them to the exact size that you want them to appear.

Director, as of version 6.5, allows you to import Flash movies as sprites. Director (or your Director-enriched Shockwave Web pages) can then play Flash's vector-based movies alongside the conventional animated bitmapped content. As of this writing, only Flash 2 movies are supported in this manner. You can use Flash 3, of course, but you have to save the files in Flash 2 format. As a result, you won't be able to take advantage of Flash 3's new graphics features such as morphing and transparency.

Creating Templates For Flash Generator

Flash Generator is yet another Macromedia application. It does not ship with Flash 3 or with the Design in Motion suite. Generator is a Web server tool that automates the creation of both Flash and standard GIF graphics according to input from users or viewers.

In laymen's terms, a Generator-based site might show one graphic if you answered "yes" to a question, another if you answered "maybe," and yet another if you answered "no."

You can't create a Generator site in Flash, but you can create a Generator template. You do this by either of the following:

- Adding text variables to a movie
- Installing Generator extensions to Flash 3

The second option requires that you own Generator; the first doesn't. All you need to do is use the Flash Text tool to place the required code inside curly braces ({}). When that movie is subsequently processed in Generator, the text in brackets will be replaced by the appropriate text from an associated text file or in the command line.

You will learn more about creating text templates for Flash Generator in Chapter 11. Operations that require you to own a copy of Generator are outside the scope of this book.

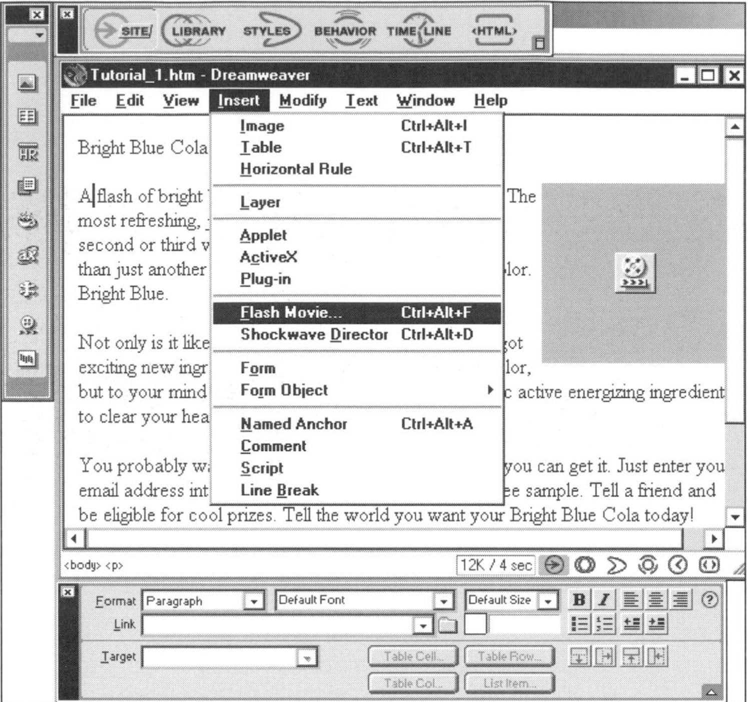

Figure 3.12 Placing a Flash movie into an HTML document in Dreamweaver.

Moving On

Well, so much for the theory and overviews. Now that you have an idea of what you can accomplish with Flash 3, it is time to get down to the specifics of creation. The next chapter will teach you the fundamentals of drawing in Flash 3.

DRAWING WITH FLASH 4

KEN MILBURN

This chapter serves two purposes. It teaches you to draw in Flash and provides you with a quick reference to all the tools, icons, and commands related to drawing.

Drawing with Flash is more like drawing on paper than is any other drawing program, such as Illustrator or FreeHand. But it's also different from drawing on paper in a big way: Flash recognizes basic geometric shapes, such as circles and squares, and straightens or smoothes your freehand lines.

This chapter will do much more than just show you how easy it is to draw with Flash. It serves as a complete guide to the drawing and editing tools you'll use. It also gives you lots of tips for controlling and refining your drawings, as well as making them look more professional.

You Don't Need Drawing Talent

Actually, even though Flash is a very useful drawing program, you don't have to be a practiced artist to produce worthwhile results. You can choose among several options to include artwork in your Flash creations. Plenty of professional-looking artwork is available at reasonable prices on CD-ROM. (Figure 4.1 shows some of the art that comes in the FreeHand 8 clip art collection.) Hundreds of similar libraries are also available from other companies, such as SoftKey and Image Club.

Another option is to hire someone else to draw your art, which can then be scanned. If you don't have a scanner, you can easily find one at your local quick-print shop (such as Kinko's or PIP). They'll scan the work for you, or you can rent time on their scanner and computer and save the work to a disk. The scanned image should be saved as a Joint Photographic Experts Group (JPEG), Graphics Interchange Format (GIF), or a Portable Network Graphics (PNG) file—all of which can then be imported into Flash. Use the Trace Bitmap command to convert the

Figure 4.1 A smattering of vector images from the FreeHand 8 collection.

scanned image into a Flash drawing. You also can hand-trace imported bitmaps; this is a technique that many animators and technical illustrators use. The sketch in Figure 4.2 was made on a napkin and scanned into Macromedia's Fireworks, then saved as a PNG file. Later, I'll show you how to turn this sketch into a Flash drawing.

Yet another option is to use the extensive library of symbols that comes with Flash. These symbols are already Flash drawings, so you'll have less editing to do.

The fourth option for using Flash without drawing is to simply modify text in a graphical way. Remember that text can be any size or color in Flash. More importantly, text can also be moved or turned into a button.

You may not have to draw in Flash, but you'll want to learn to edit in Flash—especially if you don't draw very well. The exercises that follow will show you how to adapt your drawings to your needs by tracing and editing existing art.

Before Doing The Exercises

In the next few sections you will get some hands-on practice with Flash's drawing tools and commands. In order to save space and to teach you the quickest way of doing things, I have used shortcut keys in lieu of menu commands. Flash has a shortcut key for each tool in

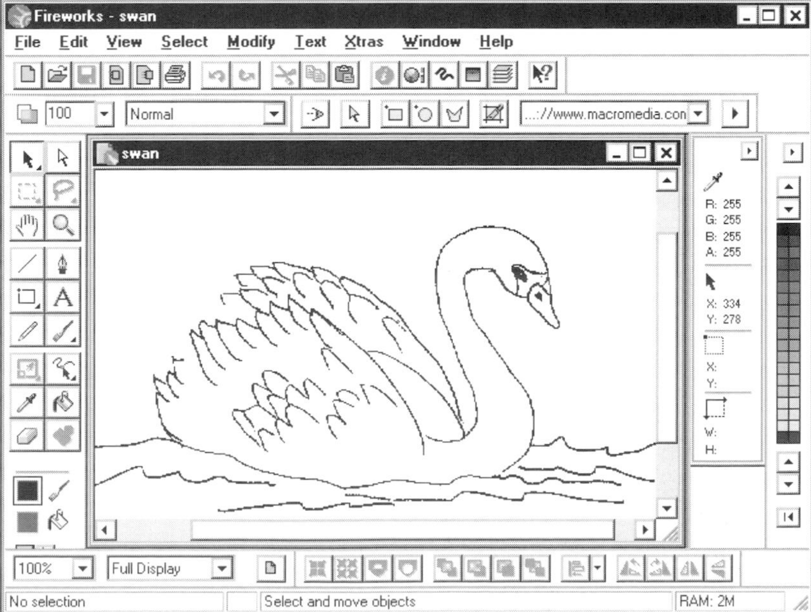

Figure 4.2 Scan of a pencil sketch.

the toolbox, all of which are listed in Chapter 2. (Remember that shortcut keys are not case sensitive.)

Also, I may not take the time to explain all the reasons for everything I'll ask you to do. My fear is that if I did, the exercises would appear to be ponderous, and you would be afraid to do them. So, you'll have to take it on faith that I'm teaching you productive habits that will serve you well in a variety of situations, and not just the one at hand. If you go ahead and finish the exercise, the reasons for a procedure will usually reveal themselves.

The other thing I should warn you about is that Flash has a number of quirks. For instance, selecting items works differently than in most Macintosh and Windows graphics programs. In Flash, you select multiple shapes by simply continuing to click with the pointer. In almost all other graphics programs, you need to press the Shift key each time you select a new item. Flash's cumulative selections may sound convenient, but it's way too easy to accidentally edit (or delete) something that you didn't realize you had selected. Fortunately, Flash 3 lets you choose the old-fashioned way of selecting as an option.

> **SELECTION TIP**
>
> I strongly recommend that you set the multiple-selection option to Shift Click and leave it that way. Choose File|Preferences. When the Preferences dialog box appears, click to check the Selection Options box. This will activate the Shift Select option. This setting will remain in effect even after you quit and restart the program. Of course, you can turn it off at any time.

Flash 3 also has some "gotchas" when making selections. If you accidentally click on the canvas (any part of the frame that's not covered with a graphic line or fill), all selections will be dropped. If you're asked to do something with a selected item and nothing happens, double-check to make sure you haven't accidentally dropped the last selection you clicked on. The simple way to check is to choose Edit|Undo (Cmd/Ctrl+Z) a few times to see if a selection marquee reappears. It's also the easy way to regain a selection if you should accidentally drop it.

The other selection quirk is that, if you make a selection with the marquee tools (Arrow or Lasso), all other selections will be dropped. So, how do you add to a selection you've made with a marquee tool? You press and hold Shift while you surround another area.

You will also have a much easier time completing these exercises if you've read Chapter 3 to familiarize yourself with the program's various functions. Pay special attention to the Timeline components: layers, frames, keyframes, pop-up menus, Onion Skin buttons, and the frame pointer.

Tracing Over A Scanned Sketch

One of the easiest ways to learn to draw is by tracing an existing drawing. The original drawing gives you a sense of where you've been and where you need to go. You also don't have to guess at shapes and proportions; you just move your pencil over what's already there.

Tracing has advantages for many professional artists, too. They can sketch on paper much faster and more expressively than they've learned to draw on the computer. (This is even true of many non-artists.)

Finally, sketches on paper are a universal and highly transportable media. If a client sketches an idea on a napkin, it's easy to digitize it into a file that can be read by any computer in the world. By the way, virtually any scanner—even handheld scanners and fax machines—can scan images with enough fidelity that you can easily trace them. It's possible, these days, to buy a workable monochrome scanner for less than $50.

In the first exercise, you will trace my sketch of a sketch, and then use Flash's "artificial-intelligence" features to make it look as though a real pro had done the job. Follow these steps:

1. From Flash's menu bar, choose File|Import. In the File dialog box, find SWAN.PNG on the CD-ROM, the sketch I scanned in Figure 4.2. If your movie is set to the default size (550 by 400 pixels), the sketch will fill most of the movie area.
2. If you import a sketch that's too large for the current movie, it's best to rescale it in your image editor, such as Fireworks, Photoshop, or another application of that type. The alternative is to increase the size of the movie in order to fit the scan. (However, if you do this, remember that all the frames in the movie will then be the same size.) To resize the movie, choose Modify|Movie and click on the Contents box to match the size of the movie to the contents of the frame. Since you probably want your drawing to fit within the

A Note About File Extensions

All of the graphics files that were created for you to use in these exercises are referred to by their file name and extension (needed by Windows versions of graphics programs). However, Windows Explorer won't show you those extensions unless you have file extensions turned on. Please turn on file extensions if you are a Windows user, and leave them that way while you're using this book. To turn on file extensions, open Window Explorers and choose View|Options. In the Options dialog box, make sure that "Hide MS-DOS file extensions" is *not* checked. (See, you're already learning good habits.) Now, you'll know which graphics file has been saved in FLA (Flash movie) or JPG format and why there seem to be two files with the same name. You'll also learn to name files so that they can be read with equal ease on both Macs and PCs. (Name everything according to the MS-DOS 8.3 convention—eight characters for the file name, a period, and a three-character extension describing the file type.)

default frame size, click on the Contents button and then click OK. The movie resizes to show the entire drawing. See Figure 4.3.

3. This image may be smaller or larger than is appropriate for its ultimate use in your Flash movie. If so, this is not a problem. Notice that the entire image has a hatched border to indicate that it is selected. (See Figure 4.4.) If this is not so, click on the image to select it.

Figure 4.3 The imported scan and the Movie Properties dialog box.

Figure 4.4 A rescaled swan. The bounding box is still active.

4. To scale the image, choose the Arrow tool, and then click on the scale modifier button. Square handles will appear at the corners of the selection frame. Press and hold Shift while dragging the corner handles to preserve the original proportions.
5. While still holding Shift, drag one of the corner handles inward until the sketch is narrow enough to fit within the current frame size. If the sketch is now too small for you to view comfortably, you can press Shift again and drag the corner handles outward to resize it.
6. Place the arrow pointer in the center of the selection and drag the sketch to where you want it in the frame.
7. Now, you want to make a new frame so that you can have a blank canvas for your drawing (the one you will trace over the scanned sketch). The quickest and easiest of the several ways to insert a new frame is to press F5.
8. You can draw or edit objects only in the currently active frame. Make the new frame the current frame by dragging the frame pointer (the down-pointing arrow slider in the frame number bar just above the Timeline) over the new frame.
9. You will use *onion skinning* to trace over the bitmap without altering it. Choose the Arrow tool (press *A*) and click on Frame 2 in the Timeline (just to the right of the blue dot indicating that Frame 1 is a keyframe). The frame in the Timeline will turn black, indicating that it is selected. See Figure 4.5.
10. Open the Frame menu for the new frame. Select the frame. Place the cursor over the selected frame. If you are using Windows, right-click. If you're on a Macintosh, click and hold. Figure 4.6 shows the Frame menu.
11. From the Frame menu, choose Insert Blank Keyframe (or just press F7). Drag the frame pointer to Frame 2, and the frame will go blank.

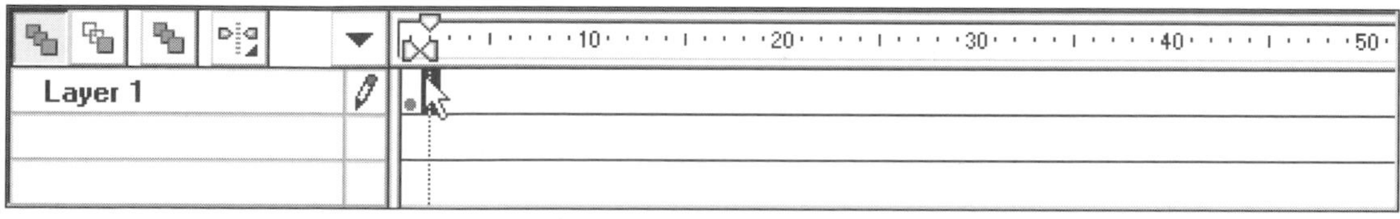

Figure 4.5 Click a frame in the Timeline (select it) to make it active.

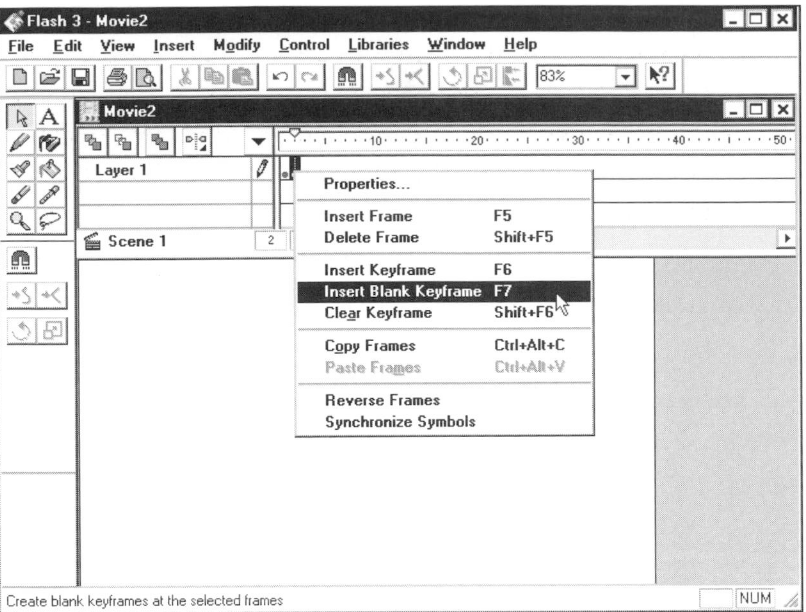

Figure 4.6 The Frame menu.

12. In the upper-left corner of the Timeline, you will see three icons that look like overlapping red pages. These are the Onion Skin buttons. Click on the first (leftmost) Onion Skin button. You now can see the sketch, but it is grayed out. (See Figure 4.7.) You can now easily distinguish your tracing from the original sketch. And, since the original scanned drawing is in a separate frame, you won't accidentally alter it, either.

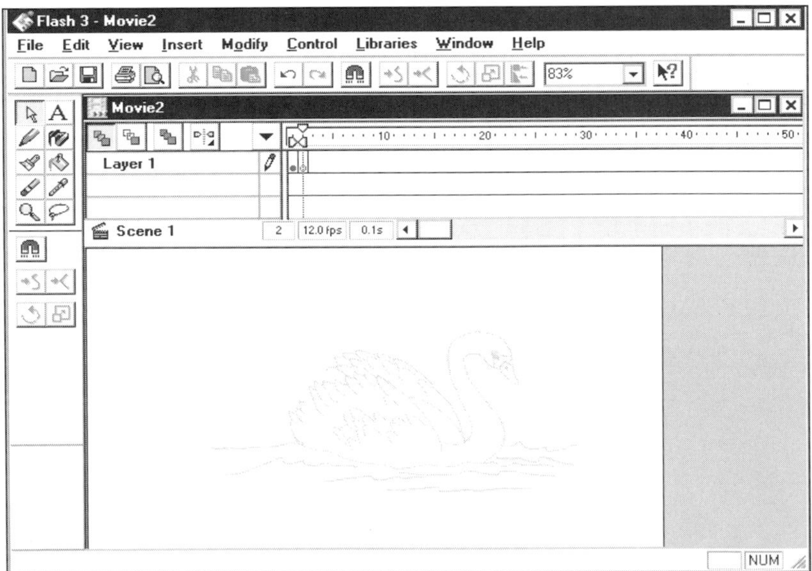

Figure 4.7 The onion-skinned sketch.

13. Now, you can start your tracing. First, freehand draw the long curves that delineate the main body and neck of the swan. Choose the Pencil tool (press *P*), and then choose Smooth from the Pencil Mode menu (under the first Pencil modifier button). This will let you see the power of Flash's smoothing capability. Don't let the ends of lines touch one another, so you can edit the lines independently. The result should look something like Figure 4.8.

14. Trace a few more of the outer lines, making sure the smooth modifier is still active.

 Choose the Arrow tool, and click on one of the lines you've traced. If your drawing was as unsteady as mine, only part of this line will be selected. Either double-click or continue clicking (or shift-clicking if you've set your Properties that way) on segments until the whole line is selected. You've selected this line so you can continue to smooth it. Click repeatedly on the smooth modifier. As you do this, the short line segments caused by your unsteadiness will merge, making the full curve both smoother and easier to edit.

15. If you still have unjoined segments (the point at which two lines converge without smoothing into a curve—often referred to as a *corner*), this step will show you how to combine those line segments into one smooth line. You can tell if you have a corner in two ways:

Note: *If you are a good artist, you may have drawn such smooth lines that only one segment can be selected with the Arrow tool. If this is the case, delete the line and intentionally draw a rougher version so you can follow this exercise.*

Figure 4.8 Freehand pencil lines with smoothing turned on.

a. Click with the Arrow tool on one end of the line. If the whole line isn't selected, you have a corner (two separate line segments) where the selection ends before the next line segment.

b. Move the arrow cursor slowly along the line and see if you always get a backward C-shaped symbol next to the arrow. (This symbol indicates a curve.) If the symbol next to the arrow cursor changes to an L-shape, you have a corner. Drag the corner(s) so the line is smoother, then reselect all the lines and click on the smooth modifier until the line is perfectly smooth. (See Figure 4.9.) Now, if you click on the line, the entire line will be selected.

16. Select and smooth the other curved lines. Click the Onion Skin button (turning it off). You now see what you've produced so far. See how clean the lines are? Okay, now we'll draw some other long curves in a much quicker way—by starting with straight lines. But first, click the Onion Skin button to turn onion-skinning back on.

17. It's sometimes easier to draw a single smooth curve by starting with a straight line, because a straight line has no segments. The next few steps illustrate this point. Choose the Pencil tool (press *P*), then the line modifier button. To make sure that your cursor doesn't jump in predefined increments, make sure that Snap is turned off. (Check in the View menu. If Snap is selected, Snap is on. Choose Snap to toggle it off.) Draw a straight line (click to start, drag to finish) for the swan's feathers. Figure 4.10 shows you how this should look after turning onion-skinning off.

18. Activate the Arrow tool. Click away from the graphic elements (in this case, lines) to deselect everything. Click the leftmost Onion Skin icon to turn onion-skinning on. Place the Arrow tool near the center of each straight line until you see a curve near the arrow, then drag to bend the line until it matches the curve in the sketch. You can see an example of this technique in Figure 4.11.

Figure 4.9 Straightening a curve.

19. With the Arrow tool, drag a rectangle around as many of the lines above the swan's body as you can without selecting any of the lines in the body. Alternatively, you could use the Lasso tool to place a freehand marquee around these lines to select them.

20. Next, click (or Shift+click if your preferences allow it) on any unselected line segments belonging to the swan's body. When all

> ***Note:*** *Be careful not to cross over any lines with the selection marquee. Doing so will segment the lines if the selection is subsequently modified in any way.*

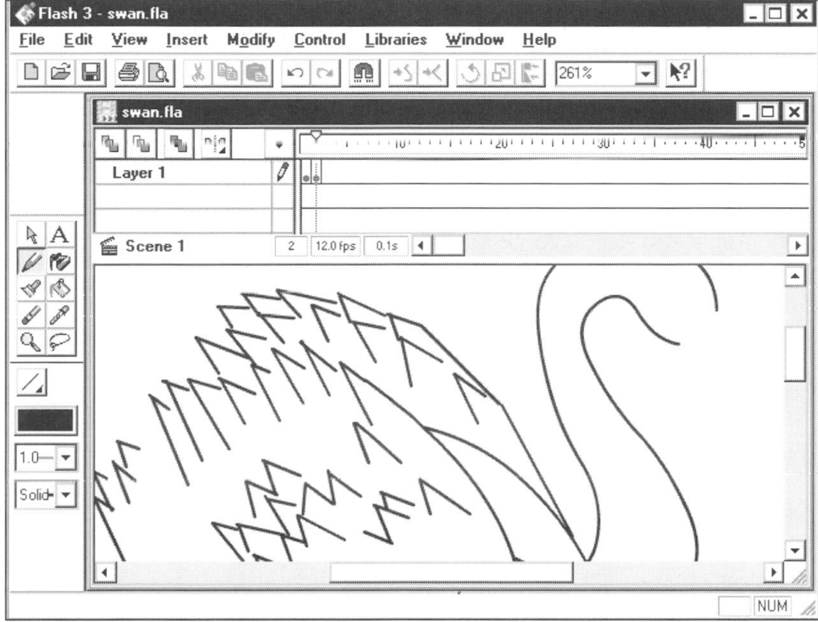

Figure 4.10 The straight lines that define the swan's feathers.

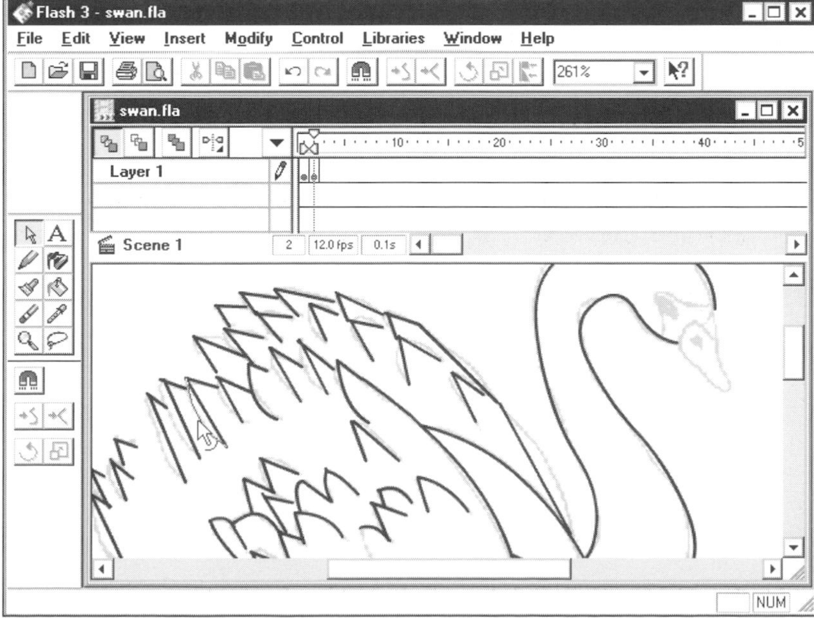

Figure 4.11 Bending straight lines to match curves.

> **Note:** *If you want to rejoin a group's lines to the other shapes on your frame's canvas, click to activate the group (the marquee will appear) and press Cmd/Ctrl+Shift. All of the shapes on the canvas, including any unselected groups will appear unghosted and no marquee will be in evidence.*

the pertinent line segments are selected, press Cmd/Ctrl+G (or choose Modify|Group from the main menu) to group them. Once grouped, the lines become an overlay, that is, they are separated from the rest of the lines so that they can be edited separately.

21. To edit the lines in the new group without accidentally editing the other lines in the image, click on one of the lines in the group. A rectangular Flash marquee will surround the entire group. See Figure 4.12.

22. To edit any of the lines within the group, double-click on the desired lines within the marquee. The marquee will disappear, and all of the lines that aren't grouped will become ghosted, indicating that you can edit them. Voila, you are now in overlay edit mode. See Figure 4.13.

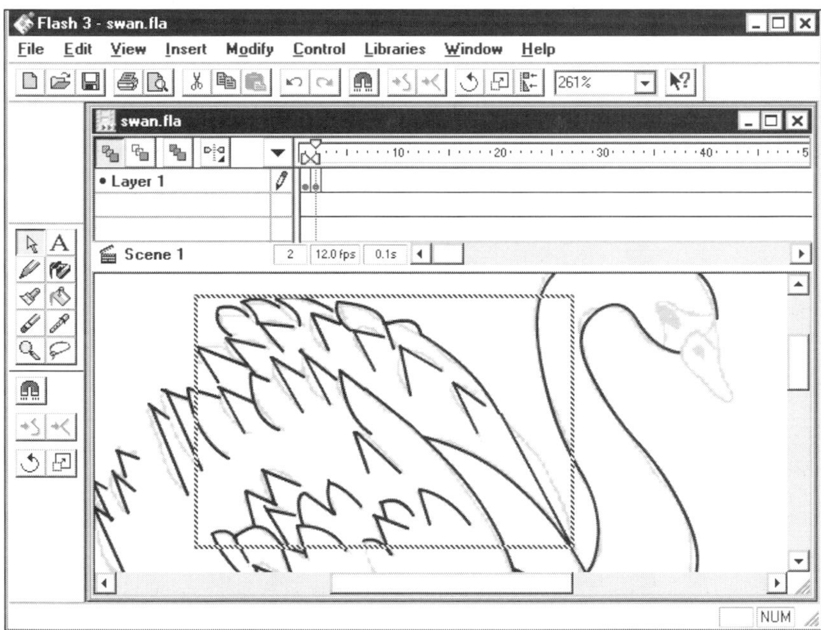

Figure 4.12 A selected group.

Figure 4.13 Editing a group.

23. Once everything is edited to suit you, click the active Onion Skin icon to turn off onion-skinning and view your standalone result.

24. Once all the lines have been shaped, you might have some unwanted segments that resulted from having lines overlap in the wrong places. If so, you need to delete the overhanging segments. Click on the segment you want to eliminate, which makes the line appear hatched. Press the Delete key, and the unwanted segment will disappear.

25. You can now eliminate the original sketch, since it is no longer needed. Click in the Timeline to select the first frame, then either press the Delete or Backspace key, or choose Delete from the Frames menu. Remember, to access the Frames menu on a Macintosh, click and hold on the frame you want to affect. To access the Frames menu in Windows, right-click on the frame.

> ***Note:*** *If this is just one of many drawings you'll use in your movie, you would be well advised to save it as a symbol. Select all the elements you want to save as a symbol, then choose Insert|Symbol from the main menu. A dialog box will appear that allows you to name and categorize the symbol. For more on symbols, see the section "Assembling And Disassembling Groups And Symbols" later in this chapter.*

Modifying Clip Art

Almost all the vector clip art in the universe can find its way into Flash. The most direct route is for the clip art to be already available on CD-ROM or via the Web in Adobe Illustrator (AI) or Encapsulated PostScript (EPS) format. Otherwise, load the clip art into the program it was designed for, export it as an AI or EPS file, and then import it into Flash. Users of CorelDRAW especially should take advantage of this route, because CorelDRAW comes with thousands of useful clip art images. If you don't have the originating program, use a graphics file-translation program, such as HiJaak Pro for Windows NT/95. Macintosh users will have a tougher time finding vector file translation; however, all of the illustration programs can translate between all of the most popular formats. The granddaddy of all graphics file translators, DeBabelizer, translates only between bitmapped image formats.

Another option is to autotrace bitmapped clip art. You can do this in Flash with the Modify|Trace Bitmap command, but you also could use the autotracing capabilities built into most illustration programs (notably FreeHand or CorelDRAW). You could also use Adobe's dedicated autotracing program, Streamline. All of these options are attractive if you want more editing control over the traced image than Flash allows with the Trace Bitmap command.

The problem with commercial vector clip art, especially if it is free or inexpensive, is that it tends to be produced as quickly as possible. So curves are made of many straight lines, and grouped objects overlap in

Note: *If you are opening files from a commercial CD, the files may often have names such as SYMB0001.EPS. This file name indicates that this is a symbol and that it's file number one. Flash will think the numbers indicate sequential frames and will ask if you want to load them all at once. Just say no—unless you want to preview a series of files before picking one. In that case, you can load them all, then use the frame pointer in the Timeline to preview each. When you have exactly the image you want, delete the remainder of the frames.*

ways that make them hard to edit, simply because it's difficult for you to see how they're constructed. Again, Flash comes to the rescue! The following exercise will show you a procedure that actually makes it easier to edit clip art than if you had imported it into a more advanced illustration program such as Illustrator, CorelDRAW, or FreeHand:

1. Choose File|Import from the menu bar. From this book's companion CD-ROM, import the file DRAGON.EPS.
2. The dragon file opens as several grouped objects. You'll know this because you'll see several overlapping selection frames. See Figure 4.14.
3. While the groups are still selected, press Cmd/Ctrl+G to group all of them into one main group. Because grouping objects puts them on a separate overlay above the canvas, any editing you do to a group will not affect anything on the canvas or in other overlays (such as text and symbols).
4. If you want the object to be a different size, this is a good time to rescale it. Choose the Arrow tool and click on the scale modifier. Press the Shift key and drag the corner handle of the group until the dragon is the size you're going to need most often in your movie.
5. Get rid of all or most of the scales. You could do this by ungrouping the dragon, but that would mean that any of its shapes would be

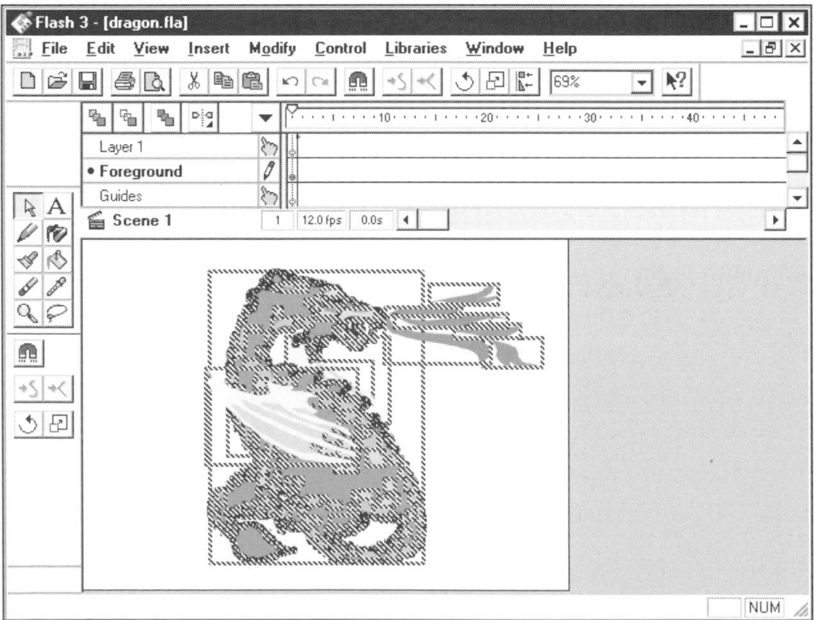

Figure 4.14 The imported dragon clip art, showing the object group selections.

automatically merged with any of the shapes already on the canvas of your movie. So, click on the dragon. Since it's a group, a rectangular marquee will surround the entire dragon to show that it's grouped into a single object. From the main menu, choose Edit|Edit Selected. Any shapes on the canvas that aren't part of the currently selected group will be ghosted.

6. Let's start simplifying the drawing by getting rid of the scales. Press Shift+click to select a number of scales, then press Delete/Backspace to eliminate them. See Figure 4.15.

7. Once you've eliminated as many scales (or objects in some other image) as you would like, it's easier to continue to simplify the drawing. Most imported vector art (especially packaged clip art) contains thousands of straight lines. You can combine these into longer curved lines by selecting a series of end-to-end lines and then using the smooth modifier to join them. This technique works only when the angle between lines is less than the amount specified in the Drawing Assistant. (See Figure 4.16.) Open the Drawing Assistant by choosing File|Assistant from the main menu.

***Note:** One of the problems often associated with clip art is that it's likely to be unnecessarily complicated. For instance, lines that could be a single geometric curve may be made of many single segments. Or, there may be a decorative pattern (such as the scales on the dragon) that just isn't needed. Remember, superfluous detail makes for larger files, which results in slower Web performance.*

Figure 4.15 Multiple objects are selected. Pressing Delete/Backspace clears the objects from the workspace.

Assistant

Snap to grid:	Normal	OK
Connect lines:	Normal	Cancel
Smooth curves:	Normal (Off / Rough / Normal / Smooth)	
Recognize lines:		
Recognize shapes:		
Click accuracy:	Normal	Help

Figure 4.16 The Flash Drawing Assistant. Each item is associated with a pull-down menu from which you can choose stricter or looser control over the various aspects of shape recognition.

***Note:** If you accidentally double-click on a scale (or any other editable object), you will have executed the Edit|Edit Selected command for that object. Everything else on the screen will fade by 50 percent, indicating that you can edit only the one small object. To resume editing the scales, choose Edit|Edit All or double-click on a portion of blank canvas that's outside the area of the group. When you're in Edit All mode, all lines and colors are shown at their normal intensity.*

Note: *If you miss the object you want to select—or you want to select another object—you may find yourself editing another group or deleting something you wanted to keep. Flash provides a wonderful solution: multiple undos. Just press Cmd/Ctrl+Z as many times as necessary to get you back to where you wanted to be.*

8. Pull down the Smooth Curves menu in the Drawing Assistant and choose Smooth. This smooth modifier joins lines whose ends meet at sharper angles than would be joined if we left the setting at Normal.
9. We now come to another problem common to modifying vector drawings imported into Flash. We want to smooth both the black outline of the dragon as well as the edges of its solid green fill. Unfortunately, there's no outline, only individual brush strokes that imitate an outline and greatly increase the file size. (The same is true of the white space between the tail and the body of the dragon.) Fortunately, Flash is capable of instantly making a new outline. We'll do that before we delete the old outline.
10. Make sure you're still in Edit|Edit Selected mode. Click in the white space between the tail and the body. It will be surrounded by a checkered marquee to indicate that it is selected.
11. From the main menu, choose Modify|Ungroup. You cannot use the Ink Bottle tool used in the next step on grouped objects.
12. Choose the Ink Bottle tool. In the Ink Bottle modifiers box, pull down the Line Thickness menu and choose 2.0. Make sure the color shown in the color sample box contrasts with the existing outline. (If the tone of the colors is too similar, click and drag on the color swatch and choose a contrasting color.) Doing this will allow you to distinguish the new outline you are about to make from the old outline, which you will want to delete.
13. Click in the white space. It is now surrounded by a two-point contrasting outline that we can select as an entity and edit to make smoother.
14. Repeat steps 11 through 13, except now select the green body of the dragon. We now also have a contrasting outline around the dragon's body. In Figure 4.17, you can see both the old outlines and the new.

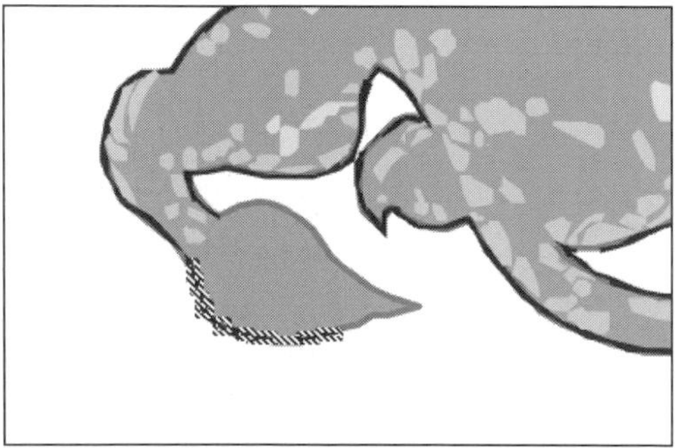

Figure 4.17 The darker outline is the old outline that you need to erase.

15. Next, delete the old outline (which really consists of a large number of individual shapes). You delete the outline in the same way you eliminated the scales: by using the Arrow tool to select the shapes, then pressing the Delete/Backspace key to eliminate them. To speed things along, after selecting the first shape, press Shift+click to select several more shapes before deleting them. See Figure 4.18.

16. Next, you want to change the color of the outlines back to their original black. This is easy. Start with the outline around the white space in the tail. Make sure the outline and fill are ungrouped. (If they appear with a rectangular marquee around them when you click with the Arrow tool, they are grouped. Press Shift+Cmd/Ctrl+G to ungroup them.)

17. Choose the Ink Bottle tool. When the Ink Bottle modifiers appear, choose black as the color. (Click in the color swatch, then drag to choose a new color.)

18. Click on the outline which color you want to change. Repeat steps 16 through 17 to change the color of the dragon's outline.

19. Now, you want to make sure that this drawing contains as few line segments as possible. Choose the Arrow tool and pass it carefully along all the edges in the image. When the sign next to the Arrow tool looks like a backward *L* rather than a backward *C*, you have found the start of a new line segment. See Figure 4.19.

20. If you think a smooth curve would do the job, drag the cornerpoint so that the two lines look almost straight.

21. Click (or Shift+click if that's the way your preferences are set) on either side of the cornerpoint to select the two lines. Next, click the smooth modifier. The two lines will join into a smooth curve

Note: *You can greatly speed up the selection and deletion of small items, such as the little shapes that make up the outline. Choose the Arrow tool and, starting where no shapes are on the current layer, drag a rectangle around some shapes. Selection rectangles will appear around those that were entirely contained within the rectangle. If you accidentally select shapes, press Shift and click with the Arrow tool to deselect them before pressing Delete/Backspace.*

Figure 4.18 The dragon with its new outlines visible and the old ones removed.

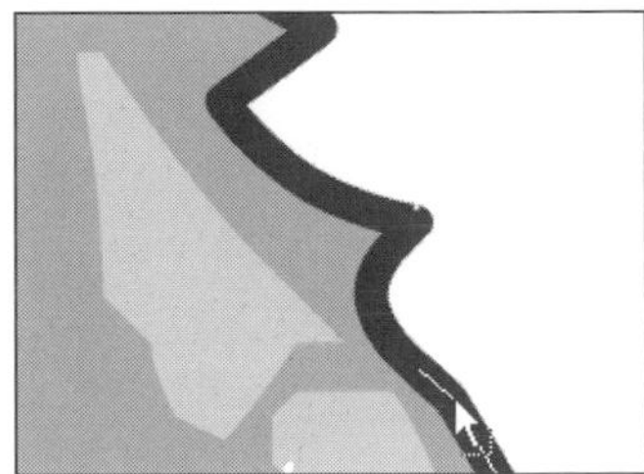

Figure 4.19 The Arrow tool indicating the start/end of a line or curve (known in illustration programs as a *cornerpoint*).

(unless you haven't dragged the cornerpoint far enough, in which case, just try again).

(unless you haven't dragged the cornerpoint far enough, in which case, just try again).

22. Continue to smooth lines as much as possible while maintaining the integrity of the drawing. The result will be the smallest possible file size, which will result in the highest-performance movie. Flash 3 also has the ability to automatically optimize drawings, but you'll find that you get the best results when you learn to combine both techniques. (Chapter 7 will provide more details about automatic optimization.)

23. When you've finished optimizing this item, select all the elements. Press Cmd/Ctrl+G to group them. Now, you will be able to introduce new shapes into the scene or frame without this group's items affecting them.

    If there is any chance that you may also want to use this same drawing (even at different sizes or orientations) in different parts of a scene or movie, you'll also want to save it as a symbol. Symbols can be used in the same movie for an unlimited number of appearances without increasing the overall file size of a movie. Also, symbols are very easy to move from one movie to another.

Note: *When you need to reduce the number of lines in objects that are touching (as are the outlines and their fills in the dragon), you may have trouble editing one object without accidentally editing the other. If this is the case, select the lines you want to smooth, then choose Edit|Edit Selected from the main menu. Now, you can smooth without affecting the neighboring image.*

Learning To Draw Freehand With Flash

If you completed the previous exercises, you already have a pretty good idea of what you can accomplish with Flash's drawing tools. This section will show you more tools and familiarize you with their uses.

If you haven't had much drawing practice, you'll have an easier time in Flash than is likely either on paper or in other programs. That's because Flash employs several means to make your drawing strokes more steady and professional. It's also because Flash has the most desirable qualities of painting and drawing programs. Paint programs seem a bit more intuitive because you draw in them simply by changing the color of the medium, just as you create an image on paper or canvas. The only difference is that in a paint program, you change the color of individual pixels on a screen and in traditional media you change the color by applying color (paint, ink, chalk, or whatever) to the surface. Drawing in Flash is like drawing on paper in that each new line or stroke alters shapes in the image that you put on the canvas. It's also unlike drawing on paper or in a paint program in that you can scale the drawing to any size without losing a speck of resolution. Also, you can easily reshape any existing shape.

To illustrate the differences among drawing programs—and to show how much easier sketching is in Flash (especially for novice artists)—I've drawn the same computer mouse and pad in three programs: Photoshop, the classic bitmap editing program (Figure 4.20); FreeHand 8, the Macromedia illustration program that is bundled with Flash 3 in the Design In Motion suite (Figure 4.21); and Flash (Figure 4.22).

Note: *It's a good idea to save all your drawings as symbols. The symbol files are more portable, more efficient, and much safer from unintentional alteration.*

Photoshop is a paint or bitmapped graphics program. When you paint with an unsteady hand, you get unsteady lines. Also, just as on paper, the only way to edit your sketch is to erase what was already there or to paint over it. There's no way to reshape lines or outlines or to erase part of the graphic without leaving gaps in the picture. If you make this image bigger, the pixels that compose the image get bigger, too.

In the FreeHand drawing in Figure 4.21, you will notice that the curved lines are perfectly smooth. The shape and direction of the lines are controlled by the location of the control points (the small squares that intersect the curves) and the length and direction of the handles. This isn't a very intuitive method for making a shape, but it offers extremely precise control. It's also harder to delete unwanted lines in FreeHand than it is in Flash. (You have to cut the line with the Knife tool, then select the unwanted portion of the line and delete it.)

In the Flash sketch in Figure 4.22, it was never necessary to painstakingly edit control points to get the desired curves. The mouse was sketched freehand with the Pencil tool while the smooth modifier was

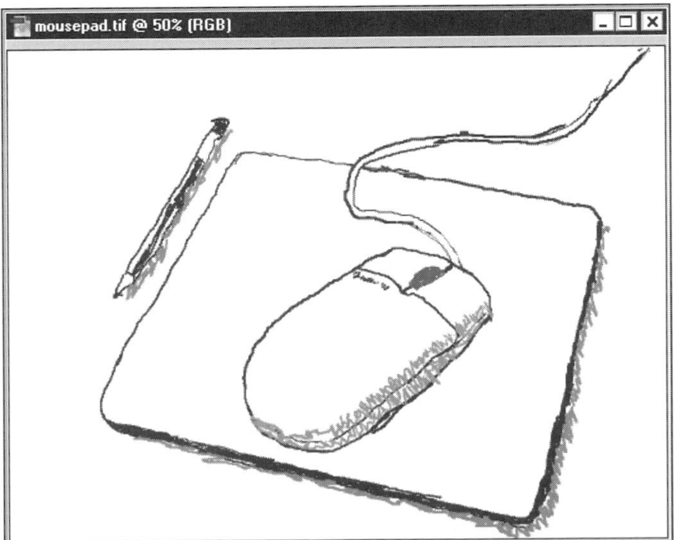

Figure 4.20 Mouse and pad sketched in Photoshop.

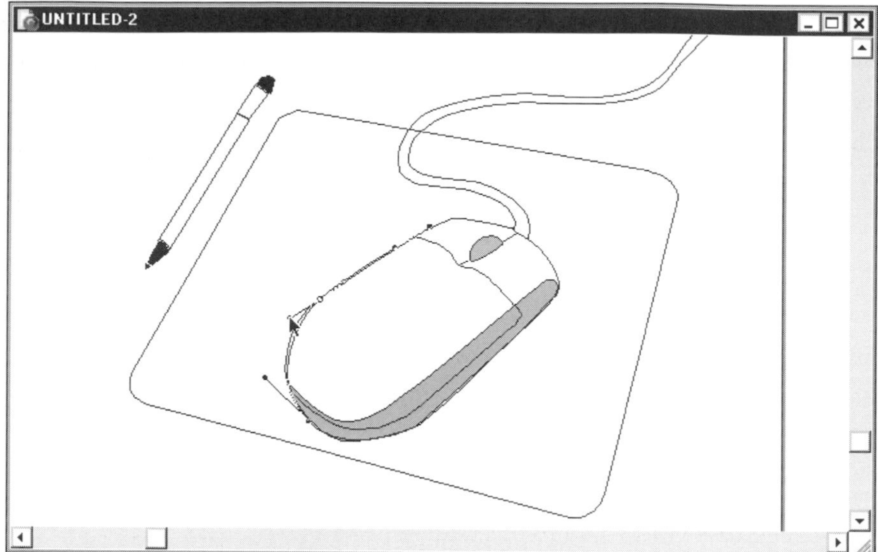

Figure 4.21 The mouse and pad drawn in FreeHand.

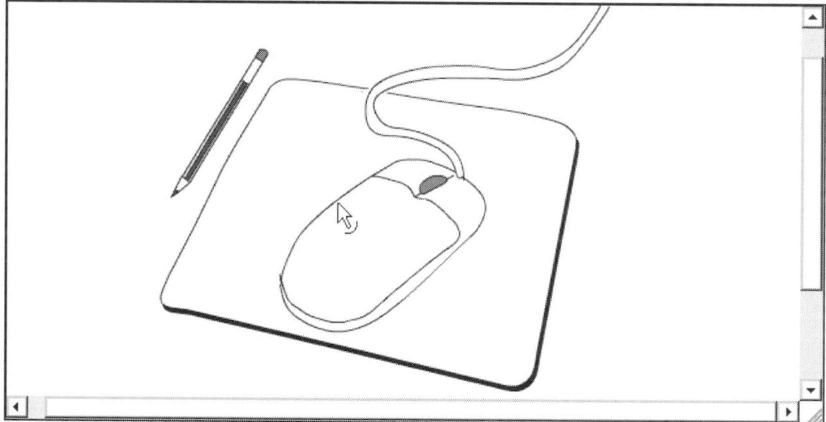

Figure 4.22 The mouse and pad sketched in Flash.

active. The mouse pad was drawn the same way, then scaled to give it the right perspective and copied to make the thick edge. Because shapes are automatically divided where they intersect one another, all you have to do to delete unwanted lines is click to select them and press the Delete/Backspace key.

The following exercise will show you how to draw a wineglass from scratch. In the process, you'll pick up some valuable clues as to how to draw quickly and effectively using Flash. First, take heed of the hints in the next section.

Hints For Drawing Efficiently

Here are some hints concerning good habits to form when drawing with Flash:

- Keep your fingers on the Cmd/Ctrl+Z (undo) and Cmd/Ctrl+Y (redo) keys. Flash can misinterpret the shape you're trying to draw and sometimes oversmooth or overstraighten lines. Also, it's easy to accidentally let a line touch another line, thereby joining it or dissecting it. The easiest cure is to undo and then start over drawing a new shape.
- To draw symmetrical shapes, draw half the unit, copy and paste it, and then flip the copy. Be sure to group the pasted unit before it's deselected to keep it from inadvertently editing any preexisting shapes.
- Group pasted shapes before you deselect them. Then, you can move, adjust, and edit them before you drop them onto the canvas.
- Always draw all the simple shapes independently on a blank canvas. You will find that you'll never have to draw those shapes from scratch again. You will build a library of subjects, drawn in your own style, that you can use over and over again.

Making A Basic Freehand Drawing

In this exercise, you'll draw a wineglass. The exercise contains just enough shapes to let you get used to the Flash drawing tools and their modifiers and to show you how to practice the good habits you are forming. Once you've learned to draw simple subjects like this one, you can draw very complex scenes by adding new simple shapes. By the way, this exercise uses simple oval shapes to let you experience the power of Flash's shape recognition. Ordinarily, it would be faster to draw these ovals with the Pencil tool's oval modifier. Follow these steps to draw the wineglass:

1. Open Flash and choose File|New from the menu bar to open a new movie. In Flash 3, you will automatically get a blank frame set to the default settings for a movie. You are now going to draw a rough geometric shape, an oval. If you're as bad at this as I am, there will be a brief moment when your oval looks something like Figure 4.23. Before you draw the oval, read the next step.
2. To draw the oval, choose the Pencil tool from the toolbox. Notice that the bottom of the toolbox changes to show the modifiers for the Pencil tool. Each tool has its own modifiers that appear in the area just below the toolbox when you choose the tool. At the top of the Pencil modifiers is a button for a dropdown menu called the Pencil Mode menu. Choose straighten (for some odd reason, straighten is the mode Flash uses for shape recognition—whether the shape is oval or rectangular) from the Pencil Mode menu. On the frame canvas, draw an oval approximately like the one shown in Figure 4.23. When you complete the loop, the line will automatically transform into a perfect oval. Well, maybe. If you've been really sloppy, press Cmd/Ctrl+Z to undo and try again. Flash has multiple undo and redo capabilities (with a default of 20 levels), so you can quickly recover from an error.
3. Let's assume that your oval is (oops) vertical instead of horizontal and that it's a bit on the chubby side. (This is going to be the profile of the top rim of wineglass, viewed from an angle slightly above). No problem. Choose

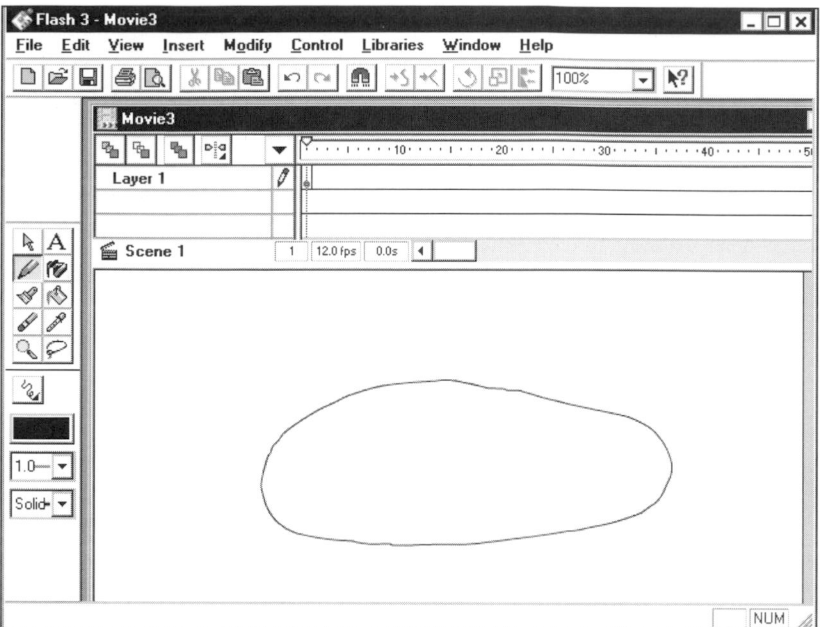

Figure 4.23 The oval before smoothing.

the Arrow tool (press *A*), and click on the oval. The entire oval becomes highlighted with a checkered pattern. Press Cmd/Ctrl+G to group the oval. (Grouping turns the shape into an overlay that floats above the main canvas.) You know this has happened when you see a single checkered selection frame around the entire group (which in this instance is only the oval but could be a drawing with any number of parts, including other overlays). Make sure the Snap icon in the Arrow modifiers is enabled. From the Arrow modifiers, choose the rotate icon. A bounding box with circular handles appears around the oval. Slowly drag the upper right-hand corner handle in a clockwise direction. The oval rotates but seems to do so in small increments. It is snapping to the grid intersections, even though you don't currently have the grid displayed. Stop when the oval has a perfectly horizontal orientation.

4. Now, you want to squeeze the oval a bit so that it looks as though you're seeing the cup from a slightly elevated viewpoint. From the Arrow modifiers, choose the scale icon. The group frame will now appear with eight square handles. You can scale the shape in all directions by dragging the corners. Right now, you want to squeeze the shape. Use the arrow to drag either the top or bottom center handle inward.

5. If you want to scale while preserving the proportions of the original shape, press Shift while dragging. Hold down the Shift key while using the corner handles to scale the oval to the overall size you want.

6. You want to make a rim for the glass. The easy way is to press Cmd/Ctrl+C to copy the oval to the operating system's clipboard and then immediately press Cmd/Ctrl+V. This pastes the grouped oval so that it won't autoedit the other oval if you accidentally deselect it. See Figure 4.24.

7. Turn off Snap. (Make sure the Snap modifier icon is not depressed—if it is, click on it.) Drag the oval up so that it is just below the top oval. You can use the arrow keys on your keyboard to move a selection (including a selected group) in one-pixel increments.

8. Now, you are going to draw the foot of the glass. Press Cmd/Ctrl+V to place another oval group above the canvas. Use the same procedures as in Step 5 to scale this new oval to about two-thirds its original size and place it exactly so that it is centered below the top oval. You can do this with absolute precision in seconds by using Flash's align command. Make sure the Arrow tool is still active and drag a rectangle around the top set of ovals.

Note: *If you want to make your drawings even more efficient, save any repeated geometric shapes (such as the oval in the wineglass drawing) as a symbol. You could then place the symbol and rescale it for each of the oval sections of the following drawing.*

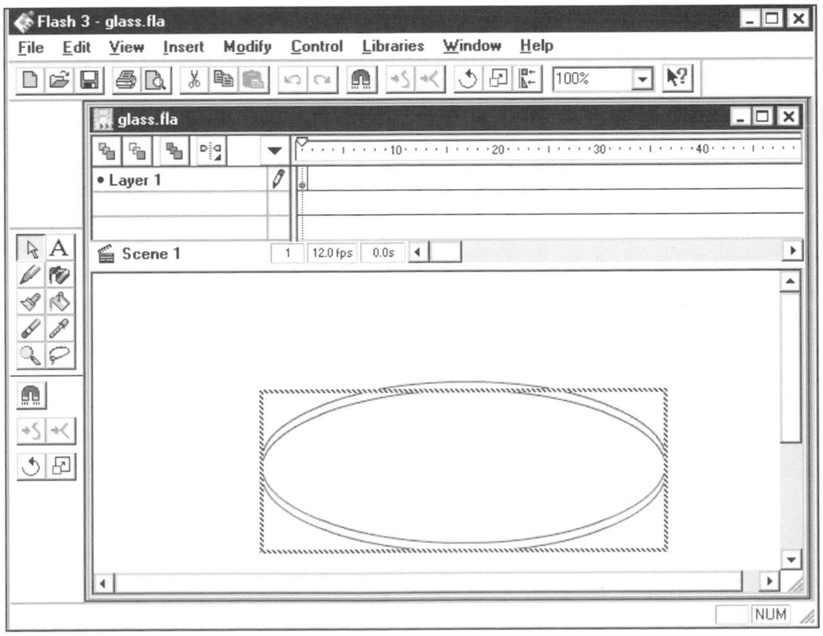

Figure 4.24 The copied oval after pasting.

When they are selected, click on the newest oval to select it. From the menu bar, choose Modify|Align. In the dialog box, click on the icon that indicates that selections will be aligned vertically at their centers. Make sure no other icons are selected and click on OK.

9. Copy, paste, group, and align another foot oval and drag it to just below the original. See Figure 4.25.

10. Once all the ovals are properly scaled and in position, either select each group individually (click on the shape with the Arrow tool) or press Cmd/Ctrl+A to Select All, then press Cmd/Ctrl+U to ungroup. Doing this drops all the shapes onto the canvas, where any overlapping shapes will autoedit one another. All you have to do to remove any superfluous lines is select them with the Arrow tool, then press Backspace/Delete. There's no need to cut lines or add control points—that happens as soon as one shape (line, paint stroke, or fill) is laid atop another. This is what is meant by *autoediting*.

11. In order to help you draw the two symmetrical sides of the glass, turn on the grid. Choose View|Grid from the main menu or press Cmd/Ctrl+Opt/Alt+Shift+G. Count grid spaces to find the center of the glass. You want to draw a temporary guideline here.

12. Choose the Pencil tool and the line modifier. Click to start the vertical line that will divide the glass and Shift+Drag (to turn Snap on so that you can draw an absolutely vertical line). See Figure 4.26.

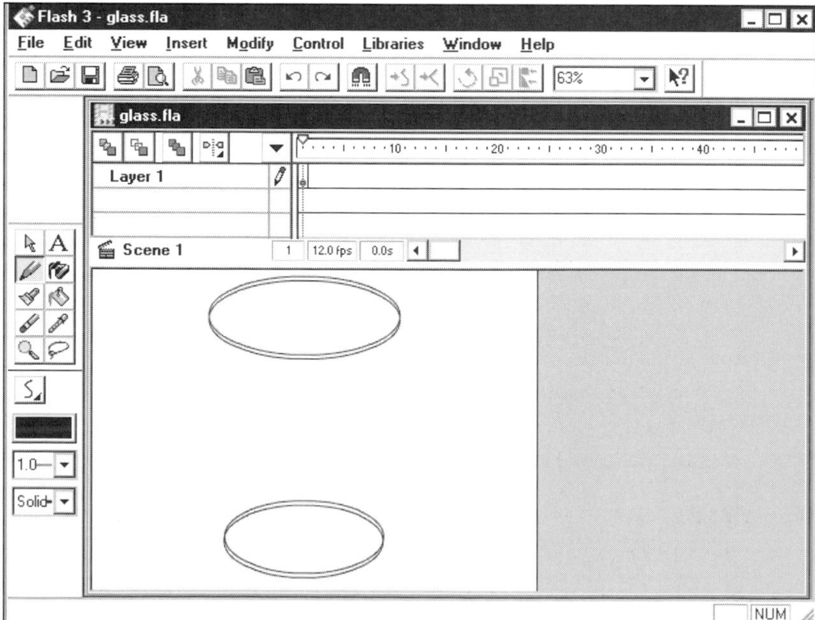

Figure 4.25 The ovals for the lip and foot of the wineglass.

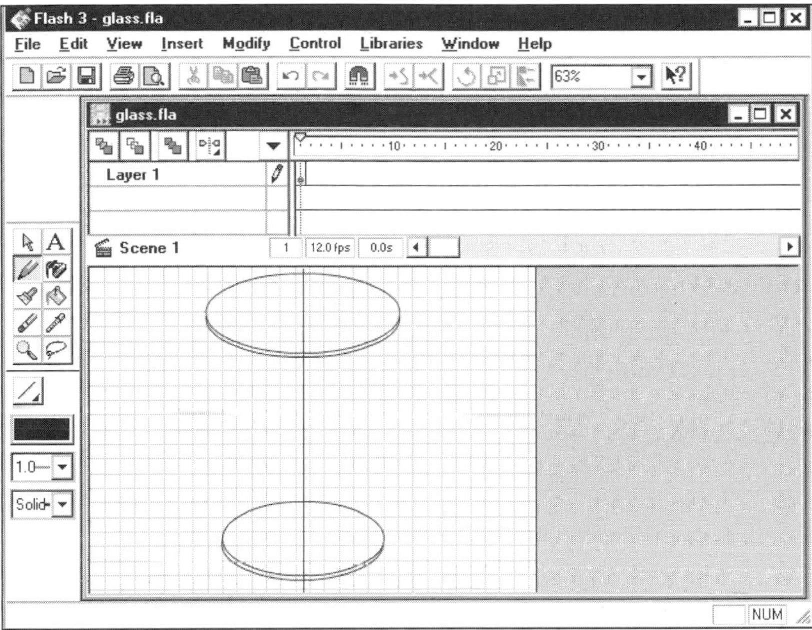

Figure 4.26 The glass with your vertical guideline in place.

13. Now, it becomes easier to draw the sides of the glass. Choose the Pencil tool and make sure that smooth is chosen from the Pencil Mode menu. With nothing selected, press Cmd/Ctrl+G. The lines you have drawn so far dim to indicate that you have created a new, blank group. Draw a curved line from near the lip of the cup to the foot of the cup. If smoothing doesn't give you the profile you want, press Cmd/Ctrl+Z to undo and try again. (It's faster than erasing pencil lines.)

14. One of the pleasant experiences of drawing with Flash is that it's so easy to edit what you draw. Place the Arrow tool cursor near the end of a line or a corner, and a corner symbol appears next to the arrow. Place the arrow anywhere else along a line, and the arrow cursor displays a curve symbol next to it. If you place the arrow inside a selection, a four-way arrow symbol appears, which indicates that dragging will move the selection. Now knowing all this, shape the line just the way you want it. If you make the line undesirably wiggly or bumpy, select it and repeatedly click on the smooth modifier button in the Arrow modifier box.

15. Once you get the line shaped exactly the way you want it, use the Arrow to drag it exactly into place. (See Figure 4.27.) From the menu bar, choose Edit|Edit All. All the shapes will return to their normal color. Click on the new edge curve to select it. The group frame will appear.

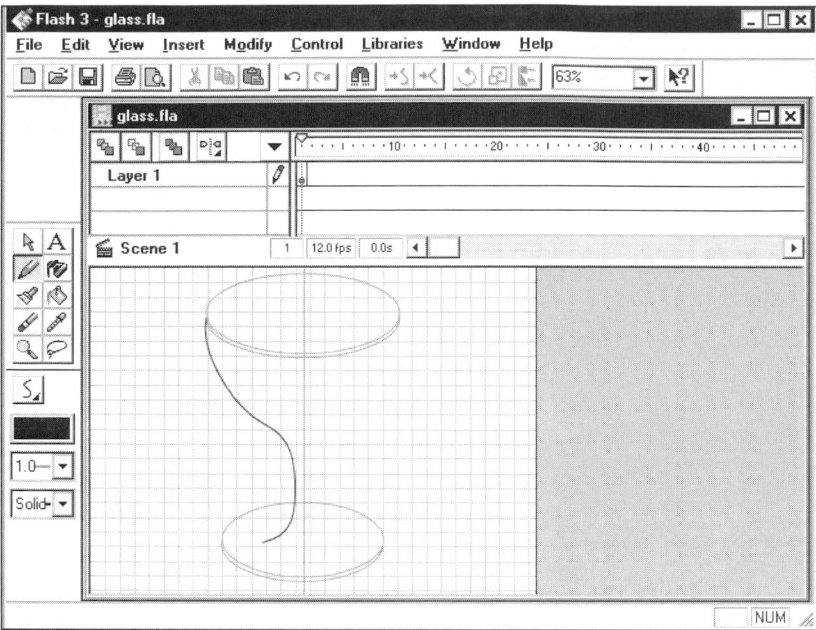

Figure 4.27 The wineglass with the side curve in place.

16. The easy way to make sure that the glass is symmetrical is to copy the left side, and then paste and horizontally flip the pasted copy. Then, join the copy precisely to the original. Flash makes this child's play. Press Cmd/Ctrl+C (or choose Edit|Copy), then Cmd/Ctrl+V (or choose Edit|Paste). A copy of the curved left edge will appear, bounded by a selection rectangle indicating that it is a group.

17. Choose Modify|Transform|Flip Horizontal. Click on the Snap modifier. While the lines are still selected, place the cursor at the left end of the topmost line and drag it until it snaps to the topmost line in the left-hand side of the glass. What you see will look like Figure 4.28. Click anywhere outside the selection to drop it onto the canvas.

18. Now, you can turn off the grid and get rid of the centerline. Choose View|Grid. The checkmark next to the grid option will disappear and so will the grid. Choose the Arrow tool and select each section of the centerline. (Use Shift+Select if you've set your preferences this way.) When all the sections have been selected, press Delete.

19. Now, you want to fill the glass with wine. Choose the Arrow tool and select the topmost curve of the glass. Press Cmd/Ctrl+C, then Cmd/Ctrl+V. A selected copy of the curve will appear near the center of the canvas. Use the Arrow tool to Drag the selection into place as shown in Figure 4.29.

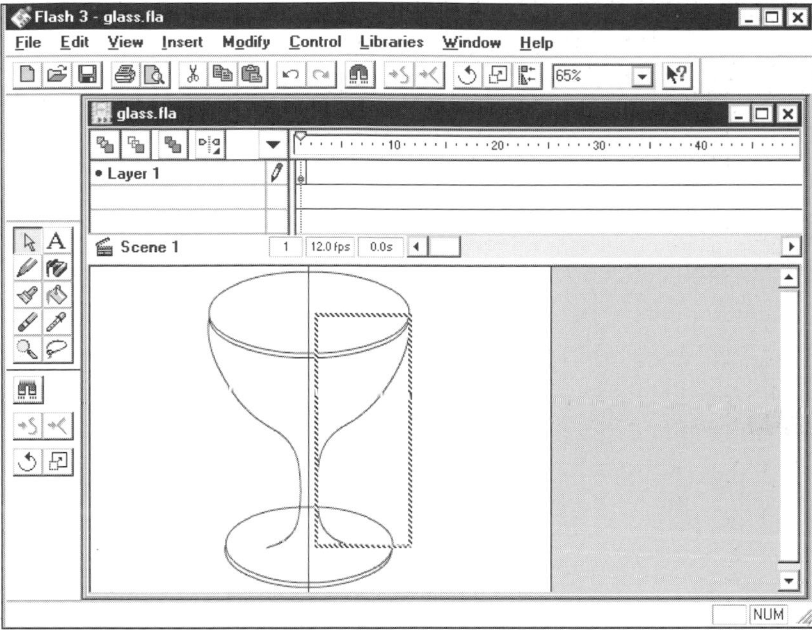

Figure 4.28 The copied and flipped left side of the glass, still selected and snapped to the original.

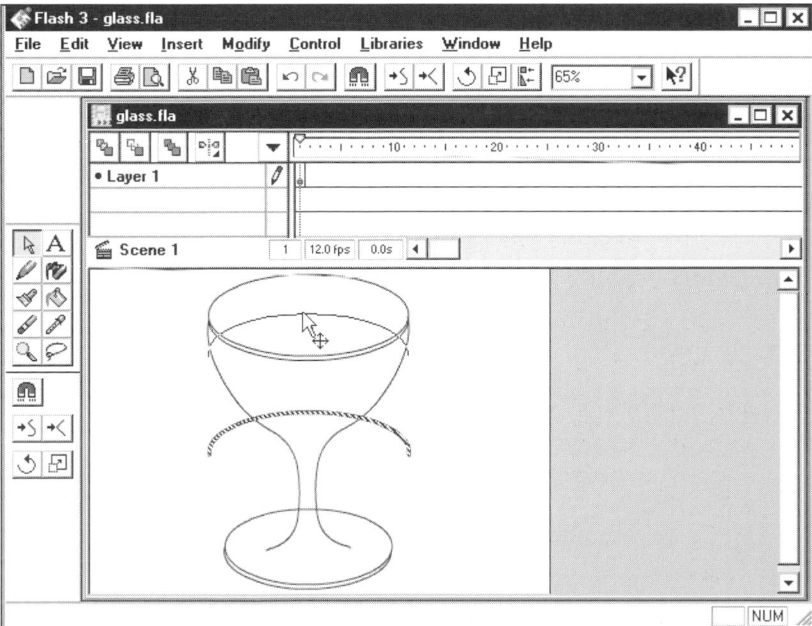

Figure 4.29 Placing a curve for the upper edge of the wine.

20. Next, you will outline the inside of the glass. Use the same techniques as you used to make the edges of the glass: Press Cmd/Ctrl+G to start a new, empty group. Choose the Pen tool with the smooth modifier. Draw one side of the inside of the glass.

21. Choose the Arrow tool and select the line you just drew. Be sure to use the smooth modifier as many times as necessary. Then, press Cmd/Ctrl+C, and then Cmd/Ctrl+V. When the copy of the left side of the line appears, choose Modify|Transform|Flip Horizontal. Finally, drag the flipped copy into place. From the main menu, choose Edit|Edit All. The drawing should now look like Figure 4.30.

22. Now, you will ungroup everything so that any overlapping lines will auto-edit one another. (This procedure makes it very easy to clean up any overlapping or unwanted lines.) Select everything in the image. Either choose Edit|Ungroup from the main menu or press Cmd/Ctrl+Shift+G to ungroup everything.

23. Click in an empty space to deselect everything. To clean up the unwanted lines, choose the Zoom tool and drag a rectangle around any areas that have the small lines you want to remove. When you find a line you want to eliminate, choose the Arrow tool, then select the line segment you want to erase. Finally, press Delete/Backspace. The selected line will disappear. Keep selecting and deleting line segments until the picture looks like that in Figure 4.31.

24. The drawing is almost done. Now, it's time to add the color that represents the wine. You can do this in two ways: with the Brush or with the Paint Bucket. Since you'll learn more by using the

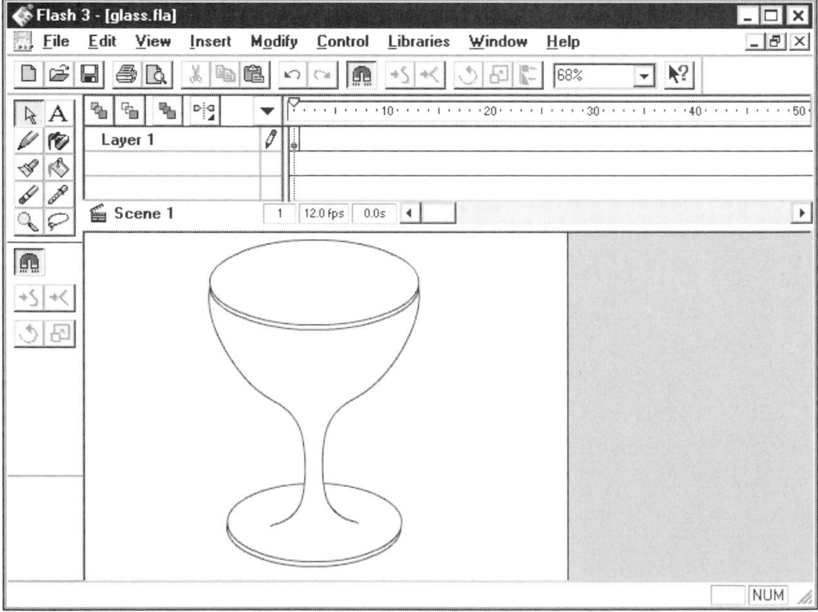

Figure 4.30 The wineglass with the finished lines.

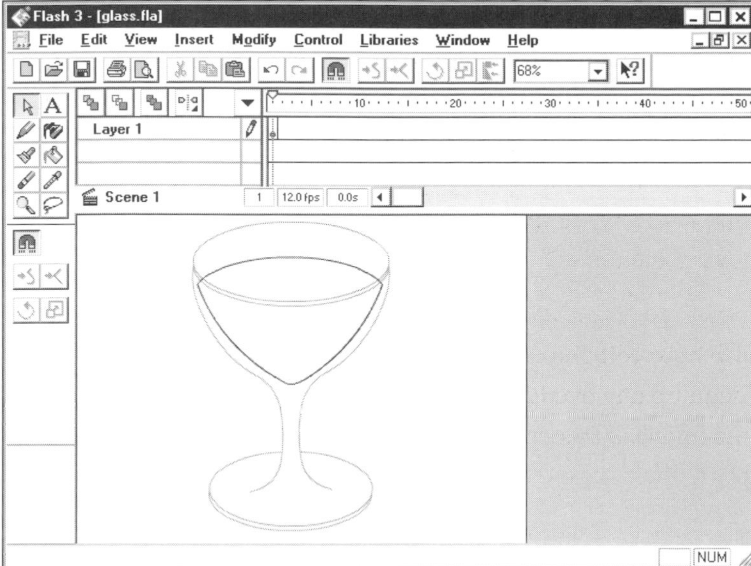

Figure 4.31 The outline for adding wine to the glass.

Brush, choose the Brush tool. Click and drag to pull down the Brush Mode menu and choose the Paint Inside mode.

25. Click on the color swatch in the Brush modifiers. Drag across the pop-up palette and choose an appropriate color for wine, such as burgundy. Now, just paint to fill. (See Figure 4.32.) As long as you start your stroke inside the lines you wish to fill, no color will

Figure 4.32 The partially painted wineglass fill.

accidentally overlap the lines. Don't you wish your mom had given you such a coloring book?

26. Okay, now try filling the glass with the Paint Bucket. Press Cmd/Ctrl+Z repeatedly until the glass is empty. Be sure not to undo any of the lines.
27. Choose the Paint Bucket tool. Choose the Close Small Gaps modifier (and you can choose to close larger gaps if you have them). This will permit a fill even if you have gaps between lines that are too small to notice.
28. Click and drag in the color swatch and choose a burgundy color.
29. Click the Paint Bucket inside the lines that enclose each area you want to fill. You can see the finished wineglass in Figure 4.33.
30. Drag a marquee around the entire drawing (or press Cmd/Ctrl+A), then group and scale it to the size you would like.
31. Now, you want to save it to the library for future use. While the group is selected, press F8 or choose Insert|Create Symbol. In the dialog box, type the name you would like to give to the symbol. Since this isn't a button (not yet, anyway), leave the Button Behavior box unchecked. From the menu bar, choose Window|Library. You'll see the wineglass. To copy the wineglass into this or any other frame, simply drag it onto the canvas. (You can do this as

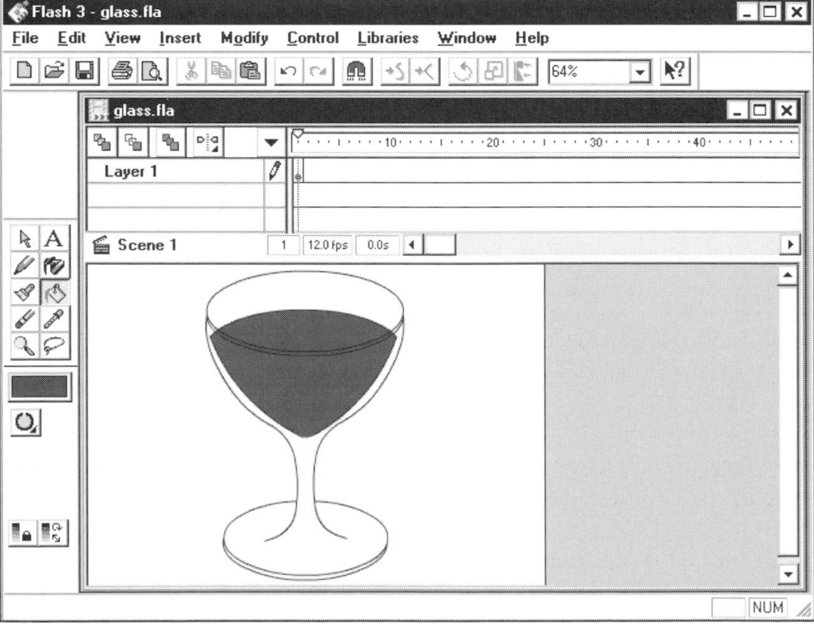

Figure 4.33 The finished, filled wineglass.

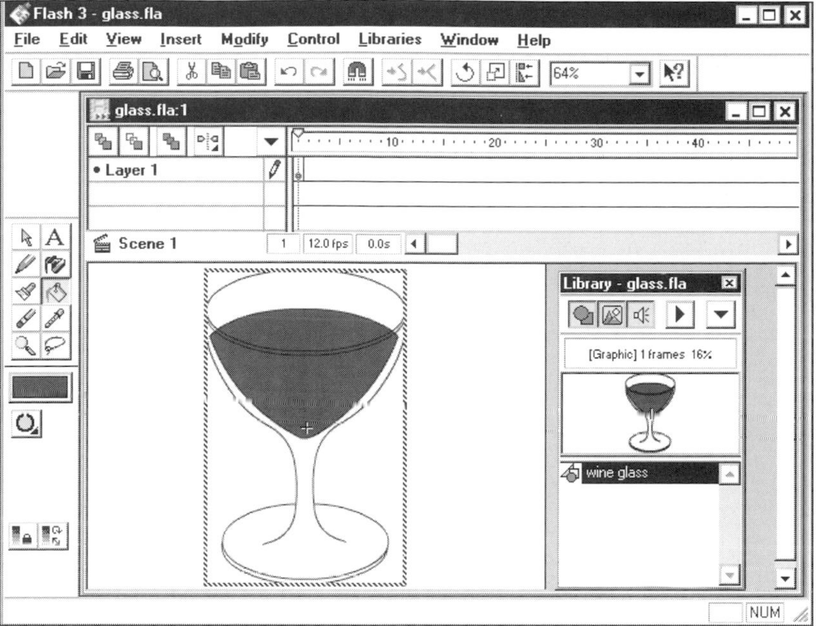

Figure 4.34 The wineglass saved as a symbol in the current library.

many times as you like without using one speck more RAM for your movie. Furthermore, you'll never have to redraw this wineglass.) (See Figure 4.34.) To open the library from another movie, all you have to do is choose File|Open As Library from the menu bar. When you open the chosen movie, all that opens is its library, and you can use any of its symbols, sounds, or bitmaps in the current movie. When you do, these items will be added automatically to your current movie's library.

Drawing With Animation In Mind

In the following exercise, you'll use a pair of very useful techniques to make drawings that you intend to animate. One of these techniques is tracing over a photo, which is useful because photos (including movie or video frame captures) can arrest movement so accurately. The other technique is to create overlays for each component of the drawing, so that you can move them from frame to frame.

In this exercise, you will trace a photo of an in-line skater. All the skater's limbs will be created as individual symbols, so that they can be animated later. We start with the photo seen in Figure 4.35.

To animate the skater in the photo, follow these steps:

1. To import a file contained in a non-Flash (but Flash-compatible) format, choose File|Import, or press Cmd/Ctrl+R and use the

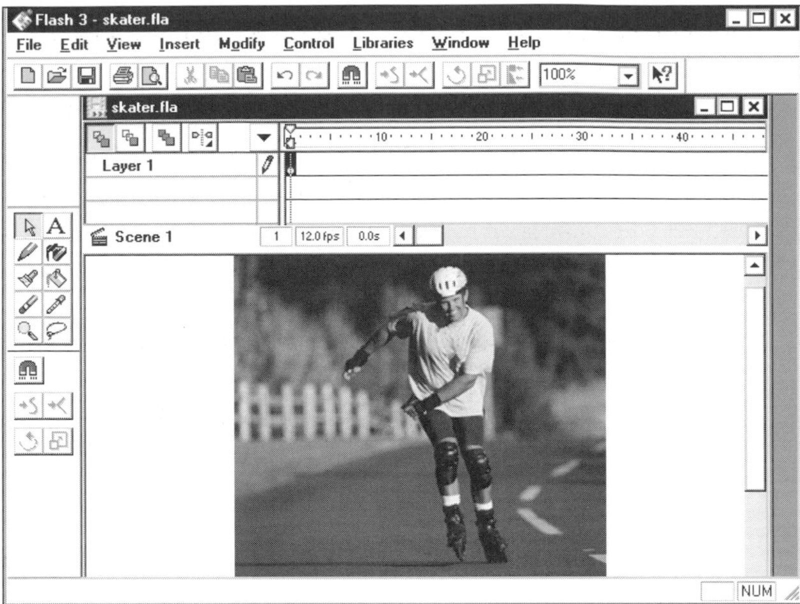

Figure 4.35 The imported PhotoDisc photo.

conventional file dialog boxes to find the desired file. Import the file SKATER.PNG from this book's companion CD-ROM. (This file is from a PhotoDisc CD, but it could just as well have been your own scanned snapshot or one from a digital camera.)

2. If you've ever worked with an illustration program, you're probably familiar with drawing in a tracing mode. In such tracing modes, the image you're tracing is on a separate, locked layer that's been dimmed so that your tracing lines will stand out. Flash doesn't officially have that feature, but you can do the same thing. Click on the second frame in the Timeline. (The frame will turn black, showing that it's selected.) To reveal the Frame menu, click and hold (Mac) or right-click (Windows). (See Figure 4.36.) When the menu drops down, choose Insert Blank Keyframe.
3. Grab the frame slider at the top of the Timeline and drag it to the second frame. The photo will disappear, and you'll see a blank frame. Click on the far-left Onion Skin button. Now you see the photo, dimmed for tracing.
4. You will be working in Frame 2. Keep in mind that you will want to group many of the shapes you draw so that you can keep them independent of the other shapes in the drawing. Choose the Pencil tool (or press *P*). In the Pencil modifiers, choose Hairline for line thickness, Solid for line style, Ink for Pencil mode, and black for the color. (If you really need to contrast your outlines, you can

temporarily make them contrast outrageously with the photo, then use the Ink Bottle later to change them to something more "normal.") Plan to keep these settings for the Pencil for all of your outline tracing. Choose the Magnifier (press *M*) and drag a marquee tight around the face and neck. Press *P* (to choose the Pencil) and trace an outline for the skater's face. You will trace the helmet separately. The result should look like Figure 4.37.

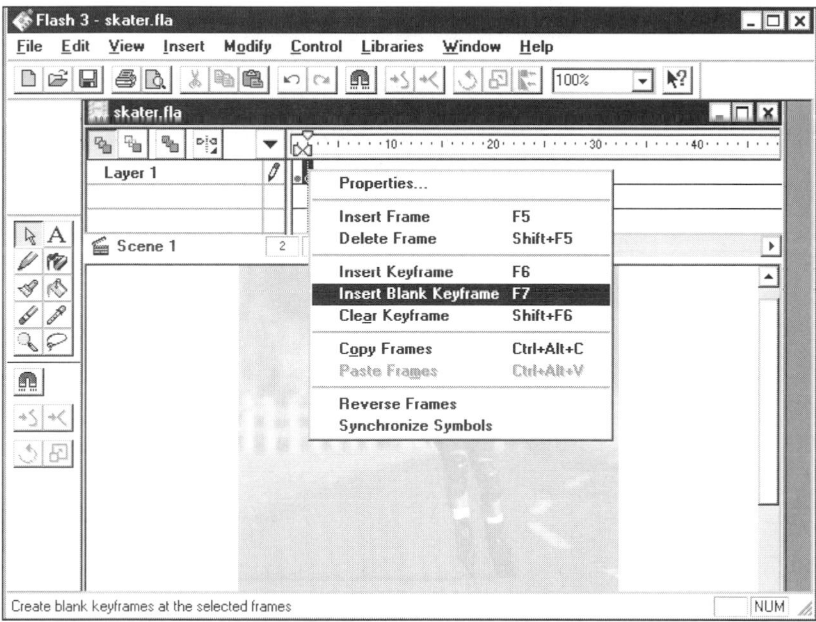

Figure 4.36 The Frame menu.

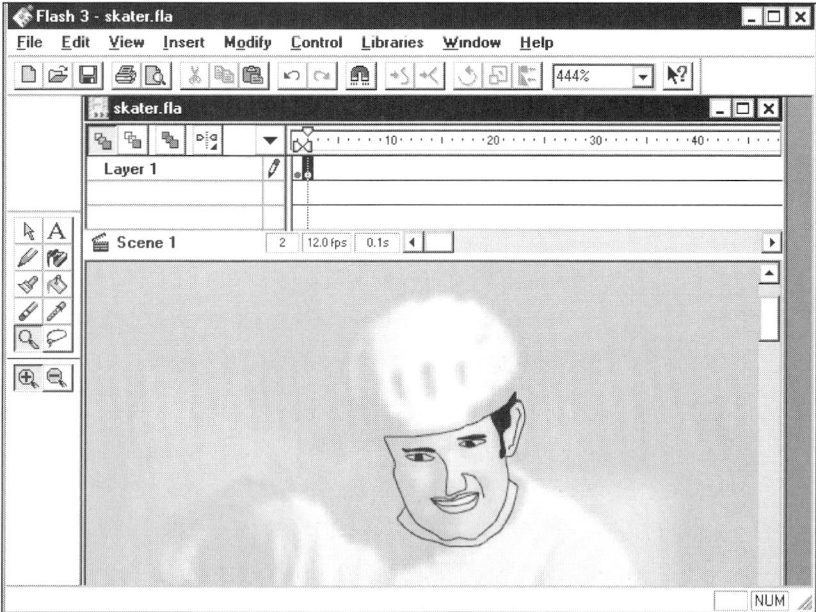

Figure 4.37 Tracing the face.

5. Choose the Arrow tool, drag a marquee around the facial lines you've traced, and press Cmd/Ctrl+G to group what you've done so far. To continue to work only within the confines of the lines in the group, choose Edit|Edit Selected.
6. Next, use the Brush to paint in shaded areas of the skin. If you have a pressure-sensitive pad, you'll want to choose the pressure toggle in the Brush modifiers. Also in the Brush modifiers, choose Paint Inside from the Brush Mode menu. Choose appropriate brush sizes (larger brushes generally make smoother shapes). To pick colors for the shading, drag the frame indicator to the first frame and turn off onion-skinning. Then, choose the Dropper and pick up the color you want to shade from the photo.
7. When you have all the shading in place, you'll want to edit it for smoothness. Zoom in (so you'll have better control over details) and use the Arrow to drag the edges of your brush strokes so that they are close to being as smooth as you'd like. Then, choose the Lasso, outline edges that need further smoothing, and then choose Modify|Curves|Optimize. In the Optimize Curves dialog box (Figure 4.38), set the slider in the middle and click on OK. A subdialog will appear, showing you how many curves have been consolidated. Optimizing curves not only makes them look smoother and more professional, but also makes file sizes smaller—very important when drawings are to be used as Web graphics or animations.

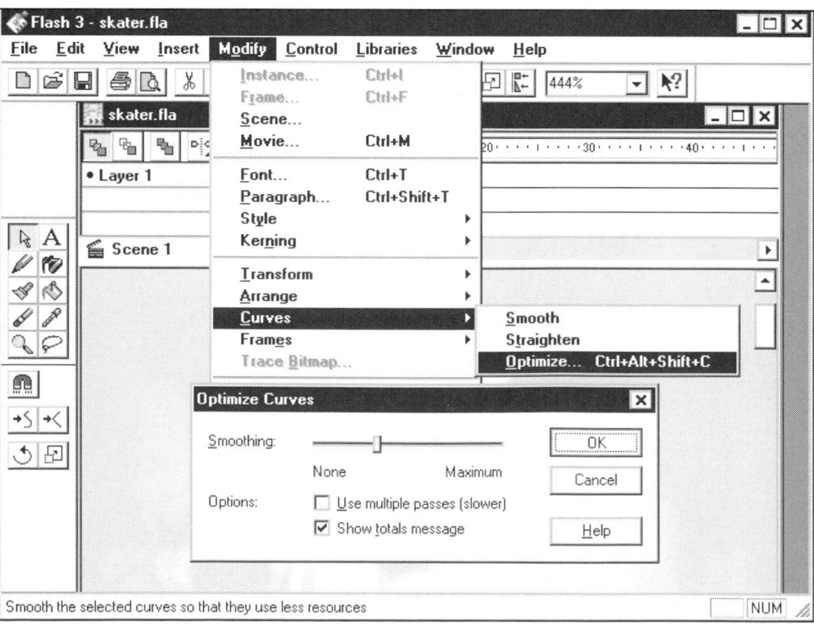

Figure 4.38 The Optimize Curves dialog box.

8. When you have finished doing all the highlight and shadow shading with the Brush, choose the Dropper (press *D*), slide the frame pointer back to Frame 1, and choose a skin tone. If you want to modify this tone, choose the color modifier to open the color palette, then choose the palette icon at the bottom of the dialog box. Now, you can type in red/green/blue (RGB) values, or move the slider up and down the intensity scale in order to lighten or darken the tone you have picked. If you want to do elaborate shading involving many shades of the same tone in a given area, leave this dialog box on screen so you have instant access to making subtle color changes. From time to time, you can choose the Onion Skin button to show or hide the bitmap in Frame 1. Figure 4.39 shows the shaded head with onion-skinning turned off. You can give quite a bit more depth to the head by shading it with a radial gradient. You will want to use lighter and darker tones of the same skin tone you chose previously. Choose the Dropper and click on the facial tone fill color. This will be the current color for all tools until you change it.

9. Choose the Paint Bucket, then the color modifier, and then the palette button. The color dialog box appears (see Figure 4.40); jot down (or memorize) the RGB values for the current color. Press the gradient tab. Click on the leftmost pointer above the gradient box to activate it, then enter the RGB values for the skin tone. Adjust

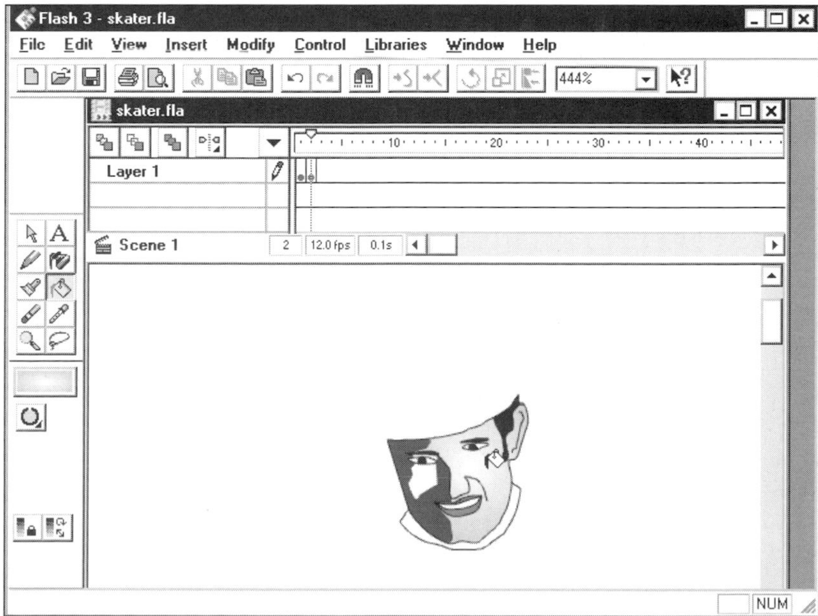

Figure 4.39 The shaded head with onion-skinning turned off.

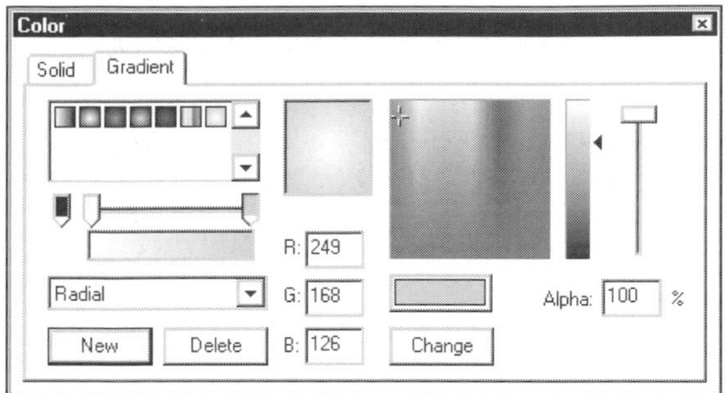

Figure 4.40 The Gradient tab in the Color dialog box.

the density slider (at far right) to a slightly lighter tone. Click on the right-hand gradient pointer, enter the same RGB values, and then slide the density slider down to a somewhat lower number. The left end of the gradient bar should now be a light skin tone, while the right end is a darker one. Choose Radial from the Gradient Type menu (just above the New button). Finally, click on the New button to keep this gradient for further use. You can click on the close box or leave the Color dialog box active for future changes. Unfortunately, the Color dialog box gobbles a big chunk of screen acreage. (What I wouldn't give for a hotkey that popped this up.)

10. Make sure the Paint Bucket is still your chosen tool. Click inside the outline of the head, then click on the Lock Gradient toggle in the Bucket modifiers. Continue to click wherever you see empty space. All the areas of the gradient should look contiguous, as though you'd filled behind all the shaded areas.

11. Now, you want to move, scale, and rotate the gradient so that you can place the shading exactly where you want it. In the Paint Bucket modifiers, click on the Scale Gradient toggle. Click anywhere in the gradient. The gradient will be surrounded with a circular selection frame with three handles. (See Figure 4.41.) The square handle makes the gradient more circular or oval. The round handle just below it scales the overall size of the gradient. The bottom round handle rotates the gradient. There's also a handle in the center of the gradient, which you'll drag to move the center. Now that you know what the handles are used for, position, scale, and rotate the gradient until it looks right to you. There are no hard and fast rules here. After all, you're an artist now.

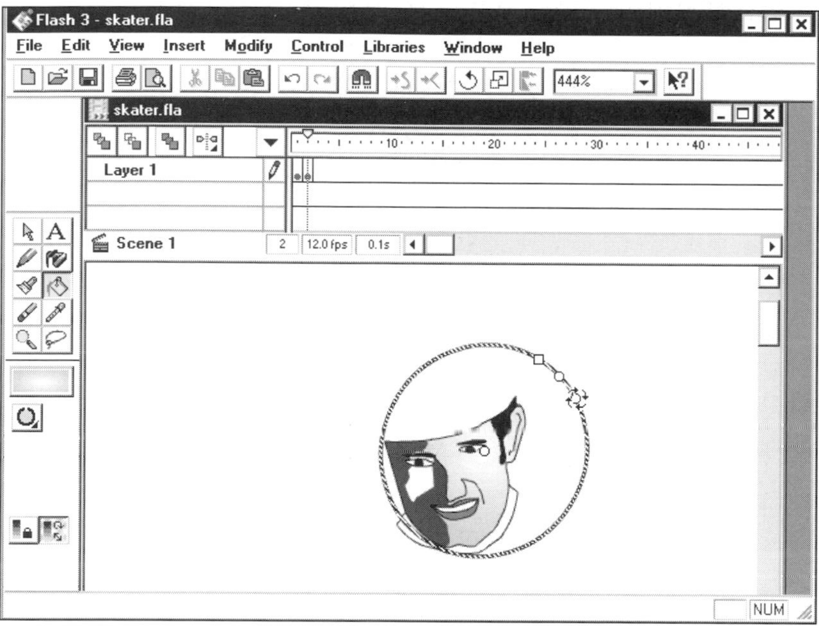

Figure 4.41 Transforming and moving the gradient to control its focus.

12. Choose the Arrow tool and drag a marquee around the entire head. Choose Insert|Create Symbol. You now have a drawing of a head that you can use for many purposes—including incorporating it into other parts of this drawing. Zoom out to full frame. Click on the first Onion Skin icon so you can see your photograph again.

13. Zoom in to the head again, but be sure to include the helmet. Select the face symbol and move it out of the way temporarily. Choose the Pencil and trace the helmet. Once the outline is drawn, reshaped, and smoothed to your liking, choose the Arrow tool and select the entire outline. Press Cmd/Ctrl+G to group. Double-click inside the group to edit the group, and fill the areas of the helmet that should be shaded. When you have finished, double-click outside the silhouette of the hair or choose Edit|Edit All.

14. Now, you want to draw the little chunk of hair that falls behind the face. Follow all the procedures in the immediately preceding step. When you have finished editing the group, choose Modify|Arrange|Send To Front. The head and helmet should now appear as in Figure 4.42. Lasso the entire head and hair and choose Insert|Create Symbol. In the dialog box, name the symbol "head and helmet."

Figure 4.42 The head and helmet.

15. Choose View|Show Frame. Click on the Onion Skin icon. Choose the Arrow tool and drag the head symbol to one side so that you get a clear view of the T-shirt. Outline the T-shirt with the Pencil. Select and group the outlines, then double-click on the outline to enter Group Edit mode. Choose the Paint Brush and set the mode to Paint Inside. Lift the color from the photo of the T-shirt in Frame 1. If you want to get fancy, gradient fill the shaded areas (but in the interest of efficient movies, keep fancy to a minimum). Then, choose a yellow and set the mode to Paint Behind. Now, paint the T-shirt. Choose Edit|Edit All. Select the jacket group and choose Modify|Arrange|Send To Back. If you've moved the head and hair symbol out of the way, drag it back into position. Choose Edit|Select All (Cmd/Ctrl+A), and then choose Insert|Create Symbol. In the dialog box, name the symbol "head and T-shirt."

16. Follow the same procedures to make the rest of the components of the drawing. If you save all the components as symbols, you'll gain four advantages:

    a. You may be able to use the symbols in other movies.

    b. It will be much easier to move body parts for animation without having to redraw them.

    c. It will be much easier to place objects over and under one another to compose the drawing.

    d. You can always edit an individual object or symbol without disturbing the rest of the drawing.

    You can see the finished drawing in Figure 4.43.

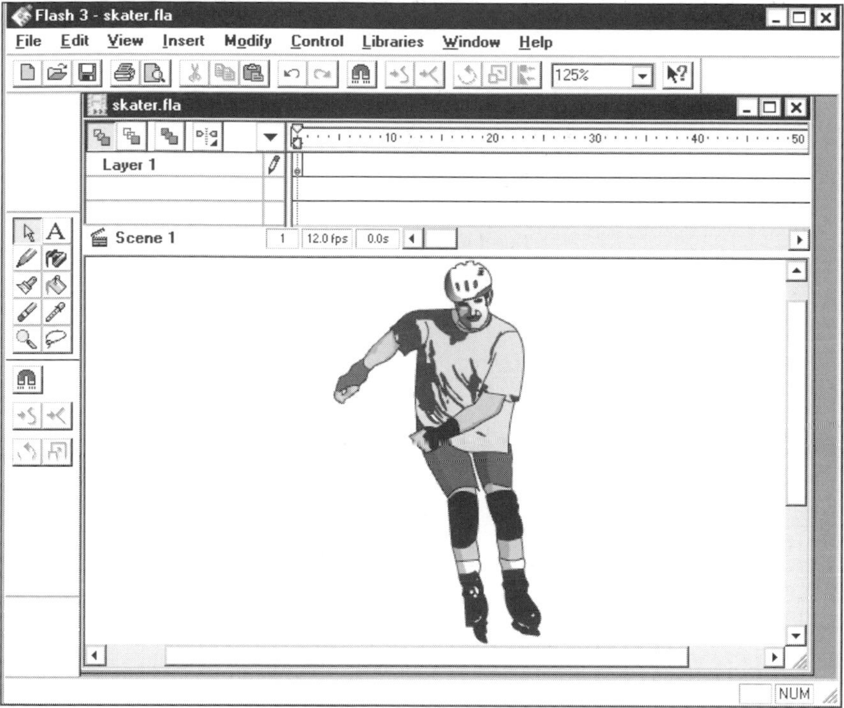

Figure 4.43 The finished traced drawing.

The Drawing Tools And Their Modifiers

Flash's toolbox looks deceptively simple. It has only 10 tools, and most of us are already familiar with their basic functions: Arrow, Text, Pencil, Ink Bottle, Brush, Paint Bucket, Eraser, Dropper, Magnifier, and Lasso. You've already been introduced to the basic functions of these tools in Chapter 2. This section will not only describe the tools in more depth but also give you some tips and tricks for using them.

The toolbox is divided into two parts: tools and tool modifiers. All the Flash tools, with the exception of the Dropper, have modifiers. Modifiers dictate the behavior of the chosen tool and their icons automatically appear in the lower half of the toolbox when you choose their parent tool. Figure 4.44 shows the toolbox.

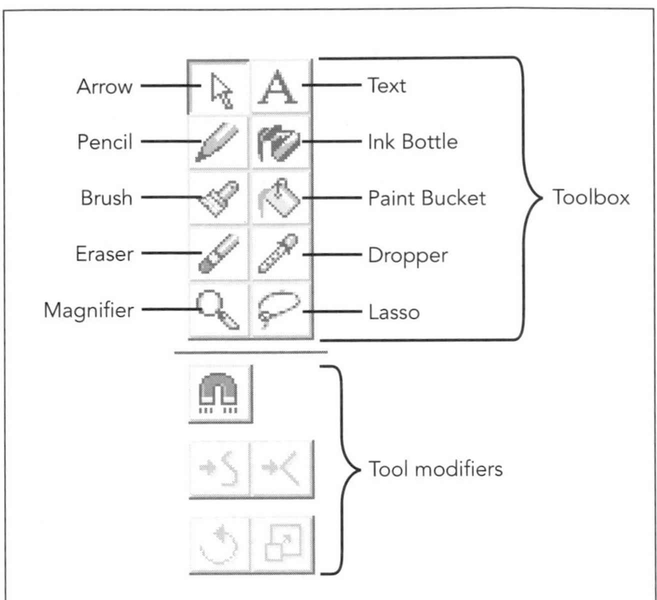

Figure 4.44 The Tools palette with the Arrow tool chosen.

Arrow Tool

To choose the Arrow tool, click on its icon in the toolbox or press *A*. When the Arrow is the chosen tool, the cursor changes to an arrow. The Arrow tool makes and edits selections. Selected entities are always identified by a checkered pattern imposed upon them. In order to modify an entity using any of Flash's commands or modifiers, you must first select it. This includes turning entities into groups or symbols. You can make a selection in one of the ways shown in Table 4.1.

Table 4.1 Arrow tool cursor functions.

Cursor	Function
	Click the arrow cursor directly on an entity (line, fill, group, symbol, and text). You can select multiple entities with multiple clicks. (If you wish to press Shift+click before adding entities, choose File|Preferences from the main menu and check the Shift Select box.)
	Double-click the arrow cursor on any entity (except overlays). All connected entities will be selected.
	Drag a marquee around a section of the drawing. If you cover only a part of the drawing, that part will be separated from the rest of the drawing, cutting all lines and fills that intersect the marquee path. (You must press Shift if you want to select multiple marquee entries.) This is very useful for isolating only a section of an entity for smoothing, straightening, or optimizing.

Arrow Tool Modifiers

When you select the Arrow tool, the Arrow modifiers appear in the lower section of the toolbox. Figure 4.45 shows the Arrow tool modifiers. Table 4.2 explains the function of each Arrow tool modifier.

Table 4.2 Arrow tool modifiers.

Name	Function
Snap	Causes the arrow's drag point to jump precisely to either a grid intersection or a particular spot on an entity, whichever is closer. You can snap an entity to another entity's center, midpoint, or endpoint. You can also make one object abut another. When Snap is on, the Snap icon is ghosted and the arrow cursor has a circle. See Figure 4.46.
Smooth	Causes the selection to have a smoother curve. Repeatedly choosing this modifier continues to make the curve smoother. Remember to experiment by using this modifier in combination with the multilevel undo and redo commands. See Figure 4.47.
Straighten	Causes the selection to have a straighter line. Repeatedly choosing this modifier continues to make the curve straighter (or the curve smoother). Remember to experiment by using this modifier in combination with the multilevel undo and redo commands. See Figure 4.48.
Rotate	Actually performs two kinds of transformations: rotating and skewing. Dragging a corner handle with the arrow cursor rotates freely. If you do this with Snap turned on, it's easy to rotate in 90-degree (and smaller) increments. Dragging a center handle with the arrow cursor slants the selection. See Figure 4.49.
Scale	Corner handles resize the selection in all dimensions simultaneously. Press Shift while scaling with the corner handles to preserve the proportions of the original. Dragging the center handle shrinks or stretches in a single dimension. See Figure 4.50.

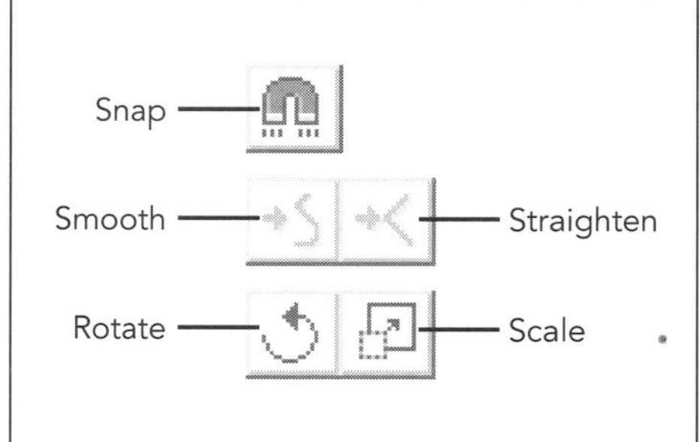

Figure 4.45 The Arrow tool modifiers.

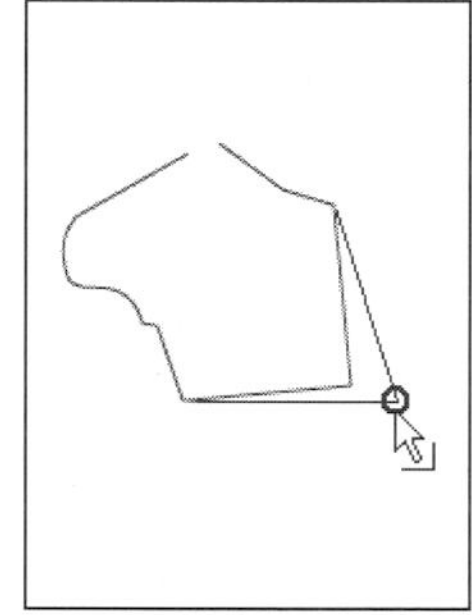

Figure 4.46 Moving a cornerpoint with Snap turned on.

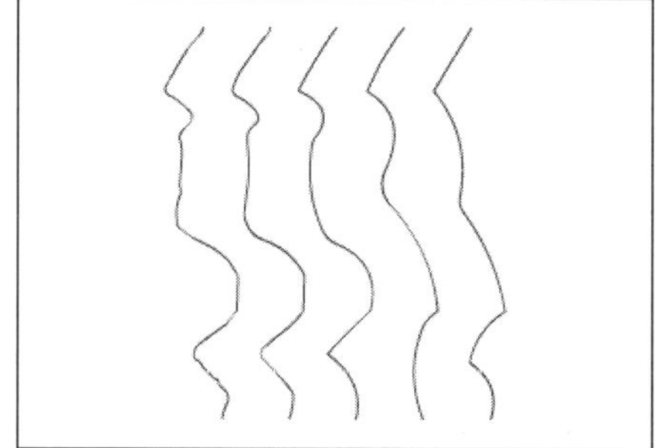

Figure 4.47 The same smoothed pencil line, copied four times. Each successive line was smoothed by one more click than its predecessor.

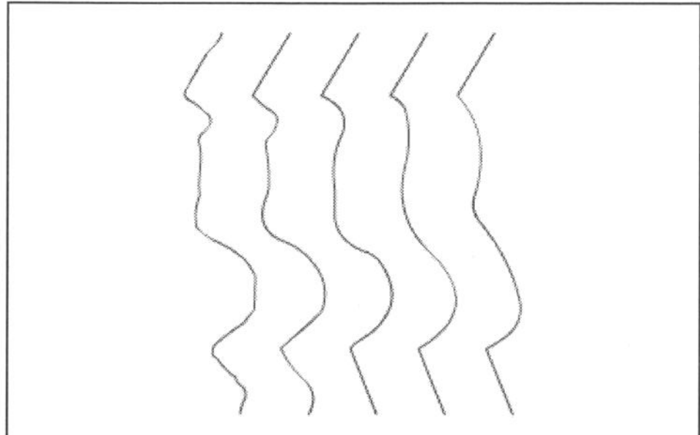

Figure 4.48 The same smoothed pencil line, copied four times. Each successive line was straightened by one more click than its predecessor.

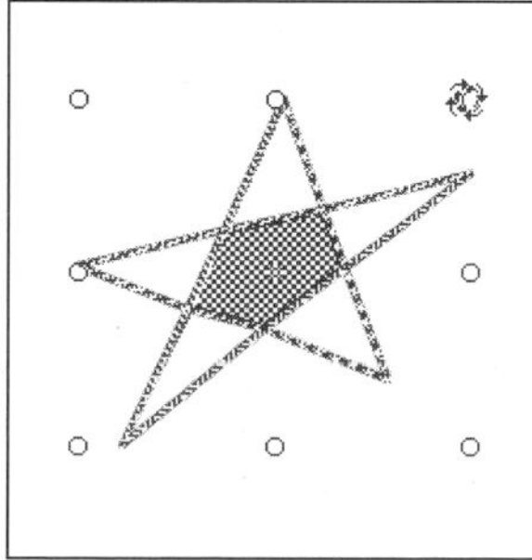

Figure 4.49 Slanting and rotating with the rotate modifier.

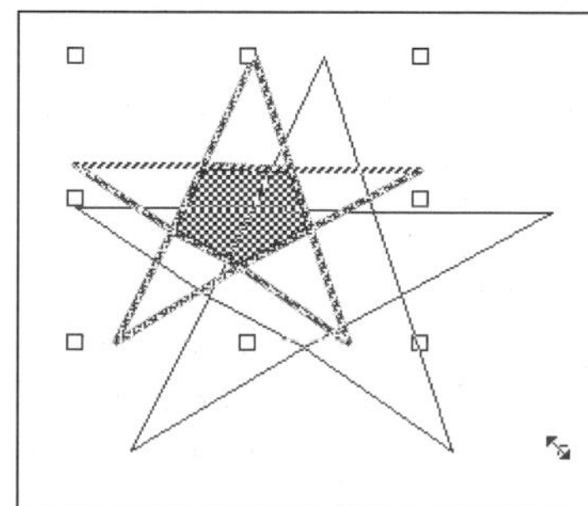

Figure 4.50 Scaling and stretching with the scale modifier.

Text Tool

To choose the Text tool, click on its icon in the toolbox or press *T*. When Text is the chosen tool, the cursor changes to an A with a cross hair at the upper left. The Text tool is used to enter text. Text is always entered as an overlay, so it won't dissect graphics on the underlying canvas (unless you break it apart).

Another advantage of text being entered as an overlay is that you can edit it anytime. Simply select it with the Text tool and drag across the portion of the text that you wish to edit. You can now enter new text, replace text, or use any of the Text modifiers to change a portion of the text. The text in Figure 4.51 was entered, the brush strokes were painted on top, then partially highlighted, and then the font size and style were changed. The brush strokes immediately appeared behind the letters, because the brush strokes were painted on the canvas and the text is always an overlay, unless it's broken apart.

As long as you don't break text apart, you can scale it to any proportionate size by dragging the handle at upper right. See Figure 4.52.

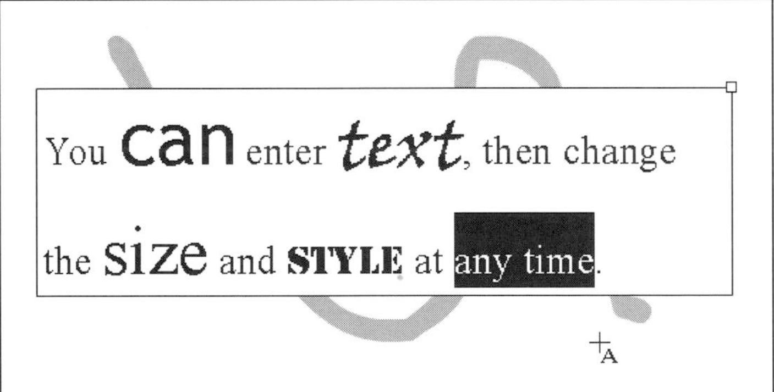

Figure 4.51 Text is automatically grouped when entered. Simply choose the Text tool to revise at any time.

Figure 4.52 Text, immediately after breaking apart.

You also can choose to edit text as shapes. To do this, simply choose Modify|Break Apart from the menu bar. The text will become checkered, to indicate that it is selected, as in Figure 4.52.

Immediately after breaking apart or ungrouping text or an object—while it is still checkered as in Figure 4.52—the shapes are still temporarily "floating" above the canvas. You can avoid autoediting the underlying shapes on the canvas by pressing Cmd/Ctrl+G or choosing Modify|Group. You then can continue to edit the group independently by selecting it and choosing Edit|Selected from the menu bar.

Once you've deselected an ungrouped or broken underlay, it immediately becomes a part of the image on the canvas. Letters have to be selected individually because dragging a marquee or using a Lasso would result in selecting other, contiguous shapes as well. See Figure 4.53.

Even if you select text individually and move it, you will leave "holes" in the shapes that were touching it. See Figure 4.54, and notice that the Arrow tool has been used to reshape an edge of the *d* in the word *and*. Once text has been broken apart, it can be edited just like any other shapes in Flash.

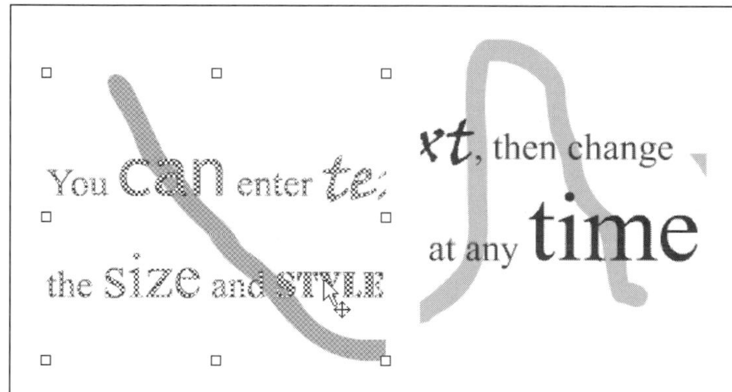

Figure 4.53 Oops. This text was selected and moved.

Figure 4.54 Moving broken-apart text after individually selecting letters.

The Text tool creates two kinds of text: label and block. Label text simply expands from the cursor to accommodate as much text as you type. (Its name comes from the fact that it's a very useful way to enter callout labels on a drawing.) (See Figure 4.55.) To enter label text, choose the Text tool from the toolbox or press *T*, then click on the point in your drawing where you want the label to appear.

Block text is also entered after choosing the Text tool, but by dragging the cursor to indicate an area large enough to accommodate the paragraph you want to enter. Block text looks like Figure 4.56, and is the mode you usually will use for creating headlines, banners, and blocks of copy.

You can change block text to label text, and vice versa, by double-clicking on the small handle at the upper-right corner of the text edit frame. If the handle is round, you are in label mode; if it's square, you are in block mode.

Flash's text can be displayed as antialiased at any time. Actually, Flash graphics can be displayed in three ways: Fast, Smooth, and Text Smooth. Only the latter displays text as antialiased. (Antialiasing gives text very smooth edges for display on the Web.) Figure 4.57 shows the result of displaying the same text as in Figure 4.56, but with Text Smooth turned on. To turn on antialiasing for text, choose View|Antialias Text from the menu bar.

Figure 4.55 Entering label text.

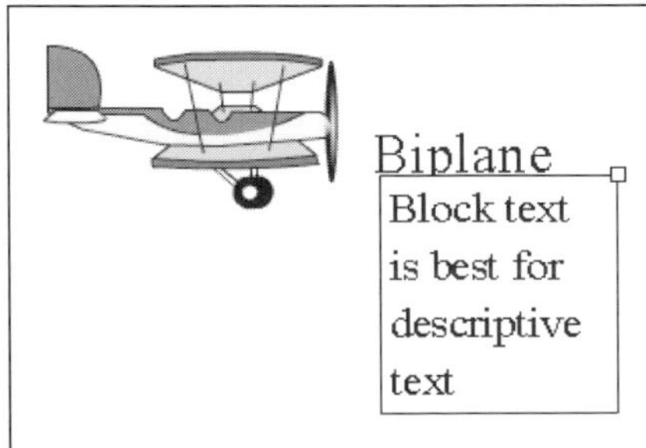

Figure 4.56 Entering block text.

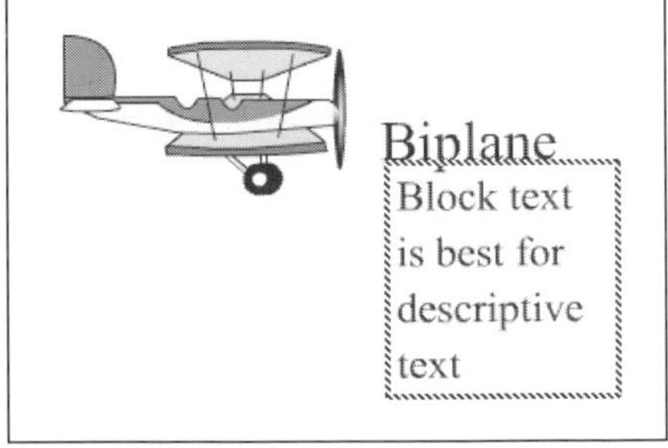

Figure 4.57 The same text with Antialias Text turned on.

It is not a good idea to use antialiasing in animations that are intended to display at a higher frame rate, because the target browser has to take extra time to render the smooth edges. It's also not a good idea to antialias text that will be exported as a GIF file with a transparent background, because the antialiasing will mix in colors from the current background that may clash with the colors in the target background, creating an unsightly halo around the text.

You can change the size and proportion of text without breaking it apart. To do this, choose either Modify|Transform|Scale or Modify|Transform|Scale and Rotate, or choose the Arrow tool and use its scale modifier. Figure 4.58 shows text that has been stretched in a single dimension. Scaling text by this method does not remove its overlay status.

Figure 4.58 Text stretched in a single dimension with the scale command.

Text Tool Modifiers

When you select the Text tool, the Text modifiers appear in the lower section of the toolbox. See Figure 4.59. Table 4.3 explains the functions of the Text modifiers.

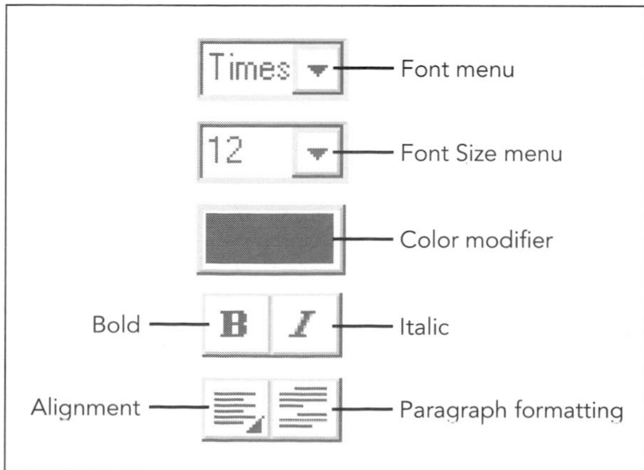

Figure 4.59 The Text tool modifiers.

Table 4.3 Text tool modifiers.

Name	Function
Font menu	The standard Windows or Macintosh font menu. It allows you to choose any font installed for your system. You can change fonts within a block or label by highlighting them and choosing a new font. You also can change fonts with the Modify|Font command.
Font Size menu	Changes the font size. If you don't find the size you want on the menu, you can enter any number you like in the menu box.
Color modifier	Brings up a palette of 216 Web-safe colors. These are the best colors to use when designing for any 256-color display, because this palette avoids colors that are used by the system or browser. You aren't limited to this palette, however. You can create your own colors by clicking on the palette icon at the bottom of the color palette and choosing them from a standard color chooser in as many colors as your display will allow. You can use this Color dialog box to change the standard palette by choosing a color and then clicking on either the New or Change buttons. Clicking on New adds a color, and clicking on Change changes the color of any selected swatch in the palette. If you want a specific RGB value, you can enter numbers directly in the RGB boxes. The Color dialog box is shown in Figure 4.60.
Bold	Toggles bold on and off. If you click on this button before you enter any text, all the text will be bold. You also can highlight any amount of text after you've entered it, then click on the button to change it to bold and vice versa. Only the highlighted text will be changed.
Italic	Toggles italic on and off. Works just like the bold toggle.
Alignment	Displays a pull-down menu that gives you a choice of aligning text to the left, center, or right, or having it justify.
Paragraph formatting	Brings up a dialog box that lets you set margins, indentation, and line spacing by any of the acceptable units of measurement. (The default is pixels.) Acceptable abbreviations for unit type are *px* for pixels, *pt* for points, *cm* for centimeters, *mm* for millimeters, and " for inches.

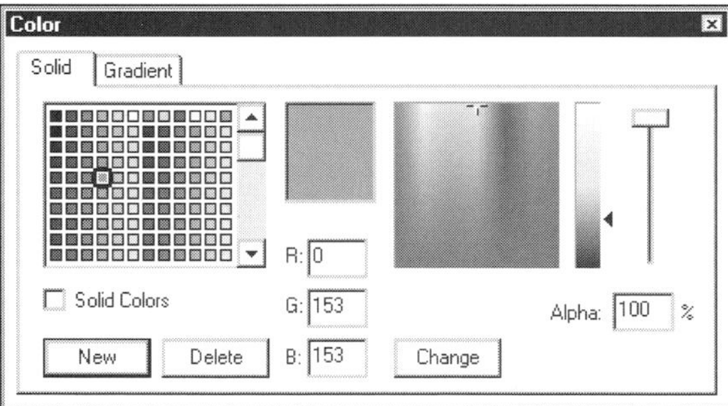

Figure 4.60 The Color dialog box.

Pencil Tool

To choose the Pencil tool, click on its icon in the toolbox or press *P*. When the Pencil tool is chosen, the cursor changes to a miniature pencil (unless Line is the chosen pencil mode, in which case the cursor changes to a small cross hair).

The function of the Pencil tool is drawing lines. One of the differences between the Pencil and the Brush is that the pencil line is always down the center of the stroke, whereas the brush stroke actually fills, outlined by an invisible pencil. When you change the shape of a line, no matter how thick, you are moving its centerline.

Pencil lines are always drawn on the canvas, unless you first enter Group Edit mode (press Cmd/Ctrl+G) while nothing is selected. Now, as soon as you draw one line across another, all lines are cut at the intersection. Also, any sharp changes in the direction of your stroke will cause Flash to terminate one line and to start another. In Figure 4.61, each line was made with a single stroke. I have selected alternate lines to show how Flash terminates and starts lines.

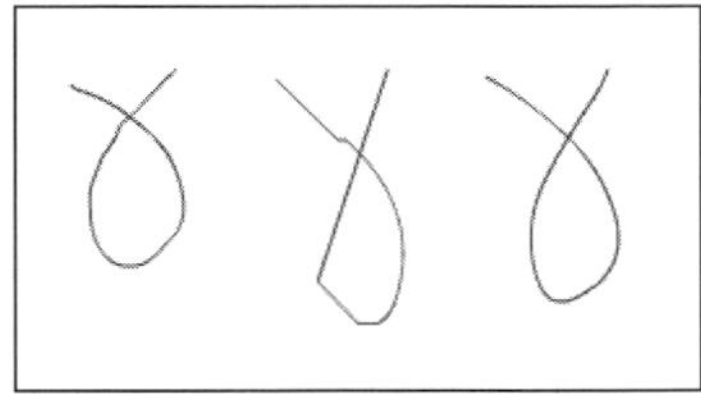

Figure 4.61 Single stroke lines made with the Pencil.

When the Pencil tool draws lines, the lines will take certain shapes, depending on several factors (each of which will be discussed in more detail in other sections of this chapter):

- The settings you have chosen in the Drawing Assistant
- The Pencil mode you have chosen
- The rough shape you indicate as you draw the line

Practice drawing lines in different modes until you get a feel for how Flash interprets strokes at various settings. A few minutes of practice will give you a pretty good (and invaluable) knowledge of what to expect.

As is true of all shapes created in Flash, you can change the course and curvature of lines at any time after drawing them. You also can change the style of existing lines at any time with the Ink Bottle tool.

Pencil Tool Modifiers

When you select the Pencil tool, the Pencil modifiers appear in the lower section of the toolbox. See Figure 4.62. Table 4.4 explains the functions for the Pencil modifiers.

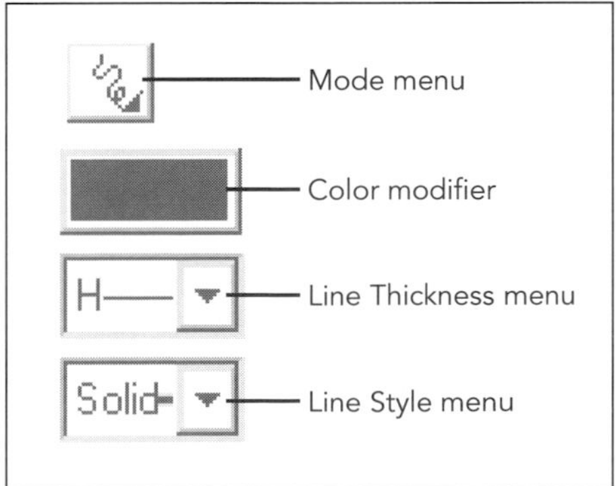

Figure 4.62 The Pencil tool modifiers.

Table 4.4 Pencil tool modifiers.

Name	Function
Mode menu	The Mode pull-down menu has several functions (see Figure 4.63): • Straighten is the most versatile mode. It recognizes shapes, straightens lines that are nearly straight, smoothes long curves, and joins any short (wavy) lines. The shapes it recognizes are rectangles, ovals, semicircles, and ninety-degree curves. • Smooth softens curves and reduces the number of wiggles in unsteadily drawn lines. Smoothing also reduces the number of line segments. • Ink leaves lines pretty much as you drew them but with some slight smoothing. • Oval draws an oval or a circle. (If you press Shift while dragging the pencil in oval mode, you will temporarily turn on Snap. When the Snap circle appears at the tip of your cursor, you are drawing a perfect circle.) • Rectangle draws a rectangle or a square in the same manner that Oval draws ovals and circles. (If you press Shift while dragging the pencil in rectangle mode, you will temporarily turn on Snap. When the Snap circle appears at the tip of your cursor, you are drawing a perfect rectangle.) • Line causes a straight line to be drawn between the start and end points of a cursor drag.
Color modifier	Works exactly the same as for the Text modifier. See the Text modifier section for details.
Line Thickness menu	Lets you draw a line of any thickness between hairline (H) and 10 points. You can choose any preset size from the pull-down menu or enter any whole number and decimal point size up to the 10-point limit.
Line Style menu	Lets you choose from a number of styles that vary from solid to dots or dashes, even a couple of artistic "natural media" styles. You also can create custom line styles.

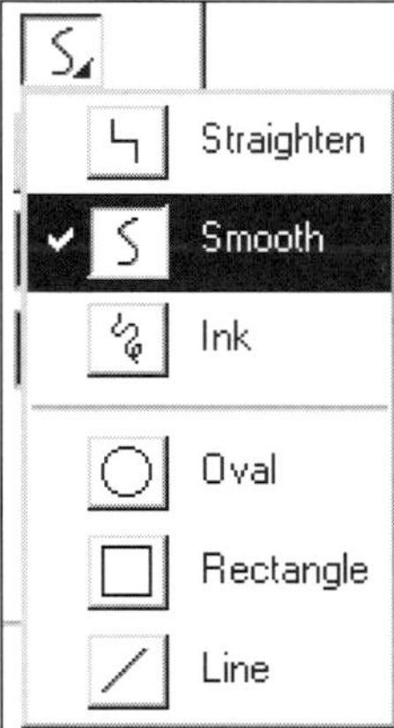

Figure 4.63 The Pencil modifier's Mode pull-down menu.

The Power Of Custom Line Styles

The Line Style dialog box (Figure 4.64) is an amazingly powerful tool for giving personality to your drawing strokes. To give you an idea of what I mean by that, the lines in Figure 4.65 are all copies of the same line, each with a customized line style applied to it. Table 4.5 explains each of the custom line styles.

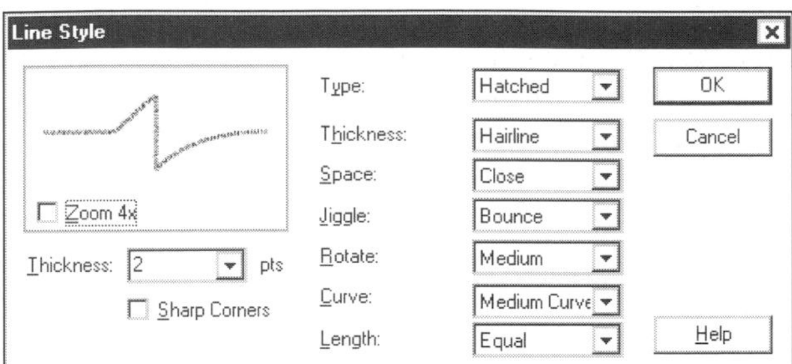

Figure 4.64 The Line Style dialog box.

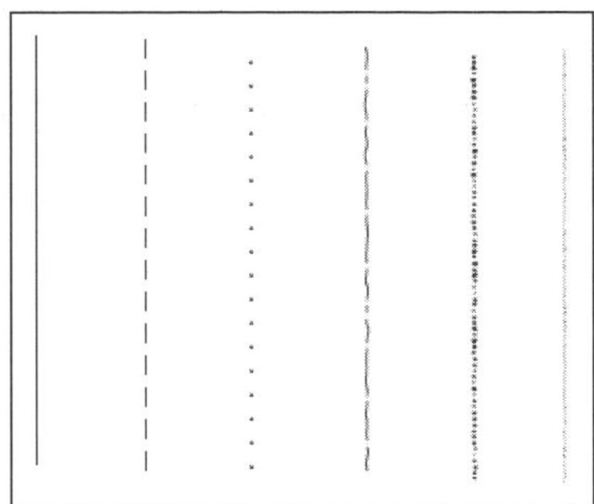

Figure 4.65 Several customizations (from left, solid, dashed, dotted, ragged, hatched, and stippled) applied to the same line style.

Table 4.5 Custom Line Styles.

Style	Variables	Description
Solid	Thickness and sharp corners only. These two variants are available for all line types.	The default line type. Simply creates a solid line. Specifying sharp corners breaks the line anytime the curve reverses direction.
Dashed	Length of dash. Space between dashes.	A steady line of uniform thickness with regular intervals between dashes of a specified length. Be sure there's enough space between dashes to accommodate line thickness.
Dotted	Dot spacing	Evenly spaced circular dots of the specified thickness.
Ragged	Pattern (7 variations), Wave Height (4), Wave Length (4).	This style gives an "unsteady hand" or arty look to your strokes. Variations are numerous enough to keep Van Gogh happy.
Stippled	Dot Size (4 variations), Dot Density (4), Variation (4).	This is also a very arty look that can resemble anything from charcoal to a mezzotint to etching.
Hatched	Thickness (4 variations), Space (4), Jiggle (4), Rotate (4), Curve (4), Length (4).	Drawn with spaced vertical line segments that can vary between very regular to a random, freehand look.

Ink Bottle Tool

To choose the Ink Bottle tool, click on its icon in the toolbox or press *I*. When Ink Bottle is the chosen tool, the cursor changes to a miniature ink bottle. The purpose of the Ink Bottle is to change existing line styles. Its use is extremely simple. When you want to change line styles, choose the Ink Bottle and use its modifiers to pick or to customize the line style (see the preceding section, "The Power Of Custom Line Styles") and click on the line or lines whose style you want to change.

Ink Bottle Tool Modifiers

When the Ink Bottle tool is chosen, its modifiers appear in the lower section of the toolbox. See Figure 4.66. Table 4.6 explains the functions of the Ink Bottle modifiers.

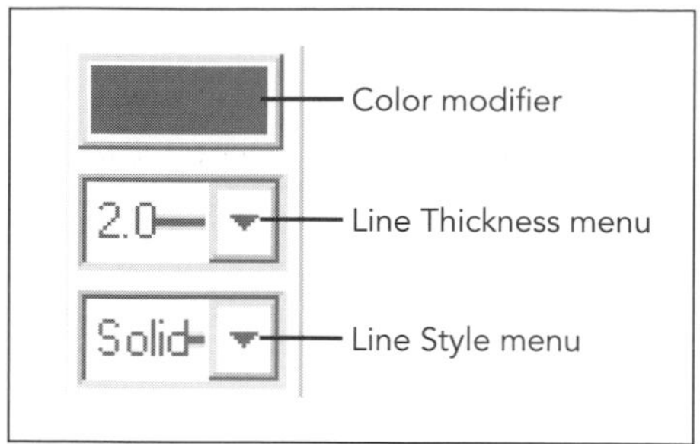

Figure 4.66 The Ink Bottle tool modifiers.

Table 4.6 Ink Bottle modifiers.

Name	Function
Color modifier	Works exactly the same as for the Text tool. See that earlier section. Basically, it brings up a a palette of 216 Web-safe colors.
Line Thickness menu	Lets you draw a line of any thickness between hairline (H) and 10 points. You can choose any preset thickness from the pull-down menu or enter any whole number and decimal point size up to the 10-point limit.
Line Style menu	Lets you choose from a number of styles that vary from solid to dots or dashes, even a couple of "natural media" styles. You also can create custom line styles.

Brush Tool

To choose the Brush tool, click on its icon in the toolbox or press *B*. When Brush is the chosen tool, the cursor changes to a brush. The Brush tool draws fills: solid color, gradient, or bitmap. (See Figure 4.67.) Each of the nine possible brush shapes can be set to 10 different sizes. Flash doesn't, however, provide any means for you to make custom brush shapes or to use brushes that are larger than 10 pixels in diameter.

Use the Brush when it's more natural and intuitive to paint a shape or colors than to outline and fill. Better yet, draw the silhouette of your subject with the Pencil tool, fill it with the Bucket tool, and then add interior details with the brush.

Remember that brush strokes can be reshaped, smoothed, straightened, and transformed with the Arrow tool.

The moment you paint a brush stroke atop another shape, you have altered (cut a hole) in the underlying shape. To avoid this, press *G* or choose Modify|Group when there is nothing selected. Then, your strokes will be overlaid. Using this method, you can overlay strokes within overlaid strokes.

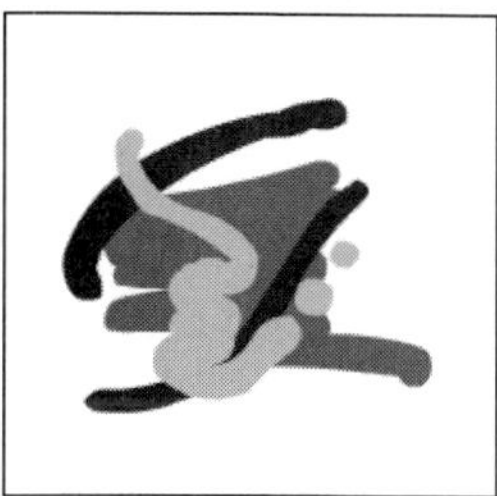

Figure 4.67 Strokes made with the Brush tool.

Brush Tool Modifiers

When the Brush tool is selected, the Brush modifiers appear in the lower section of the toolbox. See Figure 4.68. Table 4.7 explains the functions of the Brush modifiers.

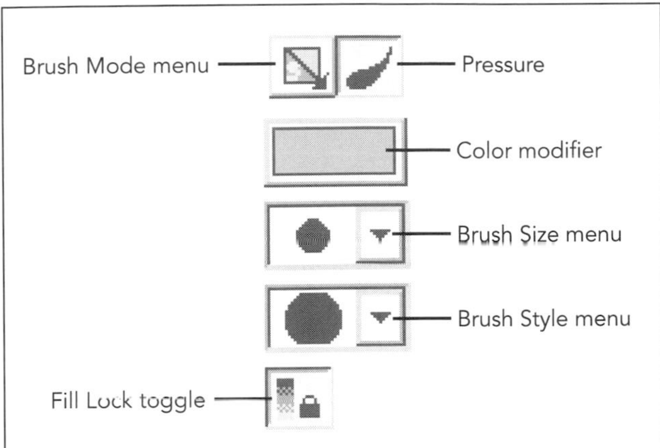

Figure 4.68 The Brush tool modifiers.

Table 4.7 Brush tool modifiers.

Name	Function
Brush Mode menu	The Brush Mode pull-down menu has several functions (see Figure 4.69): • Paint Normal paints atop and autoedits any other shapes on the same canvas or group. • Paint Fills paints on the canvas and on any fills (including brush strokes) but won't paint or otherwise affect any pencil lines. • Paint Behind paints only those parts of the canvas that aren't covered by other shapes. • Paint Selection paints only those portions of active selections covered by a brush stoke. • Paint Inside paints only inside the selected shape.
Pressure button	Click to activate variable brush size for pressure-sensitive pads.
Color modifier	This is the same color modifier picker used for the Text, Pencil, Ink Bottle, and Bucket tools.
Brush Size menu	Offers 10 different brush sizes, from 1 to 10 pixels in diameter.
Brush Style menu	Offers nine different brush shape/angle choices.
Fill Lock toggle	When on, this button locks the beginning and end points of a gradient to the full size of the movie. This makes it possible to make multiple brush strokes without restarting the gradient.

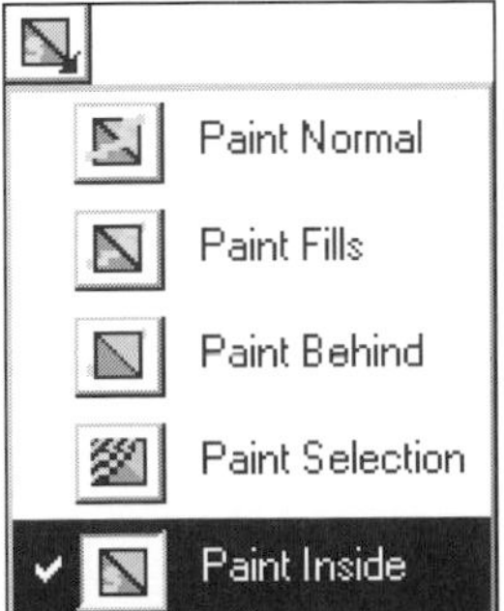

Figure 4.69 The Brush modifier's Mode pull-down menu.

Paint Bucket Tool

To choose the Paint Bucket tool, click on its icon in the toolbox or press *U*. When Paint Bucket is the chosen tool, the cursor changes to a paint bucket. The Paint Bucket is used to fill any area enclosed (or partially enclosed) by a pencil line or to refill selected strokes and fills with a different color, gradient, or bitmap.

You can fill several filled objects with a single new fill in a single click. Select all the fills (or filled objects) you want to change, then choose the Paint Bucket and fill you want to use and click in any one of the selected fills. The other selected fills will change simultaneously.

If you are filling small areas, it helps to know that the tip of the pouring paint indicates the precise point at which the fill will occur.

Paint Bucket Tool Modifiers

When the Paint Bucket tool is selected, its modifiers appear in the lower section of the toolbox. See Figure 4.70. Table 4.8 explains the functions for the Paint Bucket modifiers.

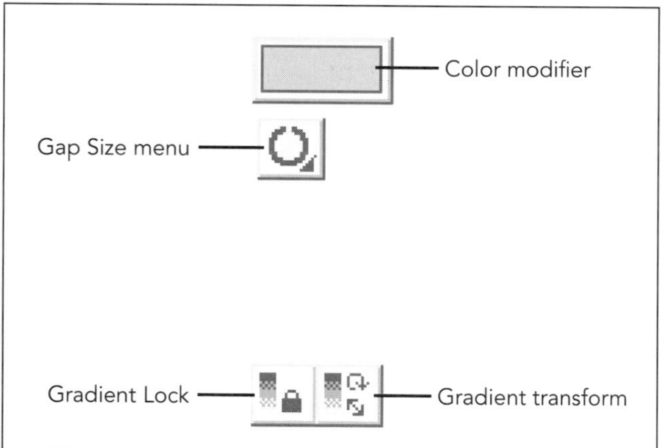

Figure 4.70 The Paint Bucket tool modifiers.

Table 4.8 Paint Bucket modifiers.

Name	Description
Color modifier	Yep, it's the same old color modifier.
Gap Size menu	The Gap Size menu has several options: • *Don't Close Gaps*—Choose this when you want to make sure that fill doesn't accidentally fill areas that were meant to be blank. This isn't always obvious in complex drawings. • *Close Small Gaps*—Similar to the previous choice, but a bit more forgiving when the artist meant to enclose an area but didn't quite make ends meet. • *Close Medium Gaps*—Good for when you've been a little sloppy about enclosures or when you want some artistic license in choosing whether or not all your fills need to be completely outlined. • *Close Large Gaps*—Near total artistic freedom.
Gradient Lock	Locks the gradient to the movie frame size.
Gradient transformation	Lets you scale and rotate the gradient.

Eraser Tool

To choose the Eraser tool, click on its icon in the toolbox or press *E*. When eraser is the chosen tool, the cursor changes to a eraser. Erasing autoedits the erased shapes, subdividing them into new shapes, as in Figure 4.71.

The Eraser tool erases lines and fills. It can be customized to erase just lines, just fills, just the selected fills, or just the fill on which you start erasing. Use the Eraser modifiers to select one of five sizes and to set the eraser shape.

***Note:** The Eraser can erase only lines and fills on the canvas; it cannot erase overlays. If you need to erase part of an overlay, either select the overlay and choose Edit | Edit Selected to edit the overlay, or Modify | Break Apart to return the overlay to the canvas.*

Figure 4.71 These were once part of the same shape, before an eraser stroke passed through.

Eraser Tool Modifiers

When the Eraser tool is chosen, the Eraser modifiers appear in the lower section of the toolbox. See Figure 4.72. Table 4.9 explains the functions of the Eraser modifiers.

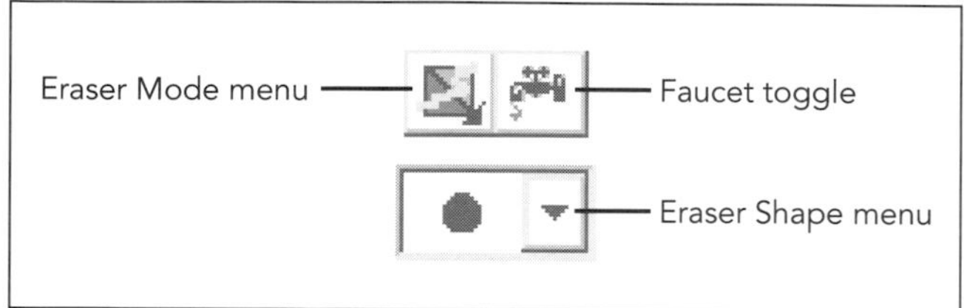

Figure 4.72 The Eraser tool modifiers.

Table 4.9 Eraser tool modifiers.

Name	Function
Eraser Mode menu	The Eraser Mode menu offers several options (see Figure 4.73): • Erase Normal erases any line or fill you brush over. • Erase Fills erases only fills; it leaves lines alone. • Erase Lines erases only lines; it leaves fills alone. • Erase Selected Fills erases only fills that have been selected, but it won't erase selected lines. If you want to erase particular lines, select the previous option and be careful. • Erase Inside erases only fills inside the enclosed area where you start erasing.
Faucet toggle	Acts like a "reverse bucket fill" by eliminating any line, fill, or selection on which you click. Multiple selections will all be erased if you click on any one of them.
Shape/Size menu	Lets you choose from one of five sizes of circles and rectangles.

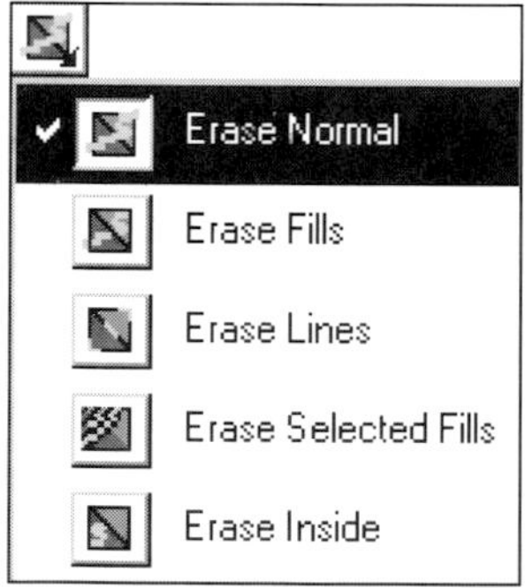

Figure 4.73 The Eraser Mode pull-down menu.

Dropper Tool

To choose the Dropper tool, click on its icon in the toolbox or press *D*. When Dropper is the chosen tool, the cursor changes to an eyedropper.

The purpose of the Dropper is to copy the properties of one entity to another. The Dropper picks up either the line style or the fill, depending on the location of the cursor. The Dropper cursor changes sub-icons to show you whether it is ready to pick up a line style (Pencil sub-icon in Figure 4.74) or a fill (Bucket sub-icon).

Once you've picked up a line style or fill, the cursor changes to either the Paint Bucket or the Ink Bottle to show you what types of entities you can change. There are no modifiers for the dropper.

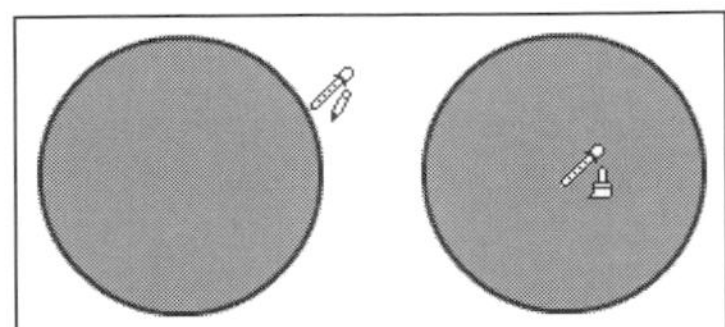

Figure 4.74 The Dropper cursor changes to show whether it is ready to pick up a line style or a fill. Note the Pencil and Bucket sub-icons.

 Magnifier Tool

To choose the Magnifier tool, click on its icon in the toolbox or press *M*. When Magnifier is the chosen tool, the cursor changes to a magnifier. At the same time, the Magnifier modifiers appear in the lower section of the toolbox. See Figure 4.75.

Figure 4.75 The Magnifier tool modifiers are zoom in (plus) and zoom out (minus).

The Magnifier tool works pretty much like similar tools in other programs. Unfortunately, there's no hand tool modifier to let you move about the screen at the press of the Space key, and you can't zoom out by pressing a modifier key (such as Opt/Alt).

To zoom in, press *M* and click to zoom in at 100 percent magnification increments, centered at the spot where you clicked. You also can drag a rectangle to indicate the area of the movie you would like to make as large as possible. As soon as you release the mouse key, the image will magnify to the degree you have indicated.

To zoom out with the Magnifier tool, you have to click on the zoom-out modifier. Dragging a rectangle with the zoom-out cursor actually zooms *in*—really.

You also can change magnifications by choosing View|100% (which scales the drawing to actual size), View|Show Frame (which shows the entire movie frame), or View|Show All (which zooms the drawing to its limits, without regard to frame size).

 Lasso Tool

To choose the Lasso tool, click on its icon in the toolbox or press *L*. When Lasso is the chosen tool, the cursor changes to a lasso. The Lasso tool lets you shape freehand selections; in other words, they can be any shape. If you don't end the selection marquee where you started it, it will close automatically. The shape you select will autoedit any shapes you encircle on the canvas, but without affecting overlays (groups and symbols).

Starting a new selection with the Lasso tool, unlike the Arrow tool, drops the current selection and starts a new one. If you need to select multiple areas, press Shift before making subsequent selections. You can deselect all by clicking anywhere in the frame with the lasso cursor.

The Lasso tool has two options that seem to have nothing whatever to do with the Lasso tool or making selections. These are the magic wand modifiers, and they work only on imported bitmapped (GIF, JPEG, or PNG) images.

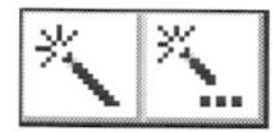

Figure 4.76 The Lasso tool modifiers are the Magic Wand (left) and the Magic Wand Options.

Lasso Tool Modifiers

When the Lasso tool is selected, the Lasso modifiers appear in the lower section of the toolbox. See Figure 4.76. Table 4.10 explains the functions of the Lasso modifiers.

Table 4.10 Lasso tool modifiers.

Name	Function
Magic Wand	Modifies color areas of a bitmap. The bitmap must first be selected, then broken apart (choose Modify|Break Apart).
Magic Wand Options dialog box	Threshold sets the range of colors that will be chosen for recoloring. Smoothing is a pull-down menu that lets you select the level of smoothing.

Flash's Drawing Aids

Flash provides you several means of helping you visualize the spacing and measurement of your drawing elements: grids, guide layers, Snap, and alignment. The following sections highlight Flash's drawing aids.

Grids

Flash's grids are beneath anything you draw. They don't print, and they aren't visible in exported movies (that is, anything your audience might see). Figure 4.77 shows a drawing where the grid is visible.

You can turn the grid off and on in three ways: choose View|Grid from the menu bar; in the Properties dialog, check or uncheck the Show Grid box; or you can press Cmd/Ctrl+Opt/Alt+G.

Flash's grids are always square and spaced according to the settings you choose in the Movie Properties dialog box. (To reach the Movie Properties dialog box, choose Modify|Movie from the menu bar.) Grids are shown in light gray by default, but you can make them any color in the Movie Properties dialog box. (See Figure 4.78.) You may want to change the color of the grid to contrast more with the content of your movie. The Movie Properties dialog box also lets you choose the units of measurement you like.

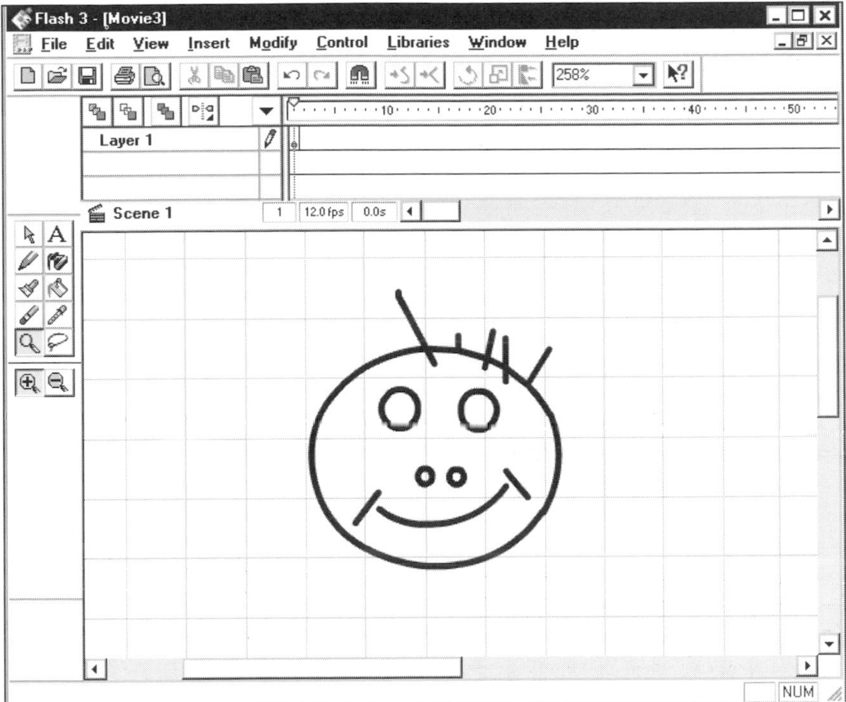

Figure 4.77 Drawing with grid visible.

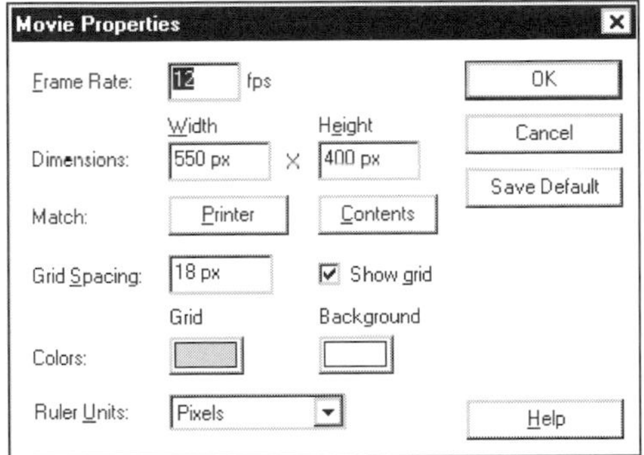

Figure 4.78 The Movie Properties dialog box.

Guide Layers

Guide layers are a special kind of layer that doesn't print, export, or interfere with anything you draw on other layers. On the other hand, you can draw anything on a guide layer, such as motion paths, asymmetrical grids, guide lines, or positioning Xs.

To create a guide layer, simply choose Insert Layer from the Layer pop-up (the button at the right end of the layer name bar). This creates a new layer. Draw any kind of guides you want on it. Then, to designate a layer as a guide layer, choose Guide from the Layer menu. You also can choose to make a guide layer into a regular layer. To convert a guide layer to a regular layer, choose Guide again from the Layer pop-up. The checkmark alongside Guide will disappear.

Snap

Snap causes tools to jump to the nearest grid point, end point, or mid-point of another line or to the edge of another entity—whichever is closer. You know when Snap is turned on because a small circle will appear at the tip of the selection tool's arrowhead. An easier way to know that Snap is on is to look at the magnet icon either at the top of the screen or in the Arrow modifiers. You toggle Snap on and off by clicking on the Snap modifier in the Arrow tool modifiers. (Turning the grid off and on simultaneously turns grid Snap off and on.) Snap is very useful to use when you want to make ends meet (talking about lines, here—not finances).

To adjust the Snap distance, choose File|Assistant and then, in the dialog box, choose from any of five levels of Snap distance ranging between Off and Always Snap from the Snap to Grid pop-up.

Alignment

Flash's alignment dialog box lets you align selections (a shape or any part of it) with one another. You can specify that they be aligned horizontally or vertically and can specify for each direction that they be aligned by their centers or sides. You also can specify that all objects be made the same size and that they be spaced evenly. Figure 4.79 shows drawings before and after they have aligned horizontally by their centers, sized equally, and spaced evenly. When you size all objects to the same size, they are sized to match the largest object selected. Another thing to watch out for is that they will all be placed inside the movie frame, regardless of how you set alignment and spacing. This can mean that all the objects end up stacked one atop another. If this happens, just press Cmd/Ctrl+Z.

To align several objects, first select them. You can use any of the selection tools and can even use the Lasso to select parts of objects. From

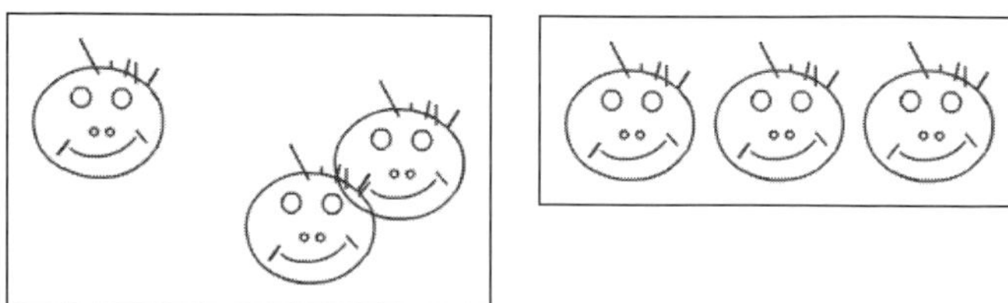

Figure 4.79 Before and after aligning, sizing, and spacing using the Align command.

the menu bar, choose Modify|Align. In the dialog box (Figure 4.80), set the parameters you want by clicking on the appropriate diagram icons and clicking on OK. The rest is automatic.

Commands And Tools For Refining Drawing Elements

Flash has quite a few ways of helping you to fine-tune the way your lines and strokes appear in the final product. These commands and tools are found in several different places in the Flash interface, and many of them duplicate functions that can be found in the tool modifiers. The next sections focus on commands and tools that will help you refine drawing elements.

Assistant

Assistant is a dialog box that lets you set preferences for drawing and shape-recognition tolerances. The options are Snap to Grid, Connect Line, Smooth Curves, Recognize Lines, Recognize Shapes, and Click Accuracy. All of these options can be set to on, off, or one of several tolerance settings, simply by choosing a setting from the appropriate pop-up menu. (See Figure 4.81.) Each of the tolerance settings doubles the value of its predecessor. Normal is the default for all tolerance settings.

The actual degree to which a tolerance setting works is entirely dependent on screen resolution. In other words, the settings function on the basis of the number of screen—not file resolution—pixels. So, one way to instantly get tighter control without resetting the Assistant is to zoom in. If you want a freehand line to be less smooth, zoom in; if you want the line smoother, zoom out.

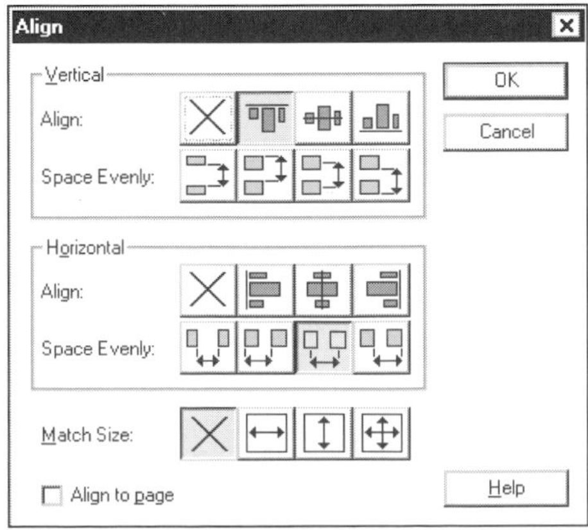

Figure 4.80 The Align dialog box.

Figure 4.81 The Assistant dialog box.

You can activate the Assistant and change its settings at any time. To do so, choose File|Assistant. The Assistant dialog box will appear.

Transformations

The Transform command on the Modify menu lets you reshape or reorient any active selection(s), including overlays. Though you can do the same thing with the scale and rotate modifiers as with the Scale and Rotate commands on the Transform submenu, other commands on this menu are unique. (See Figure 4.82.) Table 4.11 explains each of the commands on the Transform submenu.

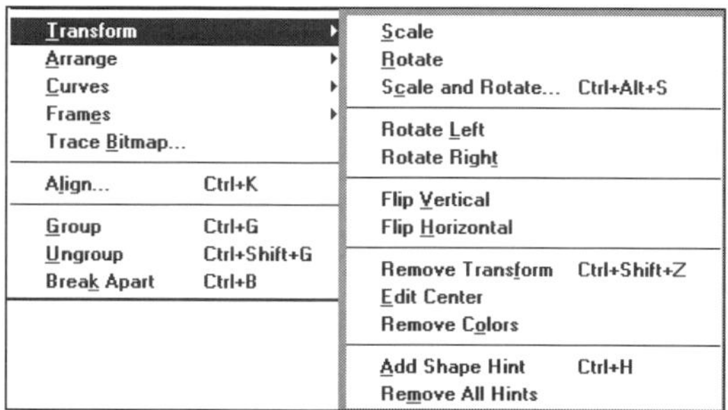

Figure 4.82 The Transform submenu.

Table 4.11 Transform submenu commands.

Command	Function
Scale and Rotate	(Cmd/Ctrl+Shift+S) Brings up a dialog box that lets you enter an exact percentage to scale and/or a precise degree of rotation. (Precede the number with a hyphen (-) to indicate counterclockwise rotation.)
Rotate Left and Rotate Right	Turns the selection by exactly 90 degrees.
Flip Vertical	Turns the selection upside down but doesn't reverse it from left to right (as rotating it would).
Flip Horizontal	Swaps left to right.
Remove Transform	Returns the selection to its original state, regardless of how many transformations (uninterrupted by other commands) you have made since the current selection.
Edit Center	Lets you move the center of an overlay. Pay attention: This means any overlay—a group, symbol, text, or (of course) a selection. This command is ghosted unless you've moved or transformed the current selection. Selections that have been moved can be considered a kind of overlay because they temporarily "float" above the drawing until they are deselected, at which point they drop back down onto the canvas and autoedit any other object they intersect. The purpose of this command is to give you more control over transformations by changing the center around which they are calculated. As soon as you choose the Edit Center command, a cross appears at the current center of the selection. Drag this cross to move the center.

Arrange

The Arrange command lets you control the stacking order of overlays. If you want to stack shapes without letting them autoedit one another, you first must make them into either groups or symbols (both are overlays).

To change the stacking order of an overlay, choose Modify|Arrange and then choose whether you want the overlay to move to the top of the stack (Bring to Front), bottom of the stack (Send to Back), up (Move Ahead), or down (Move Behind) a layer. As you can see in Figure 4.83, each of these commands has a hotkey.

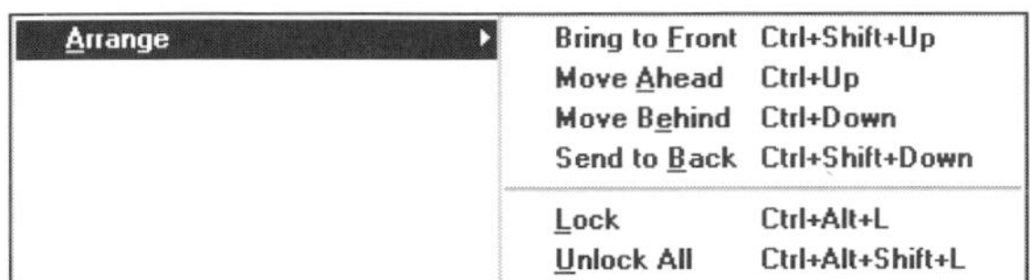

Figure 4.83 The Arrange submenu.

Curve Control

Also on the Modify menu is a command called Curves. Two of the commands on this submenu do exactly the same thing as the Smooth and Straighten buttons in the Arrow tool modifiers. Whether you choose these commands from the menu or from the Arrow tool modifiers is strictly a matter of whatever is most convenient for you.

The third command, Optimize, is both unique and powerful. The Optimize command serves two purposes:

- To make file sizes smaller by minimizing the number of curves in a drawing.
- To give you more control over the smoothing of curves and your ability to reshape them easily. It is easier to reshape a large portion of an object when fewer curves are involved, because the lines are longer.

To optimize curves, first select the shape you wish to optimize. (If it is outlined, be sure to select both the outline and the fill.) Then, choose Modify|Curves|Optimize. The Optimize Curves dialog box will appear. See Figure 4.84.

Near the top of the dialog box is a slider labeled Smoothing. Moving the slider all the way to the left introduces no smoothing (and, therefore, little to no curve optimization); moving it to the right causes

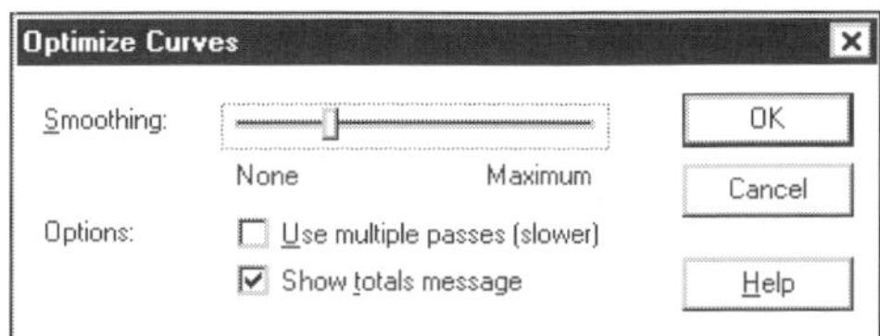

Figure 4.84 The Optimize Curves dialog box.

WEB TIP

Before exporting movies for use on Web pages, it is a good idea to optimize the curves for all the shapes in all the keyframes in the movie. (Tweened shapes will optimize themselves automatically.) This will ensure that your file sizes are as small as possible.

maximum smoothing and optimization. Too much optimization, however, can cause serious shape distortion, so you will want to experiment to find the best compromise for each shape.

Below the slider are two check boxes: Use Multiple Passes and Show Totals Message. Checking Use Multiple Passes causes the command to repeat optimization until no further optimization is possible. This is somewhat like repeated clicking of the Smooth button in the Arrow modifiers. Checking Show Totals Message displays a dialog box after optimization has terminated. The dialog box reports the number of original curves and the number of curves in the final result.

Assembling And Disassembling Groups And Symbols

It is very easy to turn selections into overlays—either groups or symbols. Both have the advantage of being editable in a space of their own, where the edit won't affect any other part of the movie.

To create a group, make your selection and press Cmd/Ctrl+G (or choose Modify|Group). To edit a group, select the group you want to edit and choose Edit|Edit Selected, or double-click on the group after it has been selected. To quit editing a group, choose Edit|Edit All, or double-click in an empty space within the frame. To disassemble a group, press Cmd/Ctrl+Shift+G, or choose Modify|Ungroup. It is possible to have groups within groups.

To create a symbol, make your selection and choose Insert|Create Symbol. A Symbol Properties dialog box opens to allow you to name the symbol and to check whether this symbol should behave like a graphic, button, or movie clip. Symbols can include multiple groups, other symbols, and even multiple frames. (There'll be much more about animated symbols in Chapter 5.) If you check the Button Behavior box, the symbol will automatically inherit four frames, the first being the current selection and the other three blank. The symbol also will know how to behave like a button when you pass the mouse over it or click on it. You then are free to add any content you like to the other three frames. Chapter 6 provides much more detail on this procedure.

Inserting Objects Created In Other Applications

You can place components from other applications, such as images, charts, or spreadsheets directly into a Flash movie. To do this, choose

Insert|Object from the menu bar, then choose the application type you want to include from the list in the pop-up.

What You Shouldn't Expect From Flash As A Drawing Program

Flash is such a strong and easy-to-use drawing program that you may come to think that there's nothing you can't do with it. That actually may be true, if you put enough effort into it, but for certain types of drawings or drawings incorporating certain types of elements, you can work faster and more efficiently in a more specialized, vector-based drawing program.

Flash doesn't have unlimited drawing sizes or the precision needed for architectural and engineering drawings. It has no 3D modeling capabilities, either.

More expensive illustration programs, such as CorelDRAW, Adobe Illustrator, and Macromedia FreeHand can accept a variety of third-party special effects plug-ins, will do morphs or blends from one shape to another, and allow you to control cyan, magenta, yellow, and black (CMYK) output to printers, color separators, and printing presses. Also, drawing in an illustration program allows you to manually control curved lines with great precision because you can use the visible control points and handles that Flash (in the interest of more intuitive sketching) eschews.

Moving On

This very long chapter has been more detailed and patient in explaining how to draw in Flash (and how to draw even if you don't know how) than the Flash manual itself. The next two chapters will do the same for the process of making animations.

In Chapter 5, I'll write about stages in the animation process and about all the procedures basic to making simple animations. Chapter 6 provides more detailed explanations of symbols, their uses, and the ways in which you can use them to optimize the size of your Flash 3 files.

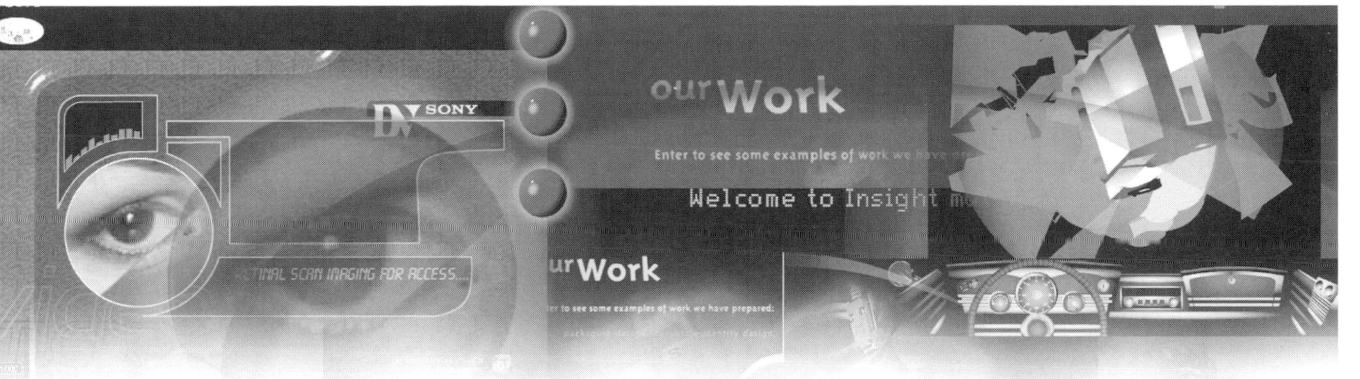

5

The Essentials of Making a Flash Animation

Ken Milburn

This chapter introduces you to the fundamentals of Flash 3 animation, including working with some of the new features. Also, brief tutorials will show you how to create the simplest and most effective types of animation.

Flash's animation capabilities are what attracted all the attention in the first place. Because Flash's animations are vector drawings rather than bitmap paintings, the animator has a great speed advantage in creating as well as displaying animations (especially on the Web).

The relatively small file size of a Flash animation is also a benefit in offline uses. You can store an entire animated and interactive presentation on a single floppy disk. Since DOS-formatted floppy disks can be read by both Windows and Mac users, you can distribute a near-universal presentation on low-cost floppy disks. This is even truer in Flash 3, since the destination computer no longer needs to have a browser. You can simply save the file as a self-running "projector."

So you can get a feel for the basics of animation and how easy it really can be, this chapter will start with an exercise that lets you create a very simple animation. The most effective Web animations are often the simplest. Furthermore, the simplest also load and play the fastest.

Next, I'll discuss the kinds of animation techniques that are equally easy and especially effective as quick attention-getters. (Are you paying special attention, Web developers?) In that section, you'll get a good idea of how you might make those animations. I'll progress to a brief discussion of the different types of animation procedures (frame by frame, tweened, and still frame) and the purpose for each. That discussion will be followed by an extensive reference section on the tools, commands, the Timeline, and hidden Timeline menus that provide Flash all its animation power.

The Basics Of Animation

Think of an animation as nothing more than a stack of still images shown to the viewer in rapid succession. (The old-fashioned flipbook is probably the best visual metaphor.) You get the illusion of movement because the drawings change slightly from page to page and because the pages are flipped quickly enough to create the illusion of motion. With the advent of the motion picture camera, these still pages became known as *frames*, and the frames are shown rapidly by sliding them past a light, lens, and shutter at high speed. Well, video and computer animations are just electronic adaptations of the same idea.

Flash creates animations by starting with a powerful but easy-to-use set of drawing tools to let you create the pictures in your frames. You can then use frames, overlays, symbols, layers, and scenes to assemble your drawings into a whole "production," which Flash calls a *movie*.

The length of a Flash movie and the number of scenes it can contain are limited only by your computer and your distribution requirements. You can use Flash to produce anything from an animated Graphics Interchange Format (GIF) animation for use on a Web page to a series of numbered stills for incorporation into other animation or video editing programs such as Macromedia Director or Adobe Premiere. Flash movies can even contain *actions* (instructions to do such things as play a specific scene or sound) and *buttons,* which means that you could use Flash to produce a multimedia application for distribution on a CD-ROM. More likely, you'll use these interactive capabilities to drive the navigation of a Web site.

Now that I've said all that, you have to start with a good idea of what it takes to put together an animation. Remember, the illusion of motion is created by making small changes in each frame. You have to make these changes in careful increments from one frame to the next, and it's important that objects must move a planned distance in a planned direction from the original. Otherwise, your movie will be amateurish and jerky. (Okay, so that can be an effect, but it's probably not the one you'll want to use most of the time.)

Movies are created in this logical order: frame by frame, layer by layer, scene by scene. Movies can be made to play continuously from scene to scene or to stop at the end of a scene while waiting for viewer interaction, such as clicking on a button or scene tab.

Making A Basic Animation

This exercise will make you realize how easy it is to grasp the basics of animation. You're going to simply change the form and size of an explosion over time. At the end of the exercise, you'll save this exercise as a symbol so that you can use it as an element in a presentation or on a Web site. Follow these steps:

1. Start a brand new movie. Choose the Pencil tool and the straighten modifier (from the Pencil mode menu). Draw an oval. It can be pretty rough—Flash probably will whip it into perfect shape as soon as you close the loop. If not, just press Cmd/Ctrl+Z and try again.

2. Choose the smooth line modifier from the Pencil mode menu and draw looping arcs all around the circle. See Figure 5.1.

3. You can edit the curvature of the arcs by choosing the Arrow tool and dragging their edges. Remember, whenever an arc intersects the oval, it divides (autoedits) the line that makes up the oval.

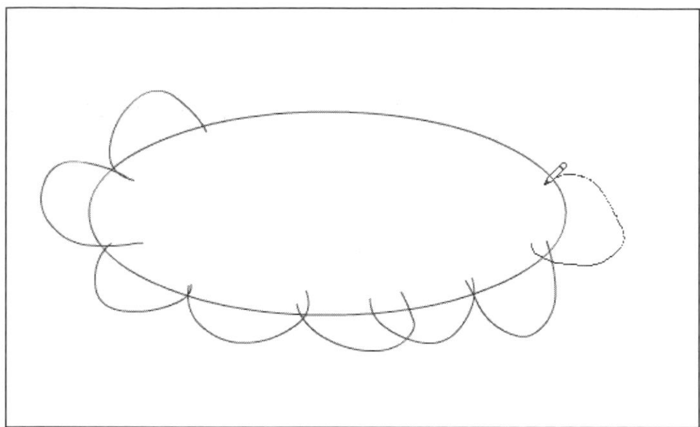

Figure 5.1 Drawing the cloud with ovals and arcs.

4. When you have the basic shape the way you want it, erase the oval. Choose File|Preferences and click Shift Select to check its box. (It's a good idea to leave this setting this way so you can make multiple selections in the same way as in your other graphics programs.) Now, Shift and click all the lines that make up the oval. (See Figure 5.2.) When you are done, press Delete/Backspace or choose Edit|Cut.
5. When you have finished the cloud shape, choose the Text tool. Click inside the cloud and enter the word *WOW!* in large type. To set the type size, click and drag the Type Size Modifier menu—or simply highlight the existing point size and enter the size you like. (I chose 72 points.)
6. To choose from any of the fonts installed on your system, pull down the Font Modifier menu and drag to highlight the font you want. I used a free Microsoft font called Comic Sans, made

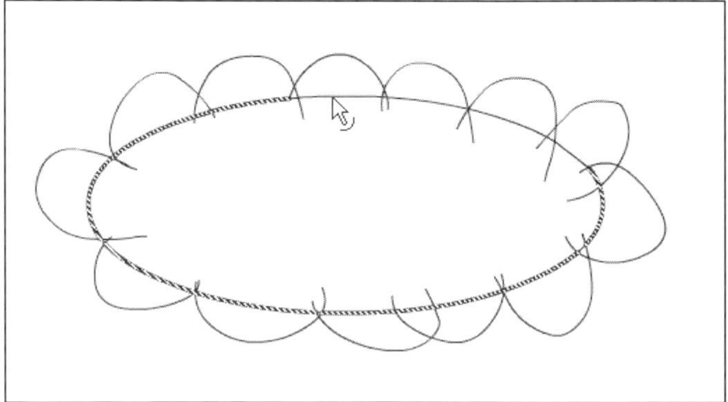

Figure 5.2 Shift and click to select the various lines that make up the oval.

especially for screen display (as on the Web), but you should feel free to pick your own favorite.

7. Since type is an overlay, it won't cut into the cloud. This will make it easy to edit and replace the type, so you can use the same cloud (or starburst, or what have you) for many attention-grabbing notices or instructions.

8. When you have finished entering the type, choose the Arrow tool and click on the scale modifier. Drag the handles until the type fills the cloud. See Figure 5.3.

9. You may also want to thicken the lines in the cloud: Double click the cloud to select all the lines at once, then choose the Ink Bottle tool. Choose a four-pixel line thickness from the Line Thickness menu in the modifiers. Click the Ink Bottle on any of the selected lines, and all their line styles will change at the same time.

10. Next, choose the Paint Bucket and a bright, light-blue color. Click inside the cloud to fill it.

11. Now, you want to group the cloud. Choose the Arrow tool. Select all the outlines and the blue fill in the cloud (but not the text). Press Cmd/Ctrl+G to group the cloud and its fill. The text will seem to disappear, because each new group is automatically moved to the top of the stack. See Figure 5.4.

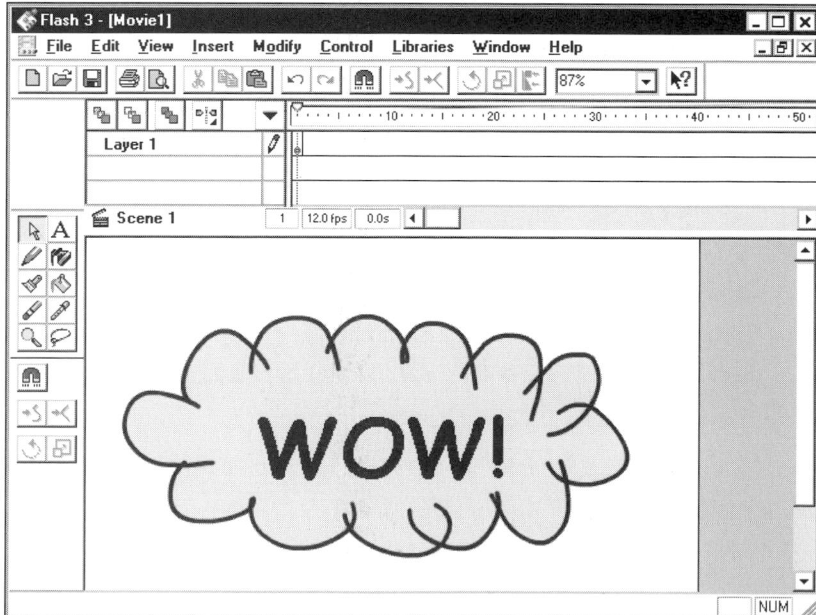

Figure 5.3 The cloud with type. The color fill seen here is done later in this exercise.

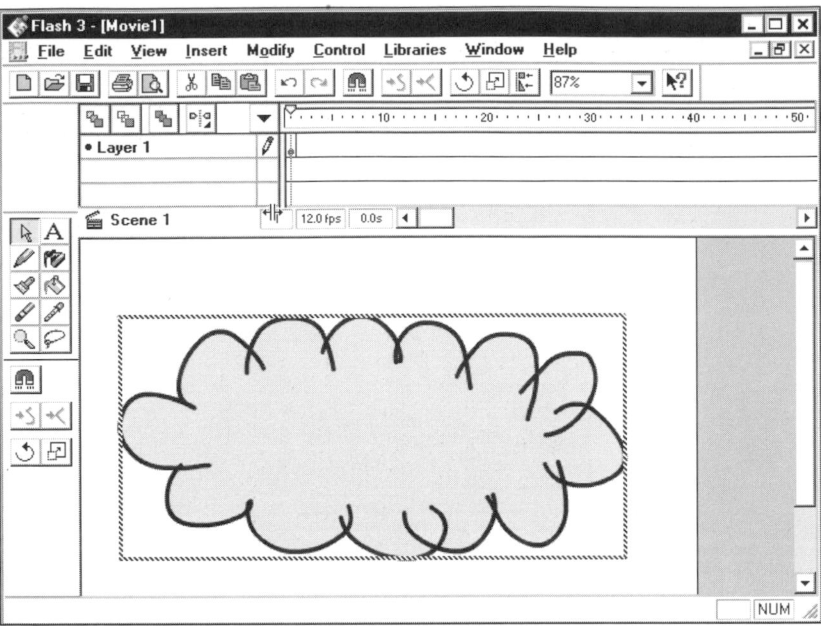

Figure 5.4 The grouped cloud, automatically moved to the top of the stack.

12. Press Cmd/Ctrl+Down arrow key—or choose Modify|Arrange|Send to Back—to place the cloud overlay beneath the text overlay.
13. Because this animation will involve transformations, you want to make sure that the centers of each overlay are aligned with one another. Unfortunately, Flash doesn't have a way for you to do this directly. For each overlay, select the overlay and then choose Modify|Transform|Edit Center. A cross hair will indicate the overlay's current centerpoint. It is now possible to drag this center, but don't do it now. The aim is to simply make the center cross hair visible when the overlay is selected. Use this procedure to turn on the center cross hair for each overlay. See Figure 5.5.
14. Choose View|Grid to turn on the grid. Turn on Snap (or simply press the Shift key while you drag a selection, which temporarily turns on Snap). Now, select one of the overlays you want to center, and drag it so that the center cross hair snaps to a grid intersection. Repeat for the other overlay, so that it snaps to the same grid intersection.
15. Press Cmd/Ctrl+A again to select all, and check the location of the centers. (See Figure 5.6.) If you see more than one cross hair, there's a discrepancy.
16. Now that you have all the basic parts in place, you can start animating. Take a look at the Timeline (shown in Figure 5.7). Place the

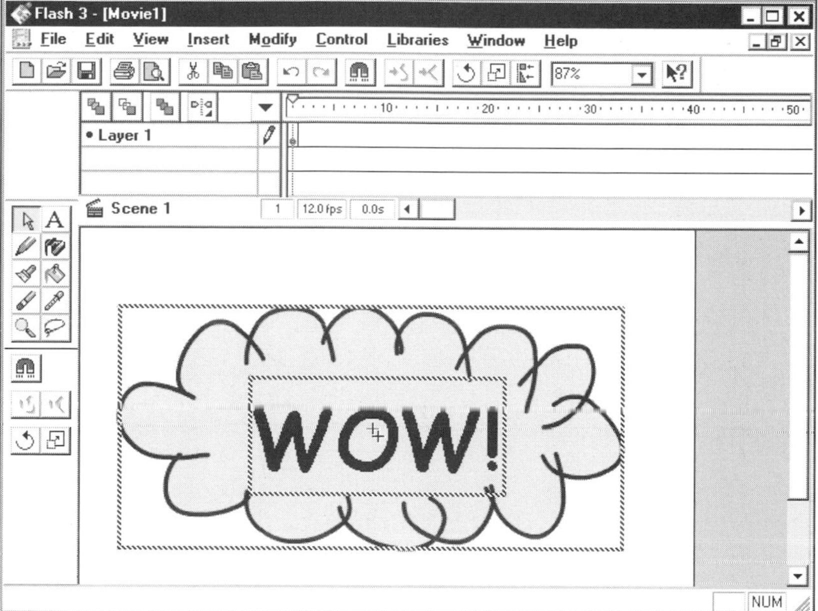

Figure 5.5 The center of both overlays made visible.

cursor in the space for the second frame and drag to frame 4. When you release, you'll see a black band. These black highlights appear any time you click on a frame position in the Timeline. To access the Frame menu, right-click (Windows) or click and hold (Mac), and a menu will drop down. (This is also shown in Figure 5.7.)

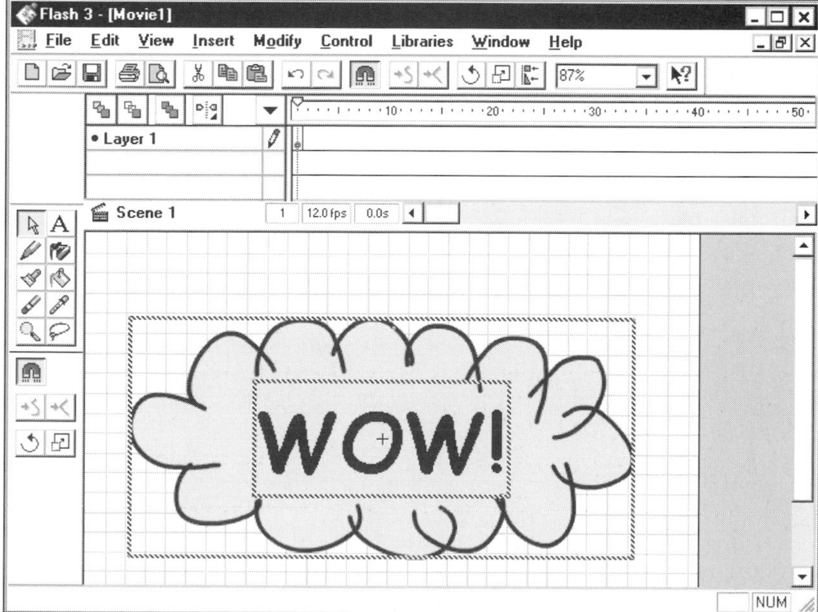

Figure 5.6 With both overlays selected, the centers are perfectly aligned.

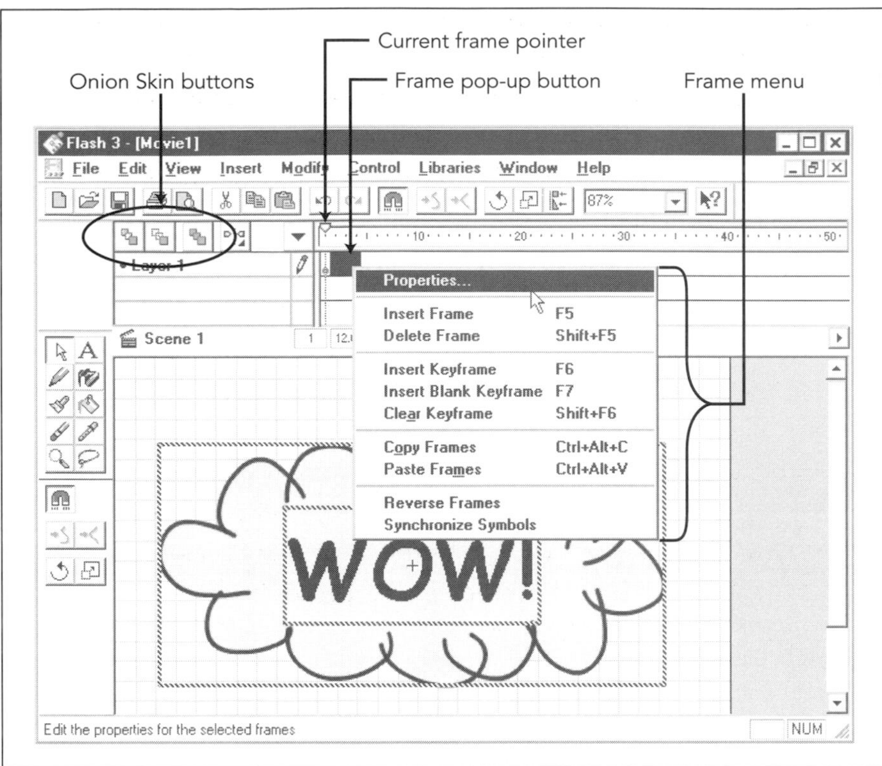

Figure 5.7 The Timeline for the cloud animation.

17. When the Frame menu appears, choose Insert Frame. New frames will be inserted for frames 2 through 4. If you move the current frame pointer across all four frames, you will see four exact copies of the cloud as we have drawn it.

18. You want each of these frames to be slightly different from all the others. In order to do that, you must make each frame a *keyframe*, frames in which something changes from the previous frame. Highlight frames 2 through 4, then press the Frame pop-up button (place the cursor on the frame and right-click (windows) or click and hold (Macintosh) and choose Insert Key Frame. (In Flash 3, you could have inserted the keyframes without first inserting frames, but this way you can see the difference between repeated static frames and keyframes.

19. Press Esc. The highlight will disappear, and you'll see a solid blue dot in each of the frames.

20. Click on the leftmost Onion Skin button. Onion markers will appear on either side of the current frame pointer. You can drag these to change the number of onion skin layers that are visible before and after the current frame.

21. Let's make the cloud vibrate in and out while the letters grow and spin. To do this, it will help to turn on the grid so that you can maintain the relative position of the two elements as they move. Choose View|Grid. Also, look at the View menu again and make sure there is no checkmark alongside Snap. If there is, choose View|Snap to toggle Snap off.

22. You are going to animate changes in one element and then the other, starting with frame 1. Make sure the frame pointer is at frame 1. Select the text overlay. From the menu bar, choose Modify|Transform|Scale and Rotate. The Scale and Rotate dialog box appears. (See Figure 5.8.) This dialog box is very handy in animation because it lets you scale, rotate, or do both at the same time and in perfectly precise increments—thus assuring smooth movement from frame to frame. Enter 25 in the Scale field and 180 in the Rotate field. Click on OK. The text will be one-fourth its original size and upside down.

23. Drag the current frame pointer to frame 2. The text overlay will still be visible, but at its original size and orientation. Select the text overlay. Press Cmd/Ctrl+Opt/Alt+S. The Scale and Rotate dialog box reappears. Enter 50 in the Scale field and 120 in the Rotate field. Click on OK. Repeat this step for frame 3, entering 75 in the Scale field and 60 in the Rotate field. In the fourth frame, the text is already upright and full sized, so you don't need to do anything.

24. Now comes the fun part. Press Enter/Return and watch the movie—that is, if you don't blink. The text starts small and simultaneously spins and zooms out. Now, you want to animate the cloud so that it moves at the same time that the text is rotating and zooming.

25. Drag the current frame pointer to frame 1 and select the cloud. Press Cmd/Ctrl+Opt/Alt+S. The Scale and Rotate dialog box reappears. Enter 90 in the Scale field and 0 in the Rotate field. Click on OK. The cloud shrinks slightly.

26. Drag the current frame pointer to frame 3. Make sure that only the cloud is selected. Press Cmd/Ctrl+Opt/Alt+S, and click on OK when the Scale and Rotate dialog box reappears. (The figures you entered last time are still in effect.) Press Return/Enter to play your movie. You can see the frames in sequence in Figure 5.9.

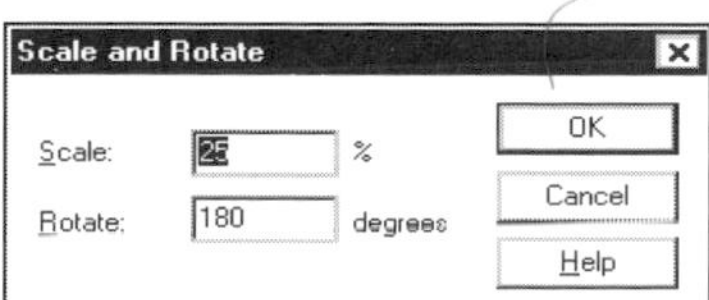

Figure 5.8 The Scale and Rotate dialog box.

Figure 5.9 The four frames of this animation

27. If the movie plays too fast, it is because Flash's default frame rate is 12 frames per second (fps). You will see that figure in the Frame Rate Setting box (the center box just below the layer names—it contains a number followed by "fps"). To change it, double-click in the Frame Rate Setting box. The Movie Properties dialog box will appear. This is a very valuable shortcut, as you can change any of the movie properties this way. (See Figure 5.10.) All you have to do to change the frame rate is enter a different number (in a range from 0.1 to 120) in the Frame Rate field. Yes, you can change many other properties for this movie at the same time, but remember that changing a movie's properties affects the entire movie and not just one frame or scene.

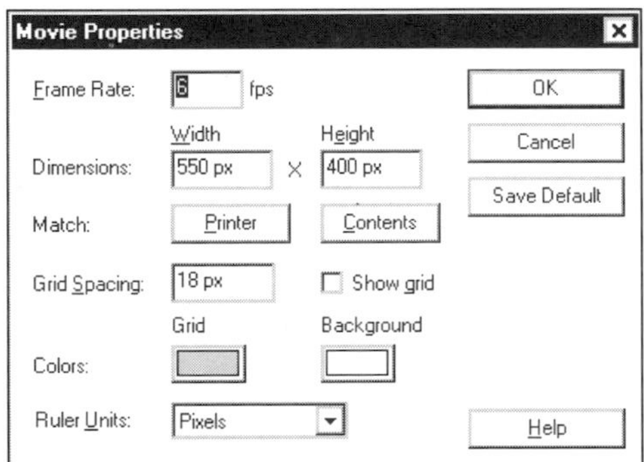

Figure 5.10 The Movie Properties dialog box.

28. When this movie ends, you want the frame to pause long enough for the viewer to read it. Flash doesn't let you control the playing time of a single frame (as animated GIFs do). This isn't a problem, really. Just insert duplicate frames after the frame you want to freeze—as many as it takes to have the frame pause for as long as you want, given the current frame rate. In this instance, we want the animation to pause for several seconds before it starts playing again. Place the cursor in the frame Timeline and drag for an additional 24 frames. From the Frame menu, choose Insert Frame. See Figure 5.11.

29. Press Esc to evaporate the I-beam and the highlighted frames. You will see a vertical bar at frame 28 to indicate the end of the movie.

Figure 5.11 Inserting frames to freeze a frame.

If you move the current frame pointer through these frames (or press the > key), Flash will propagate the same image as the one in the last frame through all the other frames. Remember, if you make any change in any of these frames, it will be reflected in all the others because these are not keyframes.

30. Okay, let's wrap this up by making the animation loop, and then save it as a symbol so that you can use it as a part of any other movie. From the menu bar, choose Control|Loop Playback. Now, press Return/Enter and watch what happens: The animation plays and then keeps repeating.

31. To save the movie as a symbol requires a little trickery. First, you have to export it to Shockwave Flash format: Choose File|Export Movie, and then select Shockwave Flash from the File Name menu. The Export Shockwave Flash dialog box appears. Accept all the defaults and click on OK.

32. Open a new movie and, with nothing selected, choose Insert|Create Symbol. A new, clean scene will open. Choose File|Import and choose the file name you just exported. All the frames in this movie will be keyframes, and the movie will play just as it did earlier.

33. From the main menu, choose File|Save As, and name the movie "MySymbols" (or whatever you wish).

Well, that was quick and easy! Now, you have a really good idea of what it takes to produce an animation in Flash. From this point on, you just ice the cake.

Easy Animation Techniques

Many animation tricks are so easy that you could put a nearly endless variety of material on a Web site or in a presentation without ever doing anything more elaborate. After working through the previous exercise and reading this list (and the few helpful hints that follow each technique), most of you will be able to employ all of them. If not, the tools and command references that follow surely will show you the way. Try to think of different types of subjects and situations to which you could apply these. The techniques are presented in the following sections.

Concentric Shapes

This technique draws attention to a static subject by having a series of concentric shapes (such as circles) radiate from it. This one is very easy. Place your shape in the center of the frame, then draw a series of shapes around the subject. Copy the frame over as many keyframes as there are concentric shapes; then, select and erase the shapes in subsequent frames.

The following example animates concentric circles. This time, we are sending out radial waves from an eye above a pyramid. I'm assuming you can draw the pyramid (or find appropriate clip art.) It should look something like Figure 5.12. Follow these steps to create radio waves:

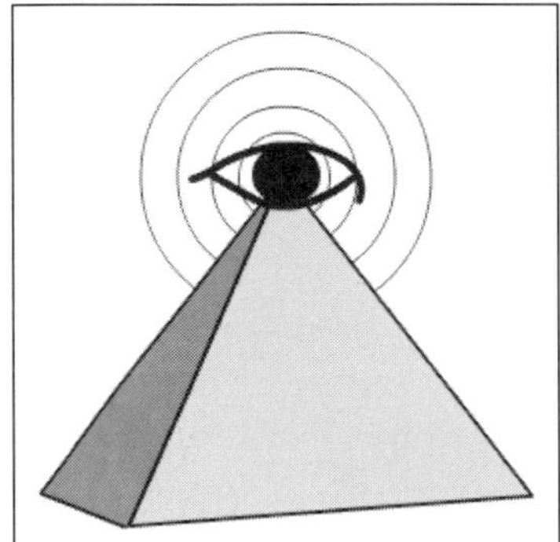

Figure 5.12 The radio waves draw attention to the eye atop the pyramid as they radiate out.

1. Start by turning on the grid so that you can snap to grid intersections. From the main menu, choose View|Grid.
2. Select all the elements that make up the pyramid (not the eye). Press Cmd/Ctrl+G to group them.
3. Select all the elements that make up the eye. Press Cmd/Ctrl+G to group them.
4. Move the Eye Group to the top of the stack. Select the Eye Group and then choose Modify|Arrange|Bring to Front.
5. You are now going to make the concentric circles. You want them in a group so that you can change the position of all of them at once and so that they don't autoedit the other shapes in the movie. Choose the Arrow tool and double-click in a blank area of the canvas. The pyramid and the eye will fade to gray.

6. Choose the Pencil tool and the oval modifier. In an area of the canvas well away from the pyramid, press Shift and drag to draw a small circle. When the shape is a circle, you will see a small circle to the lower right of the Pencil cursor. See Figure 5.13.

7. Draw three more perfectly concentric circles. Use the grid to snap the start point of each consecutive circle, placing the start point of each circle at the next farthest grid intersection that would describe the same corner of an imaginary box around the circle. The end result should look like Figure 5.14.

8. Now, you want to go back to editing the movie. The circles will automatically become a group. Either choose Edit|Edit All or simply double-click outside the group. All the elements of the movie will be seen in their regular color.

9. Move the group of concentric circles behind the pyramid and the eye. Choose the Arrow tool and click on one of the circles. The group will be selected. Drag it to the eye. If necessary, choose Modify|Arrange|Send to Back to place the circles behind the pyramid and the eye. The frame should now look like Figure 5.15.

10. Now, you start the animation. Choose the Arrow tool and, in the Timeline, drag across frames 3 through 5. Each of these frames will turn black to indicate that they have been selected.

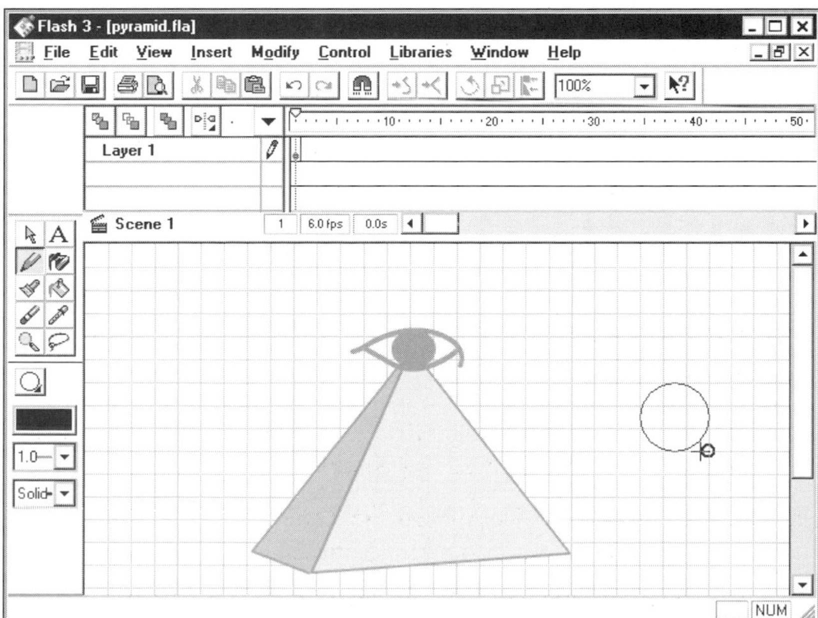

Figure 5.13 Drawing a perfect circle.

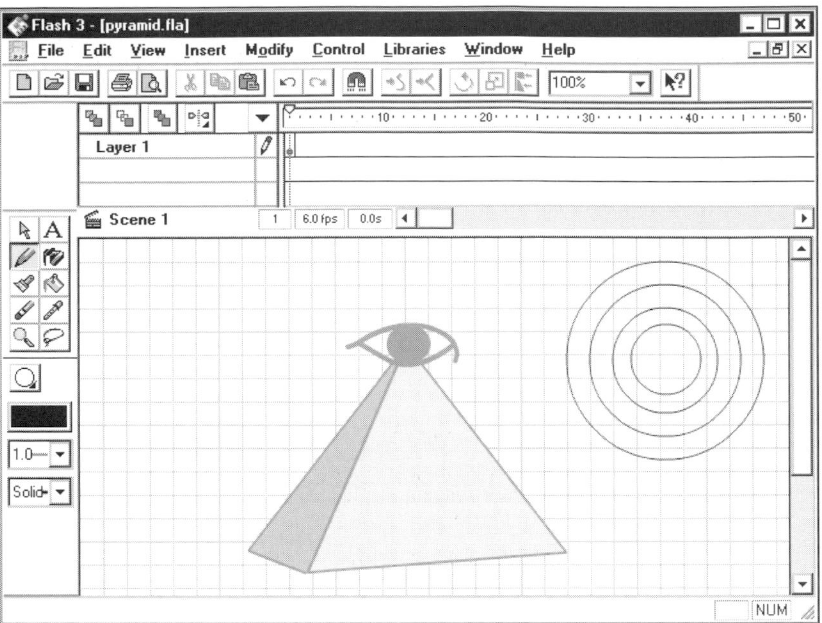

Figure 5.14 Perfectly concentric circles, drawn in their own group.

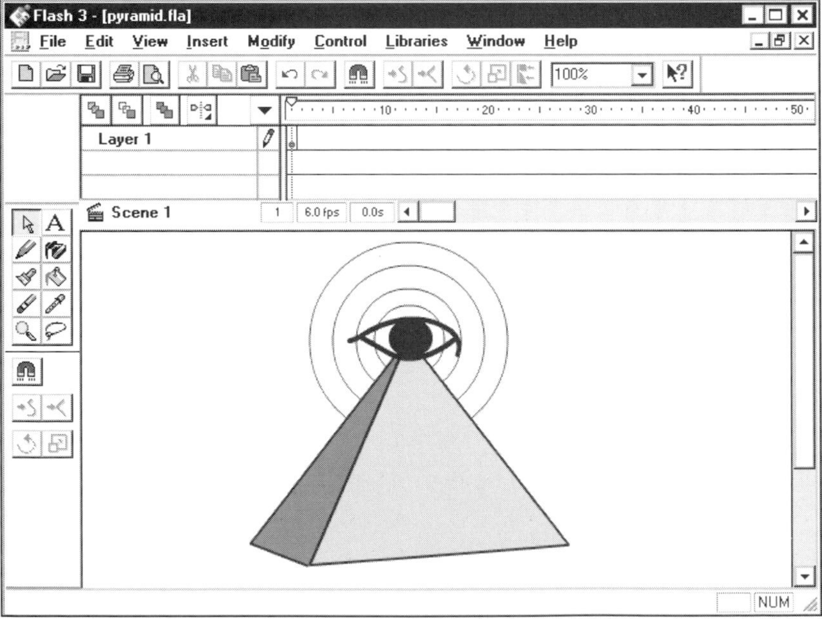

Figure 5.15 The finished pyramid and concentric circle drawing.

11. Now, insert keyframes for each of the selected frames. Place the cursor on the black bar that makes up the selected frames and right-click (Windows) or click and hold (Macintosh). The Frames menu appears. Choose Insert Keyframes.

12. Drag the Frames pointer to frame 1. Select the concentric circles group. From the main menu, choose Edit|Edit Selected. Select all the circles and press Delete/Backspace to erase them all.
13. Move the pointer to the next frame and erase all but the smallest circle.
14. Move the pointer to the next frame and erase all but the two innermost circles.
15. Move the pointer to the next frame and erase all but the three innermost circles.
16. The last frame shows all the circles. (You don't want to erase any.) Select this frame and drag across the next 20 (or so) frames. Right-click (Windows) or click and hold (Mac) on the selected frames; then, choose Insert Frames from the Frames menu. This will cause the last frame to stay still (showing all the circles) for a few seconds before the movie loops. See Figure 5.16.
17. Save your movie. Then save your movie as a symbol, based on the instructions in the preceding exercise.

Note: *You may also want to save a movie of the concentric circles as a symbol. Then, you can use these concentric circles to represent the animation of many other things, such as waves emanating from a radio tower, ripples in a pond...you get the idea. To do this, return to each of the first five frames and erase the pyramid and eye. (This is easy, because they're grouped.) Then, save the movie as a symbol under a different name.*

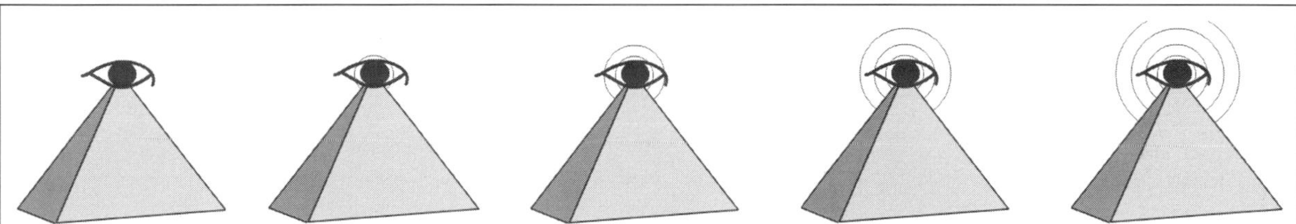

Figure 5.16 All the frames of the concentric circles movie.

Flashing Lights

Flashing lights are, oh, so easy to make and, oh, so useful. They can be the gleam in an eye, the blink of a headlight, or an idea about to be born. Actually, you would be smart to make a bunch of flashing lights and save them as a library of symbols. You could then use them all over a movie, plus they're very effective as buttons on a Web page.

Here's how to make flashing lights: Create several freeform splashes, fill them with a radial gradient, then eliminate the outlines and group each so that they can overlay one another. Then, select them all and use the align command to stack them all at their centers. Copy them all to keyframes and then move from frame to frame deleting the unneeded overlays. You can see a flashing light in Figure 5.17.

Figure 5.17 A flashing light.

This exercise will give you a quick rundown on how to make a flashing light movie. Follow these steps:

1. Place the drawing of the object from which the flashing light will emanate on the canvas. If this drawing isn't already a group or symbol, select all its components and Press Cmd/Ctrl+G to group it. (Grouping the drawing ensures that it won't be autoedited into additional shapes as you add new lines.)
2. With nothing selected, press Cmd/Ctrl+G to create a new group. Now, anything you do (until you choose Edit|Edit All) will be added to a new group.
3. Import a shape that will contain the flashing light (or draw one, if you insist on being original). Be sure that all the lines in the shape are ungrouped. Also, select and delete any lines other than the main outline or silhouette. Figure 5.18 shows the outline of a starburst that has been imported.
4. Double-click the starburst outline, or select it and choose Edit|Edit Selected. The lightbulb will fade to gray.
5. Now, we will make a radial gradient fill. Choose the Paint Bucket tool, then the color modifier. A palette will appear. See Figure 5.19.

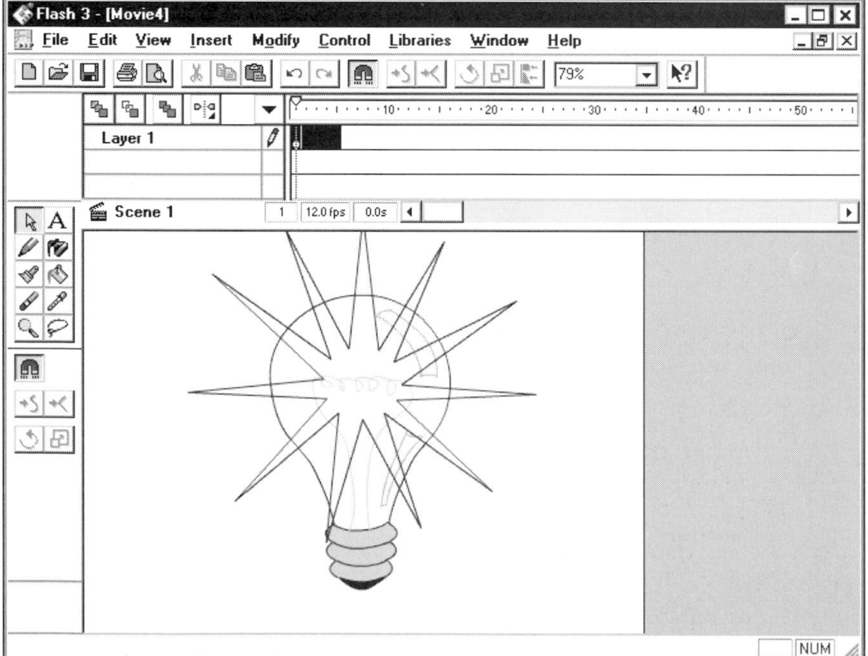

Figure 5.18 The starburst outline that will contain the flashing light.

6. Let's say you want to change one of the gradients in the row at the bottom of the palette. Click to choose the gradient you want to change. The palette will disappear, and the chosen gradient will appear as the Paint Bucket's color modifier.

7. Click in the color modifier box to reopen the palette; then, click in the palette icon at the very bottom center of the palette. The Color dialog box will open. Click on the Gradient tab. See Figure 5.20.

8. You will see a slot with two sliders on the left side of the Gradient tab. These sliders indicate the stop and start colors of the gradient. Click the color swatch inside the slider to change this color. Then, click and drag in the color modifier on the right side of the dialog box to choose the color for that slider. To the right of the color modifier you will find another slider that indicates the intensity (brightness) of the color you have chosen. Use the color modifier and the intensity slider to indicate a very light yellow (almost white).

9. Use the same procedure to pick a darker yellow for the other gradient slider. Leave the two sliders at opposite ends of the slot.

10. You'll want to be able to see through the "light," so drag the rightmost slider down until the Alpha box reads approximately 60%. (This makes the colors only 60 percent opaque, so that you can see through the "light.") When the colors are set as you like them, click the Change button. The color in the Paint Bucket color modifier will change to the gradient you have chosen. You can find more about making gradients in Chapter 4.

11. Double-click the starburst outline shape to edit its group. Choose the Paint Bucket cursor and click inside the starburst. It will fill with the gradient. Select the outline and delete it, leaving only the gradient fill. Choose Edit|Edit All.

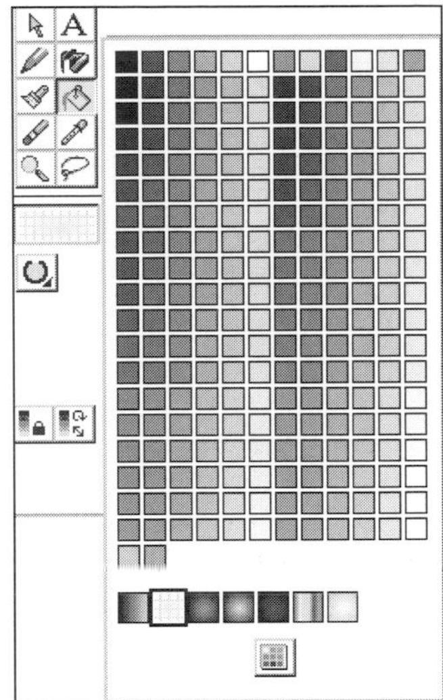

Figure 5.19 The color palette. Note the gradients in the row at the bottom of the palette.

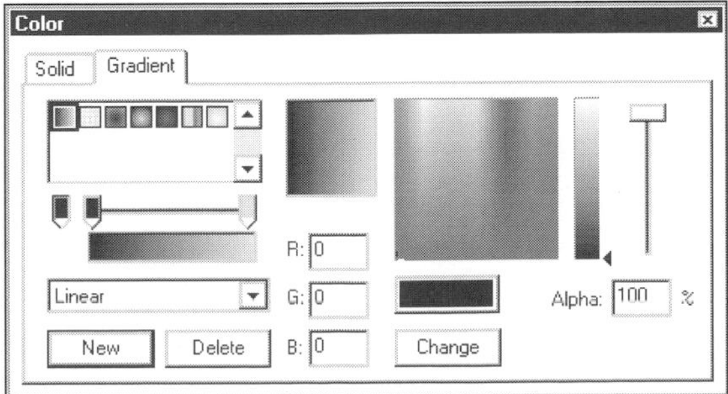

Figure 5.20 The Gradient tab of the Color dialog box lets you specify the colors and other characteristics of a gradient.

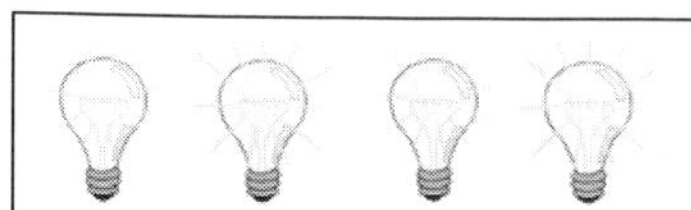

Figure 5.21 The four frames of the blinking light movie.

12. Choose the Arrow tool and drag across frames 1 through 4 to select them. Place the cursor over the resultant black bar and click and hold (Mac) or right-click (Windows) to access the Frames menu. Choose Insert Keyframes. You now have a copy of this first frame in each keyframe.
13. Select the first frame. Choose the Arrow tool and select the starburst. Since the starburst is grouped, a selection rectangle will appear around it. Choose Modify|Transform|Scale and Rotate. The Scale and Rotate dialog box will appear. Enter 75 (percent) as the scale factor and 12 (degrees) as the rotate factor.
14. Select the third frame. Choose the Arrow tool and select the starburst. Choose Modify|Transform|Scale and Rotate. The entries will be those you previously set. Since you want the light to alternate size and position in every other frame, just press Return.
15. Press Return to play the movie. You will see a pulsating light. To make this movie loop, choose Control|Loop Playback. Now, if you press Return, the light will pulsate endlessly. See Figure 5.21.

Traveling

This is the easiest animation you can make and, at the same time, one that you'll use more often than almost any other. It simply involves moving an object (such as a line of text or a speeding bullet) from one side of the frame to another. You could do traveling frame by frame—as you've done everything so far)—or you could do it the smart and easy way: by letting the computer do it through a process called *tweening*. You make a keyframe at the start of the movement. Put the item to move (it must be an overlay: group, symbol, or text) at its start point in this first keyframe. Then, choose Tweening from the Frames menu. Now, add another keyframe several frames further along the Timeline. The content of the original keyframe will appear. Select and drag it to the location where you want its movement to end. If you like, you also can scale and rotate it. The computer will automatically draw all the in-between frames. Figure 5.22 shows a simple traveling animation.

The exact steps for creating a traveling animation follow. Once again, we are using existing art, since the point of this exercise isn't to teach

Figure 5.22 An automatically tweened traveling scene.

you to draw, but to animate. Oh, we'll use some type, too. Follow these steps to create a traveling animation:

1. Place your drawing elements on the canvas and group them. Drag the group to the right side of the frame.
2. Enter some type, then scale and place it so that it is in position to be dragged by the subject of the drawing. I used a sketch of an airplane and the words "Flying Text" that you saw in Figure 5.22.
3. Press Cmd/Ctrl+A to select all (or choose Edit|Select All from the main menu). Now, press Cmd/Ctrl+G to group everything. (Only groups and symbols can be tweened.)
4. Double-click frame 1 in the Timeline. The Frame Properties dialog box will appear. See Figure 5.23.
5. Click the Tweening tab. From the Tweening pull-down menu, choose Motion. Leave the rest of the settings at their defaults.
6. Choose the Arrow tool and click in the Timeline at frame 5. Place the cursor on the highlighted frame and click and hold (Mac) or right-click (Windows). Choose Insert Keyframe from the Frames menu.
7. With the last frame still selected, select and drag the airplane and banner group clear off the canvas to the right.
8. Click in the Timeline slot for frame 1 to select it. The drawing group will appear at its original position. Drag it to the left until it is off the canvas.
9. Press Return to play your movie. If it plays too fast, you can slow the frame rate. You can also insert more frames in place of any of the non-keyframe frames. Then, the animation will play more smoothly, and the file size will remain the same. You can see the finished progression in Figure 5.24.

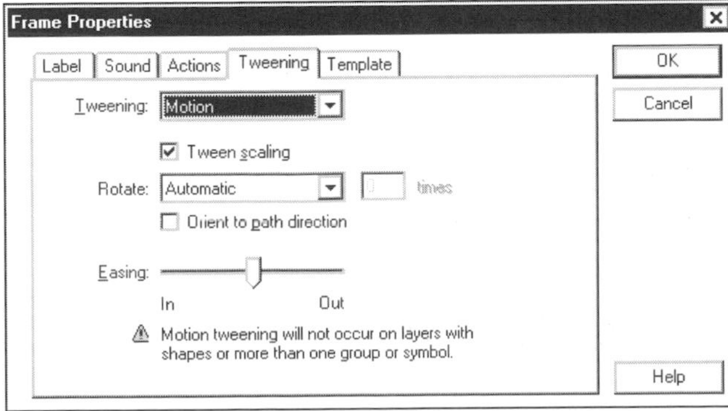

Figure 5.23 The Frame Properties dialog box, showing the Tweening tab.

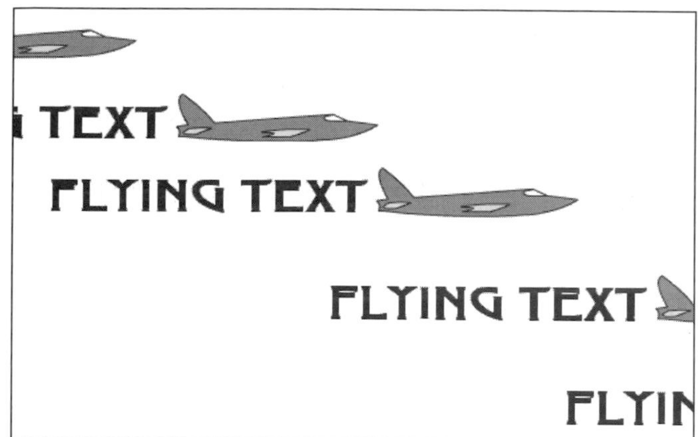

Figure 5.24 The flying banner.

Radiating Lines

Radiating lines can be used to imply that an object is outstanding, beating, bonging, or throbbing. The trick is to make the lines radiate in the right direction and along a specified path. I do this by first drawing a circle or oval with a dashed or dotted line, then scaling it at regular intervals with the Modify|Transform|Scale and Rotate (Cmd/Ctrl+Shift+S) command. Then, I align the resulting images all on a centerpoint, and make this a guide layer by choosing Guide from the layer modifier pop-up menu (the button just to the right of the layer name bar in the Timeline). Then, I can copy my original drawing to a number of keyframes, turn on Snap, and drag the lines until they snap to the next concentric circle. When I no longer need the guide layer, I simply choose Delete Layer from the layer modifier pop-up. See Figure 5.25.

Here's one possible scenario for ringing your bell. You'll think of several effective variations. Follow these steps:

Figure 5.25 The bell and radiating lines.

1. Draw or import the bell.
2. Choose the Pencil tool and the smooth modifier and draw several squiggly lines until you find one or two you like. See Figure 5.26.

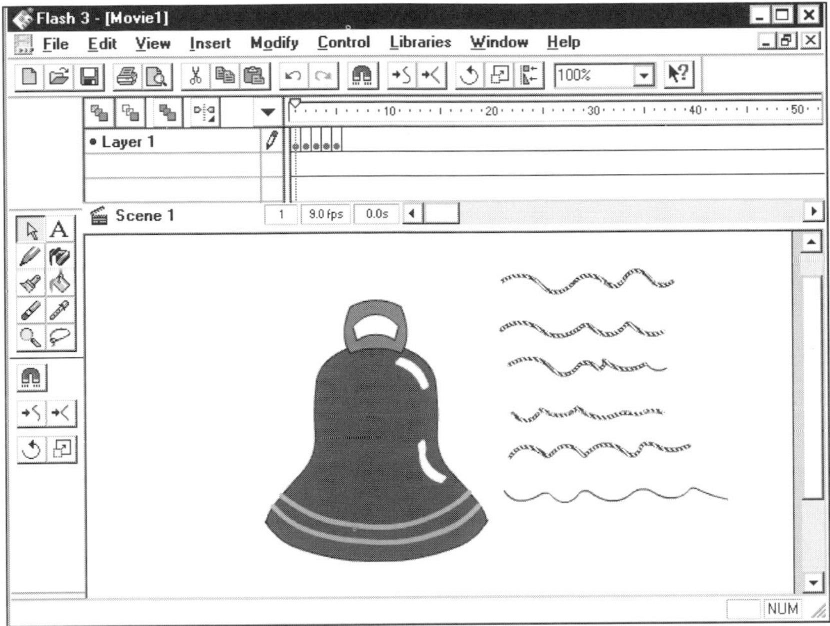

Figure 5.26 Making smoothed lines until you get one you like.

3. Erase all the lines you don't want to keep. I wanted all my radiating lines to be uniform, so I erased all but one. Drag the line into position alongside the bell.
4. Press Cmd/Ctrl+D to duplicate the squiggly line.
5. Choose the rotate modifier in the toolbox. Drag one of the corners of the squiggly line so that it rotates slightly, and then drag it into position. Repeat this step until the radiating lines surround half the bell. See Figure 5.27.
6. Select all the radiating lines. Press Cmd/Ctrl+G to group the radiating lines. Be careful not to include any of the shapes that compose the bell. Press Cmd/Ctrl+D to duplicate the radiating lines group.
7. Drag the second group of radiating lines to the opposite side of the bell. From the main menu, choose Modify|Transform|Flip Horizontal. You now have the group of radiating lines that you need for the opposite side of the bell.
8. Copy the bell and radiating lines to three more frames by inserting four new keyframes. Drag across several frames in the Timeline, then choose Insert Keyframe from the Frames menu.

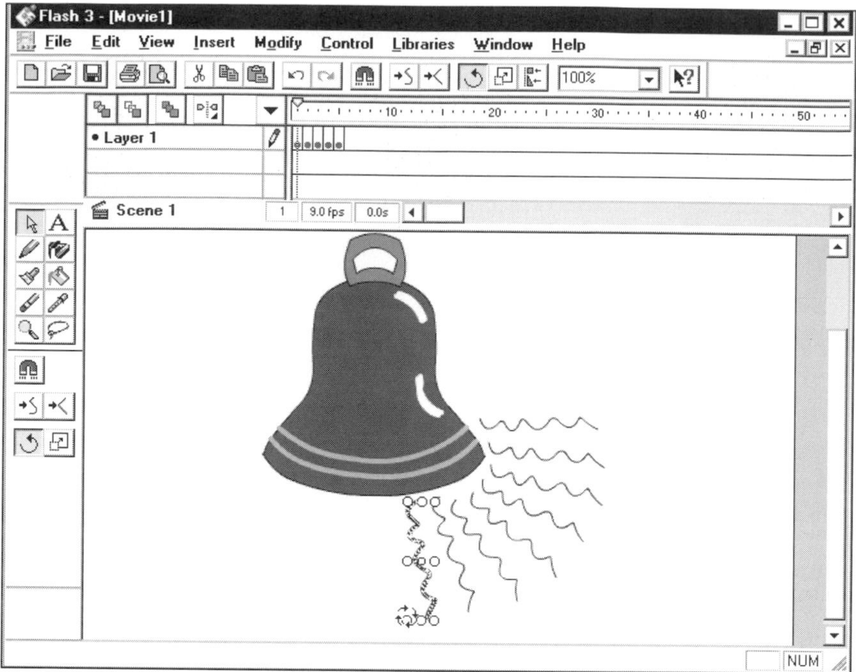

Figure 5.27 Lines radiating around half the bell.

9. Place the pointer in the first frame. Select and delete all the radiating lines. Then, place the pointer in the third frame and do the same.

10. Drag the pointer to the second frame. Press Cmd/Ctrl+A to select all, then Cmd/Ctrl+G to group the bell and radiating lines.

11. Now, you want to rotate the bell and radiating lines to the left. Choose Modify|Transform|Scale and Rotate. Enter 110 in the Scale field and -20 in the Degrees field. Click OK.

12. Move the pointer to the fourth frame and repeat the previous step, except enter 20 in the Degrees field.

13. To make the movie loop so that the bell rings continually, choose Control|Loop Playback. See Figure 5.28.

Spin And Zoom

This is another technique that can be done automatically (although it was done manually in the first exercise). You simply put the subject in the first frame, and insert a keyframe as many frames later as you want the spinning and zooming to end. Select the first keyframe, double-click it to activate the Frame Properties dialog box, and choose the Tweening tab. You can choose whether to tween motion or shape

Figure 5.28 All four frames of the bell-ringing movie.

from the Tweening pull down menu in the Properties dialog box, then choose the type of rotation from the Rotation pull-down menu. Then click OK. That's all there is to it.

In this exercise, we'll not only spin and zoom, but have tweening change the color and opacity of the text as well. Follow these steps to spin and zoom:

1. Start by entering the text you want to tween. If you want to tween an object that will move against a static background or when there are other objects moving in other directions, create a new layer and place the tween on it. For now, we'll just keep it simple and tween in a new movie with a blank canvas.
2. Select the word(s) you just typed. From the main menu, choose Insert|Create Symbol. The Symbol Properties dialog box will appear. See Figure 5.30.
3. Enter a descriptive name in the name field. Click the Graphic radio button. Click OK.
4. From the menu bar, choose Window|Library. You will see your symbol in the library. (This is just a check to make sure you have saved your symbol. You don't need to do anything with the library window at this time.)
5. Select frame 10, then click and hold (Mac) or right-click (Windows) to choose Insert Keyframe from the Frames menu.

Note: *Although you can't edit the tweened frames, you can change them into keyframes and then edit them. That way, you get automatic positioning and rescaling, but you also can make changes in the individual frames. To do this, place the I-beam on the Timeline at the frame you wish to convert to a keyframe (by clicking on a given frame in the Timeline) and then choose Insert Keyframe from the Frame menu. You then will be able to make any change or addition to this frame you like. You also could highlight all the frames and choose Insert Key Frame from the Frame menu to make all the tweened frames into keyframes. That's how I changed the color of the text in the spin-and-zoom example in Figure 5.29.*

Figure 5.29 The graphic we'll spin and zoom.

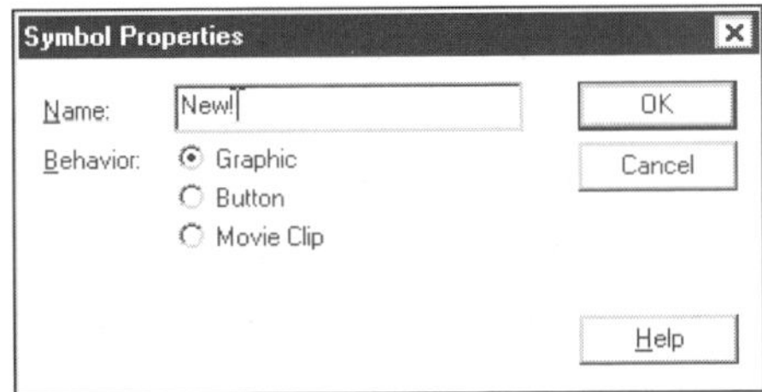

Figure 5.30 The Symbol Properties dialog box.

6. Choose the Arrow tool and select the symbol (if it's not already selected). Then, choose the scale modifier. Press Shift to enforce proportionate scaling, and drag one of the sizing boxes until the word fills about half the canvas. See Figure 5.31.

7. Double-click frame 1. The Frame Properties dialog box appears. Choose Motion from the Tweening pull-down menu and Clockwise from the Rotate pull-down menu. Make sure that Tween scaling is checked. (If not, just click in the box.) Click OK. You have just made a spinning and zooming animation. Press Return/Enter to watch the amazing effect. But wait, there's more...

8. Make sure the pointer is over frame 1. Choose Modify|Instance from the menu bar. The Instance Properties dialog box appears. (This is why you made the text into a symbol; otherwise, there would be no access to the Instance Properties, and so you couldn't tween between them.) Choose Color Effect from the pull-down menu and drag the Alpha slider to approximately 10 percent. You can see the Instance Properties dialog box in Figure 5.32.

9. Move the frames pointer to frame 10. From the main menu, choose Modify|Instance. When the Instance Properties dialog box reappears, click the Color Effect tab. The choice of settings changes. (See Figure 5.33.) Choose Tint from the Color Effect pull-down menu. Drag the amount slider to 100 percent. Use the color modifier and intensity slider to choose a bright red color. Click OK.

10. You have now made your movie tween a color change, and a transparency change—in addition to the rotation. Figure 5.34 shows you every other frame in the final sequence.

Figure 5.31 The scaled-up symbol in the last keyframe.

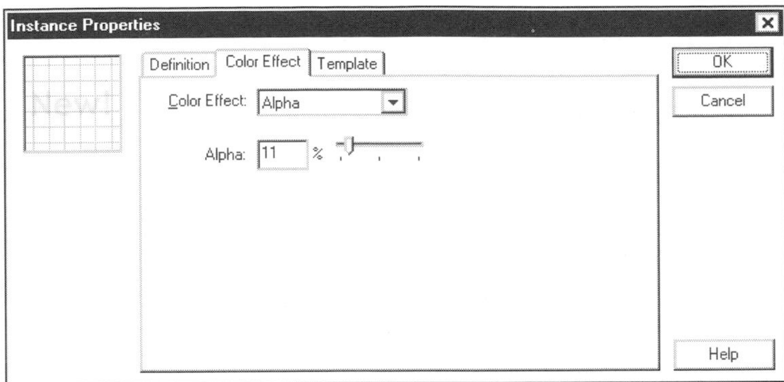

Figure 5.32 The Instance Properties dialog box, showing the setting for this exercise.

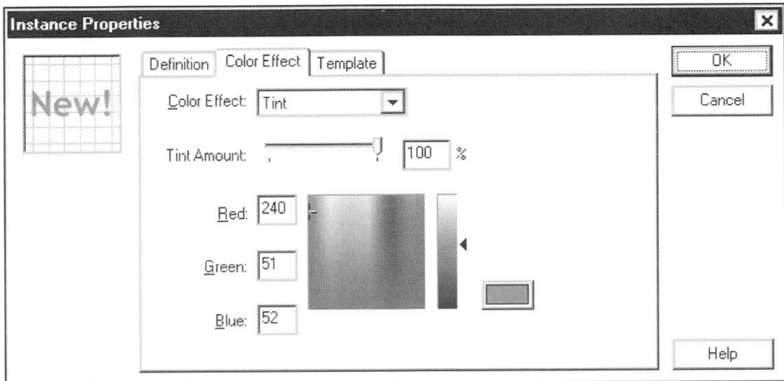

Figure 5.33 Instance Properties settings for tint.

Figure 5.34 Every other frame in the tweened sequence.

Transition Effects

Transition effects are those that move us from one scene to another. Examples are wipes and dissolves. Flash has no built-in transition effects, but you can animate them in several ways. One of my favorites is "fading in" on a drawing, an effect that has been made much easier in Flash 3. You simply save the frame you want to fade in (or out) as a symbol, then use the Symbol Instance properties to modify the transparency of the start or stop frame.

This exercise fades in a photo of a phone from PhotoDisc's Everyday Objects 1 collection. (The photo is shown in Figure 5.35.)

This one's really easy. Follow these steps:

1. Select the object you want to fade in (in this case, an imported PNG photo). Choose Insert|Create Symbol from the main menu. When the Symbol Properties dialog box appears, name the symbol, click the Graphic radio button, and then click OK.
2. While the original imported photo is still selected, choose Edit|Clear or press Backspace/Delete to erase it. The canvas is now blank.
3. From the main menu, choose Window|Library. Drag the phone symbol to the center of the canvas.
4. From the main menu, choose Modify|Instance. When the Instance dialog box appears, click the Color Effect tab. From the Color Effect pull-down menu, choose Alpha. Enter 0 in the percentage box or drag the slider to the far left. Click OK. The phone will appear to disappear.
5. Select frame 10. Click and hold (Mac) or right-click (Windows) on the selected frame and choose Insert Keyframe.
6. Select frame 1. Double-click the selected frame to bring up the Frame Properties dialog box. When it appears, click the Tweening tab. From the Tweening pull-down menu, choose Motion. Leave the rest of the settings at their defaults and click OK.
7. Press Return/Enter to see your movie. The phone will slowly fade into view, as in Figure 5.36.

Figure 5.35 The phone photo.

Figure 5.36 The phone, fading in.

Animation Fundamentals

You have now used the three fundamental types of Flash animation:

- Frame by frame
- Tweened
- Still-frame

You already have a good sense of the functions of frames and where to find commands on the Timeline. In addition to discussing the three types of animation and how to implement each, this section also will show you how to use layers to create complex animations, and how to use animated symbols to make animations even richer.

Frame By Frame

Frame-by-frame animations require that every (or nearly every) frame be a keyframe. In each keyframe, something changes, and you (not the computer) have to make the change. The walking stick figure in Figure 5.37 is an example of frame-by-frame animation.

Figure 5.37 Frame-by-frame animation of a walking stick figure.

USING STICK FIGURES AS SKELETONS

Animating stick figures is a good way to make a "skeleton" for animating complex frame-by-frame movements. It's especially common for people and animals. You then can make that layer a guide layer, start a new layer, and draw (or move) your full-bodied figure according to the way the skeleton moves. That way, you can test your movement before you have to make painstaking changes to a full drawing in each and every frame.

When animating a skeleton (stick figure), make all the lines for the left-side limbs red and all those for the right blue. It will be much easier to keep track of what moved past what. When you finish the animation, you can change the color of the limbs.

Tweening

As previously mentioned, tweening implies the drawing of two keyframes (to represent the starting and ending positions of a movement) with the in-between frames filled in by someone else. In the case of computer animation, the "someone else" is the computer software that automates the process. Flash's tweening capabilities are expanded in Flash 3. All of the following effects, except morphing, can be incorporated into the same tweening sequence:

- *Movement*—From the drawing's position in the first keyframe to the drawing's position in the last keyframe. The drawing will appear to move in a straight line.
- *Movement along a path*—You can have the tweened movement follow a line or curve in a guide layer.
- *Scaling*—Stretching or changing the size of the drawing (or part of it) from keyframe to keyframe. Flash can animate anything you can do with the Transform|Scale command or the Arrow tool's scale modifier.
- *Rotating and skewing*—Once again, you can use either the Modify|Transform|Rotate (or scale and rotate if you prefer numeric entry).
- *Morphing*—You can cause the shape in the start keyframe to gradually become the shape in the end keyframe. It is important that the two shapes be drawn starting at the same point and with lines moving in the same direction. Flash 3 provides "shape hints" to let us control the order of points in shapes so that they can be made to blend smoothly. To create a morph, double-click on the first keyframe to bring up the Frame Properties dialog box, click the Tweening tab, and select Shape from the Tweening pull-down menu.

- *Color Shifting*—You can start with one color and end up with another. The in-between frames will be progressive mixes of the beginning and ending tints. Color shifting works only on symbols and is controlled by the Modify|Instance command.
- *Fading*—A symbol can be assigned one level of transparency in the start frame and another in the end frame. You can also fade by specifying different levels of brightness for the start and stop keyframes. In-between frames will graduate smoothly between the two. Fading can also be controlled by the Modify|Instance command.

In Figure 5.38, you can see what happens to a bowling pin when it's tweened by moving, scaling, rotating, and dimming (reducing in brightness) all at the same time. Since the bowling pin is a symbol, you could animate the action of a whole rack of bowling pins after a strike.

How To Tween

The rules to remember are:

- If you want to tween something, you have to turn it into a group or a symbol first. Tweening affects only overlays.
- If you want to tween more than one overlay in a scene, you have to place each overlay in a separate layer.

Here's the step-by-step procedure for setting up a tween. I'm going to use the bowling pin I used in Figure 5.38, but you can substitute any overlay—that is, anything in the library or anything you first group.

1. From the menu bar, choose File|Open as Library and open the Book Library from this book's companion CD-ROM. Choose

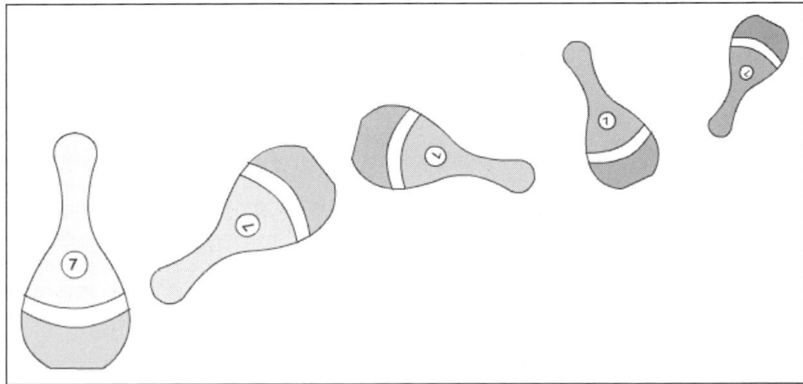

Figure 5.38 Tweening a bowling pin while moving, rotating, scaling, and dimming it.

> **Note:** *Okay, so you can't ease in and out in the same tween. But, you could add some frames to this sequence and make the last keyframe in this sequence the first keyframe in the next sequence. Then, continue your motion and have it slow down ("ease out") at the end. To your viewer, it would look exactly as though your tween eased in and out.*

Libraries|Graphics|Book to open this book's library. In the Library window, choose Bowling Pin. When the pin appears in the preview window, drag it into your movie.

2. Choose the Arrow tool and click on the bowling pin to select the symbol. Double-click in the layer 1 time strip at frame 1 (or whatever frame in your current movie you want to make the first keyframe). When the Frame Properties dialog box appears, choose the Tweening tab.
3. Choose Motion from the Tweening pull-down menu. If you plan to scale, check the Scale box. If the tween is going to follow a path, also be sure to check the Orient To Path Direction box.
4. If you want the movement to accelerate as it begins, slide the easing slider to the left. If you want the movement to brake as it ends, move the slider to the right. (Sorry, you can't do both in this program.) Click on OK.
5. Click in the Timeline several frames later (depending on how long you want it to take for the tween to occur). From the Frame menu, choose Insert Key Frame. A red arrow will appear in the Timeline between the first keyframe and the last. Move the frame pointer over the new keyframe.
6. Choose the Arrow tool (if it's not already active), and drag your overlay to its stopping point. If you want to scale or rotate, now is the time to do it.
7. Test your animation. All you have to do is press Return/Enter.

Tweening With A Path

It's really easy to make the tween follow any path you like, no matter how erratic (as long as you can draw it). The line that the overlay follows is called a *motion path,* and there's a special procedure for drawing one. The following steps assume that you've already followed the steps in the previous exercise and have created a tween.

1. Move the frame pointer to the first keyframe of your tween. From the menu for the layer in which you have created the tween, choose Add Motion Guide. A second layer will magically appear. An icon of a curved blue path and ball indicates that this is a motion guide layer. Notice that this layer has become the current layer, so anything you draw will appear on it.

2. Choose the Pencil tool and draw a zigzag path to the upper corner of the screen. Now, all you have to do is attach your overlay to the path.

3. From the main menu, choose View|Snap. Choose the Arrow tool and drag your overlay (in this case, the star) to the starting point of your motion path. A Snap circle will appear in the center of the circle when it is in the right position.

4. Move the frame pointer to the last keyframe and drag the overlay to the endpoint of the motion path.

5. Choose Tweening from the Frame pop-up for the first keyframe and then check the Orient to Path Direction box. Finally, since you don't want to see the motion path in your actual movie, choose Hidden from the layer pop-up.

Press Return/Enter to preview your movie.

Tweening Color Effects

Color effects tweening lets you create all sorts of bizarre and wondrous illusions. You can make objects fade from view, flash and pulse, or just change colors. Tweening color effects works only with symbols—not with other types of overlays and certainly not with anything you've drawn on the canvas (unless, of course, you first select it and choose the Insert|Create Symbol command).

The following exercise will take you through the not-so-painful process required to create a symbol.

1. Create a new layer by choosing Insert Layer from the layer pop-up (unless, of course, you're doing this in an already-blank movie).

2. From any library, choose the symbol you want to tween and drag it into the current frame. This is called establishing a link to the symbol.

3. Follow the same procedure you would use to create any tween: Choose Tweening from the Frame menu for the first frame, choose Motion from the Tweening dialog box, check any desired boxes, and click on OK. Wrap things up by inserting an end keyframe. (Look at the previous exercise if you've forgotten how to do any of this.)

4. Move the frame pointer back to the first frame. Select the symbol. From the menu bar, choose Modify|Instance. The Instance Properties dialog box appears. (See Figure 5.39.) Click the Color Effect tab from the Color Effect pull-down menu, and choose the effect

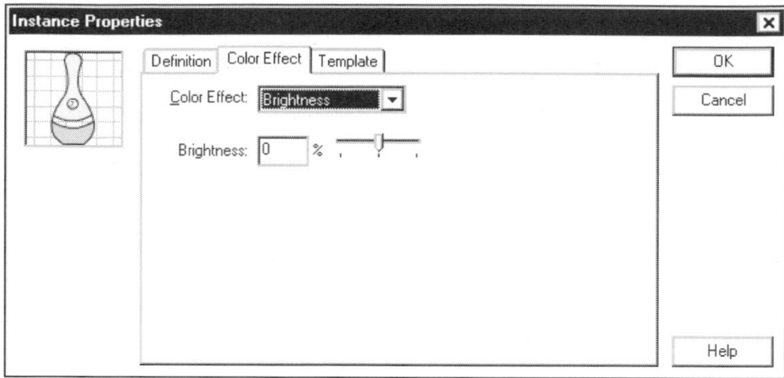

Figure 5.39 The Instance Properties dialog box.

you want (None, Brightness, Tint, Alpha, or Special). If you want the first frame to be the same as it was when you linked the symbol, don't take this step.

5. Move the frame pointer to the end keyframe. Choose Instance|Modify again and set Instance Properties Color Effect as you want your effects to appear at the end of the tween.
6. Press Enter/Return to test your movie.

You can add other tweening effects to this symbol if you like. All you need to do is move the frame pointer to the first frame of the tween, choose Tweening from the Frame menu again, and this time check Tween Scaling and/or Tween Rotation. Move to the last frame of the tween and scale, rotate, or both.

Tweening Shapes

You can't combine shape tweens (also known as morphs) with motion tweens, although the morph will move if the shapes to be tweened are in different positions on the layer. Otherwise, the steps are very similar to those described previously, except you choose Shape from the Tweening pull-down menu in the Frame Properties dialog box. The shape in the first frame will then metamorphose into the shape in the last keyframe.

Tweening shapes differs from motion tweening in two important ways:

- You can't shape tween a group or symbol. All the shapes must be independent of one another.
- It's a good idea to tween shapes on a separate layer from the rest of the movie.

Step by step, here's how you go tween shapes:

1. Unless you are starting with a blank movie, place the cursor over the icon just to the right of the active layer name. Click to pull down the Layers menu. From the Layers menu, choose Insert Layer.
2. Insert a keyframe where you want to introduce the original shape. Create or import a new shape. (I used the bowling pin.) If you import the shape, or use a library symbol, you will need to ungroup or break apart all the elements until the entire drawing is on the canvas for that frame.
3. Select a frame farther down the Timeline. From the Frames pull-down menu, choose Insert Blank Keyframe (or just press F7). Draw or import the shape you want to use as the final shape. In this case, we used the bowling ball.
4. Select the first keyframe and double-click it to bring up the Frame Properties dialog box. Click the Tweening tab and choose Shape from the Tweening pull-down menu. Click the radio button that chooses between distributive and angular tweening, and drag the ease-in/out slider to the appropriate setting. Click OK.
5. Play the movie. The resultant frames will look something like Figure 5.40.

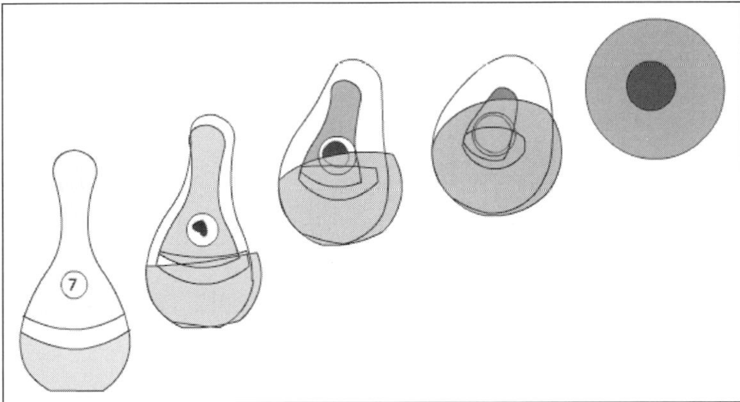

Figure 5.40 The bowling pin becomes a bowling ball over space and time.

The Instance Properties Color Effects

You can also tween instance properties of symbols, as mentioned previously. The properties you're most likely to use this way are the color effects. Changes in color effects for a given symbol affect only that instance (the place where the symbol appears) and not the symbol itself.

To bring up the Instance Properties dialog box, either double-click the instance in the movie or choose Modify|Instance from the main menu.

When you open the Instance Properties dialog box and click the Color Effects tab, you are given a choice of settings:

- *None*—This one is self-explanatory.
- *Brightness*—Changes the overall brightness of the symbol from pure white to black. Use this control to fade an item without introducing transparency.
- *Tint*—Use this to change the overall color of the symbol. You can switch it to just about any other color. This is a good choice when you want to make a symbol fade into the background color. (This doesn't work on patterned and photographic backgrounds, of course.)
- *Alpha*—Lets you enter a value or drag a slider to indicate a percentage of opacity for the given instance. This is the way you make a see-through bubble or glass of water.
- *Special*—Lets you change the saturation and brightness of each primary color (red, green, and blue) individually.

Still-Frame Sequences

It may seem an oxymoron to call a still frame a sequence, but the only way Flash lets you extend the life of a single frame is by copying it to a number of subsequent frames. So, anytime you want an object or a scene to just sit there doing nothing, you want to create a *still-frame sequence.*

The primary use for still-frame sequences is as backgrounds. You can draw or import a "set" or "location," then let your "actors" (drawings and overlays on other layers) perform in front of it.

Creating a still-frame sequence is so easy, you'll wonder why it has a special name. Insert a frame or end-of-sequence marker after any keyframe, and the keyframe will be copied to all subsequent frames.

Step by step, here's the drill:

1. Click in the Timeline under the marker for where you want to start your still-frame sequence. From the Frame menu, choose Insert Frame and then Insert Key Frame.
2. Click under the marker for the last frame in which you want your still sequence to appear. If this is the end of the sequence and nothing is to follow, you're finished. On the other hand, if you want to start a new still-frame sequence or another type of animation, choose Insert Frame and then follow the proper procedure for a frame-by-frame, tween, or still-frame sequence.

By the way, any editing changes that you make in any frame of a still-frame sequence will automatically occur in all the frames in that sequence.

You can't interrupt a still-frame sequence, either. If you insert a new keyframe anywhere in the Timeline that is occupied by your sequence, the frames after it will take on all the characteristics of the contents of the new keyframe. You can work around this seeming limitation by inserting pairs of keyframes and making changes in-between every other pair. You will find a good example of this in the next tip.

Note: *Suppose you want to create a strobe effect for your still-frame sequence. Insert blank keyframes at regular intervals along the way, and move the frame pointer to every other keyframe, in sequence. At each stop, tween a brightness effect. You could create similar effects for introducing wind or rain to your set by following this same technique.*

The Power Of Layers

So far, I've talked only about animating one sequence at a time. Truth is, Flash gives you tools that let you animate many things at once. This section is all about one of those tools: layers.

Theoretically (if you were really good at visualizing multiple-motion occurrences over time), you could hand-draw complex animations over a single span of frames. After all, Disney started out doing it that way. Imagine a scene in which six people are walking and running, all at different speeds and gaits. A flock of birds is flying overhead, moving from the opposite side of the screen. A helicopter is taking off, and the lights in the background cityscape are turning on and off. You can do all of this with Flash. All you have to do is take one step—er, layer—at a time.

With layers, you can run as many movies as you'd like, one atop the other. Since the canvas (background) for each of these layers is transparent, the activity on each of the layers seems to be taking place at the same time. You can change the stacking order of layers by dragging their name bars (just like layers in Photoshop, if you're familiar with that program). There's also a Layer menu button just to the right of the layer name box. The Layer menu hosts 20 commands for showing, hiding, and changing the properties of the layer to which it's attached. Figure 5.41 shows the Layer menu and its location in the window.

The purpose of all those commands on the Layer menu is to make it easier for you to edit the contents of layers when your movie becomes crowded with them. Layers number themselves automatically whenever you create a new one, but it's a much better idea to name them in a way that will help you to remember their contents.

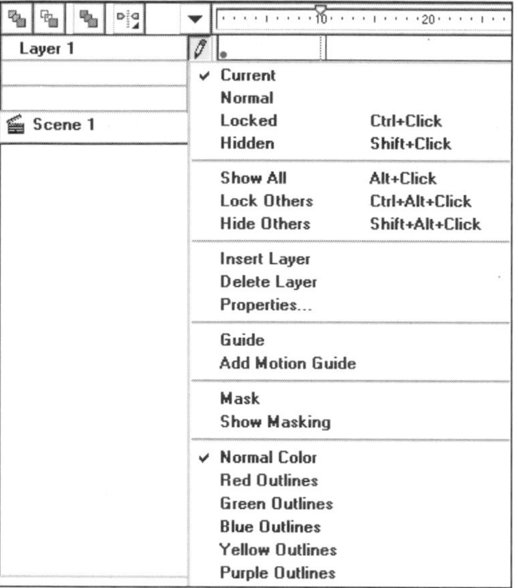

Figure 5.41 The layers section of the Timeline, showing the Layer pop-up menu.

Let's look at the commands on the Layer menu:

- *Current*—Makes this the layer you can draw on and puts a pencil icon on the Layer pop-up button.
- *Normal*—You can't draw new images on these layers, but you can edit their contents. Puts a hand icon on the Layer pop-up button.
- *Locked*—Makes it impossible to make changes to this layer, although you still can see it. This is the safest state for all layers that you aren't intentionally editing at the moment. Puts a padlock icon on the Layer pop-up button.
- *Hidden*—Makes the layer invisible and uneditable. Puts a red X on the Layer pop-up button.
- *Show All*—Shows all the layers. Saves you having to individually unhide layers. Often used in conjunction with Hide Others to check which visible elements are on the current layer.
- *Lock Others*—Locks all but the currently selected layer. Make this one a habit.
- *Hide Others*—Hides all but the currently selected layer.
- *Insert Layer*—Brings up the Layer Properties dialog box so you can name the new layer and then insert it below the currently selected layer.
- *Delete Layer*—Eradicates the current layer.

- *Properties*—Opens the Layer Properties dialog box so you can change the name of a layer.
- *Guide*—Turns this layer into a guide layer. Guide layers are not visible when printed or exported.
- *Add Motion Guide*—Attaches a new motion guide to the current layer.
- *Mask*—This new feature turns the current layer into a mask. You'll find the process of masking detailed in Chapter 7.
- *Show Masking*—This new feature shows the masking layer.
- *Normal Color*—The default mode, shows the current layer in its normal colors.
- *Red, Green, Blue, Yellow, or Purple Outlines*—Serves the same purpose that onion-skinning does for frames. Shows the current frame as outlines only, in the chosen color.

You also can view a thumbnail of each frame's image in the Timeline. This can be a great help in synchronizing the action with one frame on one layer with the action in another frame on another layer. To view the Timeline in preview mode, click on the Frame View pop-up button (just left of the Frame pop-up buttons, with a downward-pointing arrowhead). Choose either Preview or Preview-In-Context. Preview shows the extent of the drawing in each frame (as large as will fit in the thumbnail). Preview-In-Context shows the drawings in all the frames at the same size they will be in relationship to the entire movie. You can see what a preview looks like in Figure 5.42.

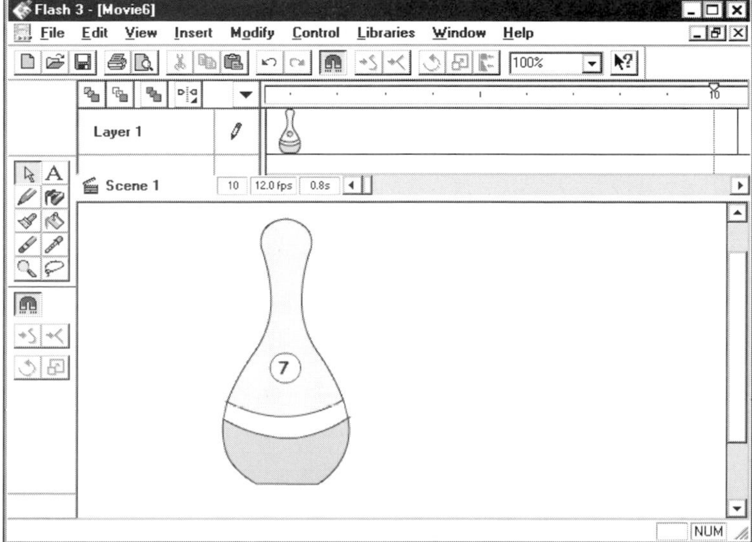

Figure 5.42 Viewing layers in the Timeline in the preview mode.

Guide Layers And Motion Guide Layers

Guide layers are layers whose only purpose is to act as a placement guide for creating the art in frames on other layers. Using the same techniques as for any other type of layer, you can draw or animate anything in a guide layer. So, you can use anything that will help you to properly visualize the movement of animated objects on other layers. For instance, you might animate a skeleton on a guide layer, then create the full-featured animation of the same creature on another layer.

To create a guide layer, choose Guide from the Layer pop-up menu for the layer you want to turn into a guide. In case you've forgotten, you access the Layer menu by clicking on the layer icon (the little picture that tells you what type of layer it is, at the right of the layer name bar).

You can turn any layer into a guide and any guide back into a normal layer by repeating the same command. The fact that a layer is acting as a guide is signaled by a blue icon of a T-square to the right of the layer name.

Motion guides at first seem similar to guide layers, but motion guides can't be animated and can't be converted to regular layers. Also, motion guides have to be attached to their parent layer. The purpose of a motion guide is to create a path for the movement of a tweened symbol to follow over a series of frames.

To create a motion guide, choose Add Motion Guide from the Layer menu for the layer to which you want to add a motion guide. The name of the motion guide layer will be the same as its parent layer, but there will be a blue icon of an arcing path with a ball at the end of it.

To create a motion path, choose the Pencil tool and draw any path you like while the motion guide is the current layer. (See Figure 5.43.)

Only symbols can be made to follow a motion path. To attach a symbol to a motion path, select it, then choose Tweening from the Frame menu. When the dialog box appears, check the Orient To Path Direction box and click on OK. Move the frame pointer to the first keyframe, then drag the symbol until it snaps to the beginning of the path. Repeat for the end keyframe.

The Symbols Of Power

If you've gotten this far, you probably know that *symbols* are a kind of overlay and are very closely related to groups. Symbols are another tool Flash provides to let you animate several things at once.

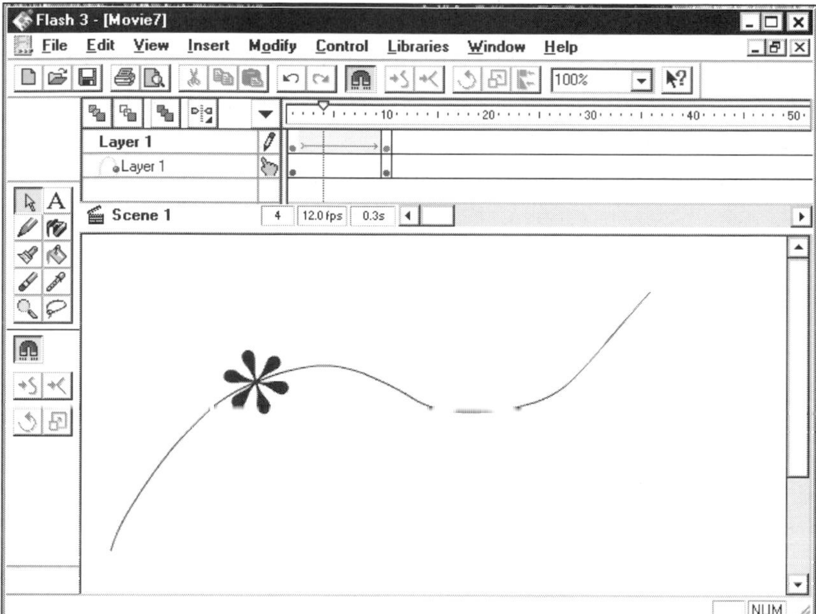

Figure 5.43 A motion path, drawn on a motion path layer.

Symbols are one of the most powerful features of Flash 3. They significantly reduce file size by making it possible to store all the data for a given shape only once, no matter how many times that shape appears in the movie. In other words, you could have a whole field of animated flowers—which appears in the background of several scenes in the movie—stored as a single flower.

Symbols also contribute to online performance because they need to be downloaded only once, no matter how many times they are used in a movie.

The chief differences between symbols and groups are:

- Symbols can be stored in the library and can be used in many different places in the same movie (different locations in the same frame, different frames in the same layer, different scenes). Symbols can greatly reduce file sizes because the symbol needs to be stored only once and simply appears in other locations via links.
- Symbols can be animated over any number of frames. In order to do this, you have to first choose Insert|Create Symbol from the menu bar when nothing is selected. A single-field dialog box appears to let you name the symbol. Inserting a symbol when nothing is selected automatically creates a *symbol scene*. Symbol scenes have all the animation capabilities available in Flash but

are created in their own space—so there's no chance of accidentally editing any other components of the movie. When you've finished animating your symbol, choose Edit|Movie from the menu bar. The symbol will instantly be stored in the Library under the name you gave it. It can then be used anywhere.

- The editing procedure is different for symbols. You select the symbol and choose Edit|Selected or Edit Symbol. Either command opens the symbol scene so that you can perform any editing operation possible in Flash 3, even add frames and animate a static graphic symbol. You can also edit symbols by choosing Window|Library, choosing the symbol you want to edit, and then choosing Edit from the Library pull-down menu. (See Figure 5.44.)
- Symbols can't be ungrouped. To drop the components in a symbol onto the canvas, you must select the symbol and then choose Modify|Break Apart from the main menu. If the subject of the symbol is a single group, it will appear as though nothing has happened. Check the Modify menu. If Ungroup is not ghosted, choose it.
- Every instance of a symbol can have its own properties and behavior. To change a symbol instance's properties, either double-click the instance as it appears on the canvas or choose Modify|Instance from the main menu.

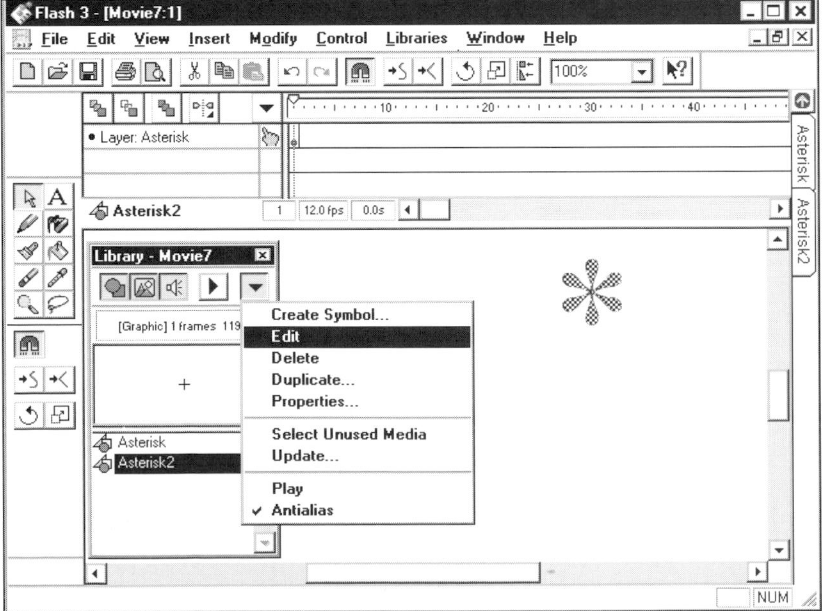

Figure 5.44 The library window showing the Library menu.

The Three Types Of Symbols

Flash 3 recategorizes symbols, dividing them into three types: graphic, button, and movie. You will need to understand the differences in characteristics and functions of each of these three symbol types. Macromedia calls each of these types a *behavior.*

Graphic

This is the preferred symbol behavior for static images. However, graphic symbols needn't be static. They have their own Timeline, and you can use any type of graphic element inside a graphic symbol, even other symbols. It differs from a movie symbol in that it is completely dependent on the main movie's Timeline. When the main movie's Timeline runs out, the graphic symbol stops animating. Also, you may not use sounds or interactive controls within a graphic symbol.

Button

Button symbols automatically respond to mouse events according to what you place in a given frame. A button symbol Timeline has only four frames, each of which has a distinct purpose: frame 1=mouse up; frame 2=mouse down; frame 3=mouse over; and frame 4=hit area. Movie symbols can be placed inside button frames in order to create animated buttons. Actions (see Chapter 7) can also be assigned to button events.

Movie

Within your movie, you can place a complete movie with an independent Timeline and full movie functionality. Movie symbols can include sounds, interactivity, and actions. It is even possible to place a movie symbol (also called a movie clip) in an animated button within a movie clip.

Note that these are the default properties of a symbol. In fact, every instance of a symbol can have its behavior reassigned through the Instance Properties dialog box.

Symbols That Aren't Symbols

Two types of elements stored in the Library aren't symbols: bitmaps and sounds. (Any scanned photo is a bitmap.)

How To Make A Symbol

You can create a symbol either from anything you can select on the canvas (including multiple symbols), or you can create an empty symbol and then place anything into it you like. The only way to create a symbol from an existing movie is to edit a symbol or create an empty one, then (while still in symbol editing mode) choose File|Import Movie.

From Existing Selections

Follow these steps to make a symbol from existing selections:

1. Select all the elements you want to include in the symbol. (These can include all types of overlays, as well as graphics on the canvas.)
2. From the main menu, choose Insert|Create Symbol. The Symbol Properties dialog box appears.
3. In the Symbol Properties dialog box, enter a name for the symbol in the name field (or simply accept the default), then click the radio button that designates whether the behavior is to be as a graphic, button, or movie clip.

Creating An Empty Symbol

Follow these steps to create an empty symbol:

1. Be positive that no elements are currently selected. The way to ensure that no invisible (or difficult-to-notice) item is selected is by choosing Edit|Deselect All from the main menu (or press Cmd/Ctrl+Shift+A). The Symbol Properties dialog box will appear.
2. In the Symbol Properties dialog box, enter a name for the symbol in the name field (or simply accept the default), then click the

radio button that designates whether the behavior is to be as a graphic, button, or movie clip. Click OK. You will immediately enter Symbol Edit mode.

3. Use any of the Flash 3 tools and features to create the contents of this symbol.
4. To finish editing and store the symbol in the current movie's library, choose Edit|Edit All from the main menu.

Makin' The Scene

Next to a movie, a scene is the most encompassing unit of construction in a Flash movie. Scenes are simply movies linked together for purposes of organization and interactivity. (You'll learn all about working with interactivity in Chapter 8.) Meanwhile, suffice it to say that organizing a movie into scenes arranged by such criteria as topic, location, or number makes it much easier to "jump" from a movie covering one topic to a movie covering another. This device alone is enough of an organizational and interactivity tool for use in many offline documentation and training applications. The lessons on using Flash that ship with the program are a prime example of how well this works. You can see a page from one of these lessons in Figure 5.45. Notice the tabs on the right side of the screen. Each tab represents a different scene (or, in this case, lesson subject).

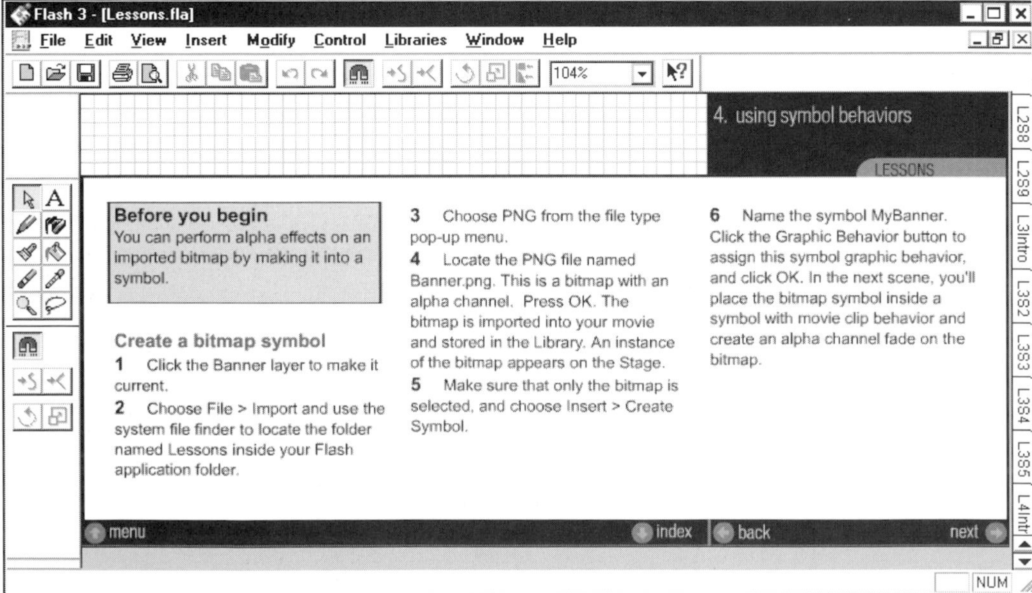

Figure 5.45 The Flash lessons. Each tab is a scene.

As soon as you create a movie, you automatically create a new scene. Remember that, in Flash, a movie can be either an animation sequence or a static image. Each scene has an associated tab that looks like the tab on a notebook divider. The name of the scene appears vertically on its tab. (Scenes are automatically named in the sequence in which they are created: Scene 1, Scene 2, and so forth.) If you want to give a scene a more meaningful name, choose Modify|Scene and name or rename the scene in the Scene Properties dialog box shown in Figure 5.46.

To create a new scene, choose Insert|Scene from the main menu. The display automatically switches to the first frame of a new movie. Don't worry; any work you've done up until now is still in the previous scene, and clicking on its tab will return you to it.

Tabs are turned on as soon as you insert a new scene. You can toggle tabs on and off by choosing View|Tabs. As I said earlier, if you click on a tab, you go directly to that scene. Double-clicking on a tab (or choosing Modify|Scene) brings up the Scene Properties dialog box so you can change the name on its tab. You can reorder the scene sequence simply by dragging a tab. If there are too many tabs (or their names are too long) to fit the vertical space on the screen, scroll arrowheads (up and down) automatically appear at the bottom of the tabs column. Clicking on one or the other moves you up or down through the tabs.

Another way to go to a specific scene, especially if you have tabs turned off, is to use the View|Goto submenu. (See Figure 5.47.) You can jump to the first, last, next, or previous scenes using this submenu. The submenu also lists the names of all current scenes, so you also can go directly to any one of them.

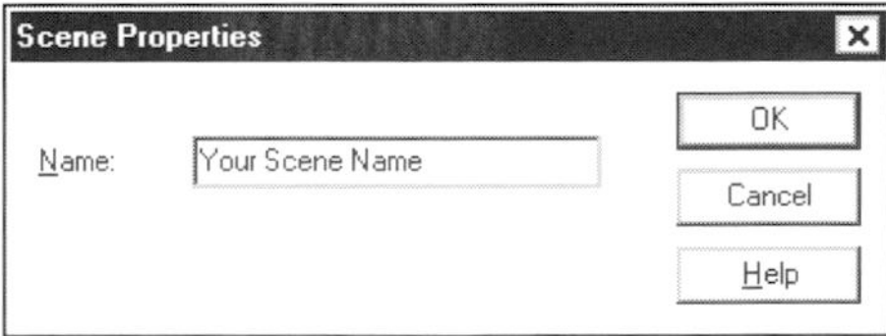

Figure 5.46 The Scene Properties dialog box.

View Insert Modify Control Libraries Window Help

Goto		First	Home
		Previous	Page Up
		Next	Page Down
		Last	End
100%	Ctrl+1	Scene 1	
Show Frame	Ctrl+2	Scene 2	
Show All	Ctrl+3	Scene 3	
Outlines	Ctrl+Alt+Shift+O	✓ Scene 4	
Fast	Ctrl+Alt+Shift+F		
✓ Antialias	Ctrl+Alt+Shift+A		
Antialias Text	Ctrl+Alt+Shift+T		
✓ Timeline	Ctrl+Alt+T		
Work Area	Ctrl+Shift+W		
Rulers	Ctrl+Alt+Shift+R		
✓ Tabs			
Grid	Ctrl+Alt+Shift+G		
✓ Snap	Ctrl+Alt+G		
Show Shape Hints	Ctrl+Alt+H		

Figure 5.47 The View|Goto submenu.

Finally, you can move from scene to scene from the keyboard. Press Home to go to the first scene, End to go to the last, or PgUp or PgDn to move up or down a page at a time.

It is also perfectly possible to play multiple-scene movies from start to finish without resorting to tabs or menus. To play a movie from start to finish, choose Control|Play All Scenes, then choose Control|Play (or press Enter/Return or choose Control|Show Controls, and click on the Play button).

Onion-Skinning

Onion-skinning is a term derived from the practice of analog animators who would use very thin and translucent paper to trace and modify drawing elements from one frame to another. Tracing the main elements of one frame's drawing that can be laid over the next ensures that things have moved the proper distance and in proper relationship to their position in the previous frame. The practice sounds tedious, but it eliminates a lot of guesswork.

Working on a computer with a program such as Flash makes life much easier. Flash automates onion-skin drawings at the push of a button—well, four buttons, really. You can see them in Figure 5.48, along with their names. Moreover, you can "onion-skin" multiple frames or onion-skin showing only the vector outlines of the preceding and succeeding frames.

Onion Skin

The first button, Onion Skin, is the one I use most often. You have already used it several times for tracing single frames. This button

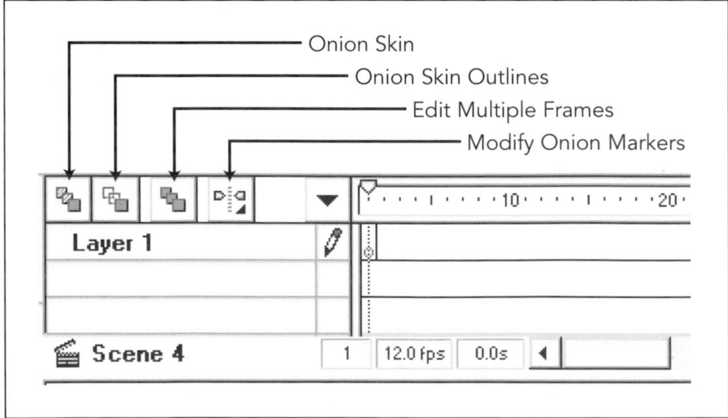

Figure 5.48 The Onion Skin buttons.

turns on onion-skinning and lets you see dimmed, full-detail images of the frames before and after the current frame. At the same time, you can use any of Flash's creating and editing tools on the current frame. The number of frames you can see before and after the current frame is dependent on where you set the markers. (See the following section called "Markers.") For an example of what onion skin looks like with two previous frames showing, see Figure 5.49.

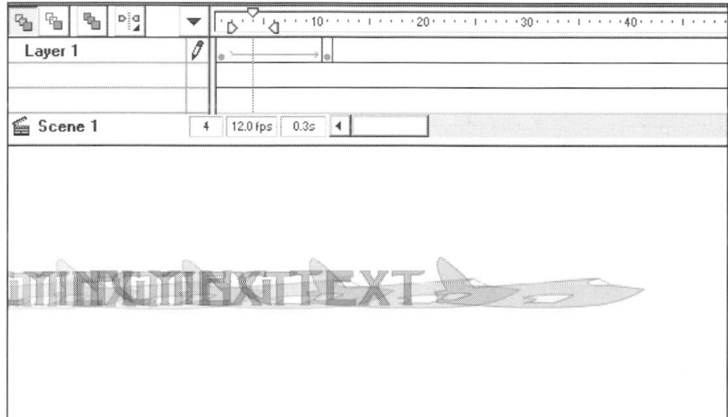

Figure 5.49 Onion Skin with two previous frames.

Onion Skin Outlines

If you have to onion-skin very complex shapes as they move, you may really appreciate this one. The onion-skin frames show only the vector outlines of their shapes, so it can be easier to distinguish the contents of the current frame from that of the onion-skinned frames. Take a look at Figure 5.50.

Edit Multiple Frames

This button lets you directly edit the frames within the current onion-skin range (whichever frames are between the markers). In Figure 5.51, notice that none of the frames is dimmed. If any of these frames were tweened, the tweened frames would be ghosted and would change in accordance with the edits made to keyframes.

Modify Onion Markers

Macromedia also calls this the *current frame button.* (After all, consistency can be boring.) This is a pop-up button used to control the behavior of the onion skin markers. You can see the pop-up in Figure 5.52. Table 5.1 explains the functions of the items on the Modify Onion Markers menu.

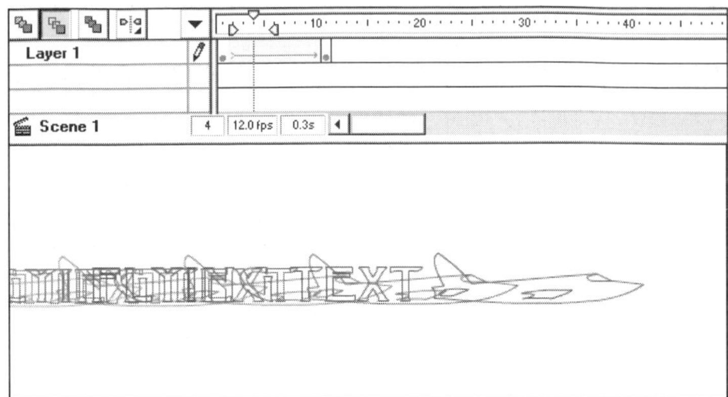

Figure 5.50 Onion Skin outlines view.

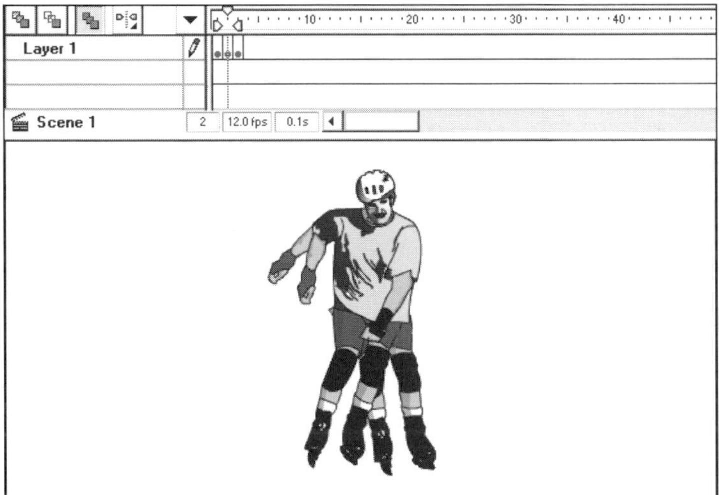

Figure 5.51 The contents of multiple frames are visible when editing multiple frames.

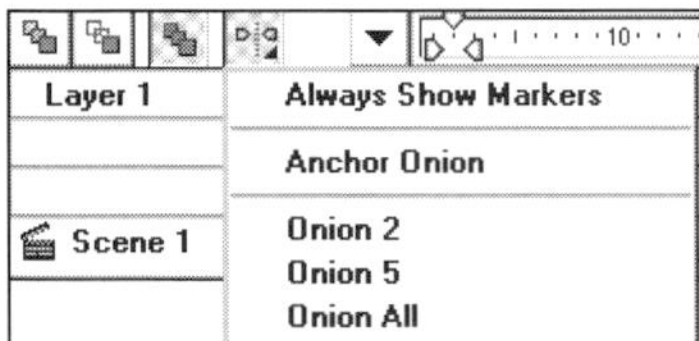

Figure 5.52 The Modify Onion Markers pop-up.

Table 5.1 Modify Onion Markers menu.

Menu Item	Function
Always Show Markers	The markers are always visible, whether or not onion-skinning is active. This command is a toggle (switches on and off).
Anchor Onion	Keeps the marker tabs in their current location, regardless of where the frame pointer is located. The result is that onion skins of the same frames are always in view, except they are lighter or darker according to the location of the frame pointer.
Onion 2	Shows two frames on either side of the frame pointer.
Onion 5	Shows five frames on either side of the frame pointer. The markers move to reflect this, regardless of where you move the frame pointer.
Onion All	Onion-skins every frame in the sequence. This can be useful for editing short scenes and sequences but could be very confusing if you apply it to a sequence of more than a few frames.

Markers

Markers bracket the frames that will be onion-skinned. (See Figure 5.53.) You can manually change the number of frames that will be onion-skinned by dragging the markers. For instance, I often find it helpful to turn off onion-skinning for frames that follow the frame I am editing. All I have to do is drag the right-hand marker to the selected frame.

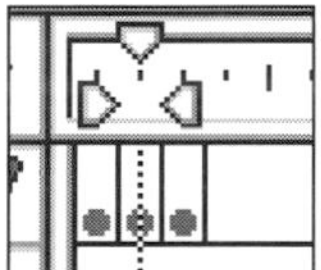

Figure 5.53 The markers.

Moving On

This chapter has shown you how to make some simple animations and has given you basic training in using the various components of Flash's animation interface.

The next chapter will dive into symbols in depth. You'll learn all about the three new symbol behaviors in Flash 3 and how to maximize their power.

6 The Symbols Of Power

Ken Milburn

This chapter will provide you with a thorough explanation of all three types of symbols: graphics, buttons, and movie clips. You will also learn how to deal with bitmaps and sounds, which are automatically placed into the symbols library.

Symbols are entities that can be repeated any number of times within a Flash movie and that can contain any and all the elements of any Flash movie. The two main advantages of using symbols, rather than re-creating entities, are that you create the symbol only once, and that the data for the symbol is stored only once for the entire movie. This results in a smaller data file that takes less time to download. Symbols are one of the main reasons (in addition to the use of vector rather than bitmapped graphics) why Flash's Web performance is so stunning.

All symbols are stored in the library of the current movie. You can drag and drop symbols into other libraries, so you can have a stockpile of symbol elements that you can use in all your movies, or in all the movies for a particular client or for a particular category. The Library window can be seen in Figure 6.1.

Flash 3 has three distinct types of symbols: graphic, button, and movie clip. Two other categories of items are stored in the library: bitmaps and sounds. Each of these categories will be discussed in-depth in the following sections. Then, you'll learn how to edit instances (the individual occurrence of a symbol in a movie), how to tween instances, how to place sounds in a symbol, and how to edit symbols.

Graphic Symbols

This is the type of symbol that you'll use most often to store static graphics (such as picture icons) and geometric elements (such as rounded rectangles). However, graphic symbols can be animated, and they have their own Timeline.

So, what's the difference between a graphic symbol and a movie clip? The animation in a graphic symbol stops when the Timeline of the containing movie stops. Also, neither sounds nor interactive controls will work within a graphic symbol.

Creating A Graphic Symbol

You can create a graphic symbol (or any other type of symbol) either from scratch or from existing selected elements.

Creating a symbol from existing elements is simple: All you have to do is to select the elements and press F8 (or choose Insert|Create Symbol from the main menu). When the Symbol Properties dialog box appears, click the Graphic radio button. Then, click OK. The symbol will automatically appear in the library. See Figure 6.2.

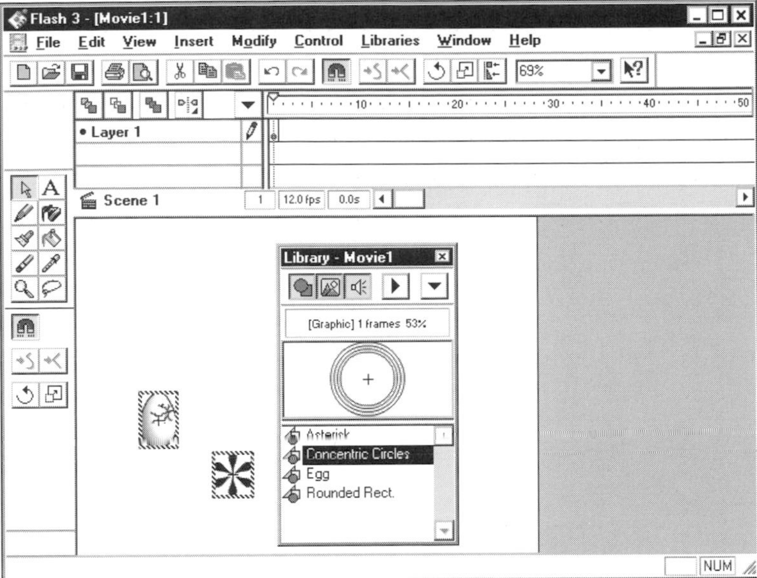

Figure 6.1 The Library window shows all the symbols stored in the current movie.

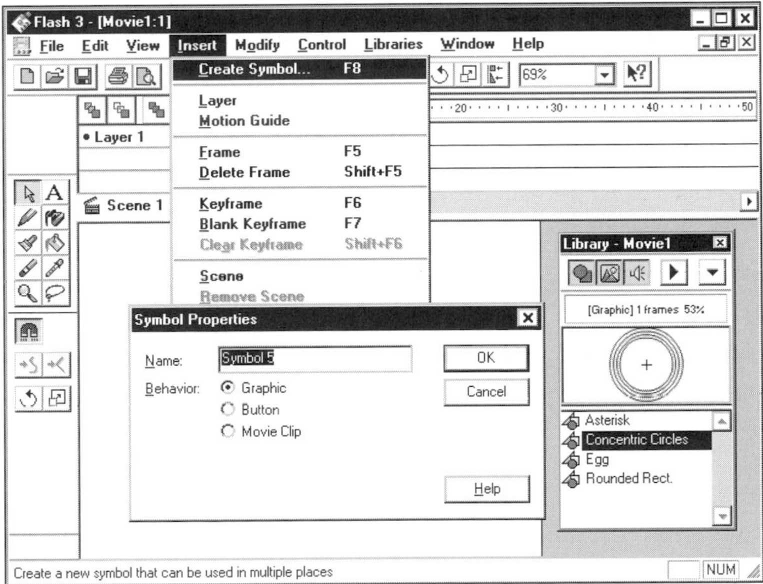

Figure 6.2 Creating a graphic symbol from existing elements.

To create a symbol from scratch, make sure nothing is selected by choosing Edit|Deselect All from the main menu (or press Cmd/Ctrl+Shift+A). Next, choose Insert|Create Symbol from the main menu. You will find yourself in Symbol Editing mode, where anything you create will then be stored as a symbol.

Buttons

Button symbols are four-frame movies, except that the playing of each frame depends on the state of the mouse. Each frame is named after a mouse state: Up, Over, Down, and Hit. The Up frame describes the mouse button that has not been pressed and that the cursor hasn't passed over. The Over frame depicts the button when the cursor passes over it, without pressing a button. The Down frame depicts the button when you click. The Hit frame is simply a graphic (which may as well be a solid color, because it will never be seen) that defines the shape of the area in which the other mouse events can occur. Figure 6.3 shows the four-frame, four-state Timeline and the four "looks" for a simple button. The figure is a composite screen shot; you won't normally see all four states of the same button on screen at once.

You can insert movie clips and graphic symbols into button frames, but you cannot insert another button. You can also assign actions to any of the first three button frames.

Here's the skinny on how to create a button from scratch:

1. Choose Edit|Deselect All from the main menu (or press Cmd/Ctrl+Shift+A) to ensure that nothing on the canvas is currently selected.
2. Press F8 or choose Insert|Create Symbol from the main menu. The Symbol Properties dialog box will appear. See Figure 6.4.

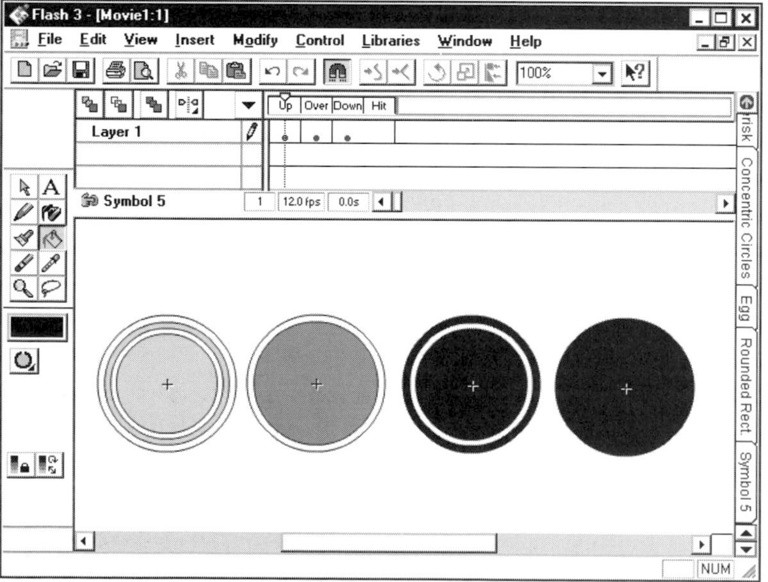

Figure 6.3 The four frames of the button Timeline and the four images for the button.

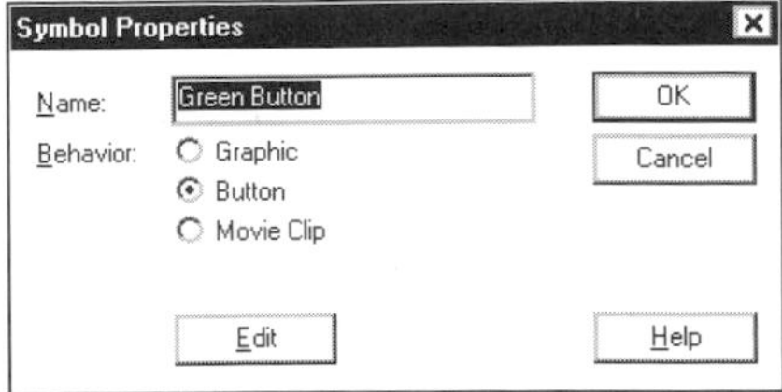

Figure 6.4 The Symbol Properties dialog box. The Button radio button has been clicked to designate this symbol as a button.

3. In the Symbol Properties dialog box, click the radio button labeled Button. You may also want to give your button a more descriptive name than the default. If so, enter the name in the name field. Click OK. The canvas clears.

4. You are in Symbol Editing mode. The Timeline shows four frames that are wider than movie frames and labeled Up, Over, Down, and Hit. Create the image for the Up state frame by using any of Flash's drawing tools or by importing graphics or symbols (but not other buttons).

5. Click the Over frame, then choose Insert|Keyframe from either the main menu or from the Frame pull-down menu. A copy of the image in the first frame will appear.

6. Select the copy of the first button and choose Modify|Break Apart from the main menu (so that you can edit the individual components). Make any needed changes.

7. Repeat Steps 5 and 6 for the Down frame.

8. Select the Hit frame. Choose Insert|Insert Keyframe. Choose the Pencil tool and the smooth modifier. Draw around the copy of the last button. Now, select and delete the elements that make up the copy of the Hit button.

9. Choose the Paint Bucket tool and click inside the outline you drew for the Hit area.

10. Choose Edit|Movie from the main menu. The button will be automatically saved in the library.

Adding Sound To A Button

You can add sound to any state of a button. Flash accepts only digitally sampled analog sounds, in the form of AIFF files on the Macintosh or WAV files in Windows. Because these aren't very efficient formats (analogous to bitmapped versus vector images), you should try to keep the sounds short. Simple clicks and beeps are most appropriate. The following steps allow you to add sounds to a button state:

1. Select the frame to which you want to add sound.
2. From the Frame pull-down menu, choose Insert Keyframe.
3. Choose Modify|Frame from the main menu. The Frame Properties dialog appears. See Figure 6.5.
4. Make sure there's a sound symbol in the library.
5. In the Frame Properties dialog box's Sound tab, choose the sound file you want from the Sound pull-down menu. From the Sync pull-down menu, choose Event. Leave Loops at zero and Effect at None. Click OK.
6. Test the button. Choose Edit|Edit Movie from the main menu. Then, choose Control|Enable Buttons. Click the button. When the mouse enters the state to which the sound has been attached, you should hear the sound.

Creating Animated Buttons

This is very simple. Just place a movie clip symbol in any (or all) of the button's four frames.

Movie Clips

Movie clips differ from graphic symbols mainly in that they will play independently of the main movie's Timeline. Any feature that can be added to a regular Flash 3 movie can be included in a movie clip. Also, both interactive controls and sounds function fully in the context of a movie clip.

One of the primary uses for movie clips is animated buttons. You can place a movie clip in any or all of the first three button states.

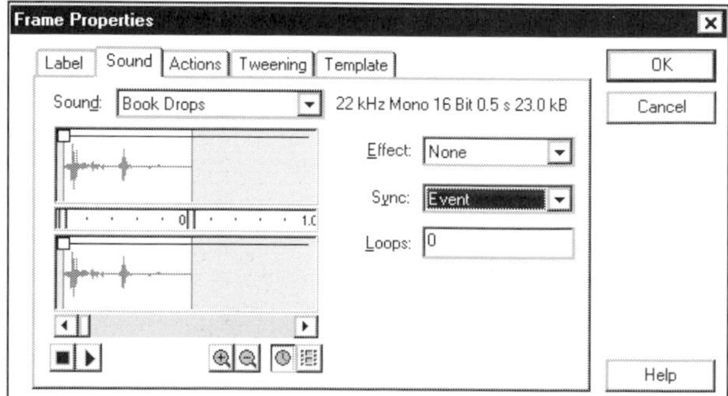

Figure 6.5 The Frame Properties dialog box's Sound tab.

Bitmaps

As soon as you import a JPEG, GIF, or PNG file, the data for that file is stored in the library. This means that you can reuse that bitmap as many times as you like in the same movie without increasing the movie's file size. Because even highly compressed bitmaps consume a lot of storage space, this is a very big deal.

Sounds

Flash accepts only analog sound files, which, like bitmaps, are memory hogs. The fact that sounds are always stored as symbols means that you can make the doorbell ring as often as you like without increasing the file size of your Flash movie.

Placing Sounds In A Movie

It's really easy to place sounds in a movie. Follow these steps:

1. Choose File|Import. The Import dialog box will appear. See Figure 6.6.
2. In the Import dialog box, choose WAV (Windows) or AIFF (Macintosh) as the file type. Browse until you find the sound file you are looking for, and click its name to enter it in the File Name field. Click OK.
3. The sound will appear in the Library window, with its file name immediately to the right of a speaker icon.

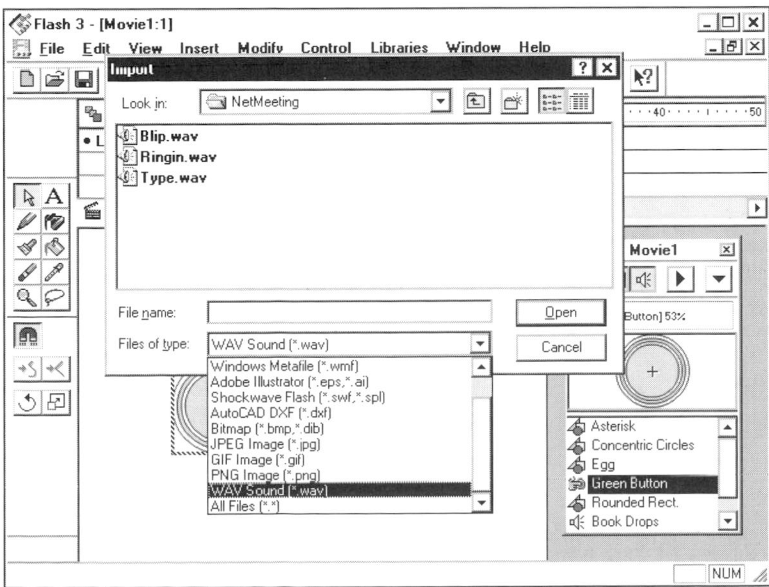

Figure 6.6 The Import dialog box, showing the Files Of Type pull-down menu.

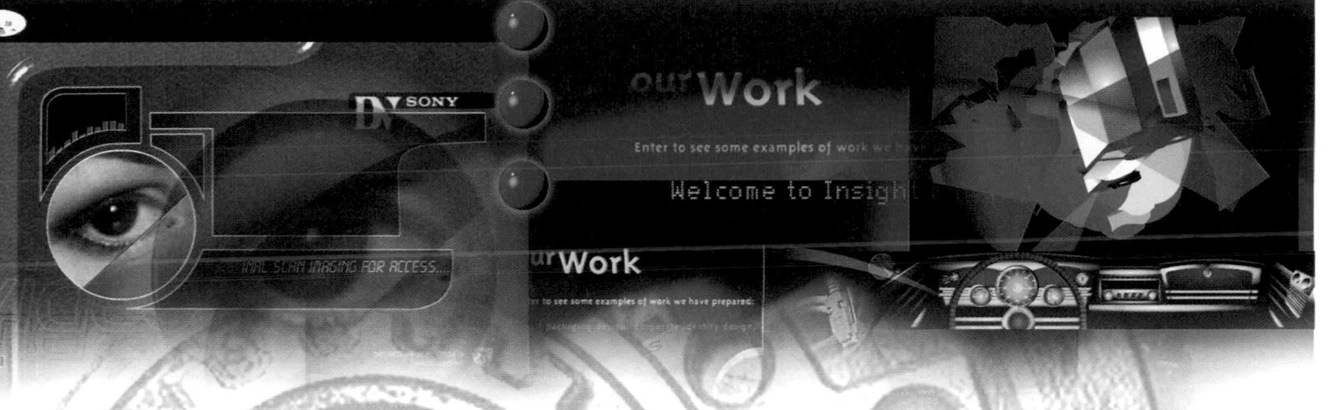

Flash Studio

This studio of outstanding Flash 3 Web sites shows you how some of the most talented Flash designers have taken advantage of this program's unique features. The purpose of the sites varies from pure entertainment to hard-nosed business.

Web Diner

Web Diner is a San Francisco-based Web site design company. Laurie and Tim McCanna head the Web Diner. (Laurie is the author of *Creating Great Web Graphics*.) The Web Diner site (**www.webdiner.com**) is a good source for free clip art and tips on creating Web sites and Web graphics. This site is especially notable for how quickly its pages load and how fast its animations run. Careful attention has obviously been paid to making the maximum use of simple shapes and to optimizing those that are used.

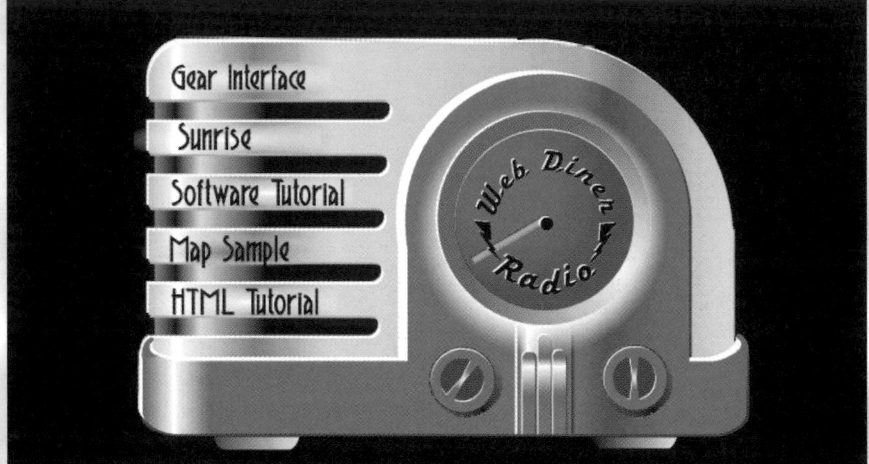

This is the main sample screen for Web Diner's Flash demos. On mouse over, the menu choices glow in red, the radio dial spins, and music plays. The music playing demonstrates Real Audio capabilities.

In this city map, blocks that contain points of interest are live buttons. On mouse over, an icon appears to identify the type of location, and a short description is shown on the notepad. Clicking on the location icon (mouse down) reveals a more detailed description of the location.

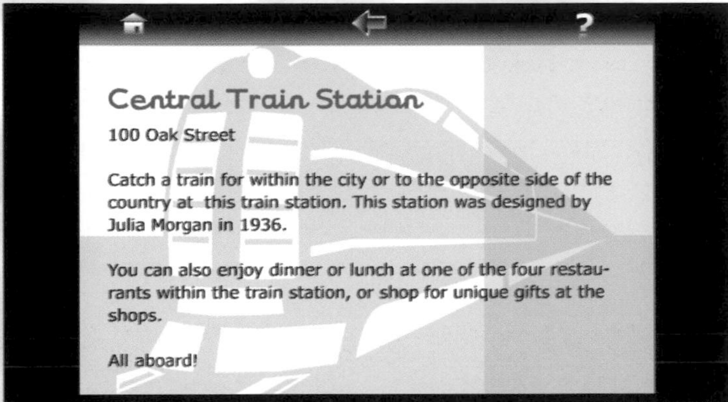

After clicking on a location in the city map, a more detailed description of the location fills the screen.

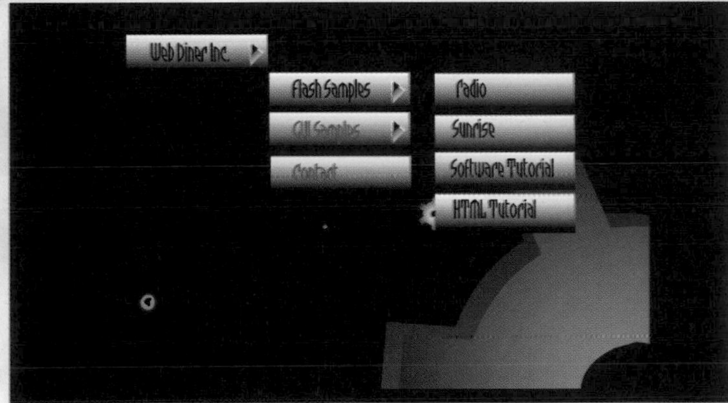

This alternative interface design from Web Diner involves hierarchical menus of buttons. Different sounds are associated with buttons that have a hierarchy and those that don't.

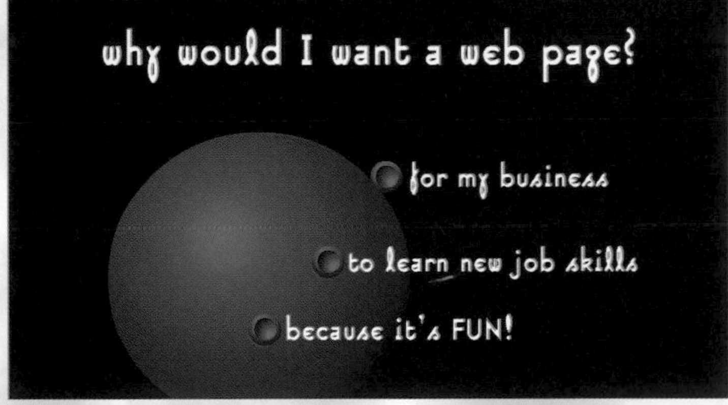

This opening animation for a dummy HTML tutorial makes excellent use of layers, tweens, and Alpha transparency.

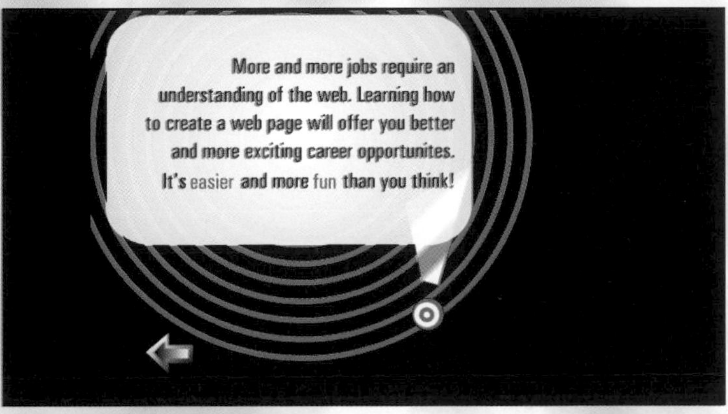

On the screens that follow the HTML tutorial's navigation screen, more tweening, layering, and transparency are used.

Suburban Lodge

USWeb is a major Web design and consulting firm located in Atlanta, Georgia. Clients include Sony, Toshiba, American Airlines, and Charles Schwab. The Suburban Lodge site, created by Robert Thompson, takes the form of an animated slide presentation that could work just as well offline as on the Web. It is especially effective on the Web, however, because of the speed that Flash brings to the full-screen animations opening the presentation. Visit the site at **www.suburbanlodge.com** to see a great demonstration of how parts of maps—in this case, a floor plan—can be used as buttons.

Robert Thompson at USWeb designed this animated Flash 3 splash screen for maximum speed and impact. Several layers of animation lead to this main screen. Clicking on any of the buttons takes you to a standard HTML page for that topic.

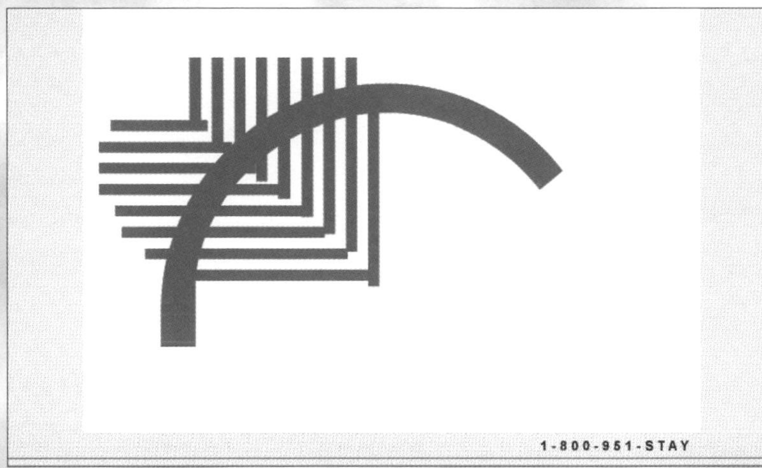

The first stage of the animation leading to the main splash screen for Suburban Lodge.

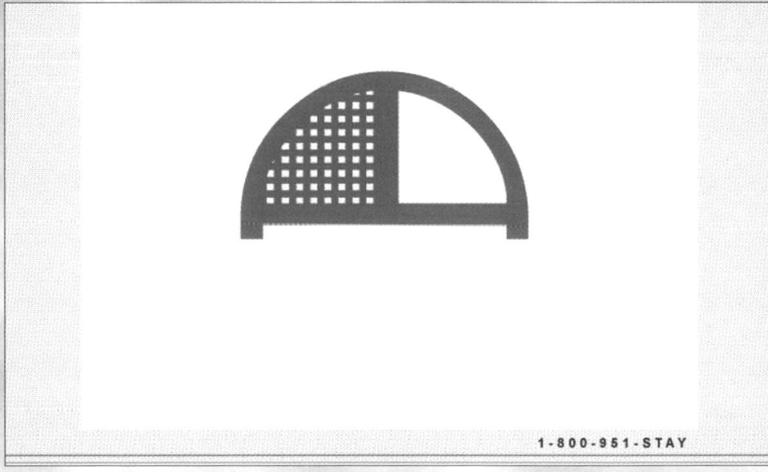

The second stage of the animation leading to the main splash screen for Suburban Lodge.

The third stage of the animation leading to the main splash screen for Suburban Lodge.

Spyplane

The Spyplane site (**www.spyplane.com**) uses Flash for its main splash screen and for many of its content pages. Designer Eric DeJesus built the site to promote the talent of Spyplane, a San Francisco-based Web design firm.

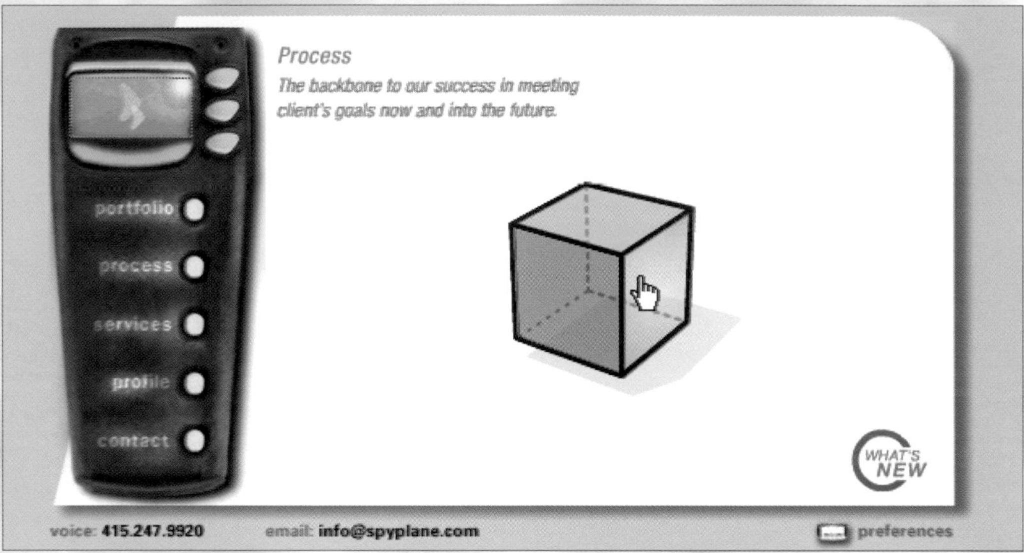

The spinning cube was animated in a 3D program, then rendered as bitmapped frames. The bitmapped frames were imported into Flash, where each frame was autotraced, then filled with outlines and solid colors. Now, here's the really good trick: Each of the cube's surfaces is a live button. On mouse over, the surface lights up and the text associated with that surface's button appears.

This is part of the animation that leads to the screen with the spinning cube. The animation uses transparent text zooms and features synchronized sound.

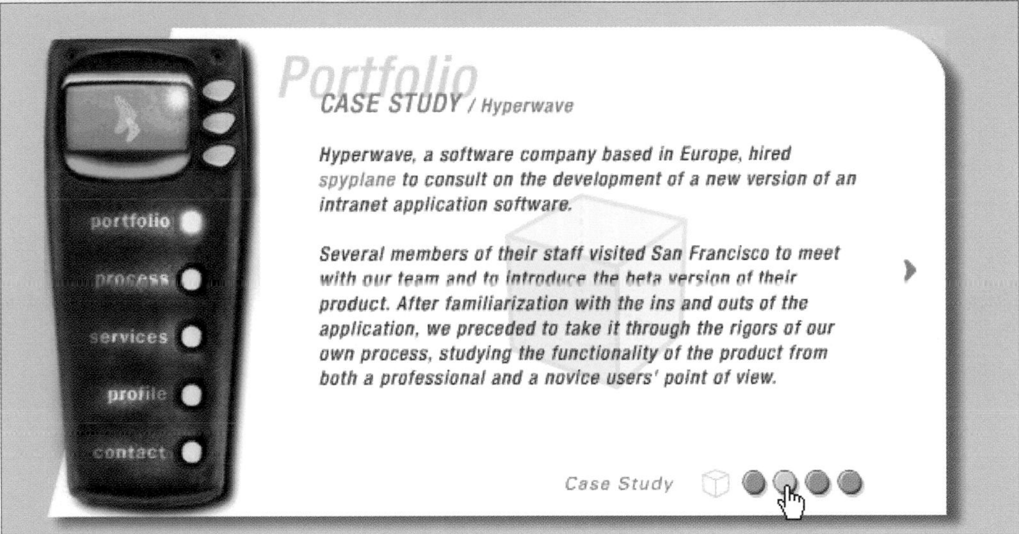

On this portfolio screen, all of the buttons lead to descriptive text.

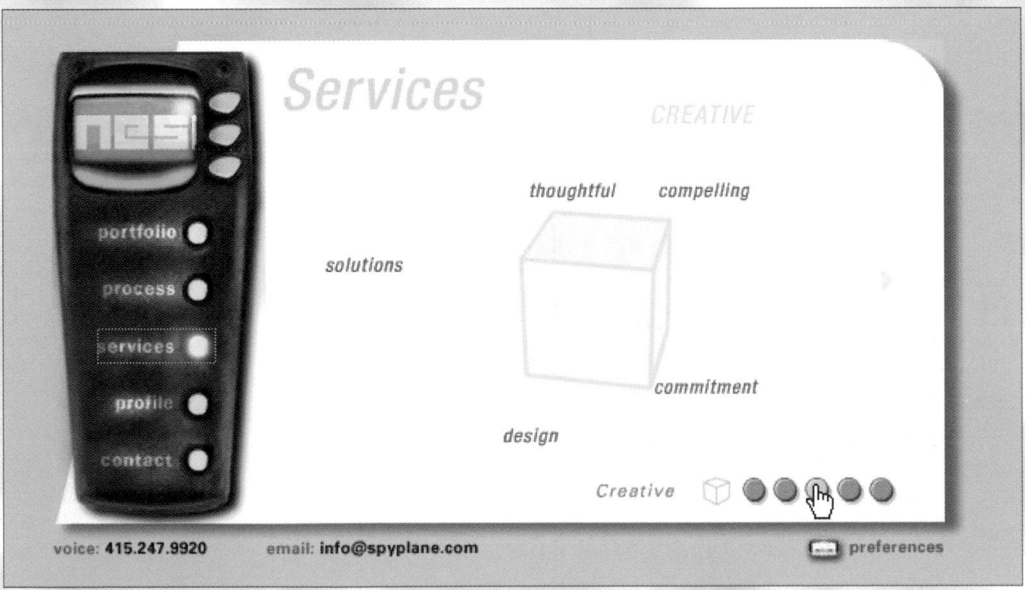

On this screen, however, all the buzzwords fly into place before it loads a text screen.

Levi's Canada Site

This entire site (**http://colinmoock.iceinc.com/webdesign/portfolio/levisite**) is an interactive animation that makes extensive use of Flash's ability to go to a particular scene and frame. All the dialog clouds pop up as a result of a mouse down event. These dialog clouds are hierarchical. Clicking on one of the arrowheads seen inside the dialog clouds leads to another set of dialog clouds for the same character.

"The goal of the strip was to guide visitors to Levi's content through the characters and narrative of the animated tavern, The Hot Spot," said Colin Moock, the site's creator.

This is the opening screen. Because this is a Canadian site, it must be bilingual.

This is one screen of a very active animation that is narrated by a voice-over. There are no interactive buttons in this scene.

This is the entrance to The Hot Spot.

This is the bartender whose voice welcomes you to The Hot Spot. The fan spins. The telephone rings on mouse over. The radio lets you turn the sound off or on.

You hear the phone ring on mouse over. On mouse down, the dialog clouds pop up.

In this scene, the hierarchical dialog clouds let you branch to a variety of scenarios.

Click the Hot Advertising line and you branch to a part of the standard Levi's site.

Click on the jukebox and you get a screen that navigates you to any of several Levi's sites. Click on the Exit door and you are taken outside to a final animation.

Andy Lim, Designer

Flash is utilized on this site (**http://andy.artdirectors.com**) in an intelligent way. JavaScript detection ensures that browsers without the plug-in will be redirected to a non-Flash page that prompts the viewer either to download the plug-in or to enter the site without it. If the user enters without the plug-in, JavaScript displays the HTML-based content only, completely bypassing the Flash introduction scenes.

The site is a showcase for Andy Lim's Web-building and Flash skills. While each section has a unique intro scene, it maintains the site identity with distinctive graphic elements. The highlight of the site is the interactive portfolio, which is also available for downloading in projector format. The visual style of this site emphasizes clean and subtle design elements, as well as a clear and logical navigation system.

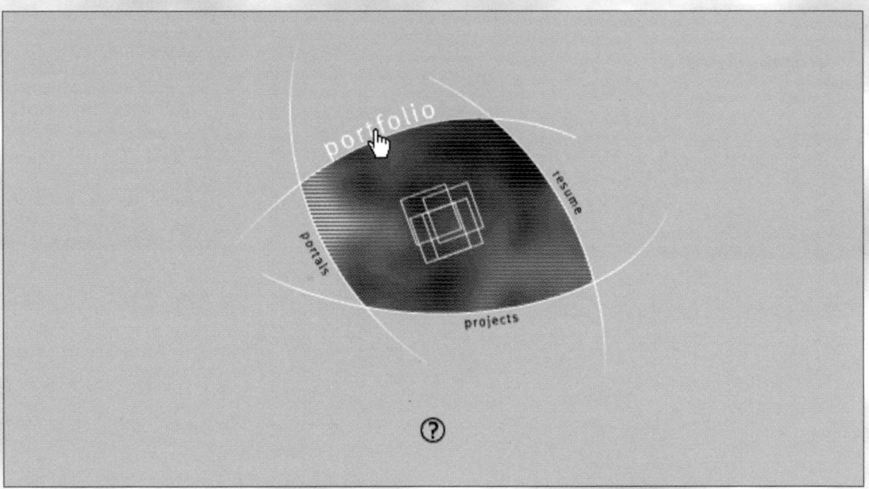

The pieces fly into place on this title page. On mouse over, the menu choices grow and turn white, while geometric shapes and type are animated in the center of the screen.

All of the elements on this first portfolio screen fade in and fly into place.

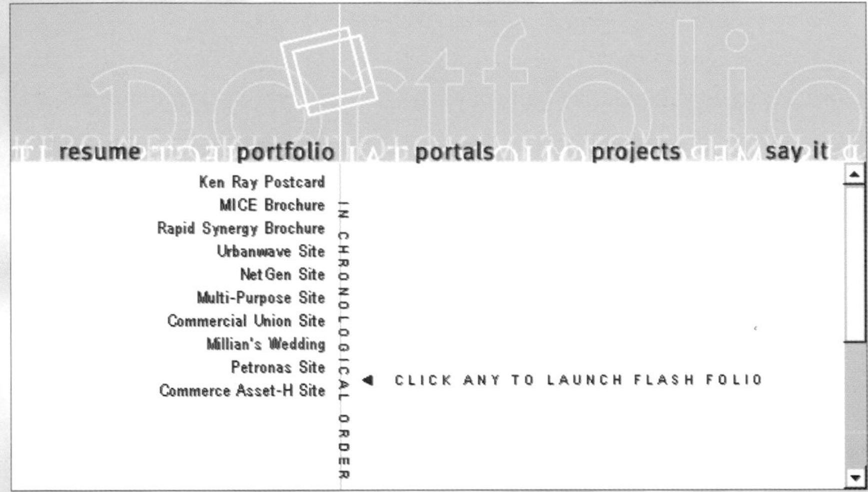

The portfolio screen finally moves to this one. Clicking on any project title leads to the next screen.

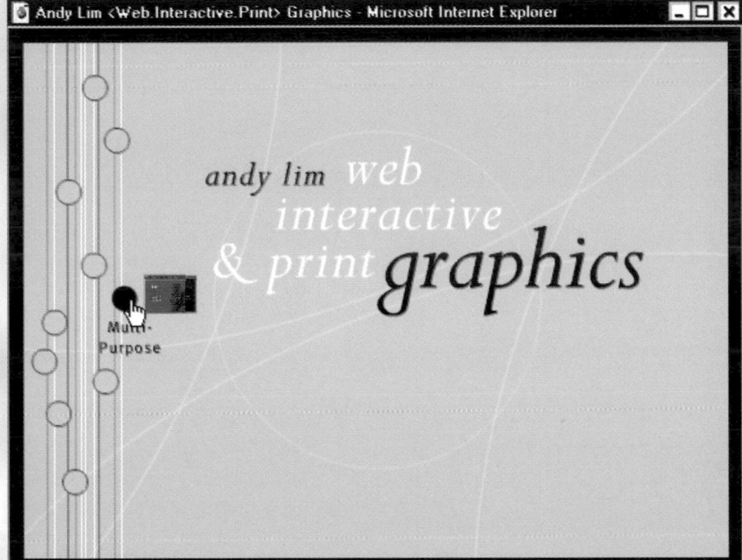

This is the lead-in navigation screen for print graphics. The circles at the left are buttons that animate into concentric circles. On mouse over, tiny thumbnails also appear. Click on a button to go the next screen.

This is the static screen for a print portfolio piece.

Poison Dart Frog Music

Marc Hoffman's Poison Dart Frog Music can be viewed at **www/jps.net/dartfrog/sampler**. Play a virtual marimba at **www.jps.new/dartfrog**. Also, get the schedule for Hoffman's band at **www.jps.net.dartfrom/littlebird**.

The elements of the title navigation screen animate into place. This design is notable for the use of a bitmapped gradient in the center of the screen, which causes a longer-than-normal download time. You be the judge of whether it's worth it.

This is one of the introduction pages for Poison Dart Frog Music.

Each of the jungle's inhabitants, as well as each of the keys of the marimba, is a button that plays music or voice effects. This allows visitors to sample the sounds from Poison Dart Frog.

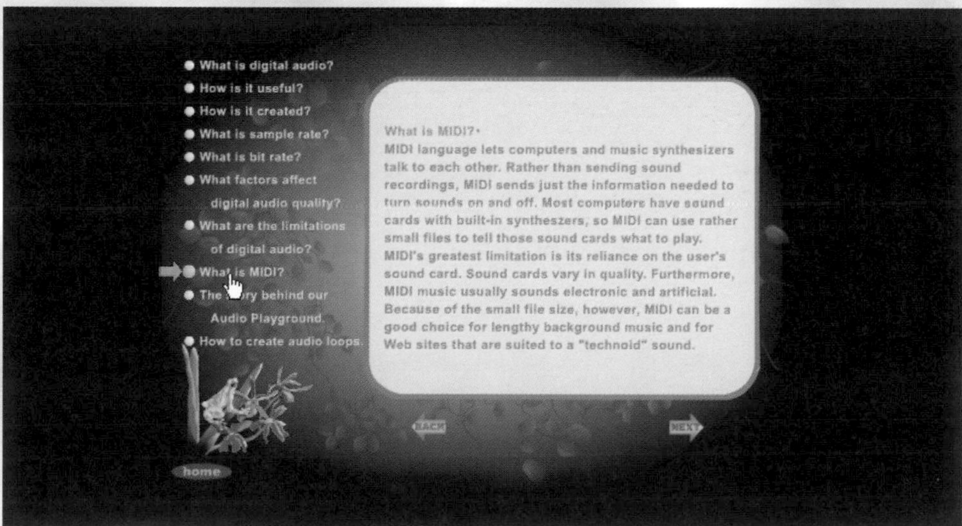

Each of the components on the audio FAQ screen animates into place. Each item on the menu is a button. Click on a button and the accompanying text is displayed instantly. Many of these text pages have buttons that reveal more material on the subject.

Flash Central

John Croteau is the mastermind and guardian of several Web sites that are devoted to providing information on developing and maintaining Web sites with Flash. Flash Tech offers advanced tips on Flash. Flash Central (**www.flashcentral.com**) is the main independent repository of information on Flash. And, the Flash Tech Resource is an archive of technical advice gleaned mostly from the Flasher mailing list. Flash Central is the gateway to the other two services. By the way, John maintains the Flasher mailing list. Instructions for joining the Flasher list can be found at **www.flashcentral.com/Tech/List/FlasherL.htm**.

This is the main menu for Flash Central. The site is a gold mine of information for designers and developers who are working with Flash. Each button (and some of the words in the introductory text) animates on mouse over.

This freeze-frame is from the opening animation for Flash Central. The logo starts at full frame, as does the flash. The logo and flash tween into place, before the rest of the information on the screen appears.

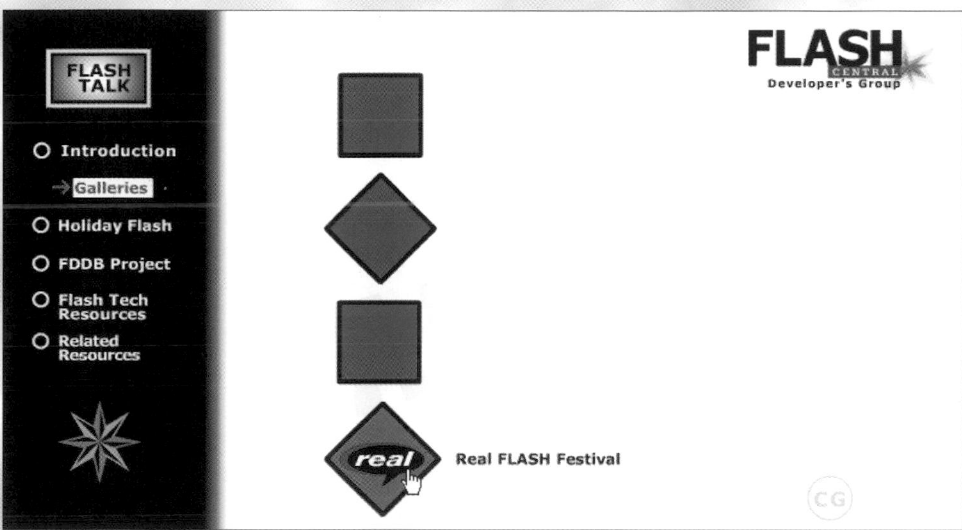

On the Galleries menu page, each of the menu buttons is shot into place by a cannon at the right of the screen. The cannonballs morph (shape tween) into their final shapes during the trajectory. On mouse over, each button lights up with the logo of its linked gallery, and the name of the gallery appears on the right.

This is Flash Central's page of links to Flash technical resources. Each of the round buttons links to a different resource site, including the Flash Tech Resource, Flash Pad, Flasher's Corner, and the Macromedia Flash Developer's Center.

Gwen

Originally created as a test movie by Colin Moock during the development of the Levi's Canada Web site, Gwen (**colinmoock.iceinc.com/qwen**) is now an animated Flash series following a young woman, Gwen, through her world. Episode 1 introduces us to Gwen and her likes and dislikes. Don't, for example, touch her cheeks! Episode 2 was developed partly in Flash 2, and then extended with the beta release of Flash 3. Posted before Flash 3 even shipped, Gwen is an early display of the increased level of interactivity developers can reach using Flash 3's movie clips and Tell Target technique. Quick, help Gwen get ready for work so she's not late!

The letters on the title screen drop down one at a time. The author's name scrolls right to left until the movie has loaded. The movie then begins to play automatically, without intervention from the user.

Gwen begins peeking into the frame, like the famous "Kilroy" character. Dialog clouds give you instructions.

Mysteriously, Gwen is bodiless in both episodes. Many, but not all, of the bottles are buttons. On mouse over, Gwen announces their color. Click on a bottle, and her hair is dyed in that color.

Ah, there, blue hair. Want to return to normal?

Click the sink and Gwen's hair gets washed.

That's better.

Dorian Nisinson

Dorian Nisinson is the principal in Dorian Nisinson Design: Design for the Internet, Print, & Multimedia. As you can see from her site (**www.bway.net/~dorian/Splash3.htm**), she specializes in designing with Flash and is one of its most knowledgeable and talented practitioners. Dorian is also a regular contributor to Flash Central.

Each menu choice flies into the title navigation screen. The opening animation tweens the geometric shapes that house the menu. Text is animated using layers, transparency, and tweening. Each navigation button animates and makes a sound on mouse over.

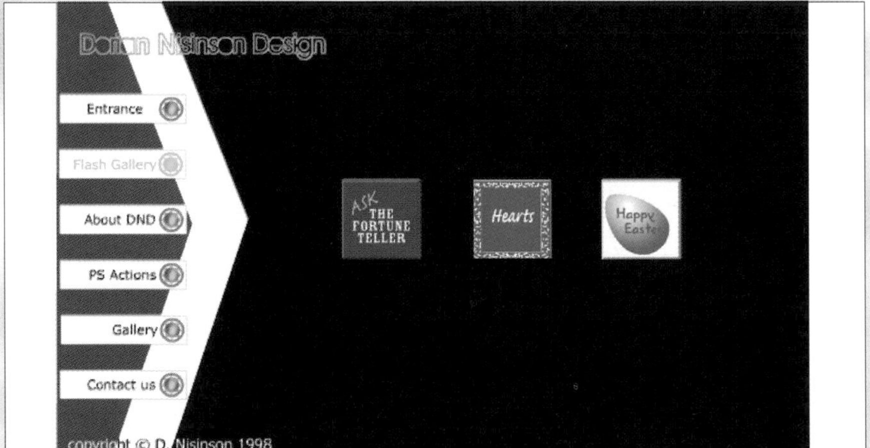

Note the color shift in the background when we click the button for the Flash Gallery. Each of the three icons changes on mouse over, and each leads to an animated greeting card designed in Flash.

Hearts can be golden.

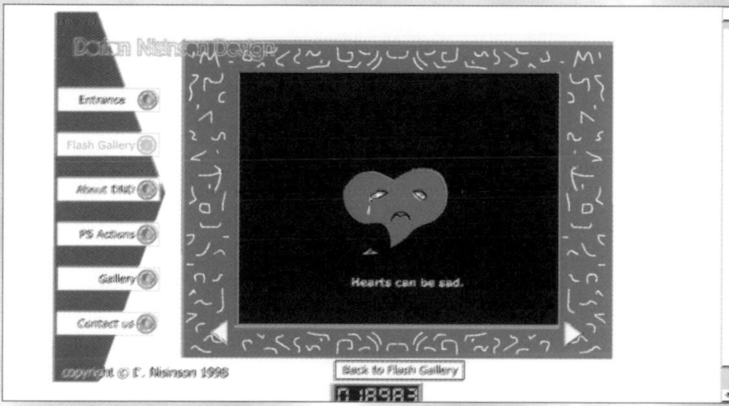

Hearts can be sad.

Hearts can be angels.

Hearts can be bad. Sorry we don't have room to finish the poem, but you can check it out for yourself on Dorian's site.

Meanrabbit

Craig Ferrante of Meanrabbit Graphic Design believes that the Meanrabbit Drive-In (**www.meanrabbit.com**) is the first drive-in done in Flash 3. You sit in the car and view old drive-in trailers created in Flash. It took Craig approximately two months to do. Most controls in the car work, and movie-goers even attach the drive-in speaker to the door. The main point of the site is to introduce the main character for MeanRabbit, an interactive Flash game that Craig is creating. It's about a genetically altered half-human/half-rabbit, but Craig can't disclose plot details until Episode 1 is complete.

The mirror, steering wheel, radio, glove compartment, and side speaker are active buttons The movie plays from start to finish, however, with no interaction possible from the audience.

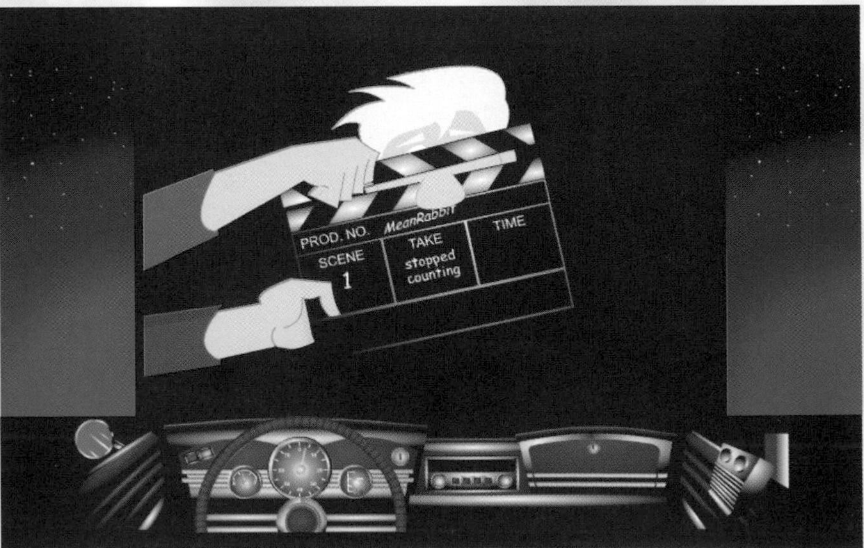

The movie begins with this animation.

Looping animations run while larger portions of the movie load. This particular one is a commercial for the snack stand.

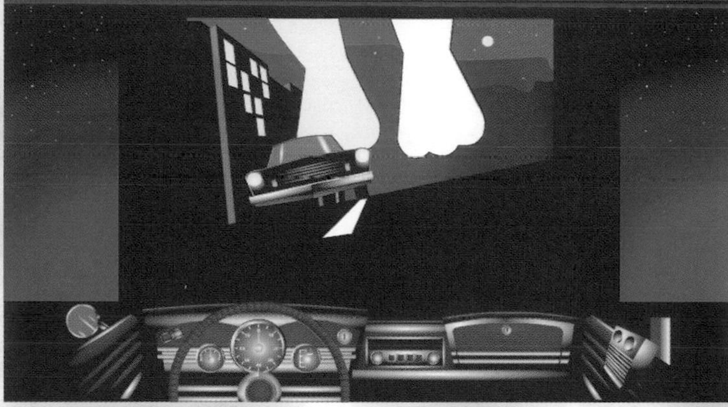

One movie involves a highly animated looping car chase.

Another animation has an exploding police car.

This is the end of the movie, as the present sample stands.

The Olympic Movement

Located at **www.olympic.org**, this is one of the most dynamic, complex, and innovative single-scene uses of Flash. The rest of the content for this Olympic site (not to mention the left column frame) is in straight HTML. As a result, visiting this site is a great lesson in what Flash and HTML—and more conventional media, such as GIFs and JPEGs—can contribute to an overall site. The site was created by Quokka Sports.

The opening navigation screen has many constantly animated text elements. The row of small photographic thumbnails across the center are buttons, and their content (as you will see in the next screens) stays consistent. This is the first stage of the animation.

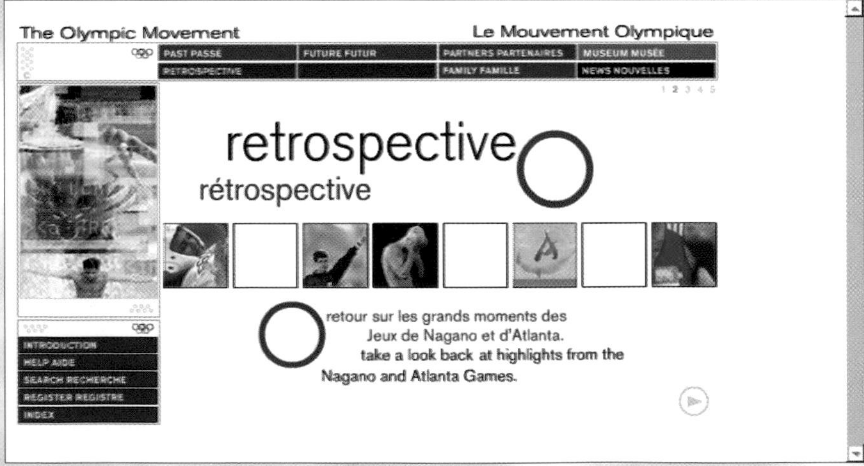

This is the second animation stage. The circles and text travel onto the screen from left to right. Each line travels at a different speed.

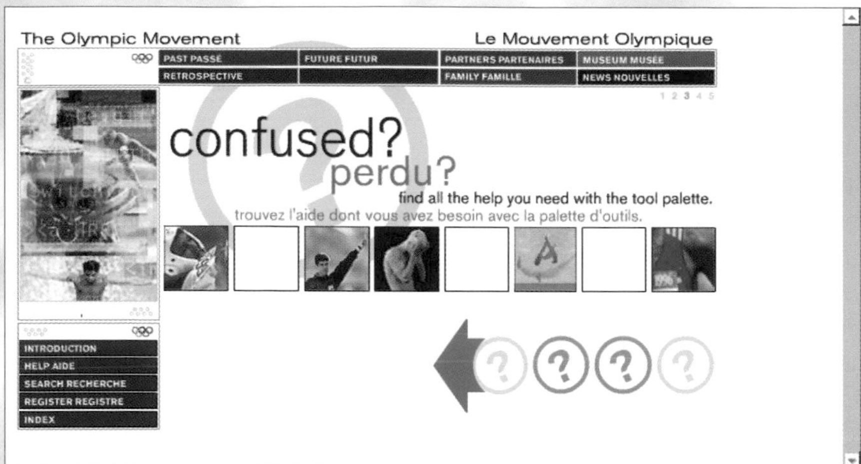

This is the third stage of animation in the title screen. The arrows and text travel from right to left and stop when they are pointing directly at the help buttons at the bottom of the left frame.

In the title screen's fourth and final animated message, the dashed circles rotate.

Flash 3 is also used in the opening screen for the upcoming Athens Olympics. The animation is much less ambitious on this screen, but the buttons light up when the mouse cursor moves over them.

WCN Exhibit Hall

This site (**www.wcnonline.com**) from Fusion Media Group is a demo simulating an online tradeshow exhibit. Its outstanding feature is an animated, lip-synched character that uses Real Audio dialog to narrate the entire presentation. He also gestures quite effectively and believably at each of the bullet points and image slides in the presentation. Flash makes this a practical working experience over a 28.8K connection. It should be a marvel over a faster connection.

As the demo opens, the spotlight fades in, the central character appears, and the sides of the lectern animate into place, one at a time.

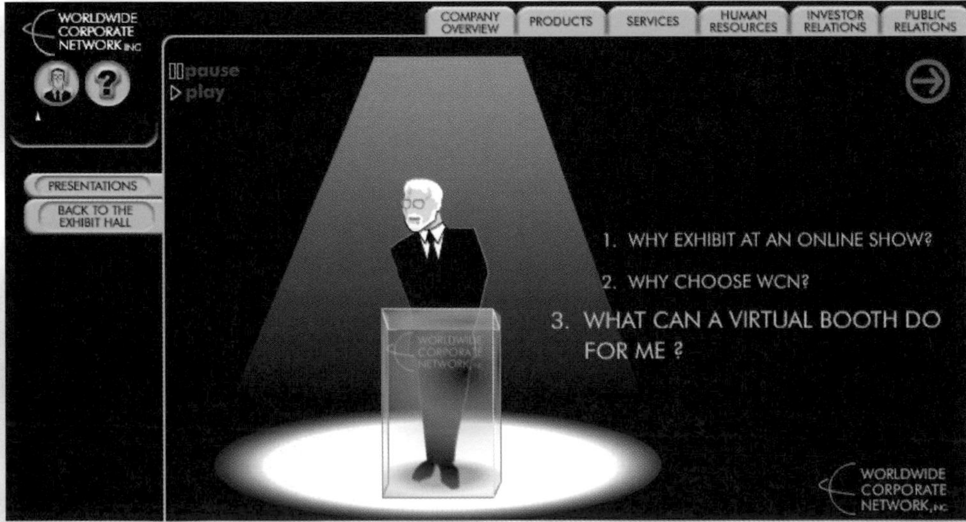

The character begins to speak. In this scene, text points appear alongside the character in a manner similar to slide-show presentations. As the character addresses each point, it enlarges.

Some "slides" fade in from time to time. These slides are GIF or JPEG bitmaps that show photographic images.

Some of the other slides are (or could be) vector drawings, such as these corporate logos.

Sony Europe DV Site

This site (**www.sony-europe.com/camcorders**) from I-D Gruppe is a great example of how Flash can be used to demonstrate a product, either online or offline. The screens shown are from the Web version of the site, which uses extensive animated bitmaps. These could be made by scanning individual frames of movie film or by saving individual frames of a captured (ideally, digital) video and then importing the frames into a movie clip symbol.

As the digital camera presentation loads, this screen animates. The geometric shapes fly in and morph into their final shapes. The positive and negative photos of the eye change as the red diagonal bar moves across the circle. The "retinal scan imaging..." marquee scrolls across the bottom.

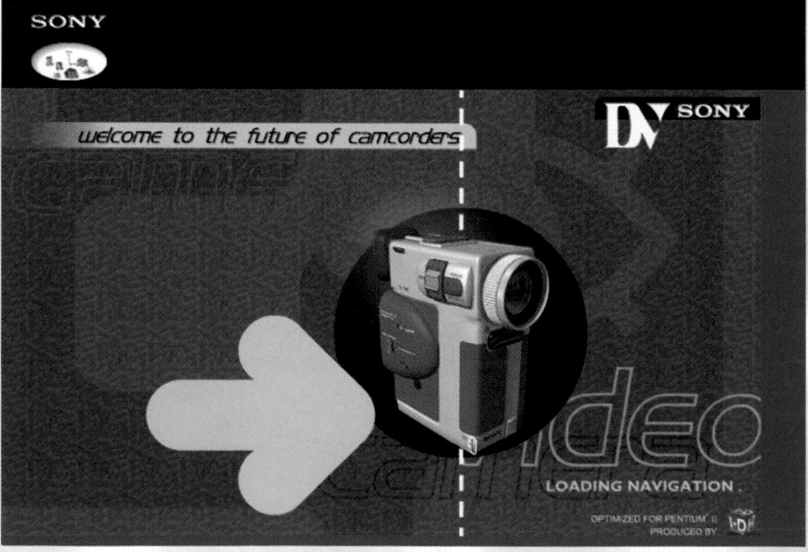

The arrow moves from left to right, while the camcorder rotates and the titles scroll into view.

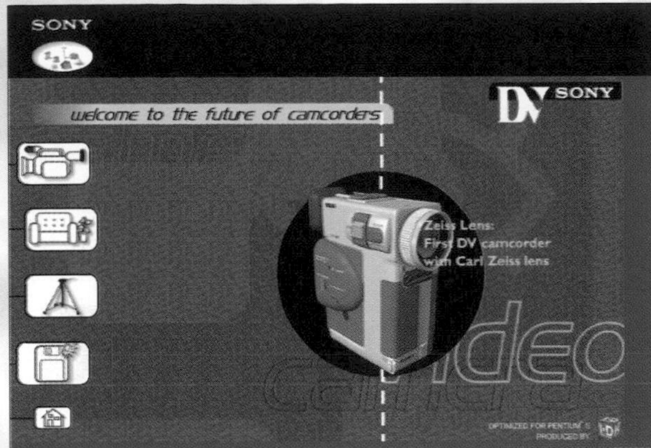

The navigation buttons appear, and various features of the camera begin to flash in front of it.

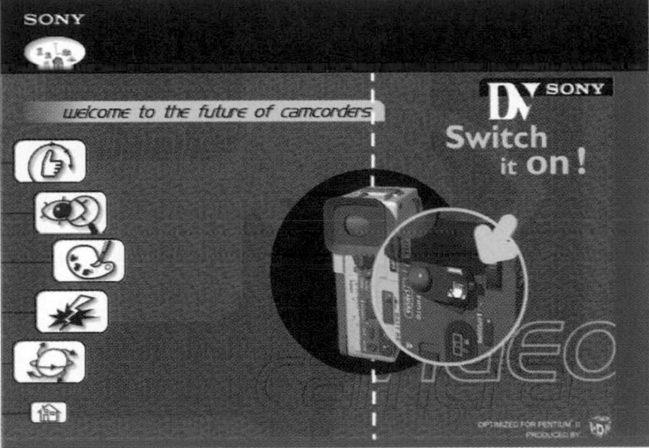

Click on the top button on the left, and the camera rotates and magnifies the "on" switch. If you click on the switch, it rocks into place.

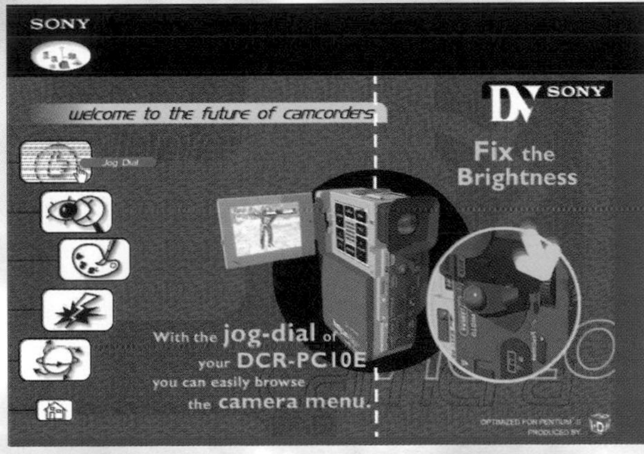

Click the jog dial and the LCD screen brightens and dims.

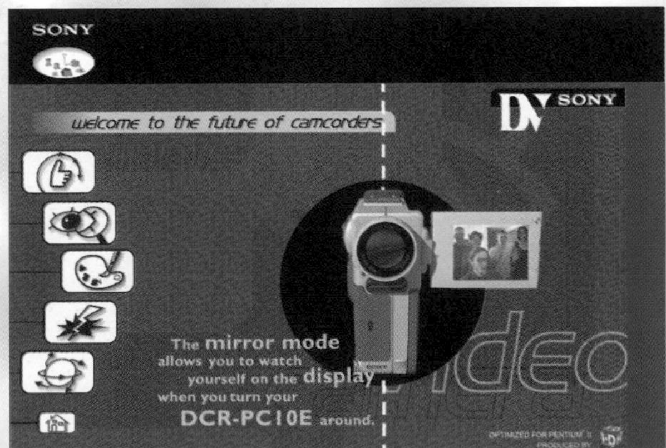

Click the second navigation icon and the camera rotates to face us, while the LCD screen rotates in the opposite direction to face us.

Diversity Corporation

Diversity Corporation of Beaverton, Oregon, is another Web design firm that works extensively (and beautifully) with Flash 3. On the Web site at **www.diversitycorp.com**, the Flash qualifying animation is the best I've seen. It consists of the animated words "Flash Installed." That's just what the viewer needs to know, with no further explanation.

Flash 3 allowed the Diversity designers to create an intuitive interface and deliver truly "interactive" content. According to Diversity's Rick Turoczy, "The site has life even as the user pauses to examine details. While driving the site, there is no point at which the screen is sitting still. Something is always happening, no matter how subdued. We were very satisfied with the balance that Flash allowed us to achieve."

This is one of the most tasteful and best-designed business sites I've had the pleasure to encounter. The first part of the animation entertains you while the movie is loading.

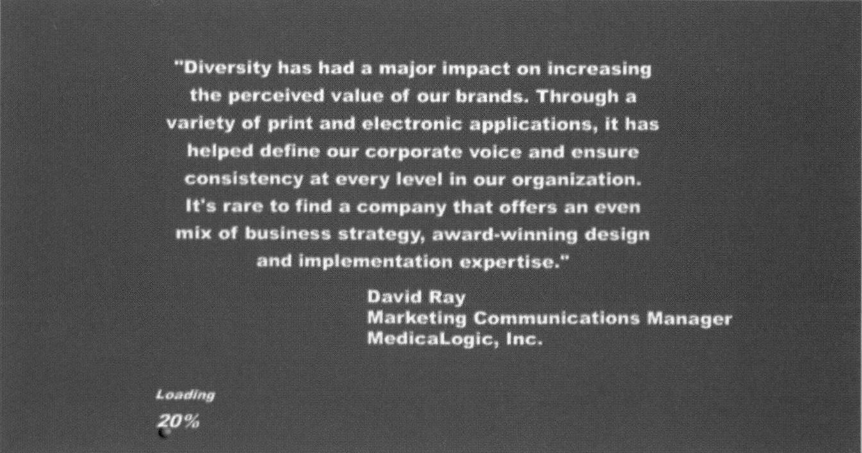

Customers' testimonials fade in from top to bottom, while the main movie continues to load. This is a great way to inform and intrigue potential clients. The designers are not wasting the viewer's time, and they don't make you stop to question the value of installing Flash.

This is the splash screen and opening navigation scene. Mouse over any of the circles and they tween into a ball that floats, then pops out the title. Click and the screen changes. The ball drops and bounces, and a new menu shows up.

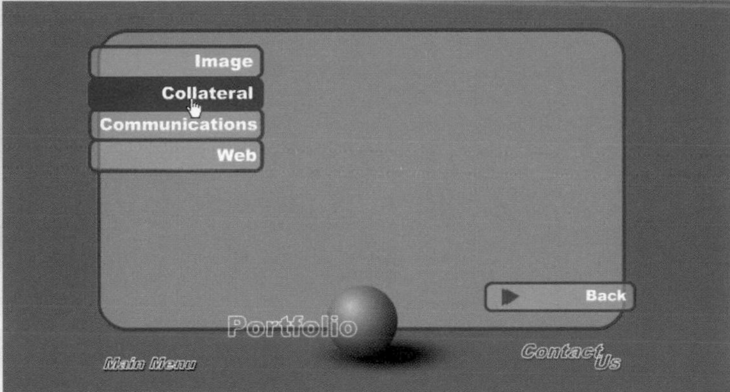

Click one of the choices and you get a text page that features a bitmapped clipping of one of Diversity's projects. By clicking the arrow at lower right, you can cycle through a series of these.

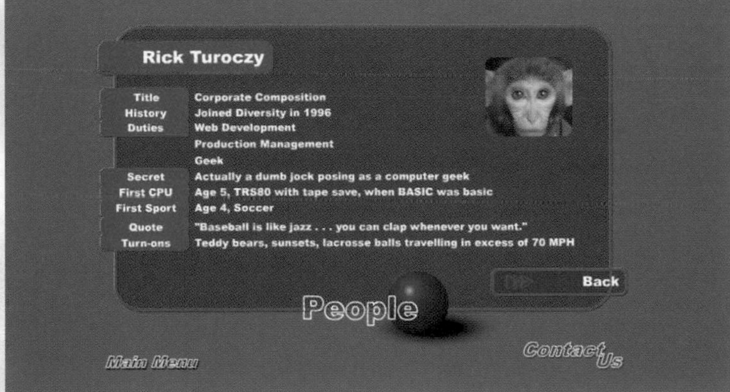

A bio screen offers information about one of the Diversity staffers.

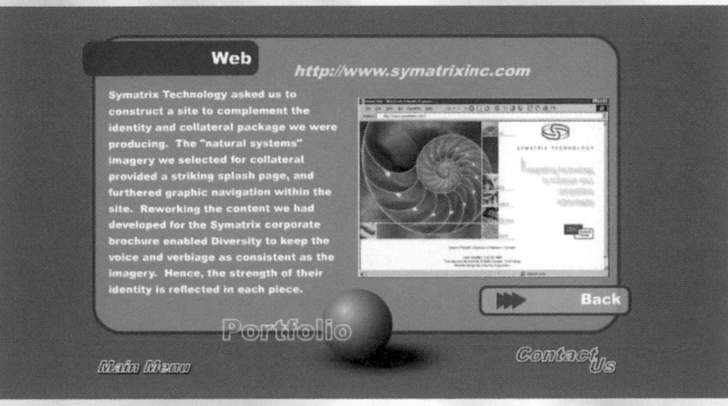

A portfolio page features one of the sites designed by Diversity.

Insight Multimedia

This Dutch Web design firm specializes in and enthusiastically promotes the use of Flash for Web site design. Jos van der Vleuten has designed a Flash version of the company's main Web site, the highlights of which are shown here. This site at **www.insight-multimedia.nl** takes a little longer to load, thanks to the inclusion of a background sound track.

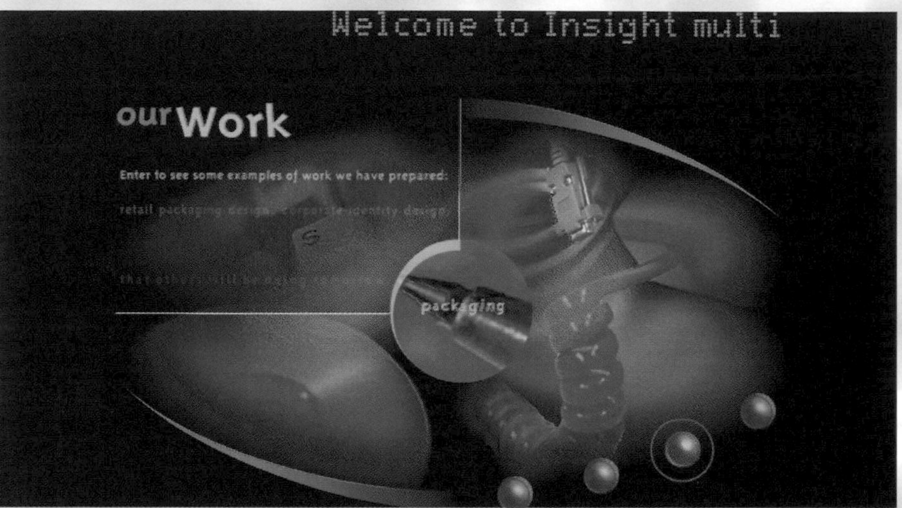

On the main splash screen for Insight's Web site, you see many of Flash's outstanding features. The "Welcome to Insight Multimedia" banner is an animated symbol that flies out of the right side of the screen. The image in the center circle is a multilayered animation, with each new animation linking to a different Web page on the site. The buttons at lower right animate on mouse over. Unfortunately, nothing appears to tell you what will happen if you click one of these buttons.

Insight's "about the company" page uses scrolling text that also fades in as it scrolls up. On this page, the animated buttons have labels that pop up on mouse over.

This is another page that is linked to the main splash screen shown previously. It links the viewer to various portfolios of Insight's work.

This is one of the portfolio pages for packaging design. Each click on the animated buttons places a new movie in the center of the screen. The symbols slide into place, pushing the previous item off screen.

These screens show the animation that evolves into the main Insight navigation screen. By using simple animation elements that perform over a fair amount of time, Insight gives the more complex bitmaps that form the main illustration plenty of time to load.

7 Advanced Techniques

Ken Milburn

This chapter shows you the techniques and tweaks to create facets of animation that are more sophisticated and complex than those previously demonstrated. I'll combine symbols and create multilayered animations with multiple scenes, transparency effects, shape tweening, masking layers, and more.

This chapter is a collection of information, tips, and subtle tricks that you'll use to create and export advanced projects in Flash 3. It includes techniques for outputting the most efficient products in terms of bandwidth.

Combining Symbols

You know by now that you can use a symbol as many times as you like within a movie without increasing the movie's file size. Symbols are even more powerful because you can make a symbol from a collection of other symbols, making it possible to create a whole new shape, animation sequence, or effect without adding any new data.

The process for combining symbols is so simple that it hardly seems worth making a fuss over. Place the symbols that you want to combine on the stage. Then, drag them and arrange them into the positions you want them to occupy in the new symbol. Finally, select all the symbols you want to combine and press F8 (or choose Insert|Create Symbol from the menu bar). Figure 7.1 shows you a symbol made by repeatedly combining the same symbol.

You can transform (scale, rotate, or skew) an instance of a symbol without affecting the symbol in the library.

You can also create combined symbols from scratch. As would be the case when creating a simple symbol, make sure nothing is selected, then press F8 or choose Insert|Create Symbol. Import or draw your first symbol, select its parts, and choose Insert|Create Symbol

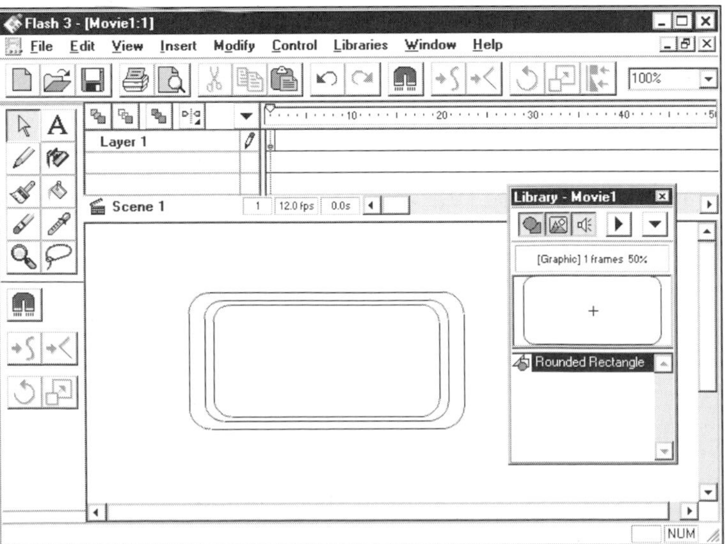

Figure 7.1 All of the rounded rectangles in this symbol are the same symbol.

again. Keep doing this until your symbol contains all the symbols you want to combine.

Of course, it can get more complicated than that. You can combine symbols that are already combined symbols.

Now, all of this is easy as long as you're dealing with static graphics. Things get a bit more complicated when you combine symbols with different behaviors or different numbers of frames.

Combining A Static Symbol With An Animated Symbol

If you want part of a symbol to move while the rest remains static, the static part of the symbol must have the same number of frames as the moving part. In Figure 7.2, I've placed a freeform animated shape inside the concentric rectangles used in Figure 7.1.

When you combine these two types of symbols, the order in which you do it is critical to your success. Keeping the example simple should help you to see the process more clearly. The following exercise shows how you combine the symbols seen in Figure 7.2:

1. Open the movie Combo.fla on this book's companion CD-ROM.
2. Choose Window|Library from the menu bar. The symbols library for this movie will appear. See Figure 7.3.
3. Next, you need to know how many frames are in the animated symbol called Blob. Select its name from the library list, and a

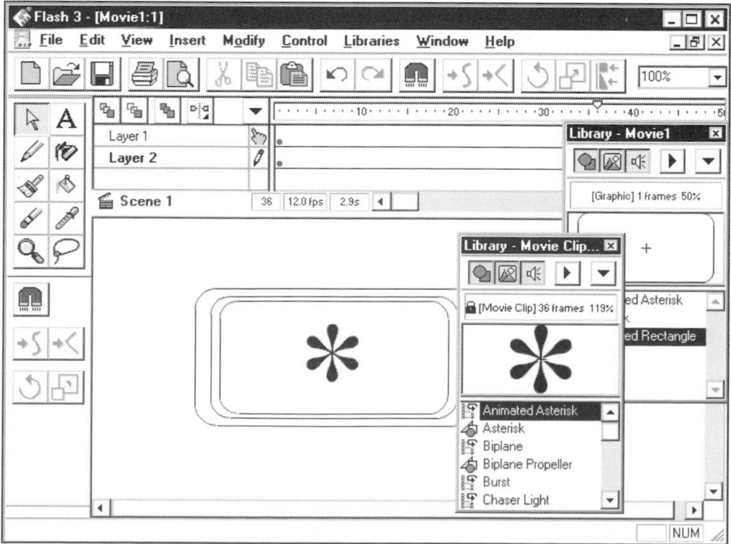

Figure 7.2 A multisymbol symbol with an added animated symbol in the center.

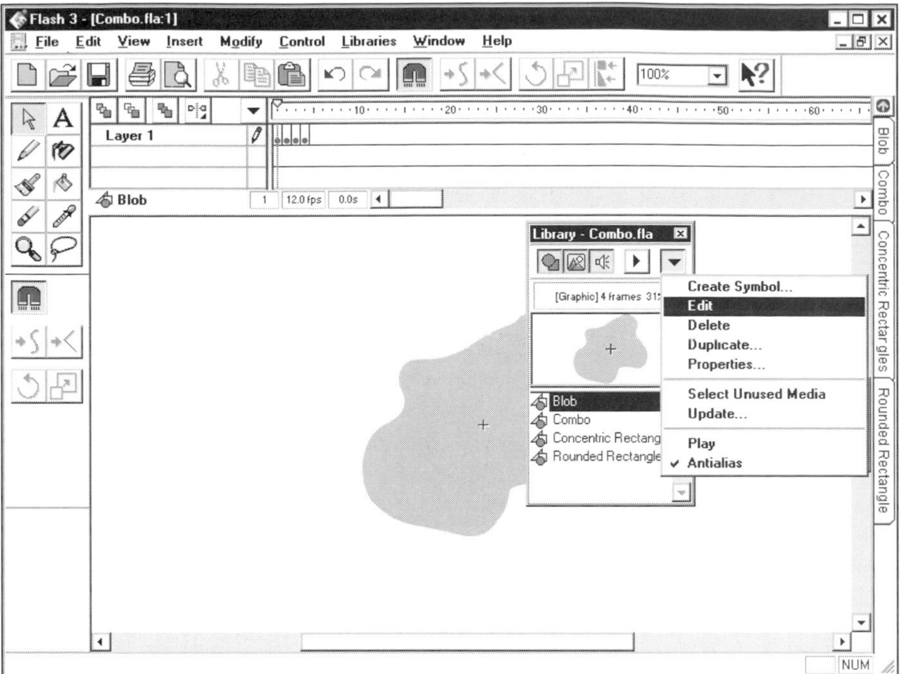

Figure 7.3 The Library window showing the Library pull-down menu. To save space, the stage is shown in Symbol Edit mode (not actually seen until after choosing Edit).

green blob will appear in the preview. From the Library pull-down menu, choose Edit. The stage and Timeline will now look as they do in Figure 7.3. Note that this symbol has five frames.

4. You don't actually need to edit the blob, so choose Edit|Edit Movie from the menu bar. You are now back to a blank stage. It would be okay if the stage weren't blank, but make sure nothing is selected and press F8 to create a symbol. You will see another blank stage.

5. Now, you're going to create a new symbol that combines the two symbols. Press F8 (again making sure nothing is selected). When the Symbol Properties dialog box appears, name the symbol "Combo2". You now have a blank movie in which to edit.

6. In the Library window, select the concentric rectangle symbol and drag it onto the stage. Click away from the symbol to deselect it.

7. Highlight the four frames following the keyframe. From the Frames menu, choose Insert Frame.

8. In the Library window, select the blob symbol. Drag its thumbnail onto the stage and into the center of the concentric rectangle. Press Return to play the symbol's movie. The rectangles will stay static while the blob throbs.

9. To save the new symbol, choose Edit|Edit Movie. Then, choose File|Save As, and give the movie a name of your choice.
10. If you want to use this symbol in another movie, open the other movie. Choose File|Open as Library. In the standard dialog box, navigate to the movie you just saved, select it, and click OK. Choose Libraries|Your Movie from the menu bar. Drag your symbol preview onto the stage, and it will become a part of the current movie's library—even if you delete the instance from the stage. You can see the five frames of the finished combined symbol in Figure 7.4.

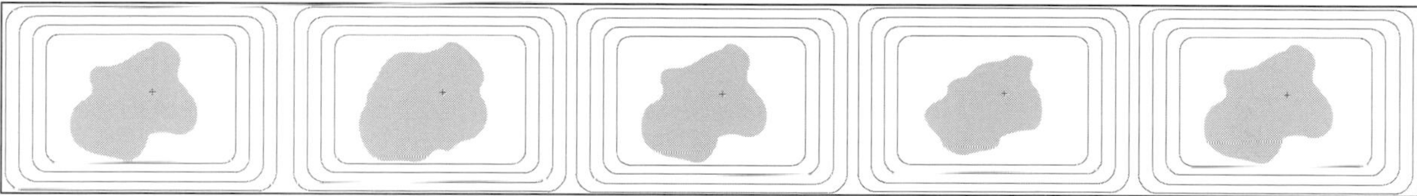

Figure 7.4 The five frames of the combined symbol.

Making Animated Buttons

A different kind of combined symbol is the animated button. In this type of symbol, movie clip symbols are combined with button symbols, because the animation needs to play inside a single frame representing a button state. Movie clip symbols will play the entire animation, regardless of the number of frames in the host symbol, so they're ideal for animating buttons.

Why would you want to make an animated button? On the simplest level, animations are fun and they draw attention to the subject. More importantly, they can be instructional and can even make the interface more intelligible. You could have instructional text zoom out when the mouse cursor passes over the animated button. Or, you could have a button transform into a directional arrow. By the way, the cursor moving over the button (mouse over) is the event that's usually used for animating a button, although you can animate any of the button states.

To make animated buttons, it's a good idea to start a new movie. Then, you can import symbols (including your buttons) from that movie into any movie in which you want to make buttons. If you choose not to start a new movie, at least make sure that nothing is currently selected by pressing Cmd/Ctrl+Shift+A. Then, follow these steps:

1. Press F8 or choose Insert|Create Symbol. The Symbol Properties dialog box will appear. In the dialog box, select the Movie Clip

radio button. Enter a name for your animation in the Name field. See Figure 7.5.

2. Create an animation for each of the button states (Up, Over, and Down) that you intend to animate. It's best to keep the animations short and simple. Tweening is the technique likely to work best, although you can do anything Flash 3 will create.

3. As you finish each animation, choose Edit|Edit Movie. This will store the animation in the library. Then, repeat the process for any other animations you want to make. When you're finished, remember to return to the main movie by choosing Edit|Edit Movie.

4. Now, you're going to create a button symbol. Once again, making sure nothing is selected, choose Insert|Create Symbol. This time, when the Symbol Properties dialog box appears, choose Button as the symbol type.

5. You get a new, blank stage. In the Timeline, there are four frames. The pointer will be over the first frame. If the Library window isn't already open, choose Window|Library. Select the symbol you want to represent the Up state, and drag it into place on the stage. The placement of the first button isn't critical. Figure 7.6 shows you how this will look.

6. For the Over and Down frames, the procedure is the same. From the Frame pull-down menu, choose Insert Blank Keyframe. From the Library window, choose the movie clip or symbol you want to

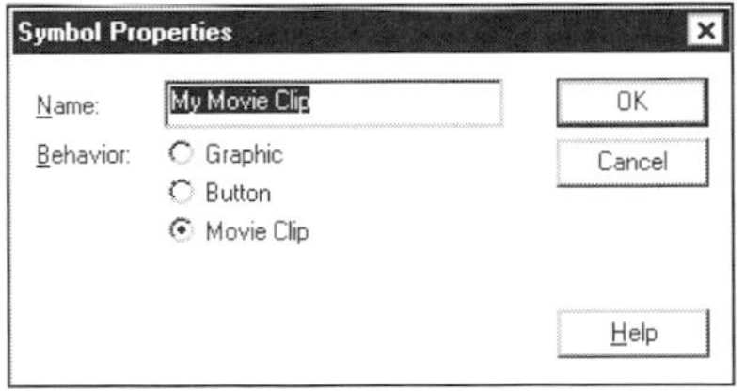

Figure 7.5 The Symbol Properties dialog box.

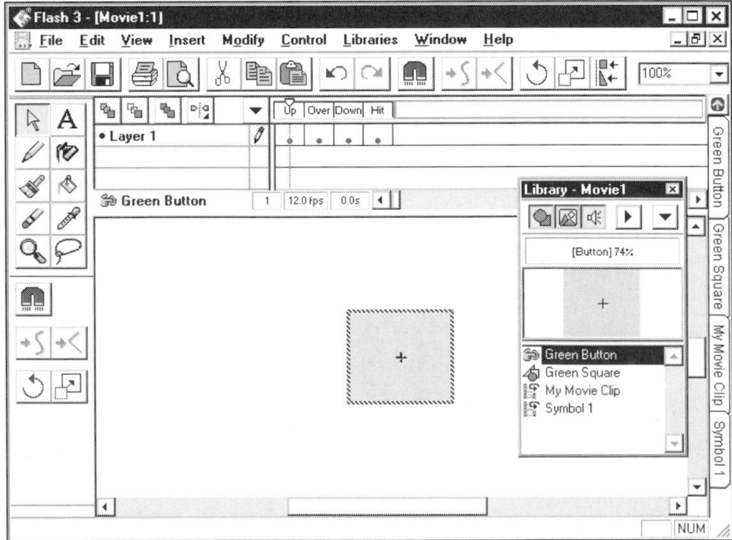

Figure 7.6 The Flash 3 stage as it looks when creating or editing a button symbol.

use for that frame and drag it into place. Be sure to place the center mark (the plus sign) in register with the existing center mark.

7. Insert a blank keyframe in the hit frame. Draw a filled shape that covers the area you want to be active when the mouse cursor passes over it.
8. Choose Edit|Edit Movie to go back to the main movie.
9. Repeat Steps 1 through 8 for as many animated buttons as you're likely to need.
10. Choose File|Save As and name your movie so that you'll recognize it as a button library.
11. Open the movie into which you want to place the animated buttons. Choose File|Open As Library. A standard-type file loading dialog box will appear. Locate the movie that contains the buttons (or any other symbols) that you want.
12. Choose Libraries|Your Button Movie (whatever it's name may be). A Library window will appear. Select the buttons you want and drag the preview onto the stage of your target movie.

Note: *You can't preview both interactivity (Control|Enable Buttons) and movie clip animation while you're actually authoring in Flash. If you want to see the result of an animated button, choose Control|Test Movie or Control|Test Scene from the menu bar.*

Creating Multilayer Animation

When you want to make different objects move with different timing and direction over the same background, layers make it easy. With layers, each object can be animated in its own movie. Since any part of the stage in a layer that isn't occupied by a shape is transparent, all you have to do is stack the movies atop one another. If one subject is supposed to move behind another, just make sure that its layer is below that on which the foreground subject resides.

It helps to envision what layers can do if you first look at a Timeline with layers, shown in Figure 7.7.

Characteristics Of Layers

In order to understand layers and their purpose, it helps to understand how their structure fits into the overall structure of a Flash movie. All

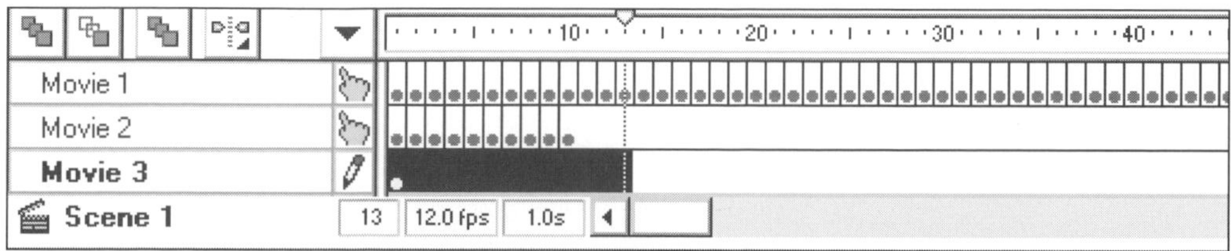

Figure 7.7 The Timeline in a movie with layers. The active (selected) layer is the one whose name is shown in boldface.

> **Note:** *Tweens must reside on their own layer. You shouldn't attempt to have stage-level (canvas) shapes on the same layer as a motion tween.*

of the other components of Flash movies—groups, symbols, and scenes—contain layers. Each of these layers has its own stage level and its own overlay (groups and symbols) levels. In any given scene of a Flash movie, each layer shares a common Timeline with the other layers.

Any portion of a layer that is not artwork (outlines and fills) is transparent. Thus, artwork that is displayed on other layers will be fully visible unless it is hidden by artwork on a higher level. You are not limited in the number of layers that can be placed into a given scene.

Creating Content On A New Layer

Regarding both organization and performance, you'll find it best to create each new animated element on its own layer. To create content on a new layer, click the Modify Layers button of the Layer Name bar. The Layers pull-down menu will appear. Choose Insert Layer. The inserted layer will appear just above the current layer (unless you clicked on the tab for an empty layer). The new layer will always be selected by default. Figure 7.8 shows the result of inserting a layer above an existing layer.

Any new content created on an active layer will remain on that layer. If you want to copy an instance, group, or selection to another layer, first make the appropriate selection. Next, press Cmd/Ctrl+C (or choose Edit|Copy), then select the target layer to make it active. (A pencil icon will appear on the Layer Menu button.) Next, press Cmd/Ctrl+V (or choose Edit|Paste).

If you import a movie, it will always be imported on a layer of its own. This is true whether you import a Flash movie in SWF format or a series of still images in any of the still-image formats that Flash 3 supports.

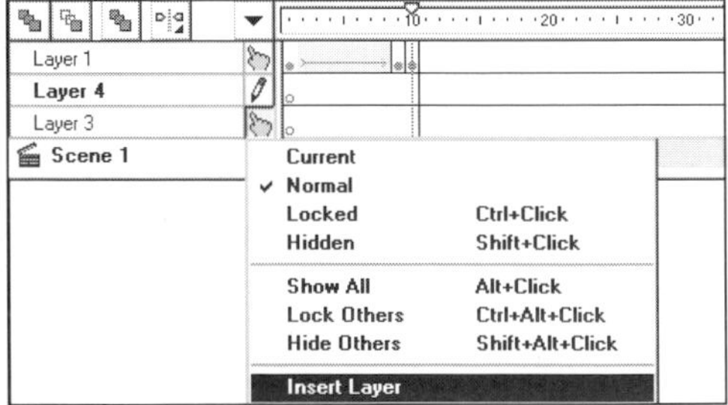

Figure 7.8 Inserting a layer above an existing layer. Note that Layer 4 was automatically inserted above Layer 3. Also, the bold type and pencil icon indicate that this layer is the active one.

More Layer Controls

The Modify Layers pull-down menu has quite a few commands that give you additional control over the behavior of layers. Included are commands for showing or hiding, locking, and specifying outline colors.

Showing And Hiding Layers

Given the facts that objects can hide one another and that you can have as many layers as you like, editing can easily become confusing. It becomes much less so when you turn layers on and off. The following are options for showing and hiding layers:

- To hide individual layers, choose Hide from the Modify Layer pull-down menu. Do this for each layer you want to hide. You cannot select anything on a hidden layer.
- To hide all but one layer, choose Hide Others from the Modify Layer pull-down menu of the layer you want to show.
- To show individual layers, choose Show from the Modify Layer pull-down menu. Do this for each layer you want to show.
- To show all the layers, choose Show All from the Modify Layer pull-down menu of any of the layers.

Locking Layers

Like hiding layers, locking a layer (or layers) will prevent accidental selection and editing of unseen objects. The difference is that you can still see the objects on locked layers. This is important if you want to check the relative position, shape, or color of the objects on the locked layers. The following are options for locking layers:

- To lock an individual layer, choose Locked from its Modify Layer pull-down menu.
- To lock all but one layer, choose Lock Others from the Modify Layer pull-down menu of the layer you want to leave unlocked.

Changing The Colors Of Layer Outlines

One way to make it easy to see which objects are on which layers is to assign different colors to given layers, then use the Show Outlines command. The Show Outlines command will hide all the fills, making shapes transparent except for their outlines. Figure 7.9 shows what this looks like.

To edit your movie in outlined mode, with a different color assigned to the layer in each outline, follow these steps. (It is assumed that your multilayered movie is open.)

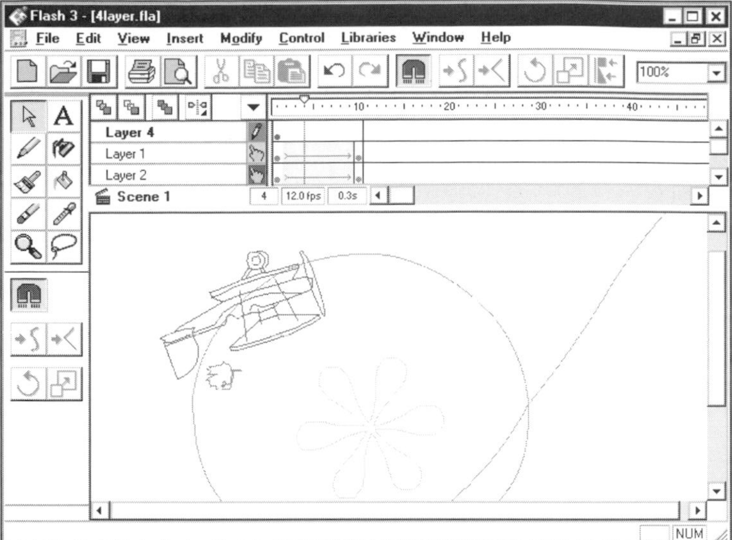

Figure 7.9 A multilayered movie with Show Outlines turned on.

1. From the menu bar, choose View|Outlines. The fills will all disappear and the outlines will all be black.
2. Now, you want to assign the colors to each layer. Select a layer to change its outline.
3. From the Modify Layers pull-down menu, choose Red, Green, Blue, Yellow, or Purple to assign that color to the outlines on that layer. (See Figure 7.10.) Repeat this step for each layer, choosing a different color each time.

Specialized Layer Types

Three types of layers—guide, mask, and sound—don't appear when the movie plays, but they serve special functions, which are explained in the following sections.

Guide Layers

Guide layers are simply layers that don't show when the movie is played or printed. Any shape you place on a guide layer can be used as a way to visually align objects on active layers.

You can use any layer as a guide layer, but most of the time you'll want to create a special layer for that purpose. To create a guide layer, follow these steps:

1. From the Layers pull-down menu, choose Insert Layer to create a new layer that will serve as a dedicated guide.
2. Click the Layers Menu tab and drag to choose Guide. A checkmark will appear to the left of the command. See Figure 7.11.

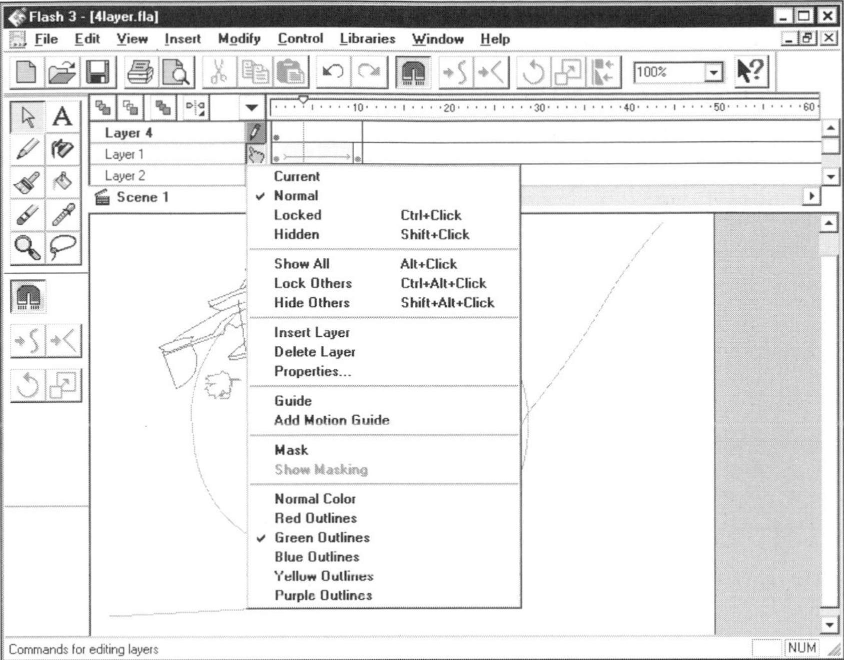

Figure 7.10 The Modify Layers pull-down menu lets you assign one of six colors to a layer's outlines.

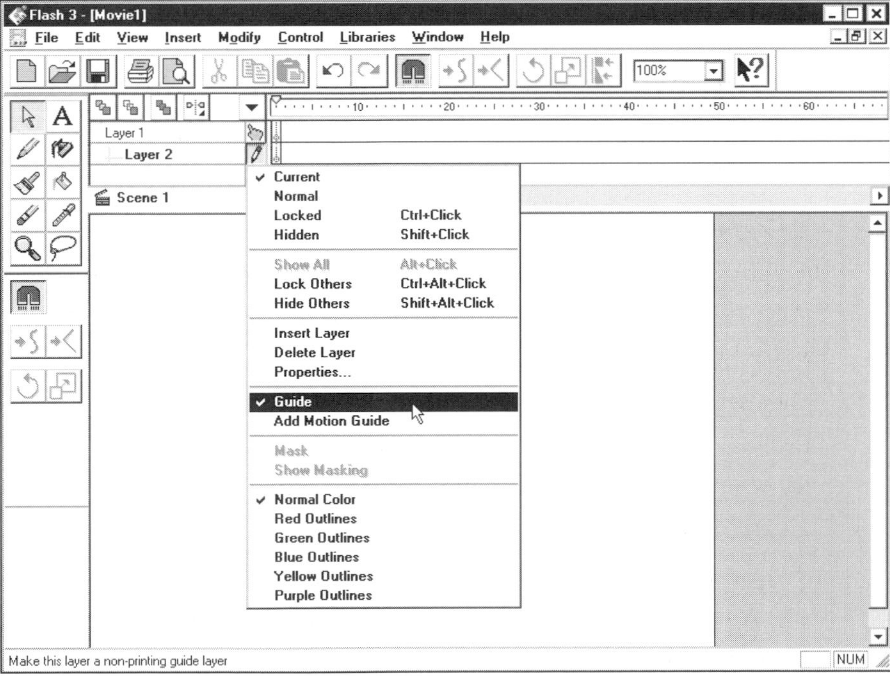

Figure 7.11 Choosing the Guide command.

Note: *It's important that you understand the following distinction between shape tweens and motion tweens: You can't move a shape tween along a motion path because you can't tween the shapes of symbols or groups. Only symbols can be attached to a motion path.*

You will know that your layer has become a guide layer because a blue T-square will appear to the left of the layer name.

3. Make sure the guide layer is selected (active). Then, use any of the Flash tools or commands to put the lines, shapes, or grids on the guide layer.

In Figure 7.12, a guide layer has been created to make it easy to snap the top center of a series of circles to the same point.

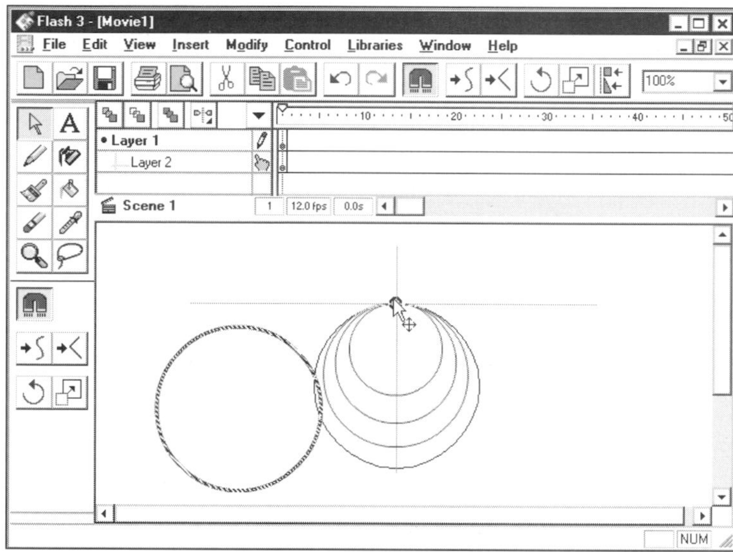

Figure 7.12 The gray cross is drawn on the guide layer to serve as a snap guide. The circles were drawn on the layer above and then dragged into place.

Motion Path Layers

A motion path layer is similar to a guide layer, but it is created with a different procedure to serve a different purpose. While guide paths strictly provide a visual placement and snap reference, motion paths are used to control the direction of tweened groups or symbols.

The process of creating a motion path is difficult to understand if you divorce it from the process of creating a motion tween. For that reason, the following exercise has you create a motion tween and then a motion path to which you'll attach the tween. Follow these steps:

1. Start with a new movie. (Choose File|New.)
2. From the menu bar, choose Libraries|Graphics. The graphics Library window will open. Select biplane from the list. You will see the biplane in the preview. See Figure 7.13.
3. Drag the biplane icon onto the stage.

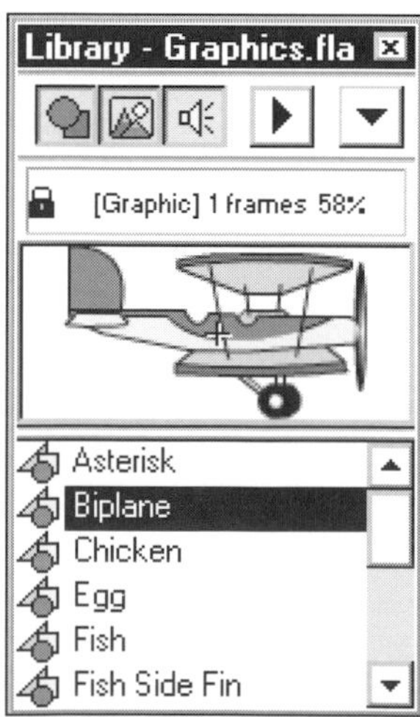

Figure 7.13 The graphics Library window with the biplane in the preview.

4. From the menu bar, choose Window|Library. The biplane is now in the symbols library of the current movie.
5. Highlight the first frame in the Timeline, which is a keyframe. From the Frames pull-down menu, choose Properties. The Frame Properties dialog box will appear. See Figure 7.14.
6. From the Tweening pull-down menu, choose Motion. (The contents of the dialog box will change to look like Figure 7.14.) The default settings shown will suffice for now. Click OK.
7. Click on a frame several frames after the first in the same layer in the Timeline. From the Frames pull-down menu, choose Insert Keyframe.
8. On the stage, drag the biplane instance to its destination. Press Return to watch the motion tween take place. The biplane will move in a straight line between its positions in the first and last keyframes of the tween.
9. Now, it is time to create a motion path. Click the biplane's layer button and choose Add Motion Guide from the Layers pull-down menu. A new layer will appear with the same layer name as the layer on which your tweened symbol resides. See Figure 7.15.
10. Choose the Pencil from the toolbox and click the smooth modifier. Draw a path similar to the one in Figure 7.15.
11. Click the biplane's layer to activate it. Click the Snap button in the toolbar. Choose the Arrow tool. Drag the center of the biplane until it snaps to the lower end (beginning) of the motion path.
12. Drag the frame pointer to the second keyframe in the tween. You will see the tween happen, but it won't be following the motion path. Once again, drag the center of the biplane until it snaps to the end of the motion path.

> ***Note:** It's very important that you specify tweening in the first keyframe, before you add the second keyframe in the tween.*

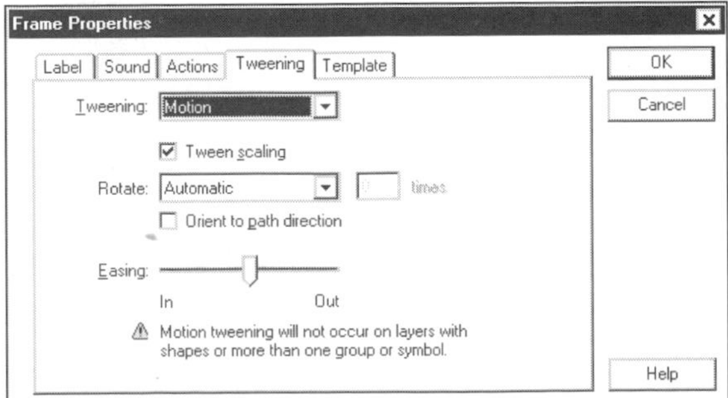

Figure 7.14 The Motion Tweening mode of the Frame Properties dialog box.

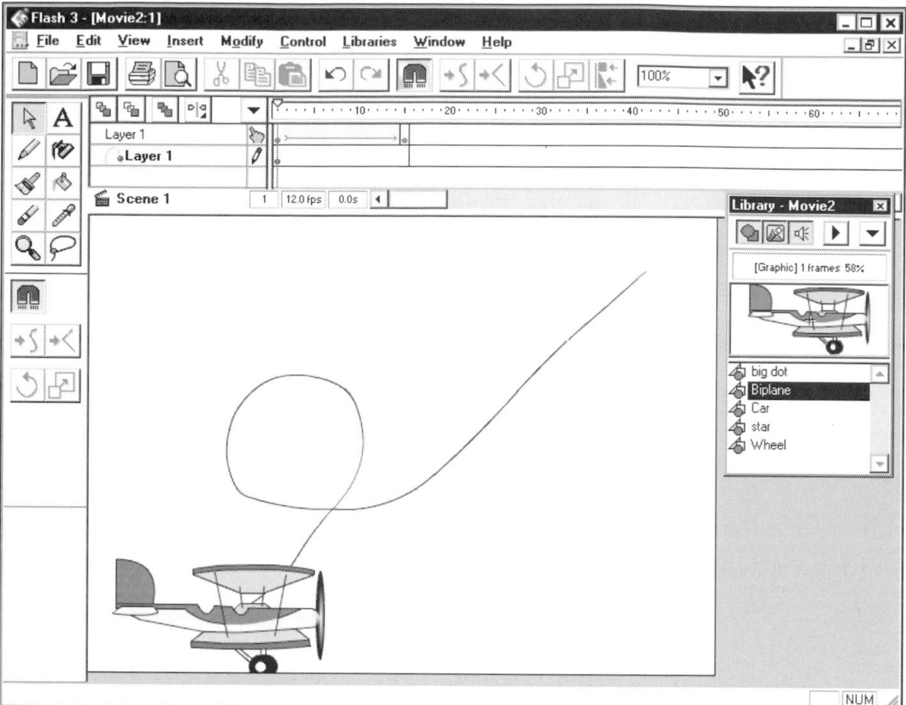

Figure 7.15 A motion path drawn with the Pencil tool on the motion layer.

13. Press Return to play the movie. The biplane should follow the motion path, but it won't turn upside down when it follows the loop. Let's fix that.
14. Drag the frame pointer to the first keyframe. From the Frame pull-down menu, choose Properties. The Frame Properties dialog box will appear. If necessary, click the Tweening tab. Click the Orient to Path Direction box. A checkmark will appear. Click OK.
15. Press Return/Enter to play the movie. The biplane will now turn upside-down when it makes the loop. See Figure 7.16.

Mask Layers

Mask layers are used to hide part of the underlying layers. The technique is often used to create a spotlight or keyhole effect. When you create a mask layer, anything you paint on that layer becomes transparent. If you animate or tween the shapes on that layer, the area that is revealed can be made to move.

When you paint on a mask layer, the normal 100-percent opacity colors will hide what you're masking. This can be annoying and imprecise, because what you are masking is actually what you want to have revealed in the final movie. Therefore, it's a good idea to change the

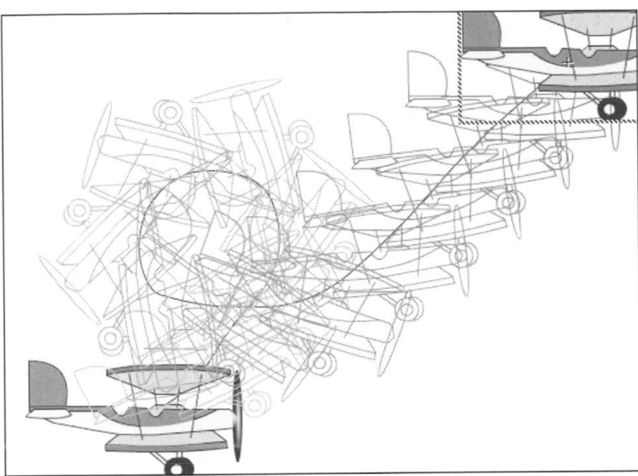

Figure 7.16 The looping biplane.

Alpha channel opacity of the color you are going to paint or fill with. I've found that an opacity of about 15 percent is clear enough to let me see what will be revealed and dark enough to let me see the area I've painted. This works because the opacity of the color used in the mask has no effect on the opacity of the actual mask. The drawback is that this means that you can't create gradient masks or vignettes.

The following exercise demonstrates making a mask under an unmasked layer. Layer masks will reveal any shapes drawn on any layers under them.

1. Start a new movie by choosing File|New. Put some content on the top layer (perhaps some text and a graphic shape). I started with the screen in Figure 7.17.
2. Next, create a new layer so that you can import an image that will be selectively revealed by the masked layer you are about to make. Do this by choosing Insert Layer from the Modify Layers pull-down menu.
3. From the menu bar, choose File|Import. The Import dialog box appears. It is a standard dialog box for opening files, so navigate to a bitmapped image you would like to use and double-click on the file name. See Figure 7.18.
4. Next, you need to insert a layer between the top and bottom layers that will become the mask layer. While Layer 2 is still active, choose Insert Layer from the Modify Layer pull-down menu. Layer 3 will appear between Layer 1 and Layer 2.

Note: *You can have as many mask layers in a movie as you like. Because you can animate the mask, you could use combinations of masks to reveal different combinations of different portions of layers over time. Try adding layers and masks to the movie you make in the mask layers exercise and you'll soon catch on.*

Figure 7.17 The top layer of the movie, which won't be masked.

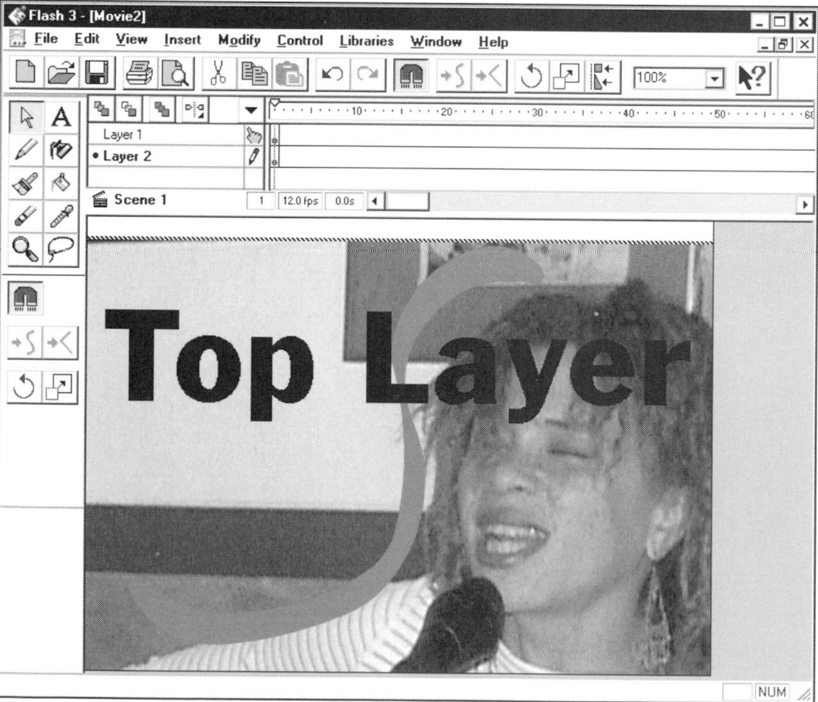

Figure 7.18 Singer Tracy Blackman's photo imported onto the second layer.

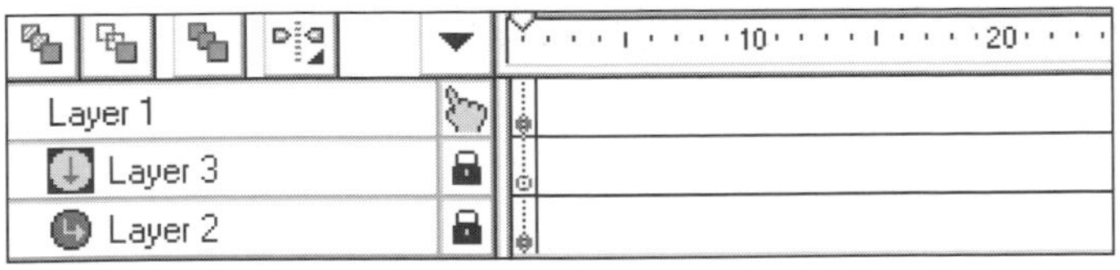

Figure 7.19 The Layer name bars show icons that indicate that Layer 3 is a masking layer and Layer 2 is a masked layer.

5. From the Modify Layer pull-down menu, choose Mask. Icons like those shown in Figure 7.19 will appear to the left of the layer names in Layers 3 and 2.

Sound Layers

Technically, a sound layer does not differ from any other layer—except that you must place all sounds on a Timeline layer of their own. This turns out to be more of an advantage than a limitation. Because Flash currently accommodates only digitized analog sounds, rather than the much more efficient computer-generated MIDI (musical instrument device interface) sounds, keeping sounds in their own layers makes it much easier to delete the sound layers in a version of the Web animation that will be seen over slower modem connections. Also, keeping sounds on their own layers makes it easy to synchronize the beginning and ending of a soundtrack with specific frames of animation on other layers.

Here are the basic steps for placing streaming sound on a Flash layer. In the section "More About Sound And Flash Animation," you'll find a more detailed discussion of sound and sound techniques as applied to Flash animations.

1. Open any multiple-frame Flash movie that you've created. If you don't have one handy, make one (following the directions previously given for creating a shape tween).

2. Select an empty layer just below the layer to which you want to add a synchronized, streaming sound. (Streaming and event sounds are explained in the "Types Of Sounds" section later in this chapter.) From the Modify Layers pull-down menu, choose Insert Layer.

3. It is a good idea to name this layer after the sound you will place there. To do so, double-click the layer name bar. The automatically assigned generic layer name (Layer N) will be highlighted, and you can simply type to enter a new name.

4. You should see a pencil icon on the Modify Layers button of the new layer to indicate that it is active. From the menu bar, choose

File|Import. The typical dialog box for importing files will open. From the Files Of Type pull-down menu, choose either AIFF (Mac) or WAV (Windows). Now, only the specified type of files will show in the file selection windows. Navigate to the sound file that you want to import (anything will do for the moment) and double-click the file name.

5. From the menu bar, choose Window|Library (unless the Library window is already open). The name of your chosen sound will appear in the list of symbols. A speaker icon will appear to the left of the name, indicating that this symbol is a sound. See Figure 7.20.
6. Drag the sound preview from the Library window to the stage. You will immediately see the sound's histogram in the Timeline (See Figure 7.20.) The histogram will occupy as many frames as it takes to play the entire sound. Later in this chapter, you'll learn how to edit sounds and animations to stop and start at specific frames.
7. To test your movie, pull down the menu bar's Control menu and make sure that Mute Sounds is unchecked. Once that's done, press Return/Enter to play the movie.

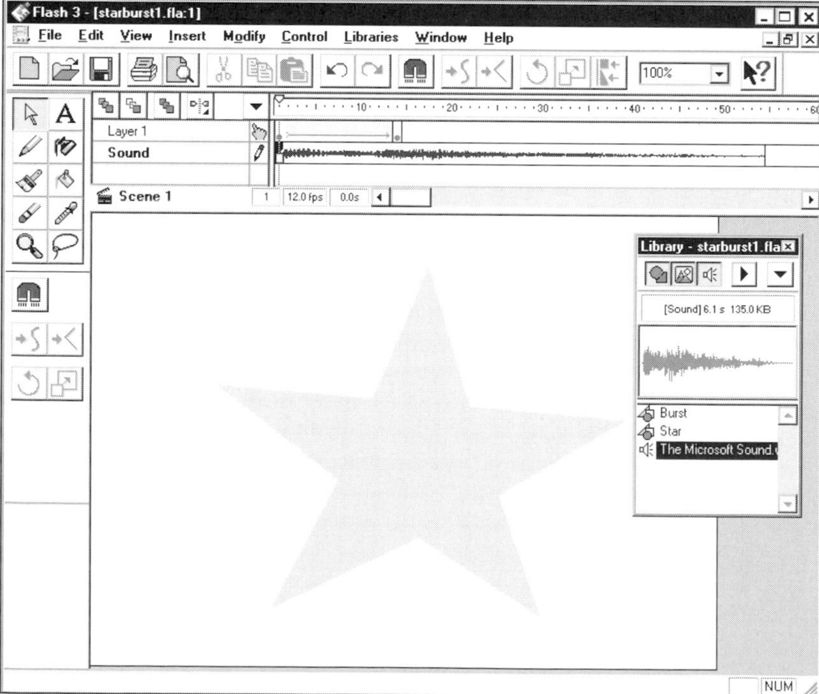

Figure 7.20 A simple animation with an imported sound. The sound's name and preview appear in the Library window at right.

Saving Time With Layers

One of the primary reasons for using layers is that they give you greater control over the bandwidth required by your animations. This is because Flash transmits the data for each layer according to how much information actually changes on that layer. So, if you have a layer in which very little changes from frame to frame (such as a background), the data for the unchanged frames does not need to be retransmitted. Small items, such as animated characters and tweened shapes, will play over the Web (or on a slow computer) at a higher frame rate if each resides on its own layer.

Changing The Stacking Order Of Layers

You can change the stacking order of layers at any time. Drag the layer name (of the layer to be moved) to the layer name above which you'd like to move the original. For instance, in Figure 7.21, Layer 1 (originally the top layer) was dragged down to Level 3. When the mouse button was released, Layer 1 appeared above Layer 3 and below Layer 2. Whew! Don't worry; it's easier to do than it is to describe.

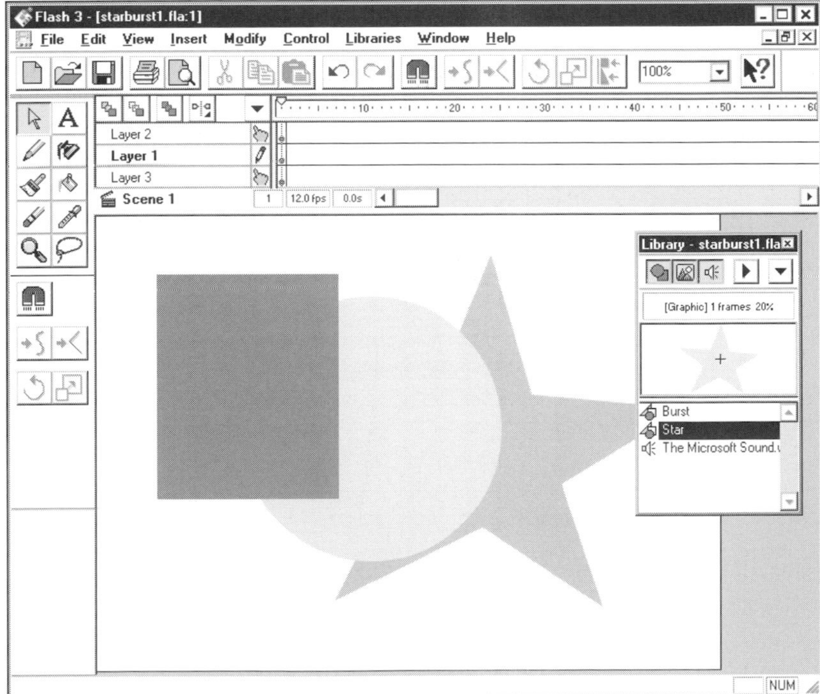

Figure 7.21 Layer 1 after repositioning. The square is on Layer 2, the circle on Layer 1, and the star on Layer 3.

Moving The Content Of Multiple Frames To A Different Layer

In Flash, the usual cut, copy, and paste operations act on whatever object you select with the Arrow tool, regardless of the layer on which that object resides. However, if you want to move the contents of a specific frame or frames on a specific layer or layers, you have to go about it a little differently, as detailed in the following steps:

1. Select the frames you want to copy. To select several sequential frames on the same layer, drag horizontally across the Timeline of the target layer. To select several frames on several layers, drag diagonally until the frames you've selected are highlighted. See Figure 7.22.
2. While the frames are still highlighted, choose Copy Frames (Cmd/Ctrl+Opt/Alt+C) from the Frames pull-down menu.
3. To place the copied frames elsewhere in the movie, select the target scene. Choose View|Tabs from the menu bar, then click the tab of the target scene. (Skip this step if you want to place the frames elsewhere in the same scene's Timeline.)

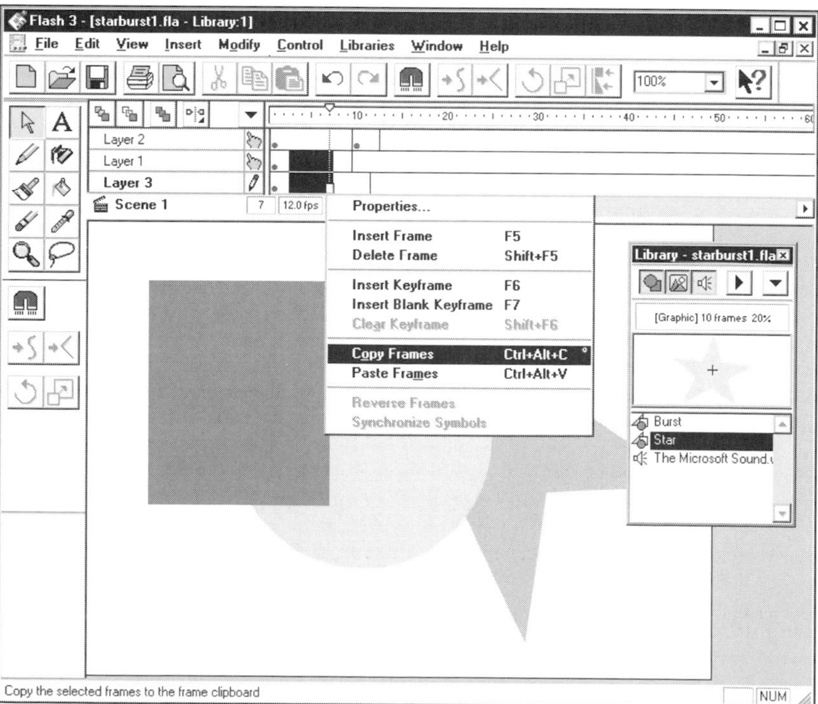

Figure 7.22 Copying the contents of the highlighted frames.

4. Select the frame where you want to paste the copied contents. From the Frames pull-down menu, choose Paste Frames (Cmd/Ctrl+Opt/Alt+V).
5. Of course, the frames you copy are still in their original locations. If you want to remove the originals, highlight them, then choose Delete Frame from the Frames pull-down menu.

> ***Note:** Any time you want to know how many scenes are contained in a movie, choose View|Tabs from the menu bar. You will see an index tab for each scene in the movie on the right side of the stage.*

Combining Interactivity And Multiple Scenes

We have already discussed the basics of assigning actions to frames and buttons. You can maximize the power of these actions when you combine them with multiple scenes.

Structurally, the only difference between a scene and a movie is that you can have several scenes within a single movie. Just as in regular movies, scenes are a useful way to organize the specific events within a movie. Scenes also make it much easier to locate and change the order of events.

Scenes can share any of the symbols stored in the parent movie's library. If you have objects appearing in more than one scene, be sure to convert them to symbols. Otherwise, the movie will store the same data for each scene in which that object appears.

When you play a movie to test it while still in the workspace, only one scene will play at a time. When movies are played in the Flash player, all scenes are played without interruption, unless you insert frame or button actions that tell them to do otherwise.

To test how all the scenes in a movie will play (with or without being influenced by actions), choose Control|Test Movie from the menu bar.

Each scene is automatically named as it is created. The name assigned is Scene N, N being the total number of scenes that have been created thus far in the same movie. If you create four scenes, delete two scenes, and then create another, it will still be named Scene 5. If you create (insert) a new scene between Scenes 1 and 2, the automatically assigned name will still be Scene 5. To rename a scene, double-click its tab. The Scene Properties dialog box, shown in Figure 7.23, will appear.

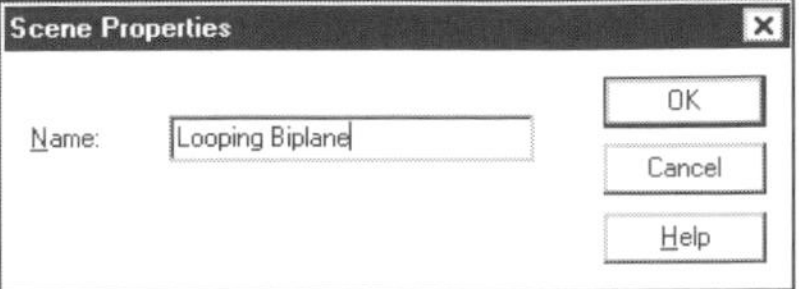

Figure 7.23 The Scene Properties dialog box. You can enter any name you like in the Name field.

Enter any name you like in the Name field. Generally, you will want to enter a name that is descriptive of the scene's purpose, contents, or category. Doing so makes it easy to organize the parts of a long movie.

To create a new scene, choose Insert|Scene from the menu bar. To import an existing movie into the new scene, choose File|Import and then import the Flash movie or still-frame sequence of your choice. All imported movies will be interpreted as keyframes. In other words, such data-saving devices as symbols, layers, and tweens will be lost. You can, however, move the frames from one scene to another by using the Copy Frames and Paste Frames commands in the Frames pull-down menu. You could also use the same method to move frames between two open movies.

Using Frame Actions And Scenes

Actions give you (and, with the addition of buttons, the end user) control over the sequence of the movie. Aside from the interactivity that you can achieve with buttons, the most important advantage of this control is that you can use actions to conserve file size and loading time. Remember, a frame action can direct any frame in any scene to start, stop, or change scenes. Thus, you can reuse complete, multilayered, many-symbol scenes (in whole or in part) as many times as you like within the overall movie.

Frame actions don't require any participation on the part of the user; they simply execute when the frame that they are attached to plays. Attaching an action to any frame on any layer in any scene is simply a matter of picking the needed action from the Action pull-down menu on the Frames tab of the Frame Properties dialog box, shown in Figure 7.24.

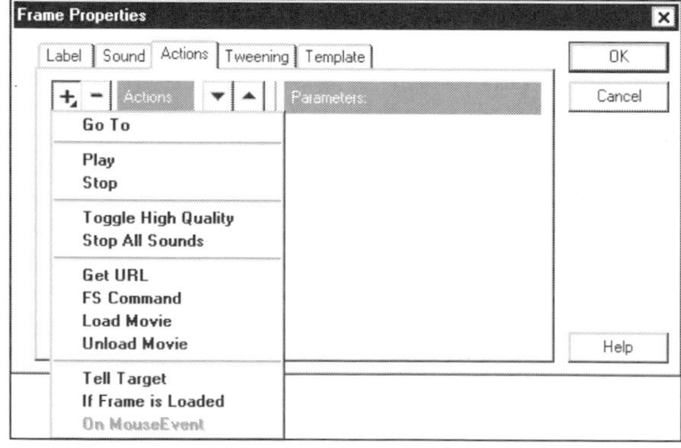

Figure 7.24 The Actions tab of the Frame Properties dialog box.

To reach the Frame Properties dialog box, either double-click the target frame or choose Properties from the Frames pull-down menu. Table 7.1 lists the names of all the frame actions and their purposes.

Table 7.1 Frame actions.

Action	Purpose
Go To	Jumps directly to the named scene and frame. The frame can be specified as a label, number, or next/previous frame. The movie will freeze at the target frame unless you check the Go To and Play box.
Play	Sets a frame to start playing any time an action jumps to it.
Stop	Sets a frame to stop playing any time an action jumps to it.
Toggle High Quality	Toggle antialiasing.
Stop All Sounds	Turns off any sound associated with that frame.
Get URL	Loads an HTML document into a browser window. Options for target windows are Self (the current window), Blank (new window), and Parent (of the current window).
FS Command	Sends strings to any host that the scripting environment (for example, JavaScript, VBScript, and Lingo) supports. This is not an option for nonprogrammers.
Load Movie	Loads another Flash movie from the specified URL. You can also specify the stacking order of the movie with respect to the current movie.
Unload Movie	Turns off a movie being played by the Load Movie command.
Tell Target	Sends one of the other actions in this table to the specified instance of a symbol.
If Frame Is Loaded	Prevents an action from executing unless and until the player or browser has loaded the specified frame. The most frequent use for this action is to play an entertaining or informative short animation while waiting for the main movie to download.
On Mouse Event	Ghosted unless the action is being applied to a button.

Creating Transparency Effects

Alpha channels mask or partially mask artwork so that it becomes more or less transparent. Flash 3 can apply transparency effects to imported bitmaps (GIF and PNG files), gradients, and solid colors. You can even set the level of transparency for an instance of a symbol. If that's not enough to suit you, you can tween the transparency of a color, gradient, or symbol instance over time. This section will discuss the uses and methods for each of these applications of transparency.

Figure 7.25 shows several of the types of transparency that Flash 3 supports. The swish on the background is opaque and is on the canvas level. The two psychedelic *A*s are bitmaps, one GIF and the other PNG. (JPEG doesn't support transparency.) The big round dot is a symbol instance at 50 percent transparency.

Bitmaps And Alpha Channels

Flash 3 now supports the transparent color assigned to GIF indexed-color files as well as that defined by the first Alpha channel (mask) stored in a true-color PNG file.

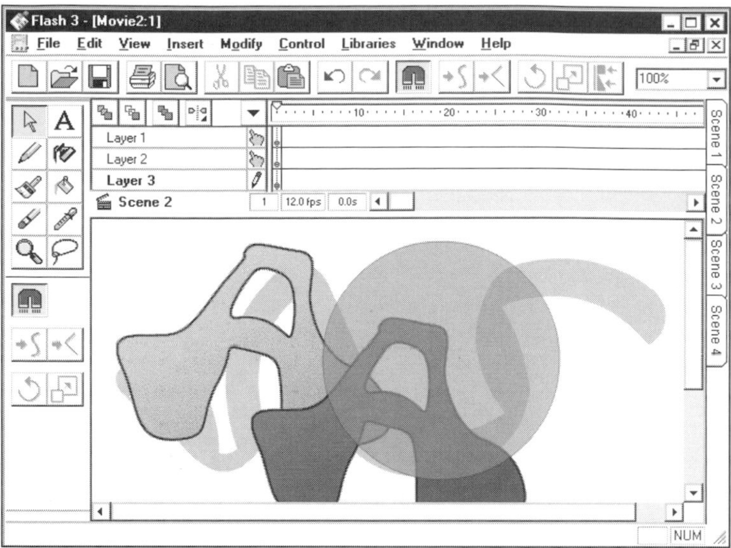

Figure 7.25 Some different types of transparency supported by Flash.

This is a blessing because it allows photo cutouts and other irregularly shaped artwork to have a transparent background. Thus, you can "float" such art over other art, just as you always could with Flash's native vector artwork. You see this effect demonstrated clearly in the way the two A-shaped graphics are overlapping one another in Figure 7.25.

Symbol Instances

Flash also makes it possible to control the overall level of a bitmap's transparency (or opacity, depending on whether you consider the glass half empty or half full). Well, not really, but here's a cheap trick that works. The following procedure will let you control the overall transparency of any symbol, regardless of how many shapes, colors, and other components that symbol may host:

1. Select the bitmap that you want to make partially transparent.
2. Press F8 to make it into a "real" Flash symbol. (I know, you thought it already was one, but even though it's already stored in the library, it doesn't meet all Flash's requirements for qualifying it as a symbol until you do this.)
3. While the new symbol is still selected, choose Modify|Instance from the menu bar. The Instance Properties dialog box will appear.
4. Click the Color Effect tab. See Figure 7.26.
5. From the Color Effect pull-down menu, choose Alpha. The contents of the dialog box will now show the Alpha field and slider seen in Figure 7.26.

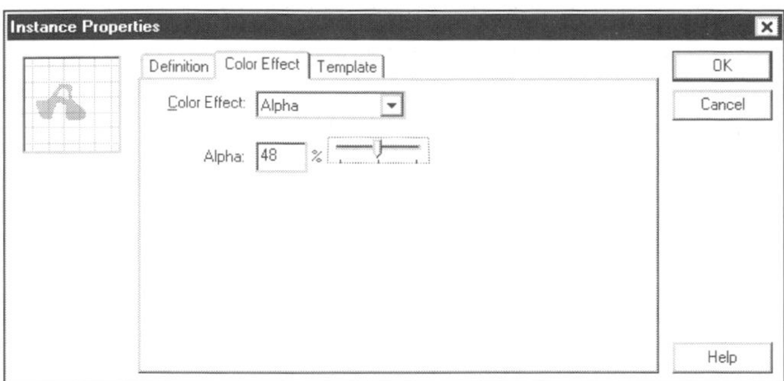

Figure 7.26 The Color Effect tab of the Instance Properties dialog box after choosing Alpha from the Color Effect menu.

6. Either enter a percentage of transparency in the Alpha field or drag the slider to indicate a transparency level. When you think you've got it, click OK. You can see the result in Figure 7.27.

Solid Colors

You can also control the transparency of a color that you use in a line or fill. The brush stroke in Figure 7.28 was made on the top layer of the movie, and its swatch color has been designated as 60 percent transparent, so you can see all the shapes below it.

Here are the steps needed to create a partially transparent color:

1. Click the Color Swatch in the chosen tool's modifier section of the toolbox. The Swatches menu appears. Click one of the swatches to select a color.

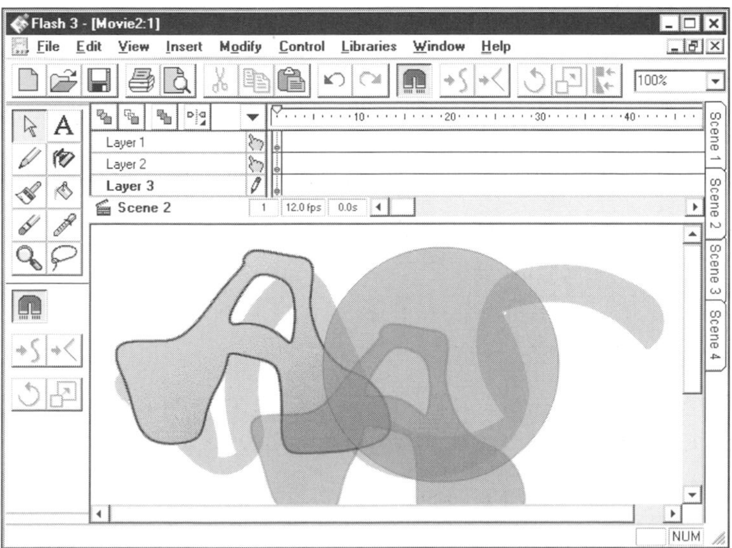

Figure 7.27 The bitmap image of the *A* on the right is set at about 50 percent transparency.

Controlling Transparency of a Layer

You can't control the overall transparency of a layer, but you can copy all the frames in that layer into a new symbol. Highlight all the frames, then choose Copy Frames from the Frames pull-down menu. Press F8 when nothing is selected to create a new, empty symbol. Select the first frame in the Timeline of the first layer. From the Frames menu, choose Paste Frames. Now, place the symbol on its own layer and use the procedure in the "Symbol Instances" section to control its transparency.

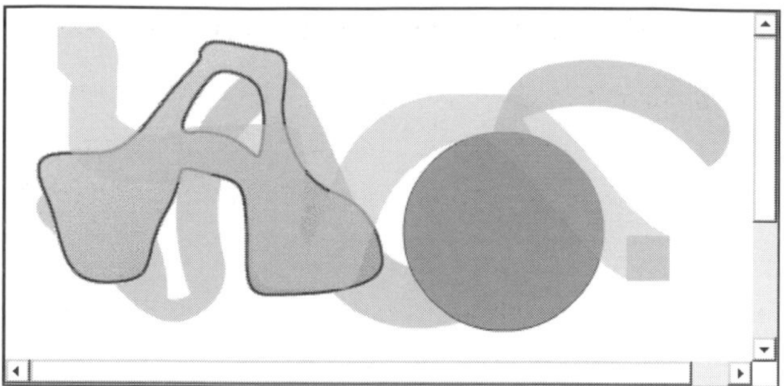

Figure 7.28 A partially transparent solid-color brush stroke on the top layer of the movie.

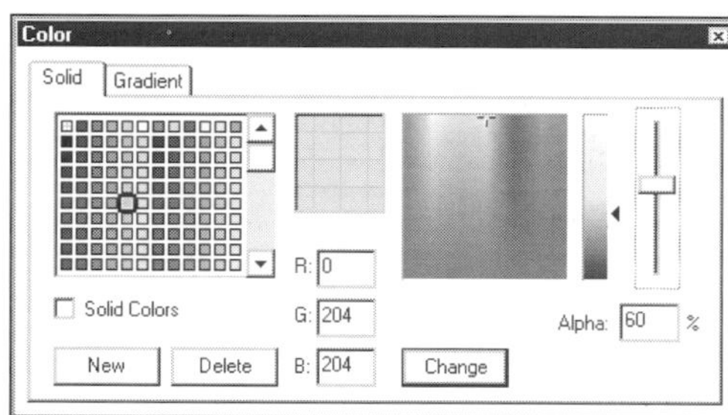

Figure 7.29 The Color dialog box Solid tab contents.

2. Click the Color Swatch again so the Swatches menu reappears. This time, click the edit icon at the bottom of the swatches box. The Color dialog box appears. See Figure 7.29.

3. Drag the slider at the far right. You will see the color in the sample swatch change slightly. The lower you drag the slider, the more the grid underlying the color will be revealed. You will also see the percentage of transparency change in the Alpha field. Click the Change button if you want to change the current color. If you want to add a new transparent color to the Swatch menu, click the New button.

4. Paint as you wish using the transparent color.

Gradients

A gradient is a smooth blend from color to color. You can have many colors in a gradient (a rainbow is an example of a multicolor gradient), or only two. You can use the same kind of controls as previously demonstrated to determine the level of transparency of any or all of the principal colors in a gradient.

Making a gradient can be as easy as choosing one of the gradients that come with Flash 3. To fill a shape with a custom gradient, follow these steps:

1. Draw the outline of the shape you want to fill with a gradient.
2. Choose the Paint Bucket tool. Click and drag on the Fill Color swatch to bring up the color palette, and drag down to the Colors window icon at bottom center (or choose Window|Colors from the menu bar).
3. The Color window opens. Click the Gradient tab. The Gradient dialog box will look like Figure 7.30.
4. From the Gradient Type pull-down menu, choose a Linear or Radial (circular) gradient.
5. To change the colors in the gradient, click the Color Pointer for the color you want to change. Next, click in the Color Space to indicate the color you want to choose for that pointer. Adjust the intensity of that color by dragging the Hue Bar slider. The color change will simultaneously appear in the pointer's swatch, in the Gradient Definition bar, and in the Gradient preview box. Repeat this step to change the color assigned to any of the other pointers.
6. To change the center point of a color in the gradient, drag it's pointer.

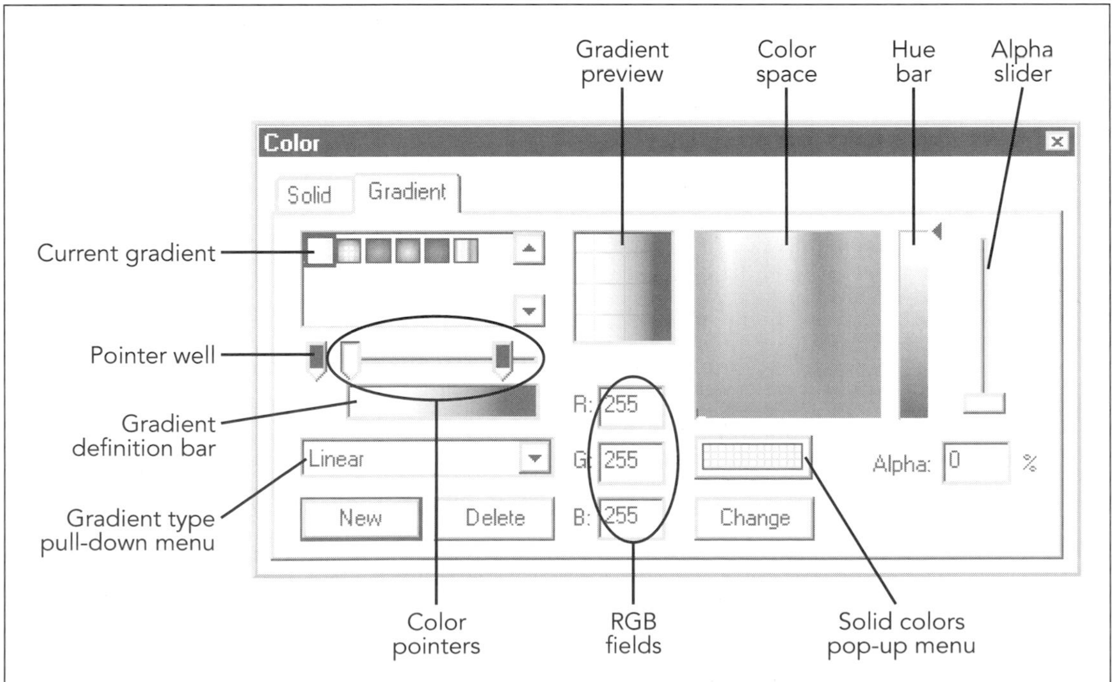

Figure 7.30 The Gradient tab dialog box.

7. To add a new color to the gradient, drag the Pointer Well to the position over the Gradient Definition bar where you would like the new color to appear.
8. To fill with your new gradient, drag the Bucket Fill cursor in the direction of the fill. The first color will start where your drag line starts. Any space within the shape preceding the start of the drag line will be filled with the starting color. The last color will end where the drag line ends and will fill the rest of the shape.

The following steps are for changing the transparency of a color in a gradient:

1. Click in the Color Swatch to bring up the Swatches menu. Click on the Edit box at the bottom. The Color dialog box will appear. Click the Gradient tab.
2. Click one of the gradient swatches at upper left to select the gradient you want to change. (I chose the one at far left.)
3. Choose Linear or Radial from the Gradient Type pull-down menu (just under the Gradient Definition bar).
4. Click the pointer for the principal gradient color you would like to change. This will make it the active color for editing.
5. Drag the Alpha slider at far right (or enter a percentage of transparency in the Alpha field).
6. Click the Change button to change the currently selected gradient or the New button to create a new gradient. You may now paint with the partially transparent gradient.

In Figure 7.31, I have filled a rectangle with a black-to-clear gradient. Repeat this process for any additional colors whose transparency you would like to change.

Tweening Transparency

It is possible to change the transparency of an area or item over time. One of the most frequent reasons for wanting to tween transparency is to simulate a fade-in, fade-out, or flashing effect. Flashing effects are made by fading in a symbol over a few frames, fading out the same symbol over a few frames, and then looping the effect. It is best done when an object is created as a new animated symbol.

You will often want to fade text in or out over time. In order to tween transparency, you must use a motion tween, which works only on symbols and doesn't include text. So, you must first enter the text, break it apart, and then save it as a symbol.

Here's a simple example of tweening transparency so that text fades in a motion tween. Follow these steps:

1. Paint a simple background so that you can see the transparency effect when you create it.
2. In the Timeline, highlight the next 15 frames and then choose Insert Frames from the Modify Frames pull-down menu.
3. From the Modify Layer pull-down menu, choose Insert Layer. Make sure the new layer is above the background layer. (This will happen automatically if you have only two layers; otherwise, just drag the background layer's name bar below the new layer's name bar.)
4. Click the Layer name bar of the new layer to make sure that it is active.
5. Choose the Text tool. From the text modifiers, choose a contrasting color for the text and choose a sans-serif font (such as Arial, Helvetica, or Trebuchet). Enter 90 in the Front Size field. Click the Bold button.
6. On the stage, click at lower left to indicate the start point for entering text. Type "Fade-Out".

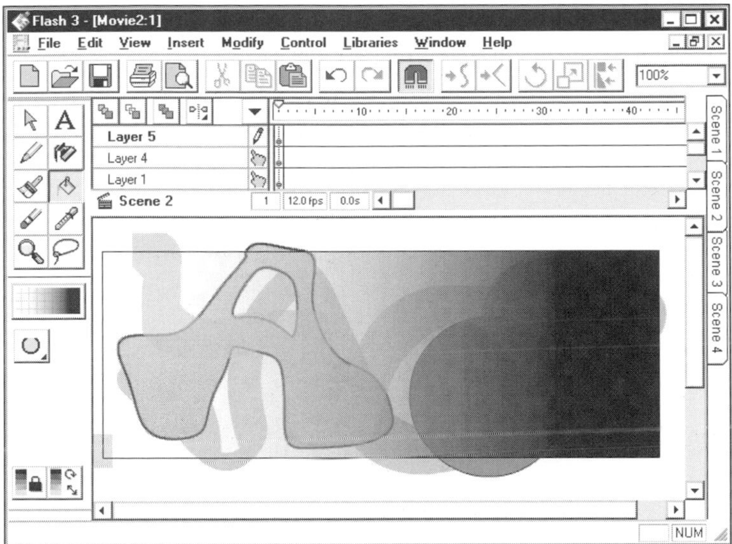

Figure 7.31 A black-to-clear gradient is now on the top layer.

7. Choose the Arrow tool, and use it to select the newly entered text. From the menu bar, choose Modify|Break Apart. Each letter of the text will be checkered to show that it has been selected. See Figure 7.32.

8. Choose Insert Symbol from the menu bar while the text is still selected. The Symbol Properties dialog box will appear. You can enter a descriptive name for the text if you like. Leave Graphic as the chosen symbol type and click OK. A selection marquee will appear around all of the text to show that it is now an overlay.

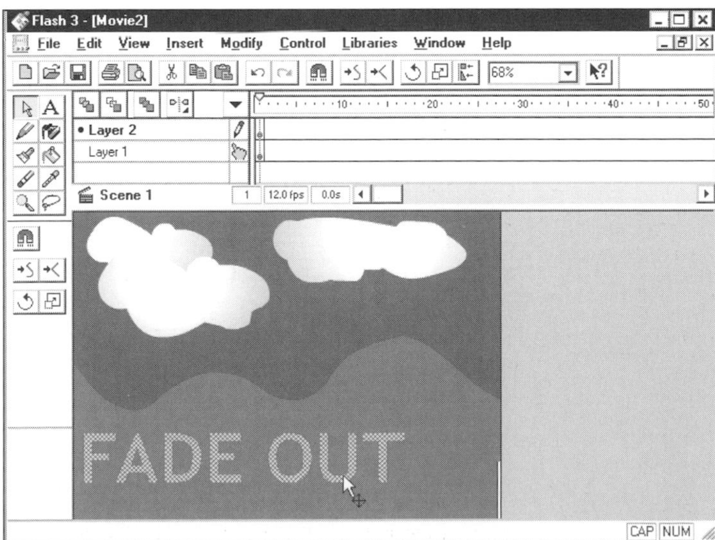

Figure 7.32 Text after the Break Apart command. Each shape is now individually selected.

9. Select the first frame of the text layer. From the Modify Frames menu, choose Properties. The Properties dialog box appears.
10. Click the Tweening tab. From the Tweening pull-down menu, choose Motion. You may leave all other settings at their defaults. Click OK.
11. Select a frame several frames farther along the text layer's Timeline. From the Modify Frames pull-down menu, choose Insert Keyframe.
12. This step isn't absolutely necessary, but it shows you that you can combine transparency tweening with motion, scaling, and transformation tweening: Drag the text symbol to the upper-right corner of the frame. While it is still selected, choose the scale modifier. Hold the Shift key to maintain the proportions while scaling, and then drag one of the corners inward so the text becomes much smaller.
13. Now, for the transparency tween, choose Modify|Instance from the menu bar. The Instance Properties dialog box appears.
14. Click the Color Effect tab. From the Color Effect pull-down menu, choose Alpha. Enter 25 percent in the Alpha field or drag the slider left until the Alpha field reads approximately 25 percent. Click OK.
15. That's all there is to it. Press Return/Enter to play the scene. Figure 7.33 shows the scene after playing about three-fourths of the frames.

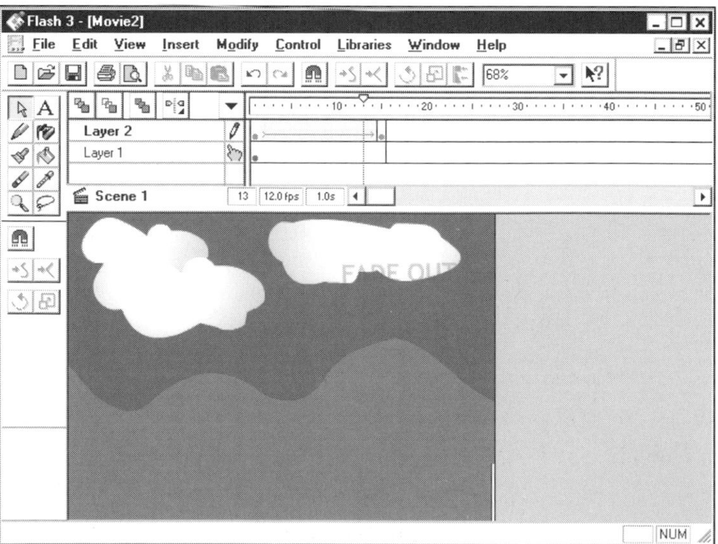

Figure 7.33 The finished transparency tween.

More About Sound And Flash Animation

The exercise on sound layers earlier in this chapter introduced you to the basics of adding sound to a Flash animation. This section will detail some of the tweaks and variants you can use.

The first thing you should know about using sound in Flash is the limitations you are faced with. The glaring shortcoming is that only sampled sounds (analog sounds that have been digitally recorded) can be used. You can't use computer synthesized sounds, which are far more efficient in terms of bandwidth (but not very good at voice and natural sound effects). Flash doesn't provide any way to create or record sounds internally. All sounds have to be imported. Furthermore, only one file type is legal for the operating system you are using: AIFF for the Macintosh and WAV for Windows.

With those limitations aside, there is some good news. You have quite a bit of control over sound in Flash. Sounds can be synchronized to specific frames in the Timeline or they can be made to play continuously. You can also edit the start and stop points of sounds as well as make them fade in and out. You can even attach sounds to buttons, in much the same way that you can animate a button by attaching a button state to a movie clip symbol. Finally, you control the tradeoffs between the quality of a sound and its file size and resulting performance.

Types Of Sounds

Behavioral types of sounds are divided into two categories: event and streaming.

Event sounds are assigned to a keyframe or mouse event. They start and stop based on the keyframe or event to which the sound is assigned. Event sounds must download completely before they can begin playing. Short sounds (such as beeps, clicks, and shots) tend to work best as event sounds.

Streaming sounds are synchronized to the frames of the movie that occur over the same stretch of frames in the Timeline. Streaming sounds begin playing as soon as enough frames have downloaded to allow the whole file to play in synchronization with the assigned frames in the movie's Timeline. The movie (or scene) will pause until that has happened. Longer sounds, such as speech and music, tend to work best as streaming sounds.

To designate a behavioral type to a sound, select the keyframe in the sound's layer where the sound begins. Then, follow these steps:

1. From the Modify Frames pull-down menu, choose Properties. The Frame Properties dialog box appears. Click the Sound tab. The Sound Properties dialog box appears. See Figure 7.34.

2. Choose Event or Stream from the Sync pull-down menu. (The purpose of the Start and Stop choices will be explained later in this chapter.)

Importing Sounds

The only way to get sounds into a Flash 3 movie is to import them. Importing sounds is only slightly more complicated than choosing File|Import from the menu bar. Here's the drill:

1. It's not absolutely necessary to put sound on its own layer, but it ought to be. Select the first empty layer in your movie. From the Modify Layers pull-down menu, choose Insert Layer.

2. Double-click the layer name. The name will be highlighted and you can enter a new name. It's advisable to use a name that contains the word "sound," just so you'll know that this is a sound layer even if you don't see the sound's waveform in the Timeline (because it doesn't start early enough).

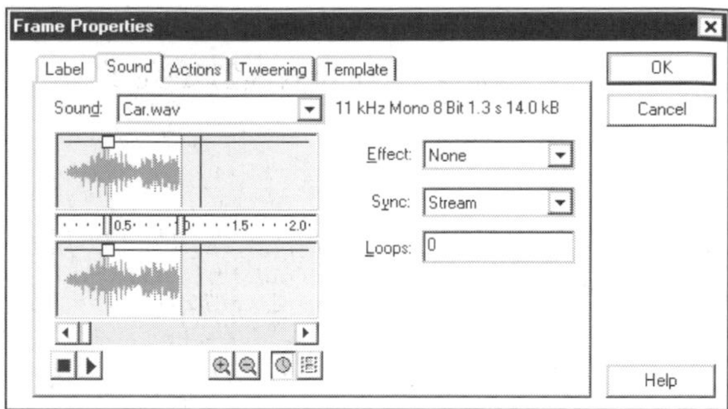

Figure 7.34 The Frame Properties Sound tab dialog box.

3. Now, from the menu bar, choose File|Import. The Import dialog box will appear. From the Files Of Type pull-down menu, choose AIFF (Mac) or WAV (Windows). Find and choose the file you want to import, then click OK. Nothing appears to have happened, and you won't see a waveform in the Timeline.

4. From the menu bar, choose Window|Library. The Library window will appear. If necessary, scroll down until you see the sound and choose it. The sound's waveform will appear in the preview. Drag the waveform from the preview onto the stage, and presto, the waveform appears in the Timeline.

Sound Settings Options

You can choose the settings for an imported sound only after the sound has been placed in the Timeline. If you've read all of this chapter so far, you'll know this is because the settings are found in the Frame Properties dialog box under the Sound tab. These settings are shown in Figure 7.35.

To make settings for an instance of a sound, select the frame where the sound starts, and choose Properties from the Frame Modify pull-down menu. The sound properties will appear, as shown previously. The function of each item in the dialog box (shown in Figure 7.35) is described in the following paragraphs.

Sound Pull-Down Menu

This menu lists all the sounds that have already been imported into the current movie's library. You can change the sound assigned to this frame (or button) simply by choosing a different item from this menu.

Sound Quality Statistics

This line of text merely reports on the quality of the current sound, and you cannot use this dialog box to change it. The sample rate and other

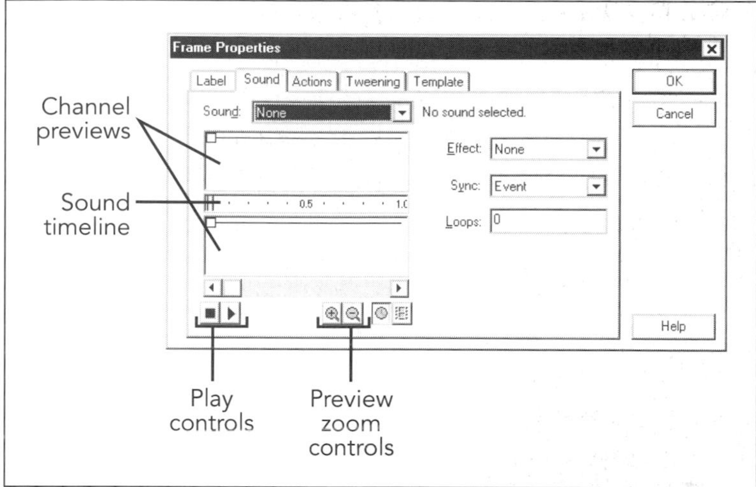

Figure 7.35 The Sound tab of the Frame Properties dialog box.

settings that control the bandwidth of a sound are controlled by the Sound Properties dialog box (detailed in "The Sound Properties Dialog Box" section later in this chapter).

Channel Previews

The left and right sound channels have separate previews, and you can view the waveform for each channel in the preview window. (Mono sounds will have identical waveforms for both channels.) You can also see the volume controls and the in-and-out demarcations in the previews. Here are your options:

- To add a new volume control point, click anywhere in the preview.
- To raise or lower the volume at a volume control point, drag the volume control point up or down.

Sound Timeline

The sound timeline resides in-between the two channel previews and represents the number of frames needed to play both channels of the sound simultaneously. Double bars at either end of the Timeline represent the In Point (start of the sound) and Out Point (end of the sound).

To edit the starting and stopping points of the sound, drag the In Point to the start, then drag the Out Point to the end. You will see a gray "bar" covering the portions of the waveform that have been cut. Click the Play button at the bottom left of the dialog box to hear what the edited sound is like. The portion of the sound that has been removed will not upload for that instance, which saves file-loading time.

Play Controls

These play controls are fairly basic: Stop (the square) and Start (the arrowhead). They let you hear the sound, as edited, complete with the fade-in/out volume control effects. To play the sound, click the Play button. To stop playing, click the Stop button.

Preview Zoom Controls

These controls let you enlarge or reduce the waveform in the preview. To see more frames at a time, click the zoom-out magnifier (-). To see fewer frames at a time, click the zoom-in magnifier (+).

Effect Pull-Down Menu

The Effect pull-down menu (shown in Figure 7.36) lets you choose from eight preset volume level effects. The result of each effect is as follows:

- *None*—Both channels are played at full volume from start to finish. This is the setting you should use if you want to clear any previous settings, because there is no way to erase an individual volume control point.
- *Left Channel*—Full volume on the left channel, no volume on the right channel.
- *Right Channel*—Full volume on the right channel, no volume on the left channel.
- *Fade Left To Right*—Fades sound from the left to the right channel. This setting is very useful for making the sound seem to travel across the screen with the subject of the animation. The volume for the left channel decreases at the same rate that the volume for the right channel increases.
- *Fade Right To Left*—Fades sound from the right to left channel. Again, this setting is good for making the sound seem to travel across the screen with the subject of the animation. The volume for the right channel decreases at the same rate that the volume for the left channel increases.
- *Fade In*—Starts the sound at zero volume for both channels and rises to maximum volume for both channels.
- *Fade Out*—Starts the sound at current volume for both channels and drops to zero volume for both channels.
- *Custom*—Lets you click anywhere in the preview to place a volume control point. You can then drag the points anywhere you like.

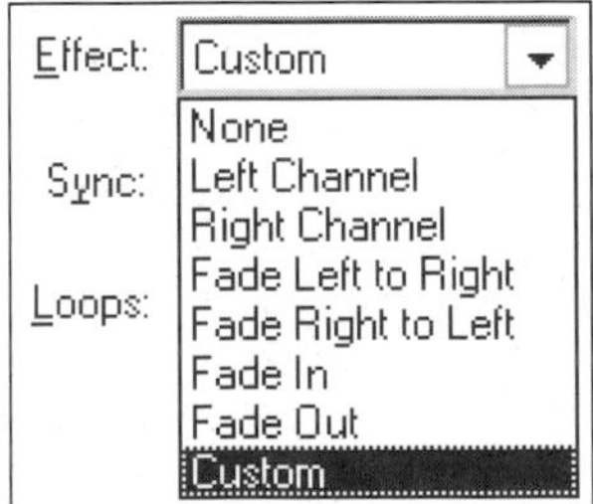

Figure 7.36 The Effect pull-down menu, showing the eight effects you can choose from.

(You don't really have to choose this mode. You can start with any mode, and if you click to add a new volume control point, the mode automatically switches to Custom.)

> **Note:** *In order to hear the results of start and stop sounds properly, you must export the movie or choose Controls | Test Movie from the menu bar.*

Synch Pull-Down Menu

As you may have deduced from what you read earlier in this chapter, the Synch pull-down menu lets you designate the behavior of sound instances as either event or streaming. You also have two other choices, start and stop. Start and stop are used to start a streaming sound at a particular frame and to stop that same sound at a particular frame.

To start a sound at a particular frame, follow these steps:

1. Select the frame in the sound layer Timeline where you want the sound to start. From the Modify Frames pull-down menu, choose Insert Blank Keyframe.
2. Choose the sound you've imported from the Library window and drag its preview onto the stage. The waveform will appear in the Timeline, starting where you inserted the blank keyframe.
3. From the Modify Frames pull-down menu for the blank keyframe, choose Properties and then click the Sound tab in the Properties dialog box. From the Sync pull-down menu, choose Start.

To stop a sound at a particular frame, follow these steps:

1. Select the frame in the sound layer Timeline where you want the sound to stop. (This can be any frame after the point at which the waveform ends.) From the Modify Frames pull-down menu, choose Insert Blank Keyframe.
2. From the Modify Frames pull-down menu for the blank keyframe, choose Properties and then click the Sound tab in the Properties dialog box. From the Sync pull-down menu, choose Stop.

> **Note:** *When you assign the start behavior to a frame, you ensure that the sound will start at that particular frame, even if the movie has to slow down to wait for the sound to load (usually because of a slow or impaired Web connection). The same is true when you place a stop behavior in the sound layer's Timeline: The movie stops at that frame, regardless of how much of the sound has played given the "real world" frame rate.*

Loop Field

The default entry in the Loop field is zero, which means that the sound will play only once, as edited. If you want the sound to repeat, enter the number of repeats here.

The Sound Properties Dialog Box

The Sound Properties dialog box controls how the sound is stored in the library, as opposed to the Sound tab of the Frame Properties dialog box, which controls the behavior of the instance of a sound.

The Sound Properties dialog box is accessed from the Library pull-down menu. First, select the sound whose properties you want to access. Then, choose Properties from the Library pull-down menu. The Sound Properties dialog box will appear. See Figure 7.37.

The following are the parts of the Sound Properties dialog box:

- *Name field*—You can enter any name you like to describe the sound. It won't change the name of the sound file itself, only the title of the sound as it appears in the Library window.
- *Path name*—You can't alter this. It reports the path and name of the file imported for this sound.
- *Date of creation*—This is the date of the last modified version of the imported sound file.
- *Sound quality stats for the original*—This reports the sound's sample frequency, whether it's stereo or mono, the playing time in seconds, and the size of the file in kilobytes.
- *Export Rate pull-down menu*—This menu allows you to choose the sample rate to be exported. You should choose the minimum sample rate that remains consistent with an acceptable sound quality. Choosing a higher rate will not have any effect on the exported file, because Flash doesn't do anything to improve the quality of the original.
- *Export Compression pull-down menu*—This menu lets you set the number of bits per sample for the export.
- *Sound quality stats for modification*—This reports the specifications for the sound file that will be exported with the movie.

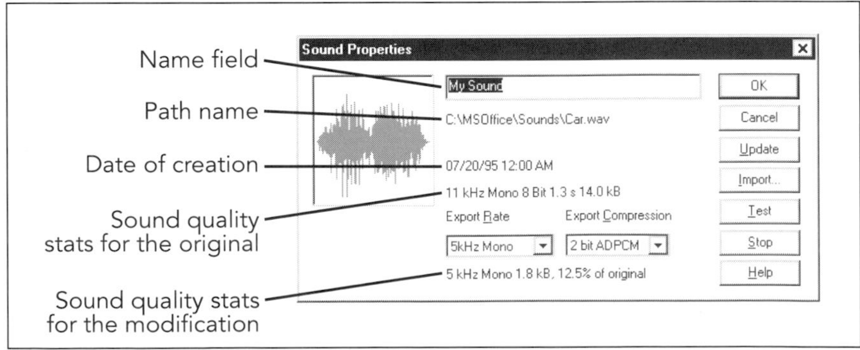

Figure 7.37 The Sound Properties dialog box.

- *Update button*—This button restores the copy of the sound file stored in the library to the quality of the original file.
- *Import button*—This button lets you substitute any compatible-format sound file on disk for the currently selected library sound file.
- *Test button*—This button lets you play the sound specified for export.
- *Stop button*—This button stops playing the sound you're testing.

Reusing Sounds

Because sounds are stored as symbols, you can place a given sound file into any number of different Timelines in any number of scenes and symbols without increasing the overall data space required by the movie. Any changes you make to a given instance of a sound will not affect the sound stored in the library or any other instances of the same sound.

Adding Sounds To Buttons

You want to keep two things in mind when you think about adding sounds to button events:

- Always use event behavior for the sound.
- Buttons are always symbols, so you will have to choose Edit|Edit Symbols in order to access the frames that constitute the button events.

You can attach sounds to any of the first three button events (Up, Over, and Hit). For this example, the Over event is used because it's the one most frequently used to call attention to the fact that the cursor has passed over something that is clickable. Here's the step-by-step procedure for adding sound to a button event. (For the purposes of learning, this example will use a button and sound that are in Flash 3's built-in libraries.) Follow these steps:

1. From the Modify Layer pull-down menu for the top layer in your movie, choose Insert Layer. (It's always best to place buttons on their own layers for editing and organization purposes.)
2. From the menu bar, choose Libraries|Buttons. The Buttons Library window will open. Scroll down to and select Dial. A dial will appear in the preview. Drag the preview to the stage. It will appear with a selection marquee surrounding it.
3. From the menu bar, choose Edit|Edit Symbol (or press Cmd/Ctrl+E). You will find yourself in Symbol Edit mode, and the Timeline will display four frames labeled Up, Over, Down, and Hit.
4. Because you want to place sounds on their own layer, pull down the Modify Layer menu for the layer immediately under the current layer and choose Insert Layer.
5. Double-click to highlight the second name and enter "sound" as the name of the new layer.
6. Select the Over (second) frame in the sound layer. From the Frame pull-down menu, choose Insert Blank Keyframe.
7. From the menu bar, choose Libraries|Sounds. The Sounds Library window will open. Scroll down and select Camera Shutter 35mm. A waveform will appear in the preview. Drag the preview to the stage, and a waveform will appear in the Timeline, starting with the Over frame. The screen should now look like Figure 7.38.
8. To continue working on other aspects of your movie, choose Edit|Edit Movie from the menu bar.

Note: *You can use the same process to add sounds to any of the first three frames. The sounds will play for as long as that event is true. When the next event occurs (for instance, you click the button and cause the Down event to be true), the sound assigned to that event will occur.*

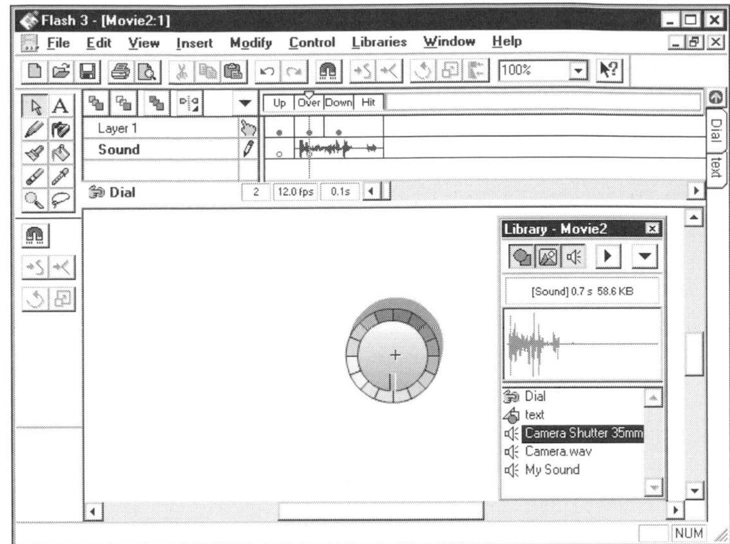

Figure 7.38 The dial button in Symbol Edit mode with a sound attached to the Over event.

Optimizing Sound Files

Before you put your sound-filled Flash movie on the Web, it's a good idea to make sure that your sound files are as efficient as the other parts of your movies. The three following tasks are essential:

- Edit each instance of your sounds to the shortest possible length.
- Set the export rate and export compression of each sound to the lowest acceptable value, which will depend on your individual requirements for a given sound situation.
- Eliminate all unused sounds. This last step doesn't actually make any of the included sounds play any faster, but it will make your movie load and perform much faster.

Testing Sound Before Export

Many factors can influence the way sound synchronizes with your movie and how sound affects the frame rate of the animation. Some of these factors are overall file size (and, therefore, download time), the speed of the browsing computer, whether other programs are also running, the effect of heavy traffic on the performance of the network, and the degree to which you've optimized your animations. So, unless you set up a routine for testing your animations before you publish, you're liable to get some unpleasant surprises.

Here's a workable routine for testing the performance of a sound-enriched Flash 3 movie:

1. Open your movie and select the scene that contains the sound you want to test. You want to make sure that the settings will cause the movie to play on your machine with the worst possible performance.
2. From the menu bar, choose View|Show Frame. This fits all the frame's information into the current window.
3. Choose View|Antialias to ensure that the image will play at maximum quality.
4. From the menu bar, choose Test Scene. The movie will start playing. Press Return/Enter immediately. You may not have noticed, but you are now in the Player window and the menus have changed slightly. (See Figure 7.39.) From the menu bar, choose Control|14.4.
5. If the sound doesn't start or stop playing at the right time, close the Player window and retweak your scene using the three steps outlined in the "Optimizing Sound Files" section.

Finalizing And Publishing The Movie

Most of the time, you will want to export your movie in the Shockwave Flash 3 format, because it is the format that will give your movies the best performance and will allow you to take advantage of all the current features.

It is possible to save Flash movies in older Flash formats: Flash 2, Flash 1, and FutureSplash (the program from which Flash evolved). The

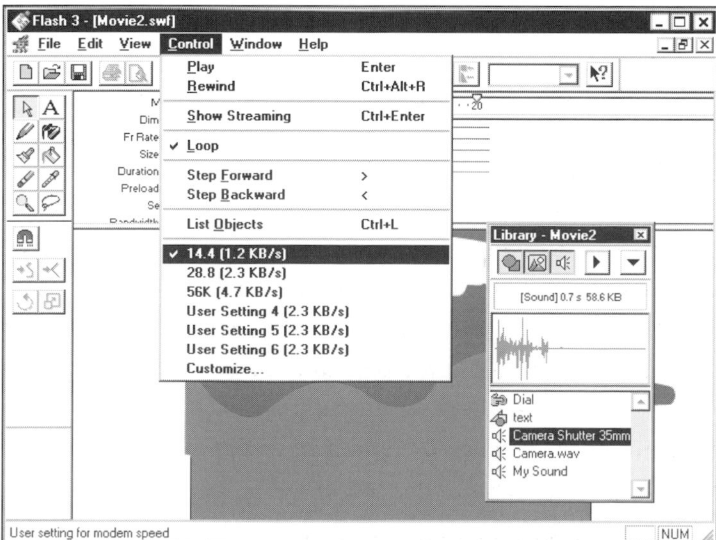

Figure 7.39 Testing your movie in the player window by choosing the slowest modem connection.

Note: *Saving a movie in the Shockwave Flash format automatically optimizes the movie in several respects. All unneeded sounds, bitmaps, and symbols are deleted. Compression is applied according to a default formula or according to the export settings you employed when inserting or optimizing sounds and bitmaps. All bitmaps are compressed as JPEG images.*

advantage is that the movies will play in browsers that are equipped only with older versions of the plug-in. The disadvantage, however, is twofold:

- Older versions do not have a standalone player, so they aren't as well suited for offline presentation, such as on floppy or CD.
- Several of the Flash 3 features won't work in older versions. For instance, sound won't work in versions prior to Flash 2. Other features that won't work in any non-Flash 3 version are shape tweening, transparency, most button actions (except On Release), and the Load Movie action.

The following steps show you how to save a movie in Flash 3 format:

1. From the menu bar, choose File|Export Movie. The Export Movie dialog box will appear. See Figure 7.40.
2. In the File Name field, enter the name you would like to save the movie as.
3. From the Save As Type pull-down menu, choose Shockwave Flash and click OK. The Export Shockwave Flash dialog box will appear.
4. Make the appropriate settings to maximize the performance and meet the requirements of your publishing media (Web, CD, hard drive, floppy). The choices for each of these settings are explained in the next section.

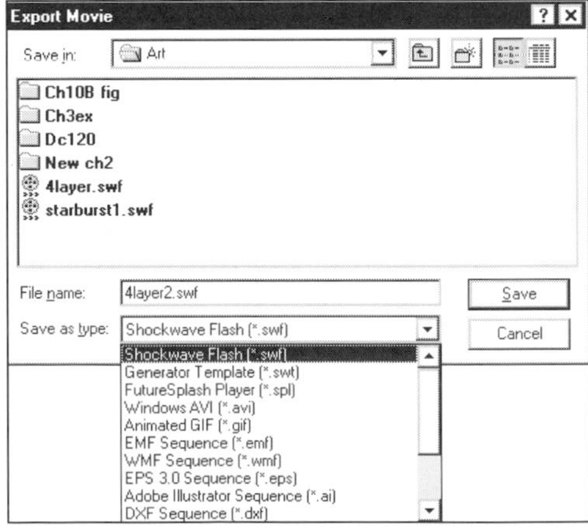

Figure 7.40 The Export Movie dialog box showing the Save As Type pull-down menu choices.

The Export Shockwave Flash Settings

The Export Shockwave Flash dialog box is pictured in Figure 7.41. The features of this dialog box are labeled. The following explain the meaning, purpose, and use of each of these settings.

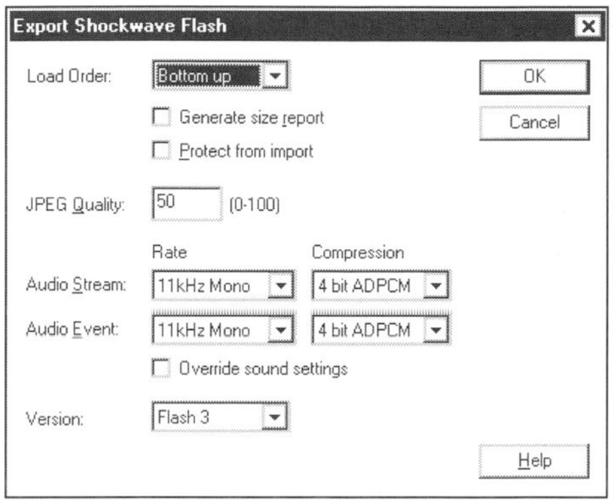

Figure 7.41 The Export Shockwave Flash dialog box.

Load Order Pull-Down Menu

This menu lets you choose whether to load levels and layers from the background up (Bottom Up) or in the order received, which is generally the top overlay starting with the top layer (Top Down). Even if you specify Top Down, any background color assigned to the movie will display first. However, movies that are viewed in the standalone player or as a standalone project ignore the load order.

Generate Size Report Checkbox

If checked, this box causes Flash to save a text report on the exact size of each frame, scene, symbol, bitmap, sound, and font used in the subject movie. The report is printed as four columns: Frame #, Frame Bytes, Total Bytes (for the movie up to that point), and Scene. You can easily spot which frames contain a disproportionate amount of data, so you'll know which frames to concentrate on when manually optimizing the movie.

Protect From Import Checkbox

If this box is checked, viewers will be prevented from downloading your artwork. (However, because imported Flash movies don't transfer actions, layer, buttons, or symbols, people aren't going to be able to "steal" your movies off the Web anyway.)

JPEG Quality Field

Flash 3 automatically converts all bitmaps to JPEG format. Since JPEG loses some of the original information in a file during compression, you want to use as little compression as is consistent with delivering images

USE TRACE BITMAP

JPEG format is not well suited for flat-color or sharp-edged artworks, such as that typically found in logos, buttons, or cartoons. If you have bitmaps of that nature, convert the images to Flash's vector format with the Trace Bitmap command, then delete the original bitmap from the library. You'll have a much smaller movie with much cleaner graphics.

of acceptable quality. Flash 3 does not yet provide a preview of the result of changing settings, so you may want to export the movie in several versions with different settings, then throw out those that don't provide either acceptable performance or acceptable quality.

Audio Stream Rate

The audio stream rate is the time interval between samples, expressed in kilohertz. The higher the kilohertz, the higher the fidelity of the sound to the original. However, higher stream rates also produce much larger files. If the Web is the intended destination, this can mean poor synchronization. It can also mean distorted sound if the sound can't upload in time to play the segment needed for the next frame.

Audio Stream Compression

With this feature, you can set the bit rate for all streaming audio in the movie. Use a high bit rate when realism is required of a sound effect or when you need high-fidelity music. Use the lowest bit rates when telephone-quality speech is okay or when you want to use sound effects primarily for emphasis.

Audio Event Rate

The audio event rate is the sampling rate as applied to sound events. See "Audio Stream Rate."

Audio Event Compression

This feature lets you set the bit rate for all event audio in the movie. Compression considerations are the same as for audio stream compression.

Override Sound Settings Checkbox

If checked, this feature overrides all sound settings made for individual frames in the movie.

Version Pull-Down Menu

This menu lets you choose in which version of Flash you want to export this movie. Your choices are Flash 3, Flash 2, and Flash 1. Flash 1 and Future Splash are functionally identical.

Playing Flash Movies

Aside from simply opening an FLA file in Flash and clicking the Play control, you can play your Flash 3 movies in three ways: use the standalone Shockwave Flash player, create a standalone projector, or embed it an HTML file. All three of these methods, which are explained in the following paragraphs, require you to first export the movie from Flash as an SWF file:

- Use the standalone Shockwave Flash player. This is the option you would usually choose if you were playing the movie from a local drive (because the Flash player will open the file as soon as you double-click the file icon). The reason that happens is because the Flash player is automatically installed on your system when you install Flash. You are also licensed to copy the standalone player to other systems, but the next option makes more sense.
- You can create a standalone projector. This is different from the standalone player in that all the software needed for playback of the Flash movie is embedded in the movie file itself. The result is that—no matter what disk or what computer (as long as it's the same platform—Macintosh or Windows)—you can play the movie simply by double-clicking it.
- You can embed it in an HTML file. This is the way you publish Flash movies to the Web, but this method requires that the receiving browser have an ActiveX (MS Internet Explorer) or Netscape plug-in. However, these plug-ins are included in all current versions of Internet Explorer and Netscape Communicator. Folks using other or older browsers can download and install the plug-in in less than two minutes. (This playback option is the only one of the three that supports the Get URL Action.)

The Standalone Player

Use the standalone player option if you don't want to worry about performance and file-size constraints and don't need to use the features of a browser or to link to HTML pages. This is especially true if you are going to play the movie on computers that have Flash 3 already installed, because the player won't have to be installed separately. Another advantage of saving to the player's SWF format is that the same file can be played as part of an HTML document through a browser.

The interface for the standalone player looks much like the interface for the standalone projector. (See Figure 7.42.) The one difference is that you can create a standalone projector by first playing the movie in the standalone player.

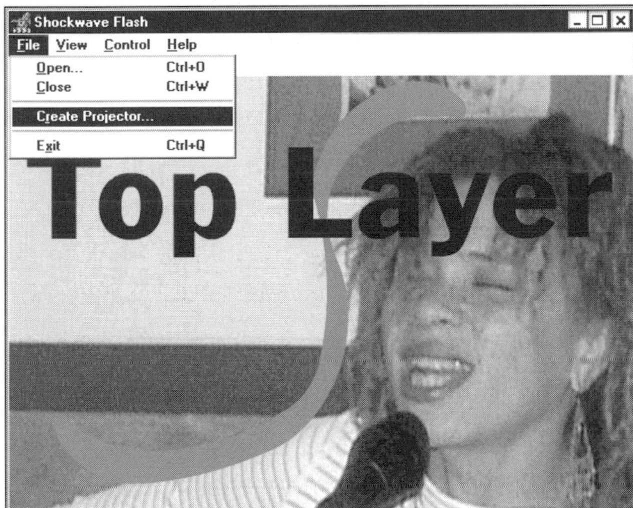

Figure 7.42 The standalone player/standalone projector interface.

The Standalone Projector

Standalone projectors are saved as executable (application) files, and they can be transported to any other computer of the same platform type without requiring the additional installation of any player software. Beyond that, they share the advantages and disadvantages of SWF standalone player files.

To create a standalone projector, follow these steps:

1. Export the movie to SWF format.
2. Locate the file in your computer's directory system and double-click it.

3. The movie will open in the standalone player. From the menu bar, choose File|Create Projector. The standard file-saving dialog box will appear. Browse to locate the drive or folder where you want to save the file, name it, and click OK.

Embedding In An HTML File

This is the way to prepare your SWF files for publication on the Web. Many reasons can be given for embedding Flash into HTML documents that will be published offline, but they all boil down to the fact that HTML environments can use the Get URL Action. This means that your movie can interact with browser scripting languages, such as JavaScript and VBScript. It also means that your Flash movie can use the Get URL Action to open other Flash and non-Flash sites.

The procedure for embedding Flash files in HTML documents is detailed extensively in Chapter 10.

Exporting To Other File Formats

As was emphasized in the beginning of this book, Flash is quite good at exporting its movies to file formats that are more conventional. Unfortunately, there is no way to export synchronized sound or interactivity (that is, actions).

You can, however, export whole movies, scenes, or the current contents of a frame (as either the whole frame or only that part of the frame that actually contains art).

To export a movie, follow these steps:

1. Choose File|Export Movie from the menu bar. An Export Movie dialog box will appear that behaves just like the Save As dialog box typical of your operating system.
2. Enter a name for the file in the File Name field.
3. Choose the destination file format from the Save As Type pull-down menu, then click OK. Another export dialog box, specific to the format to which you are exporting, appears. See Figure 7.43.

To export a still image, follow these steps:

1. Choose File|Export Image from the menu bar. The Export Image dialog box will appear that behaves just like the Save As dialog box typical of your operating system.
2. Enter a name for the file in the File Name field.
3. Choose the destination file format from the Save As Type pull-down menu, then click OK. Another export dialog box appears. See Figure 7.44.

A full discussion of the settings for all the movie export formats can be found in Chapter 9. One thing especially worth noting is the Include pull-down menu that is found in the settings of all of the Export Image dialog boxes. You can use it to choose whether you want to save only the artwork in the image or the entire frame.

Creating Generator Templates

Flash Generator is a Macromedia program designed to supply database material to a Flash movie as specified by an audience member's prompted input. This input can either take the form of typed-in text or the response to a button.

(Unfortunately, a discussion of all that it takes to successfully author Flash Generator applications is a subject more advanced than the scope of this book.)

Assuming you already know—or are willing to learn elsewhere—how to design a Flash movie as a creator template, here's how to export a movie that will behave in that manner:

1. From the menu bar, choose File|Export Movie. The Export Movie dialog box will appear. (Again, it behaves just like the Save As dialog box typical of your operating system.)

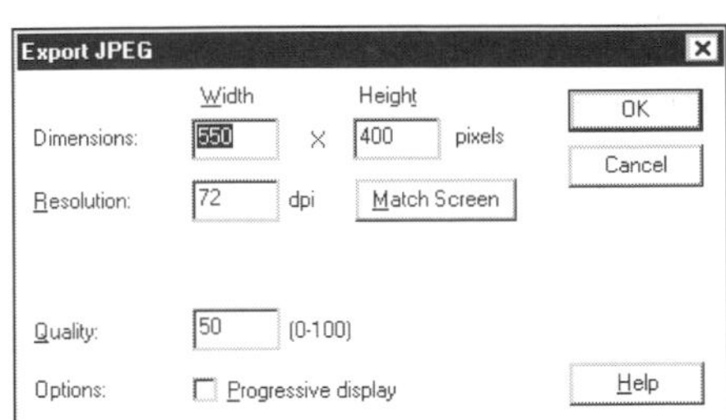

Figure 7.43 The Export JPEG movie dialog box.

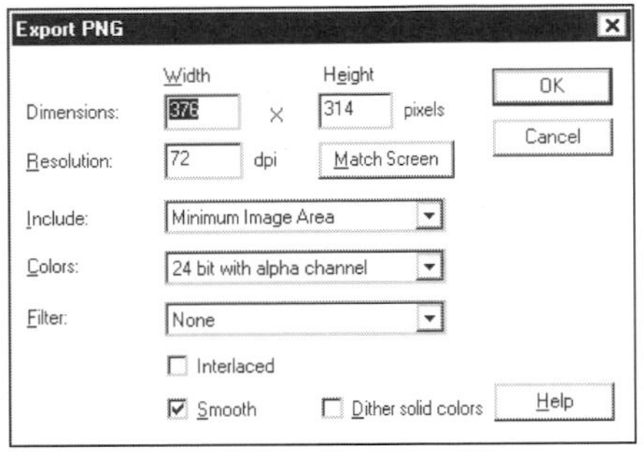

Figure 7.44 The Export PNG image dialog box.

2. Enter a name for the file in the File Name field.
3. From the Save As Type pull-down menu, choose Generator Template, then click OK. The Export Generator Template dialog box appears. (See Figure 7.45.) Its settings are identical to those of the Export Movie dialog box and the considerations for using those setting are the same as discussed previously.

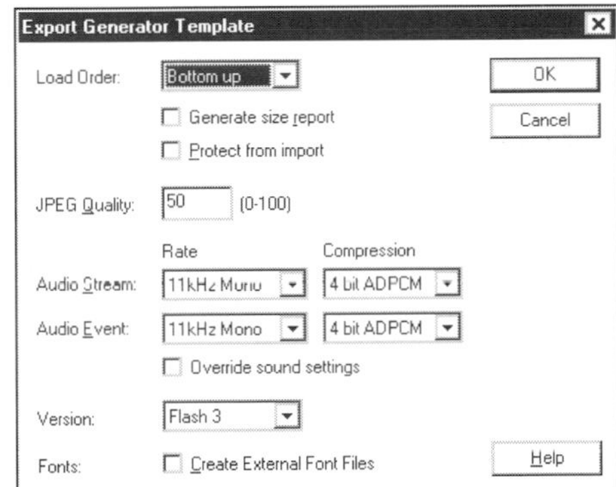

Figure 7.45 The Export Generator Template dialog box.

Moving On

The next chapter will tell you about creating interactivity within your Flash movies. You'll learn the ins and outs of creating button symbols, including how to make animated buttons. Then, you'll discover how to apply Flash's actions to button events, including how to apply multiple actions to a single button event.

8 Buttoning Up Flash And Interactivity

Ken Milburn

This chapter will not only teach you how to make buttons, but it will also explain all the kinds of actions that you can associate with them. You'll also learn how to associate interactivity with the playing of specific frames.

Buttons make interactivity possible in multimedia. We usually think of buttons as looking like, well, buttons. The fact is that they can look like anything, as long as clicking on them causes something to happen (usually branching to another part of the application or moving to another Web page or site). Buttons in Flash are especially versatile, because anything you can draw can be turned into a button.

A Flash button is a subgenus of an animated symbol. Button symbols always have four frames, and each frame is associated with a specific mouse event.

Creating Buttons

If you've read the chapters preceding this one (particularly Chapter 7), you already know most of what it takes to create a button. Basically, you can choose between two techniques.

If you have a graphic element or symbol that you would like to turn into a button, the following steps will show you how:

1. Draw the item (object, character, shape) that you want to turn into a button, or copy something that you drew for another purpose.
2. Select the object and turn it into a symbol.
3. Designate the symbol as a button.

If you would like to start from scratch, take the following steps:

1. With nothing selected, choose Insert|Create Symbol and, in the Symbol Properties box that appears, name the symbol and choose the Button radio button.
2. Import, draw, or copy the artwork for each frame (mouse state) in the button. See Figure 8.1.

You can find complete instructions for each method of creating buttons later in this section under the heading "Editing Symbols As Buttons." The section "Attaching Actions to Buttons" will show you what can be done with a button once you've created it. First, however, we'll review a few tips for drawing simple buttons.

Drawing Techniques For Buttons

Because anything can be a button, there are endless drawing techniques for creating buttons. Naturally, all the techniques can't be shown here. On the other hand, simple buttons that anyone can draw (and their endless variations) are likely to be the ones that are used most often and are most likely to get the job done without appearing

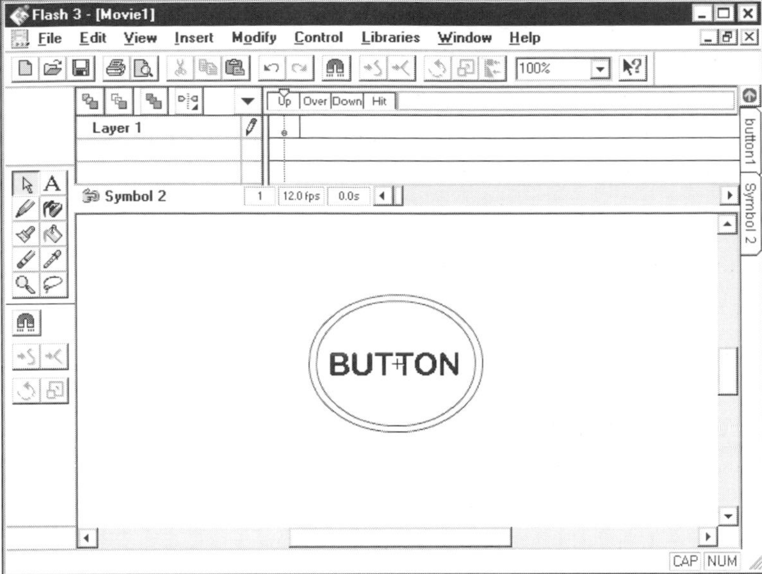

Figure 8.1 Creating a button symbol. Note the four labeled frames in the Timeline.

affected or pretentious. Each of the following sections will show you a quick-and-easy way to create either a button or an effect, which can enhance the appearance of buttons.

Simple Shapes For Simple Buttons

The three shapes most commonly used for buttons are circles, ovals, and rounded rectangles. Plain rectangles are used, too, but they tend to look less suggestive of a push button. You don't really need any additional instruction on how to draw a circle or an oval, but these shapes tend to look more buttonlike if they consist of a pair of concentric shapes, as shown in Figure 8.2.

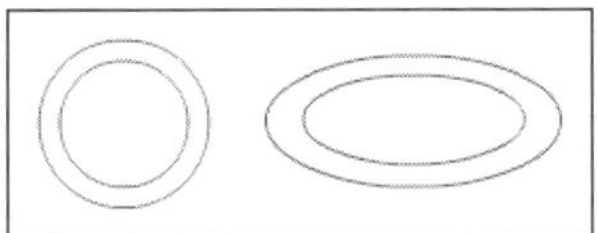

Figure 8.2 A concentric circle and concentric oval that will be used as buttons.

The procedure for making concentric objects is as follows:

1. Draw the object. Practice with a simple shape, such as an oval.
2. Next, you will duplicate the object. Select the object by double-clicking on it, so that its entire outline is selected, then press Cmd/Ctrl+D. A slightly offset duplicate will appear. The duplicate will be selected.
3. Choose the Arrow tool, and use it to drag the selected duplicate to one side of the stage. The duplicate should be completely clear of the original. Keep the selection active.
4. Choose the scale modifier. Handles will appear around the corners and sides of the shape. Shift+drag one of the corner handles to scale the duplicate shape to a size smaller than the original.

5. Now, you will fit the smaller shape inside the larger (original) shape. Select both the original shape and its duplicate. From the menu bar, choose Modify|Align. The Align dialog box will appear. See Figure 8.3.
6. In the Align dialog box, choose the Center button for both the Horizontal and Vertical rows.

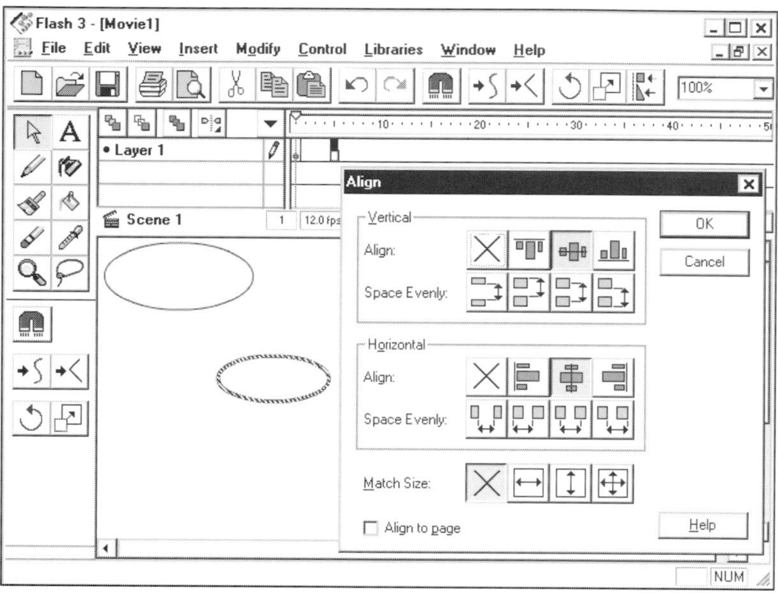

Figure 8.3 The Align dialog box.

One of Flash 3's few shortcomings is that it has no command for drawing round-cornered rectangles. (I call these rounded rectangles.) If you have FreeHand, which is included in the Design In Motion Suite, you can draw these automatically and import them into Flash. If you don't have FreeHand, here's a not-too-painful way to draw rounded rectangles in Flash:

1. Draw a rectangle.
2. In an area that doesn't overlap anything else, draw a circle with the same radius as the corner you want for your rounded rectangle.
3. Duplicate the circle (Cmd/Ctrl+D) three times. Each time you create a duplicate, drag it near the corner it is going to "round." See Figure 8.4.
4. Select the top-left circle and then the left and top sides of the rectangle. Choose Modify|Align.

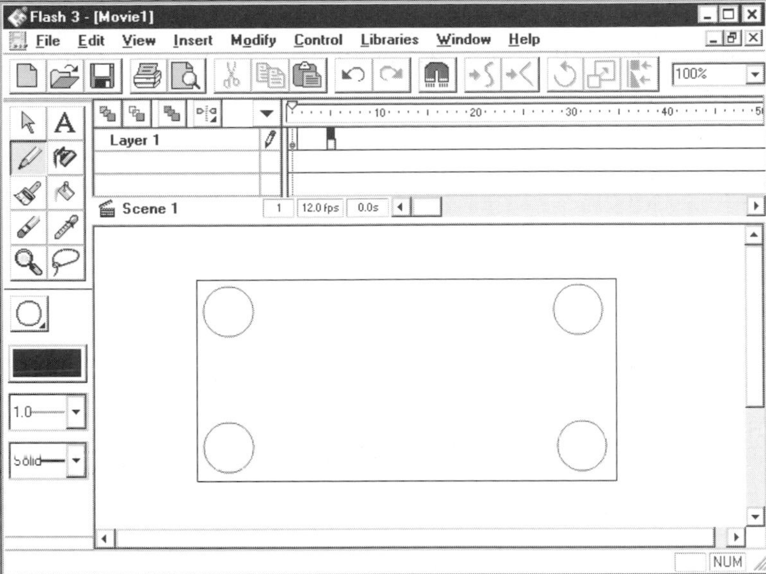

Figure 8.4 The rectangle and four copies of the same circle.

5. When the Align dialog box appears, choose the Top icon in the Horizontal row and the Left icon in the Vertical row. Click on OK.
6. Select the top-right circle and then the right and top sides of the rectangle. Choose Modify|Align.
7. When the Align dialog box appears, choose the Top icon in the Horizontal row and the Right icon in the Vertical row. Click on OK.
8. Select the bottom-right circle and then the right and bottom sides of the rectangle. Choose Modify|Align.
9. When the Align dialog box appears, choose the Bottom icon in the Horizontal row and the Right icon in the Vertical row. Click on OK.
10. Select the bottom-left circle and then the left and bottom sides of the rectangle. Choose Modify|Align.
11. When the Align dialog box appears, choose the Bottom icon in the Horizontal row and the Left icon in the Vertical row. Click on OK. Your rectangle should now look like Figure 8.5.
12. Select all of the parts of the drawing you want to eliminate: the rectangle's corners and the unneeded parts of the circles.
13. Press Delete/Backspace. Presto! You have a rounded rectangle. Select the new shape, and save it as a graphic symbol. You can use this symbol any time you need a rounded rectangle button.

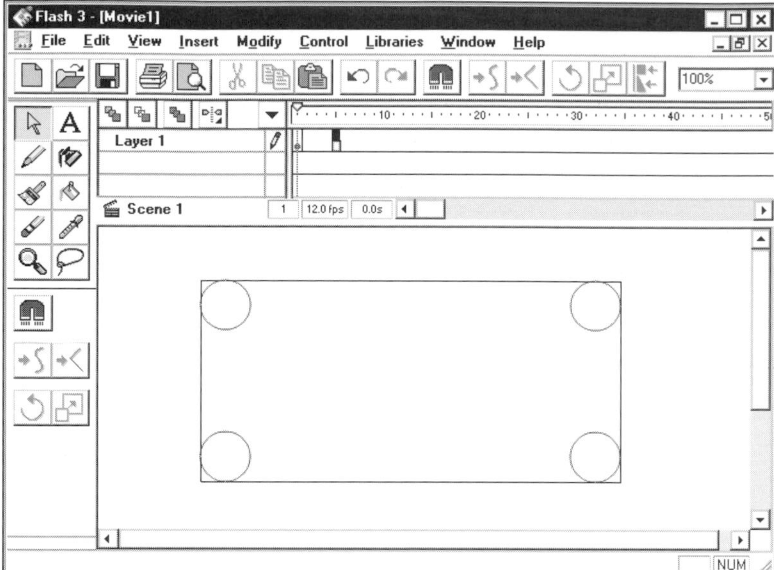

Figure 8.5 The rectangle with four identical circles aligned to the corners.

Gradient Fills

If you want a button that looks concave or convex, you can fill it with a gradient. Round and oval buttons tend to look most convincing, because they can be filled with radial gradients. If you want the button to look convex (raised in the center), make the center color of the gradient lighter than the outside color. If you want it to look concave (bent inward), place the darker color in the center. See Figure 8.6.

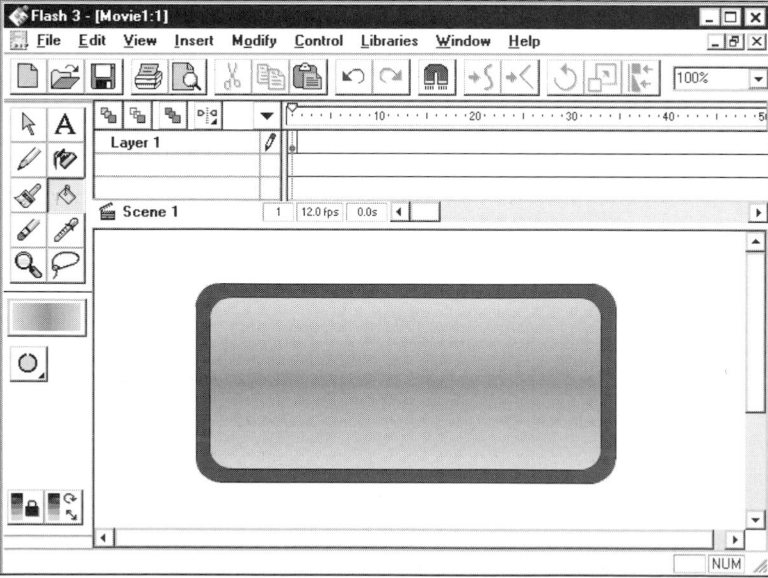

Figure 8.6 A rounded rectangle with a gradient fill that looks concave.

Drop Shadows

Flash 3 doesn't yet provide an automatic way to make drop shadows. As long as you don't insist on realism to the extent of having the shadow fade as the light moves away from the subject, it's fairly easy to create your own. Follow these steps:

1. Select the outline of the object for which you want to make a drop shadow. If there is no outline, create one with the Ink Bottle tool, then select the outline.
2. From the menu bar, choose Insert|Create Symbol.
3. Reselect the outline. (It is now a symbol, so you'll see a square selection marquee surrounding it). Choose Edit|Edit Symbol.
4. Use the Paint Bucket tool to fill the outline with black or dark gray.
5. Choose Edit|Edit Movie. Double-click on the new symbol (the black shape that will become the shadow). The Symbol Instance Properties dialog box will appear. Click on the Color Effect tab. See Figure 8.7.

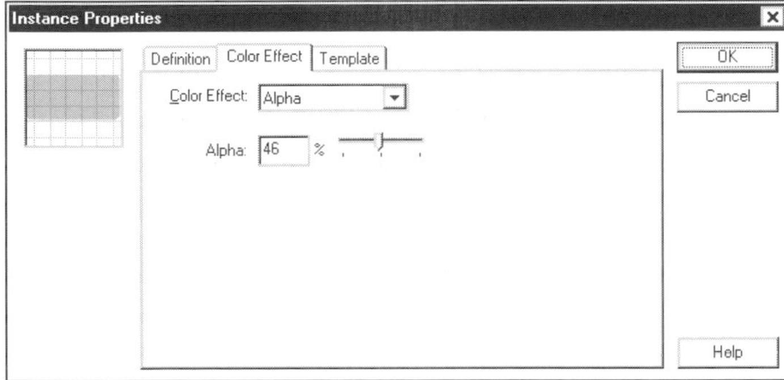

Figure 8.7 The Instance Properties Color Effect tab.

6. From the Color Effect pull-down menu, choose Alpha. Drag the Alpha slider to about 50 percent, and click on OK. The drop shadow is now a medium gray, and you can see through it.
7. Make sure the drop shadow is selected. Choose Arrange|Modify|Move To Back. Your drop shadow will now be behind your button. You can see the result in Figure 8.8. The asterisk was placed on the layer below the button so that you can see the transparency effect in the shadow.

Editing Symbols As Buttons

As mentioned previously, you can create a button in one of two ways: starting from scratch or making one from an existing graphic element

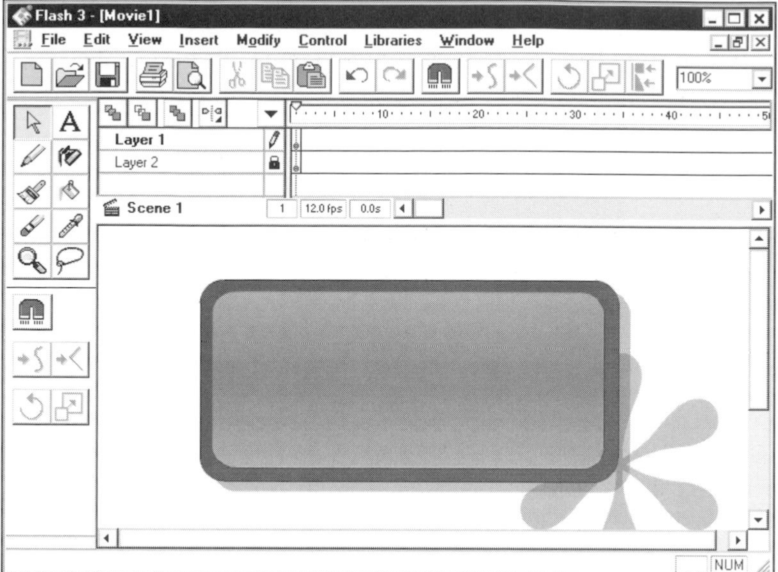

Figure 8.8 The finished drop shadow

or symbol. Remember, all buttons have four stages, and the static appearance of each of these stages is entirely up to you. You can see the four stages of one button in Figure 8.9.

Starting From Scratch

The advantage with starting from scratch is that you get to create your button entirely in the context of its own scene. You don't have to worry about accidentally editing other graphic elements in your movie. Follow these steps to create a button from scratch:

1. With nothing selected, choose Insert|Create Symbol from the menu bar. A Symbol Properties dialog box is displayed to let you name the button anything you like. (All buttons are symbols, but not all symbols are buttons.) Enter the name, check the Button Behavior box, and click on OK. A new scene opens. If you were working within the context of an existing movie, everything seems to disappear. Notice the Timeline has a unique appearance: In place of the

Figure 8.9 The four stages of one button.

frame markers it now has four tabs—Up, Over, Down, and Hit. (See Figure 8.10.) The names of these tabs describe the state of the cursor when the mouse is over the button.

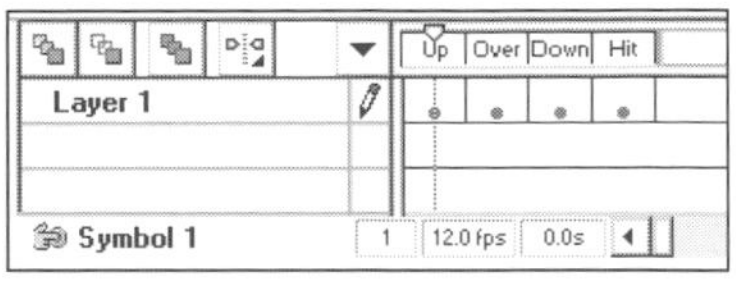

2. Draw the graphic element that you want to represent the first stage (no mouse event) of your button. At this point, you also can elect to import a graphic or an existing symbol.
3. Click on the second frame (Over), and choose Insert Frame from the menu. Place the cursor at the point in the active layer's Timeline where you want to add a frame. Again, from the menu, choose Insert Keyframe. When the mouse is over a button, it can change in any single frame way. Edit the symbol to incorporate any change, or delete it and draw, import, or paste anything you want the user to see. You could even type in a set of instructions. The button doesn't even have to be the same size, so you could have the instruction appear off to one side.
4. Click in the third frame (Down), and choose Insert Frame from the menu. Place your cursor in the third frame. Again, from the menu, choose Insert Keyframe. Edit the symbol to incorporate any change, or delete it and draw, import, or paste anything you want the user to see. You also can assign actions to what happens at a mouse click. Actions can do many things, such as jumping to another scene or playing a sequence starting at a specific frame. See the section "Attaching Actions To Buttons" later in this chapter.
5. Click in the fourth frame (Hit), and choose Insert Frame from the menu. Place your cursor at the fourth frame. Again, from the menu, choose Insert Keyframe. Draw a solid-color shape that encompasses the area to which you want to assign an action. The area can be any size or shape you want. Most often, though, you just want to draw a rectangle with the Pencil tool and fill it with a solid color.

Figure 8.10 The scene Timeline when editing a button.

Once you have finished making the button, return to working in the main movie by choosing Edit|Movie from the menu bar.

***Note:** In Flash 3, you can also choose Insert Blank Keyframe from the Frames menu. This saves time if you want to draw or import a completely different button picture for any (or all) of the four states.*

Turning An Existing Object Into A Button

Let's suppose you want to import a graphic and then make it a button. Perhaps you have already drawn a shape for another part of the movie, and suddenly, it dawns on you that it would make a good button. Follow these steps to turn an existing object into a button:

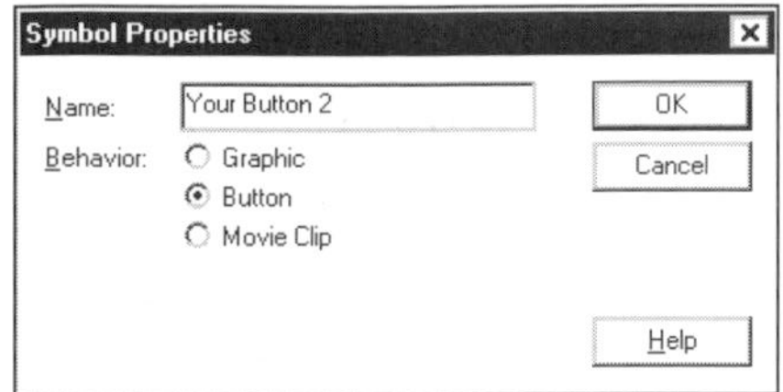

Figure 8.11 The Symbol Properties dialog box.

1. Select the shape and choose Insert|Create Symbol from the menu bar. The Symbol Properties dialog box (Figure 8.11) appears. Name the button and check the Button Behavior box. Click OK.
2. You now have a symbol that can be animated as a button. To finish making the button, you will need to edit each of its four frames. Select the symbol, then double-click on one of its elements (not in an unfilled space). You'll now be editing in the button's scene. (The Symbol Properties dialog box won't appear, as it did in Flash 2.)
3. Click in the second frame (Over), and choose Insert Keyframe from the menu. Now, select the second frame. When the mouse is over a button, the button can change in any way. For example, it can change shape and color, become animated, or pop-up text instructions. Edit the symbol to incorporate any change, or delete it and draw, import, or paste anything you want the user to see.
4. Click in the third frame (Down), and choose Insert Keyframe from the pop-up menu. Edit the symbol to incorporate any change, or delete it and draw, import, or paste anything you want the user to see. You can even import a movie clip symbol. You also can assign actions to what happens at a mouse click. Actions can do many things, such as paging to another scene or playing a sequence starting at a specific frame. See the section "Attaching Actions To Buttons" later in this chapter.
5. Click in the fourth frame (Hit), and choose Insert Keyframe from the menu. Draw a solid-color shape that encompasses the area to which you want to assign an action. The area can be any size or shape you want; most often, though, you just want to draw a rectangle with the Pencil tool and fill it with a solid color.

You've now finished making the button. To return to working in the main movie, choose Edit|Movie from the menu bar.

Testing Buttons

You can see your button in action in two ways: in the library or within the movie scene frame.

To test a button within the library, choose Window|Library, and then scroll (if necessary) to choose the button you want to test. The button will appear in the Library preview window. Click on the play button, and watch your button play all four frames (including the Hit area, which you won't see when the button is actually in use). Figure 8.12 shows the Library window. Alternatively, you could choose Play from the Library pull-down menu.

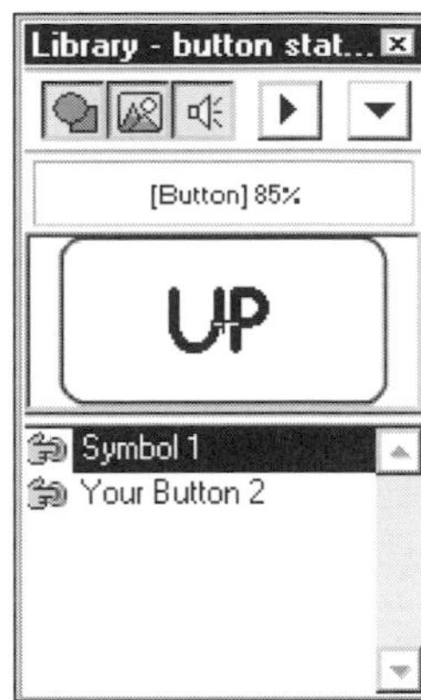

Figure 8.12 The Library window.

To test within a movie scene, choose Control|Enable Buttons. Now, whenever the cursor passes over a button, it will behave as a button. You won't be able to edit buttons (or other symbols) until you go back and choose Control|Enable Buttons again, which toggles you back to the normal editing mode.

Placing Existing Buttons Into Scenes

Since buttons are symbols, you can use them over and over again without using a single extra byte of storage or memory space. When you see a button on a page, it is actually just a link to the button in the library.

To place a button into a frame, choose Window|Library. The Library window will appear. Choose the desired button from the scroll list, and the button will appear in the preview window. Choose the Arrow tool and drag the preview image into the scene frame. Continue dragging, scaling, and rotating until the button is placed as you like it. You can repeat this routine for any other frame of this or any other layer and in as many scenes as you like.

Interactivity And Assigning Actions

You can assign actions to buttons and also to frames. (See Table 8.1.) When you assign an action to a button, the action doesn't occur until you move the mouse over or click on the button. When an action is assigned to a frame, the action occurs when the frame is played.

The method for attaching actions to a frame is described in the section "Attaching Actions." It's a good idea to understand what the actions do, however, before attaching them.

Table 8.1 Actions and what they do.

Name	Description
None	Nothing happens. Choose this action when you want to defeat a previously assigned action.
Play	Executes the Play command; same as choosing Control|Play from the menu bar.
Stop	Executes the Stop command; same as choosing Control|Stop from the menu bar.
Next Frame	For buttons only. This action is useful for still-frame offline presentations. It simply takes you to the next frame.
Previous Frame	For buttons only. This action takes you to the previous frame.
Next Page	For buttons only. This action takes you to the next scene or tab.
Previous Page	For buttons only. This action takes you to the preceding scene or tab.
Toggle High Quality	For buttons only. This action switches you between unsmoothed (nonantialiased) fast play mode and smooth text mode.
Goto	Takes you to a specific scene and frame. You can choose the scene from a pop-up menu (so you don't have to remember scene names).
Get URL	Replaces the current movie with the contents of another. The URL can be either local or remote and may or may not contain Flash content. The Get URL command effectively terminates the current movie, because the current page is replaced by the new page. For more information on interfacing Flash actions with Hypertext Markup Language (HTML), see Chapter 10.
Goto and Play	Just like Goto, except the movie automatically starts playing at the specified frame.
Get URL and Goto	Replaces the current page and also goes to a specific movie in another frame. To be used in conjunction with HTML framesets, for example, when you want a navigation bar on the left side of the screen, and you want another page to come up in the main frame. For information on interfacing Flash actions with HTML, see Chapter 10.
Get URL, Goto, & Play	To be used in conjunction with HTML framesets. Replaces the current page and also goes to a specific movie in another frame, then starts playing that movie at a specific frame. For more information on interfacing Flash actions with HTML, see Chapter 10.
Stop all Sounds	Stops all sounds.

Filling In Action Forms

Some actions, notably those that start with Goto or Get, ask you to provide more information once you've chosen them. The forms for those actions are illustrated in Figures 8.13 through 8.20.

Goto

The Goto form is shown in Figure 8.13. The following actions are available on the Goto form:

- *Scene*—The menu lists all scenes in the movie. Just choose one. If left blank, you will stay in the current scene.
- *Frame*—Enter the specific frame where you want to start.
- *Label*—Takes you to a named label rather than a numbered frame. You choose the label from the pull-down menu to the right.
- *Next Frame*—Takes you to the next frame.

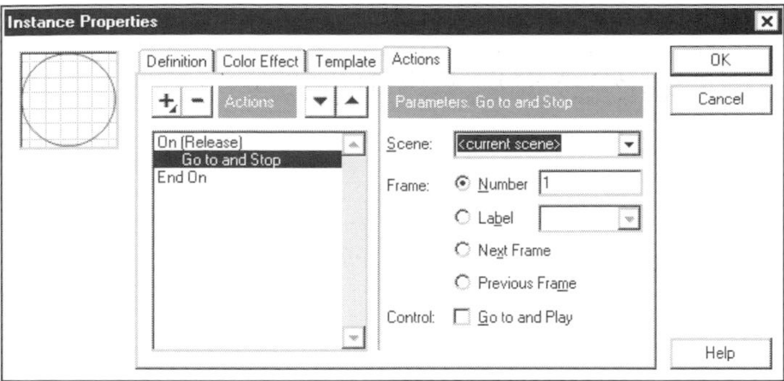

Figure 8.13 The Goto form.

- *Previous Frame*—Takes you to the previous frame.
- *Go To And Play*—Checking this box changes the Goto action from Goto And Stop to Goto And Play.

Get URL

The Get URL form is shown in Figure 8.14. The following actions are available on the Get URL form:

- *URL*—Enter the URL you want to activate with this action.
- *Window*—The menu shows all available frame windows for the current URL. If you'll be entering a network URL, you need to enter a specific target window.

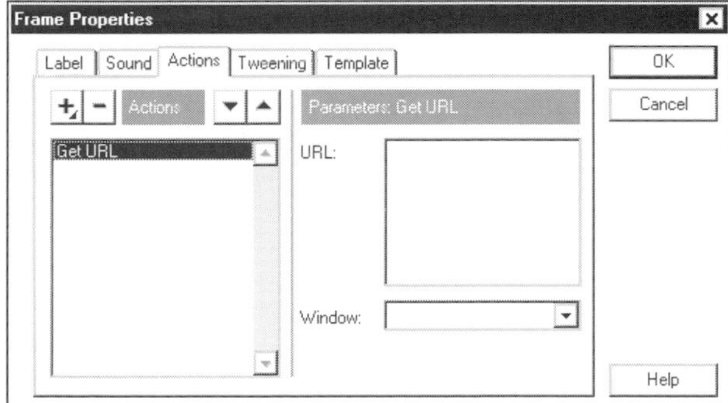

Figure 8.14 The Get URL form.

FS Command

The FS Command form is shown in Figure 8.15. The following fields are available on this form:

- *Command*—Enter the name of the FS command here.
- *Arguments*—Enter any parameters for command arguments here.

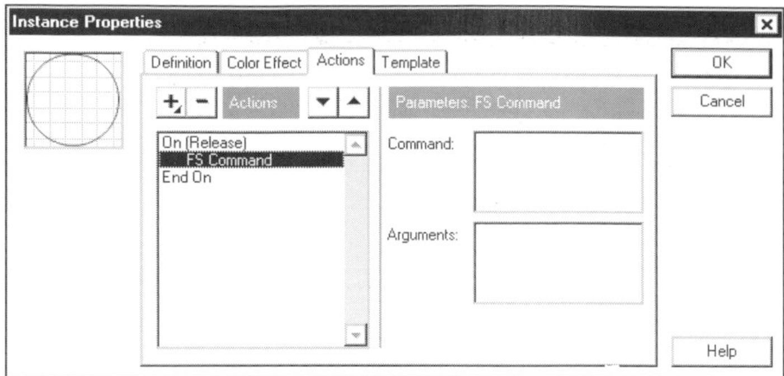

Figure 8.15 The FS Command form.

Load Movie

The Load Movie form (shown in Figure 8.16) allows multiple movies to be loaded on a single HTML page or player instance. The following fields appear on this form:

- *URL*—Enter the name of the URL that contains the movie to be loaded.
- *Level #*—Enter a number that indicates the stacking order in which the movie will be played. Level zero (0) is the bottom of the stack.

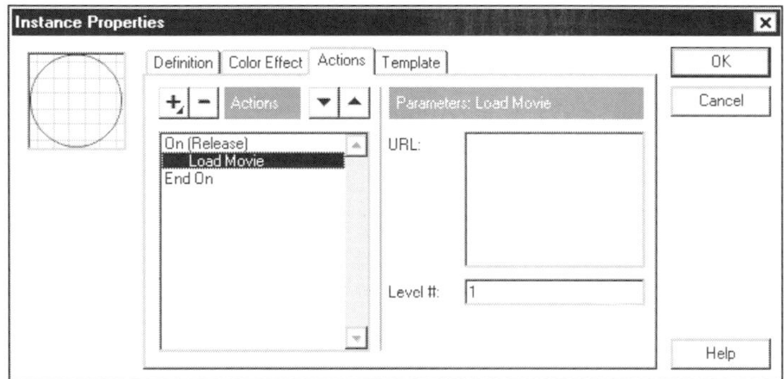

Figure 8.16 The Load Movie form.

Unload Movie

The Unload Movie is shown in Figure 8.17. This form lets you drop the movie that's playing on a specific stacking level. In the Level # field, enter the number of the level that contains the movie you want to quit playing.

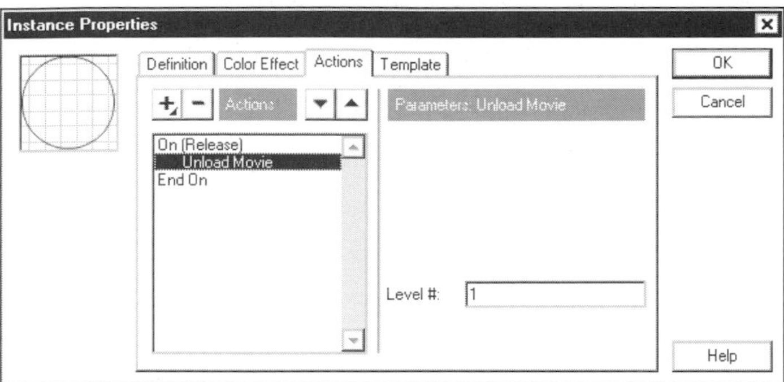

Figure 8.17 The Unload Movie form.

Tell Target

The Tell Target form lets you stop and start movies that are playing in specific positions on the stage. In Figure 8.18, enter the parameters for actions the target will take under Parameters: Begin Tell Target. In the Target field, enter the path and instance name of the target.

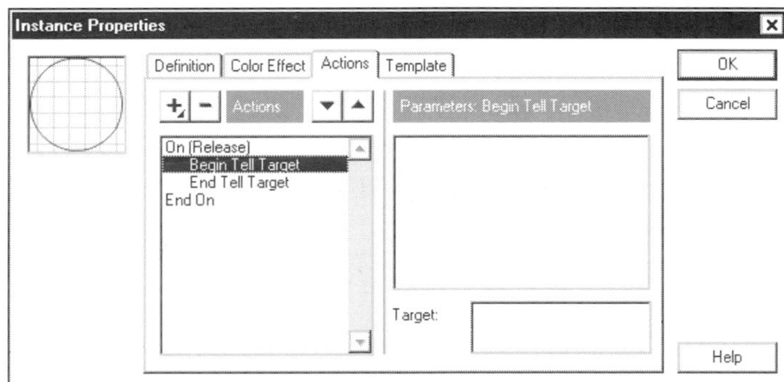

Figure 8.18 The Tell Target form.

If Frame Is Loaded

The If Frame Is Loaded form is used to ensure that a specific frame's contents are ready before an action is executed. (See Figure 8.19.) The following fields appear on this form:

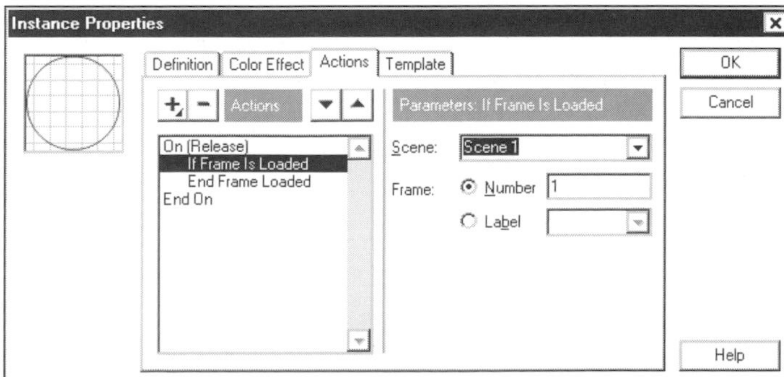

Figure 8.19 The If Frame Is Loaded form.

- *Scene*—A pull-down menu chooses the scene that must be loaded.
- *Frame Number*—Shows the frame number that must be loaded.
- *Frame Label*—A pull-down menu can be used to choose a frame label.

On MouseEvent

The On MouseEvent form lets you specify what mouse event must occur before an attached action can occur. In Figure 8.20, the event boxes allow you to check the pertinent event.

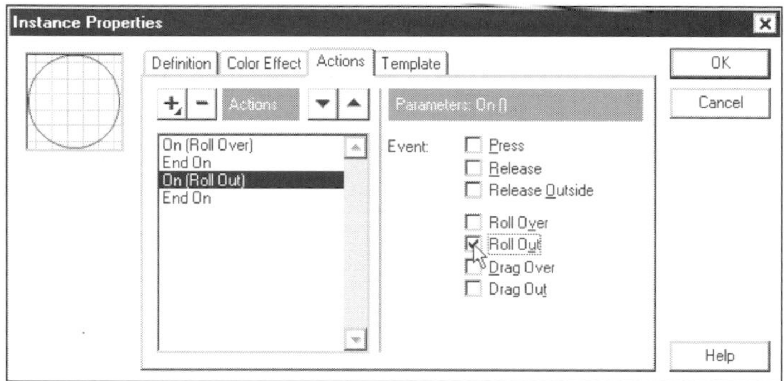

Figure 8.20 The On MouseEvent form.

Attaching Actions To Buttons

In order to take advantage of the range of interactivity that you can inject into Flash movies, you need to be able to attach actions to buttons. Macromedia has made this process almost painless. Follow these steps:

1. Make sure the button to which you want to attach the action is placed in the scene and frame where you want it. Choose the Arrow tool and use it to select the target button.
2. From the menu bar, choose Modify|Instance. The Instance Properties dialog box appears (see Figure 8.21). Click the Actions tab. Drop it

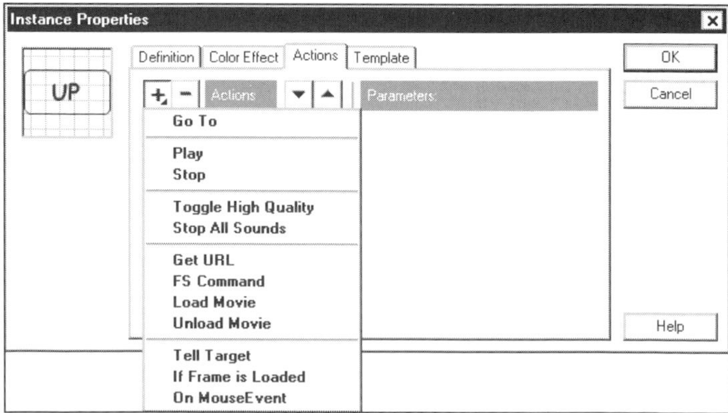

Figure 8.21 The contents of the Actions tab in the Instance Properties dialog box.

down and select the action you want the button to perform. If your choice is a Goto, Get URL, or one of their variants, you will be asked to enter information in some fields and to make further choices.

That's all there is to it. If you have questions about what the various forms are asking for, see the preceding section, "Filling In Action Forms."

Attaching Sounds To Buttons

Buttons are the only type of symbol to which you can attach sounds (although you can import sounds into a movie clip's Timeline). The limitations and considerations for attaching sounds to buttons are the same as for attaching sounds to frames. More detail on attaching sounds is available in Chapter 7. Any sound you attach to a button is associated with that particular button—not just to a specific link to it.

The procedure for adding sound effects to a button is detailed in the following steps:

1. Select the button, either in a specific scene or in the library.
2. If you've selected the button in the library, choose Edit from the symbol pop-up menu (the button at upper right with the downward arrowhead). If you've selected the button's link in a scene frame, choose Edit|Edit Selected from the menu bar. As soon as you do either of these, you will be switched to the button's scene.
3. From the layer pop-up menu for the layer just below the active layer, choose Insert Layer. This will insert a new layer into which you can place the sound.
4. Activate the new layer and click in the Timeline under the frame with which you want to associate the sound (probably frame 2). From the Frame pop-up menu, choose Insert Keyframe.
5. Select the new keyframe and choose Modify|Frame. The Frame Properties dialog box will appear. Click the Sound tab. See Figure 8.22.

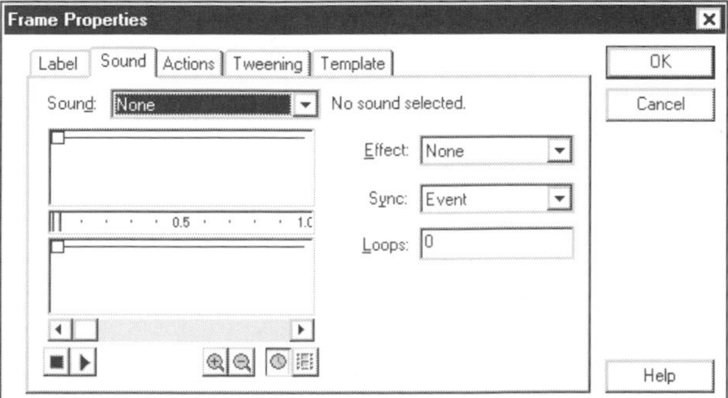

Figure 8.22 The Sound tab of the Frame Properties dialog box.

Using Actions With HTML Offline

One of the biggest advantages of being able to attach actions to frames is that you can "cascade" events. For instance, in the same scene and on the same Timeline, you can have any number of keyframes taking you to various points on that Timeline and, at each of those points (frames), a different thing could happen. You also should remember that Flash interfaces with HTML and that you don't have to be online in order to take advantage of HTML. You can put a browser on a CD-ROM, and then, program a whole interactive application that uses actions to create new browser windows, to open new instances of the browser, and to do anything else that HTML will allow you to do on a Web page. Furthermore, HTML is constantly evolving. Netscape Navigator and Microsoft Internet Explorer—both compatible with Flash 3—are constantly incorporating more built-in capabilities for playing other kinds of media and for capabilities such as cascading style sheets. See Janine Warner's lucid explanation of how to interface Flash and its actions with HTML in Chapter 10.

6. In the dialog box, use the Sound pull-down menu to navigate to a sound file that's present in the current library. Choose Event from the Sync pull-down menu. (If you need to know how to put a specific sound file there, or if you want details on using the Effect, Sync, and Loops settings, see Chapter 7.)
7. Repeat this procedure for each button frame (Up, Over, Down, Hit) for which you want to associate a sound. If you associate a sound with the Up frame, the sound will play as soon as the frame containing the button plays (because the button is visible, but the mouse is nowhere near it). If you associate a sound with the Hit frame, the sound will play after the sound (if any) that plays after a click (the sound associated with the Down frame).

Attaching Actions To Frames

Frame actions can be assigned to any keyframe anywhere in a Flash 3 movie. It's nearly as simple as attaching an action to a button. Although there are fewer kinds of actions for frames than for buttons, the behavior of those that you can use and the procedure for filling in forms are exactly the same. Follow these steps to attach an action to a frame:

1. Place the I-beam in the Timeline layer at the frame where you want to attach the action. From the main menu, choose Modify|Frame. The Frame Properties dialog box will appear. Click the Action tab.
2. From the Action pull-down menu in the Frame Properties dialog box, choose the action you want to occur when this frame plays.

If you want to play your movie to test frame actions, you won't see anything happen until you choose Control|Enable Frame Actions. While you're working on your movie and editing the contents of frames that contain actions, you'll want Enable Frame Actions off. Otherwise, the movie will jump as instructed by the action before you get any chance to edit other contents of the frame.

Cool Button Tricks

I want to encourage you to do all in your power to be creative and inventive in your design and use of buttons. Imaginatively crafted buttons can attract a lot of favorable attention to your Web site and to your message(s). They can make working with your presentation or Web site pleasurable and fun. Remember, a Flash button can be any size or shape and can be associated with any sound (although for online use, you'll want to keep sound files short and highly compressed for the sake of loading time).

If you want to see one of the ultimately creative uses of buttons, visit Jim Curry's Virtual Museum Tour, an interactive experience created entirely in Flash 3: **home.twcny.rr.com/jcurry/museum.html**.

The entire tour is a showcase of what buttons can do. The obvious buttons are the ones that guide you into various rooms and down hallways, simply by pointing to them. Many of the room props and decorations (such as drawers, newspapers, and framed paintings) are also buttons that animate, scroll a text instruction, or make something happen. This is almost a museum of buttons. The first room you see in the museum tour is shown in Figure 8.23.

The following sections present more suggestions for some really cool ways to treat buttons.

Inverting Colors In A Gradient

Make a pair of radial gradients (or three-color linear ones) using the same colors but reversing their positions. Then, you can fill the Frame 1 button (the Up event) with one version of the gradient and the Frame 2 button (the Over event) with the other. When the mouse passes over the button, it will seem to reverse its curvature. You can see one such treatment of buttons in Figure 8.24.

INTERACTIVITY FOR ADVANCED PROGRAMMERS

You can pass messages from any keyframe in Flash to JavaScript; you can also use certain JavaScript functions. This is a highly technical subject, and workable routines were just being discovered as this book was going to press. Experienced JavaScript programmers will have a good idea of what to do and where to do it if they reference the Flash Developer's pages on the Macromedia Web site: **www.macromedia.com**. Of course, Flash lends itself to experimentation, so if you know JavaScript, testing is not a problem.

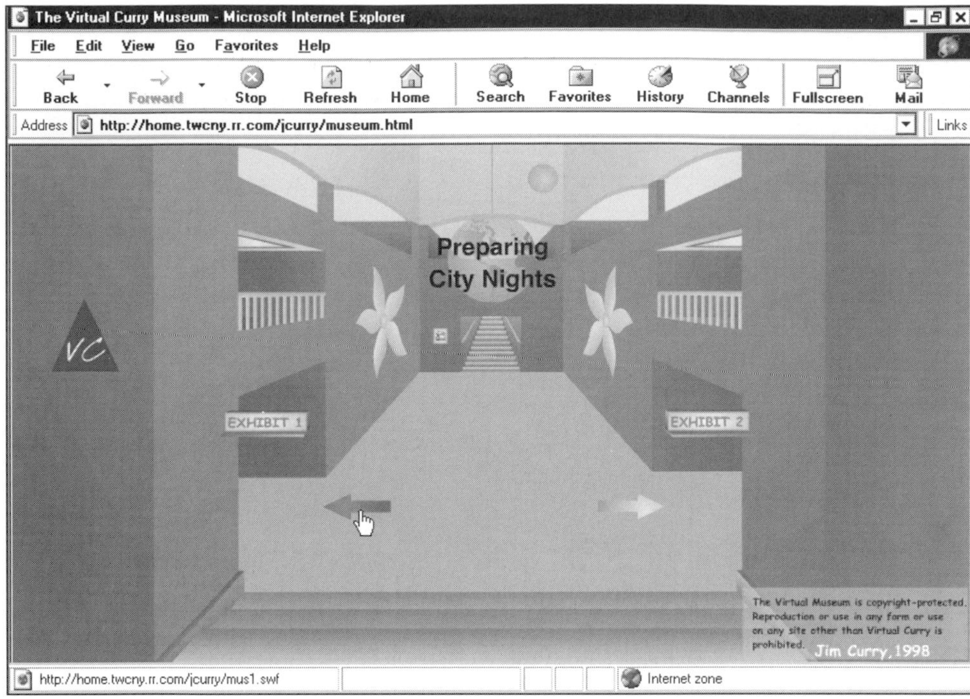

Figure 8.23 The first room in Jim Curry's Virtual Museum Tour.

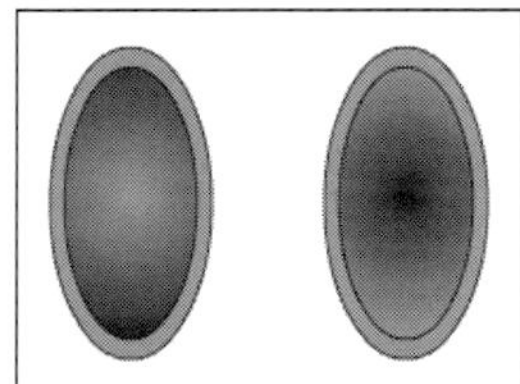

Figure 8.24 Inverting buttons with reversed gradients.

Bringing Up A Banner Or Panel Off To One Side

The image in one frame doesn't have to match the image in another. So you can have a row of buttons and have their functions described in an entirely different place on the screen, as in Figure 8.25.

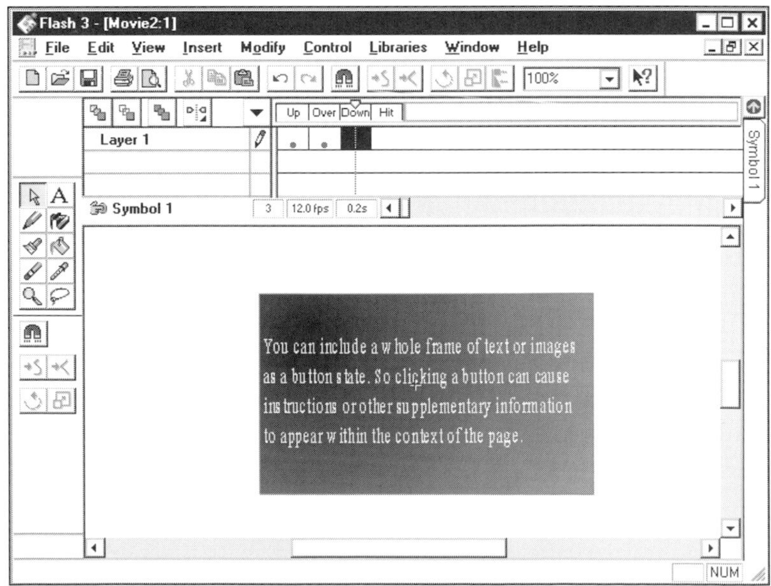

Figure 8.25 Whenever the mouse passes over a button, its function appears in the panel.

Moving On

Now that you've learned the basics of what you can do with Flash 3 alone, this seems a good time to learn what sort of power you can add to your arsenal by spending another $100 on the Macromedia Design In Motion suite. In addition to Flash 3, the package includes FreeHand 8 and Insta.HTML.

9 Using The Design In Motion Suite (And Other Macromedia Software)

Ken Milburn

Macromedia is deliberately reinventing itself as a Web-focused company. In the course of doing so, all of its products have been upgraded to make them more useful to Web designers in general and to Flash authors in particular.

This chapter introduces you to some of the most helpful Web-specific features in other Macromedia programs, especially those that can help you to create sophisticated Flash movies (or those that let you do it faster).

This chapter emphasizes two applications that are also a part of the bargain-priced Macromedia Design In Motion suite: FreeHand 8 and Insta.HTML. Because you can buy Flash with these two very powerful programs for a mere $100 more than the cost of Flash 3 alone, I suspect many of the readers of this book will have made that investment without really knowing its worth.

The chapter ends by discussing the advantages to Flash 3 users of two of Macromedia's other Web-specific programs, Dreamweaver and Fireworks. Dreamweaver is an HTML authoring tool that is aimed at serious Web designers. Fireworks is designed specifically for manipulating bitmapped graphics to make them look and perform better on the Web.

Using FreeHand 8.01 With Flash

FreeHand, like Flash, is a program that allows you to create vector shapes. FreeHand isn't nearly as easy to learn as Flash, but its drawing capabilities are much more powerful. Besides, many of you already have considerable experience with illustration programs, or maybe you already work primarily in FreeHand. The important thing to remember is that, even if you're not an illustration whiz, FreeHand can save you a lot of drawing time because it is capable of making a large number of geometric shapes automatically.

Exchanging Graphics With FreeHand 8.0.1

FreeHand 8.0.1 is an upgrade to FreeHand 8 that made it easier to create in FreeHand and then display in Flash. The following enhancements have been made:

- You can now drag drawings from a FreeHand window to a Flash window—even in Windows 95 and 98.
- A Flash 3 export extra has been added that significantly optimizes the size of FreeHand files when exported to Flash 3 SWF format. Repeated elements are now stored once as symbols.
- You can choose to export only those objects that have been selected.
- Transparency effects created in FreeHand will translate to Flash 3 Alpha channels.

- Any export settings you make are automatically saved so that they can be applied to the next export.
- Handling of included bitmapped graphics has been improved. LZW-compressed TIFF and Photoshop 5 files can now be imported.
- You can now export files that contain clipping paths that mask underlying graphics (both vector drawings and bitmapped).
- Lens fill effects are converted to clipping paths before translation to Flash.
- CMYK TIFFs are automatically converted to RGB format when exported to Flash.
- Grayscale TIFF images are automatically sampled between 72 and 143 dpi and converted to 8-bit RGB files.

Drag-And-Drop From FreeHand To Flash

As noted previously, you can now select any part of a FreeHand drawing and drag it into an open Flash 3 window without having to go through an elaborate export procedure. This *sounds* wonderful, but it doesn't really work as well as you'd wish. On either Macintosh or Windows computers, you get an error message warning that certain elements of the drawing may not translate properly. What it means is that the drawing better not be too complicated, and that fills, transparency, and gradients will more than likely get lost or be reinterpreted. Macromedia is constantly improving its products, so we can hope that this will change over time. Be sure to occasionally check the Macromedia Web site (**www.macromedia.com**) to upload any updates that may follow version 8.0.1.

Caveats aside, drag-and-drop is still a useful capability. FreeHand can create all sorts of basic geometry (stars, polygons, rounded-corner rectangles, shape blends) that would take several times longer to create in Flash. So you can open both programs, create the shape in FreeHand, and then just drop it into the appropriate Flash frame.

To drag and drop from FreeHand to Flash, follow these steps:

1. The FreeHand window that contains the desired drawing must be open and visible (not minimized). Select only those parts of the drawing that you want to incorporate in a Flash frame.
2. Draw or import the shapes you want to put into Flash. Since you drag and drop only what is selected, you can draw several shapes on the same page. Then, just drag what you want to a specific Flash frame.
3. Open Flash (if it isn't already open) and the movie into which you want to place the new shapes.
4. Select the frame in the layer where you want to place the FreeHand drawing.
5. In the FreeHand window, select the shape(s) you want to place in the Flash frame.
6. Drag the selected shapes from the FreeHand window to the Flash window. See Figure 9.1.
7. Make any needed (or desired) changes in the imported shape. The dropped drawing is always treated by Flash as an overlay. To avoid mixing shapes in the overlay with shapes that might already be on the canvas, be sure the shape is selected, then press F8 (or choose Insert|Create Symbol from the menu bar).
8. From the menu bar, choose Edit|Symbol.
9. Select the object. (All its parts will still be grouped.) From the menu bar, choose Modify|Break Apart. Now, you can treat each shape individually.
10. When you've finished your editing, choose Edit|Edit Movie from the menu bar.

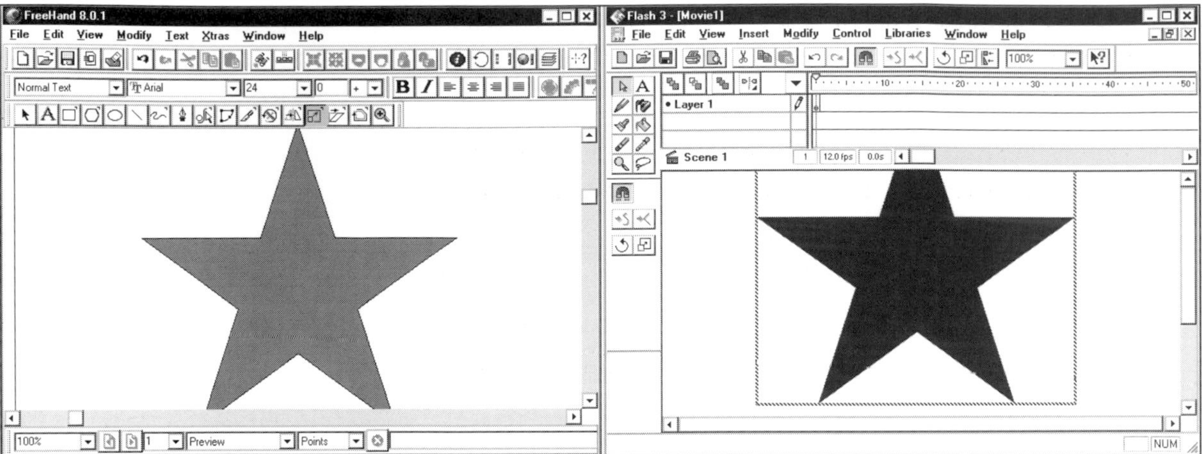

Figure 9.1 The shape shown at left is in FreeHand. The one on the right has been dragged to Flash 3.

Import A FreeHand Drawing Into Flash 3

If you want to import all the characteristics of your FreeHand drawing into Flash, the best way is to export the drawing as an Adobe Illustrator 88 file from FreeHand. Figure 9.2 shows a drawing that incorporates three properties that don't translate at all to Flash 3 via drag-and-drop or cut-and-paste: blends, transparency, and gradient fills. They only partially translate if you import a Flash 3 movie exported from FreeHand.

To move all of these elements into a Flash 3 frame, follow these steps:

1. Create, import, or open the drawing in FreeHand. From the FreeHand menu bar, choose File|Export. The Export Document dialog box will appear. (This is a standard Save As dialog box.) From the Save As Type pull-down menu, choose Adobe Illustrator 88.

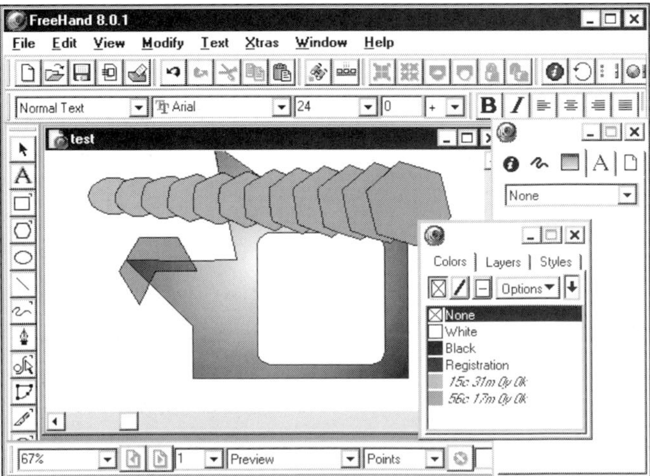

Figure 9.2 A FreeHand drawing showing blends, transparency, and gradient fills.

2. Locate the folder/directory in which you want to save the file. Enter the file name in the File Name field of the Export Document dialog box. Click on OK.

3. Switch to Flash 3 (or open a window in it). From the menu bar, choose Import, and the Import dialog box will appear. From the Files Of Type pull-down menu, choose Adobe Illustrator. Locate the file you exported and double-click on it.

4. The imported file will open in Flash 3. In Figure 9.3, you can see that each entity is selected and has been automatically saved as a symbol.

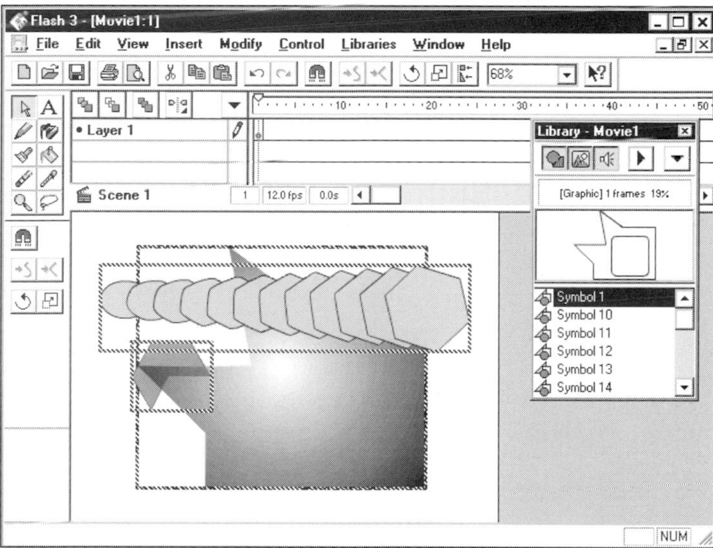

Figure 9.3 The same FreeHand drawing seen in Figure 9.2, after importing to Flash 3.

Export Layered FreeHand Drawings As Flash Animations

A FreeHand drawing that has been created on multiple layers can be exported directly to Flash as an animation. You can then import that animation into an existing Flash movie, either as a new scene or as a continuing part of an existing scene.

This technique can be a very handy way to animate existing drawings done in FreeHand or other illustration programs. You can copy the drawing (or only those shapes that you want to animate) to new layers, edit each layer to suit the animation, then choose File|Export from FreeHand's menu bar, select a couple of options, and then import the result into Flash 3.

In order to keep the basics of this procedure easy, you will create in the following exercise a very simple three-layer drawing, export it as a Flash movie, and then import it into a Flash movie. Here's the dance:

1. Open FreeHand 8. (If you don't own the program, you'll find a demo version on this book's companion CD-ROM.) If a new file isn't already open, choose File|New.
2. You need to size your FreeHand document to match the size of the movie to which you want to import the files (or in which you want the movie to appear on a Web page). From the menu bar, choose Modify|Document. The Document Inspector will appear. See Figure 9.4.

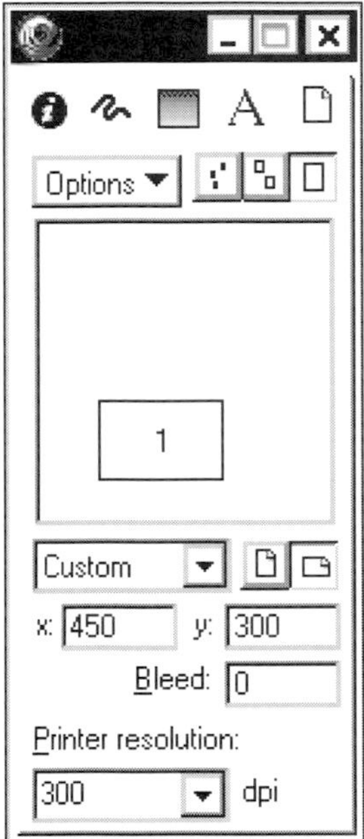

Figure 9.4 The FreeHand Document Inspector.

3. Click the Page button at the upper right of the Document Inspector. Then, choose Custom from the Page Size pull-down menu. Click the Landscape button. Enter 450 in the X field and 300 in the Y field. Press Return/Enter. Leave the rest of the entries at their defaults (shown in Figure 9.4).
4. Double-click on the Polygon tool in the Toolbar. A Polygon Tool dialog box will appear. See Figure 9.5.
5. In the Polygon Tool dialog box, enter 5 as the number of sides and click on the Star radio button. Click the Automatic radio button in the Star Points box and click on OK.
6. Drag a star that fills the center of the page.
7. From the menu bar, choose Window|Panels|Layers. The Layers panel will appear. The screen will now look something like Figure 9.6.

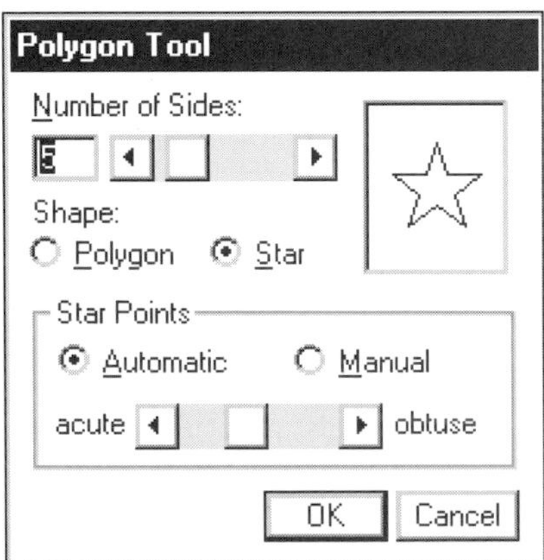

Figure 9.5 The Polygon Tool dialog box.

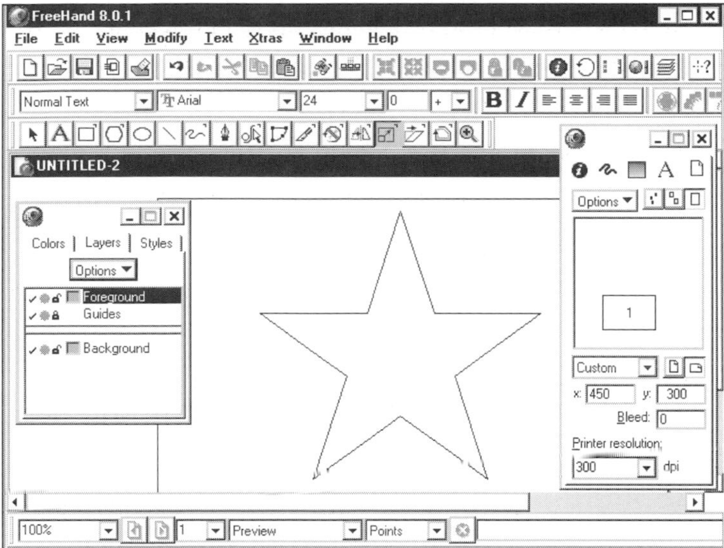

Figure 9.6 The FreeHand illustration environment. Note the five-point star in the center of the pasteboard and the Layers Panel at far left.

8. Now, you are going to copy the star twice and place each copy on a new layer. Choose the Arrow tool and click on the star to select it. Press Cmd/Ctrl+C to copy the selection to the clipboard. Now, press Cmd/Ctrl+V twice. Drag the second copy slightly away from the first copy, so that the copies are easier to select. You will now see three stars all of which are currently placed on the foreground layer.

9. From the Layers panel's Options pull-down menu, choose New. Now, do it again. You now have two new layers labeled Layer-1 and Layer-2.

10. Now, you want to move one copy of the star to Layer-1 and another to Layer-2. It doesn't matter which copy is moved to which layer at this point. In the Layers panel, select the foreground layer by clicking on its name. A layer whose name is thus highlighted is the active layer.

11. Select one of the stars. Control points will appear at each intersection of a line. To move the selected shape to another layer, select Layer-2 in the Layers panel. Drag the copy of the star so that it registers directly on top of the original star.

12. In the Layers panel, click on the Lock icon. This layer is now locked so that you won't accidentally move or edit the shape(s) on that layer. Now, repeat Steps 8 through 11 to move another star from the foreground layer to Layer-1.

13. Lock all the layers except the foreground layer. Choose the Arrow tool and drag each of the star's five inside points inward toward the center.
14. Lock all the layers except Layer-2. Drag each of the star's inward points outward. Your screen should now look similar to that in Figure 9.7.
15. Now you have a pulsating star on three layers. When you export this file as a Flash movie in SWF format, each layer will become a keyframe in an animation. From the menu bar, choose File|Export. The Export Document dialog box will appear. See Figure 9.8.
16. Click on the Setup button. Make sure that Animate Layers is checked and that Animate Pages is unchecked. Leave other settings at their defaults, as shown below in Figure 9.9 Click on OK. Then, click on Save in the Export Documents dialog box.

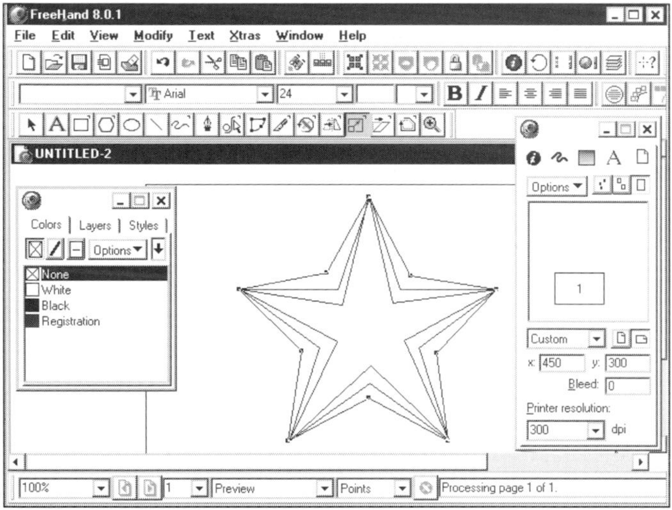

Figure 9.7 A differently shaped star on each of three layers in FreeHand.

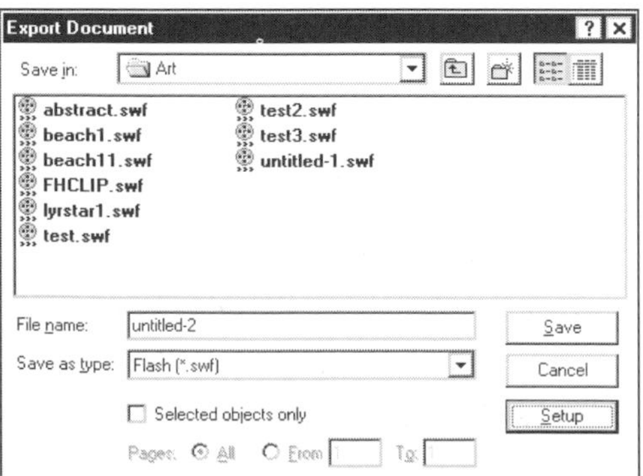

Figure 9.8 The Export Document dialog box.

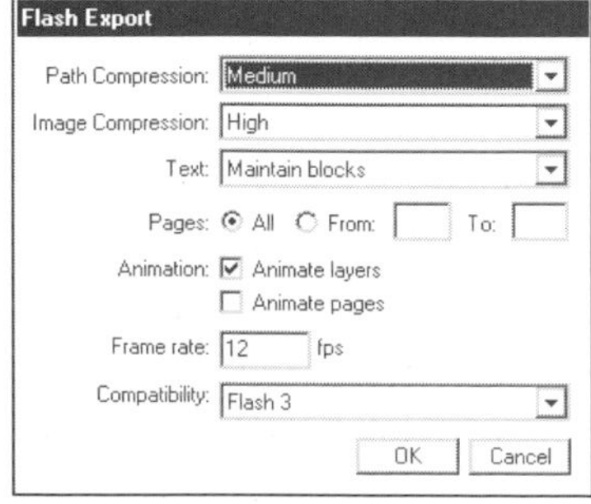

Figure 9.9 The Flash Export Settings dialog box.

17. Now, let's pretend we are adding the Flash SWF file we just exported from FreeHand to an existing Flash 3 movie. Open Flash and open a new file.

18. Select the layer and frame to which you want to start importing new frames (not actually necessary when working with a new file with only one layer).

19. From the menu bar, choose File|Import. The Import dialog box appears. (Again, it is a standard File Open dialog box.) From the Files Of Type pull-down menu, choose Shockwave Flash. Locate STAR.SWF and double-click on the file name. You will see the image of the first frame on the stage and will find new keyframes appearing after the originally selected frame. See Figure 9.10.

20. Play the movie by pressing Return/Enter.

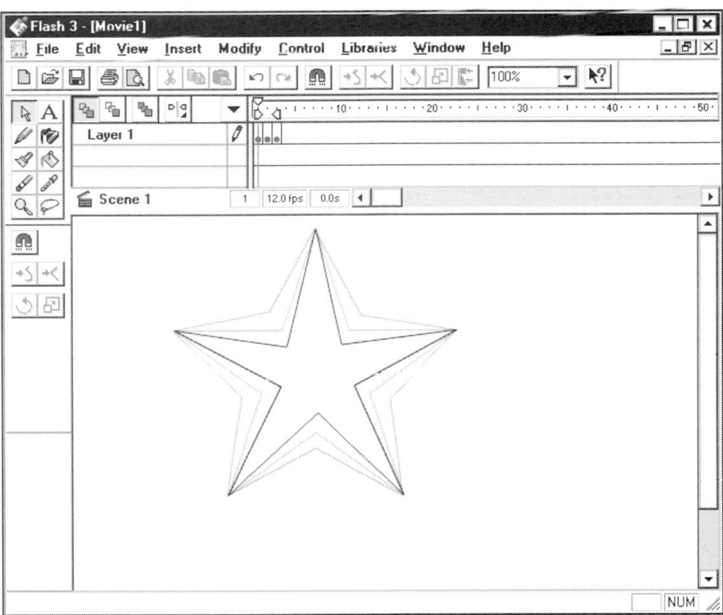

Figure 9.10 The imported FreeHand movie (with Onion Skinning turned on to show all three frames).

Using FreeHand's Precision And Advanced Drawing Capabilities

Illustration programs, such as Macromedia's FreeHand, are loaded with powerful vector-drawing capabilities. This often means being able to create better-designed, more sophisticated graphics than you might have taken the time to create using only the tools afforded by Flash 3.

Not least among these capabilities is the one typical of illustration programs in general: Bezier control points. Control points determine whether the lines in shapes are straight or curved, exactly how curved and where, and how these lines meet. Lines can meet at sharp angles (cornerpoint), in a smooth curve (symmetrical point), or in a curve that is more severe on one side of the point than on the other (asymmetrical point). The degree of control inherent in Bezier curves makes it possible for you to draw shapes with fewer control points and, therefore, smaller data files. Figure 9.11 shows a curve being reshaped by moving one control-point handle.

FreeHand also has many other time-saving drawing features. Some that you're most likely to use frequently are blends, text along a path, rounded rectangles, variable point polygons and stars, embossing, envelope distortion, and automatic animations. Each of these is described and demonstrated below.

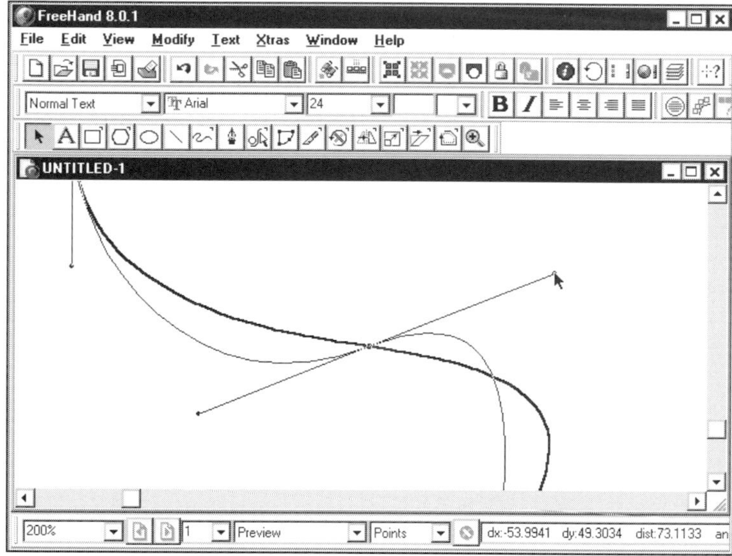

Figure 9.11 Reshaping a curve with a control-point handle.

Blends

Blends are similar to Flash's shape tweens. The difference is that all of the in-between shape and fill transitions are drawn on the same layer. Figure 9.12 shows two blends between a star and a pentagon. The blend at the top occurs between shapes placed at different locations and outlined with a stroke. The blend at the bottom uses many more steps and occurs between superimposed shapes.

One thing that you can create with blends in FreeHand that you can't do at all in Flash 3 is smooth gradients between shapes, as shown in the blend at the bottom of Figure 9.12.

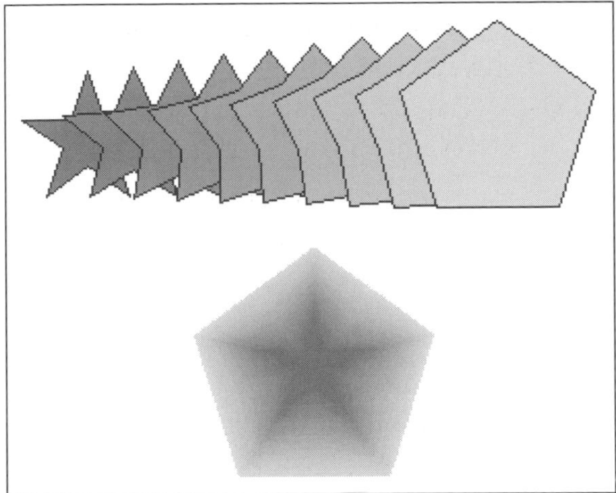

Figure 9.12 Two different blends between a star and a pentagon.

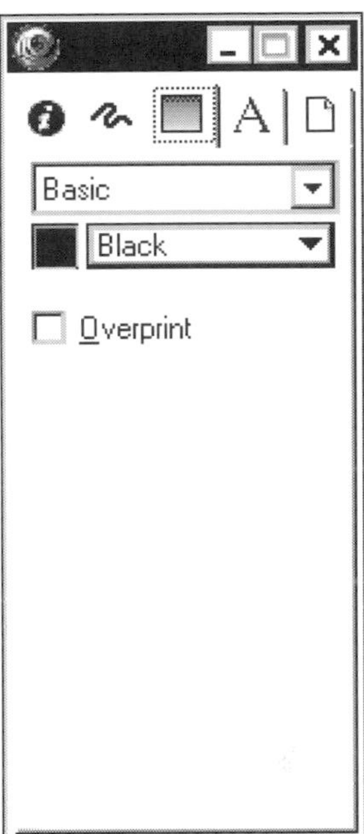

Figure 9.13 The Fill Inspector.

Creating a blend in FreeHand is amazingly quick and easy. FreeHand will blend any two shapes, regardless of whether they have the same number of control points or whether the control points were entered in the same sequence from top to bottom. However, the smoothest blends are between shapes with the same number of control points and whose direction matches. Here's the basic procedure:

1. Double-click on the Rectangle tool and, when the Rectangle Tool dialog box appears, drag the slider all the way to the left (no corner radius).
2. On the pasteboard, drag a rectangle.
3. Choose the Pen tool and draw a four-point oval in the center of the rectangle. Be sure to place the first point at upper left and to move in a clockwise direction until the oval is completed. If the oval's a little eccentric, you can drag the control points and handles to make it more regular.
4. Select the rectangle. From the menu bar, choose Window|Inspectors|Fill. The Fill Inspector will appear. (See Figure 9.13.) From the Fill Type pull-down menu, choose Basic. The rectangle will fill with black.
5. To change the color of the fill, double-click on the color swatch to the left of the Colors pull-down menu. The Mixer panel will appear. (See Figure 9.14.) Click the RGB button, and drag the three sliders to mix a blue color. Click the Tints tab and choose a light shade of the blue you mixed. Click the Add To Colors button (just above and to the right of the Colors pull-down menu).

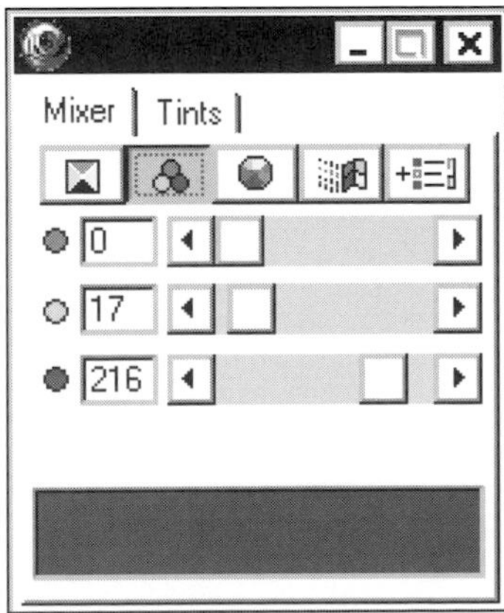

Figure 9.14 The Mixer panel.

Exporting Blends To Flash

You can export a blend to Flash in two ways: as an AI file (Illustrator 7 or 88) or as a bitmapped file. If you have few blend steps or if you want to place each of the blended shapes into a separate frame, the AI vector format will be most appropriate. Shade blends, such as the one shown in Figure 9.15, generally contain 25 or more shapes and would be more efficient if first converted to a bitmap by exporting the blend as a PNG file.

6. The Colors List panel will appear. Select the rectangle and then select light-blue color in the color list. The fill color will change. Repeat these last three steps to fill the oval but this time with a bright red.
7. Select both the rectangle and the oval shapes. (Their control points will appear to let you know that they are selected.)
8. At the top of the Fill Inspector you will see an icon of an S-shaped stroke, the Stroke icon. Click on it, and the Stroke Inspector will appear. Choose None from the Stroke Type pull-down menu.
9. From the menu bar, choose Xtras|Create|Blend. You will see a smooth color shift between the shape of the oval and the shape of the rectangle. You can see the result in Figure 9.15.

Figure 9.15 The finished blend from oval to rectangle.

Text Along A Path

FreeHand allows you to place text along the curve of any vector path. Text arranged in this manner can be a very strong design element. The only way you could do this within Flash 3 would be to convert each letter to an outline, then transform and position each letter individually. Figure 9.16 shows the effect of placing text around an oval.

Figure 9.16 Text placed along the path of an oval.

Here's the routine:

1. In FreeHand, open a new document (File|New). Choose the Text tool from the toolbar.
2. Choose a font style to your liking from the Font Name pull-down menu, and select 48 point as your font size on the Font Size pull-down menu.
3. Click on the pasteboard location where you'd like your text to begin. (This isn't critical, since you're probably going to move it later, anyway.) Enter your text.
4. From the menu bar, choose Window|Inspectors|Text. Your screen should look similar to Figure 9.17. Make any needed adjustments in leading, kerning, and justification.
5. Just to show you how powerful FreeHand can be when dealing with text, choose Zoom from the Text Effect pull-down menu in the Text Inspector window.
6. From the toolbox, choose the FreeHand tool. Draw a loose S-curve on the pasteboard. Then, use the Arrow tool to select the curve and to drag the control points and handles into the S-curve you'd really like to see. The shapes on the pasteboard should look something like those in Figure 9.18.
7. From the menu bar, choose Text|Attach to Path. The selected text will immediately flow along the path, starting at the first control

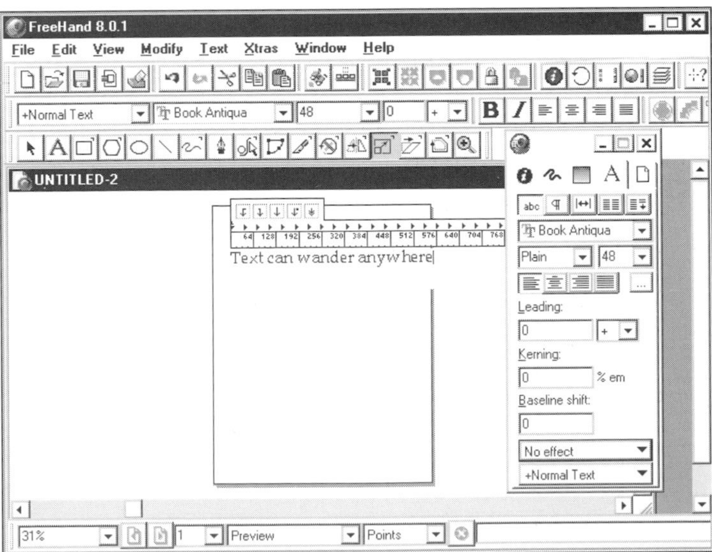

Figure 9.17 Text that has been entered. The Text Inspector window is shown at right.

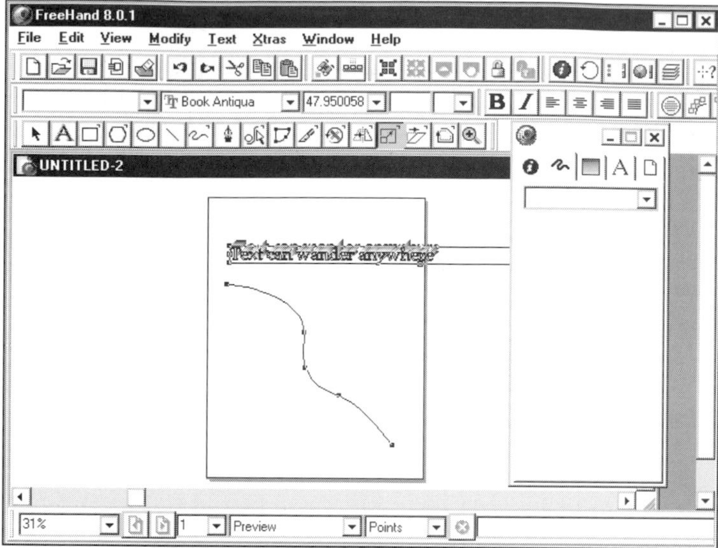

Figure 9.18 The zoomed text and the finished S-curve, both selected.

point and continuing for as long as the text and its assigned spacing will allow. You'll notice in Figure 9.19 that the text doesn't extend the full length of the path.

8. To stretch the text to the end of the path, change the kerning (spacing between letters). Choose the Text tool and drag it across the whole text path, so that all the letters are highlighted. In the Text Inspector window, enter 12 in the Range Kerning field and then press Return/Enter. You can see the result in Figure 9.20.

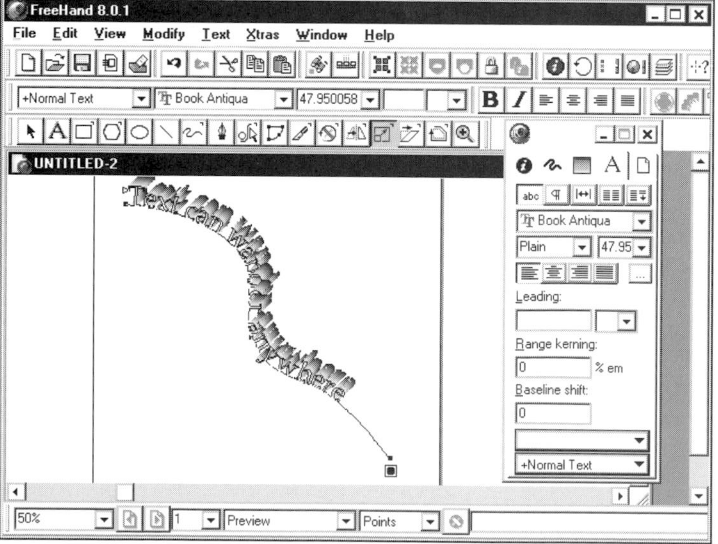

Figure 9.19 The text when attached to the path. Text and path are selected here, so you can see the path.

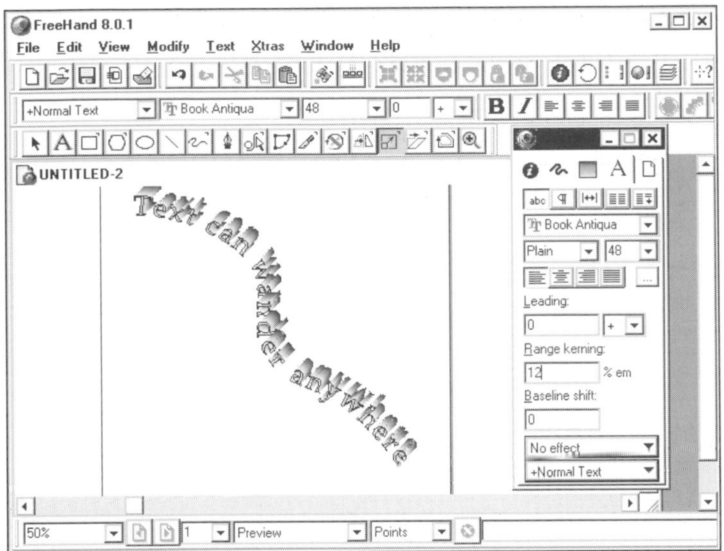

Figure 9.20 The text stretched along the path.

MAKING PRECISION-SIZED RECTANGLES

If you need to make the rectangle a specific size, draw the rectangle. Then, from the menu bar, choose Window|Inspectors|Object. The Object Inspector window will appear, and here you can enter precise horizontal, vertical, and corner-radius measurements. Press Return/Enter to apply any changes.

Rounded Rectangles

Rounded-corner rectangles are one of the most useful geometric shapes for Web design because the shape is frequently used for banners and buttons. You can make rounded rectangles fairly easily in Flash by drawing a rectangle and a circle, copying the circle four times, turning on Snap, and placing each circle in a different corner of the rectangle. Then, select all the unneeded lines and press Delete/Backspace to eliminate them.

If you own the Design In Motion suite, you'll find it's much faster and more flexible to create your rounded rectangles in FreeHand. Figure 9.21 depicts some rounded rectangles made in FreeHand 8.0.1.

Making a rounded rectangle is a matter for true non-artists. Follow these steps:

1. Double-click on the Rectangle tool in the toolbox. The Rectangle Tool dialog box will appear. See Figure 9.22.
2. Drag the Corner Radius slider to indicate the number of points for the radius of the corner curve. (You can actually use this dialog box to make an oval. Feel free to experiment.) Click on OK.
3. Drag to make the rectangle the desired size.

Variable Point Polygons And Stars

Making truly geometric shapes such as regular-sided polygons and stars is a painstaking process in Flash—but a no-brainer in FreeHand.

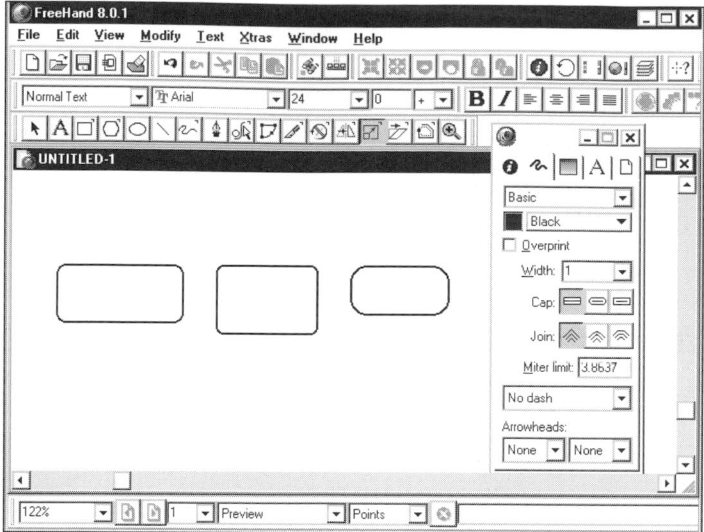

Figure 9.21 Rounded rectangles made in FreeHand

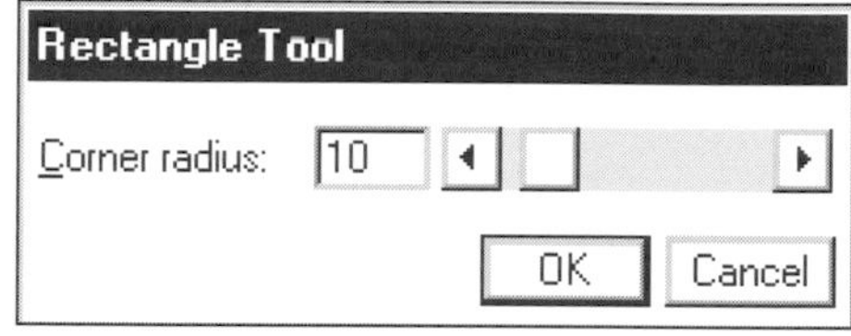

Figure 9.22 The Rectangle Tool dialog box

Figure 9.23 shows a number of shapes that can be made with absolute accuracy in FreeHand, using only two or three steps.

To make a star, follow these steps:

1. Double-click on the Polygon tool. The Polygon Tool dialog box will appear. Select the Star radio button (unless it's already selected). The dialog box should now have all the settings shown in Figure 9.24.
2. Enter 5 in the Number Of Sides field, or drag the slider until 5 is the value shown.
3. Just so you can see the power of this dialog box, select the Manual radio button and drag the Star Points slider from left to right. Notice

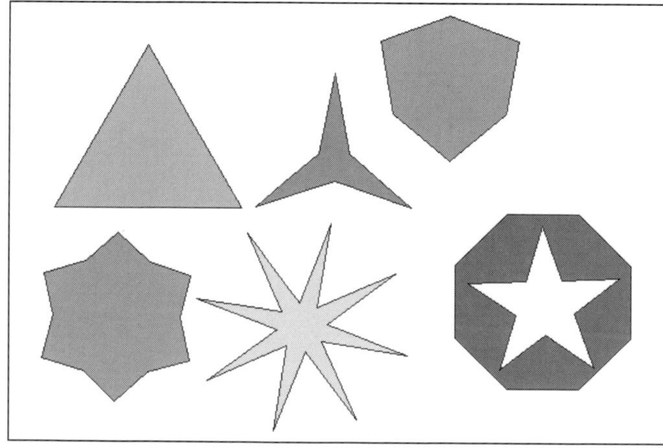

Figure 9.23 Just a few of the stars and polygons you can make automatically in FreeHand.

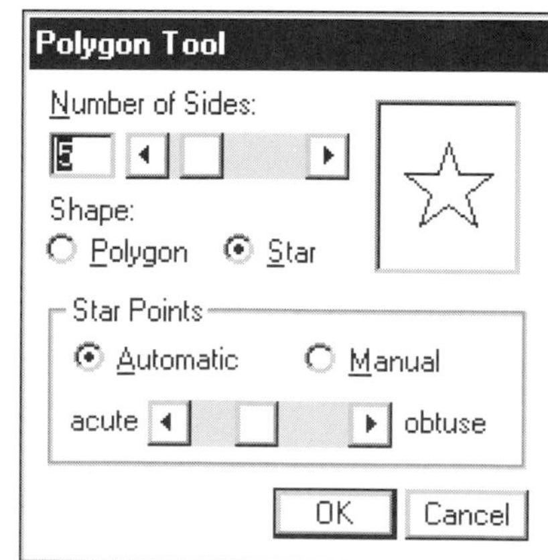

Figure 9.24 The Polygon Tool dialog box with the Star radio button selected.

the changes in the star shape in the preview box (upper-right corner of the dialog box).

4. To make this the standard, five-point star, select the Automatic radio button and then click on OK. Press Shift to constrain the rotation of the star to 15-degree angles and drag diagonally until the star is the size you want it to be. The star will look like Figure 9.25.

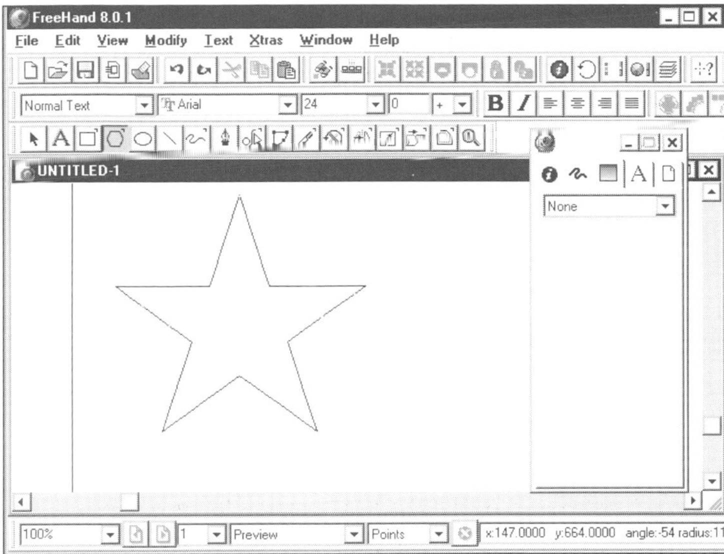

Figure 9.25 The automatically drawn five-point star.

Embossing

Embossing can give your buttons and geometric shapes a dimensionality that can't be simulated in Flash without endless tedium. FreeHand adds this dimensionality to shapes in several different ways. You can also control the depth of the 3D effect and whether it is rendered in colors or in shades of gray. Examples of an embossed star are shown in Figure 9.26.

To emboss the star, follow these steps:

1. Draw a star or use the one you made in the previous exercise. Fill it with a solid color.

2. Select the star by clicking on it with the Arrow tool. All the points should be black.

3. From the menu bar, choose Xtras|Create|Emboss. The Emboss dialog box will appear. See Figure 9.27.

Figure 9.30 The drawings of the two stars, each filled with a different color.

Here are the exact steps for turning a blend into a Flash movie:

1. Draw two shapes (in this case, stars) and fill them with different colors. See Figure 9.30.
2. Superimpose one shape over the other. This is an optional step. It is done here so that the shape will seem to change shape and color over time without moving in space. The effect will be a flashing star.
3. From the menu bar, choose Edit|Select All, then Xtras|Create|Blend. A blend will occur, although you won't be able to see it because the larger star is superimposed over the smaller one.
4. From the menu bar, choose Xtras|Animate|Release to Layers. Choose Window|Panels|Layers. The Layers panel will open. (See Figure 9.31.) You will notice that there are now many layers in your document (one for each step in the blend).
5. From the menu bar, choose File|Export. The Export dialog box will appear. From the Save As Type pull-down menu, choose Flash (SWF). Click the Setup button and make sure that Animate Pages is unchecked. Leave all other settings at their defaults. Click on OK to close the Flash Export dialog box, then choose Save to close the Export Document dialog box.
6. Open Flash and choose File|Import. From the Files Of Type pull-down menu, choose Flash and click on OK. Press Return to play the file.

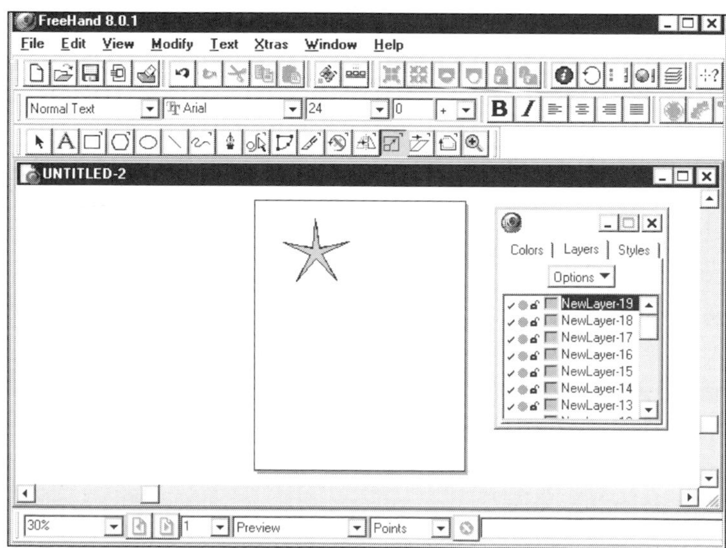

Figure 9.31 The Layers panel after running the Animate Xtra on a blend.

Using Insta.HTML

Insta.HTML is another application that is included with the Design In Motion suite. It is capable of taking layouts and drawings made in FreeHand and automatically turning them into HTML documents.

Of course, Flash creates vector animations and not HTML. So, what's the advantage of Insta.HTML to Flash animators? If you're creating from scratch, you'll work more quickly and efficiently by using the combination of Dreamweaver to create your HTML pages and Flash 3 to do your vector graphics, graphical layout pages with animated buttons, and maps and technical drawings.

Insta.HTML isn't very well documented and has a ways to go before it will be sophisticated enough to produce an accurate representation of FreeHand pages that contain such ordinarily commonplace items as overlapping graphics or fonts that are not commonly used on the Web.

On the other hand, if you're used to working in an illustration program, you may find it handy to lay out your Web page design in FreeHand and automatically convert it to HTML using Insta.HTML. Then, you could open the resulting code in Dreamweaver (or any other capable WYSIWYG (What You See Is What You Get) HTML editor for fine-tuning.

Converting A FreeHand Page To HTML

This chapter is no more a manual for Insta.HTML than it is for the other programs mentioned in this chapter. The example below is meant only to give you a quick feel for the process. It does not go into detail about what illustration components will and won't translate successfully. For the moment, suffice it to say that it's best to use the fonts built into most operating systems (such as Times and Helvetica), to avoid overlapping graphics, and to convert your illustrative graphics to a bitmapped format (such as GIF). You can always substitute more sophisticated graphics and Flash graphics and animations when you are working in your HTML editor.

Thus forewarned, here are the basic steps for using Insta.HTML. In the following exercise, you will start by creating a Web document that has the basic elements you would want to have on most Web pages: a graphic headline, a line drawing, a photograph, some body text, and some interactive buttons. Follow these steps:

1. Open FreeHand 8 and choose File|New from the menu bar.
2. Select an exotic font (one unlikely to be found on most browsers) and a large point size. Enter a big headline.
3. So that the headline font won't be reinterpreted by a browser, change the headline to a graphic. To do this, select the headline. From the menu bar, choose Text|Convert To Paths.
4. Since the text is a graphic, you can change its color and emboss it. Don't use a gradient for the fill unless you plan to convert your graphics as Flash graphics. If they are converted as GIFs, they are more likely to show banding.
5. Import a decorative FreeHand or Illustrator vector graphic. (In the example, it's the flower.) To do this, first choose File|Import from the menu bar. The Import dialog box will appear. Locate the file you want to import and double-click on its name in the directory. The image will appear on the pasteboard. Scale it to the desired size and drag it into position.
6. Now, you want to enter a paragraph of text that won't require reinterpretation by most browsers. Choose Arial, Helvetica, or Times in 10 or 12 points. Choose the Text tool and drag a rectangle the size of the space you want your text to occupy on the page. Type the text. Finally, choose the Pointer tool and click on a blank area on the pasteboard to unselect the text.

7. Import a photograph with an Alpha channel mask. (For practice purposes, a PNG-format photo called “Guitar” can be found in the Art folder of this book’s CD-ROM.) The procedure is the same as that outlined in the previous step.
8. Finally, we want to create a pair of buttons. Draw a small rectangle. (Choose the Rectangle tool and drag.) Select it and press Cmd/Ctrl+C, then Cmd/Ctrl+V. An identically sized rectangle will appear. Drag the rectangles so that they are close together. From the menu bar, choose Modify|Align. The Align dialog box will appear. Choose None for one of the directions and either Top or Side for the other. Fill one rectangle with red and the other with green.
9. Now, you need to use Insta.HTML to assign URLs to the two buttons. Normally, you’d type in real URLs. (See Chapter 10.) Since you’re just practicing, you’ll just pick any two that are already in the list. Select one of the “buttons.” From the menu bar, choose Window|URL Editor. The URL Editor window will appear. See Figure 9.32.

Figure 9.32 The URL Editor.

10. The currently selected URL will be None. From the list of URLs in the editor, select Page 1. Now, select the other “button” and select **http://www.macromedia.com** from the list. Click on the pasteboard to deselect everything and close the URL Editor.
11. Now, here comes the good part: instant (almost) HTML. From the menu bar, choose Xtras|HTML|Insta.html. The Insta.html dialog box will appear. See Figure 9.33.

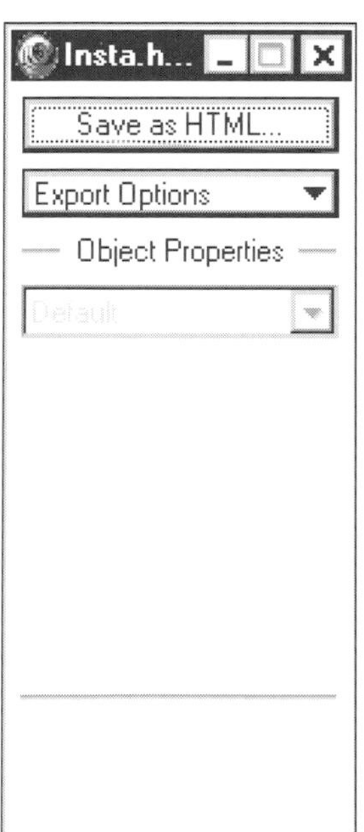

Figure 9.33 The Insta.HTML dialog box.

12. In the Insta.HTML dialog box, click on the Save As HTML button. The Save As HTML dialog box will appear. See Figure 9.34.
13. In the Save As HTML dialog box, you can choose which pages of your FreeHand 8 document to save to HTML, whether to convert the file to Dynamic HTML (DHTML) or HTML 3.2, and whether to convert images to GIFs or Flash. Because you have only one page, leave the All radio button selected.
14. If you want to save your file in a format that can be read by virtually all contemporary browsers, choose the HTML 3.2 and GIF radio buttons. The result is shown in Figure 9.35.
15. If you want to save your layout in a format that supports image overlays, precision placement, and Flash graphics, choose the DHTML and Flash radio buttons. Virtually all browsers that

Save As HTML
Pages: All
From: To:
Save
Cancel
HTML Output: DHTML HTML 3.2
Image Default: GIF Flash
Process Images
View Result in Browser
Insta.html

Figure 9.34 The Save As HTML dialog box.

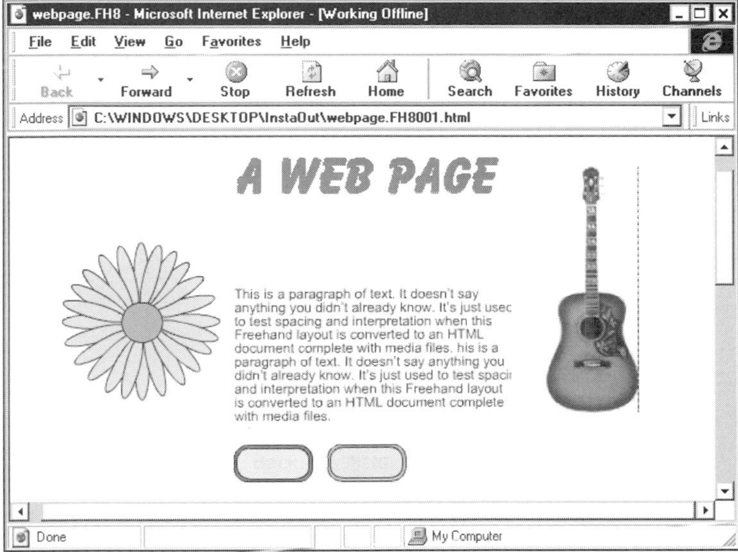

Figure 9.35 The FreeHand test page interpreted as HTML 3.2 with GIF graphics.

support DHTML also support Flash. Thus, you will also be able to place Flash animations on those pages. The results of this second choice are shown below in Figure 9.36.

Using Fireworks With Flash

For all that I've boasted about the speed, efficiency, and cleanliness of the vector-based graphics that Flash produces, there are occasions when bitmapped graphics simply work better:

- Photographs that need a full range of tonal values in order to be effective. (Think of photographer's or artist's portfolios.)
- Many Web designers like to create a standard HTML site that parallels the Flash site. When the first page opens, the viewer is given a choice of which version to tour. Or, at least, there's an HTML home (index) page that gives the viewer the opportunity to download and install Flash before proceeding.

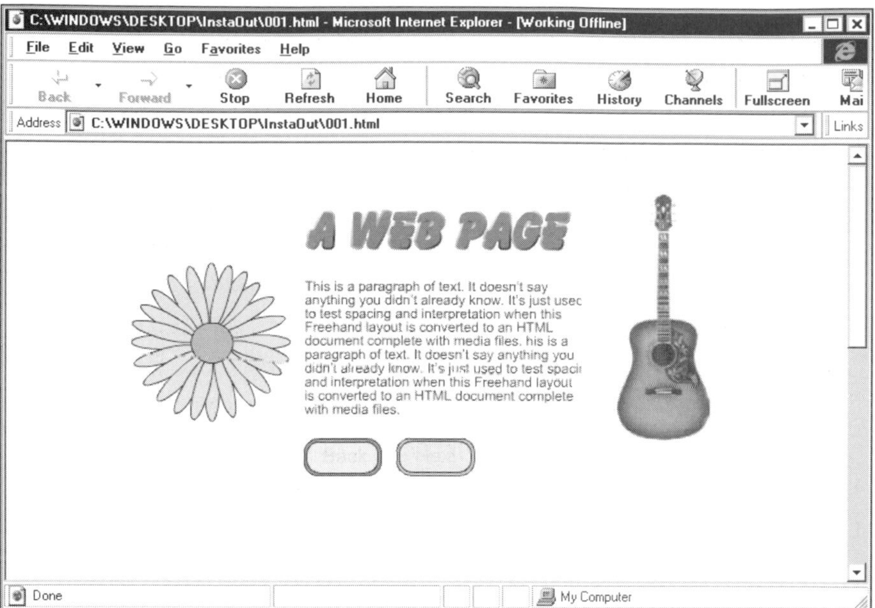

Figure 9.36 The FreeHand test page interpreted as HTML 3.2 with GIF graphics.

- Photos that need to be "floated" may need the partial transparency that Alpha channels provide. Some examples of this might be wispy hair in a portrait, soft edges on drop-shadowed text, or a fishbowl. Fireworks' native cross-platform PNG format is ideal for that.
- Graphics with gradient (smoothly blended transitions between colors) fills often have smaller file sizes as bitmaps than when created in an illustration program.

You probably already own image-processing software that is capable of producing Web-standard GIF, JPEG, and PNG graphics. Furthermore, the software you already own is probably capable of sophisticated darkroom and retouching operations, also.

So why use Fireworks?

- Fireworks is designed specifically for optimizing bitmapped Web graphics, and you can export to any of the Web-standard file formats. For every Web export format, you have extensive controls for transparency, Alpha channels, compression levels, palettes, dithering algorithms, and the number of colors. So you can "try before you buy," large preview windows let you compare the appearance of files exported to different formats or at different levels of compression—all before you actually export them. (You can have as few as one preview window or as many as four.) At the bottom of the preview window is a report on the size of the file and how long it will take to download over a typical modem. (You can even set the baud rate.) This means that you don't have to go through an endless cycle of testing and trying in order to find the most effective formula for exporting a given image.

- Fireworks makes it very easy to do a brilliant job of creating vector-based shapes and then automatically converting them to bitmapped graphics. Instead of having to employ the usual route of creating logos, drawings, and buttons in a vector program (such as Flash or FreeHand)—and then exporting them as bitmaps—Fireworks gives you the vector-drawing tools that let you control the precision of your shapes. Fireworks then automatically converts them to bitmapped graphics formats. In other words, you don't have to waste time switching from tool to tool. As soon as you create the shapes, you see the bitmap representation of the stroke, fill, and effect. You see exactly what you're getting. Even more important, you can change any of these characteristics at any time before you export the finished graphic. Figure 9.37 shows a pair of shapes that have been created with the Pen and Brush tools, filled or textured with a bitmapped pattern, and given bevel effects.
- Fireworks comes with a variety of fill textures, patterns, and gradients. Because you can change any of the characteristics of any shapes created in Fireworks at any time after their creation, you can create basic objects to which you can quickly give many looks. I've done just that with copies of the same rectangle in Figure 9.38.

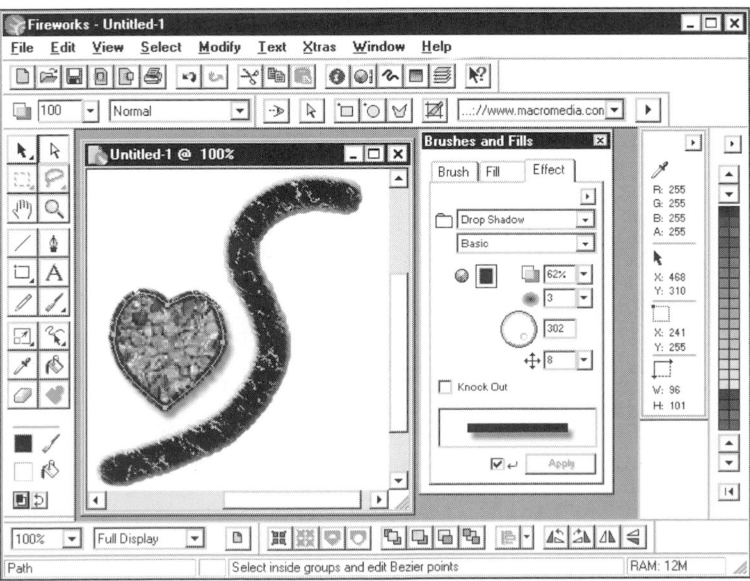

Figure 9.37 A pair of shapes created with the Pen and Brush tools. Any time you select a shape, the path and control points appear so you can change the shape.

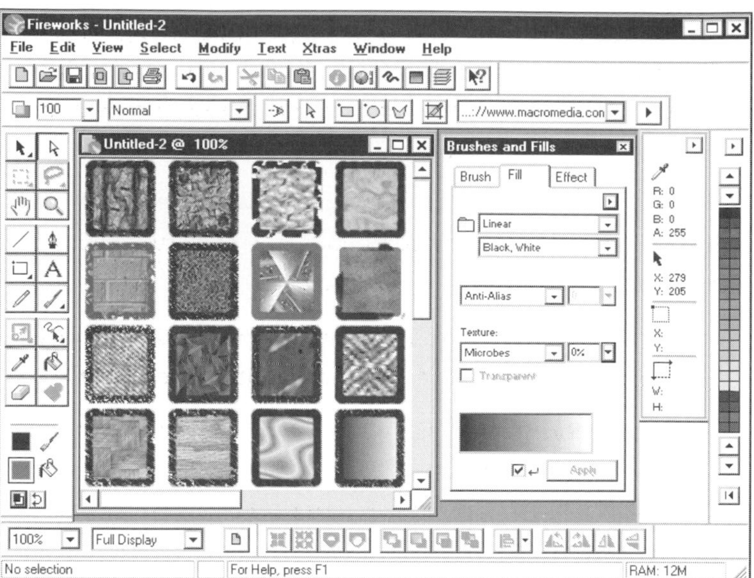

Figure 9.38 Multiple copies of the same rectangle using some of the stroke textures and fill patterns.

- Fireworks automatically creates Web effects that have traditionally required a much higher level of programming expertise or the use of separate tools. These effects include sliced graphics, JavaScript rollover buttons, and image maps.

Using Dreamweaver With Flash

Dreamweaver is a visual Web design tool that automatically creates the needed HTML tags to incorporate Flash 3 graphics and movies. It automatically does this in a form that is compatible with both major browsers. It also makes it just as easy to further enrich the site's design with cross-platform Dynamic HTML (DHTML) and cascading style sheets.

Dreamweaver is Macromedia's WYSIWYG HTML authoring tool. With it, you can visually and interactively create Web pages and sites with highly professional design and content without having to understand the complexities (or even anything at all) of the HTML language and its ever-changing permutations. However, unlike other products that allow you to do this, Dreamweaver creates professionally clean and accurate HTML code that any pro would find easy to tweak. It even comes with—and lets you automatically switch to—the most popular HTML code editor for the platform you're working with. (That would be BBEdit on the Macintosh or HomeSite in Windows.) At any time while composing your Web pages, you can switch to the HTML editor in a single command.

Placing a Flash (SWF) movie onto a Web page is easy enough if you just follow Janine's instructions in Chapter 10. It's even easier using Dreamweaver. The process is the same whether the Flash content is only a graphic or animation on a page full of other Web media, or whether you've designed your entire site as a Flash movie:

1. Open Dreamweaver. Next, open (or create) the document into which you want to place your Flash movie.
2. (Optional) If you're familiar with the use of tables as a means of forcing placement on a page, you may want to insert a table.
3. Click to place the cursor at the upper-left corner of the spot where you want the Flash movie to appear. From the menu bar, choose Insert|Flash Movie. The Insert Flash Movie dialog box appears. See Figure 9.39.
4. Enter the directory path and file name of the Flash movie you want to insert. If you'd rather search your directories and choose the file visually, click on the Browse button and a standard File Open dialog box will appear. Find the file and double-click on its name.
5. A Flash movie icon will appear on the page. Drag the scaling handles to give the Flash movie the space you want it to occupy on the page. (Remember? Flash movies are scalable; they look equally good at any size.)
6. At the same time that the Flash movie icon appears on the page, the Flash Properties Inspector, a floating window, will appear. You can see both the Flash movie icon and the Flash Movie Properties Inspector in Figure 9.40.
7. Enter all the properties you want to assign to your Flash movie. Properties are the parameters that make the movie behave in respect to how you intended the movie to relate to the other contents on this page.

That's it. A full explanation of all the properties and what they mean follows. These are the same properties that Janine discusses in Chapter

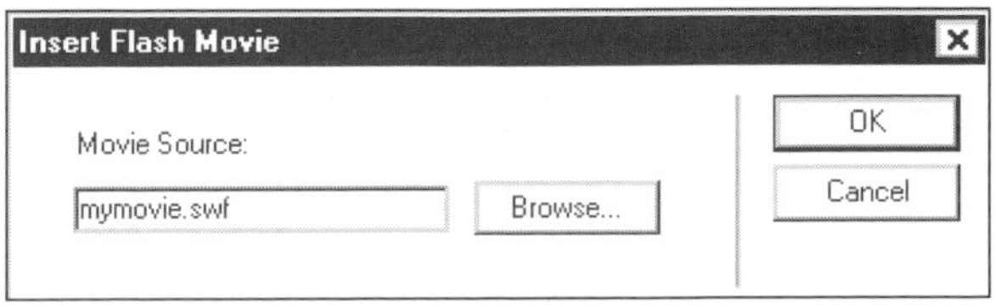

Insert Flash Movie

Movie Source:

mymovie.swf

Browse...

OK

Cancel

Figure 9.39 The Insert Flash Movie dialog box.

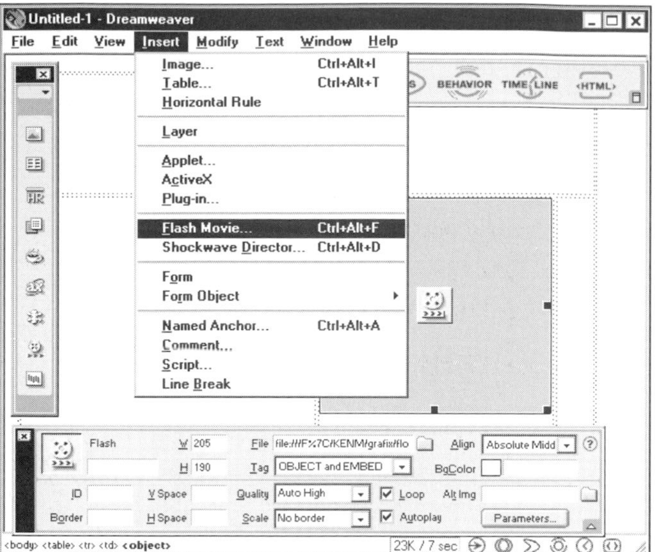

Figure 9.40 Inserting a Flash movie into a Dreamweaver page.

10, but they're explained there more in the context of how they relate to HTML code.

Dreamweaver's Flash Movie Properties

This section will briefly explain the meaning of each of the fields and buttons in the Property Inspector:

- *Name*—What you enter (if anything) is entirely up to you, as long as it fits the field. The only purpose of entering a name is to identify this movie to any script you might want to attach to this page.
- *W (Width)*—If you want to force a specific width for the movie, enter it here. The default unit is pixels, but by adding any of the following abbreviations immediately after the number, you can specify picas (pc), points (pt), inches (in), millimeters (mm), cm (centimeters), or % (percentage of the original file's value).
- *H (Height)*—The preceding explanation of width applies here, only now it's related to the forced height of the movie.
- *File*—The path and name of the movie file will be automatically entered here. Any time you want to change the movie that's playing in this spot, just enter a new path and file name.
- *Tag*—A pull-down menu that gives you three choices of HTML tags to identify the Flash file to a browser: both **<OBJECT>** and **<EMBED>**, **<EMBED>**, or **<OBJECT>**. (Both is almost always the best answer.)

- *Align*—Defines how the movie will be aligned with other elements on the page.
- *BgColor (Background Color)*—The color of any transparent area assigned to the size of the Flash movie. Suppose you've assigned a width and height that is disproportionate to the size of the actual movie. You'd see a border on either side that was the background color.
- *ID*—The entry field for the ActiveX identifier.
- *Border*—Forces an open area around the file. The color of the border will be the page color, not the background color.
- *V Space*—The number of pixels above and below the height measurement.
- *H Space*—The number of pixels on either side of the width measurement.
- *Quality*—The manner in which antialiasing is applied to the movie when playing. Choose from four possible settings:
    - *Low*—No antialiasing. Fastest playback.
    - *High*—Forced antialiasing. Quality always takes precedence over speed.
    - *Autohigh*—Starts with antialiasing on, but turns it off whenever the frame rate drops below the rate you specified when building the movie.
    - *Autolow*—Turns antialiasing on only when the browser figures that download times and processor power will permit quality without forcing a slowdown in playback.
- *Scale*—You can choose to tell the browser to display the Flash movie at a specific pixel size or percentage of the screen. If you use the percentage parameter, the Flash movie will always use the same proportionate space in the window, regardless of what size you make the window. If you use the size parameter, the movie will stay the same size no matter what size the viewer makes the playback window. If you use percentage, you can apply any of the following three controls in order to avoid such problems as cropping or distorting:
    - *Showall*—The movie's proportions will be maintained, but a border may appear.
    - *Noborder*—Same as above, but no border will appear.
    - *Exactfit*—Proportions may be distorted to fit the specified size parameter.
- *Loop*—Checking this box forces the repeat playing of the movie. You cannot specify the number of loops.
- *Autoplay*—Checking this box forces the movie to play as soon as the page is loaded. Otherwise, the movie won't play until whatever conditions you've set in making the movie (such as the call from an action) have been met.
- *Alt Image*—The path and file for the location of a GIF or JPEG image that will be automatically substituted at this location if the visiting browser doesn't have Flash.

3D Tools And Flash

A fair amount of interest exists for using 3D animations within Flash. Virtually any 3D modeling program that does animation is capable of exporting the animation as a series of sequential stills. So you can use the animation power of the 3D program to create the animation, export it as sequential GIFs or JPEGs, import the series as frames in a Flash movie, and then use the Trace Bitmap command to convert each of the frames into a drawing. Once you've done that, be sure to delete the imported bitmaps in order to optimize your file sizes and download times.

When you create your animations in the 3D program, try to keep the shapes, colors, and shading

IMPORTING 3D ANIMATIONS AS SYMBOLS

If you want to import a small 3D animation that will be used in more than one place in the movie, import it as a symbol. To do that, make sure everything is unselected. (Press Cmd/Ctrl+D.) Then, choose Insert|Create Symbol from the menu bar. A new symbol movie will open and you can then import your 3D animation.

as simple and clean as possible. If you do, they will autotrace into much cleaner vector files that you're much less likely to have to edit by hand. Of course, there's nothing (except for the fact that time is money) to stop you from enhancing the autotraced drawings by changing the line weights, fills, gradients, and transparency.

Moving On

The next chapter is Janine Warner's elegant explanation of how to incorporate Flash into HTML documents. She even gets into a discussion of state-of-the-art HTML techniques, such as cascading style sheets and DHTML. On top of all that, you'll get a bit more information (and from a different point of view) on using Dreamweaver to incorporate Flash movies and stills into HTML documents.

10 Placing Flash On An HTML Page

Janine Warner

6. Click OK. A small icon appears on the Web page, representing the Flash movie.
7. If the Property Inspector is not already open, choose Window|Properties.
8. Click to select the Flash file. The Property Inspector displays the <**EMBED**> and <**OBJECT**> options shown in Figure 10.7.
9. Enter the height and width of the Flash file. Height and width are the only required attributes for most multimedia file types. (Consult the height and width options in the "Attributes And Parameters" section later in this chapter to better understand these options.)
10. To ensure the best results in both Internet Explorer and Netscape, choose Object and Embed from the Tag pulldown menu. This causes Dreamweaver to use both <**OBJECT**> and <**EMBED**> tags when inserting the Flash files.
11. Click to place a checkmark next to Loop if you want the movie to repeat indefinitely.

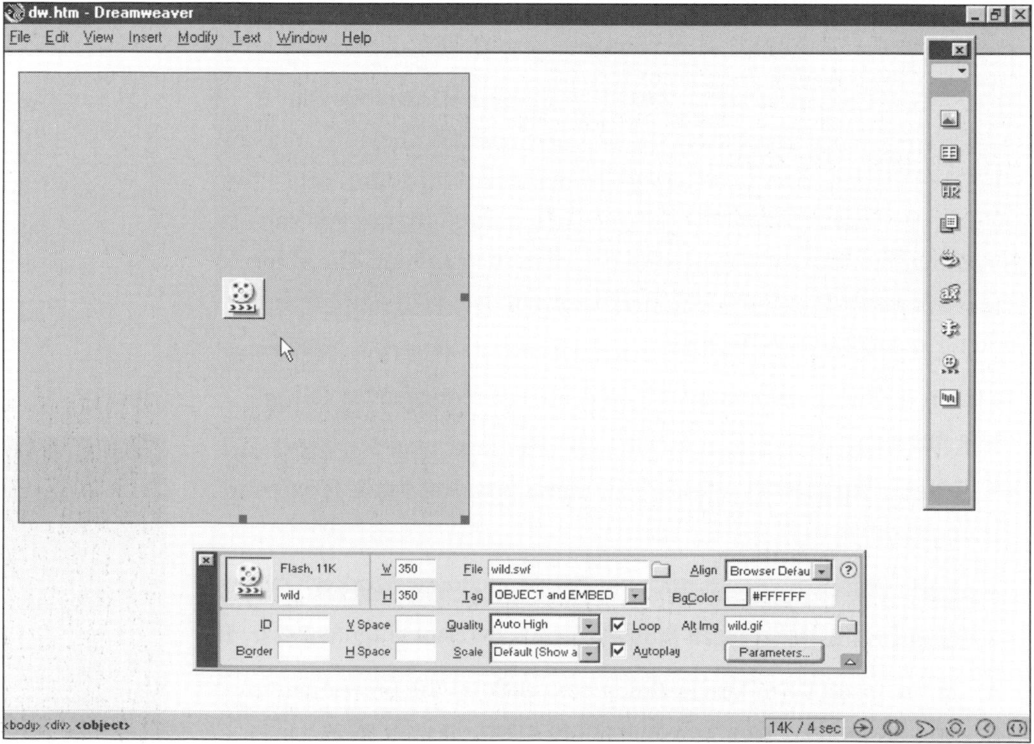

Figure 10.7 The Property Inspector in Dreamweaver lets you specify the attributes and parameters for the **<EMBED>** and **<OBJECT>** tags.

12. Click to place a checkmark in the Autoplay box if you want the animation to automatically start when the page is loaded.
13. Save the page and choose File|Preview in Browser to test your work.

Note: Consult Dreamweaver's Help files for more information about the options available when using Dreamweaver to place a Flash file in an HTML document.

Using Dreamweaver's Check Plug-In Option

Dreamweaver includes a feature that enables you to direct visitors to your site's best page on the basis of the viewers' software. For the most part, this option is necessary only if you are concerned about visitors using browsers that are so old or limited that they don't support plug-ins at all. You may also choose this feature if you don't want your users to have to download the plug-in. When you add this feature, called a *behavior*, to your pages, you insert a JavaScript at the top of your HTML page. When the page is being loaded by your viewer's browser, the script checks for the availability of the Flash plug-in before loading the page. If the plug-in is not available, the script directs the browser to an alternate page, based on your specifications. Usually, you will provide an alternative design that uses a static image or animated GIF. This sounds a little complex, but as you'll see in the following exercise, Dreamweaver makes it very easy to set this up. You'll find the Check Browser option in the Behavior Inspector available under the Window menu. The Behavior Inspector features a variety of behaviors, but we'll limit ourselves to the Check Browser feature for now. Refer to Dreamweaver's Help files to learn more about applying other behaviors.

To use Dreamweaver to apply the Check Plug-in option to a page, follow these steps:

1. Open the HTML file you want to work with.
2. Choose Window|Behaviors to open the Behavior Inspector.
3. In the pulldown menu at the top of the inspector, choose 3.0 and 4.0 Browsers.
4. Click the + sign at the top of the Events pane (the one on the left) and select OnLoad.
5. Click the plus sign (+) at the top of the Actions pane (the one on the right) and choose Check Plug-in as shown in Figure 10.8.
6. In the Check Plug-in dialog box, select the radio button next to Enter and type in "Shockwave Flash 3.0", as shown in Figure 10.9.
7. Use the Browse button next to the URL text field and find the page that contains the Flash file. Double-click to select the page.

Note: Dreamweaver cannot automatically create a static image or animated GIF from a Flash movie the way Aftershock can. If you choose to provide this type of option, you should use Aftershock to create the HTML pages and then use Dreamweaver to add the JavaScript to check for the plug-in and to direct the user to the correct page.

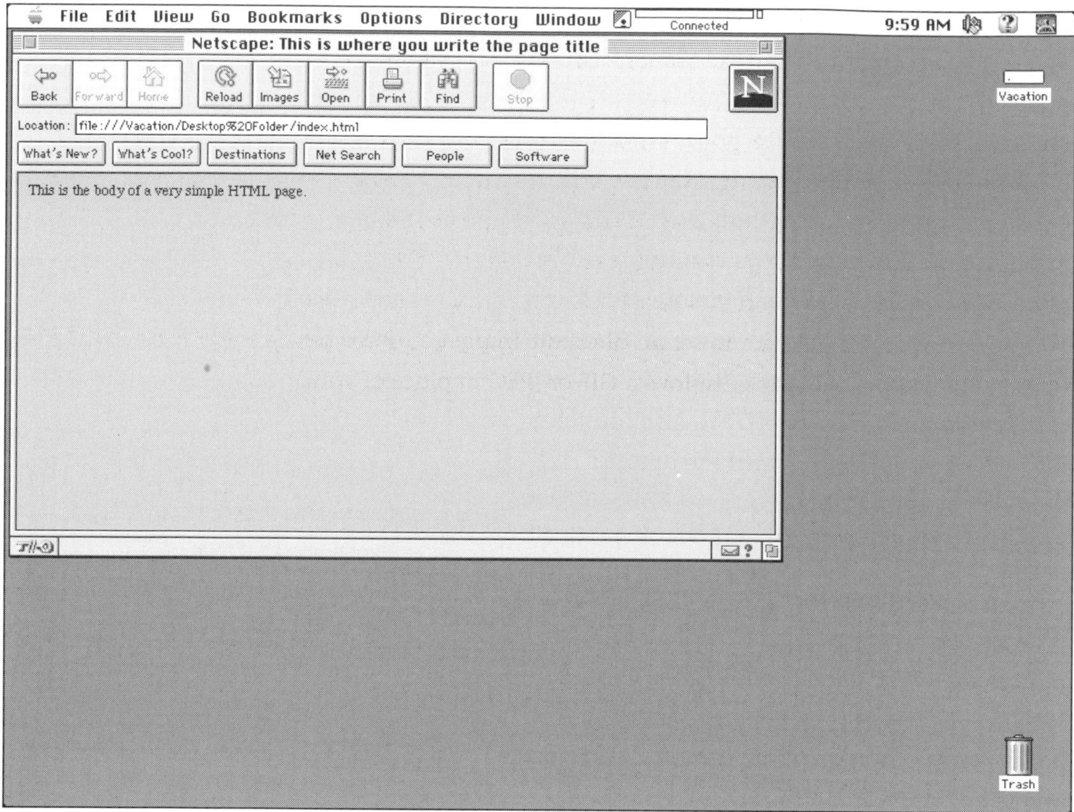

Figure 10.10 This is how that simple HTML code displays in Netscape Navigator.

attributes and parameters you can set in the HTML code (such as background color, height, and width).

Multimedia files, such as Flash movies, can be placed on a Web page using the **<OBJECT>** or **<EMBED>** tags. But how do you know which to use on your pages? If you are on an intranet or other limited system in which everyone will be using the same browser, you can choose the tag that is best suited to that browser. If you are designing Web pages for the broader audience of the Web, however, the best choice is to use both tags.

The main reason to use these tags in combination is that Netscape and Microsoft have gone off in two different directions, each providing different features for their own tags. (Netscape created the **<EMBED>** tag, and Microsoft created the **<OBJECT>** tag.) Unfortunately, the two companies have made it more complicated for developers because they've adopted different standards. Fortunately, you can use both tags in combination so that you can maximize your results in both browsers with the same HTML page.

HTML tags can be used in combination because browsers were designed to ignore HTML tags they don't recognize. So, if a browser doesn't support a tag, such as **<OBJECT>**, it won't display it. But, if there is no other code that the browser does understand, then the browser may just display an ugly gray square, and nobody wants that on their Web pages. Using these tags in combination ensures that, if one tag is not recognized by a browser, another option will be displayed. For example, in the following HTML code sample, you'll see how to use the **<EMBED>** tag to set an alternate image so a browser that doesn't support plug-ins displays a GIF or JPEG in place of your Flash movie.

The <OBJECT> Tag

Created by Microsoft, the **<OBJECT>** tag is supported by Internet Explorer 3 and later versions on any computer running Windows 95, 98, or NT4. Since other browsers may support this technology by the time you read this, let me generally say that the **<OBJECT>** tag will work in any browser that supports the use of the Flash ActiveX control.

One of the biggest advantages of the **<OBJECT>** tag is that, by using ActiveX controls, you can instruct the browser to automatically download the Shockwave Flash plug-in, install it, and use it to display your animation. This is a big deal on the Web; many developers have avoided features that required plug-ins because they didn't want to force users to download a separate application, install it, restart their browser, and then return to the page before they could access an animation, sound, or other multimedia feature. Because the Shockwave Flash plug-in is so small (approximately 150K), this automatic download is done in the background and happens so quickly that most users will just think they are waiting for your Flash movie to load.

The <EMBED> Tag

Originally created by Netscape, the **<EMBED>** tag is supported by Netscape Navigator 2 or later, as well as any browser that supports the use of the Shockwave Flash plug-in (just about any browser that supports plug-ins).

The **<EMBED>** tag has two cool features. One feature is that you can include instructions for users to get the needed plug-in if they don't already have it. (This is important because, although it's cool to use ActiveX to automatically download the plug-in, many Web surfers are still using computers and browsers that don't support that feature.) If

Avoiding Problems With Tables

Netscape Navigator 2 does not properly display the HTML **<EMBED>** tag when it is inserted into table cells. This can be frustrating, but if you want to ensure that people using Navigator 2 or earlier can view your pages without problems, it's best not to place an **<EMBED>** tag inside a table cell. Later browser versions, Netscape Navigator 3 and up, as well as Microsoft Internet Explorer 3 and up, should display the **<EMBED>** tag properly in table cells.

you use the **PLUG-INSPAGE** attribute, you can direct users to a Web page where they can download the Flash Player.

The other advantage to the <**EMBED**> tag is the <**NOEMBED**> tag. Netscape created the <**NOEMBED**> tag because the company realized that not all browsers on the Web support plug-ins and there should be an alternative to an empty gray box or a puzzle piece with a question mark for those users. Using the <**NOEMBED**> tag, you can display alternate content, such as a GIF or JPEG.

Combining The <OBJECT> And <EMBED> Tags

To ensure that the maximum number of users will be able to view your Flash files, use the <**EMBED**> tag nested within the <**OBJECT**> tag as in the following example:

```
<OBJECT classid="clsid:D27CDB6E-AE6D-11cf-96B8-444553540000"
codebase="http://active.macromedia.com/flash2/cabs/
swflash.cab#version=3,0,7,0" width=100 height=80>

<PARAM name="Movie" value="myflashfile.swf">

<EMBED src="moviename.swf" width=100 height=80 plug-
inspage="http://www.macromedia.com/shockwave/download/
index.cgi?P1_Prod_Version=ShockwaveFlash"> </EMBED>

<NOEMBED>

<IMG src="myalternative.gif" width=100 height=80>

</NOEMBED>
</OBJECT>
```

The preceding HTML code is written exactly as it should be in an HTML page, with the exception that the file names and attributes have to be changed to the specifics of your Flash files. To place a Flash movie on a page, simply copy the preceding HTML code into your HTML document, and then customize it. You'll learn more about customizing, especially how to use attributes and parameters, in the following section. If you want to put up your file right away, you just need to change the file name (they always have an .SWF extension), the width, and the height attributes in both the <**OBJECT**> and <**EMBED**> tags to reflect the name and exact size of your Flash file. If you want to provide an alternate image, change the image file name in the <**NOEMBED**> tag.

The **classid** (that long series of numbers and letters at the beginning of the <**OBJECT**> tag) must be written exactly as it is in this example.

The **CODEBASE** attribute must also be written exactly as it is previously. These specifications tell the browser where to find the Flash Player for automatic download using ActiveX.

Attributes And Parameters

HTML tags—such as **<EMBED>** and **<OBJECT>**—include attributes and parameters that provide information about the behavior of the multimedia file described in the tag. Some attributes or parameters, such as those that specify the height and width of the file, are required; others, such as **BGCOLOR** (which enables you to specify a background color), are optional.

Although there is some overlap, the **<EMBED>** and **<OBJECT>** tags each have their own features which are listed separately in the following sections for easy reference.

<EMBED> Attributes

The **<EMBED>** tag, which is supported by Netscape Navigator and other browsers that support plug-ins, has many attributes. The attributes are detailed in the following sections.

BASE

The **BASE** attribute specifies the directory path that will be used for all relative path statements in the Shockwave Flash movie. Although this attribute is not required, it can be helpful when your Flash files are in a different directory from your other files and you want to be able to set links from a particular reference.

For example, the statement:

```
BASE=http://www.yourname.com/flash
```

would instruct the browser that all of the paths in the Flash file are relative to the "flash" directory at **http://www.yourname.com**. Thus, if you linked a file called "main.html", it would be resolved to **http://www.yourname.com/flash/main.html**.

BGCOLOR

The **BGCOLOR** attribute sets the background color using a hexadecimal color code. This background color will fill the area defined by the **WIDTH** and **HEIGHT** attributes and can be used to provide a colored area around a Flash movie. The background color can also be set while you are editing a Flash file in the development tool by selecting Modify|Movie and using the pop-up color selector to assign a background color. If you haven't done this or you want to change it, you can use the **BGCOLOR** attribute in the **<EMBED>** tag. The **BGCOLOR** attribute overrides the background color set in the Flash movie.

HEIGHT And WIDTH

Because Flash movies are scalable, you can specify the original dimensions in pixels or in percentages of a browser window. If you want to force the Flash movie to be a specific size, use a measurement in pixels for the height and width. If you want a Flash movie to be scaled to the same proportion of any browser window, use a numeric value with a percent sign, such as 25% (to fit a fourth of the screen) or 100% (to fill the entire screen).

LOOP

The **LOOP** attribute enables you to specify whether an animation will continue to play repeatedly (loop) or stop after the movie reaches the last frame. The values are TRUE (loop) and FALSE (don't loop). The default is TRUE.

Setting **LOOP=TRUE** causes the movie to return to the first frame and play again when it reaches the last frame. Playback is continuous until another page is loaded or another option is selected.

Setting **LOOP=FALSE** causes the movie to stop when it reaches the last frame. The last frame will remain visible in the browser window until another page is loaded or another option is selected.

Don't Make Your Viewers Reload The Page

Here's a JavaScript trick you can use with the **PLUG-INSPAGE** attribute to save your viewers the hassle of restarting their browsers after they download a plug-in. This works only with Netscape Navigator 3 and later, but it's a nice thing to do for your users. The technique involves creating a link for the user to click after downloading and installing the plug-in. When the user clicks on the link, the JavaScript reloads the plug-ins from Netscape's plug-ins folder on the user's hard drive. This also automatically refreshes the current page the user is viewing.

The following is an example of the JavaScript for the additional link:

```
<A HREF="javascript:navigator.plug-
ins.refresh(true);
parent.location.reload()">click here</A>
```

After you finish downloading and installing the Shockwave Flash plug-in, you will not need to re-start your browser to use the plug-in.

MENU

The **MENU** attribute enables you to specify the type of menu users will see when right-clicking on a Windows computer or command-clicking on a Macintosh. Again, the options are TRUE (show all applicable options in the menu) and FALSE (show only the About Flash option). The full menu allows users a variety of options to enhance or to control playback in the browser. In some cases, such as interactive games, you may want to limit the user's control. In other cases, you will want to give the user the option to alter how the Flash movie plays.

PLAY

The **PLAY** attribute enables you to determine whether a Flash movie starts as soon as it is down-loaded to the viewer's computer or whether a user must click on a button (or take some other action) to play the movie. Again, the options are TRUE (begin the movie immediately) and FALSE (load the first frame and then wait for a viewer action). The default is TRUE. If you do not set the **PLAY** attribute, the Flash movie will start as soon as it is downloaded.

PLUG-INSPAGE

The **PLUG-INSPAGE** attribute specifies where the plug-in can be found if a user doesn't already have the plug-in needed to view a Flash movie. This can also be used for other file types that require plug-ins. For Flash movies, this should be set to: "**http://www.macromedia.com/shockwave/download/index.cgi?P1_Prod_Version=ShockwaveFlash**".

QUALITY

The **QUALITY** attribute enables you to specify the quality (antialiasing options) of your images versus the speed of playback. Using the LOW, HIGH, AUTOHIGH, and AUTOLOW options, you can con-trol whether speed or image quality gets priority.

This attribute will help compensate for the fact that the Smooth options, which you may have used to eliminate the jagged edges when you cre-ated your Flash movie, are not stored as playback settings in the exported SWF file. This will also help you control the fact that playback slows down when the Smooth option is selected.

Antialiasing, which makes your files look smoother, can slow down the rendering of each frame because the computer must first smooth the edges. The **QUALITY** attribute enables you to make a choice about how much your Flash movie will be slowed down by prioritizing the importance of appearance versus playback speed. The default setting is AUTOHIGH.

The following are the results of the **QUALITY** setting options:

- *LOW*—Antialiasing is never used, and playback speed is given priority over appearance.
- *HIGH*—Antialiasing is always used, and appearance is given priority over playback speed.
- *AUTOHIGH*—A somewhat more sophisticated option, AUTOHIGH sets playback to begin with antialiasing turned on, but if the actual frame rate supported by the user's computer drops below your specified frame rate, antialiasing is automatically turned off to improve playback speed. This option emphasizes playback speed and appearance equally at first, but then sacrifices appearance for the sake of playback speed, if necessary.
- *AUTOLOW*—With this option, playback begins with antialiasing turned off. If the Flash player detects that the processor can handle it, antialiasing is turned on. Use this option to emphasize speed at first but to improve appearance whenever possible.

SALIGN

The **SALIGN** attribute enables you to specify how a Flash movie is positioned within a browser window when you use the **SCALE** attribute (explained next). This alignment option is important because, if you specify the NOBORDER value for the **SCALE** attribute, portions of your movie may be cropped—and if you specify SHOWALL, unwanted borders may appear. **SALIGN** enables you to control which areas of the Flash movie are cropped or where borders will appear.

The **SALIGN** attribute has the following value options:

- *L*—Aligns the movie along the left edge of the browser window and crops the top, bottom, and/or right sides as necessary.
- *R*—Aligns the movie along the right edge of the browser window and crops the top, bottom, and/or left sides as necessary.
- *T*—Aligns the movie along the top edge of the browser window and crops the bottom, left, and/or right sides as necessary.
- *B*—Aligns the movie along the bottom edge of the browser window and crops the top, left, and/or right sides as necessary.
- *TL*—Aligns the movie at the top-left corner of the browser window and crops the bottom and/or right sides as necessary.
- *TR*—Aligns the movie at the top-right corner of the browser window and crops the bottom and/or left sides as necessary.
- *BL*—Aligns the movie at the bottom-left corner of the browser window and crops the top and/or right sides as necessary.
- *BR*—Aligns the movie at the bottom-right corner of the browser window and crops the top and/or left sides as necessary.

SCALE

The **SCALE** attribute is needed only if you use percentages for the **HEIGHT** and **WIDTH** attributes. The **SCALE** attribute enables you to define how the Flash movie is placed within the boundaries of percentage specified in the browser window.

Use the **SCALE** attribute controls to specify whether borders appear around the edges of your movies, whether edges are cropped to fill the entire area, and whether the movie is distorted (stretched or shrunk) to fit exactly into the area specified by the percentage. Because using a percentage can lead to undesired effects, the following options enable you to set preferences controlling how the Flash movie will display:

- *SHOWALL*—This option enables the entire movie to be displayed in the specified area. The width and height proportions of the original movie are maintained and no distortion occurs, but borders may appear on two sides of the movie.
- *NOBORDER*—This option enables you to scale a Flash movie to fill a specified area. Again, the original width and height proportions are maintained and no distortion occurs, but portions of the movie may be cropped. (See the preceding information on the **SALIGN** attribute to control which margins are cropped.)
- *EXACTFIT*—This option allows the entire movie to be displayed in the specified area. However, the Flash movie may be distorted because the width and height proportions may be stretched or shrunk in order to fit the movie in the specified area.

Table 10.1 provides a quick reference to the <EMBED> tag attributes.

<OBJECT> Parameters

When used with the <**OBJECT**> tag, the following are called parameters, but they serve the same function as attributes with the <**EMBED**> tag. Note these carefully. Although many parameters of the <**OBJECT**> tag are the same as the attributes for the <**EMBED**> tag, there are some important differences.

BASE

The **BASE** parameter—which can also be used in the HEAD section of any HTML page—specifies the directory path that will be used for all relative path statements in the Shockwave Flash movie. This parameter is not required but can be helpful when your Flash file is in a different directory from your other files and you want to be able to set links from a particular reference.

For example, the statement

```
BASE="http://www.yourname.com/flash"
```

would instruct the browser that all of the paths in the Flash file are relative to the "flash" directory at **http://www.yourname.com**. Thus, if you linked a file called "main.html", it would be resolved to **http://www.yourname.com/flash/main.html**.

BGCOLOR

The **BGCOLOR** parameter sets the background color using a hexadecimal color code. This background color will fill the area defined by the **WIDTH** and **HEIGHT** parameters and can be used to provide a framed area around a Flash movie. Background color can also be set while you are editing a Flash file in the development tool by selecting Modify|Movie and using the pop-up color selector to assign a background color. If you haven't done this or you want to override it, you can use the **BGCOLOR** parameter in the <**EMBED**> tag. The **BGCOLOR** parameter overrides the background color set in the Flash movie. The following is an example:

```
<EMBED src="filename.swf" BGCOLOR="#000000"
width=100 height=80 plug-inspage="http://
www.macromedia.com/shockwave/download/
index.cgi?P1_Prod_Version=ShockwaveFlash">
</EMBED>
```

CODEBASE

The **CODEBASE** parameter is unique to the <**OBJECT**> tag because it is used only by browsers that employ ActiveX controls. This is an exciting feature because it enables a browser to automatically download and install a plug-in, such as

Table 10.1 <EMBED> attributes.

<EMBED> Attribute	Description
BASE	Specifies a base directory or URL.
BGCOLOR	Specifies a background color using a hexadecimal color code.
HEIGHT and **WIDTH**	Specifies the height and width of the animation and can be set in exact pixels or as a percentage.
LOOP	Can be set to TRUE (continue looping) or FALSE (stop after one play). The default value is TRUE.
MENU	Can be set to TRUE (show all applicable options in the menu) or FALSE (show only the About Flash option).
PLAY	Can be set to TRUE (begin play upon download) or FALSE (wait for user action, such as button click). The default value is TRUE.
PLUG-INSPAGE	Specifies where the plug-in can be found if a user doesn't already have it. For Flash movies, this should be set to: **"http://www.macromedia.com/shockwave/download/index.cgi?P1_Prod_Version=ShockwaveFlash"**.
QUALITY	Can be set to LOW, HIGH, AUTOHIGH, or AUTOLOW to specify a preference for quality versus playback speed. The default value is AUTOHIGH.
SALIGN	Can be set to L, R, T, B, TL, TR, BL, or BR.
SCALE	Can be set to SHOWALL, NOBORDER, or EXACTFIT. The default value is SHOWALL.

Shockwave Flash, making it possible for a user who doesn't have the plug-in to download and install it in the background and then to view your Flash movie. The **CODEBASE** parameter must be entered exactly as it appears in the following code to work properly for the Shockwave Flash 2 viewer:

```
CODEBASE="http://active.macromedia.com/flash2/cabs/
swflash.cab#version=3,0,7,0"
```

CLASSID

The **CLASSID** parameter is important because it identifies the ActiveX control specified in the **<OBJECT>** tag. The **CLASSID** should be entered in the first part of the **<OBJECT>** tag exactly as written in the following:

```
CLASSID="clsid:D27CDB6E-AE6D-11cf-96B8-444553540000"
```

HEIGHT And WIDTH

Because Flash movies are scalable, you can specify the original dimensions in pixels or in percentages of a browser window. If you want to force the Flash movie to be a set size, use a measurement in pixels for the height and width. If you want a Flash movie to be scaled to the same proportion of any browser window, use a numeric value with a percent sign, such as 25% (to fit a fourth of the screen) or 100% (to fill the screen).

LOOP

The **LOOP** parameter enables you to specify whether an animation will continue to play repeatedly (loop) or stop after the movie reaches the last frame. The values are TRUE (loop) and FALSE (don't loop). The default is TRUE.

Setting **LOOP=TRUE** causes the movie to return to the first frame and continue to play again when it reaches the last frame. Playback is continuous until another page is loaded or another option is selected.

Setting **LOOP=FALSE** causes the movie to stop when it reaches the last frame. The last frame will remain visible in the browser window until another page is loaded or another option selected.

MENU

The **MENU** parameter enables you to specify the type of menu users see when right-clicking on a Windows computer or command-clicking on a Macintosh. Again, the options are TRUE (show all applicable options in the menu) and FALSE (show only the About Flash option). The full menu allows users a variety of options to enhance or control playback in the browser. In some cases, such as interactive games, you may want to limit the user's control. In other cases, you will want to give the user the option to alter the Flash movie.

MOVIE

The **MOVIE** parameter specifies the name of the movie to be loaded by the **<OBJECT>** tag. When you use this with your files, simply replace "filename.swf" with the relative path and file name of the Flash SWF file you want to display on your page.

PLAY

The **PLAY** parameter enables you to determine whether a Flash movie starts as soon as it is downloaded to the viewer's computer or whether a user must click on a button (or make some other action) to activate the Flash movie. Again, the options are TRUE (begin the movie immediately) and FALSE (load the first frame and then wait for a viewer action.) The default is TRUE. If you do not set the **PLAY** option, the Flash movie will start as soon as it is downloaded.

QUALITY

The **QUALITY** parameter enables you to specify the quality (antialiasing options) of your images versus the speed of playback. Using the LOW, HIGH, AUTOHIGH, and AUTOLOW options, you can control whether speed or image quality is given priority.

This parameter will help compensate for the fact that the Smooth options, which you may have used to eliminate the jagged edges when you created your Flash movie, are not stored as playback settings in the exported SWF file. This will also help you control the fact that playback slows down when the Smooth option is selected.

Antialiasing, which makes your files look smoother, can slow down the rendering of each frame because the computer must first smooth the edges. The **QUALITY** parameter enables you to make a choice about how much your Flash movie will be slowed down by prioritizing the importance of appearance versus playback speed. The default setting is AUTOHIGH.

The following are the results of the **QUALITY** setting options:

- *LOW*—Antialiasing is never used, and playback speed is given priority over appearance.
- *HIGH*—Antialiasing is always used, and appearance is given priority over playback speed.
- *AUTOHIGH*—A somewhat more sophisticated option, AUTOHIGH sets playback to begin with antialiasing turned on, but, if the actual frame rate supported by the user's computer drops below your specified frame rate, antialiasing is automatically turned off to improve playback

speed. This option emphasizes playback speed and appearance equally at first, but then sacrifices appearance for the sake of playback speed, if necessary.

- *AUTOLOW*—With this option, playback begins with antialiasing turned off. If the Flash player detects that the processor can handle it, antialiasing is turned on. Use this option to emphasize speed at first, but to improve appearance whenever possible.

SALIGN

The **SALIGN** parameter enables you to specify how a Flash movie is positioned within a browser window when you use the **SCALE** parameter (explained next). This alignment option is important because, if you specify the NOBORDER value for the **SCALE** parameter, portions of your movie may be cropped—and if you specify SHOWALL, unwanted borders may appear. **SALIGN** enables you to control which areas of the Flash movie are cropped or where borders will appear.

The **SALIGN** parameter has the following value options:

- *L*—Aligns the movie along the left edge of the browser window and crops the top, bottom, and/or right sides as necessary.
- *R*—Aligns the movie along the right edge of the browser window and crops the top, bottom, and/or left sides as necessary.
- *T*—Aligns the movie along the top edge of the browser window and crops the bottom, left, and/or right sides as necessary.
- *B*—Aligns the movie along the bottom edge of the browser window and crops the top, left, and/or right sides as necessary.
- *TL*—Aligns the movie at the top-left corner of the browser window and crops the bottom and/or right sides as necessary.
- *TR*—Aligns the movie at the top-right corner of the browser window and crops the bottom and/or left sides as necessary.
- *BL*—Aligns the movie at the bottom-left corner of the browser window and crops the top and/or right sides as necessary.
- *BR*—Aligns the movie at the bottom-right corner of the browser window and crops the top and/or left sides as necessary.

SCALE

The **SCALE** parameter is needed only if you use percentages for the **HEIGHT** and **WIDTH** parameters. The **SCALE** parameter enables you to define how the Flash movie is placed within the boundaries of percentage specified in the browser window.

Use the **SCALE** parameter to specify whether borders appear around the edges of your movies, whether edges are cropped to fill the entire area, and whether the movie is distorted (stretched or shrunk) to fit exactly into the area specified by the percentage. Because using a percentage can lead to undesired effects, the following options enable you to set preferences controlling how the Flash movie will display:

- *SHOWALL*—This option enables the entire movie to be displayed in the specified area. The width and height proportions of the original movie are maintained and no distortion occurs, but borders may appear on two sides of the movie.
- *NOBORDER*—This option enables you to scale a Flash movie to fill a specified area. Again, the original width and height proportions are maintained and no distortion occurs, but portions of the movie may be cropped. (See the preceding information on the **SALIGN** parameter to control which margins are cropped.)
- *EXACTFIT*—This option allows the entire movie to be displayed in the specified area. However, the Flash movie may be distorted because the

width and height proportions may be stretched or shrunk in order to fit the movie in the specified area.

Use Table 10.2 as a quick reference to <**OBJECT**> parameters.

Table 10.2 <OBJECT> parameters.

<OBJECT> Parameter	Description
BASE	Specifies a base directory or URL.
BGCOLOR	Specifies a background color using a hexadecimal color code.
CODEBASE	Should be set exactly to: **CODEBASE="http://active.macromedia.com/flash2/cabs/swflash.cab#version=3,0,7,0"**.
CLASSID	Should be set exactly to: **CLASSID="D27CDB6E-AE6D-11cf-96B8-444553540000"**.
HEIGHT and **WIDTH**	Specifies the height and width of the animation and can be set in exact pixels or as a percentage.
LOOP	Can be set to TRUE (continue looping) or FALSE (stop after one play). The default value is TRUE.
MENU	Can be set to TRUE (show all applicable options in the menu) or FALSE (show only the About Flash option).
MOVIE	Specifies the name of the movie to be loaded by the **<OBJECT>** tag.
PLAY	Can be set to TRUE (begin play upon download) or FALSE (wait for user action, such as button click). The default value is TRUE.
QUALITY	Can be set to LOW, HIGH, AUTOHIGH, or AUTOLOW to specify a preference for quality versus playback speed. The default value is AUTOHIGH.
SALIGN	Can be set to L, R, T, B, TL, TR, BL, or BR.
SCALE	Can be set to SHOWALL, NOBORDER, or EXACTFIT. The default value: is SHOWALL.

Moving On

This chapter has given you an overview of the HTML tags and attributes you can use to put your Flash movies on the Web. Although it takes a little more effort to use this combination of HTML tags, taking the time to do so will help ensure that all of your users have the best experience on your Web site.

Chapter 11 will introduce you to techniques and technologies that will ensure that your Flash-created content can be viewed, at least at some level of quality and speed, by anyone using a graphical browser. You'll also learn how to export your Flash movies into conventional Web graphics formats, and how to use JavaScript to identify whether a visitor's browser is equipped with the ability to play Flash.

In Chapter 12, you'll learn how other companies have used Flash to create dynamic and interactive Web sites. You'll also learn more about the unique features of Flash and how companies have pulled it all together, integrating Flash, HTML, and other Web features to create some of the coolest sites on the Web.

11 Expanding Flash and Your Audience

Ken Milburn

By now, you should be familiar with the tools and capabilities of Flash 3. You've probably even started to expand on the techniques explained in this book and to develop a few of your own. This chapter tells you where you can go from there.

This chapter will introduce you to some techniques and technologies that will ensure that your Flash-created content can be viewed—at least at some level of quality and speed—by anyone using a graphical browser. I mean *anyone*, even if they haven't downloaded and installed the Flash plug-in. (This chapter also covers which browsers have built-in Flash capability.) You'll learn how to export your Flash movies into conventional Web graphics formats (such as animated GIFs), and how to use JavaScript to identify whether a visitor's browser is equipped with the ability to play Flash. Another small section of this chapter will show you how to predict the performance of a specific Flash movie at different modem speeds. Finally, you'll be introduced to two technologies that expand the power of Flash to new horizons: Flash Generator and RealFlash.

Making Sure You Have The Biggest Possible Audience

The fact that Flash 3 movies look better and perform faster than ordinary Web content matters little if no one sees them. If you are developing with Flash, you want to make sure that as many people as possible can get your message. This section reveals several ways you can be assured of a surfer's ability to utilize your Flash sites. If you employ all of these methods, you will have a Flash-created site that is virtually universally accessible.

Browsers With Flash Built In

The vast majority of the Web-surfing public accesses the Web using one of four browsers: Netscape Navigator, Microsoft Internet Explorer, the AOL browser, or the Web-TV browser. Another browser that is growing in popularity is the one distributed to subscribers of the @Home Web cable service. As of summer 1998, all current releases of these browsers include a built-in Flash player.

So, millions of viewers can access your Flash 3 files without being required to download and install a plug-in. However, it takes time before a majority of viewers are using the latest version of any browser. In other words, there are still millions more folks who can't view your Flash 3 creations without first downloading and installing a plug-in. However, they can still see and hear your Flash movies...if you'll just read on.

Exporting To Conventional Formats

Flash can export its movies to formats that can be read by virtually any graphical browser. So, if you want to create Web sites that can be seen by anyone, simply create parallel sites. This is not *nearly* as much work as it sounds; you just need to start by designing the site in Flash. Then, using the Flash site as a guideline, you can create a similar site in HTML. (Dreamweaver is strongly recommended for that purpose.) Continue by inserting the graphics and animations created in Flash. You can then create a parallel site by making a copy of the original and substituting conventional Web-format graphics and animations. All of the content for those files can be the very same Flash content, but just exported to the needed conventional formats.

Note: *You could also design a "splash" (introductory) page that provides a button for downloading the Flash plug-in. Viewers will then have a choice as to whether to view the content with all the Flash characteristics intact (such as scalability, automatic antialiasing, actions, and animated buttons) or to stick with conventional content.*

Because Flash files are so small, all the Flash vector files and Flash-generated conventional graphics should consume only approximately 20 percent more space than it would have taken to store the HTML site alone.

Now, all you need for universal playback is a means by which a viewer's browser can automatically determine which version of the graphics and animations should be loaded.

Using JavaScript To Identify Browsers

In Chapter 10, Janine Warner gives you sample JavaScripts (and instructions for their use) that can be inserted into your site's HTML code to allow the viewing browser to identify whether the Flash plug-in has been installed (or is built in). At that point, the script can be made to display a message advising the viewer that this site would look best with Flash and then ask if the viewer wants to download and install the player. If the viewer answers "yes," either the player is automatically downloaded and installed (Internet Explorer 3 or later) or the browser connects to the appropriate URL at the Macromedia site. (See Figure 11.1.) If the viewer answers "no," the conventional site can be made to play.

Note: *How closely the conventional site resembles the Flash site's capabilities will depend greatly on the tools used to design the conventional site and on the site designer's expertise in such matters as Java, JavaScript, and Dynamic HTML. It is possible to create DHTML without programming in Dreamweaver and to do such graphics tricks as slicing images, creating image maps, and creating JavaScript button rollovers in Fireworks.*

The URL for the Macromedia Flash download page is **www.macromedia.com/shockwave/download**.

Monitoring Download Performance

This topic may seem a little out of place at first. It's true that it's here partly because I couldn't find any other place for it. But it's also true that, if you're going to reach the widest possible audience, you have to know whether your Flash movie will meet your audience's performance expectations.

You can test the performance of movies either as you create them or after they're completed. You also have a choice of testing either the

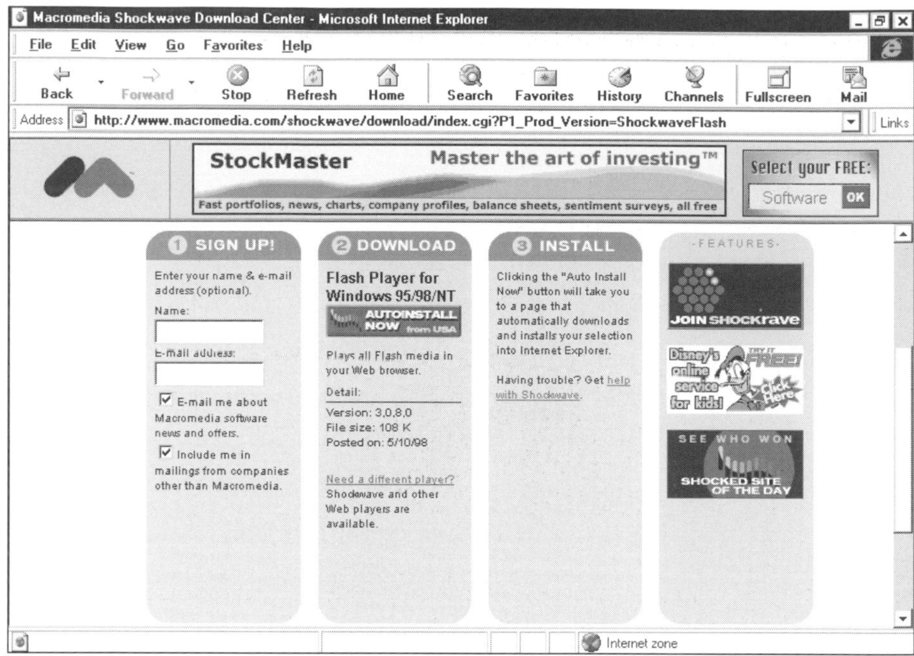

Figure 11.1 The Flash 3 player download page provides complete installation instructions.

frame-by-frame performance of the movie or the streaming performance of the movie. Finally, you can simulate the performance of any modem speed, including the predominant 14.4K, 28.8K, and 56K as preset menu choices.

To test a completed movie, follow these steps:

1. Choose File|Open and select the movie you want to test from the proper directory. When the movie opens, it will begin playing automatically.
2. First, you want to set the speed of the modem connection you want to simulate. From the menu bar, choose Control|28.8 (or any other speed of your choice). You can also create and save a custom setting for any upload speed you choose).
3. Now, decide whether you want to choose to profile the streaming or frame-by-frame performance of the movie. From the menu bar, choose View|Frame-By-Frame Graph (or Streaming Graph).
4. From the menu bar, choose View|Bandwidth Profiler. The Bandwidth Profiler will appear in the timeline. See Figure 11.2.
5. Press Return/Enter or choose Control|Play to play the movie. It will simulate running at the modem connection/upload rate you have chosen in the settings.

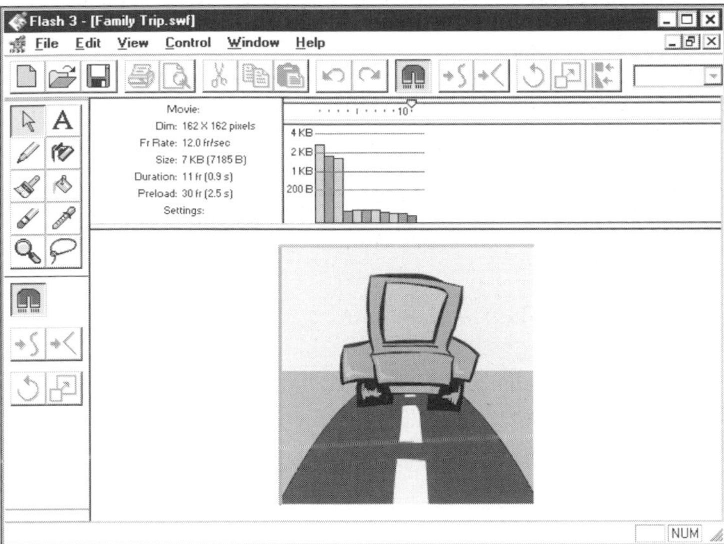

Figure 11.2 The Bandwidth Profiler shown in frame-by-frame mode as it displays in the Timeline. Each alternating gray bar represents a single frame.

If you discover that the movie pauses in places, you will be able to spot the specific frames by looking at the performance graph in the Bandwidth Profiler Timeline. Frames whose graph bar extends above the red line must pause to catch up. Try to find ways to reduce the size of these frames in order to make the playback of your movie work better in a wider variety of browsers.

The playback performance of the movie will be the same regardless of whether you choose a streaming or frame-by-frame graph for the Bandwidth Profiler. The difference is that the streaming graph divides each frame into regions that show how much of each frame's allotted time is used for streaming and how much for playing.

Macromedia's documentation claims that, if you click an individual frame's bar in the chart, the data displayed to the left of the graph will change. This was not true in early versions of Flash 3. Check with Macromedia to see when this bug has been corrected.

Expanding Flash To New Horizons

Macromedia has been working with other companies and in new ways to enhance the power of Flash by making it even more versatile. Along those lines, Macromedia has made the SWF file format an open specification. So far, Microsoft, IBM, RealNetworks, Associated Press, and Broderbund have begun working on products that incorporate that specification. Although just how these companies are using this specification is still secret, two such products have already arrived:

RealNetwork's RealFlash Player and Macromedia's own Flash Generator.

Flash With Sound, Voice, And Music: The RealFlash Generator And Player

If you've experienced or heard of the RealNetworks server systems for streaming audio and video on the Web, you know that these systems offer faster, higher-quality performance for a given modem rate for any other. So it is intriguing, to say the least, to consider that there is a "marriage" between RealNetworks RealSystem 5 and Macromedia Flash. The technology, called RealFlash, is being jointly marketed by both companies.

What this marriage boils down to is a workable way of creating long animated cartoons and demos with fully synchronized voice and music that can be expected to play well over a 28.8 connection. Unfortunately, there's no way to demonstrate the effectiveness of this combination within the static, two-dimensional confines of this book. Don't take my word for it that RealFlash is a worthwhile extension of Flash's capabilities, though. Go to the Web site and get a live demo on your own system. If you haven't done so already, you'll have to download and install the RealPlayer 5 (or later). It will take about 15 minutes of your time, but you'll find your experience of many news and entertainment sites a richer one as a result. The URL is **www.real.com/devzone/library/stream/flash/index.html**.

If you want to implement RealFlash, you'll need all of the following:

- Flash 2 or later from Macromedia or RealNetworks.
- The RealFlash Content Creation Kit (either Macintosh or Windows).
- The RealEncoder for audio encoding (Free from RealNetwork's site).
- A RealServer from RealNetworks, or have your content hosted by an ISP with a RealServer installed. One such ISP is GalaxyNet Telecom in Campbell, California. You can contact them at **www.galaxy-net.net/streaming.html**.

If your interest in Flash is in Web entertainment, online multimedia portfolios, training applications that include visual demonstrations of complex procedures, or online infomercials, you definitely owe it to yourself to check out RealFlash.

Authoring for RealFlash isn't a totally alien activity. The visuals are created in Flash. The biggest difference is that you need to place all the animation on a single layer and all the sound on a single layer. The sound is also placed into the Flash file for synchronization.

Once you've finished authoring and synchronizing the sound, the animation and audio are separated. The animation is exported to a Shockwave Flash (SWF) file. Audio is exported to the RealAudio (RM) format. Finally, a metafile is created that links the SWF and RM files to one another.

RealFlash currently has some drawbacks, but remember that these may change in future versions:

- Only Flash 2 files are supported. You can export these from Flash 3, but you won't be able to take advantage of any of the new Flash 3 features.
- You are limited to single layer animations.
- RealFlash productions must be linear—no buttons or actions.

The Importance Of The Flash Generator

Flash Generator is a separate (and separately priced) package of tools that, together with Flash 3, make it possible to automate and personalize Web sites that use Flash content. Such graphics and animations as banners, calendars, charts, headlines, maps, and item-specific descriptive text can be automatically and instantaneously inserted at a specific location in a Flash site according to a viewer's input or according to other criteria (such as the viewer's location or time zone).

Macromedia suggests thinking of Generator as a "mail-merge" for graphics. The program comes in two parts: the Generator Developer's Studio (Flash Edition) and the Generator Dynamic Graphics Server. The Generator Developer's Studio is used to create Flash movies as templates. These templates are placeholders for graphical data, which can be in the form of Flash movies (SWF files), GIF, animated GIF, JPEG, or PNG files. The advantage is that the format can be designed once, leaving designers more time for creating a wider variety of graphics for specialized viewer segments. Applications for this technology range from individualized stock market reports to games tailored to meet an individual player's preferences.

Many other products offer database connectivity with Web sites, but Generator is the first such product to be graphically, rather than textually, oriented. Generator can also work in conjunction with other database connectivity systems.

Currently, the Generator Dynamic Graphics server runs only on Windows NT 4 running IIS and on Windows 95/98 running Personal Web Server (PWS). A release for the Solaris operating system was imminent at the time of this writing. Macromedia says it is also considering other operating systems.

The price and requirements of Generator, as well as the fact that it is a separate product aimed at serious Web design professionals, places any detailed discussion of Generator's operations outside the boundaries of this book. If your curiosity is piqued and you want to know more, point your browser to **www.macromedia.com**.

Moving On

For much of the time that I have known her, Janine Warner gets the last word. So it seems fitting that she close this book with case studies of a few major and trend-setting Flash 3 sites.

12 Case Studies

Janine Warner

It is easy to forget the limits of bandwidth when you are captivated by an animation made nimble by vector technology. In a flash, the Web is forever changed, enhanced, enriched. As you move from site to site, pages that use Flash jump out at you, drawing you in with motion, sound, and interactivity—and all without making you wait.

No matter how large or small your screen, or how slow your modem, Flash sites consistently look great as they stream across the Web. As more and more creative developers apply their skills to this powerful technology, the Web dances and sings in more places. Some of the biggest names on the Web have adopted Flash as an integral part of their development arsenals. What's made Flash so appealing to designers working on sites for the Olympics, Sony, MSN, NBC, and so many others? How have they used this new feature to add interactivity and enhance their Web sites?

In this chapter, you'll learn how some of the hottest sites on the Web have used Flash as a fundamental tool in creating their designs. You'll discover why developers chose Flash, how they used it, and some of their favorite features. Best of all, you'll learn some great tips these experts have developed after working on large, complex projects with Macromedia's Flash. Keep in mind as you view the images in this chapter that they are only highlights of these Web sites. (See Figures 12.1, 12.2, and 12.3.) It's nearly impossible to convey the animation and interactivity possible with Flash in a still image on the page of a book. Make sure you visit these sites to see what they really have to offer.

Interview With Josh Ulm, Quokka Sports (www.quokka.com)

In late 1997, Quokka Sports, a San Francisco-based digital sports media company, called Josh Ulm and asked if he would be interested in leading the design of the Web site for the international Olympics committee. In September, he traveled to the Bay Area and joined Michael Gough, Alex Pineda, and Brett Gardiner to develop a Web presence that would launch with the 1998 Nagano games. When the site launched in February, the team had grown to include: Gough as creative director, Gardiner as executive producer, Ulm as lead designer, designers Pineda and Ammon Haggerty, and production designers Mark Buccella and Josh Draper.

Quokka Sports has used Flash on a variety of Web sites, including the Olympics (**olympic.org**), the Remedi Project: Redesigning the Medium Through Discovery (**www.theremediproject.com**), and Around Alone Race Coverage (**www.aroundalone.com**). Ulm was interviewed recently about his work at Quokka Sports.

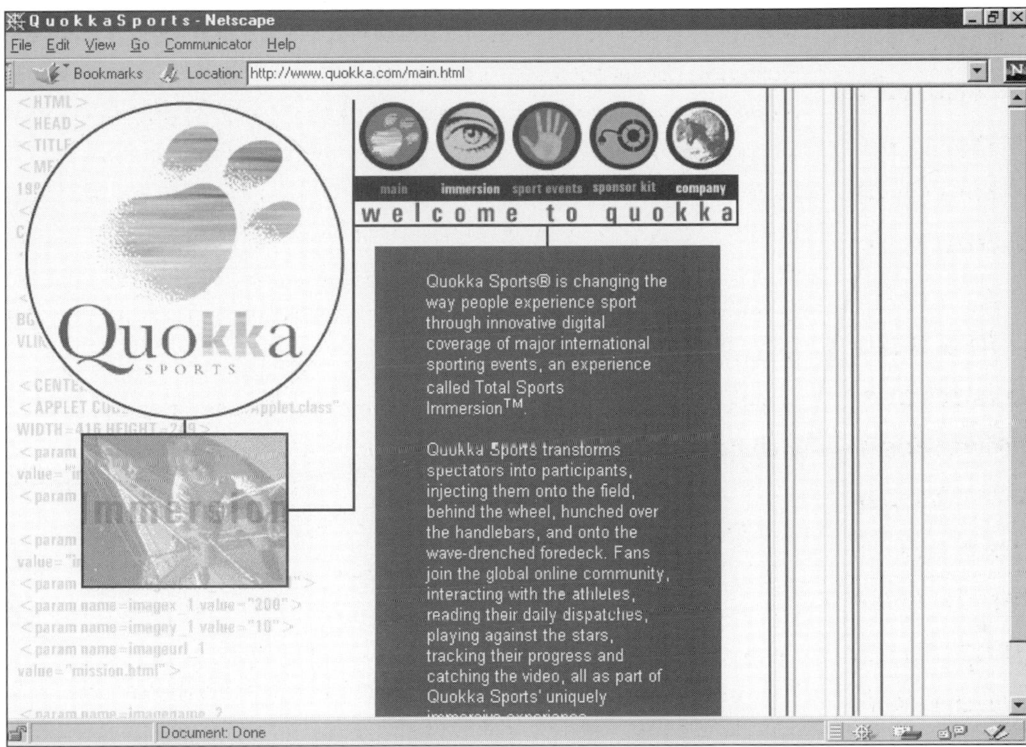

Figure 12.1 Lead Designer Josh Ulm, of Quokka Sports **(www.quokka.com)**, used Flash to make the Olympic Web site an international showpiece.

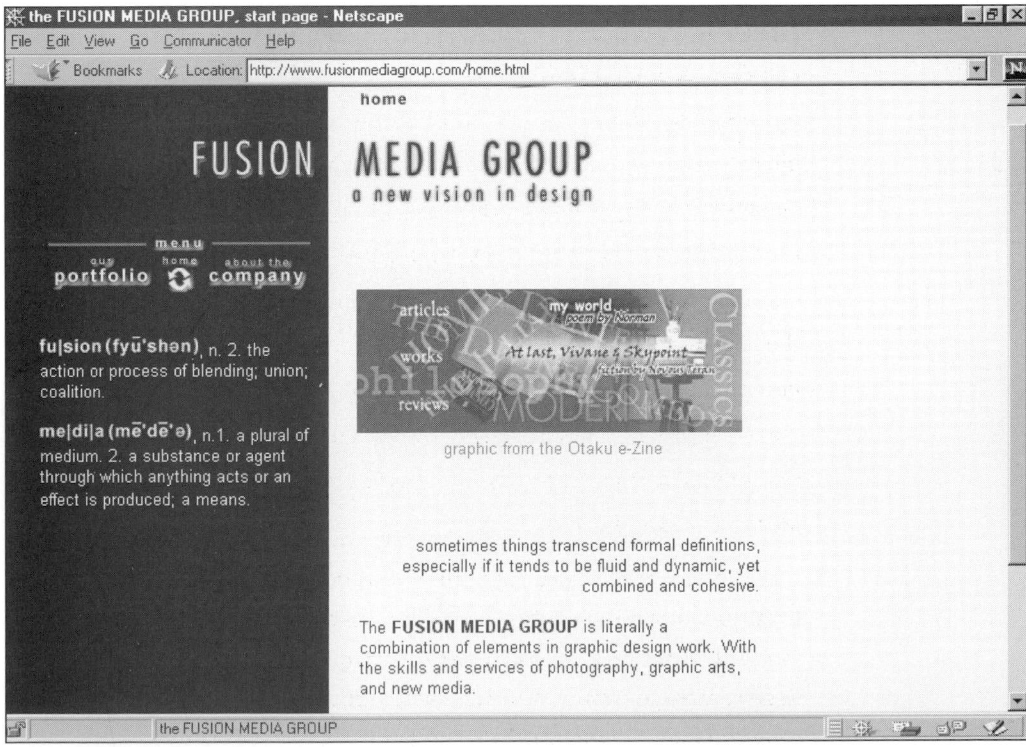

Figure 12.2 The Fusion Media Group, Inc., **www.fusionmediagroup.com**.

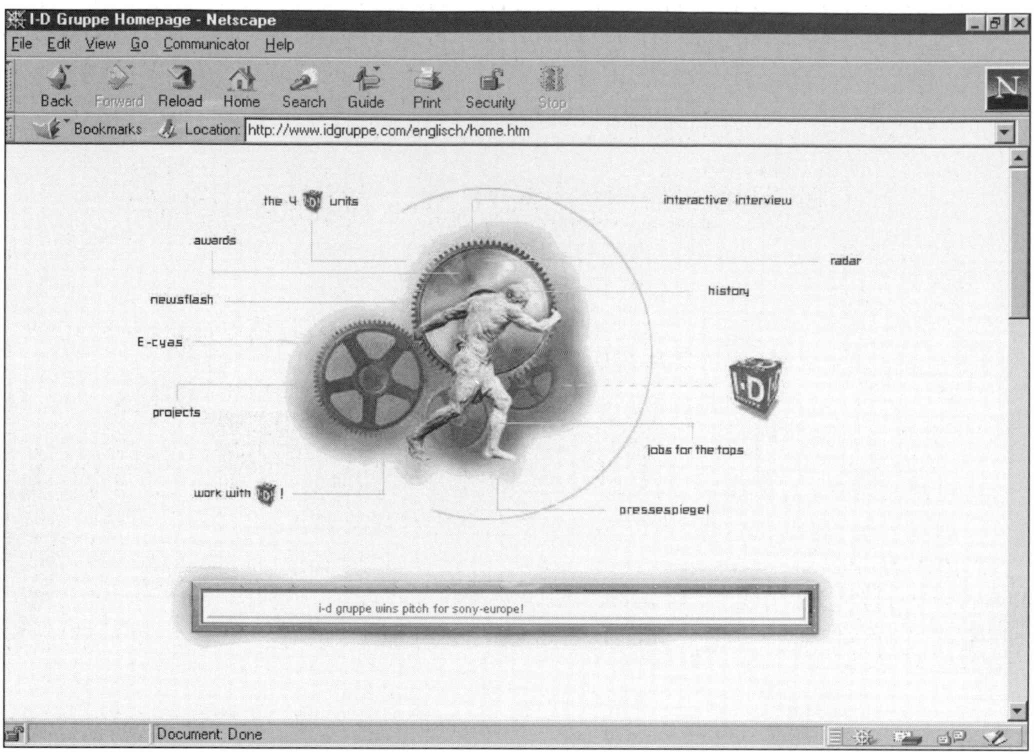

Figure 12.3 I-D Gruppe, **www.idgruppe.com**.

Why did you choose Macromedia's Flash?

I had had quite a bit of experience already with Flash. Working with an art collective back on the East Coast called Combine (**www.combine.org**), myself and a group of talented artists started playing with what we thought at the time was an incredible new trend in Web design. Flash brought the interactivity and dynamic movement of Director to the Internet while improving all the issues of speed, performance, and file size. Experimenting with Flash—and at that time, Future Splash—back in early 1997 led to a view of the future of the Internet, at least for the next few years. I brought that experience into the Olympics project and fought hard to use the technology to create a truly unique use of the Web.

The Olympics site, shown in Figure 12.4, was created using Flash because it offered the following important features: small file size, superior playback speed, and the ability to scale to fit different monitor sizes. In general, we chose Flash because we wanted to create a Web site that came alive, quickly, over any connection speed. Flash allowed us to create emotional and immersive multimedia presentations that were fast and engaging.

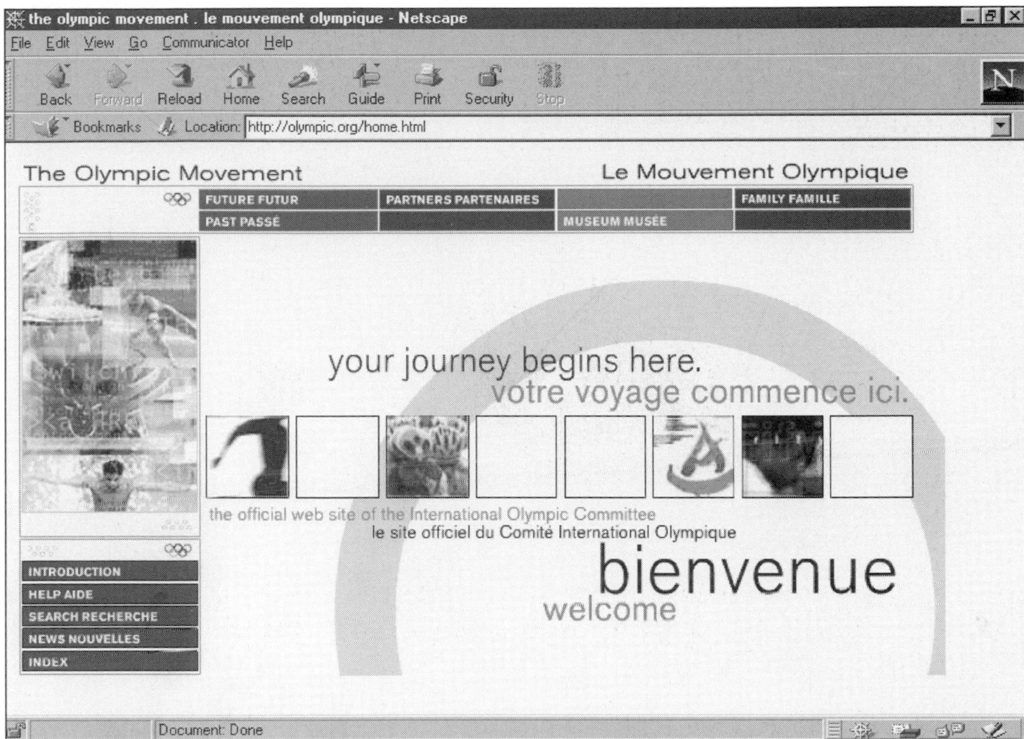

Figure 12.4 The Olympics Web site comes to life with Flash technology.

What's your favorite new feature in Flash 3?

Looking ahead there are two features that stand out. The first is transparency. This attribute will enable much more organic effects. Hopefully, people will use it to make effects more subtle and natural instead of just *more*. The second outstanding feature is the incorporation of Generator. The added functionality support goes a long way to making Flash a much more robust tool for creating technically powerful applications.

What have you been able to do with Flash that would not have been possible with other tools?

It's really the speed and the beauty of the rendering that makes Flash such a wonderful program to design in. (See Figure 12.5 for an example.) The vectors are responsive and clean. Traditional Web graphics and DHTML just don't allow the same level of fluid design that Flash accomplishes. Authoring in a timeline, object-oriented environment is intuitive and simple and improving with newer versions (namely version 3).

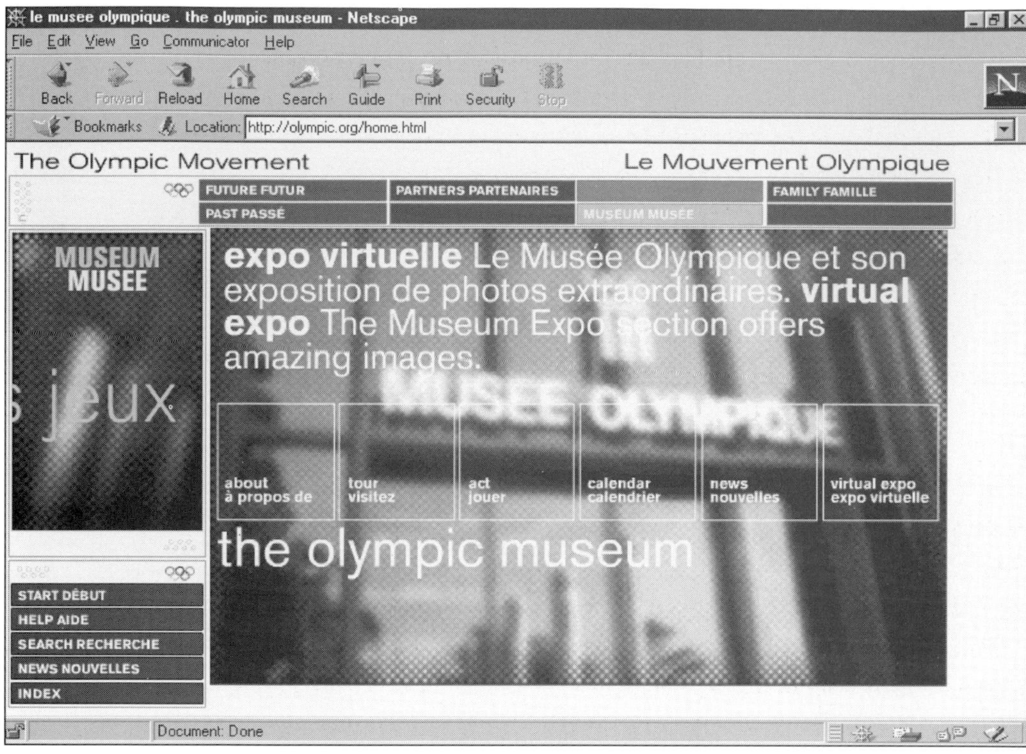

Figure 12.5 Quokka Sports used Flash to create the interactive museum section of the Olympics Web site.

Have you used Flash for drawing, or do you import images from other programs? If so, which ones, and have you encountered any stumbling blocks?

Both. When I teach Flash, I try to show people the advantages and disadvantages of drawing in the program as to drawing outside. The way Flash handles drawn objects is very awkward at first as it doesn't conform to the way most drawing programs deal with objects. Most people hate it at first, as did I. But once you understand the behavior of objects, people usually find it even more intuitive. Because of the behavior of the vectors, complex shapes and objects can be created quickly and altered over time easily. Once they are used to the tools, I recommend that users build moderately simple shapes right in Flash. For more-complex images, FreeHand interfaces with Flash fairly well, and I use that to develop anything that I think is beyond the ability of Flash to develop quickly.

Have you used Flash for storyboarding or drafts of designs?

Not for the Olympics as much, but now—and I get teased about it incessantly—I do all my design work right in Flash. Whether I'm designing a Web site, a postcard, typeface, whatever. Gone are the days of layout in Photoshop, because Flash works with objects much more intuitively. I can change type and move objects quickly. I still use Photoshop to fix my images, but then I bring them directly into Flash to work them into the layout. (See Figure 12.6 for an example.) No other program to date has offered the ease of use of design that Flash offers. I can create a design quickly, export it, take a screen snap of it or change the resolution instantly without affecting the design at all, and output to print or screen on the fly. It's disturbing how much of my work I actually do inside Flash now, even if it will never see the Web.

Have you used Flash in combination with other programs, such as Director, Authorware, Java, and so on?

Not any of those three, but of course I use Flash with nearly every program. I'm constantly jumping in and out of Photoshop, Flash, the 3D application of the day, Director, Premiere, etc. They all play. Because I can just paste nearly anything into Flash, or import pictures and sounds, it's all part of a process. More and more in this industry, the valuable designer isn't the one who knows the apps; it's the designer who looks

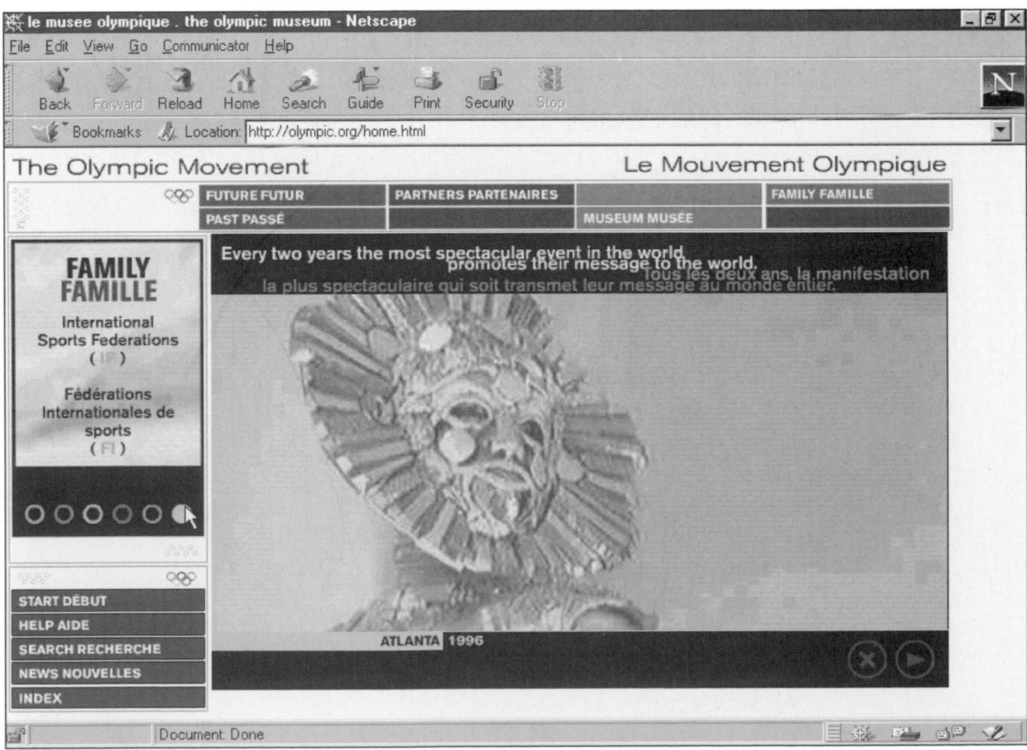

Figure 12.6 Quokka Sports used Flash to create the family section of the Olympics Web site.

beyond the app and sees the bigger picture being created. Then, you go off and find the right tool for the job. Too many designers today try and make the tool fit their idea, but the idea should always dictate the direction. Flash is just one tool in the process. It just happens to be a very powerful tool.

Have you simultaneously set up animations of multiple objects? What was the desired effect? Was Flash a good tool for this?

Yes, the Olympics site has several animations going simultaneously throughout the site. The way Flash sets up a timeline is key to its power. Flash isn't about creating basic animation, it's about creating interactive, animated environments that evolve over time. If it didn't do that, we wouldn't be talking about it.

Who is your target audience, and what are you doing to ensure that they are able to view your site (for example, using Aftershock, the <OBJECT> and <EMBED> tags, ActiveX, Java, and so on)?

We used a version of Macromedia smart installer scripts, but tweaked them to suit our own purposes. Basically, what happens is that there is a JavaScript detect script that looks to see if a browser is Java and Flash enabled. Depending on the intelligence gleaned from that, we send the browser to the appropriate page, either a Flash download page, a flat version of the site, or the Flash site itself.

What's the coolest thing you've done with Flash?

Another site I developed using Flash is the Remedi Project: Redesigning the Medium Through Discovery. The site, **ww.theremediproject.com**, is shown in Figure 12.7. It uses Flash's ability to incorporate bitmaps to give a wonderful illusion of integrated motion images. A butterfly comes to life on the canvas and moves throughout the environment, which really breaks down the dimension of space on the screen. The experimental nature of the work on the site (most of which was also done in Flash) makes it a wonderful place to open your mind about the limits of design on the Web today.

Interview With Elmer Erana, Fusion Media Group, Inc. (www.fusionmediagroup.com)

Fusion Media Group is a custom design house that creates projects for print, CD-ROMs, and the Web. Elmer Erana is the group's creative director. The animation studio division of the Fusion Media Group is a Flash

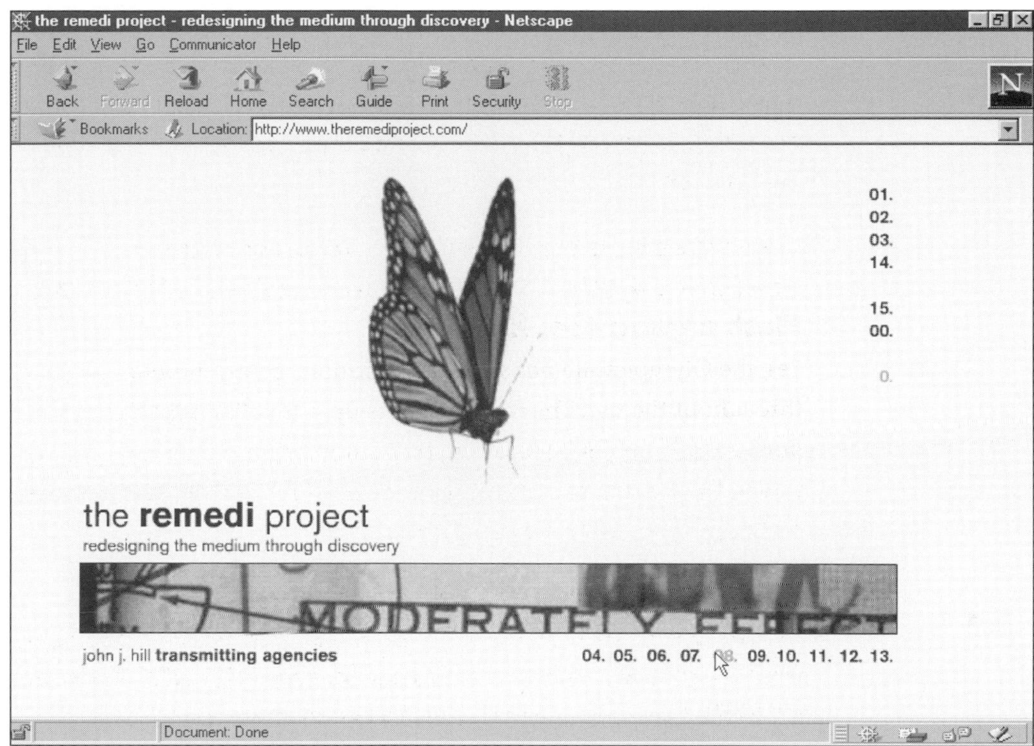

Figure 12.7 The Remedi Project is an innovative and powerful exploration of the Web as a design medium. Experience it at **www.remediproject.com**.

Leading Edge Partner and two-time winner of Macromedia's Shocked Site of the Day. The group specializes in Shockwave and created the E3 DIREKTIV project (shown in Figure 12.8) to showcase what could be done with multimedia on the Web. Fusion Media Group also created the Otaku e-zine site, an e-publication covering such topics as technology, subculture, visual arts, film, fashion, and literature—all with a new media edge. The site, located at **www.otakuezine.com**, also features Flash animations.

Why did you choose Macromedia's Flash?

Initially, we discovered the first version of Future Splash at MSN. Following the link revealed Macromedia with Flash 2 beta. Upon a single day's testing, it seemed so very straightforward that we prepurchased it online the next day, and have been using it since.

What's your favorite new feature in Flash 3?

I think the alpha channel support is high on the list. It provides a familiarity in layout to regular graphics, allowing more conventional methods to be employed during authoring. It also offers a level of broadcast quality, bringing the Internet closer to the television technology and

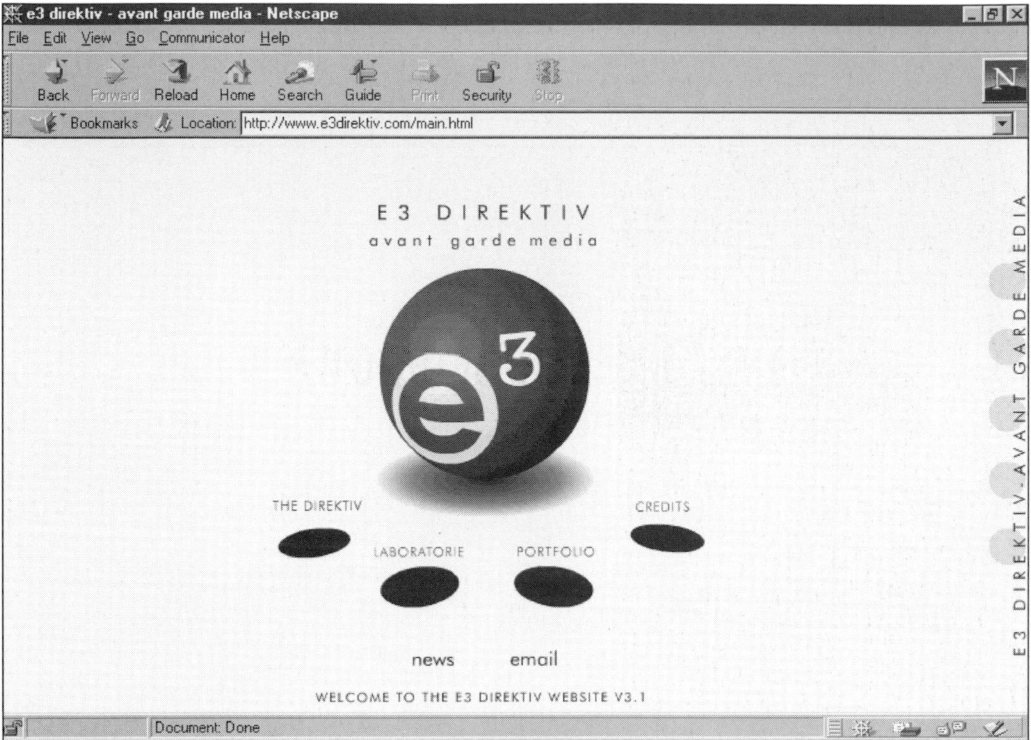

Figure 12.8 E3 DIREKTIV—Avant Garde Media at **www.e3direktiv.com/main.html**.

techniques already practiced. But the movie clip is quite a coup also, and thus would be a close tie. There are too many tricks and functionality additions... to not make a note of it.

What have you been able to do with Flash that would not have been possible with other tools?

Flash in general provides incredibly fast performance that is hard to beat for the file size. (See Figure 12.9 for an example.) It combines all the aspects of multimedia—dynamic transitions, streaming sound, and interactivity—into an inexpensive software.

Have you used Flash for drawing, or do you import images from other programs? If so, which ones, and have you encountered any stumbling blocks?

I personally am more adept drawing inside of the Flash program and often use it to illustrate for formats outside of Flash, although there are others in the design group who are more comfortable with Adobe Illustrator. Illustrator tends to have some unpredictable results importing into Flash when dealing with color accuracy, as well as sometimes the AI files wind up rather large in the Flash program, likely due to certain groupings or organized options in Illustrator.

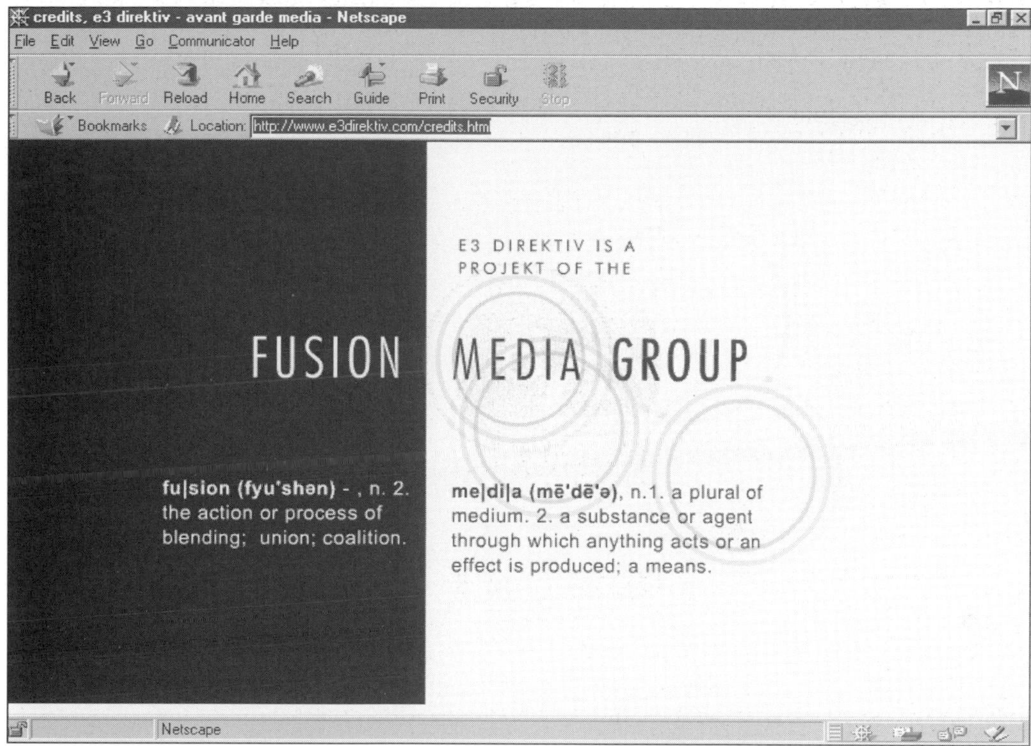

Figure 12.9 Fusion Media shows off a variety of Flash features in the site's credits at **www.e3direktiv.com/credits.html**.

Have you used Flash for storyboarding or drafts of designs?

We do use Flash for roughings, but we still resort to paper storyboarding for the artistic or visceral feel of the pencil in hand. I personally find, since Flash has some fast and simple drawing tools, it gets things done quickly for rough ideas.

Have you used Flash in combination with other programs, such as Director, Authorware, Java, and so on?

Currently, we have just been experimenting with Flash and Beatnik for alternative sound/music generation, and have dabbled with real Flash.

Have you simultaneously set up animations of multiple objects? What was the desired effect? Was Flash a good tool for this?

Yes, in a discarded movie, "TSR Wireless—Life of a Page Reject," the intent was to simulate the fantastic visuals of something like the movie *Hackers* or *Johnny Mnemonic*, with several moving objects, just perceptible to human eyes, to simulate an overload of information in the environment the user sees.

Flash was the only tool that would have allowed this to work on the Web at all; standard AVI or MOV production could have done the effect easily, but would have had a file size at least 100 times larger. (Figure 12.10 shows a Flash animation used to explain a complex concept with a very small file size.)

Who is your target audience, and what are you doing to ensure that they are able to view your site (for example, using Aftershock, the <OBJECT> and <EMBED> tags, ActiveX, Java, and so on)?

Our target audience is the more adventurous client, willing to do something different with their company or organization. After all, Flash is still a leading-edge technology, and thus shows initiative on the part of the client. If they can demonstrate that they are well-apprised of what is available, it seems they would appear wiser to their own clients also. These types of clients would likely have the latest browsers (as they are free now), and would see the most features, but we try not to diminish the experience to older browsers, thus dynamically write the code for the individual visitor. Flash also offers so much flexibility to the artistic quotient, as well as the interactivity that others can share in.

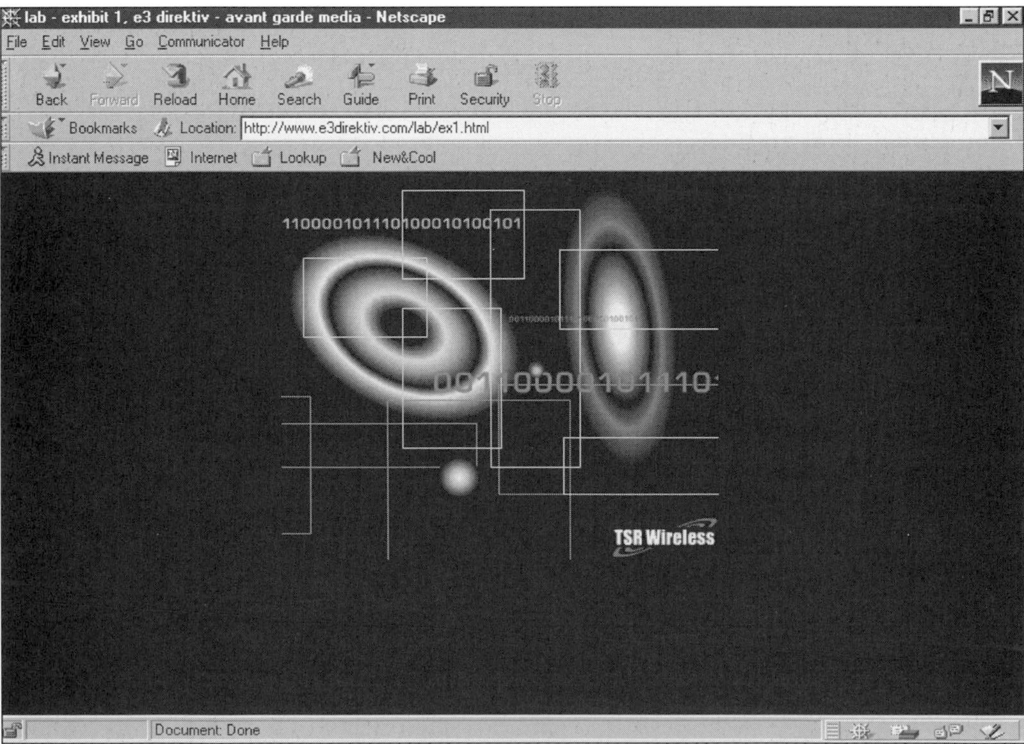

Figure 12.10 The TSR Wireless site uses Flash animations and transitions to provide a comprehensive demonstration of wireless technology.

We currently use comprehensive JavaScript detection routines to ensure current versions of plug-ins, combined with step-by-step install instructions for lower-version browsers. Smart Shockwave, as well as ActiveX, are utilized for the ease of the client. We are waiting for the Java player for Flash 3 to be functional, to offer the widest exposure.

What's the coolest thing you've done with Flash?

Well to date, the v3.1 E3 DIREKTIV 'DIREKTIV section' (shown in Figure 12.11) might have to be the coolest thing currently, as we have received many emails that attest to it. I personally have a short attention span, thus what is cool one second is replaced by something else the next. I really think the coolness is in the small details, and it's littered all over the place at the e3direktiv.com site, so it's like a small game of "where's the next thing" at DIREKTIV.

Do you have any favorite tricks for getting the most out of Flash?

"Tricks," in that context, I would word better as "techniques." The key thing would be to think in reverse when making Flash movies. Not only does it streamline planning of your movie functionality, it can start to

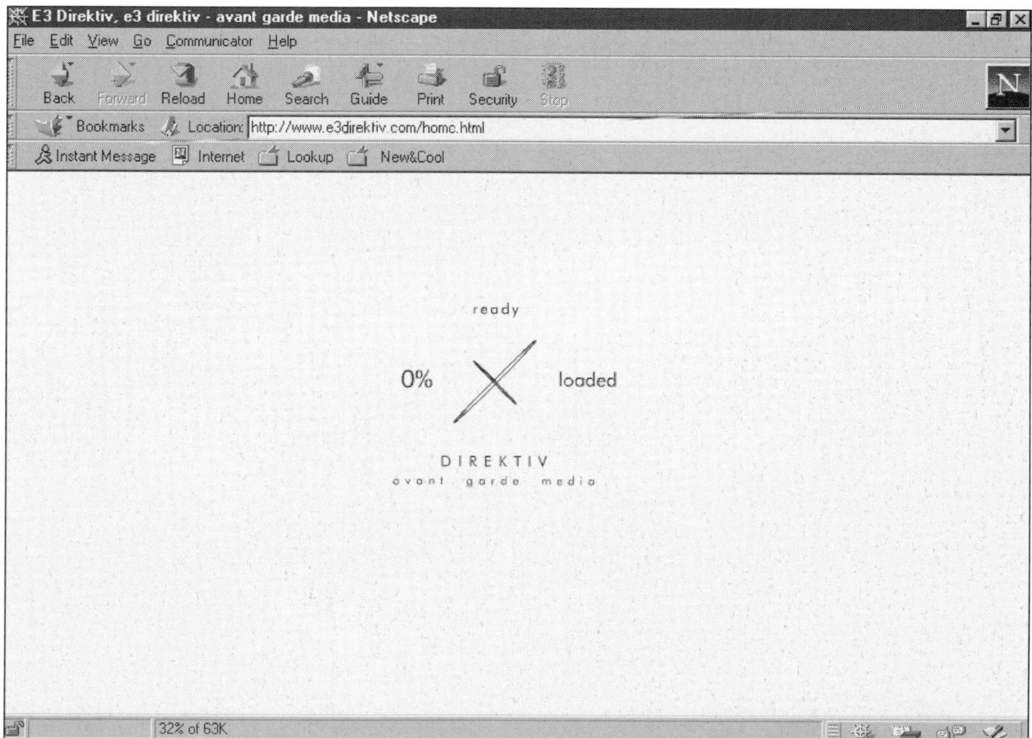

Figure 12.11 The opening animation at E3 DIREKTIV sets the tone for the variety of Flash techniques you'll find throughout the site.

adopt other schools of design. What I mean is to lay out the animation, for example, in the final positions it would be at (using graphic design layout), then start imagining the transitions for each component. This way, it's easier to visualize conflicts in motion before doing it. At least I think so. Lately, we have started to make single movies just as scrap layout sheets and are taking and pasting useful stuff into separate active movies. This is very helpful in using the newer "load movie" commands.

Briefly explain some solutions Flash provided for you and the steps you had to take to put them into effect.

Solutions-wise, it was easy and didn't require any effort on our part. The resolution-independent graphics solve many of the layout difficulties of HTML—of dealing with relative font sizes, faces, and graphics and text placement. All it took was the use of the percentage values to keep a controlled, universally common look to Web content.

Tell us anything else about your work with Flash technology that you think has been interesting, unique, or fun.

I think working with Flash is a very effective method of expressing creativity, without being so very highly technical. (Figure 12.12, a

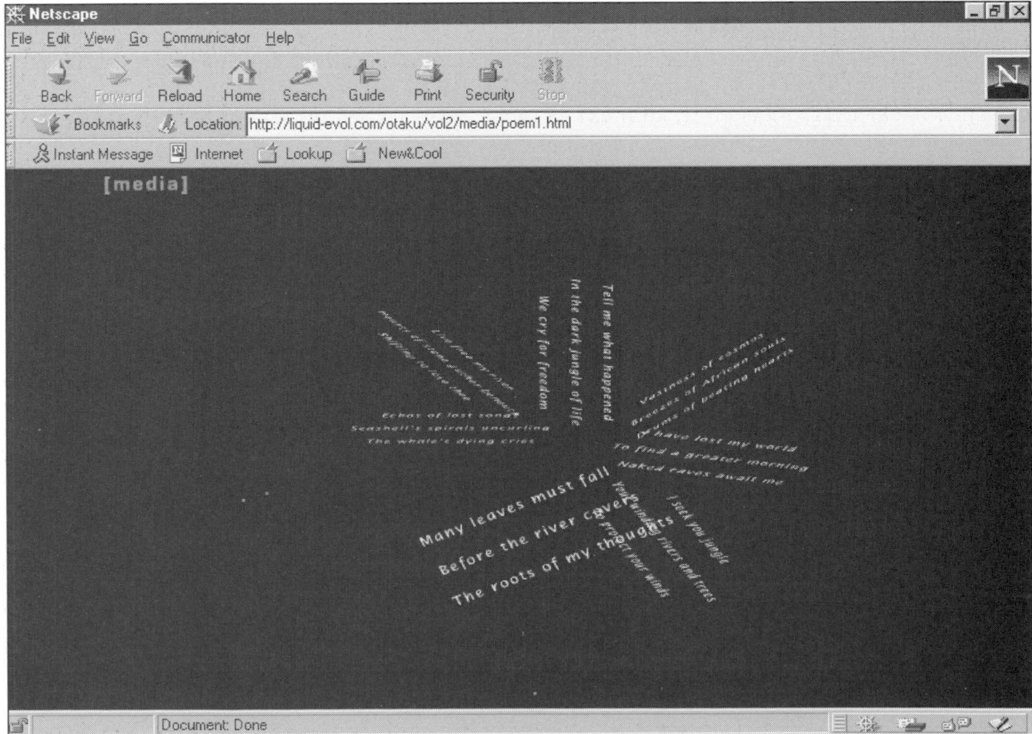

Figure 12.12 Visit **liquid-evol.com/otaku/vol2/media/poem1.html**, and you'll find Flash multimedia used to bring nontraditional poetry to life on the Web.

nontraditional poetry site, is a great example.) The program is easy enough to use so that anyone can make things with it and express more vividly what lurks in their souls. With this program, it seems that one can think purely and not be distracted by heavy technical issues, much like the spirit of how HTML and homepages became popular. Everyone can do it. I personally find it to be an outlet of cinematic or theatrical imagery that emerges in my thoughts, and Flash offers the perfect vehicle to express it more accurately than most mediums, with the purity of art.

Interview With Christopher Colshorn, I-D Gruppe (www.idgruppe.com)

I-D Gruppe is one of the world's leading multimedia agencies. I-D Gruppe has worked successfully on creative marketing concepts for international customers, including Swatch, West, Sony Europe, Peter Stuyvesant Travel, Bertelsmann Club, Metro, Hewlett Packard, and so on. Through the realization of Radar, the first European e-zine for cyberculture on CD-ROM, and the development of E-Cyas, a virtual megastar, I-D Gruppe has become a pioneer in cyberspace. (See Figure 12.13.)

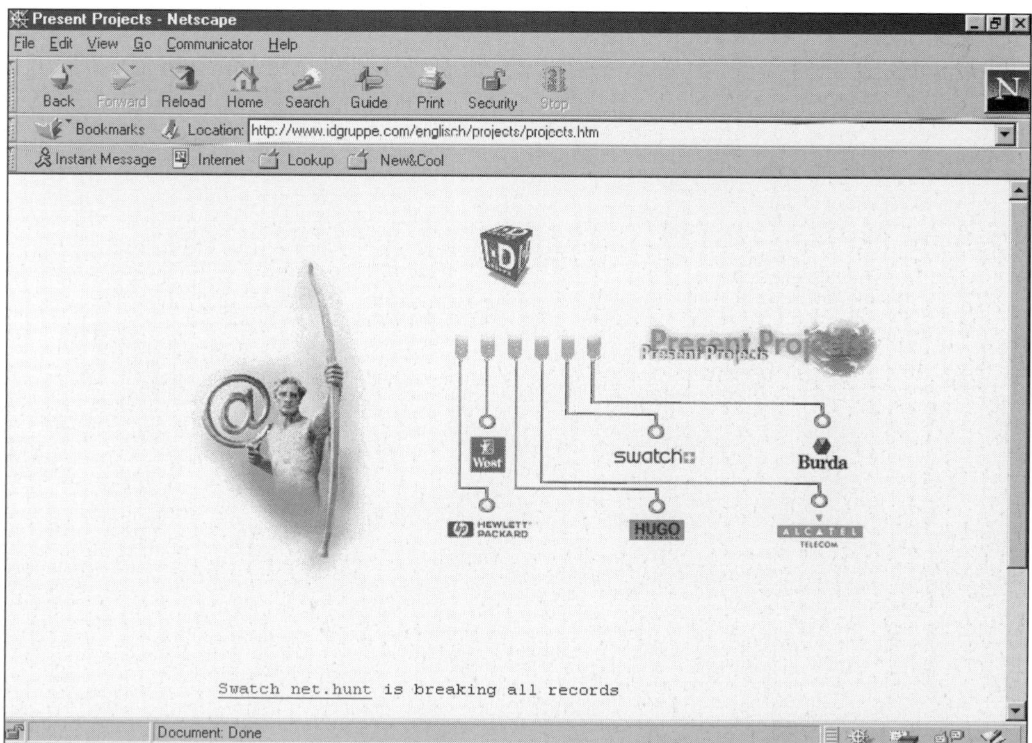

Figure 12.13 I-D Gruppe has developed sites for many clients, including Swatch, Hugo, and Sony Europe.

Why did you choose Macromedia's Flash?

We have used Flash since early 1997. Flash offers more possibilities for the presentation of multimedia on the Internet than any other tool on the market.

What's your favorite new feature in Flash 3?

The Flash technology is an outstanding innovation among all the new graphic possibilities. It enables Internet applications that convey completely new aesthetics compared to the usual page-orientated applications.

What have you been able to do with Flash that would not have been possible with other tools?

Large-scale animations and graphic effects in several new presentation forms in connection with object-oriented interaction. (Figure 12.14 is an example.)

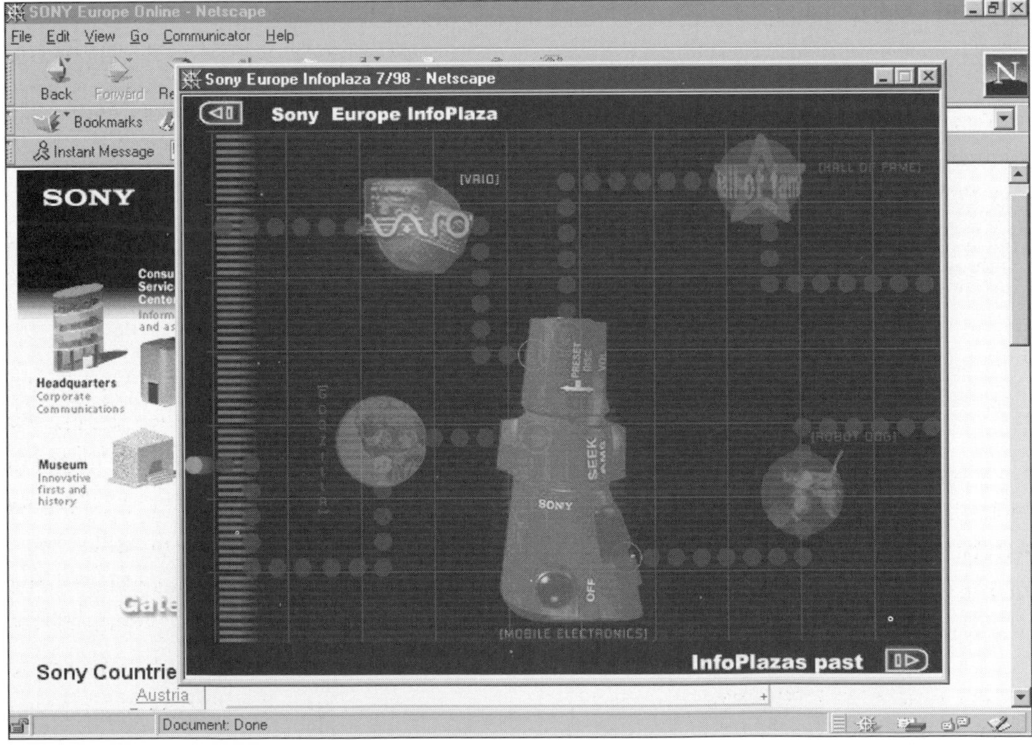

Figure 12.14 The Sony-Europe site (**www.sony-europe.com**) combines startling sound files with animation techniques.

Have you used Flash for drawing, or do you import images from other programs? If so, which ones, and have you encountered any stumbling blocks?

The editing and production of vector graphics is simple but very effective. The majority of vector graphics in our applications were produced directly in Flash. FreeHand is, of course, also used. PNG graphics are realized in Photoshop, are then imported to Flash, and some of them are processed further after break-apart.

Have you used Flash for storyboarding or drafts of designs?

Due to its simple user interface, we use flash frequently for storyboarding.

Have you used Flash for any non-Web purpose, such as offline presentations, sketching ad layouts, illustration, or CD-ROM content?

Yes, for the Sony-Europe Environment Center we produced a CD-ROM application in three languages that will be presented on several terminals at Expo 1998, where it will also be given to the visitors. This application will also be on the Internet.

Have you used Flash in combination with other programs, such as Director, Authorware, Java, and so on?

We are working on it. The combination of Flash and Director is currently being planned for a project.

Have you simultaneously set up animations of multiple objects? What was the desired effect? Was Flash a good tool for this?

Yes, of course. The animation of multiple objects is one of the strongest features of Flash 3. Flash 3 actually demands an object-oriented construction of the animations.

Who is your target audience, and what are you doing to ensure that they are able to view your site (for example, using Aftershock, the <OBJECT> and <EMBED> tags, ActiveX, Java, and so on)?

In our opinion, Flash is one of the Internet technologies of the future. Today, Internet surfers expect high quality, an interesting design with interaction possibilities, and a short loading time for the Web sites. These users have the Flash plug-in already or want it immediately. Our target is the user who's looking for entertainment and information. Smart Shockwave is the technology that we use in the main site as it offers the user a comfortable installation of the Flash plug-in. For some projects, we are currently also offering an HTML version for users without the Flash plug-in.

What's the coolest thing you've done with Flash?

The Web site for Sony camcorders at **www.sony-europe.com/camcorder/** (shown in Figure 12.15) and the CD-ROM for the Sony Europe Environment Center.

Do you have any favorite tricks for getting the most out of Flash?

By combining all Flash possibilities—depending on the importance of the individual feature—new applications become possible. The challenge is that these applications at first sight cannot be realized with Flash. These alleged weaknesses of the tool, however, can be compensated for by an open concept. This approach makes Flash exciting and enables surprising applications.

Tell us anything else about your work with Flash technology that you think has been interesting, unique, or fun.

There is so much to tell, lots of workarounds, the fun of creating applications never seen before. A

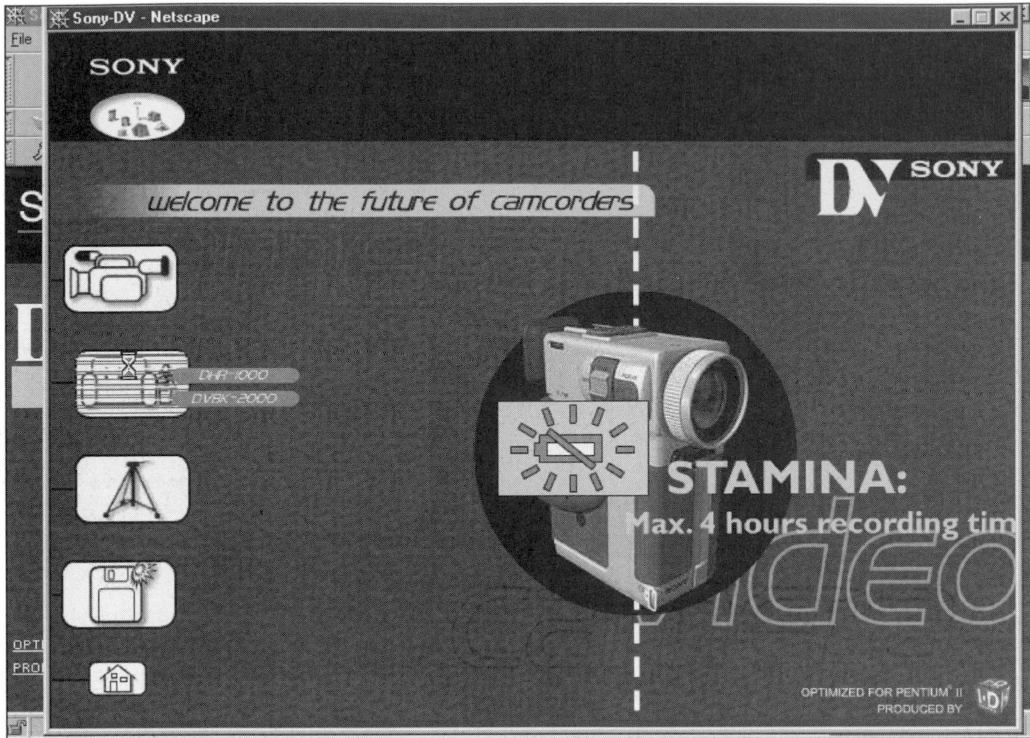

Figure 12.15 The camcorder section of the Sony-Europe Web site at **www.sony-europe.com/camcorder**.

year ago, I started to build a Flash team in our company. Now, six people are working in this exciting group. There is a lot of fun and great development in this group. This makes it fun because they have a tool that gives all of them a chance to show their different skills and to create group projects.

Moving On

The case studies described in this chapter demonstrate a range of uses for Flash. Whether you are sharing the spirit of the Olympic games with the world, or demonstrating a technical concept, or putting poetry on the Web, Flash provides an excellent development solution.

Throughout this book, you learned tips and techniques for creating Flash animations. For more ideas, spend some time on the Web visiting sites like the ones in this chapter, as well as others featured at Macromedia's site at **www.flash.com**.

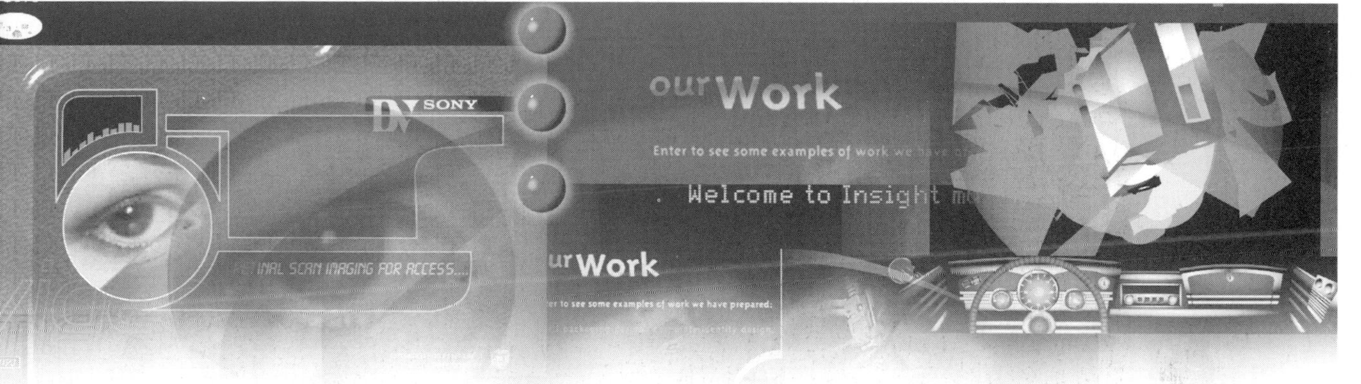

Appendix: Using Tell Target

Ken Milburn

One of the most powerful new features of Flash 3 is the Tell Target action found in the Frame Properties dialog box. Yet, the feature is so sparsely documented in the manual that users are just now discovering how to take advantage of it. This appendix presents the basic facts about using Tell Target and provides a tutorial that will help you understand the feature and its potential.

Tell Target is such a useful and powerful feature because it adds interactivity and provides yet another way to optimize performance.

Tell Target allows one movie to direct the playing of any frame in another movie. The other movie is stored as a movie clip symbol, so that the entire main movie loads before the symbols do. Different symbol instances can also be used multiple times without increasing download times. In addition, the main movie can point to different topics, each of which is a different movie clip.

Tell Target Tutorial

This tutorial will give you only the basics of how to employ Tell Target. (Beyond that, I could write another book on the possible uses of this feature alone. In the meantime, use your imagination, go to work, and give me lots of good ideas for that book.)

The following steps will guide you through a Tell Target action:

1. Start by opening a movie into which you want to incorporate a Tell Target action. (For practice's sake, this can be any movie of several frames.)
2. First, we'll make a symbol that is going to be the target of this action. Make sure nothing is selected and choose Insert|Create Symbol (or press F8).
3. The Symbol Properties dialog box appears. (See Figure A.1.) Enter "Blip" as the name for this symbol, and then click on the Movie Clip Behavior radio button. Click on OK. A new, blank movie will appear in the form of a blank stage.
4. Now, we'll make a simple animation so that you can see that your action is working. Choose the Pencil tool and the straighten modifier. Draw a rectangle.
5. On the Layer 1 Timeline, highlight the first frame and press F6 (or choose Insert|Insert Keyframe from the Frame pull-down menu). A new frame will be entered with an exact copy of the rectangle in it. Repeat this step.
6. Select Frame 3 and choose the Arrow tool, then distort one side of the cube.
7. Highlight the next two frames and insert keyframes in them by pressing F6.

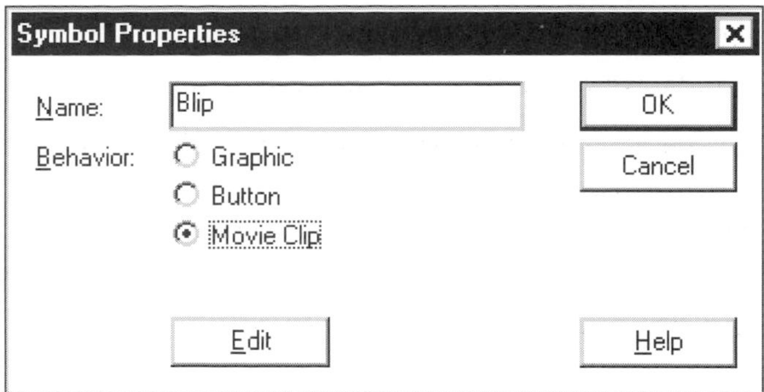

Figure A.1 The Symbol Properties dialog box.

8. Select Frame 5 and distort the next side of the rectangle in a clockwise rotation.
9. Highlight the next two frames and insert keyframes in them by pressing F6.
10. Select Frame 7 and distort the next side of the rectangle in a clockwise rotation.
11. Highlight the next two frames and insert keyframes in them by pressing F6.
12. Select Frame 9 and distort the next side of the rectangle in a clockwise rotation. In the last two frames, all four sides of the rectangle will be distorted.
13. Move the frame pointer to the first frame, choose the Text tool and choose a large font size. (I used 72 points.) Type the letter *A* in the center of the rectangle. Now, skip to Frame 3 and place a large *B* in the center of the rectangle. In every other frame, place a consecutive letter of the alphabet. You have now created a nice little movie clip for practicing actions; you'll be able to see whether the frames you've targeted are the correct frames.
14. From the menu bar, choose Edit|Edit Movie. Your symbol will disappear.
15. Click on the Layer button for the first empty layer, and choose Insert Layer from the Layers menu. Double-click on the automatically assigned layer name and enter "Movie Clip" as the new layer name.
16. Choose Window|Library (unless the Library window already happens to be in view). Scroll until your Blip symbol is visible in the

Preview window, then drag it from there onto the stage (or canvas, to those familiar with earlier versions of Flash).

17. From the menu bar, choose Control|Test Movie. Your movie should open in the Player, and the new symbol will be playing in the background. When you're satisfied that everything is working, close the Player window.

18. Make sure the Timeline's Frame pointer is over Frame 1. Choose the Arrow tool and double-click on the Blip symbol. The Instance Properties dialog box will appear. (See Figure A.2.) In the Instance Name field, enter "InstanceOne". Click on the Edit button.

19. Now, here comes a very important trick. You often want to keep your movie clips invisible until your Tell Target action dictates otherwise. Select the first frame and, from the Frame pull-down menu, choose Insert Frame. Unfortunately, you can't insert a blank frame before the first frame, so we'll have to work around that limitation.

20. Select the first frame again. From the Frame pull-down menu, choose Copy Frames. Now, select the second frame and choose Paste Frames from the Frame pull-down menu. The first frame has been copied into the blank second frame.

21. Select the first frame again. From the menu bar, choose Edit|Select All and press Delete/Backspace. The first frame is now empty.

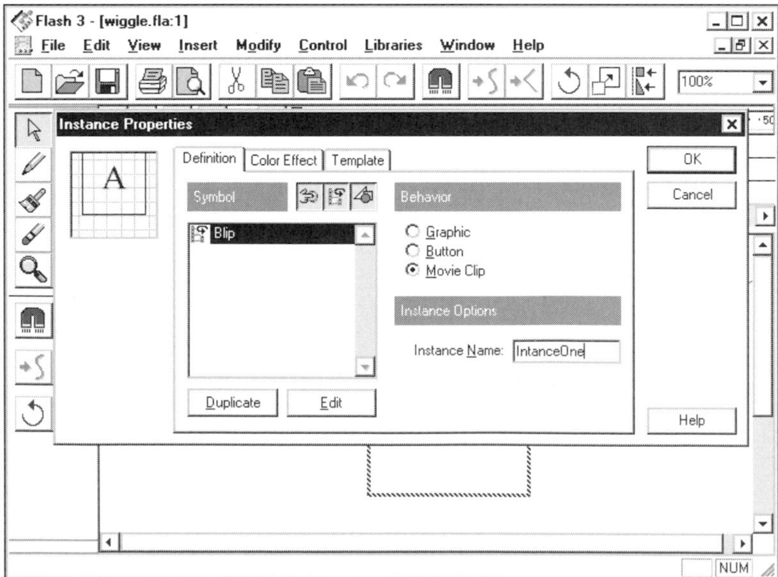

Figure A.2 The Instance Properties dialog box.

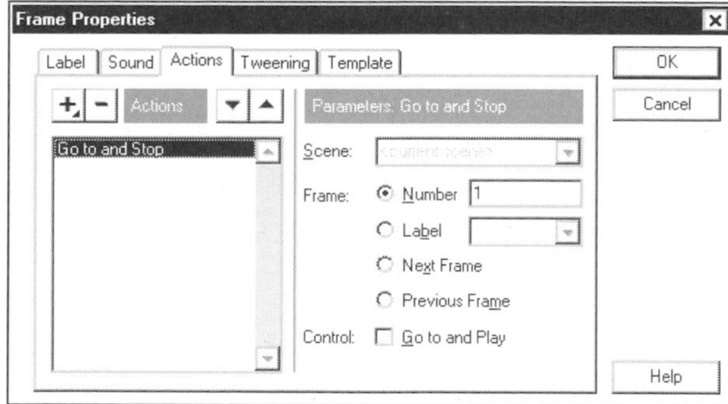

Figure A.3 The Frame Properties dialog box.

22. Now, you're going to attach an action to a frame. With the first frame still selected, choose Properties from the Frames menu. The Frame Properties dialog box will appear. (See Figure A.3.) Click on the Actions tab.

23. Click and hold the plus sign (+) button, and choose Go To from the Add Actions menu. The parameters you want are automatically chosen in this case. Note that the Action reads Go To And Stop. Take a minute to look over your other choices; you may have many reasons to use them in the future. Click on OK.

24. Now, test your movie. Choose Control|Test Movie. Your original movie will play, but there will be no sign of the movie clip instance you just placed. It's there, but it's frozen onto the blank frame, making it invisible. Close the Player window.

25. Next, you'll make a new symbol. This will be a button that controls the playback of Instance One of your movie clip. Press F8 (or choose Insert|Create Symbol). The Symbol Properties dialog box will appear.

26. In the name field, enter "Button". Also, select the Button Behavior radio button and click on OK (or Edit).

27. Select the Up frame. On the stage, draw a shape that will be your button. A simple rectangle will do for now. Fill the button with a color and superimpose "Stop/Start" in white text over it.

28. In the same spirit of keeping things simple, select the frames for the other three states and press F6 (or choose Insert Keyframe from the Frame pull-down menu). Edit the copied graphic in the Over and Down frames so that you will see a change when the different states occur.

29. When you've finished, choose Edit|Edit Movie.

30. Drag your Stop/Start button from the library to where you want it to appear on the stage and then double-click on it. The Instance Properties dialog box will appear. (See Figure A.4.) Click on the Actions tab.

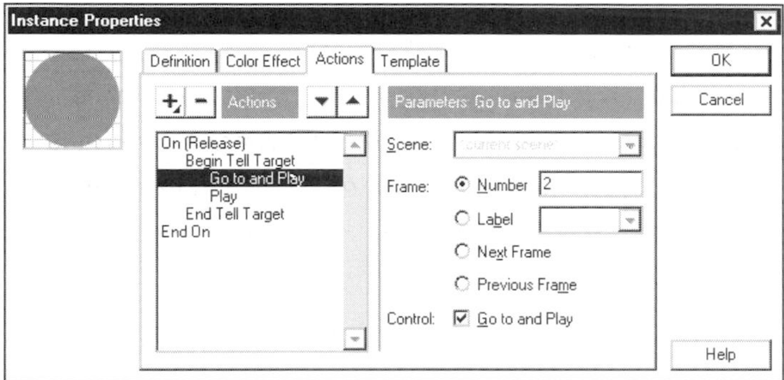

Figure A.4 The Instance Properties dialog box.

31. From the Add Actions menu, choose (finally!) Tell Target. Click on the line Begin Tell Target. InstanceOne (the Instance name of this occurrence of the Blip symbol) will appear in the window below Parameters. Double-click on the instance name, and it will appear in the Target field as InstanceOne.

32. With Begin Tell Target still selected, choose Go To from the Add Actions (+) menu. The default parameter will be Go To And Stop. Click on the Control checkbox and the parameter will change to Go To And Play.

33. Click on the Frame Number radio button and enter "2" in the adjacent field. Click on OK.

34. From the Menu Bar, choose Control|Test Movie. Test your movie and the buttons to see that they are working properly.

Wow! If you have paid careful attention, you have made a Tell Target action work properly. It's not a forgiving process, so if your test isn't working, you're leaving out something.

Things You Should Remember About Tell Target

Creating successful Tell Target actions becomes a lot easier if you just remember a few simple rules.

- *Target Instances, not the movie clip.* Remember, a single movie clip can appear in any number of places and variants. So, unless you target a specific instance, Flash has no way of knowing which of these occurrences you want to affect—therefore, nothing happens. Also, you must name each instance. (Otherwise, there will be nothing to target in the Begin Tell Target parameters.)
- *Remember the blank first frame trick.* If you want your movie clip to be invisible until a frame or button requests it, make sure the first frame contains nothing (or, that the objects it contains are transparent). Then, all you have to do is put a Stop action in the first frame of the movie clip. The movie clip will then remain invisible until another action plays it.
- *You can have one target tell another target, which tells yet another target, and so on.* Any frame in any movie clip can have an action attached to it. This is an excellent way to have your movie download only what is needed, when it's needed.
- *Tell Target works by making Timelines communicate.* It's easy to forget that a Flash movie can contain virtually any number of Timelines. First, any movie can contain any number of movie clips. Each of these clips has its own Timeline and can also contain other movie clips...and each of these has its own Timeline. Also, you can attach a Load Movie action to any of these Timelines.
- *Timelines must overlap one another in order to be targeted.* In other words, if you want the Timeline for a 25-frame movie that starts at Frame 1 to target the Timeline for a 15-frame movie or movie clip that doesn't start until Frame 40 (or even 26), you're out of luck.
- *You can place any of the other actions between Begin Tell Target and End Tell Target.* The other actions are Go To, Play, Stop, Toggle High Quality, Stop All Sounds, Get URL, FS Command, Load Movie, Unload Movie, Tell Target, If Frame Is Loaded, and On MouseEvent.

Note: *Actions, including Tell Target, will execute properly in all Flash Players that are compatible with Flash 3. They will not work (yet) in browsers that have only the Flash 2 plug-in installed, or in the Java Player, or in the Real Flash Player. Macromedia says that upgrades to the aforementioned players are just a matter of time.*

Some Suggestions On Ways To Use Tell Target

I don't know if anyone's figured out every possible Tell Target trick. I suspect we've just begun to scratch the surface. As a start, though, here are some cool applications for the action that might trigger your imagination to reach for even greater heights.

Use Tell Target To Control Sound

Remember, you can store sounds as movie clips. So you can have a sound effect come in over a particular range of frames, while a different sound effect (say the background music) continues to play under it.

Scroll Text At A Particular Frame Or The State Of A Button

Scroll your text in a movie clip and insert a blank frame at the beginning. Then, when a particular frame plays or a given button state is reached, use a Tell Target action to Go To and Play the scrolling text.

Hide Buttons Until You Need Them

If you place buttons in the main movie, they'll be there even when you don't want to look at them. You could hide them temporarily by placing an opaque layer over them, but there's a slicker way: Place the buttons in a movie clip with a blank first frame. Then, have the appropriate frame in the main movie target the movie clip with a Go To and Play starting at Frame 2. When you want the buttons to disappear again, assign a Go To and Stop that targets Frame 1 of the buttons' movie clip.

Make The Same Item Change With Each Click Of A Button

You can make a movie clip that consists of a series of still frames, each of which could contain an entirely different subject. Then, create a button and assign the click event to a Tell Target action that includes a Go To And Play with Next Frame as the parameter. Be sure to also assign a Stop action to each of the frames in the movie clip. Then, when you click on the button, the targeted movie clip jumps to the next frame and freezes until you click on the button again. You could use a variation of the same technique to change the wording on a sign or change the score on a scoreboard.

INDEX

3D effects, 291-292
3D tools, 303-304
100% command, 36

A

About Flash command, 46
Action calls, tracking, 45
Action forms
  FS Command, 265-266
  Get URL, 265
  Goto, 264-265
  If Frame Is Loaded, 267-268
  Load Movie, 266
  On MouseEvent, 268
  Tell Target, 267
  Unload Movie, 266-267
Actions
  attaching to buttons, 268-269
  attaching to frames, 270-271
  new features in Flash 3, 7
  specifying mouse events for, 268
ActiveX controls on HTML pages, 322-323
Actors. *See* Symbols.
Add Motion Guide command, 59
Aftershock, 70-73
AIFF files, 12
Align button, 49
Align command, 41
Align dialog box, 41, 132-133
Aligning objects. *See also* Grids; Guide layers; Rulers.
  Align button, 49
  Align command, 41
  Align dialog box, 132-33
  Grid command, 36
  Rulers command, 36
  Snap button, 49
  Snap command, 36
  Snap tool modifier, 115
  snapping to grid lines, 132
Alignment, tool modifier, 120
Animation. *See also* Scenes (pages); Symbols.
  buttons
    Flash 2, 13
    graphic, 191-192, 211-213
    new features in Flash 3, 7, 13
    Onion Skin, 182-185
    from symbols, 179, 191-192, 211-213
  color, 161-163
  color changes, 12
  color shifting, 167
  concentric shapes (exercise), 150-153
  creating (exercise), 141-150
  data streaming, 16
  dissolves, 163-165
  drawing (exercise), 105-113
  fading in/out, 163-165, 167, 169-170
  flashing images, 169-170
  flashing lights, 153-156
  frame by frame, 165
  frames
    definition, 140
    viewing thumbnails of, 175
  FreeHand, 293-295
  guide layers, 176, 216-218
  layers
    definition, 173
    Layer menu, 174-175
  looping, 319
  maximum movie length, 141
  morphing, 166, 170-171
  motion guide layers
    creating, 37, 59
    definition, 176
    description, 131-132
  motion paths, 168-169
  moving along a path, 166
  multilayer, 213
  Onion Skin buttons, 182-185
  onion-skinning, 182-185
  opacity, 161-163
  playing over a modem, 16
  pulsing, 169-170
  radiating lines (exercise), 158-160
  radio waves (exercise), 150-153
  rotating, 166
  scaling, 166
  skewing, 166
  spinning (exercise), 160-163
  stick figures, 166

still-frame sequences, 172-173
strobe effects, 173
transition effects, 163-165
traveling images (exercise), 156-158
tweening
color effects, 169-172
definition, 166-167
editing frames, 161
exercise, 156-158
with a path, 168-169
setting up a tween, 167-168
shapes, 170-171
wipes, 163-165
zooming (exercise), 160-163
Antialias command, 36
Antialias Text command, 36
Antialiasing
Antialias command, 36
Antialias Text command, 36
automatic, 16-18
definition, 4
GIF format, 26
graphics, 16-18
on HTML pages, 320, 324-325
text, 16-18
turning off, 36
Antialiasing command, 196
Arrange All command, 44
Arrange command, 38, 134-135
Arrow, cursor shape, 114
Arrow tool
definition, 50
description, 114
modifiers, 115
selecting objects, 114-115
Artifacts, 4
Artificial intelligence, tuning, 33
Assistant command, 33
Assistant dialog box, 133-136
Authorware program, 27-28
Autotracing. *See also* Tracing.
bitmap graphics, 22
photographs, 24

B

BASE attribute, 319
BASE parameter, 322
Behaviors
assigning to symbols, 7
on HTML pages, 313-314
Bezier curves, 283-284
BGCOLOR attribute, 319
BGCOLOR parameter, 322
Bitmap graphics
advantages of, 297-298
autotracing, 22
converting from vector graphics, 299
definition, 3-4
drawing, 93
exporting as, 69-70
in Fireworks, 298-300
minimizing size of, 22
as symbols, 193
Blank Keyframe command, 37
Blends, 284-286
Bold, tool modifier, 120
Borders, HTML pages, 325
Break Apart command, 41
Brush, cursor shape, 124
Brush, tool modifier, 125
Brush Size menu, tool modifier, 125
Brush Style menu, tool modifier, 125
Brush tool
definition, 50
description, 124
modifiers, 125
Buttons, graphic. *See also* Action forms.
adding sound to, 191-192
animation
Flash 2, 13
graphic, 191-192, 211-213
new features in Flash 3, 7, 13
Onion Skin, 182-185
from symbols, 179, 191-192, 211-213
attaching actions to, 268-269
attaching sounds to, 269-270
cascading events, 270
changing properties of, 200
concave/convex appearance, 258
concentric shapes as, 255-256
creating, 190-191
creating from existing objects, 261-262
creating from scratch, 260-261
definition, 190
describing functions of, 272

drawing, 254-255
drop shadows, 259
editing symbols as, 259
enabling, 42
Flash 2 features, 13
going to a specific frame or scene, 264-265
gradient fills, 258
interactivity, 263-268
inverting gradient colors, 271
movie URLs, specifying, 265
new features in Flash 3, 7
online examples of, 271
placing in scenes, 263
rounded rectangles as, 256-258
status, 360
testing, 263
Web site about, 271
Buttons, mouse. *See* Mouse buttons.
Buttons, toolbar. *See* Toolbar buttons.
Buttons command, 43

C

Canvases, 53-54
Cascade command, 45
Cascading events, 270
Case studies
Colshor, Christopher, 349-352
Erana, Elmer, 342-349
Fusion Media Group, Inc., 342-349
I-D Gruppe, 349-352
Quokka Sports, 336-342
Ulm, Josh, 336-342
Characters. *See* Symbols.
CLASSID parameter, 323
Clear command, 34
Clear Keyframe command, 37
Clip art. *See also* Graphics.
from commercial CDs, 88
editing (exercise), 87-92
including in movies, 76-77
sources for, 76-77
Close command, 32
CODEBASE parameter, 322
Color, tool modifier
Brush tool, 125
Paint Bucket tool, 127
Pencil tool, 122
Text tool, 120
Color palette, displaying, 45
Color shifting, animation, 167
Colors
animation, 161-163
changes, animating, 12
changing, 201-202
controls for, 202
distinguishing layers with, 215-216
dithering in GIF format, 27
fading in/out, 202-204
HTML backgrounds, 319, 322
layers, 59
painting, 50
setting number of in GIF format, 26
tint effects over time, 204-205
tweening, 169-170, 202
Colors command, 45
Colshor, Christopher, 349-352
Commands
100%, 36
About Flash, 46
Add Motion Guide, 59
Align, 41
Antialias, 36
Antialias Text, 36
Arrange, 38
Arrange All, 44
Assistant, 33
Blank Keyframe, 37
Blue Outlines, 59
Break Apart, 41
Buttons, 43
Cascade, 45
Clear, 34
Clear Keyframe, 37
Close, 32
Colors, 45
Controller, 45
Copy, 34
Copy Frames, 35
Create Symbol, 37
Current, 59
Curves, 41
Cut, 34
Delete Frame, 37
Delete Layer, 59
Deselect All, 35

Duplicate, 34
Edit All, 35
Edit Selected, 35
Edit Symbols, 35
Enable Buttons, 42
Enable Frame Actions, 42
Exit, 33
Export Image, 32
Export Movie, 32
Fast, 36
Flash Developer's, 46
Flash Help Topics, 46
Font, 38
Frame, 37-38
Frames, 41
Goto, 36
Graphics, 43
Green Outlines, 59
Grid, 36
Group, 41
Guide, 59
Guided Tour, 46
Hidden, 59
Hide Others, 59
Import, 32
Insert Layer, 59
Insert Object, 35
Inspector, 45
Instance, 38
Kerning, 38
Keyframe, 37
Layer, 37
Lessons, 46
Library, 45
Links, 35
Lock Others, 59
Locked, 59
Loop Playback, 42
Mask, 59
Motion Guide, 37
Movie, 38
Movie Clips, 43
Mute Sounds, 42
New, 32
New Window, 44
Normal, 59
Normal Color, 59
Object, 35
Open, 32
Open Library, 32
Outlines, 36
Output, 45
Page Setup, 32
Paragraph, 38
Paste, 34
Paste Frames, 35
Paste In Place, 34
Paste Special, 34
Play, 42
Play All Scenes, 42
Preferences, 33
Print, 33
Print Preview, 32
Properties, 59
Purple Outlines, 59
Red Outlines, 59
Redo, 34
Register Flash, 46
Remove Scene, 37
Rewind, 42
Rulers, 36
Samples, 46
Save, 32
Save As, 32
Scene, 37-38
Select All, 34
Settings, 42
Show All, 36, 59
Show Frame, 36
Show Masking, 59
Show Shape Hints, 36
Snap, 36
Sounds, 43
Step Backward, 42
Step Forward, 42
Style, 38
Tabs, 36
Template Command, 37
Test Movie, 42
Test Scene, 42
Timeline, 36
Toolbar, 45
Trace Bitmap, 41
Transform, 38, 134-135
Undo, 34
Ungroup, 41

Work Area, 36
Yellow Outlines, 59
Concave buttons, 258
Concentric shapes, animating, 150-153
Control menu, 42-43
Controller command, 45
Convex buttons, 258
Copy button, 48
Copy command, 34
Copy Frames command, 35
Copying properties of objects, 128-129
Copying to the Clipboard. *See* Cut, copy and paste.
Cornerpoints, new features in Flash 3, 9
Create Symbol command, 37, 196
Cropping HTML pages, 325
Cross hair, cursor shape, 116
Current command, 59
Cursor shapes
arrow, 114
brush, 124
cross hair, 116
eraser, 127
eyedropper, 128
ink bottle, 123
lasso, 129
magnifier, 129
paint bucket, 126
pencil, 120
Curves
customizing, 41
optimizing, 135-136
Curves command, 41, 135
Cut, copy and paste, 34, 48
Cut button, 48
Cut command, 34
Cutting to the Clipboard. *See* Cut, copy and paste.

D

Data streaming, 16
Delete command, 196
Delete Frame command, 37
Delete Layer command, 59
Deselect All command, 35
Dialog boxes
Align, 41, 132-133
Assistant, 133-136
Export GIF, 26
Export Shockwave Flash, 247-248
Font, 40
Frames Properties, 39-40
Insert Object, 35
Instance Properties, 39
Magic Wand Options, 130
Movie Properties, 40
Optimize Curves, 40
Paragraph Properties, 40
Paste Special, 35
Scene Properties, 40
Sound Properties, 241-243
Trace Bitmap, 41
Director, 27-28, 73
Dissolves, 163-165
Drawing. *See also* Drawing tools; FreeHand; Sketching.
for animation (exercise), 105-113
bitmapped graphics, 93
buttons, 254-255
clip art
from commercial CDs, 88
editing (exercise), 87-92
sources for, 76-77
copying properties of objects, 128-129
erasing, 127-128
Flash 3 limitations, 137
gradients, 124
line styles, specifying, 123-124
lines, 120-122
optimizing curves, 135-136
with Photoshop, 93
saving as symbols, 93
selecting multiple objects, 78, 89-91
selecting touching objects, 92
setting preferences for, 133-136
shape-recognition tolerances, specifying, 133-136
tips for efficiency, 95
tracing an existing drawing (exercise), 78-87
zooming in/out, 129
Drawing Assistant, 33
Drawing tools
Arrow
definition, 50
description, 114
modifiers, 115

Brush
definition, 50
description, 124
modifiers, 125
Dropper
definition, 50
description, 128-129
Eraser
definition, 50
description, 127
modifiers, 128
Ink Bottle
definition, 50
description, 123
modifiers, 123-124
Lasso
definition, 50
description, 129-130
modifiers, 130
Magnifier
definition, 50
description, 129
Paint Bucket
definition, 50
description, 126
modifiers, 126-127
Pencil
definition, 50
description, 120-121
modifiers, 121-122
Text
definition, 50
description, 116-119
modifiers, 119-120
Dreamweaver
checking plug-ins, 313-314, 315
creating HTML pages, 300-303
definition, 73
as HTML editor, 311-313
inserting movies on Web pages, 311-313
Web site about, 315
Drop shadows, 65, 259
Dropper tool
definition, 50
description, 128-129
Duplicate command, 34, 196

E

Edit All command, 35
Edit command, 196
Edit menu, 34-35
Edit Selected command, 35
Edit Symbols command, 35
Editing
clip art, 87-92
Edit All command, 35
Edit command, 196
Edit menu, 34-35
Edit Selected command, 35
Edit Symbols command, 35
frames, 161
groups, 57-58
HTML, 310-313
layers, 59
links, 35
photographs, 93
shapes, 22-25
symbols, 35, 56, 197, 259
text, 50
video, 27-28
<EMBED> tag
attributes of, 319-322, 323
BASE attribute, 319
BGCOLOR attribute, 319
combining with **<OBJECT>** tags, 318
definition, 317-318
HEIGHT attribute, 319
LOOP attribute, 319
MENU attribute, 320
PLAY attribute, 320
PLUG-INSPAGE attribute, 320
QUALITY attribute, 320
SALIGN attribute, 321
SCALE attribute, 321-322
WIDTH attribute, 319
Embossing, 291-292
Enable Buttons command, 42
Enable Frame Actions command, 42
Envelope distortion, 292-293
Erana, Elmer, 342-349
Eraser, cursor shape, 127
Eraser Mode menu, tool modifier, 128

Eraser tool
    definition, 50
    description, 127
    modifiers, 128
Erasing objects
    drawings, 127-128
    Eraser Mode menu, tool modifier, 128
    Eraser tool
        definition, 50
        description, 127
        modifiers, 128
Events, cascading, 270
Exit command, 33
Export file types, 21
Export GIF dialog box, 26
Export Image command, 32
Export Movie command, 32
Export settings, specifying, 42
Export Shockwave Flash dialog box, 247-248
Exporting
    animations from FreeHand, 279-283
    drawings from FreeHand, 278-279
    to GIF format, 25-27
    images, 32
    to JPEG format, 27
    movies, 32
    for Web browsers, 328-329
Eyedropper, cursor shape, 128

F

Fading in/out, 163-165, 167, 169-170
Fast command, 36
Faucet toggle, tool modifier, 128
File extensions, 21, 79
File menu, 32-33
File types for import/export, 21
Files
    closing, 32
    opening, 32, 48
    saving, 32, 48
Fill Lock toggle, tool modifier, 125
Fills
    Brush tool, 50, 124-125
    Paint Bucket tool, 50, 126-127
Fireworks, 297-300
Flash 2
    AIFF files, 12
    animated buttons, 13
    animated color change, 12
    automatic antialiasing, 16
    cutting a sound, 12
    data streaming, 16
    MIDI files, 12
    plug-in, installing, 14-15
    synchronized sound, 12
    WAV files, 12
Flash 3
    ease of use, 4-5
    exiting, 33
    new features
        actions, 7
        animated buttons, 7
        assigning behaviors to symbols, 7
        automated HTML creation, 10
        cornerpoints, 9
        displaying shape properties, 8
        frame comments, 8
        frame label, 8
        frame selection, 8-9
        FreeHand support, 11
        Inspector window, 8
        interactive Web sites, 9
        layer masks, 7
        morphing, 7
        movie clips, 7
        performance reporting, 10
        PNG graphics support, 10-11
        selecting multiple objects, 8-9
        standalone projector, 11
        templates, 9
        transparent graphics, 6
        tweening, 7
    registering, 46
    registration information, displaying, 46
    speed, 3-4
    universal playback standard, 3
    versatility, 5-6
Flash Developer's command, 46
Flash Generator
    definition, 73-74
    templates, 73-74, 250-251
Flash Help Topics command, 46
Flashing effects, 153-156, 169-170
Flipping graphics, 134-135
Font command, 38

Font dialog box, 40
Font menu, tool modifier, 120
Font Size menu, tool modifier, 120
Fonts. *See* Text.
Frame command, 37-38
Frame-by-frame animation, 165
Frames
    adding to layers, 37
    animation, 140
    attaching actions to, 270-271
    checking if loaded, 267-268
    comments, 8
    copying, 35
    definition, 140
    deleting, 37
    displaying current, 36
    enabling actions in, 42
    going to a specific, 264-265
    keyframes, 37
    label, 8
    naming, 38
    pasting, 35
    reversing order of, 41
    selecting, 8-9
    synchronizing, 41
    tweened, editing, 161
    viewing thumbnails of, 175
Frames command, 41
Frames Properties dialog box, 39-40
FreeHand
    3D effects, 291-292
    animations, automatic, 293-295
    Bezier curves, 283-284
    blends, 284-286
    converting to HTML, 295-297
    drag-and-drop with Flash 3, 277-278
    drawing, 283-284
    embossing, 291-292
    envelope distortion, 292-293
    exchanging graphics with Flash 3, 276-277
    exercise, 95-105
    exporting animations, 279-283
    exporting drawings, 278-279
    Flash 3 support for, 11
    overview, 93-94
    polygons, 289-291
    rectangles, precision, 289
    rounded rectangles, 289
    stars, 289-291
    text, curving, 286-289
    Web site about, 277
FS Command form, 265-266
Fusion Media Group, Inc.
    case study, 342-349
    Web site about, 342

G

GalaxyNet Telecom, Web site about, 332
Gap Size menu, tool modifier, 127
Get URL form, 265
GIF format
    antialiasing, 26
    colors, dithering, 27
    colors, setting number of, 26
    definition, 70
    exporting to, 25-27
    image dimensions, 25
    interlacing, 26
    versus JPEG, 25
    resolution, 26
    transparency, 26
Goto command, 36
Goto form, 264-265
Gradient colors, inverting, 271
Gradient fills, buttons, 258
Gradient Lock, tool modifier, 127
Gradient Transformation, tool modifier, 127
Gradients, 124
Graphics
    animating. *See* Animation.
    autotracing photographs, 24
    changing properties for, 199-200
    creating, 188-189
    definition, 188
    displaying shape properties, 8
    editing shapes, 22-25
    exporting, 32
    flipping, 38, 134-135
    image dimensions, GIF format, 25
    import/export file types, 21
    importing, 32
    outlines, 36
    page dimensions, setting, 22-25
    rotating, 38, 134-135
    scaling, 38, 134-135

shape recognition, tuning, 33
smoothing edges of. *See* Antialiasing.
tracing bitmaps, 41
transforms, 38, 134-135
transparency, 6

Graphics command, 43
Grid command, 36
Grids
aligning objects on, 36, 49
definition, 52
description, 130-131
toggling on/off, 36, 130

Group command, 41
Groups
breaking apart, 41
creating, 41, 57
definition, 56-57
editing, 57
leaving Group Edit mode, 57-58

Guide command, 59
Guide layers, 176, 216-218. *See also* Motion guide layers.
Guided Tour command, 46

H

HEIGHT attribute, 319
HEIGHT parameter, 323
Help
Help menu, 46-47
In-Context Help, 49
samples, 46
shape hints, 36
tech support, 46
tutorials, 46

Help menu, 46-47
Hidden command, 59
Hide Others command, 59
HTML attributes
BASE attribute, 319
BGCOLOR attribute, 319
HEIGHT attribute, 319
LOOP attribute, 319
MENU attribute, 320
PLAY attribute, 320
PLUG-INSPAGE attribute, 320
QUALITY attribute, 320
SALIGN attribute, 321
SCALE attribute, 321-322
WIDTH attribute, 319

HTML pages
ActiveX controls, 322-323
antialiasing, 320, 324-325
background color, 319, 322
base directory, specifying, 319, 322
borders, 325
converting FreeHand pages to, 295-297
converting movies with
Aftershock, 306-311
Dreamweaver, 300-303
Insta.HTML, 70
creating automatically, 10
cropping, 325
editing with Aftershock, 310-311
height and width, 319, 321-323, 325
looping animations, 319
movies
looping, 324
playing, 324
positioning on the page, 321, 325
starting on download, 320
and multimedia, 315
right mouse button, menu for, 320, 324
scaling, 319, 321-323, 325
specifying plug-ins for, 320
tables, 318

HTML parameters
BASE parameter, 322
BGCOLOR parameter, 322
CLASSID parameter, 323
CODEBASE parameter, 322
HEIGHT parameter, 323
LOOP parameter, 324
MENU parameter, 324
MOVIE parameter, 324
PLAY parameter, 324
QUALITY parameter, 324-325
SALIGN parameter, 325
SCALE parameter, 325
WIDTH parameter, 323

HTML tags
<EMBED>
attributes of, 319-322, 323
combining with **<OBJECT>** tags, 318
definition, 317-318

<**OBJECT**>
combining with <**EMBED**> tags, 318
definition, 317
parameters of, 322-326

I

I-D Gruppe
case study, 349-352
Web site about, 349-352
If Frame Is Loaded form, 267-268
Images. *See* Graphics.
Import command, 32
Import file types, 21
Importing
graphics, 32, 136-137
sounds, 237-238
In-Context Help button, 49
Ink bottle, cursor shape, 123
Ink Bottle tool
definition, 50
description, 123
modifiers, 123-124
Insert Layer command, 59
Insert menu, 37
Insert Object command, 35
Insert Object dialog box, 35
Inspector command, 45
Inspector window
activating, 45
definition, 8
Insta.HTML
converting from FreeHand, 295-297
definition, 295
exporting to, 70
Instance command, 38
Instance Properties dialog box, 39
Interactivity
buttons, 263-268
scenes, 227-229
Web sites, 9
Interlacing, GIF format, 26
Italic, tool modifier, 120

J

Jim Curry's Virtual Museum, Web site about, 271
JPEG format
definition, 70
exporting to, 27
versus GIF, 25

K

Kerning, 38, 65
Kerning command, 38
Keyboard shortcuts. *See* Shortcut keys.
Keyframe command, 37
Keyframes
clearing, 37
creating, 37
Keyhole effects, 220-223

L

Lasso, cursor shape, 129
Lasso tool
definition, 50
description, 129-130
modifiers, 130
selecting objects, 129-130
Layer command, 37
Layer masks, new features, 7
Layer menu, 58-59, 174-175
Layers
adding, 37
characteristics of, 213-214
coloring outlines, 215-216
colors, 59
creating content on, 214
definition, 58, 173
deleting, 59
displaying, 59
distinguishing between, 215-216
editing, 59
guide, 176, 216-218
hiding, 59, 215
inserting, 59
keyhole effects, 220-223
Layer menu, 174-175
locking, 59, 215
mask layers, 59, 220-223
motion guide, 176
creating, 37, 59
definition, 176
description, 131-132
motion path layers, 218-220

moving contents between, 226-227
renaming, 59
selectively displaying outlines, 59
showing, 215
sound layers, 223-224
spotlight effects, 220-223
stacking order, 225
and tweens, 214
Leading, 65
Lessons command, 46
Library command, 45
Library menu
adding libraries to, 196-197
Antialiasing command, 196
command summary, 43-44
Create Symbol command, 196
definition, 12-13
Delete command, 196
Duplicate command, 196
Edit command, 196
opening, 32, 45
Play command, 196
Properties command, 196
Select Unused Media command, 196
Symbol menu, 196
symbols, 196
Update command, 196
Line spacing, 65
Line Style menu, tool modifier, 122
Line Thickness menu, tool modifier, 122
Lines
drawing
brush, 50
pencil, 50, 120-122
rotating, 49
scaling, 49
smoothing, 49
straightening, 49
styles, specifying, 123-124
Links, editing, 35
Links command, 35
Load Movie form, 266
Lock Others command, 59
Locked command, 59
Locking layers, 215
LOOP attribute, 319
LOOP parameter, 324
Loop Playback command, 42

M

Macromedia, Web site about, 6, 271
Magic Wand, tool modifier, 130
Magic Wand Options dialog box, 130
Magnifier, cursor shape, 129
Magnifier tool
definition, 50
description, 129
Magnifying. *See* Zooming in/out.
Margins, 65
Mask command, 59
Mask layers, 220-223
MENU attribute, 320
Menu bar
Control menu, 42-43
definition, 30
Edit menu, 34-35
File menu, 32-33
Help menu, 46-47
illustration, 31
Insert menu, 37
Library menu, 43-44
Modify menu, 38, 41, 135-136
View menu, 36-37
Window menu, 44-46
MENU parameter, 324
MIDI files, 12
Mode menu, tool modifier, 122
Modify menu
Arrange command, 134-135
command summary, 38, 41
Curves command, 135
Optimize command, 135-136
Transform command, 134-135
Morphing
new features in Flash 3, 7
tweening, 166, 170-171
Motion Guide command, 37
Motion guide layers
creating, 37, 59
definition, 176
description, 131-132
Motion path layers, 218-220
Motion paths, 168-169
Mouse buttons
menu for right button, 320, 324
Movie area, 52

Movie Clips command, 43
Movie command, 38
MOVIE parameter, 324
Movie Properties dialog box, 40
Movies
- audio event compression, 248
- audio event rate, 248
- audio stream compression, 248
- audio stream rate, 248
- bitmaps, converting to JPEGs, 247
- changing properties for, 201
- controlling sequence of, 228-229
- converting to HTML with
  - Aftershock, 70-73, 306-311
  - Insta.HTML, 70
- creating, 48
- definition, 192
- in existing HTML documents, 73
- exporting, 32, 69-70, 245-248, 250
- frame actions, 229
- height and width on HTML pages, 319, 321-323, 325
- inserting sounds in, 193
- loading/unloading, 266
- looping, 324
- maximum length, 141
- maximum number of scenes, 30
- maximum size, 30
- modifying, 38
- new features in Flash 3, 7
- in new HTML documents, 72
- overriding sound settings, 248
- playing
  - from an HTML file, 248, 250
  - on different Web browsers, 3
  - frame by frame, 42
  - on HTML pages, 324
  - from a local drive, 248
  - in a loop, 42
  - with a standalone player, 248, 249
  - with a standalone projector, 248, 249-250
  - start to finish, 42
  - from Web browsers *versus* offline, 63-64
- positioning on HTML pages, 321, 325
- preventing download of, 247
- samples, 46
- scaling on HTML pages, 319, 321-323, 325
- selecting a Flash version for, 248
- size statistics, creating, 247
- specifying URLs for, 265
- starting on download, 320
- starting/stopping, 267
- testing, 42

Moving along a path, 166
Music. *See* Sounds.
Mute Sounds command, 42

N

New command, 32
New Movie button, 48
New Window, 44
New Window command, 44
Normal Color command, 59
Normal command, 59

O

Object command, 35
<OBJECT> tag
- **BASE** parameter, 322
- **BGCOLOR** parameter, 322
- **CLASSID** parameter, 323
- **CODEBASE** parameter, 322
- combining with <EMBED> tags, 318
- definition, 317
- **HEIGHT** parameter, 323
- **LOOP** parameter, 324
- **MENU** parameter, 324
- **MOVIE** parameter, 324
- parameters of, 322-326
- **PLAY** parameter, 324
- **QUALITY** parameter, 324-325
- **SALIGN** parameter, 325
- **SCALE** parameter, 325
- **WIDTH** parameter, 323

Objects. *See also* Symbols.
- aligning, 36, 41, 49
- copying properties of, 50
- erasing, 50
- inserting, 35
- selecting
  - Arrow tool, 114-115
  - clearing selected objects, 34-35
  - Deselect All command, 35
  - duplicating selected objects, 34

Edit Selected command, 35
freehand, 129-130
Lasso tool, 50, 129-130
multiple at once, 78, 89-91
Select All command, 34
when objects touch, 92
On MouseEvent form, 268
Onion Skin buttons, 182-185
Onion-skinning, 182-185
Opacity, 161-163
Open command, 32
Open File button, 48
Open Library command, 32
Optimize command, 135-136
Optimize Curves dialog box, 40
Outlines command, 36
Output command, 45
Overlays. *See also* Groups.
breaking apart, 41
definition, 56-57
stacking order, 38

P

Page Setup command, 32
Pages. *See* Scenes (pages).
Paint bucket, cursor shape, 126
Paint Bucket tool
definition, 50
description, 126
modifiers, 126-127
Paragraph command, 38
Paragraph formatting, tool modifier, 120
Paragraph Properties dialog box, 40
Paragraphs, 38, 65
Paste button, 48
Paste command, 34
Paste Frames command, 35
Paste In Place command, 34
Paste Special command, 34
Paste Special dialog box, 35
Pasting from the Clipboard. *See* Cut, copy and paste.
Pencil, cursor shape, 120
Pencil tool
definition, 50
description, 120-121
modifiers, 121-122
Performance reporting, 10
Photo-editing programs, exporting to, 69-70
Photographs
autotracing, 24
editing, 93
Photoshop, 93
Pictures. *See* Clip art; Graphics; Photographs.
Play All Scenes command, 42
PLAY attribute, 320
Play command, 42, 196
PLAY parameter, 324
Playing movies
from an HTML file, 248, 250
on different Web browsers, 3
frame by frame, 42
on HTML pages, 324
from a local drive, 248
in a loop, 42
over a modem, 16
with a standalone player, 248, 249
standalone projector, 11
with a standalone projector, 248, 249-250
start to finish, 42
from Web browsers *versus* offline, 63-64
Plug-ins
checking with Dreamweaver, 313-314, 315
installing, 14-15
specifying, 320
PLUG-INSPAGE attribute, 320
PNG format
definition, 70
Flash 3 support, 10-11
Polygons, 289-291
Preferences, setting, 33
Preferences command, 33
Pressure button, tool modifier, 125
Print button, 48
Print command, 33
Print preview, 32
Print Preview button, 48
Print Preview command, 32
Printing
from the File menu, 33
page setup, 32
print preview, 48
from the toolbar, 48
Properties
button, changing, 200

- displaying for shapes, 8
- Frames Properties dialog box, 39-40
- Instance Properties dialog box, 39
- movie clip symbol, changing, 201
- Movie Properties dialog box, 40
- object, copying, 50, 128-129
- paragraph, setting, 38
- Paragraph Properties dialog box, 40
- Properties command, 59, 196
- Property Inspector, 302-303
- Scene Properties dialog box, 40
- shape, displaying, 8
- Sound Properties dialog box, 241-243
- symbol, changing, 198-199

Properties command, 59, 196
Property Inspector, 302-303
Pulsing effects, 169-170

Q

QUALITY attribute, 320
QUALITY parameter, 324-325
Quokka Sports
- case study, 336-342
- Web site about, 336

R

Radiating lines, animating, 158-160
Radio waves, animating, 150-153
RealFlash Generator, 332-333
Rectangles
- rounded, 289
- square, precision of, 289

Redo button, 49
Redo command, 34
Redoing actions, 34, 49
Register Flash command, 46
Remove Scene command, 37
Resolution, GIF format, 26
Rewind command, 42
Rotate, tool modifier, 115
Rotate button, 49
Rotating graphics, 134-135
Rotating in animations, 166
Rounded rectangles as buttons, 256-258
Rulers
- definition, 52
- toggling on/off, 36
- units of measure, specifying, 64

Rulers command, 36

S

SALIGN attribute, 321
SALIGN parameter, 325
Samples command, 46
Save As command, 32
Save command, 32
Save To Disk button, 48
Scale, tool modifier, 115
SCALE attribute, 321-322
Scale button, 49
SCALE parameter, 325
Scaling
- animations, 16, 166
- automatic, 16
- definition, 4
- graphics, 16, 134-135

Scene command, 37-38
Scene Properties dialog box, 40
Scenes (pages)
- actions, 228-229
- buttons in, 263
- creating, 180-182, 228
- deleting, 37
- displaying tabs, 36
- going to a specific, 264-265
- inserting, 37
- interactive, 227-229
- *versus* movies, 227
- naming, 227
- navigating, 36, 181
- rewinding, 42
- tabs, toggling on/off, 181
- testing, 42, 227

Select All command, 34
Select Unused Media command, 196
Selected objects
- clearing, 34
- deselecting, 35
- duplicating, 34

Selecting frames, 8-9
Selecting objects
- Arrow tool, 114-115
- clearing selected objects, 34-35

Deselect All command, 35
duplicating selected objects, 34
Edit Selected command, 35
freehand, 129-130
Lasso tool, 50, 129-130
multiple at once, 78, 89, 90, 91
Select All command, 34
when objects touch, 92
Settings command, 42
Shape hints, 36
Shape properties, displaying, 8
Shape recognition, tuning, 33, 133-136
Shape/Size menu, tool modifier, 128
Shortcut keys
Control menu, 42-43
Edit menu, 34-35
File menu, 32-33
Help menu, 46-47
Insert menu, 37
Library menu, 43-44
Modify menu, 38, 41
View menu, 36-37
Window menu, 44-46
Show All command, 36, 59
Show Frame command, 36
Show Masking command, 59
Show Shape Hints command, 36
Sketching. *See also* Drawing.
autotracing, 22
comprehensives, 19
simple shapes, 66-68
storyboards, 19-20
tracing a bitmap image, 22
Skewing in animations, 166
Smooth, tool modifier, 115
Smooth button, 49
Smoothing the edges of. *See* Antialiasing.
Snap button, 49
Snap command, 36
Snap tool modifier, 115
Snapping to grid lines, 132
Sound files, optimizing, 244
Sound layers, 223-224
Sound Properties dialog box, 241-243
Sounds
attaching to buttons, 269-270
on buttons, 242-244
channel previews, 239
cutting, 12
event *versus* streaming
description, 237
selecting, 241
fading, 240
importing, 237-238
looping, 241
muting, 42
play controls, 240
quality statistics, 238-239
reusing, 243
setting options for, 238
Sound pull-down menu, 238
special effects, 240-241
starting at a frame, 241
stopping at a frame, 241
synchronized, 12
Tell Target, 360
testing, 244-245
timelines, 239
Web browsers, 332
zooming, 240
Sounds command, 43
Specifying plug-ins for, 320
Spinning effects, 160-163
Spotlight effects, 220-223
Sprites. *See* Symbols.
Stages. *See* Canvases.
Standalone projector, 11
Star shapes, 289-291
Step Backward command, 42
Step Forward command, 42
Stick figures and animation, 166
Still-frame sequences, 172-173
Straighten, tool modifier, 115
Straighten button, 49
Strobe effects, 173
Style command, 38
Symbol menu, 196
Symbol palette. *See* Library menu.
Symbols. *See also* Objects.
animating, 197
assigning behaviors to, 7
bitmaps, 193
breaking apart, 41
buttons
adding sound to, 191-192
animating, 179, 191-192, 211-213

changing properties for, 200
creating, 190-191
definition, 190
as buttons, 259
color effects
changing, 201-202
controls for, 202
fading in/out, 202-204
tint effects over time, 204-205
tweening, 202
combining, 208-211
creating, 37, 55-56, 179-180
definition, 55
from drawings, 93
editing, 35, 56, 197
graphic
animating, 179
changing properties for, 199-200
creating, 188-189
definition, 188
versus groups, 177-178
instances of
changing, 198-199
creating, 197-198
definition, 197
modifying, 38
movies
animating, 179
changing properties for, 201
definition, 192
inserting sounds in, 193
properties, changing, 198-199
saving. *See* Library menu.
using, 56

T

Tables on HTML pages, 318
Tabs
definition, 52
toggling on/off, 181
Tabs command, 36
Tech support, 46
Tell Target
buttons
hiding, 360
status, 360
stepping through a movie, 360
controlling sounds, 360
definition, 354
rules for using, 358-359
scrolling text, 360
tutorial, 354-358
Tell Target form, 267
Template Command, 37
Templates
Flash 3 new features, 9
Flash Generator, 73-74, 250-251
Template commands, inserting, 37
Test Movie command, 42
Test Scene command, 42
Testing
buttons, 263
movies, 42
scenes, 42, 227
sounds, 244-245
Test Movie command, 42
Test Scene command, 42
Text
curving, 286-289
drop shadows, 65
entering, 116-120
kerning, 65
leading, 65
line spacing, 65
margins, 65
paragraphs, 65
typing and editing, 50
typographic effects, 38, 65
Text tool
definition, 50
description, 116-119
modifiers, 119-120
Timeline
definition, 51
toggling on/off, 36
Timeline command, 36
Tool modifiers
Alignment, 120
Arrow tool, 115
Bold, 120
Brush Size menu, 125
Brush Style menu, 125
Brush tool, 125

- Color
  - Brush tool, 125
  - Paint Bucket tool, 127
  - Pencil tool, 122
  - Text tool, 120
- definition, 51
- Eraser Mode menu, 128
- Eraser tool, 128
- Faucet toggle, 128
- Fill Lock toggle, 125
- Font menu, 120
- Font Size menu, 120
- Gap Size menu, 127
- Gradient Lock, 127
- Gradient Transformation, 127
- Ink Bottle tool, 123-124
- Italic, 120
- Lasso tool, 130
- Line Style menu, 122
- Line Thickness menu, 122
- Magic Wand, 130
- Magic Wand Options dialog box, 130
- Mode menu, 122
- Paint Bucket tool, 126-127
- Paragraph formatting, 120
- Pencil tool, 121-122
- Pressure button, 125
- Rotate, 115
- Scale, 115
- Shape/Size menu, 128
- Smooth, 115
- Snap, 115
- Straighten, 115
- Text tool, 119-120

Toolbar, definition, 48-49

Toolbar buttons
- Align, 49
- Copy, 48
- Cut, 48
- In-Context Help, 49
- New Movie, 48
- Open File, 48
- Paste, 48
- Print, 48
- Print Preview, 48
- Redo, 49
- Rotate, 49
- Save To Disk, 48
- Scale, 49
- Smooth, 49
- Snap, 49
- Straighten, 49
- Undo, 49
- Zoom Pull-Down Menu, 49

Toolbar command, 45

Toolbox, 50

Tools. *See* Drawing tools.

Trace Bitmap command, 41

Trace Bitmap dialog box, 41

Tracing. *See also* Autotracing.
- an existing drawing (exercise), 78-87
- bitmaps, 22, 41

Transform command, 38, 134-135

Transforming graphics, 134-135

Transition effects, 163-165

Transparency
- Alpha channels, 229-230
- bitmaps, 229-230
- fading in/out, 234-236
- flashing effects, 234-236
- GIF format, 26
- gradients, 232-234
- JPEG format, 229
- new features in Flash 3, 6
- solid colors, 231-232
- symbol instances, 230-231
- tweening, 234-236

Traveling images, 156-158

Tutorials, 46

Tweening
- color effects, 169-172
- definition, 166-167
- editing frames, 161
- exercise, 156-158
- new features in Flash 3, 7
- with a path, 168-169
- setting up a tween, 167-168
- shapes, 170-171

Tweens. *See also* Blends.
- in layers, 214
- shape *versus* motion, 218

Type. *See* Text.

Typographic effects, 38, 65

U

Ulm, Josh, 336-342
Undo button, 49
Undo command, 34
Undoing actions, 34, 49
Ungroup command, 41
Units of measure, specifying, 64
Universal playback standard, 3
Unload Movie form, 266-267
Update command, 196
URLs mentioned in this book. *See* Web sites of interest.
User interface. *See also* Commands; Dialog boxes; Drawing tools; Menu bar; Shortcut keys; Toolbar buttons; Windows.
    canvases, 53-54
    grids, 52
    illustration of, 31
    Layer menu, 58-59
    movie area, 52
    rulers, 52
    tabs, 52
    Timeline, 51
    tool modifiers, 51
    toolbar, 48-49
    toolbox, 50

V

VCR control window, controlling playback, 45
Vector graphics
    converting to bitmap graphics, 299
    definition, 3-4
Video editing programs, 27-28
View menu, 36-37
Voices. *See* Sounds.

W

WAV files, 12
Web browsers
    built-in Flash 3, 328
    designing movies for, 306-311
    download performance, monitoring, 329-331
    exporting for, 328-329
    identifying, 329
    music, 332
    playing Flash 3 movies, 3
    RealFlash Generator, 332-333
    sound, 332
    universal playback standard, 3
    voice, 332
Web sites, interactive, 9
Web sites of interest
    buttons, graphic, 271
    Dreamweaver, 315
    FreeHand, 277
    Fusion Media Group, Inc., 342
    GalaxyNet Telecom, 332
    I-D Gruppe, 349-352
    Jim Curry's Virtual Museum, 271
    Macromedia, 6, 271
    Quokka Sports, 336
    RealFlash Generator, 332
WIDTH attribute, 319
WIDTH parameter, 323
Window menu, 44-46
Windows
    arranging, 44-45
    list of open, 45
    magnifying, 36
    resizing. *See* Scaling.
    zooming in/out, 18. *See also* Scaling.
Wipes, 163-165
Work area, as active window, 36
Work Area command, 36

X

Xtras Menu. *See* Library menu.

Z

Zoom Pull-Down Menu button, 49
Zooming in/out. *See also* Scaling.
    animation, 160-163
    definition, 18
    drawings, 129
    Magnifier tool, 50, 129
    sounds, 240
    windows, 18
    zoom level, setting, 36

Colophon

From start to finish, The Coriolis Group designed *Flash 3 Web Animation f/x and design* with the creative professional in mind.

The cover was created on a Power Macintosh using QuarkXPress 3.3, Adobe Photoshop 5, Alien Skin Black Box 2 filters, and the Trajan and Futura font families. It was printed using four-color process, metallic silver ink, and spot UV coating.

The interior layout was also produced on a Power Macintosh with Adobe PageMaker 6.52, Microsoft Word 98, Adobe Photoshop 5, and Adobe Illustrator 7.0.1. The body text is Stone Informal, heads are Avenir Black, and chapter titles are Copperplate 31ab.

Flash 3 Web Animation f/x and design was printed by Courier Stoughton, Inc., of Stoughton, Mass.

What's On The CD-ROM

The companion CD-ROM for *Flash 3 Web Animation f/x and design* contains elements specially selected to enhance the content of this book, including:

- ***Flash 3 (trial version)*—Flash is the standard for interactive vector graphics and animation for the Web. Web designers use Flash to create beautiful, resizable, and extremely compact navigation interfaces, technical illustrations, long-form animations, and other dazzling effects for their sites.**
- ***Dreamweaver 2 (trial version)*—See what makes Dreamweaver 2 the most powerful solution for professional Web site design and production.**
- ***Fireworks (trial version)*—Fireworks is the premier production tool for creating Web graphics.**
- ***FreeHand 8 (trial version)*—FreeHand is the tool of choice for designers producing illustrations and layouts for print and the Web.**
- ***Universal Animator*—This product allows you to create animations in any application.**
- ***Plug-ins*—Experiment with demo versions of Page/Edges 3, Photo/Graphic Edges 3, Photo/Graphic Patterns 1, Typo/Graphic Edges 3, and the Ultimate Texture Collection 1.**
- ***WebVise Totality*—These Photoshop plug-ins and standalone applications offer JPEG and GIF compression engines, digital watermarking, color correction software for GIFs, and more.**
- **Ulead Gif Animator 3—This is a GIF animation construction set.**

System Requirements

PC:

- 486 processor or faster recommended, including Intel Pentium processor, with Windows 95, 98, Windows NT4, or later
- Windows 95 with 16MB of RAM (24MB recommended)
- Windows NT4 with 24MB of RAM (32MB recommended)
- CD-ROM drive

Macintosh:

- Power Macintosh with System 7.5 or later
- 16MB of RAM (32MB recommended)
- CD-ROM drive

Both platforms require an 8-bit (256-color) VGA graphics card as well as a mouse, pen tablet, or compatible pointing device. See the readme files on the CD-ROM for acknowledgments, descriptions, installation instructions, and other important information.